HERMENEUTICS

Studies in the History of Religions

1. Stephan Beyer, CULT OF TARA
2. Edward A. Armstrong, SAINT FRANCIS: NATURE MYSTIC

THE
CULT
OF
TĀRĀ

Fig. 1. White Tārā. From a wood-block print by Roger Williams.

THE CULT OF TĀRĀ

Magic and Ritual in Tibet

by
STEPHAN BEYER

UNIVERSITY OF CALIFORNIA PRESS
Berkeley Los Angeles London

University of California Press
Berkeley and Los Angeles, California

University of California Press, Ltd.
London, England

ISBN: 0-520-02192-4
Library of Congress Catalog Card Number: 74-186109

Designed by W. H. Snyder
Printed in the United States of America

Foreword

The real history of man is the history of religion." The truth of the famous dictum of Max Müller, the father of the History of Religions, is nowhere so obvious as in Tibet. Western students have observed that religion and magic pervade not only the *forms* of Tibetan art, politics, and society, but also every detail of ordinary human existence. And what is the all-pervading religion of Tibet? The Buddhism of that country has been described to us, of course, but that does not mean the question has been answered.

The unique importance of Stephan Beyer's work is that it presents the vital material ignored or slighted by others: the living ritual of Tibetan Buddhists. The reader is made a witness to cultic proceedings through which the author guides him carefully. He does not force one to accept easy explanations nor does he direct one's attention only to aspects that can be counted on to please. He leads one step by step, without omitting anything, through entire rituals, and interprets whenever necessary without being unduly obtrusive. Oftentimes, as in the case of the many hymns to the goddess Tārā, the superb translations speak directly to the reader, and it is indeed as if the reader himself were present at the ritual.

If any blame attaches to this book, it is that it presents itself too modestly. It is, in fact, the first major work on the core of Tibetan life. I do not want to imply that all the most meaningful things in Tibetan culture or religion have been overlooked by others. The author begins his work with a discussion of great Western scholars who have studied Tibet before him. Few students, however, have been able or willing to deal extensively with the cultic procedures of Tibetan Buddhism. Instead they have focused on other subjects, such as the sublime paintings and sculptures of Tibet, the philosophical texts, the biographies of saints. These subjects are no doubt important, but their treatment has too often left the general impression of Tibetan religion as a collection of primitive customs and odd superstitions.

Tibet has retained an aura of mystery and fascination for travelers; and, as it happens, scholars have been slow in demystifying Tibetan religion. While most Asian traditions have become almost the exclusive domains of learned specialists, who sometimes seem to make it their chief concern to dampen loose enthusiasms, the history of Tibetology, in contrast, is rich in romantic details. In 1820, Alexander Csoma of Körös set out from Hungary in quest of the original homeland of the Hungarians. In the end, his journey—for the most part by foot—brought him to Tibet, and this wanderer became one of the founders of Tibetology. Our own century has seen the travelogue of Alexandra David-Neel, the fearless lady who journeyed across Tibet from one marvelous adventure to another. In spite of great political changes in our age, it is not impossible that Tibet will continue to appeal to travelers. Nevertheless, the romantic zeal that has accompanied the study of Tibet has not succeeded in unveiling Tibetan religion.

Tibet, indeed, may present one of the last great religious traditions to be interpreted. The word "last" should not sound fatalistic. I mean only that Tibet is a latecomer on the horizon of our religio-historical understanding. Perhaps we may say: Tibetan religion gives us an extraordinary opportunity for a genuine understanding of religious data. The peculiar place of Tibet in the history of Western scholarship may even be a novel chance for an understanding of *man*, for in our approaches to various religious traditions we have to face the fact that our understanding of man must strive to be unified if it is to be anything at all.

The search for a unity in our understanding of religious man is not an idle dream. The stimulus for such a search comes from the religious data themselves. For indeed, every religious tradition has a center, and no serious interpretation is possible if that center is ignored. Stephan Beyer has rendered us a great service by pointing to what can truly be regarded as central in Tibetan Buddhism: ritual forms, especially those in the worship of Tārā.

Beyer shows Tibetan religious ritual and magic in their mutual relationship as set forth in the Tibetan documents themselves, and not by relying on familiar biases concerning magic and religion. The ritual forms of religion and the practice of magic are very different from what the reader might imagine beforehand. They are different also from what most experts—often victims themselves of biases that made Tibetan religion "harmless" before it was confronted in earnest—have led us to believe. Magic and ritual as defined in the Tibetan Buddhist sources complement each other. They do not contrast in the way most of us have assumed. In particular, they are *not opposed* to each other in the manner of a psychological attitude of reverential submissiveness ("religion") versus the will to manipulate the sacred for one's own ends ("magic"). In Tibetan tradition, it would be meaningless to speak of an individual's control over anything empirical or mental, if such control did not depend on something else. This "something else" is the perfection of a being far beyond random individual wishes. Such a being is either a Buddha, who is free from the endless chain of finite existences, or a Bodhisattva, who is perfect in every way, is "almost a Buddha," yet chooses to relate to the world out of compassion. Such a being is Tārā, the great Goddess. Whatever reality is seen or "made up," whatever is done religiously or magically, and, ultimately, what is done, whether with good or evil intentions, can be realized only when it is directed toward the pure goal manifest in those beings. Stephan Beyer records the story concerning the king Langdarma, who *had* to be killed by a type of magic that seems "black" indeed. Yet the act was necessary in order to prevent the king from accumulating still more evil deserts than he had already. This little episode is a vivid instance of Beyer's ability to select data that illuminate religious structures and at the same time nullify extraneous assumptions. (Obviously, the story makes a very different point from the ideal of Calvin's democracy that might come to the mind of a Western intellectual looking for reasons to justify a rebellion. . . .) Elsewhere in the manuscript there is an eloquent example where a "ritual of subjugation" (magic, obviously!) has in its later stages a sort of meditation or prayer in whose expression the practitioner becomes, in all important ways, like a Buddha himself; hence the concrete object of subjugation seems itself lifted up and spiritually transformed in the process. The magic while being performed—the devotees in full awareness of its magic character—turns into universal bliss. The subtlest, hardly fathomable Buddhist lore—that of skill in means (upāyakauśalya)—becomes manifest, tangible in the ritual.

The image of the goddess Tārā, the focus of this work, is of great importance to our understanding of Tibetan religion. Tārā is the principal superhuman being in Tibet who might be called *divine* without further qualification. She is prayed to by millions; her help in all adversity is divine.

How may a person be sure that his need is observed by a higher power? A real fear in Tibet's Mahāyāna Buddhism was that the most qualified more-than-human powers might pass into nirvāṇa and thus disappear from the world in which need was felt. These more-than-human beings are the Bodhisattvas, the beings who are able to become Buddhas, yet are still present in the world. With Tārā, the fear that she would pass beyond this world did not seem to exist. It does not help much to search for "causes" to explain this trust in Tārā and her eternity. It would be misleading to think, for instance, of the widely held Indian tradition that only a male birth can be a last birth. Such rationalizations are too thin, especially if the *cause* for the formation of a deity is the issue. The help provided by Tārā was real. She was real, she was divine. Tārā was, had always been, and still is the almighty support of her devotees who address her. In fact, she is mightier than Buddhas and Bodhisattvas. The author convinces us that "Tārā in all her forms transcended any monopoly" (p. 15). And we hear that in a hymn she is addressed as ". . . mother who gives birth to all the Buddhas of the three times" (p. 215). To understand something of her cult is to understand something of the mainstay of Tibetan culture and religion.

Certainly, no study of magic can be undertaken from now on that does not take the present study into full account. A serious beginning has here been made on a deep understanding of Tibetan religion, and the general history of religions will profit by it. Locating the vital center of a religious tradition prepares the ground for a unified, structured, meaningful understanding of all religious phenomena. Obviously, this is no task that can be completed overnight. Rather, we are encouraged on the road we travel and we are surer of our direction. The time is past in which historians of religions might think themselves capable of writing complete histories of the religion of all mankind. The framework of ideas for such undertakings turned out to need more generous dimensions than even the most far-seeing minds could envision. Many historians of religions in the last couple of decades have reacted by addressing themselves to the safer studies of specific religions, ignoring the demands of a *general* history of religions. Ultimately, such modesty provides no solutions. It seems to me that the right direction will be provided by *essays*, not in the sense of small, safe studies, but in the sense of endeavors at interpretation of specific phenomena, done with full awareness of the great task of the general history of religions. The perennial aim of the history of religions is the interpretation of man as a religious being. The awareness of this aim must be reflected in the essays which in turn will inform that gigantic task. I feel honored to present Stephan Beyer's book as the first such essay in a series devoted to the interpretation of religious phenomena.

Kees W. Bolle

Preface

This paper represents a first attempt to formulate the processes and presuppositions of Tibetan Buddhist ritual, a field that has been left relatively untouched by Western scholars. One finds oneself almost immediately intimidated by the vast amount of material to be covered, even though there remains only a decimated literary debris carried from Tibet by refugees of the Chinese occupation. Here the problem of organization becomes acute. Ferdinand Lessing, in his often neglected classic *Yung-ho-kung*,[1] attempted to deal with the unwieldy mass of material at his disposal by discussing the rituals that took place in the various halls of this large temple complex, but the promise of this projected multivolume series remained unfulfilled at his death. David Snellgrove, taking a similarly localized approach in his *Buddhist Himalaya*,[2] discussed the ceremonies he had seen performed at Chiwang Monastery. René de Nebesky-Wojkowitz, on the other hand, in his brilliant compendium *Oracles and Demons of Tibet*,[3] organized his material around the cult and iconography of the Tibetan protective deities, approaching the problem through the rituals of a class of deities rather than of a particular place.

These works together constitute a standard of presentation which is difficult to meet. All three authors clearly felt deep bonds of affection for and sympathy with the Tibetans, and their works are important in their attempt to capture the spirit of a living tradition and to describe a practice of Buddhism which is still a vital force among an entire people.

The present work is an extension of their approach, for Snellgrove's concern for the history of Buddhism, and Lessing's and Nebesky-Wojkowitz's concern for its iconography, limited the space they had available in their books for detailed analyses of the complexities of Tibetan ritual. As Lessing himself said, "A book could well be written describing in detail these rites alone, with the ritual books translated, annotated and illustrated by sketches, drawings and photographs."[4] This is, in essence, what I have tried to do, and I have further attempted to throw light on the basic ritual structures that underlie the relatively few rituals with which I deal, hoping that these patterns may be extended and used as formulas in the interpretation of other Tibetan rituals.

The problem of organization remains. This paper began originally as a history of the goddess Tārā, but once in the field I found myself growing more and more engrossed in the actual practice of Buddhist ritual as a study in itself; a scholar from our secular society, I discovered, may too easily ignore the fact that Buddhism is basically a performing art. Still, the cult that centers on this goddess provided an organizational nucleus around which my paper could be written, limiting my choice of ritual material to a bulk none the less intimidating but at least yielding a hope of manageability.

Thus, too, the primarily Indian historical problems with which I had originally intended to deal seemed, finally, irrelevant to the main point of the paper, and these researches I plan to cover in a separate article. For the historical problems involved, the reader may refer to the works by Tucci[5] and Shastri,[6] to the textual studies published sporadically since the late nineteenth century,[7] and to the articles collected under the aegis of a seminar on Tārā held at the University of Calcutta in 1965, these last being of the most dizzyingly varied quality.[8]

Further, there are many iconographic questions I studiously ignore: the various Sanskrit anthologies of "evocations" contain numerous descriptions of deities who are almost totally unimportant in Tibet, which the original editors and their Tibetan translators included for the sake of simple comprehensiveness; this indiscriminate approach was then copied by the Tibetans themselves, and it has been faithfully followed by many Western scholars in their iconographic handbooks. All these anthologies tend to sacrifice implicit information as to relative importance rather than quit their quest for all-inclusiveness, reminding us of our own overstuffed anthologies of English poetry; we might paraphrase a piece of doggerel from e. e. cummings:

> mr u will not be missed
> who as an anthologist
> sold the many to the few
> not excluding mr u

The Indian anthologies, like our own, doggedly persevere in setting down the limited and personal revelations of minor masters alongside the great lineages that exercised much more influence both in India and in Tibet, a practice not culpable in itself were it but accompanied by some indication of which lineages were, indeed, the important ones. For example, the various minor goddesses, occasionally assimilated to forms of Tārā, who may be grouped together as one or another type of snake goddess (e.g., Jāṅgulī, Parṇaśabari), evoked almost no response in the hearts of any but the most scrupulously studious Tibetans; all these "minor Tārās" are so minor indeed that I could find no artist who knew offhand what any of them looked like, nor did any of the most learned monks at the great institutions of Sera or Jütö know where one could easily locate a text devoted to them, except, as has happened to me, by accident. The Tibetan artists with whom I worked could draw these deities only after I had provided them with the canonical Tibetan translation of the *Garland of Evocations*, which I had brought with me from America! Similarly, the anthologies give several evocations of a four-armed White Tārā, a revelation granted to the master Cintāmaṇirāja,[9] which simply did not catch on to form a school, and which was completely overshadowed in Tibet by the two-armed form revealed to Vāgīśvarakīrti and transmitted by Atīśa.[10] With these minor and idiosyncratic deities I do not deal.

Many of the Indian iconographic lineages did take hold in Tibet, however, though there are iconographic fads and styles in that country as well as everywhere else in the world, and many of these lineages seem simply to be out of fashion at the moment and have been replaced by others. Very few artists nowadays, for example, depict the Twenty-one Tārās according to the canonical school of Sūryagupta, but rather they follow the school attributed (without canonical warrant) to Nāgārjuna, which is claimed, again, to have been transmitted by Atīśa; and many artists follow a Nyingma or "ancient" tradition embodied in the "hidden text" *Heart's Drop of the Great Long*, which makes no claim at all to canonical authenticity.[11] As we shall have occasion to note, it seems a good idea not to be too engrossed in the iconographic externals of color, hand gesture, or emblem, for such typologies as have been attempted along these lines in the West appear, finally, to be castles built on the shifting sands of the personal revelations, the unique dreams and visions of the different masters and their disciples.

There seems to be little standardization in Tibetan bibliography. In this paper I cite sources from the canonical *Kajur* and *Tenjur* collections by their sequential numbers in the *Catalogue and Index to the Tibetan Tripitika, Peking Edition* (Tokyo: Suzuki Research Foundation, 1962), hereafter abbreviated as "P.," since the Japanese photographic reproduction of this edition is available in many libraries that could not ordinarily acquire an original Tibetan xylograph edition of the canon. The citation consists of the author; the Sanskrit title (where given); the catalogue number; the volume, page, folio, and line of the photographic edition; and the section, volume, folio, and side of the original block print (e.g., Dipaṃkaraśrījñāna, *Ārya-tārā-stotra*, P. 4511, vol. 81, 94.5.5-95.2.1, Rgyud-'grel DU 425a-425b). The citation of noncanonical works should be self-explanatory; and, with the expansion of the P.L. 480 program to include Tibetan texts, even those works not published in Western-style editions are becoming increasingly available in libraries. Many of the noncanonical works were lent me by my Tibetan friends or come from my own collection; but many Gelug sources were obtained from the magnificent collection of Tohoku University in Sendai, and I would like here to thank the members of the Department of Buddhist Studies for helping me gain access to the library.

There has as yet been very little agreement upon the phonemic transcription of Tibetan, owing in part to the intransigency of scholars and in part to the innate profligacy of the Tibetan language in producing dialects. Classical Tibetan texts, like those in Chinese or Mongolian, are read with considerable regional variation in pronunciation; but I use in the body of my text a much simplified transcription of the central Tibetan koine, based in large measure upon Roy Andrew Miller, "The Independent Status of the Lhasa Dialect within Central Tibetan" (*Orbis*, 4 [1955,] 49-55), modified for the maximum possible ease of pronunciation by non-Tibetologists. Scholars will find the literary Tibetan spellings of these words in the index; the footnotes use the standard classical orthography. The phonemic transcription is as follows:

vowels:		i	ü	u	
		e	ö	o	
		a			
consonants:	k	k'	g	ng	h
	tr	tr'	dr		r

ch	ch'	j	ny	y	sh	zh
ts	ts'	dz				
t	t'	d	n	l	s	z
p	p'	b	m	w		

The research on which this paper is based was carried out under a grant from the Foreign Area Fellowschip Program and was conducted in the hill station of Dalhousie, Himachal Pradesh, where the remnants of many of the great Tibean monastic centers have gathered.

Here my wife and I lived with a group that calls itself the Tibetan Craft Community for the Progress of the Dharma, earning its living mainly by the production of Tibetan handicrafts and centering upon the charismatic person of K'amtrü Rinpoch'e VIII Dönjü nyima, the Precious Incarnation of K'am, Sun of the True Lineage. This community consists of about 50 monks and about 250 lay people, preserving among themselves—perhaps better than any other refugee group I have encountered—their traditional practices and community relationships. I would like to express my deep gratitude to K'amtrü Rinpoch'e for his kindness to us, which sprang spontaneously and openly from a nature "precious" by more than title. I would like to thank the manager of the lay community, Geleg namje, and his brother, the gifted artist Ts'ewang tobje, for opening their house and their hearts to us, and all the monks and lay people who became our friends.

My major informant in this group was the young Chöje jats'o, head of the monastery of Drugu and the eighth in his line of incarnations, whose natural graciousness, scholarship, and quick grasp of what I as a Western scholar was attempting to accomplish made him both an ideal informant and a good friend. My major informant for the various artistic traditions was Tendzin yongdü, a venerable and learned lay artist who has been depicting these deities on painted scrolls for all the Tibetan sects for more than fifty years. Some of his drawings are reproduced in this book. For information on the actual performance of ritual—hand gestures, chants, and offerings—I am grateful to Kajü drugje, the head monk of the monastery, who, I think, got as much delight from my singing as I got from his, though for different reasons.

I would further like to express my indebtedness to Miss Diane Perry (Ani Tendzin Pemo) for her advice and encouragement, and especially for her Perfection of Forbearance in the face of infuriating scholarly nit-picking; to my late teacher Richard Robinson, of the Department of Indian Studies, University of Wisconsin, who constantly challenged me with his own fierce intellectual honesty; and to Roger Williams, who drew the frontispiece for this book. And especially I want to thank my wife Judy, who did not type up my manuscript, renew my library books or correct my spelling, but who rather performed the much more important function of constantly reminding me, in India and in America, that a Buddhologist does not deal with Buddhism so much as he deals with Buddhists.

Contents

ILLUSTRATIONS
xix

I
WORSHIP: OFFERINGS, PRAISES, AND PRAYER
1

II
APPLICATION: PROTECTION AND ATTACK
227

III
ACQUISITION: INITIATION AND RITUAL SERVICE
361

NOTES
469

BIBLIOGRAPHY
503

INDEX
521

Illustrations

Figures

1 White Tārā. From a wood-block print by Roger Williams. Frontispiece
2 Songtsen gampo with Tr'itsün (left) and Wen-ch'eng kung-chu (right); note the national costumes. From an iconographic sketch by Tendzin yongdü. 5
3 Green Tārā. From an iconographic sketch by Tendzin yongdü. 9
4 Sketch map of K'am, according to Ch'öje jats'o. 16
5 The type of Heruka: Cakrasaṃvara and Vajravārāhī. From an iconographic sketch by Tendzin yongdü. 41
6 The type of fierce patron: Yamāntaka in the "ancient" form of Quicksilver, the black poison-faced. From an iconographic sketch by Tendzin yongdü. 44
7 The type of ḍākiṇī: Vajravārāhī, the diamond sow. From an iconographic sketch by Tendzin yongdü. 45
8 The "ancient" ḍākiṇī Lion-faced, the guardian of hidden texts. From an iconographic sketch by Tendzin yongdü. 46
9 The type of Mahākāla: the Four-handed Lord. From an iconographic sketch by Tendzin yongdü. 49
10 The "ancient" protectors: Ekajaṭā, guardian of mantras. From an iconographic sketch by Tendzin yongdü. 50
11 The "ancient" protectors: Za. From an iconographic sketch by Tendzin yongdü. 51
12 The "ancient" protectors: Damchen Doje legpa, the oath-bound excellent diamond. From an iconographic sketch by Tendzin yongdü. 52
13 The type of Glorious Goddess: Magic Weapon Army. From an iconographic sketch by Tendzin yongdü. 53
14 The mantras and the gestures that (1) summon, (2) absorb, (3) bind, and (4) dissolve the knowledge being. 102

15 The outer offerings. 147
16 The precious gems of sovereignty. 152
17 The signs of good fortune. 155
18 The secret offerings. 160
19 The secret offerings, continued. 161
20 The maṇḍala gesture. 168
21 The tormas for the Four Maṇḍala ritual. 174
22 Palms joined in reverence. 178
23 The diamond-lady-of-the-mind gesture. 179
24 The bell and vajra. 183
25 The flying-bird gesture. 218
26 The torma gesture. 220
27 The asking-to-depart gesture. 224
28 Drawing the hearth. 266
29 Ladles for liquids (top) and solids (bottom). 267
30 A protection against gossip and slander: a figure whose lips are locked. 285
31 A protection to bind malevolent spirits. 293
32 A peaceful *lu* and a fierce *lu*. From a sketch by Tendzin yongdü. 296
33 A *tsen*. From a sketch by Tendzin yongdü. 297
34 Mach'en pomra, a mountain deity. From a sketch by Tendzin yongdü. 298
35 Kurukullā, goddess of subjugation. From an iconographic sketch by Tendzin yongdü. 301
36 The lingam effigy in its iron house—the black triangular box—surrounded by the weapons of its destruction; the syllabes NṚ TRI on its body cast the demons "down into form" to be "liberated". From a Tibetan woodblock print. 311
37 The tormas for the thread-cross ritual. 325
38 A proof sheet pulled from a *zen par*, a wooden mold for making small substitutes. The block is carved in intaglio, hence the peculiar appearance of the paper print. 326
39 *P'otong* and *motong* offered as substitutes. 328
40 The full-blown-lotus-flower gesture. 338
41 The six gestures that generate the substitutes. 347
42 White Tārā. From an iconographic sketch by Tendzin yongdü. 364
43 A metal initiation torma (left) and a flask of life (right). 376

44 The working flask (left) and the chief flask (right). 409
45 Solitary contemplation: a yogin in meditative posture, shoulders thrown back, elbows turned in, and arms locked on the thighs. From a Tibetan wood-block print. 459

Plates

Following page 260

1 Coating the food tormas with butter.
2 Setting up the altar for the Four Maṇḍala Offering.
3 Offering up the maṇḍala to Tārā.
4 Wayside shrine in Dalhousie, Himachal Pradesh.
5 The Lady of the Goring Yak.
6 The burnt offering.
7 A complex thread-cross used in the large annual evocation of the Four-handed Lord.
8 Winding the five-colored threads on the frame of the thread-cross.
9 Putting butter flowers on the torma.
10 The portrait molded of barley flour, in deep relief.
11 Four-tiered Mount Meru and the excellent house.
12 Planting shrubbery on the surrounding iron mountains.
13 The portrait complete with house, servants, livestock, and property.
14 The entire structure tied around with thread and set on the altar facing the assembly.
15 Carrying the thread-cross down the mountain.
16 The multitude tormas.

I

WORSHIP

Offerings, Praises, and Prayer

I read somewhere of a shepherd who, when asked why he made, from within fairy rings, ritual observances to the moon to protect his flocks, replied: "I'd be a damn' fool if I didn't!"

—*Dylan Thomas, note to* COLLECTED POEMS

The Eternal Body of Man is The Imagination, that is, The Divine Body . . . (In Eternity All is Vision).

—*William Blake,* LAOCOÖN

THE WORSHIP of the goddess Tārā is one of the most widespread of Tibetan cults, undifferentiated by sect, education, class, or position; from the highest to the lowest, the Tibetans find with this goddess a personal and enduring relationship unmatched by any other single deity, even among those of their gods more potent in appearance or more profound in symbolic association. This fact in itself means that her cult may repay scholarly interest, for Tārā's rituals differ from those of the "high patron deities" of the monastic cult in that they eschew much of the deeper—primarily sexual—symbolism which has so upset many Western researchers, and yet they conform to the basic patterns of all Tibetan ritual. Their straightforward avoidance of the textual complexities of the highest Tantras is an advantage, because we can direct our attention to their structure rather than to the "meaning" of their symbolism. Once these structures have been established, they may be generalized to include the most profound Tantric revelations; but we must first ask, simply, what the Tibetans are doing before we can go on to decide the "real" reason they do it.

Perhaps the most immediately impressive aspect of these rituals is the true devotion with which the Tibetans approach the goddess: she guards and protects her people, they say, from the cradle to beyond the grave, and her devotees cry out to her in their distress and share with her their joys. This fundamental attitude of worship, however, is inevitably channeled through a ritual process of "offerings, praises, and prayer" and is directed to the goddess by the ceremonial forms of the monastic community. Thus to understand something of her cult is to understand something of the whole structure of Tibetan culture and religion.

LEGENDARY BEGINNINGS

This universal veneration for the goddess was the result of a gradual process which began with the charismatic devotion of Atīśa, became a potent religious force by the fourteenth century, and culminated in the early seventeenth century with the great Tāranātha, from whose time the cult as we know it has emerged. And yet this goddess, though everyone knows that her cult was imported from India, is related by myth to the very beginning of things in Tibet.

One of the early pre-Buddhist myths relating the origins of the Tibetan people holds that "a devil and an ogress held sway, and the country was called Land of the Two Divine Ogres. As a result, red-faced flesh-eating creatures were born."[1] These demonic offspring were gradually given the crafts of culture by successive generations of culture-hero kings, and they became the civilized Tibetans. Other versions of the myth say that the Tibetans were originally the simian descendants of a union between a rock ogress and a monkey. This latter account was eventually adopted as the official Buddhist version, and the monkey became identified first as a disciple and then as an incarnation of Avalokiteśvara. But, surprisingly enough, the fierce ogress—"lustful and lascivious, under the sway of desire"—became identified as an incarnation of Tārā. As the *Red Annals* succinctly says, "Then, from the monkey Bodhisattva, an incarnation of Avalokiteśvara, and the rock ogress, an incarnation of Tārā, there sprang the Tibetan people."[2]

The point to be noted in the evolution of this myth is the influence upon it of the developing cult of Tārā, for so pervasive had her worship become by the time of the *Red Annals* in 1346[3] that the author could give this final version of the tale as a received tradition; so popular was the goddess that the Tibetans sought to relate her to their very origins, at whatever price in logic. Though there is, after all, good reason to consider the monkey ancestor related to Avalokiteśvara—the ogress threatened to eat up thousands of sentient beings every day until the monkey agreed to assuage her lust, so his act in fathering the Tibetan people might indeed be considered to be one of universal compassion—the identification of the ogress who seduced him with the goddess Tārā appears gratuitous, for in no version is her divine nature made obvious in her actions, even in the late and expanded retelling of Sumpa k'enpo.[4] But the pious intention of the attribution is clear, and the devotees of the goddess, looking at the history of their people, find more than rhetorical cause to call her "mother."

THE EARLIER SPREAD OF THE LAW

A further and historically more important tradition relates the actual introduction of Tārā's cult into Tibet to the Nepalese princess Tr'itsün, daughter of Aṃśuvarman and wife of the first great Tibetan king Songtsen gampo (617-650, according to the calculation of Roerich).[5] It is claimed in the various chronicles that this princess brought with her, among other images, a sandalwood statue of Tārā, which was placed in the Temple of Miraculous Manifestation

Fig. 2. Songtsen gampo with Tr'itsün (left) and Wen-ch'eng kung-chu (right); note the national costumes. From an iconographic sketch by Tendzin yongdü.

constructed at the princess's orders.[6] There is some doubt as to the final disposition of this image. The great lama and geographer Jamyang ch'entse wangpo (1820-1892) gave an account of the temple and described a miraculous image of the goddess which was named "Lady who Accepts the Ceremonial Scarf";[7] but in the seventeenth century the fifth Dalai Lama had already reported, in his guidebook to the temples of Lhasa, that the original sandalwood image was no longer there.[8]

It is thus problematical whether the image currently enshrined is the same as the one brought from Nepal in the early or middle seventh century (the chronicles periodically report the shuffling of images from one temple to another, according to the religious policy of the court), and it is difficult to tell at this late date how much of a cult developed around any of these early images in Tibet, whether those brought by Tr'itsün or the much more famous Jowo rinpoch'e—an image of Śākyamuni as a twelve-year-old prince —brought by the king's Chinese wife Wen-ch'eng kung-chu.[9] There is no particular evidence that Tārā received any special veneration at this time (indeed, the Chinese image of Śākyamuni seems from the chronicles to have received much the larger share of attention, being considered the original image made in the time of the Buddha himself), or in fact that any particularly Buddhist cult spread far beyond court circles. Tārā's image was to the king most likely a piece of political magic, an alien god to be treated with respect for its sacred (and diplomatic) potency, to be put in a special shrine where it could do little harm to the native gods and might perhaps do some good, especially for an imperial policy in the process of consolidating a centralized government. The image represented both religious and political forces to be dealt with, but not necessarily to be worshiped.[10]

Whatever doubts there may be about the whole tradition of Songtsen gampo's marriages, there is nothing chronologically improbable in the original contention that such an image of Tārā was brought from Nepal, or that at least some knowledge of the goddess was carried to Tibet about this time, even though the precise date of origin of Tārā's cult in India is still very much a vexed question: the earliest epigraphical document relating to her worship is a Javanese inscription of 778,[11] and it is difficult to place with assurance any text devoted to her much earlier than the early eighth century, which is too late by far to verify the Tibetan tradition. But there does exist one reference to the goddess prior to these dates, found not in any Buddhist manual of worship but, perhaps even more valuable because independent, in a pun provided by the illustrious Sanskrit author Subandhu in his romance *Vasavadattā*,[12] a source not previously adduced, as far as I know, in any discussion of the problem. In this long prose poem we find the following play on words: *bhikṣukī 'va tārânurāgaraktâmbaradhāriṇī bhagavatī saṃdhyā samadṛśyata* "The Lady Twilight was seen, devoted to the stars and clad in red sky, as a Buddhist nun [is devoted to Tārā and is clad in red garments]."

The pun centers on the ambivalence of two words: *tārā* as either "star" or "Tārā," and *ambara* as either "sky" or "garment." This sort of pun is perhaps the foremost embellishment of Subandhu's work; indeed, he himself says that he is a "storehouse of cleverness in the composition of works in which there is a pun in every syllable."[13] In his handbook of poetics, the *Kāvyâdarśa,* the theoretician and author Daṇḍin defines "pun" as follows [2.310]: "We consider a 'pun' to be a speech of a single form but of many meanings." And he says further [2.363]:

> The pun, as a rule, enhances the beauty in all ambiguous statements: the speech is divided into two parts, the inherent statement [the "manifest content"] and the ambiguous statement [the "latent content"].

Examples of this rhetorical adornment abound in Subandhu's romance, and they are usually intimated, as in the present instance, by *iva*; selection could be made ad nauseam, but perhaps it will be sufficient, to demonstrate that the present instance is indeed a pun on Tārā's name, if we give a few more examples from the whole series of puns Subandhu uses, as he did this one, to describe the Lady Twilight: *vārayoṣid iva pallavânuraktā* "reddened with blossoms, as a courtesan [is devoted to her lover]," *kāminī 'va kāleyâtāmrapayôdhara* "having vermilion clouds, as a beautiful woman [has breasts reddened with saffron]." Or again, to show the play on proper names: *vānarasenām iva sugrīvâṅgadôpaśobhita* "adorned with a beautiful throat and bracelets, as the army of monkeys [was adorned with Sugrīva and Aṅgada]."

This pun raises certain problems: *bhikṣukī* is not necessarily a Buddhist nun, and *tārā* may refer to Lady Star, the wife of Bṛhaspati; but it would be curious, after all, to find a nun of any order being devoted to the stellar heroine of a minor epic episode, the wife of Jupiter stolen by the Moon.[14] If we do accept that Subandhu was making a pun on the name of a Buddhist goddess before what was a primarily Hindu audience in his courtly circle—and playing with the name as casually as he played with those of the Brahmanic legends—it seems reasonable to suppose that this goddess was fairly well known by his time, else the pun would be without effect. And even if we concede that he might have been showing off an esoteric knowledge of Buddhism, at least he himself was acquainted with some sort of cult of Tārā, a goddess whose popular devotion extended beyond the bounds of minor legend. Though Subandhu's exact date is by no means a closed question, we would probably be not too far wrong to place him about the middle of the seventh century,[15] that is, at just about the time that Tr'itsün is said to have carried Tārā's image into Tibet.

To this we may add as one further consideration the testimony of the great Chinese pilgrim Hsüan Tsang, who traveled in India between 633 and 645, and who reports, in the offhand manner he reserves for things he is not quite sure are orthodox, the existence of two different images of a *to-lo* Bodhisattva, sex unspecified. One of these images, located about twenty miles west of Nālandā, accompanied Avalokiteśvara to form a triad with a central Buddha image;[16] the other image, in its own temple nearer to Nālandā, he reports as being a "popular object of worship."[17] There is every reason to believe that this *to-lo* is our Tārā, and his remarking upon its popularity reinforces the probable validity of the Tibetan tradition.

This native tradition, we may add, is actually quite conservative in its bestowal of venerable antiquity upon images. The geography text *A Complete Explanation of the World*[18] reports only one other image of the goddess attributed to this period of history:

> Then to the east is the region called Mark'am, where there are some Sacha and Gelug monasteries, and a temple and image of Tārā erected at the time of the Righteous King Songtsen gampo. The people of that region are quite fierce, and they speak something like the Minyag language.

It is, after all, surprising that more images have not been sanctified with age, with all the attendant benefits in increased pilgrimage trade. But later piety expressed itself in another form, for legend holds that King Songtsen gampo was an incarantion of Avalokiteśvara himself—according to Pema karpo, the king covered up his ten extra heads with a silken cloth[19]—and that his two wives were incarnations of Tārā. Among Western sources, Grünwedel[20] and Waddell[21] consider the Chinese wife Wen-ch'eng kung-chu to

Fig. 3. Green Tārā. From an iconographic sketch by Tendzin yongdü.

be an incarnation of White Tārā, and the Nepalese wife Tr'itsün to be an incarnation of Green Tārā, an attribution defensible from an ethnic point of view, since the epithet *śyāma* applied to Green Tārā can mean either "green" or "dark, swarthy." Bacot[22] and Sato,[23] on the other hand, reverse the identification, maintaining that the tradition holds Wen-ch'eng to have been Green Tārā and Tri'tsün to have been White Tārā.

When we examine the old Tibetan chronicles, however, we find no such identification of either princess with White Tārā; rather, those sources that report the tradition—Butön, for example, does not mention it, while Kunga doje, in the *Red Annals*, does—are unanimous in asserting that the Chinese wife was an incarnation of Green Tārā (or just Tārā, without qualification) and that the Nepalese wife was an incarnation of the goddess Bhṛkuṭī, the "Lady with Frowning Brows."[24] Thus, by the time of the earliest chronicles, we can see taking place an iconographization of the king and his wives, considering them a historical embodiment of the canonical triad of Avalokiteśvara, Tārā, and Bhṛkuṭī. This iconographic arrangement of the Bodhisattva with his two female companions is found as early as the *Mañjuśrī-mūlakalpa*;[25] it is found in the *Mahāvairocana-sūtra*[26] and is placed by the Japanese Shingon sect in their great Garbhakośa—"embryo receptacle" or "womb"—maṇḍala;[27] there are many evocations of Avalokiteśvara in this form in the canonical anthologies.[28] The discrepancies between this classical arrangement and the description in modern works may be resolved by considering, simply, that this triad has dropped out of iconographic style in recent years, and informants other than historical scholars might be unaware of its historical application (although my informants tended, in the main, to report the older tradition); yet the firm traditional identification of the Chinese queen with Green Tārā leaves them only the option of considering the Nepalese queen to have been White Tārā, as she is the only other iconographic form readily available to replace the little-known Bhṛkuṭī. I have a suspicion that the earlier Western works that reversed this attibution did so on their own, so that it might conform better to ethnological expectations.

We can follow this original identification with Tārā backward in time only as far as the fourteenth-century chronicles that record it; and we can say little more about this earliest development of Tārā's cult beyond the fact that there was possibly an image of Tārā in Tibet in the mid-seventh century. It is not until the second half of the eighth century that we can say for certain that at least some texts on Tārā had been translated into Tibetan, for there is preserved in the *Tenjur* a catalogue from the reign of King Tr'isong detsen (ruled 755-797)[29] of "translations of scripture and commentary in the palace of Denkar, in the Töt'ang."[30] This catalogue and its authors have been discussed by M. Lalou, who sees no reason to doubt the date attributed to it.[31] This list of translations includes only three works on Tārā: the *Spell called "Mother of Avalokiteśvara,"* the *108 Names of the Goddess Tārā*, and Candragomin's *Praises of the Noble Tārā Who Saves from All Great Terrors.*[32]

None of these works, however, can be considered of really central importance to the cult as it later developed (the spell translated, for example, is not a particularly significant one); and these works seem all but buried in the list of more than 700 texts. It is thus almost impossible to say whether during this period of the earlier spread of the Law the cult of Tārā took root in Tibet at all, or whether it exerted any influence outside court or scholarly circles; there certainly seems to be little evidence that the great mass of people in Tibet ever heard of Tārā. Repachen, the last of the great "Righteous Kings" (assassinated in 836),[33] in the same edict that sponsored the compilation of the Sanskrit-Tibetan vade mecum *Mahāvyutpatti*, decreed that "secret charms were not to be translated";[34] and the dark ages that followed upon the great persecution by the apostate King Langdarma (beginning probably ca. 840)[35] deprive us of any information beyond that.

THE LATER SPREAD OF THE LAW

It is thus perhaps justly recorded that it was the great Atīśa, the "venerable master" Dīpaṃkaraśrījñāna, arriving at Ngari in 1042[36] who brought the cult of Tārā to Tibet, despite the prior existence there of texts and images. "From the time he was a child," writes Sumpa k'enpo, "he was preserved by Tārā, the patron deity of his former lives."[37] Atīśa's life was filled with visions of the goddess; when he was young, she induced him to leave behind thoughts of royal power and seek a teacher in another country.[38] It was the goddess who persuaded him to go to Tibet, in spite of his advanced age: "And when Atīśa asked Tārā, she prophesied: 'If you go, your life will be shortened; but you will advance the teachings and benefit many beings, and chief among them a certain devotee.' And so he agreed."[39] The "certain devotee" was Atīśa's chief disciple, Jewe jungne, the Teacher from the Clan of Drom; the temple he built for Tārā still exists in Nyet'ang.[40]

It must have been Atīśa's personal devotion to the goddess—an enthusiasm that seems to have been caught by almost everyone he met—which more than anything else provided the impetus for her cult in Tibet, for he himself did not devote an inordinate amount of effort to the composition of texts dealing with her: out of his total of 117 works, only four are devoted specifically to Tārā. On these four, however, was built almost the entire structure of her Tibetan cult, and they include one of the most popular of her hymns, which is inserted somewhere in almost every one of her rituals. Atīśa wrote an evocation of White Tārā, based on the tradition of Vāgīśvarakīrti, and two evocations of Green Tārā; these works established the pattern of her evocation and outlined her basic functions for all future generations of writers.[41]

Of the seventy-seven Indian texts that Atīśa helped to translate into Tibetan, only six deal with the goddess. Among these are two devotional works by Candragomin and one minor hymn whose author is not given. But much more important and influential than these was his translation of three works on White Tārā, written by "the master and great scholar Vāgīśvarakīrti, empowered by the goddess Tārā," which together make up the cycle of texts known as *Cheating Death*; it is from these three translations that all the Tibetan lineages of White Tārā derive.[42]

We may note the pecular fact, however, that Atīśa did not translate any of the "scriptures" (ascribed as the "word of the Buddha") dealing with the goddess, which form the textual authority for her cult; these basic scriptures all describe the appearance, mantras, and rites of Green Tārā, the original form of the goddess, but they were considered "Tantric" and thus proscribed as incompatible with burgeoning Tibetan neoorthodoxy. But White Tārā was a personal revelation of Vāgīśvarakīrti, and her cult was not based upon his exposition of a Tantric scripture; thus the translation and transmission of his texts constituted the beginning of an "unbroken bridge of the lineage" in Tibet, since her cult began with him. Atīśa could transmit his own practices and evocations, for his charisma guaranteed their purity: but the textual foundation for the cult of Green Tārā consisted of Tantras that might be misapplied, which, according to tradition, Atīśa was not permitted to promulgate:

> In this world era, amidst numberless Buddhas, Bodhisattvas, and "holders of the mantra" on Potala Mountain, the Noble Avalokiteśvara spoke ten million Tantras of [Green] Tārā. The venerable Nāropa was, as it were, the owner of these Tantras, which are the source for Tārā, but at the time of his disciple Lhodrag Marpa they were not transmitted to Tibet. The great and venerable Atīśa, too, was the owner of these Tantras, and he also possessed their commentaries; but because the Tibetans did not let him preach the Tantras they were not promulgated.[43]

This prohibition was often ascribed to Atīśa's disciple Jewe jungne; the historian Zhönnupe says: "Drom suspected that these teachings might have a bad influence upon the morals of the Tibetans, and he abstained from preaching them much." The followers of the Kajü sect especially have never quite forgiven him for this;

the same author quotes the poet-saint Mila repa as saying: "Because a demon had penetrated the heart of Tibet, the venerable master Atīśa was not allowed to preach the Diamond Vehicle."[44] In any event, the result of this proscription, imposed to prevent misunderstanding and spiritual malpractice, was that scriptural authority for the cult of Green Tārā (as opposed to the personal authority of Atīśa) worked its way piecemeal into Tibet only gradually over the next hundred years, as the original puritan impulse wore off; and, indeed, "it was not until later that, from among the disciples of the great magician Rātnākaraśanti, the reverend Jonangpa [i.e., Tāranātha, born in 1575][45] diffused these Tantras widely here in Tibet, and he alone."[46]

The second half of the eleventh century did see an efflorescence of interest in Tārā, much of it due to the direct personal influence of the "venerable master." Darmadra, the Translator of Nyen, brought back from India traditions concerning what was to become the single most important canonical text of the Tārā cult, the *Homages to the Twenty-one Tārās*;[47] it is not clear whether he himself translated this text into Tibetan, since the *Kajur* catalogue gives no translator, but in Dragpa jets'en's commentary on the text, published a hundred years later, Darmadra is given credit for the translation.[48] Meanwhile, Rinch'endra, the Translator of Bari (born 1040), was translating texts on Tārā; he had met Atīśa when he was only fifteen,[49] and he too seems to have fallen under the spell of the master's devotion; when he took over the see of Sacha after the death of its founder K'ön Könch'og jepo in 1102 he brought with him an image of the goddess.[50] There was thus a flourishing tradition of Tārā at Sacha Monastery by the time Dragpa jets'en (1147-1216)[51] became abbot in 1172, and he himself was the author of no fewer than thirteen works on the cult of the goddess.[52] About the same time, in the late twelfth century, Ch'öchi zangpo helped translate another central text of the cult, the *Tantra Which is the Source for All the Functions of Tārā, Mother of All the Tathāgatas*.[53]

A century and a half later, when the *Red Annals* were written, Tārā had become indisputably the mother of the Tibetan people.

THE SECTS

The cult of Tārā, reintroduced into Tibet during the later spread of the Law, did not become the exclusive property of any of the various sects that developed out of the Buddist renaissance. All three of the major "new" sects (so-called as opposed to the "ancient" sect of the Nyingma) considered themselves at least collaterally descended from Atīśa; each sect could point in its lineage to holy men of former times who had been famous devotees of the goddess, although each may have stressed one or another portion of the original transmission.

The Gelug sect—the "Virtuous Ones"—considered themselves especially the heirs of Atīśa's Kadam lineage, the lineage "Bound to the Proclamation," and of its special devotion to Tārā; indeed, they style themselves the "New Kadam." "The holy Tārā made a vow," says Yeshe jets'en, "to preserve all the friends of the Kadam who followed after Atīśa; as she says in the *Book of the Kadam*:

> I will protect your followers:
> when you have obtained these my counsels
> teach them to your followers."

"Accordingly," he continues, "all the disciples of Atīśa and of the Conqueror Tsongk'apa [the founder of the Gelug sect, 1357-1419][54] took the holy Tārā as their highest deity, and prayed to her alone; especially the Omniscient Gedündrub [the first Dalai Lama, 1391-1475][55] would do whatever he did only after he had prayed to the holy Tārā, and thereby his active power to augment the aims of the teachings and of beings became as great as infinite space. Indeed, the majority of holy men in former times took the holy Tārā as their highest deity, and by the power of their prayers the quality of their understanding of the precepts was greatly increased in the stream of each of their hearts: and they succeeded in augmenting the aims of the teachings and of beings, just as it is related in their various biographies."[56]

The Sacha sect, too, as we have seen, took an early and active interest in the goddess—she was their patron saint of scholars—but they also felt that Tārā in her form of Kurukullā, the magically potent goddess of subjugation, was a special patron and protector of the sect. Her mantra was given in the *Hevajra Tantra*, a text of whose revelation they deemed themselves the foremost guardians and exponents, and her special rituals of domination had been transmitted to their lineage through Dragpa jets'en.[57] But all the sects would call upon this goddess when the need for her rather specialized services arose, and any sect might include individuals who were her special devotees.

Similarly, the Kajü sect—the "Lineage of the Proclamation"—were especially reverent toward White Tārā, tracing her relation with them back to their founder Gampopa (1079-1153)[58] in direct descent from Atīśa, and chronicling the personal revelations she granted preeminently to the incarnation lineage of the Karmapa. And yet a member of any sect would call upon her when he felt that the time of this death was drawing near, and the lamas of all sects regularly bestowed upon their followers her "initiation into life."

THE MONASTERY

All these sectarian lineages are more traditional preferences than exclusive preserves, for Tārā in all her forms transcended any monopoly, and a devotee would seek her teachings from any who possessed them. With the establishment of sectarian traditions, however, it becomes more and more difficult to trace the complex ramifications of the transmission; here and there in the lineages a few well-known names stand out, but the very popularity of her cult created crisscrossing branches among the sects which are almost impossible to follow. (To the Tibetans, too, many of these lineages are just lists of names, accessible only to specialists.) It is one thing to trace the almost paradigmatic growth of Tārā's worship in Tibet; but in order to understand how her cult fits into the ritual pattern of Tibetan life, it is important to review the entire ritual cycle of a particular sect in a specific monastery and to consider the lineages of her rituals as they are there presented, as guarantees of efficacy, to those who worship her. It is only against the background of the constantly recurring themes of ritual life that we may gain the perspective that shows the cult of Tārā, in all its individuality, as yet an integral part of the Tibetan religious world; and it is in terms of the totally ritual life of the monastery that this religious pattern is ultimately expressed.

Most of my informants in India belonged to the subsect of the Kajü called *Drug* or "Dragon"; when Tsangpa jare (1161-1211)[59] founded the head monastrery in Tsebola, "nine dragons appeared in the sky and spoke several times with the sound of thunder."[60] So popular did the sect become that people said: "Half the people

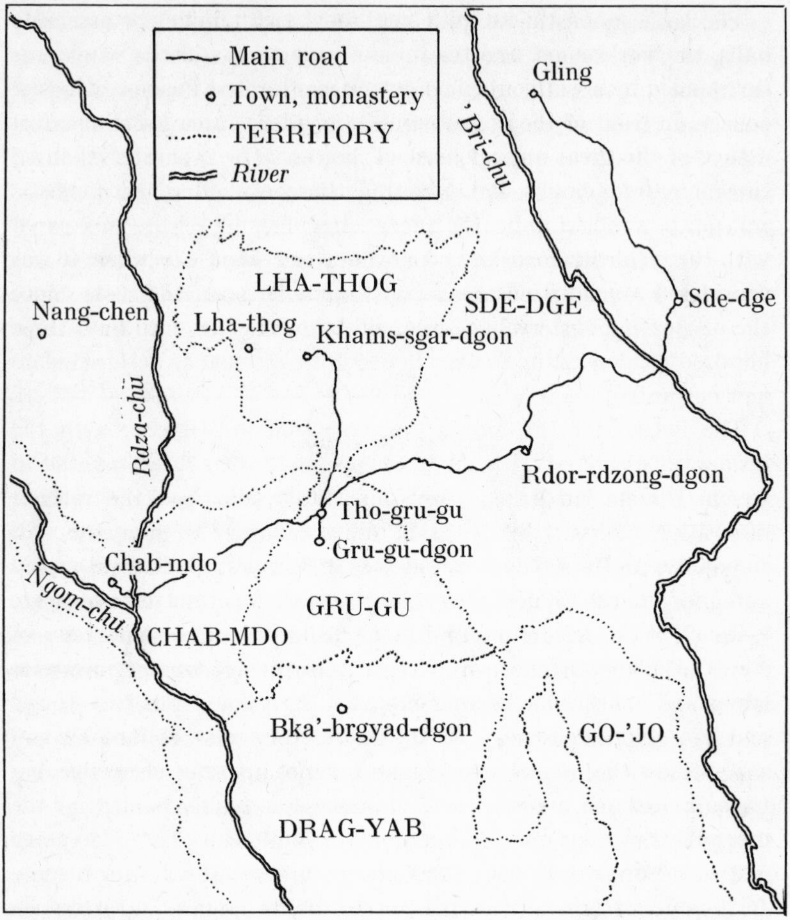

Fig. 4. Sketch map of K'am, according to Ch'öje jats'o.

are Dragons, half the Dragons are wandering ascetics, half the wandering ascetics are saints."[61] In K'am, in eastern Tibet, the head monastery of this sect was Pe p'ünts'og ch'ök'or ling, the "Glorious Divine Isle of the Wheel of the Law"—called, for short, K'amgargön, the "Monastery of the Camps of K'am"—which was at the head of almost two hundred branch monasteries. It had been founded near the beginning of the nineteenth century by Ch'öchi nyima, the fourth K'amtrü rinpoch'e; it was located in Lhat'og, surrounded by thin forest and low-lying grassy mountains whose summits were of bare white rock, and it nestled between the mountains and the river flowing through the valley beneath.

The large monastic complex contained two temples or assembly halls, the workrooms, and the monks' quarters, and the whole was surrounded by a wall, outside of which was located the new monastic college; in front of the main temple was a large area for the performance of the great annual masked dances. The monastery housed three hundred monks, not counting those attending the monastic college; it was certainly not a large establishment when compared with the gigantic monastic corporations of central Tibet, but it was considered a good-sized monastery among those of the east. Since the original monastery had been constructed with more than three hundred residences, no further housing was needed to accommodate new entrants.

The houses for the monks were built of local stone, with the inside walls covered with mud, whitewashed, and often painted in fresco; though the houses were outwardly identical, the interior decoration varied with the taste and means of the occupant. All the roofs were flat except for those of the temples, which were curved and gilded in the Chinese style. Each monk was allotted a separate house in these residences (which looked rather like short rows of New York brownstones), and there was one section for incarnate lamas and another for ordinary monks; each house was two-storied and had up to six rooms. In the lower story were storerooms and a stable for the monks' *dzomo* (the female offspring of a cross between a yak and a cow); these animals were highly valued for the creaminess of their milk, and a monk would usually try to keep one or two to supply him with dried cheese and with butter for his tea. In the upper story were a sitting room with windows—covered with imported glass if the monk could afford it or else with oiled paper—and a bedroom-shrine room where the monk would keep his books and his personal altar. Each house had its own kitchen with a smoky, wood-burning clay stove. Each row of houses had a narrow strip of garden and a wide pathway, and these complexes were scattered up and down the mountain within the cyclopean monastic wall.

The monks did their own cooking except during large monastic rituals, when they were served by the communal cooks; but usually three or four monks would arrange to eat at one another's houses. A monk too poor to provide for himself was taken care of by the older monks and the monastery, but a young monk could avoid many of the small indignities of communal life if he had a relative either inside or outside the monastery to look after his welfare. Sometimes a monk would take in a young relative, or a boy from one of the nearby villages or camps, whom he would instruct in reading or the religious arts of wood carving or painting in return for cooking and tending to what animals the monk might possess.

In addition to the milk, butter, and cheese supplied by their dzomos, the monks during the summer would lay out vegetables on their flat roofs to dry for winter stores. Breakfast would usually consist of buttered tea mixed with parched barley flour, and perhaps some cheese. At midday there would be rice or Chinese vermicelli with black mushrooms, and especially the small brown native potatoes and curd, as these were most plentiful and cheap. If the monk was well off there might be dried meat or fruit, and sometimes the staple Tibetan treat of steamed dumplings, either plain, stuffed with meat, or simmered in a sauce of cheese, butter, and sugar; another popular dish was flat fried bread stuffed with chopped meat and spices. Dinner would almost invariably be noodle soup, and between all the meals would be interspersed the consumption of an incredible amount of buttered tea, during the morning and afternoon assemblies and before and after almost every other activity. A high lama, constantly waited upon and unable to refuse his servitors the merit of serving him, would drink upward of a hundred cups a day.

A monk did not renounce his right to a share of his family's wealth or income when he entered the monastery, and he was to a greater or lesser extent responsible for his own upkeep; but the monastery as a whole was also supported by the king of Lhat'og, who had ceded several villages to the various incarnations of K'amtrü rinpoch'e, as well as by continuous donations from the wealthier families of the district. The monastery as a whole, too, would engage in trading ventures, sponsoring or investing in caravans to other districts, and it would also use the interest on the capital it lent to merchants for financing the large monastic rituals, which were not privately endowed by a lay sponsor.

All finances—income, investment, and disbursal of endowments—were in the hands of a committee headed by the storekeeper, who looked after the monastery's commercial interests and acted as the steward of its property. He was a businessman rather than a scholar, and it helped if he was rich, for at the end of his three-year appointment he was expected to make up any deficit out of his own pocket, and give a banquet for the monks as well.

The storekeeper, in turn, was part of the general structure of the monastery's administrative offices, which were divided into three general sections: one was responsible for the maintenance and supply of houses, temples, and workshops; another was in charge of the monks and their food and clothing; and a third looked after the materials for and the administration of monastic rituals. Each administrative section employed nine monks in a rotational sequence of three years, and each monk was expected to work his way through all these offices. His career thus took him through every phase of the monastery's life, and every monk could find a place in its structure for his own talents, whether scholarly, contemplative, or commercial. He might be appointed storekeeper for three years, or take a three-year turn at being one of the three communal cooks, preparing the tea and occasionally the soup for monastic rituals. He might spend a period as the altar server, responsible for the maintenance of the temple altar and the proper distribution of ritual implements to the participating monks, or he might be called upon to protect the monastery by reciting the daylong prayers in the "house of the Lord." He might be chosen as the head monk to lead the chanting in the ritual and play its complicated liturgy on the cymbals, or as the disciplinarian to maintain decorum in the assembly hall and see to the quiet progress of daily life. Even after a monk retired from his three-year appointment to any of these positions to devote himself to other tasks, his experience and advice were sought after by the new incumbent, and a man of talent might well continue to serve as an unofficial adviser to his old administrative section.

The monastry as a whole also administered two monastic colleges, supported through its commercial activity and by donations from the lay community and participating monks. The old college, founded by Ch'öchi nyima, lay about a day's journey by horse from the monastery; it was quite large, practically a monastery in itself with 120 students. The new monastic college, beside the monastery but outside the walls, was built by Dönjü nyima, the present K'amtrü rinpoch'e, as the fulfillment of a dream he had cherished over several lifetimes. The main building had three stories, contained a large library, and had eighty rooms for the students, who came either from the main monastery or from any of its two hundred branches.

A monk was expected, between the ages of fourteen and twenty, to have acquired enough knowledge of reading and writing, as well as of classical Tibetan grammar, to pass the preliminary examination and be admitted into the monastic college as a scholar. His course there lasted for eight to ten years, depending upon his ability. Those who were not too intelligent could extend the period of education for an additional five to eight years, or they could drop out altogether, though doing so could easily prejudice the remainder of their careers; those who decided to choose the scholarly calling could remain in the college their entire life, working their way by examination through the academic degrees and the hierarchy of teaching positions, gathering honor and respect.

Advancement came through active and spirited debate, punctuated by stylized gestures of intellectual attack, the clapping of hands and the stamping of feet, and stock phrases of challenge and contempt; the basis was a thorough knowledge of textual sources, literally thousands of memorized pages, but it was the monk's ability to think quickly and cleanly under pressure which was tested in these examinations. The standard curriculum consisted of five major divisions: (1) ecclesiastical law, (2) natural philosophy, (3) psychology and logic, (4) metaphysics, and (5) the "wisdom" literature. A devoted scholar could obtain his all-important *geshe* degree, comparable to the doctorate, before he was thirty, and with this degree in hand he could progress from a teaching assistant to the honor-laden heights of being a *k'enpo*, or professor.

This was certainly not a hard life by the standards of the country, and it adequately fulfilled the monastic system's fundamental role of lifting from the monk's shoulders all the cares of secular existence—apart, of course, from the inevitable conflicts and frictions that attend a group of three hundred men living together, and the small sorrows of daily life (the failed exam, the missing money, the dying relative) which afflict all dwellers in this world—and allowing them to perform the rituals that were the ultimate function of their monastic life.

From the time a young man passed through the gates of the monastery, whether as an incarnate lama or as an ordinary monk, he was surrounded by the constant sound and excitement of the rituals; every time he was initiated into the evocation of a deity, he committed himself to so much time spent in private ritual contemplation, to so many hundreds of prostrations when he awoke in the morning. Each monk owed a duty to the monastery, to the lay community and the king that supported it, and, by the strength of his vows as a

Bodhisattva, to the entire realm of sentient beings, all of whom, at one time or another in his past lives, had borne him as his mother; his debt was paid by the performance of ritual, by the study of ritual techniques, and by his increase of understanding in the monastic college.

"Perhaps what is most impressive about these people," writes Snellgrove,[62] "is their strong sense of personal responsibility and their wide freedom of action. The monks are all there on their own responsibility, subject only to their obedience to an older monk, if they choose to ask him to be their master. They meet normally every morning, take tea together, intone prayers, and separate to go about their own affairs, namely attendance on their chosen divinity in their own rooms, invocation and meditation, reading, copying and in some cases composing of texts, laughing and talking together, visiting relatives and acquaintances, either on family affairs or to perform ceremonies in private houses. Part of the year (again the time is self-imposed or imposed by one's chosen master) may be spent in solitary contemplation in the hermitage above the monastery."

THE RITUAL DAY

Every day at K'amgargön, for example, Bongpa trüku would rise before dawn to perform his private ritual contemplations and prostrations for an hour and a half. Then, after breakfast, he would join the rest of the monastery in the morning assembly for the evocation of the high patron deities of his sect and monastery and for the recitation of any special "earnest wishes" or "verses of good fortune" which had been requested by the lay people or other monks; this ritual lasted another two hours. He spent the morning employed as the monastery's librarian, locating books for the monks, rewrapping them in their rich brocade covers, and making sure that they were properly filed. His spare time went toward reading from the shelves or perhaps, with other monks, copying out the valuable manuscripts.

Bongpa trüku was served lunch by an older monk—as an incarnation he was waited upon at meals—and then went to the monastic workshops where he also worked as a supervisor and an artist (he was a very talented painter). This shop was a four-story building within the monastery compound which had been originally intended to serve as a monastic college, until the present K'amtrü rinpoch'e constructed the new college outside the walls. It contained more than fifty medium-sized rooms, used mostly for storage, and several large windowed workrooms where the monastery employed more than forty people from the surrounding districts of Lhat'og, Dege, Ch'amdo, and Nangch'en. Some monks were employed in the printing of texts, but the workers were mostly lay people, including a few women, who lived in a small village supplied for them on the other side of the river; single men were allowed to stay within the monastery after the gates closed for the night. They were silversmiths, goldsmiths, molders of images in clay and casters of images in bronze, painters, wood-carvers for the blocks from which the books were printed, carpenters, and tailors—all employed in making the ritual equipment, the costumes, the paintings, and the texts used in monastic rituals. Everything was paid for from K'amtrü rinpoch'e's own funds on behalf of the monastery.

Then came the afternoon tea break, and Bongpa trüku would once again join the other monks in the evening assembly for two hours, this time making offerings to the "protectors of the Law" and the lesser and local spirits who had been bound by oath to its service, reciting prayers to them and "entrusting them to their function." After dinner he would do more private ritual contemplation until it was time to retire.

All these rituals and ritual-oriented activities formed the thread that bound together not only Bongpa trüku's daily tasks but also almost every aspect of his monastic career, from the time he had been discovered as an incarnation, through the monastic college and his training in all phases of his ritual and communal life; these rituals bound the monastery itself to the surrounding lay community more effectively than any economic bonds could have done. If a monastery engaged in trade—almost all of them did—and even if it managed to acquire lands and riches, the ultimate aim was the performance of ritual: the gold and silver stores of the wealthiest monastery took the form of religious implements, and the Chinese brocades, the paintings, and the images were ultimately in the service of its deities. Linguistic usage did not even allow an individual person or monastery to "buy" an image; the word for its purchase price was "ransom fee," a rental paid on something owned by the whole world. The voluntary lay support of a monastery was given for the performance of ritual, and royal grants of land and villages were made to maintain the monastery in its ritual function as the protector of the country. A pilgrimage to the most holy of persons would have been incomplete without having obtained his services as a ritual expert, and a traveling lama was expected by monks and lay people alike to perform rituals and bestow initiations for the welfare of every community he visited. The life of a resident lama, especially in a small community, was often a succession of demands for the cure of disease, the prevention of hail, or the expulsion of evil spirits; all these functions were the ritual manipulation within his person of the power of the deities to whose service he had particularly devoted himself, the signs of whose favor he had received, and whose true nature he understood.

Thus, aside from the large monthly and annual monastic rituals, the monastery functioned further as a service organization in the performance of rituals sponsored by individuals or groups in the lay community. The monks, and especially the high lamas, had become ritual experts through their long professional training in ritual techniques, and even the most basic attitudes of worship toward the deities were focused through the monastery. This functional relationship between lay and monastic communities was furthered by the fact that the proper application of magic in Tibetan society was conditioned by the necessity of professional training and a long course of contemplative preparation, and even destructive magic was sanctioned if it furthered religious ends. But the lama was more than merely a Buddhist shaman; he was also involved, ideally, in his own quest for enlightenment and the spiritual preparation for his own death. It was this personal search that rendered him capable in the first place of performing his service function for others.

RITUALIZATION

A young child in the lay community went through a process of socialization during which he absorbed his basic attitudes to life just as he would absorb the steps of his folk dances or the tunes of his native songs, by the imitation of his elders and the reward of their approval, and by the often quite vocal pressure of his peers. Analogously, a young monk went through a process of "ritualization" in his monastic environment, although this process was more formally structured and had more coherently formulated ends. His first three years in the monastery were spent in learning how to read and write, and he had to commit to memory all the texts of his ritual profession: prayers and earnest wishes, confessions and offerings of the morning and evening rituals, all the incidental verses that might conceivably be introduced at the discretion of the head monk, and all the large ritual texts used monthly or annually at the great monastic ceremonies. It was a prodigious feat of memory for a nine- or ten-year-old child to be called upon to perform, though the learning was spread over a number of years. I can remember every day after breakfast hearing the young monks chanting aloud in the peculiar singsong that marked the word boundaries in the dimly understood classical Tibetan texts they were reading, and which alerted the teacher to appropriate punitive action when a break in its rhythm signaled him that a student had made a mistake in his recitation.

These younger monks also helped clean the temple before the large rituals and served the tea during their progress. For the young monk, his early training was a time of whippings and ear pullings, but it was also a time of pleasure in learning, of mastering the monastic environment, helping the older monks to fashion the delicately wrought offerings, to fill the butter lamps, and to set out the implements of the ritual.

Tibetan Buddhism has a ritual structure of its own, a syntax that has been imposed upon the experiential "given" of the contemplative experience. This structuring of meditative experience is part of a tradition that goes back to India, where the raw data of contemplation were ordered into ritual patterns, and these were the structures that made up the framework of the basic Tantras. But in Tibet this structure enclosed a basically Tibetan experience, and the Indian prototypes were transfigured into an irreducibly Tibetan expression. The interstices of the Indian outline were filled in with the fierce and vibrant movements of the Tibetan shamans' dance, and the drone and roar of Tibetan chant and music; and the flat Indian offering cake became the refined and brilliant *torma*, made of barley flour and decorated with intricate designs of colored butter, reminding one of nothing so much as the farthest flight of a Max Ernst.

Traditionally, three years were spent later in the young monk's life, after monastic college, in learning in a formal course the technical details of this ritual. The three-year sequence had six parts: (1) ritual hand gestures, (2) chanting, (3) making maṇḍalas, (4) making tormas, (5) playing the musical instruments, and (6) dancing. But in actuality the young monk began learning these skills long before his formal course, for he sat in the assembly hall with the older monks, desperately trying to get his voice low enough to chant with them, trying to keep his place in the text he had perhaps not yet memorized quite well enough, and simultaneously attempting to follow the monks across from him in their rapid sequences of hand gestures and the manipulation of their vajras and bells. His reward might be an approving glance from an older monk or perhaps from the head monk himself, of whom the young monks stood in great awe; and his punishment for losing his place in the midst of all this might be a reproof from the disciplinarian, whose fierce glance was backed up by the threat of corporal punishment. I have heard him yell at the young monks, in the middle of a ritual, "Pay attention to your books!" and create thereby a flurry of page-flipping and attention; he has been known to fling his vajra the length of the assembly hall to fall like the thunderbolt it represents upon the head of a dozing monk. Yet to be allowed to blow the conch shells or beat the drums during the ritual was a treat relished by a young monk, given as a reward for good behavior or offered as an inducement for wakefulness during a long ritual, which might last fourteen hours a day for nine days; and it was a treat despite the fact that it might earn him a pulled ear if he did not pay attention to what he was doing.

This process of ritualization thus worked upon the young monk in many ways; the most important factor was that he and his elders actually enjoyed the monastic rituals, for they provided an outlet for his creative talents in the manufacture of their accessories, the maṇḍalas and tormas, as well as in the chanting, the music, and the occasional dancing of their actual performance. From the very beginning of a monk's monastic career the rituals provided him, in the assemblies, with a feeling of communal support and common effort, they challenged his capabilities, and they provided, in their administrative structure, clearly defined and possibly attainable goals for his endeavors. He could look forward to the day when he had learned the procedures and cultivated his talents well enough to be himself appointed the head monk.

CONTEMPLATIVE TRAINING: THE PRELIMINARY PRACTICES

As early as possible every monk was expected to spend some part of his life in solitary contemplation at the hermitage associated with the monastery, and some monks would return there periodically throughout their lives. There, in constant contemplation, lived neither more nor less than thirteen yogins (literally, in Tibetan, those "possessed of understanding"); when one died, another monk volunteered or was chosen from the main monastery. When a monk became a yogin permanently, he took a vow to remain within the limits of the hermitage for the remainder of his life (except for certain specified ritual occasions); indeed, "limits" is the Tibetan word for solitary contemplation. He would neither cut nor wash his hair, nor cut his beard or fingernails, nor ever wear any garment other than the red-fringed white cotton robes that had been the dress of the "cotton-clad brothers" since the time of Mila repa. The hermitage had a main temple, and the separate houses were scattered over the top of the mountain. Other yogins lived in caves in the mountain, but they were not supported by the monastery.

Ideally, the young monk's period of solitary contemplation would last for three years, three months, and three days, during which time he would be trained in the basic contemplative techniques of the monastic rituals and given instruction in the visualizations that were their central procedure. Before he was allowed to embark upon any of these ritual procedures he had first to gain the power of the god through ritual service; and before he began this service he had first to purify himself through the preliminary practices.

To arouse his energies toward the task of contemplation which lay ahead, therefore, he began with the four common preliminaries, spending—ideally—one week each on four short meditations upon (1) the difficulty of attaining human birth, (2) death and impermanence, (3) the cause-effect pattern of karma, and (4) the horrors of this world. These meditations are called "common" because they are considered to be general to both branches of the Great Vehicle: the Vehicle of the Perfections and the Vehicle of the Mantra.

Then, when the young monk was aware of the necessity for making the utmost effort to use his precious human birth to liberate himself from worldly attachments, he purified and empowered himself for his future contemplations with the four uncommon preliminaries, here beginning the first of the peculiarly Tantric visualizations whose basic technique would be used in all his later ritual practices. These preliminaries began with his "going for refuge," which included also the formal acceptance of his vows as a Bodhisattva—his intentional awakening of the thought of enlightenment—before the eyes of the "field of hosts," the assembly of the deities and lamas of the Dragon Kajü, whom he visualized in the sky before him and to whom he prostrated himself 100,000 times in the course of his basic training. Next he "cleansed away his obscurations" by visualizing Vajrasattva above his head and reciting the 100-syllable mantra 100,000 times. He "offered the maṇḍala" 100,000 times to the lineage of his gurus. And finally he "made their empowerment enter into him" through his prayers and "yoga [union] with the gurus" another 100,000 times. After each of these four visualizations he absorbed into himself the particular "field" he was visualizing.[63]

THE MORAL BASIS OF CONTEMPLATIVE TRAINING

If he worked steadily at this program, a monk might finish it within three or four months; if he really attempted to form the visualizations, rather than mechanically going through the gestures and automatically reciting the mantras and prayers, he would by the end of that period have established a firm foundation for all his future contemplations. But perhaps even more important than just simple practice in visualization—the young monk would get plenty of practice in that during the ritual service that came next—was the conscious inculcation of certain basic and quite characteristically Buddhist attitudes with which the monk would approach his future rituals and the power, the "magical attainments," he would gain through them. This is the reason Tsongk'apa, for example, places so much emphasis in the following discussion on the necessity for these purificatory practices, including the common preliminaries:[64]

> This process of purification is absolutely essential in the path common to both the Vehicle of the Perfections and the Vehicle of the Mantra. This is stated in the following verse, which Lama Ngogpa (who held the lineage of exposition of the Tantras from the holy Marpa) quoted from the *Hevajra Tantra* [II.viii.10]: "First are given the rules of public confession . . . and then one is taught metaphysics." Both types of the Great Vehicle hold that the disciple should first be taught the "ordinary studies," and this appears to be the implication of the Tantra also. The holy Mila said: "If led with the teachings of liberation through the narrow pass between life and death, one first begins by going for refuge and awakening the 'intentional' and 'actual' thoughts of enlightenment. Led by a deep ravine which presages destruction, yoked yaks fall together into the abyss." This means that whenever a disciple does not keep the vows he has taken, both he and

his master fall into the abyss: should one hope to see only personal benefit in taking these vows, this is to be led by the nose to destruction. . . .

But then how actually does one purify oneself on this path common to both types of Great Vehicle? It should be done according to what is given in the precepts of Atīśa.

First one should find a virtuous friend in the Great Vehicle, one who has all the requisite qualities, and serve him properly by heeding his words and cleaving to him. He explains the great importance and difficulty of obtaining human birth: and he who is purifying his mind conceives a fervent desire to get the utmost use from his human body. The best way to get the utmost use from it is to set out in the Great Vehicle: and the gate through which one does so is the thought of enlightenment. If that thought in one's stream is pure, one becomes a genuine follower of the Great Vehicle; but if it is but a thing of mere words, one's following the Great Vehicle is a thing of mere words. Hence the wise man meditates step by step on all the obstacles to obtaining such a human birth, until he awakens the thought of enlightenment in all its essential characteristics.

Furthermore, if he does not, right at the beginning, turn his thoughts away from this life, then he will meet obstructions, whether it be on the path of the Great or Little Vehicle: hence he should meditate on the brevity of this life and his inevitable death at its end, and on the way in which he will wander lost through evil destinies after he dies, that he may turn his thoughts away from this life.

Then he should meditate thoroughly upon the horrors of the infinitude of this world, even if one be reborn in a heaven beyond: and he should turn his back upon it and direct his mind toward liberation.

After that, in order to turn his back upon the thought of this world, he who has thus calmed himself purifies at length his friendliness and compassion, and the thought of enlightenment whose roots they are, until he purifies a genuine thought of enlightenment.

Then, knowing the conduct of a Bodhisattva, he conceives a desire to undertake its study and performance. If he is able to take on the responsibility of conducting himself as a son of the Conqueror, he takes the vows of a Bodhisattva: he studies the six perfections in general, and in particular he studies to make his mind fit for the Calm which is the essence of contemplation, and he studies the Insight—the understanding that all events are illusory and space-like—which is the essence of the Perfection of Wisdom.

Then, if he is able to take on the responsibility of the Vehicle of the Mantra, to carry out its vows and pledges, he should serve a master such as is described in [Aśvaghoṣa's] *Fifty Verses on the Guru*, and thus set out upon the Tantra.

If the disciple does not purify himself in this process of the path common to both types of Vehicle as we have described, he cannot disentangle himself from this life, so that his desire to practice the Law is unsteady. Since he awakens no unfeigned faith, he cannot abandon his mind in the place of refuge. Since he gains no firm certainty about karma and its effects, he is nothing but a vulgar Buddhist who neither takes nor keeps his vows. Since he awakens no disgust at this world, his prayer for liberation is meaningless talk. Since he awakens no genuine intentional thought of enlightenment whose roots are friendliness and compassion, he is a follower of the Great Vehicle in name only. Since he lacks a fervent desire to study the conduct of a Bodhisattva, he does not awaken any real tranquility. Since there comes to him no understanding of Calm or Insight, he is confused at the subtleties of deep contemplation, and he awakens no certainty in the view that there is no 'self.'

But if the disciple wishes to avoid these things, he first purifies himself in the path which is common to both types of Great Vehicle. This practice is by the great Atīśa, whose precepts mix together three streams of traditional lineage—that given to Asaṅga by the holy Maitreya, that given to Nāgārjuna by the holy Mañjughoṣa, and that of Śāntideva—and who maintained that this must be performed whether one is setting out through the gate of the Vehicle of the Mantra or the Vehicle of the Perfections.

THE RITUALIZATION OF MORAL ATTITUDES

Any society that regards magic as a real and potent force would certainly desire its magicians to possess the attitudes of renunciation and benevolence outlined above. Tibetan culture has erected a system wherein the very exercises that allow the acquisition of magical powers guarantee their proper use; and it is interesting to note how these basic attitudes are perpetuated and constantly reiterated in the contemplative rituals themselves. Not only do many rituals begin, for example, with a contemplation and recitation of Vajrasattva to purify the practitioner, but also every ritual must contain what are called the "three holy things": the "holy awakening of the thought of enlightenment during the preparations," the "holy nonobjectifiable [i.e., the contemplation of Emptiness] during the main part of the ritual," and the "holy dedication of merit at the ritual's conclusion." The first of these three is often considered the "intentional" thought of enlightenment (equivalent to the formula "I will save all beings . . ."), as opposed to the second, which is the "actual" thought of enlightenment (equivalent to the formula "I will seek only perfect enlightenment . . .")—here "real" or "actual" in the sense that it is constituted of the "absolute truth" of Emptiness. Similarly, under the first of the holy things are subsumed all the acts of homage, devotion, and benevolence which go to make up a practitioner's stock of merit, and under the second is his apprehension of the truth which makes up his stock of knowledge; these are often compared to two wings that lift him to enlightenment.

Thus far this is standard "Great Vehicle" Buddhism, but here these common elements are placed within a ritual environment, a dramatic setting that lends immediacy to what might otherwise be a mere moral abstraction. The ritual act takes on the dimensions of the entire Bodhisattva Path; in effect the actual evocation of the deity from Emptiness is performed by one who is already a true Bodhisattva, the preliminaries of the ritual being a magical simulacrum of the path itself.

Thus every ritual begins with the psychological preparation of the vivid visualization of the field of hosts, before whose eyes the practitioner goes for refuge and awakens his intentional thought of enlightenment; afterward he prays that they depart from the sky in front of him (or he visualizes that they dissolve into his body, depending upon the ritual), and he contemplates the "four immeasurables" or "abodes of Brahma" to "purify his friendliness and compassion." These are, as Tsongk'apa said, the roots of his thought of enlightenment, which he now actualizes by the dissolution of everything into Emptiness with the recitation of the mantra. All this takes place before the ritual proper begins, and the deity is thus evoked "from the realm of Emptiness" by one whose merit and knowledge have taken him to the very brink of his own divinity.

Again, the "refuge and thought" may be expanded into the "sevenfold office" whose canonical source is the Indian text *All-Beneficent's Vow of Conduct*;[65] many editions of the *Homages to the Twenty-one Tārās* also include a special sevenfold office for the goddess. The list given therein may be considered standard, though the formula varies occasionally from ritual to ritual:[66] (1) homage, (2) offerings, (3) confession of sins, (4) rejoicing in the merit of others, (5) entreaty that the deity "turn the wheel of the Law," (6) prayer that the deity not pass away into nirvāṇa, and (7) the dedication of one's own merit.[67] All these elements may perhaps be made clearer by the following table:

Holy Thing	*Thought of enlightenment*	*Stock*	*Ritual element*	
thought of enlightenment	intentional	merit	refuge "thought" / sevenfold office; four immeasurables	preliminary
nonobjectifiable	actual	knowledge	Emptiness	
			evocation	ritual proper
dedication of merit			dedication of merit	conclusion

Perhaps, too, this ritual structuring of basic Buddhist attitudes will be clarified if, before we go on, we devote several pages to a translation of the beginning of an actual evocation, composed by Anupamarakṣita:[68]

> First the practitioner arises from his bed and washes his face and feet; then, purified, he should go to a solitary, pleasing place, sprinkled with sweet scents and strewn with flowers, and there sit in a comfortable posture. In his own heart he visualizes the first of the vowels, the syllable A, which transforms into the orb of the cold-rayed moon. In the center thereof he visualizes a beautiful blue lotus flower, on whose corolla is another orb of the hare-marked moon; and upon that is the seed, a yellow syllable TĀṂ. Then hosts of light issue from the seed, the yellow syllable TĀṂ, destroying the darkness of the ignorance of beings, reaching to the farthest limits of the worldly realms in the ten directions, illuminating them for the practitioner and inviting the numberless, the countless Buddhas and Bodhisattvas who dwell therein, arraying them in the sky before him.
>
> And then he should make offerings to the loving Buddhas and Bodhisattvas who sit in the sky, with great offerings of divine flowers, incense, perfume, garlands, ointments, powders, clothing, umbrellas, flags, bells, and banners.
>
> Then he should confess his sins: "Whatever sins I have committed, caused to be committed or at whose commission I was pleased, throughout my beginningless whirling in this world—all those, each one, I confess." And having confessed each one with this ritual, he should take a vow to do them no more.
>
> Then he should rejoice at the merit of others: "I rejoice in all virtue whatever, of the Well-gone Ones, the solitary Buddhas, the disciples and the Bodhisattvas, sons of the Conqueror, and of all the world with its gods and Brahmas."

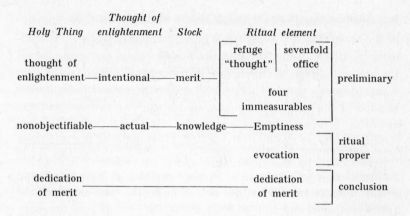

Then he should go for refuge to the Three Jewels:

Until I reach the terrace of enlightenment
I go for refuge to the Buddha,
until I reach the terrace of enlightenment
I go for refuge to the Law,
until I reach the terrace of enlightenment
I go for refuge to the Assembly.

After that he should take recourse to the path [here a variation on the thought of enlightenment]: "Let me take recourse to the path spoken by the Tathāgatas, and to no other!"

After that he should pray: "I pray the blessed Tathāgatas and their sons to remain for the sake of beings as long as this world shall last, and not to pass away into nirvāṇa."

After that he should entreat them to teach: "I pray the blessed Tathāgatas to teach the supreme Law, so that all the beings in this world may be freed from their bondage to becoming."

After that he should dedicate his merit: "Whatever merit I may have accumulated through this supreme sevenfold offering, this confession of my sins, all of it I dedicate to the attaining of complete enlightenment."

Or else the practitioner may abbreviate the above and recite these verses to represent the supreme sevenfold offering:

I confess all my sins
and rejoice with the greatest happiness at virtue;
I pray that the Blessed Ones remain forever
and teach the holy precious Law;
into the presence of the three precious Jewels
I go for refuge until I gain enlightenment;
I take recourse to this path
and dedicate to perfect enlightenment
the virtue I have gained.

With these verses he should perform the sevenfold supreme offering, and then pray that the field of hosts depart with OṂ ĀḤ HŪṂ MUḤ! Or [he may absorb them into an image, for example, thus "consecrating" it, or into himself] by reciting this verse:

Your bodies anointed with the sandalwood of morality,
clothed in the garments of meditation,
strewn with the lotus flowers of the portions of enlightenment,
remain here as long as you wish!

After that he should contemplate the four "abodes of Brahma" [the four "immeasurables"] called "friendship," "compassion," "symptahetic joy," and "equanimity"—according to the following explanations.

What, then, is "friendliness"? Its characteristic is the love that all beings have for their only son, expressing itself in providing for his welfare and happiness.

Again, what sort of thing is "compassion"? Compassion is the desire to extricate all beings from their suffering and from the causes of their suffering, the intention to extricate all those persons who have entered the iron prison of this world, which blazes with the unbearable fire of the suffering of the three sufferings. It is the wish to extricate from the ocean of this world beings who are tormented with the suffering of the three sufferings.

"Sympathetic joy" means rejoicing [in the merit and happiness of others]. Sympathetic joy is also the intention to place in unequaled Buddhahood and in the means thereof all beings now in this world. It is the mental attraction felt toward all the virtue in the world and toward the enjoyment and mastery thereof.

What is "equanimity"? Equanimity is doing good for others, for beings whether they are good or bad, disregarding motivations of repugnance or friendliness. Equanimity is devoting oneself—endeavoring through one's own inclination alone—to the natural doing of good for all others, with no feelings of love or hatred. Equanimity also is the indifference to doing anything for the sake of any of the "eight worldly things"—gain or loss, fame or disgrace, praise or blame, happiness or suffering—or similar ends.

THE RITUALIZATION OF METAPHYSICS

These ritual preliminaries have fulfilled, within a dramatic and magical context, the moral requirements of the Bodhisattva, but the practitioner must still perfect his actual thought of enlightenment—his immersion in Emptiness—before he can proceed to enter the sacred world of the ritual proper. "Those are the accumulation of one's stock of merit," says Tsongk'apa,[69] "and the contemplation of Emptiness . . . is the accumulation of one's stock of knowledge. Hence one's stock of knowledge is the contemplation of the meaning of the mantras OṂ ŚUNYATĀ-JÑĀNA-VAJRA-SVABHĀVÂTMAKO 'HAṂ! 'OṂ! I am the very self whose essence is the diamond of the knowledge of Emptiness!' and OṂ SVABHĀVA-ŚUDDHĀḤ SARVA-DHARMĀḤ SVABHĀVA-ŚUDDHO 'HAṂ! 'OṂ! Pure of essence are all events, pure of essence am I!' Here the practitioner visualizes the beings who are bound within the net of reification, and he thinks: 'Alas! These beings, by the darkness of ignorance, do not understand by themselves that they have the essence of nirvāṇa; and so I must make them understand their own essence.' And he contemplates the 'actual' thought of enlightenment." Thus Anupamarakṣita continues his ritual:

> After he has contemplated the four "abodes of Brahma," he should contemplate the perfect inherent purity of all events. He should realize that all events are perfectly and inherently pure of essence, and that he too is perfectly and inherently pure: and he establishes this perfect and inherent purity of all events with the mantra OṂ SVABHĀVA-ŚUDDHĀḤ SARVA-DHARMĀḤ SVABHĀVA-ŚUDDHO 'HAṂ! But if all events are perfectly and inherently pure, from whence is this world produced? From being obscured by the dirt of "subject" and "object" and so on. The means to the cessation thereof is the contemplation of the True Path, for thereby it ceases: it is thus that one accomplishes the apprehension that all events are perfectly and inherently pure.
>
> Then, having contemplated the perfect inherent purity of all events, he should contemplate the Emptiness of all events. Here, this Emptiness means that he should reflect upon the fact that everything, animate or inanimate, is inherently but an appearance of a wondrous non-duality upon which have been imposed mental constructions and fabrications such as "subject" and "object" and so on: and he establishes this Emptiness with the mantra OṂ ŚŪNYATA-JÑĀNA-VAJRA-SVABHĀVÂTMAKO 'HAṂ!

This mantra (which Anupamarakṣita does not explain) is held to contain within itself the most profound doctrines of the Great Vehicle, here placed again within a dramatic and magical context; these words dissolve the "construed and fabricated" universe into omnipotent Emptiness, an intense and personal actualization of the thought of enlightenment rendered all the more effective as an incantation. Tsongk'apa explains the meaning of this mantra as follows:[70]

> Therein, ŚŪNYATĀ is Emptiness: because events are free of any "essence" or "cause and effect," they are "empty" thereof. JÑĀNA ["knowledge"] is a mind of one taste with Emptiness: it is empty, unlabelable, wishless. VAJRA ["diamond"] is simply the indissolubility of the "Emptiness" of the objective world and the "knowledge" of the subjective viewer: it is "diamond" because it is unchanged by adversity, it overcomes adversity, it is beginningless and endless. These same words ["diamond of the knowledge of Emptiness"] are used, again, to describe a mind focused on the Dharma realm, which is likewise beginningless and endless, because a mind focused on Suchness takes on the form of its object. SVABHĀVA is "essence": any "essence" which is without adventitious defilement is essentially pure. ĀTMAKA is the self, and AHAṂ is "I": hence, "Any self which is essentially pure, that is I!"

But this mantra ("OṂ! I am the very self whose [intrinsically pure] essence is the diamond of the knowledge of Emptiness!") is an expression of power with connotations beyond its literal translation, and these too form a backdrop of psychological affect in its recitation. Thus, for example, Tsongk'apa goes on to interpret the mantra in terms of several basic Buddhist metaphysical formulations:

> In the syllable OṂ there are three letters, A, U and M: and these are one's own body, speech and mind: the word "self" refers to that wherein the Emptiness and the Compassion of those three are inherently a single taste.
>
> Furthermore, as it says in the *Evocation called "All-Beneficent"*:[71]
>
> Because free from any inherent nature it is empty,
> and because free from any cause it is without a label,
> because free from any imposed mental constructs,
> its substance is certainly free of all wishes.
>
> After it has explained these three "Gates of Deliverance," the text gives the above mantra and explains its meaning in terms of the quoted verse: contemplating the meaning of mantras such as ŚUNYATĀ is thus a way of contemplating the meaning of the three Gates of Deliverance. Vaidyapāda[72] says that though these are distinguished verbally as "empty," "unlabelable," and "wishless," from the absolute point of view the last two are naturally included in "empty" alone. The master Nāgārjuna says in his *Discourse on the Thought of Enlightenment*:[73]
>
> Since essenceless, it is empty. Since it is empty,
> how can it have any "label"?
> Since it is reluctant to accept any "label"
> why should a wise man make a wish?
>
> It is in conformity with this that—although they are expressed as three things—the last two are included in the Deliverance of "empty" proper.
>
> Furthermore, Vaidyapāda and Śrīphalavajra[47] explain the meaning expressed in the phrase "the essencelessness of events" in terms of freedom from constructs such as "one" or "many." Thus, while reciting the mantra, one bears in mind the correct view as to the meaning of "the essencelessness of events." To wit: first the "object" is ŚUNYATĀ and the "subject" is JÑĀNA; but then [on the third word of the mantra] one turns away from such distinctions of "subject" and "object" as are made under the sway of ignorance, and their indissolubility—like water poured into water—is VAJRA. And though it is necessary here to awaken anew [with the mantra] one's understanding that

events are thus essentially indissoluble and unfabricated, there *is* an "essence" which possesses that knowledge, which is pure, undifferentiated through "cause" or "effect," wherein one cannot distinguish a "subject" or "object": this is SVABHĀVA, and the fact that this dwells essentially in oneself, that one is never turned away from it, is the meaning of ĀTMAKA and AHAṂ.

Now the meaning of the mantra has been explained in terms of the three Gates of Deliverance; but it is also explained as the "mantra of the three diamonds." OṂ is the Diamond of Body, and "the essence which is the diamond of the knowledge of Emptiness" indicates the Diamond of Mind—there is no difficulty with this. But the reason for classifying "I am . . ." as the Diamond of Speech is that the "self," having no concrete referent, is only a verbal designation.

Furthermore in terms of the meanings of the mantra already explained, it is clear that OṂ indicates the Mirror-like Knowledge, "Emptiness" the Knowledge of Equality, "knowledge" the Intellectual Knowledge, "diamond" the Knowledge of the Carrying Out of Duty, and "essence" the Knowledge of the Purity of the Dharma realm. The last two words indicate the "self" as inherently the great Bearer of the Vajra, who is the essence of these five knowledges.

Thus it is from the "realm of Emptiness" created by this mantra that the ritual evocation of the deity takes place, and this divine generation is the beginning of the ritual proper. To whatever use this deity may be put thereafter, the ritual structure itself strives to guarantee that his sacred power will be aimed at virtue.

CONTEMPLATIVE TRAINING: RITUAL SERVICE AND INITIATION

The ritual structuring of these basic attitudes of benevolence and understanding gave the young monk the emotional and intellectual framework that would be reinforced almost continuously through his ritual career; and with these attitudes he proceeded to the actual acquisition of power, for the remainder of his period of solitary contemplation in the hermitage was spent in the ritual service of the deities whom he would later evoke and employ in his monastic and private rituals. Before he could direct the deity's power to any end, he had to render his own person a fit vessel to contain it, a requirement that involved not only the proper moral preparation and purification of the prelimary practices but also the vivid visualization of himself *as* the deity, the exchange of the deity's pride or ego for his own, and the recitation of the deity's mantra as many as ten million times. Only a god can employ a god's omnipotence, and only after this extended period of self-generation can the monk evoke the deity before him, request the magical attainments, and be capable of directing the divine power. In this connection, Tsongk'a-pa quotes the *Questions of Noble Subāhu*:[75]

> After first reciting 100,000 times according to the ritual,
> one should set out upon the actual effectuation of the mantra,
> for then one will quickly gain the magical attainments
> and by the various mantra rituals long be without misfortune.

This verse marks the distinction between the actual "*effectuation* of the mantra"—its recitation as a means of directing the deity's power—and the "*contemplation* of the mantra" which takes place during the ritual service ("100,000 times according to the ritual . . .") as a means of acquiring the capacity to direct the deity's power. "It is only after one has done the ritual service," glosses Tsongk'apa, "that one may employ the deity, evoking his functions of pacifying, increasing or destroying (to increase, for example, one's life or wisdom)."[76]

During this period a keen monk would try to get through the recitation of the mantras of as many deities as possible, each, ideally, with the appropriate visualization, beginning with those deities regularly evoked in the monastic ritual and those whom he had taken as his own personal deities, and then proceeding to those whom he might at any time in the future be called upon to evoke. An incarnate lama might have to perform the ritual service for an immense number of different deities, and by the time he was finished he would hope to be quite expert at "vivid visualization"; and any monk might well return periodically to the hermitage for the ritual service of a new deity whose initiation he had received.

Again, Tsongk'apa glosses the *Great Tantra on Proper Evocation*:[77]

> In investigating the functions and powers
> inherent in the various families,
> we will begin with the ritual service in the mantra
> which is in harmony with their respective minds.

"According to this," he says, "a wise man who has gained the proper initiations . . . and who has taken the Bodhisattva vows of the thought of enlightenment and the Tantric pledges of the mantra in their proper sequence, will first find a habitation and a friendly guide of the proper characteristics . . . and then, in short, he should perform the ritual service of the 'contemplation of the mantra.'"[78] Thus, even before the ritual service, the young monk must have received the proper initiatory authorization for each deity; it is during this period that he begins what will be a lifelong accumulation of these initiations, from his own masters, from those whom he visits on pilgrimage, and from traveling lamas who pass through his monastery. Incarnate lamas receive literally thousands of initiations, keeping a record in a special book of the date, the initiation, and the lineage of the master who bestowed it; and if a lama achieves fame in this life, his record of the traditional lineages he has acquired may be published as his "book of acquisitions" or "book of what was heard." The Longdö lama Ngagwang lozang says: "Obtaining the four initiations, dwelling in one's vows and pledges, and going through the prior ritual service—these are special doctrines of the Tantra: all of them are surely necessary."[79]

THE MONASTIC CULT AND CALENDAR

The objects of this continual attention, in the monk's private contemplations and in the assembly hall with his fellows, are generally subsumed by the Tibetans under the heading of the "Three Basic Ones," a classification that in daily life and in ritual importance supersedes even that of the "Three Jewels": these are (1) the lamas or the gurus of the lineage, (2) the high patron deities, and (3) the ḍākiṇīs, and to this list are added the "protectors of the Law," often generically called, simply, the "Lords."

The Gurus

To the Dragon Kajü, the chief of all lamas is Padmasambhava, the "Second Buddha," called most often the "Precious Guru." The tenth day is sacred to him, and on the tenth of every month there is a special "ancient" daylong ritual in his honor, the "evocation of his heart"; every year, on the tenth day of the fifth month, there begins the nine-day evocation and masked dance of the "eight earthly manifestations of the Guru."

Every ritual in the monastery begins with one or more prayers to the entire lineage of the gurus, which is either printed as part of the ritual text or recited by memory from a separately printed page, in which they are asked to empower the practitioners to the effective performance of the ritual. In K'amgargön the prayer most often recited before the rituals was written by Lord Lhak'ab Jigten lötang; known simply as "the prayer calling the gurus from a distance," it further describes itself as "the prayer to be recited at the beginning and end of the contemplative period when evoking in solitary contemplation." This prayer was recited at the beginning of every ritual the monks performed for me; and since it is of inherent aesthetic interest for its rhythmic variations, a translation is here given. The prayer begins with a section in 8-syllable meter (x́ x x́ x x́ x x́ x):

Dispelling the darkness of ignorance, glorious guru,
teaching the path of freedom, glorious guru,
saving from the waters of this world, glorious guru,
dispelling the disease of the five poisons, glorious guru,
the wish-fulfilling gem, glorious guru!

The meter then becomes 6-syllable (x́ x x́ x x́ x):

Master of all families,
head of all maṇḍalas,
pervading master of the animate and inanimate,
glorious lord of this world and of nirvāṇa,
essence of the four bodies and five knowledges,
inherent nature of the sixth Buddha, Bearer of the Vajra!

Then the prayer reverts to 8-syllable meter, but with a caesura on the fourth syllable (x́ x x́ —x́ x x́ x):

Inherent nature of unchanging Dharma-body,
inherent nature of all-pervading Dharma-body,
inherent nature of great bliss of the Dharma-body,
inherent nature of knowledge of nonduality,
inherent nature of knowledge of the Innate!

And then once again the meter becomes 6-syllable (x́ x x́ x x́ x):

The lineage of the unequaled Gampopa,
the fathers and sons of the glorious Dragons,
the gracious personal guru:
look with eyes of compassion.
Look with eyes of compassion
upon us, beclouded with the darkness of ignorance.
Look with eyes of compassion
upon us, tormented with the disease of the five poisons.
. . . upon us, who think brief life is long.
. . . upon us, with no place of refuge.
. . . upon us, unaware of approaching death.
. . . upon us, clever in the eight worldly things.

. . . upon us, attached to food and clothing.
. . . upon us, who are forgetful and confused.
. . . upon us, bound with the straps of "subject" and "object."
. . . upon us, blundering in the pit of hypocrisy.
. . . upon us, who audaciously speak what we have not heard.
. . . upon us, abandoned in space-vast heedlessness.
. . . upon us, who flee impiously from contemplation.
. . . upon us, who cannot even agree together.

Then follows one 8-syllable line (x́ x x́ x x́ x x́ x):

We have nowhere else than you to be a lord of refuge . . .

And then two 6-syllable lines (x́ x x́ x x́ x):

look with the eyes of compassion !
May our glorious holy gurus . . .

And then, finally, the meter becomes 9-syllable (x́ x x́ x x́ x x́ x x́—):

empower us, that we may free our minds of clinging to a "self,"
empower us, that in our streams we may awaken trust,
empower us, that we may cut off covetousness from within,
empower us, that now we may root out our firm attachments,
empower us, that we may be versed in the lives of our gurus,
empower us, that we may succeed as they spoke in their counsels,
empower us, that we may stroll the rugged mountains
empower us, that we may be able to evoke one-pointedly,
empower us, that we may bear aloft the banner of evocation,
empower us, that we may make the evocation our lives,
empower us, that we may evoke without hindrance,
empower us, that we may understand our True Nature,
empower us, that we may set up an encampment in nondelusion,
empower us, that we may act as friends to the unfortunate,
empower us, that we may achieve our own and others' aims,
empower us, that we may gain the highest magical attainment ![80]

In addition, the Dragon Kajü periodically perform rituals of offering to the gurus on the anniversary of the death of one of their lineage, a previous K'antrü rinpoch'e, for example, or one of his teachers. This sect is noted for the music its members play for these rituals on the oboe-like *jaling* and the large pot-shaped clay drum, a wailing and impressive dirge that echoes over the mountain in memory of a master.

The High Patron Deities

The Dragon Kajü classify the high patron deities into two major types, *general* and *particular*. The former class consists of the high

Fig. 5. The type of Heruka: Cakrasaṃvara and Vajravārāhī. From an iconographic sketch by Tendzin yongdü.

patrons of the Tantras, the deities who preside over the great Tantras of the Highest Yoga; since each sect tends to consider itself the special guardian of a particular Tantric tradition, to whose study its adherents especially devote themselves and whose lineage they take as their own, we find that the Gelug devote their rituals to Guhyasamāja, the Sacha to Hevajra, and the Kajü to Cakrasaṃvara. All the sects consider Kālacakra particularly noble and important as both a Tantra and a deity. All the Tantras of the Highest Yoga, even the minor ones, have their patron deity: Mahāmāyā, Buddhakapāla, Caturpīṭha, all of whom have a developed iconography and are depicted in art, in the huge contemplative assemblies called the "field of hosts" after the visualization they represent, but who do not enter into the monastic cult. Although there are iconographic variations among these general high patron deities, they share instantly recognizable similarities: they are all derived from the same cultic stock that produced the Indian Śiva figure; and they belong to the type of Heruka—multitudinous arms bearing attributes of power and ferocity, three-eyed faces distorted in scowls of rage, and in the sexual embrace of their naked consorts (in the special cases of being depicted alone they are called "solitary heroes"). These Herukas are perhaps the most potent and symbolically evocative of all the Tibetan deities.

The twenty-fifth day is, for the Dragon Kajü, the day of Cakrasaṃvara, and every month on that day they hold his daylong evocation: on the twenty-fifth day of the tenth month they begin the five-day ritual devoted to him.

These general high patron deities are all taken to be forms of Akṣobhya, head of the vajra family, but the Dragon Kajü arrange their *particular* high patron deities under all five families of Buddhas, according to a scheme they borrowed from the "ancient" Nyingma tradition. Each of these families has a peaceful patron—that is, the Buddha normally at the head of that family—and a fierce patron, who ranks as high as a Buddha in enlightenment but manifests himself in the same wrathful form as the "protectors of the Law." Some of these fierce patrons have, it is true, their own individual Tantras of the Highest Yoga (Yamāntaka has several) but they are distinguished from the high patrons of the Tantras by their appearance: whereas the general high patrons have Buddha faces twisted in anger, the fierce patrons have round-eyed and fearsomely lumpy faces, their fanged mouths open to reveal a curling tongue, their bodies bulging in the containment of their wrath. The arrangement of the particular high patron deities is shown below.[81]

Hayagrīva, the "horse-headed," is (like Vajrapāṇi, who is also considered a fierce patron) an Indian heritage shared by all the sects but not entering significantly into the Dragon Kajü monastic cult or its great rituals (he is evoked annually at some Gelug monasteries, and by the Mongols as their god of horses). Perhaps the most important of these high patron deities is Yamāntaka, the "Slayer of Death," worshiped by the Dragon Kajü once a year in a nine-day ritual at the beginning of the second month, as well as in the daily

family	*padma*	*vajra*	*buddha*	*ratna*	*karma*
impurity	lust	hatred	delusion	pride	envy
purity: peaceful patron	Amitābha	Akṣobhya	Vairocana	Ratna-sambhava	Amogha-siddhi
fierce patron	Hayagrīva	Yamāntaka	———	———	*Vajra-kīla
Tibetan:	Tamdrin	Shinjeshe	Ch'emch'og	Yangdag	Doje p'urpa

morning evocations, where he takes the "ancient" Nyingma from of Quicksilver, the "black poison-faced," who is three-headed and six-armed, with the bottom half of his body in the shape of a magic dagger impaling a corpse. This form of worship sets off the Dragon Kajü from their cousins the Karma Kajü, who worship Yamāntaka in the form of Black Master of Life. Both these forms of Yamāntaka are winged and solitary, and they appear to be native Tibetan developments of this divine type; but the Gelug typically evoke this deity in the canonical form of Vajrabhairava, the "diamond terrifier," with sixteen feet, thirty-four arms, and nine heads (the main head being that of a bull), embraced by his consort. This form is better known in the West than the others because of its occurence, in this and cognate forms, in Indian texts.

The remaining three fierce patrons in this arrangement are also found in another "ancient" classification, the famous "eight doctrines"[82] of the Nyingma Tantras. These consist of five classes of supramundance deities—(1) Mañjuśrī the deity of body; (2) Amitābha the deity of speech; (3) Yangdag the deity of mind; (4) Ch'emch'og the deity of quality; and (5) P'urpa the deity of function—and three classes of the mundane families: (6) the deities to bring down visitations of the *mamo* demonesses; (7) the deities of fierce mantras and maledictions; (8) the deities of worldly offerings and praise.

Among these, Yangdag, the "perfect one," is pictured by the Dragon Kajü as three-headed and six-armed. Ch'emch'og, the "most high," is considered the special fierce patron of K'amgargön, and the altar of the main temple contained a large image of him in his nine-headed and eighteen-handed form, though he occurs also with three heads

Fig. 6. The type of fierce patron: Yamāntaka in the "ancient" form of Quicksilver, the black poison-faced. From an iconographic sketch by Tendzin yongdü.

and six hands, or with twenty-five heads and forty-two hands. Perhaps the most interesting of these is Doje p'urpa, the "diamond dagger," for here we find some scattered clues to Indian antecedents for this very Tibetan deity: he has a miniscule and uninformative Tantra of his own in the canonical *Kajur* collection, and he seems to be described in passing by Nāgārjuna, in his *Short Evocation* of the maṇḍala of Guhyasamāja.[83] In Tibet, Doje p'urpa is also titled the "diamond prince": he has three heads and six arms, and in his main hands he "rolls the magic dagger" between his palms, a venerable Tibetan means of casting a curse upon an enemy. All these "ancient" deities are winged and embrace their consorts; all of them could be included, at the discretion of the head monk, in the morning evocations; and Doje p'urpa, one of the most important of them, receives an annual five-day ritual on the eighth day of the fourth month.

The Ḍakiṇīs

The ḍākas (male) and ḍākiṇīs (female) form a class of allusive and significant deities for whom Guenther appositely uses Karl Jasper's expression "ciphers of transcendence."[84] They could not be better described than by Snellgrove:[85]

Fig. 7. The type of ḍākiṇī: Vajravārāhī, the diamond sow. From an iconographic sketch by Tendzin yongdü.

Fig. 8. The "ancient" ḍākiṇī Lion-faced, the guardian of hidden texts. From an iconographic sketch by Tendzin yongdü.

> There is frequent reference to them in the tantric texts, where they appear as the partners of the yogins, flocking around them when they visit the great places of pilgrimage. Their presence was essential to the performance of the psycho-sexual rites and their activities generally are so gruesome and obscene as to earn them quite properly the name of witch. They enter Tibetan mythology in a rather more gentle aspect, and ceasing altogether to be beings of flesh and blood, they become the bestowers of mystic doctrines and bringers of divine offerings. They become the individual symbols of divine wisdom with which the meditator must mystically unite . . . although iconographically they retain their fierce and gruesome forms.

Among these ḍākiṇīs, the Dragon Kajü hold special reverence for Vajravārāhī, the "diamond sow" (or Vajrayoginī, the "diamond yogin lady"), who is the consort of Cakrasaṃvara, their high patron of the Tantras; in some Kajü monasteries she has an annual ritual on the twentieth day of the sixth month. Some Dragon Kajü, too, have conceived a devotion to Nāro K'achöma, the "celestial lady of Nāropa," although she is generally considered more of a Sacha deity; and they share with the "ancient" sect the ḍākiṇī "Lion-faced," who is for both their "guardian of hidden texts." Some, again, are devotees of Yeshe ts'oje, the Tibetan consort of Padmasambhava; the sexual partner of a great yogin, like that of a great deity (and they are often the same thing), is frequently assimilated into this class of deity, and the terms "yoginī" and "ḍākiṇī" are often used almost interchangeably. It is interesting to note here a peculiar Tibetan attitude toward women: Tibetans share the general Buddhist disapprobation of the moral character of women, and yet they add that a woman contemplative, if she is any good at all, is more often than not the superior of a man; many Dragon Kajü exhibit the deepest reverence for Machig labdrön ("the one mother, the lamp of practice"), the consort of Father Dampa sangje and the founder of the contemplative ritual of *chö*, the "cutting off" of one's body. She is pictured in art as a naked white ḍākiṇī, beating a drum and blowing a thighbone trumpet, one leg raised and turned in the posture of the yogic dance.

The Protectors of the Law

The highest of the protecting deities is called simply the "Lord," or sometimes the "Lord of Knowledge," to indicate his status as a fully enlightened Buddha and to distinguish him from the lesser oath-bound guardians who are also occasionally addressed as lords; this generic distinction is sometimes expressed as the difference between mundane and supramundane deities. One of the holiest rooms of the monastery is the house of the Lord, from which there echoes throughout the day the sound of cymbals and of the great drum (or "drum of the Law"), a large flat drum hung up in a frame and struck with two sticks. Here sits the "lama of the Lord," his texts lit only by the butter lamps on the altar, surrounded by representations of the fierce deities whose worship is his only function. The walls are covered with paintings of their offerings, skullbowls filled with blood and the flayed skins of human corpses for them to wear; their huge images dominate the altar; in the corner might be stacked piles of ancient arms long used in warfare and presented to the deities to be their weapons. Perhaps we may best approach the dark power of this room by reading of the effect it produced on the traveler Fosco Maraini, who wrote the following indignant account of its potent symbolism:[86]

> . . . a dark, crypt-chapel such as is to be found in every monastery . . . a mysterious recess, where the stink of the rancid butter of the offerings on the altars is even more sickening than usual. At the entrance are hung the decomposing bodies of bears, wild dogs, yaks, and snakes, stuffed with straw, to frighten away the evil spirits who might desire to pass the threshold. The carcasses fall to pieces, and the whole place is as disgusting as a space under a flight of stairs with us would be if it were full of rubbish covered with cobwebs, ancient umbrellas that belonged to great-grandfather, and fragments of bedraggled fur that had been worn by a dead aunt. On top of all, of course, there is the rancid butter. Pictures of the gods are painted on the walls. At first sight you would say they are demons, monsters, infernal beings. They are, however, good spirits, protectors, who assume these terrifying shapes to combat the invisible forces of evil. . . .
>
> . . . a dark, dusty pocket of stale air, stinking of rancid butter, containing greasy, skinless carcasses, with terrifying gods painted on the walls, riding monsters, wearing diadems of skulls and necklaces of human heads, and holding blood-filled skulls in their hands as cups.
>
> . . . She spoke of bones and dances, the sacred knife, the thunderbolt, of garlands of skulls, of sceptres of impaled men. In her was Tibet, the secret and untranslated Tibet; Tibet, land of exultation, beauty, and horror.

Here the lama of the Lord and his two companions sit twenty hours a day, echoing the rituals of the assembly hall; the morning evocations of the high patron deities and the afternoon worship of the protectors. Upon them falls the responsibility of continually protecting the monastery, its surrounding districts, and all sentient beings; theirs is a ritual with which all the monks have been in daily contact throughout their lives, whose importance they deeply feel and to whose service they may be appointed.

The most important of these Protectors is the Indian Mahākāla (the "great black one," a designation almost never used except when quoted from an Indian text), in all his many forms and lineages; here again the course of time allowed Tibetan sectarian influences to partition these forms, each sect considering one of Mahākāla's aspects to be its special and traditional guardian. Thus the semiofficial protecting deity of the Dragon Kajü is the Four-handed Lord, once again in contradistinction to the Karma Kajü, whose teachings are guarded by the misshapen and dwarflike Black-cloaked Lord; similarly the Sacha devote their rituals to the two-handed Lord of the Tent, bearing across his bent arms the magic stick, and the Gelug worship the Hastening Six-handed Lord of Knowledge.

Fig. 9. The type of Mahākāla: the Four-handed Lord. From an iconographic sketch by Tendzin yongdü.

The pervasive "ancient" influence upon the Dragon Kajü (as in the case of Yamāntaka) may be noted here: in the afternoon assemblies and in the "house of the Lord" they address their prayers as well to the traditional Nyingma protector, the Four-headed Lord. Indeed, the Dragon Kajü share the entire panoply of "ancient" guardians, who lie completely outside the range of the Mahākāla type and incorporate into the pantheon the native gods of Tibet. Here we find the protectress and "guardian of mantras" Ekajaṭā, the goddess "with a single plait of hair," one-eyed, one-toothed, sometimes one-breasted; the god Za, half a serpent, covered with a thousand eyes, a fierce face gaping from his belly; and Damchen Doje

Fig. 10. The "ancient" protectors: Ekajaṭā, guardian of mantras. From an iconographic sketch by Tendzin yongdü.

legpa, the "oath-bound excellent diamond," colored red and riding upon a lion, but whom the Dragon Kajü worship as black, holding a hammer and a blacksmith's bellows, crowned by a bird and riding on a snarling goat.

Ranged below these highest deities are the Five Bodies headed by Pehar, the five Long-Life Sisters, the twelve guardian goddesses of the teachings headed by the Lady of the Turquoise Lamp; the God of the Great Northern Plain and all the hosts of mountain-gods; and the protecting Father-Mother Lords of the Cemetery in the form of dancing skeletons, sometimes called "gingkara" [from Sanskrit

Fig. 11. The "ancient" protectors: Za. From an iconographic sketch by Tendzin yongdü.

kiṃkara "servant, attendant"?], a term in Tibet often abbreviated simply to "ging" and prefixed to the names of the native guardians.

These subsidiary "ancient" deities are the gods of the Tibetan earth who enter into the monastic cult of all the sects, but always, except for the Nyingma, firmly subordinated to the leadership of the Lord. These gods are worshiped daily by the Dragon Kajü, but the Lord himself comes always at the end of things: he is worshiped at the end of the day, his daylong ritual is performed on the twenty-ninth of every month, and the special nine-day evocation of his eight forms comes at the very close of the year.

Fig. 12. The "ancient" protectors: Damchen Doje legpa, the oath-bound excellent diamond. From an iconographic sketch by Tendzin yongdü.

Ranking as high as the Lord as a protecting deity is the Glorious Goddess, riding upon a mule covered with the flayed skin of her own son, adorned with skulls and the signs of ferocity. She guards the Dragon Kajü in her emaciated, four-handed form of Smoke-eater; a different four-handed form, the Self-born Lady, is propitiated by the Karma Kajü, and a two-handed form, Magic Weapon Army, by the Gelug and Sacha. Here too we may include Ekajaṭā of the ancient sect; and another Glorious Goddess, Firm Diamond Lady, is often included in this standard series as the special protectress of the teachings of Butön.

Some of this sectarian information may be tabulated as shown below. We must recognize, of course, that this sort of mechanical breakdown is not quite accurate. We have already seen that the Dragon

Fig. 13. The type of Glorious Goddess: Magic Weapon Army. From an iconographic sketch by Tendzin yongdü.

Kajü worship the Nyingma Lord and Goddess as well as their own, and this overlap is found in other sects that have had a close historical relationship. The Gelug sect grew out of the Sacha, and the important canonical triad of the high patron deities—Guhyasamāja, Cakrasaṃvara, and Vajrabhairava—is a common inheritance of both; the Sacha perform annual evocations of Mañjuvajra and Akṣobhyavajra, two deities derived from the cycle of the *Guhyasamāja Tantra,* as well as of their own general high patron Hevajra. Perhaps the sharpest difference between these two sects is that the Gelug systematically rejected those deities whose authorization was not clearly found in Indian texts; the famous Gelug reformation in Tibet was basically cultic rather than doctrinal, and it was perhaps

<table>
<tr><th>Sect</th><th></th><th>High patron of the Tantra</th><th>Yamāntaka</th><th>Lord</th><th>Goddess</th></tr>
<tr><td colspan="2">Gelug</td><td>Guhyasamāja</td><td rowspan="2">Vajrabhairava</td><td>Six-handed</td><td rowspan="2">Magic Weapon Army</td></tr>
<tr><td colspan="2">Sacha</td><td>Hevajra</td><td>Lord of the Tent</td></tr>
<tr><td rowspan="2">Kajü</td><td>Karma</td><td rowspan="2">Cakrasaṃvara</td><td>Black Master</td><td>Black-cloaked</td><td>Self-born</td></tr>
<tr><td>Dragon</td><td rowspan="2">Quicksilver</td><td>Four-handed</td><td>Smoke eater</td></tr>
<tr><td colspan="2">Nyingma</td><td></td><td>Four-headed</td><td>Ekajaṭā</td></tr>
</table>

more a canonical fundamentalism than a reformation. Thus, for example, the Sacha join the other sects in holding an annual evocation of the problematically orthodox Doje p'urpa, a practice the Gelug do not follow.

All these objects of the monastic rituals, Indian or Tibetan—the high patron deities and their consorts, the mystic ḍākiṇīs, and the fierce protectors of the Law—are the powerful deities who symbolize currents of cosmic force to be tampered with only at one's peril. They constitute the monastic cult because they are best left to the ritual experts. It is not that their cult is particularly secret, just as there is nothing esoteric about the workings of a television set; but in both instances the forces involved are too potent to be played with by a layman, and in both instances the same warning applies. The secret rituals performed only by the yogins, for example, are simply those aspects of the rituals for these deities proven by experience to be dangerous to anyone without the proper contemplative training, the ability to manipulate through one's own body the tremendous power that is thus unleashed. I told one lama of the tragic and untimely death, in an automobile accident, of Nebesky-Wojkowitz, author of a work on the cult of the Tibetan demons and protective deities. My informant just nodded wisely; he was not a bit surprised.

THE CULT OF TĀRĀ

Where, then, among these fierce and potent deities, their weapons and their sexual embraces, comes the cult of the loving Tārā? In the morning assembly, among the long series of rituals evoking the patron deities, every Kajü monastery inserts a short Four Maṇḍala Offering, a hidden text of the goddess which had been revealed in contemplation.[87] K'amgargön supported a Tārā temple where there was performed throughout the day the long Four Maṇḍala Offering to be considered later in this chapter. But the goddess has no great monastic rituals or dances; her special rituals of protection and life are enacted in the monastery or the house of a devotee only upon the request of an individual, monk or lay, who endows their performance as a thanks offering or when an emergency arises. The protection of the monastery is in the hands of the Protectors and the fierce patron deities; for an "initiation into life" there is available the full-fledged Buddha Amitāyus and his maṇḍala of nine deities,[88] or the "three deities of life" whom he heads and of whom White Tārā is but a subsidiary member.[89] Indeed, for any of the rituals considered here there are deities more ferocious, more visibly potent, and more profound in symbolic associations than Tārā.

To her devotees, however, Tārā is an abiding deity, her constant availability perhaps best symbolized by the daily repetition of her ritual rather than by any great ceremony taking place only once a year; I have seldom seen a personal altar, monk or lay, without her picture prominently displayed somewhere, though it may be surrounded by a host of representations of other deities. She is a patron deity in a second sense of the word, a personal deity rather than a monastic patron, a mother to whom her devotees can take their sorrows and on whom they can rely for help; she might appear before one in a dream or bestow other tangible signs of her favor, and many stories are told of her miraculous and spontaneous intervention in the lives of those who follow her. The popular cult of the goddess is one of trust and reverence, of self-confident reliance upon the saving capacity of the divine and upon the human capacity to set in motion the divine mechanism of protection.

THE POPULAR CULT: DRAMA

This cult is promulgated and its premises are sustained not only by an informal folktale tradition (examined in chap. ii) but also by a more formalized tradition of native drama, where wandering troupes of actors perform indigenous tales of Tārā's patronage. Indeed, one of the most popular of these masked folk dramas in central Tibet is the *Story of Nangsa öbum,*[90] an account of the trials and tribulations of one of Tārā's best-known devotees. This type of "opera" is known as *ach'e lhamo,* so named after the goddesses who are almost invariably represented therein and who must often act as deus ex machina when the plot becomes so complicated that there is no other way to resolve it. The drama is performed in the open air before enthusiastic and often vocal audiences, sung in a strangely impressive warbling chant and enlivened by ad-lib buffoonery and dance. The major part of the story is recited by a narrator (at almost unintelligible speed), with each character coming forward to sing his set speeches in a tableau, which breaks up and reforms in a new pattern to the rhythmic clash of drums and cymbals. The actual performance may take several days, depending upon the elaborations of the troupe. Following is a translation of the didactic prologue and the account of Tārā's intercession in the heroine's miraculous conception and birth.

[Narrator:]

Skilled in means, compassionate, born in the house of Śākya,
unconquerable conqueror of Mārā,
his body shining like a pile of gold:
homage to the king of the Śākyas!

In the highest dwelling of Potala,
born from the green syllable TĀṂ,
saving beings with the light of the syllable TĀṂ
homage to mother Tārā!

In the language of the gods, the serpents, and the spirits,
the languages of celestials and men,
the languages of all beings, however many there may be:
in the languages of all we will teach the Law!

Now our Teacher, skilled in means and full of compassion, had pity for all, making no distinction of near or far; and he taught 84,000 kinds of the Law, agreeable to the minds of all the different beings whom he took in hand. These are classified, briefly, under the "three stages of the Wheel of the Law."

Now for people like you or me, who do not understand these expressions of the Divine Law, he made both anecdotes and legends agreeable to a Worldly Law: among these are the Anecdotes of Ja, the Anecdotes of Re, the Anecdotes of the Monkey Alö, the Royal Anecdotes of Gesar Lord of Ling, and so on; and also the Legend of King Rāma, the Legend of Ravishing Goddess, the Legend of the Righteous King Drime künden and so on.

Among all the tales recounted in the religious commentaries on the monastic Law, the most important nowadays are those about royal gatherings and masters who save from danger, as a sample of which we offer you this portion, the Biography of Nangsa öbum, as a means to awaken avaricious people to a disgust at wordly life and to turn their minds toward the Law. Now there are many different biographies of people named Nangsa, such as Nangsa the Lady of the Land of the Gods, Nangsa with the Body of a Deer, and so on; but today we offer you a recitation, in accord with the Law, of the ancient story of how the holy ascetic, the beautiful ḍākinī Nangsa öbum took birth in a human body, and hence I pray you all listen with your undivided attention.

Now here in Tibet the parts of the country are divided among the three districts of Ngari in upper Tibet, the six districts of Amdo and K'am in lower Tibet, and the four banners of Ü and Tsang in central Tibet; and it was in this country called Nyangtö jetse, in Yaje of Tsang, the right hand banner, that there dwelt an ordinary Buddhist household called Jangp'ek'ur. Therein were both a man, named Künzang dech'en, and his wife, named Nyangts'a sedrön; and both man and wife sang the praises of Tārā of the Khadira Forest continually, all day and all night, with no greed for any gain from it.

One evening, after they had recited Tārā's mantra 100,000 times, the wife, by the strength thereof, had some exceedingly wondrous dreams, and in the following words she asked her husband about them.

[Nyangts'a Sedrön:]

Devotion and homage to Tārā of the Khadira Forest,
the active power of all the Conquerors,
the goddess who lets herself be seen!
My husband for life, ever since our destinies were ordained,
my lord Künzang dech'en: listen to me.
When I was asleep last night,
I had the most wondrous dreams:
in the Holy Realm of Turquoise Leaves,
from above a jeweled throne of blazing conch-white leaves,
from the syllable TĀṂ in the heart of Tārā
(mother of the Conquerors,
mother of the Buddhas of the three times,
protector from all terrors)
light radiated forth. It entered through the top of my head,
it traveled down the central channel, I dreamed
that it dissolved in the center of my heart.
In my body a lotus flower grew,
I dreamed that ḍākiṇis made offerings to its stem.
From all directions there gathered a host of bees;
I dreamed they were satiated with its nectar.

A dream like that must certainly be auspicious:
but I pray my husband tell me what it signifies.

[Narrator:]

When she told him this, the man was overjoyed, and he answered her in the following words.

[Künzang dech'en:]

My fair-faced wife through all my former lives,
my lady Nyangts'a sedrön: listen to me.
Although there are, indeed, false and frenzied dreams,
this one is a prophecy of the future.
The light from the syllable TĀṂ in the heart of the holy Tārā
which dissolved in the center of your heart
is a sign that within your heart dwells the blessing of Tārā,
who is the active power of all the Buddhas of the three times.
The growth of a lotus flower in your body
is a sign that this will grow into the foremost of all ḍākiṇīs.
The gathering of a host of bees from all directions
and their finding a promised treasure of nectar
are signs that she will serve the aims of beings,
all the hosts, pure and impure, whom she will take in hand
with body, speech, and mind.
Though we had no son in our youth, when our teeth were white,
we shall have a daughter in our old age, when our hair is white.
And when she is born, surely she will be better than a son,
so let us pay homage to the gods in all directions.
This dream is good, Nyangts'a sedrön;
let your mind rejoice, Künzang dech'en!

[Narrator:]

And so they made offerings upward to the Three Jewels, gave gifts downward to those in the evil destinies, and paid reverence in between to the assembly of monks; and they did so abundantly. By the power thereof a daughter was born in the Earth-Male-Horse year, in the bright half of the Month of the Monkey, during the Holiday of the Assembly of Ḍākiṇīs, the tenth day, a Thursday, when the Two Kings were in conjunction in the sky.

No sooner had she been born than she joined the palms of her hands together and, as though casting skyward a first offering of her mother's milk, she spoke the following words.

[Nangsa öbum:]

I make offering and homage to the holy Tārā,
the most excellent mother,
giving birth to the Conquerors of the three times!

I am an apparition [*nang*] for the benefit of beings;
over all the earth [*sa*] may there be grace and happiness,
may the light [*ö*] of your power shine in all directions,
may a hundred thousand [*bum*] beings be established in the Law!

[Narrator:]

And as a name for their daughter, they abbreviated these verses she had spoken; and all the people of the country, with a single voice, declared the girl's name to the Nangsa öbum.

THE POPULAR CULT: POETRY

The popular sentiments of devotion to the goddess also find expression in the praises composed in her honor, as an exercise in reverence or to commemorate her intervention on a devotee's behalf. The colophon of one such praise, for example, tells that when the author was staying in Ü, during the winter of the Water-Male-Monkey year, there arose many omens of his approaching death; so on the 15th of December he went to the Great Temple of the Four Manifestations in Lhasa,[91] and there he prayed one-pointedly before the miraculous talking image on the second story, joining to the praises and prayer he had composed the mantra AMARA-ĀYUḤ-SIDDHIR ASTU! "Let there be accomplished deathless life!" which he repeated 108,000 times. That night he had a dream about the time of dawn; in it he saw a young girl, who spoke quite clearly the following verse:

> If you visualize [the mantra] within your central channel
> and perform diamond recitation 10,000 times,
> you will surely avert untimely death . . .

As he awoke the last line faded away, and he could not remember it.[92]

These praises are often of scant literary merit from the Western point of view, being a collection of traditional epithets and a display of pyrotechnic virtuosity in the handling of stock metaphors. Frequently the verses are constructed upon an iconographic catalogue of the deity, using more or less predictable similes for each of her features, though even here poetic talent may be brought to bear on the subject, as in the following stanzas from a hymn by the fifth Dalai Lama:[93]

> Upon the orb of a moon in the center of the anthers
> of a soft and tender lotus, its petals full blown,
> the body of the goddess, sensuous, ravishing,
> mother of all the Conquerors: there I direct my prayer.

Your blazing light is embraced by a hundred thousand suns
shining upon a piled heap of powdered emerald;
your smiling face is the giver of the highest gift,
bestowing encouragement and blessing upon all beings.

The length of your eyes, spread out unscattered as a rainbow,
stretches forth with love to beings;
in a matchless grove of blue lotus flowers
dance the waving vines of your eyebrows.

Black as bees are the plaits of your hair,
falling in fine and pliant strands to your waist;
red are your lips, which smile slightly,
as though content with your forty fine-textured teeth.

Your right hand with its gift-bestowing gesture
preserves all beings from the eight terrors;
the lotus clusters held by your left thumb and finger
sway above your ear, bent with the weight of their blossoms.

Some of the works seem to be more than pious exercises in poetics, and some (which by classical Tibetan standards are rather mediocre) seem inspired by a real religious feeling. Though less embellished with classical flourishes, they manage to achieve a more immediate impact of sincerity; and though they are composed by the literate elite, they sometimes speak with the true and simple voice of a folk-song. Such a poem is the *Cry of Suffering to Tārā* by the lama Lozang tenpe jets'en:[94]

From my heart I bow to the Holy Lady, essence of compassion,
the three unerring and precious places of refuge gathered into one:
until I gain the terrace of enlightenment
I pray you grasp me with the iron hook of your compassion.

From the depth of my inmost heart and bones I pray to you
(the Three Jewels bear witness this is not just from my mouth):
think of me a little, show me your smiling face,
loving one! grant me the nectar of your voice.

Great lamas and little lamas fool us with their made-up teachings
or preach for money the Law that all things are impermanent,
knowing nothing that they claim to know,
haughty in their concern for the eight wordly things.

But since I do not turn my mind to things of this shabby age
you are the chief of my lamas:
empower me, essence of love!
show the strength of your compassion, and think of me.

If I go for refuge, no Buddha would fool me,
yet seeing the evil practices of this shabby age
most Buddhas have passed away into peaceful repose:
some may have compassion, but what can they do?

But since I have no other patron deity
you are the chief of my patron deities:
grant me the magical attainments, essence of love!
show the strength of your compassion, and think of me.

The protectors of the Law do not show their power,
despise those who evoke them, do not perform their function:
true, some wordly spirits, in pride at their ferocity,
will suffice for a while, but desert you in the end.

But since I do not turn my mind to other protectors
you are the chief of my protectors:
fulfill your function, essence of love!
show the strength of your compassion, and think of me!

The name of wealth [*nor*] is the same as its meaning [*nor* "error"]:
it produces affliction and binds to the world:
when it is time to die, unless you have True Wealth,
can a wishing gem let you carry even a sesame seed?

But since I do not turn my mind to illusory wealth
you are the chief of my wealth:
grant me my desires, essence of love!
show the strength of your compassion, and think of me.

You can't trust unvirtuous friends for even a day:
they pretend they are close to you
and all the while bear in mind the opposite:
they are friends when they wish and enemies when they don't.

But since I do not turn my mind to shabby friends
you are the chief of my friends:
be close to me, essence of love!
show the strength of your compassion, and think of me.

You are my lama, my patron, my protector,
my refuge, my dwelling, my wealth, my friends, my retinue;
since you are all things to me
let me achieve easily all that I wish.

Empower me to stop this willful mind of mine
and to awaken that compassion that does not weary
though I spend millions of lives
for the sake of each and every living being.

Empower me to root out the clinging that casts me into the world
and to understand the pure doctrine:
the deep difficult middle way
casting aside the errors of extremes.

Empower me to practice as a Bodhisattva, turned from the world,
dedicating all my virtue to the teachings and to living beings,
never for an instant thinking of my own happiness:
let me wish to attain Buddhahood for the sake of others.

Empower me to become quickly a son of the Conqueror,
able to keep the subtlest of the Conqueror's ordinances,
never to say "Oh the hell with it,"
rich with the True Wealth of faith.

Let me practice the outward rules of a Disciple
and inwardly believe in the deep Diamond Vehicle:
empower me to gain enlightenment quickly
by contemplating the path of the two Processes.

O holy Tārā! you know
everything that I have done,
my happiness and suffering, my good and evil:
then think lovingly of me, my only mother!

O holy Tārā! I give to you
myself and all who trust in me:
you are our owner: in the highest Pure Land
let us be born, set us there quickly with no births between.

With the iron hook of your compassionate skill in means
I pray you turn toward the Law the minds
of all beings, whoever they are: they have all been my mother,
the mother of one unable to follow the Conqueror's teachings.

I recite this lament at the three times of the day
and think upon the holy Tārā:
may all the beings who depend on me
be born again in the Pure Land they desire.

May the three precious Jewels
and the Holy Lady whose essence is compassion
cleave to me until I gain the terrace of enlightenment:
let me quickly conquer the realm of the four Māraṣ!

The author adds in a postscript: "If as long as you live you recite this at the three times of the day (and not just from your mouth but from the depth of your inmost heart and bones) and leave everything to Tārā, knowing that she knows all about you, just as it says, then the holy Tārā will cleave to you, and you will see her face; no obstacle will harm you, and you will gain all your desires; the Buddhas and their sons will cleave to you, because you will have pleased them. . . . This is my heartfelt belief."

THE POPULAR CULT: RITUAL

In K'am the sixth month was summer, and summer was the time for picnics. When the hills were covered with flowers and the weather was good, each village—as many as two hundred tents—would camp in a valley among the flowers and worship Tārā, thanking her for past favors and praying for future kindness. Each family set up its own tent, forming a circle around the large tent in the middle; the main tent, white with blue decorations, was for the performance of the ritual, and the smaller tents were for cooking food, for playing knucklebones and Mah-Jongg, and for reading stories. There was a space for dancing the interminable lines and circles of the K'am dances and, outside, an area where the men could race their horses and shoot at targets from horseback; inside the main tent was a circular table before the altar where the women and children piled up the flowers they had brought from the hills. For the first two days the villagers worshiped Avalokiteśvara, and then, for three to six days, they performed the ritual of the Four Maṇḍala Offering to Tārā.

There would be only a half-dozen monks performing this ritual, monks unattached to a monastery who lived permanently in the village; the rest of the tent was filled with lay people. Every day the same ritual was performed, lasting from about eight to ten o'clock in the morning, for the people could not eat meat or drink sharp liquor and sweet still beer until the performance had been completed. All the children sang and shouted together, and when each maṇḍala was offered up there was a rain of flowers as everyone threw in the air what he had gathered from the hillsides. There were no monastic strictures on this holiday; when the ritual reached a part that everyone knew, such as the *Homages to the Twenty-one Tārās*, all the people repeated it together. Then, after lunch, came the games, the races, the children wrestling and playing tug-of-war, the drinking of large quantities of beer, and the calm and gossip of the old people sitting by the tents with their prayer wheels.

THE PARADOX OF POWER

The celebration of this ritual is perhaps the most evocative expression of the Tibetans' devotion to the goddess Tārā. Yet in their devotion lies one of the basic paradoxes of the Tibetan religion: in spite of her close touch with the lives of her people, Tārā shares in the essential nature of the deities of the monastic cult. She, too, is basically alien to the human experience, ultimately "other," without personality, appearing and dispensing her miraculous favors as unapproachable and impersonal light. She, too, is a cosmic force which may be manipulated by an expert in her ritual or may be directed to one's benefit by the recitation of her mantra, the sonic reverberation of her power.

In this ritual Tārā's devotees express their love for and their personal relations with the goddess in the offerings, praises, and prayers with which they seek to "arouse her heart." They have complete confidence in the effectiveness of the ritual, fostered by their reliance upon the basic paradox of Tārā's divine nature: for she is kind and loving, ready to help them in any affliction; and the monks who perform her ritual have imbibed her power, have completed all the recitations of her ritual service, and are empowered not only to arouse her heart but also to employ her, to direct her divine energy by the impersonal recitation of her mantra.

To understand the nature of this basic duality of the Tibetan religious and devotional attitude we must first seek to understand the sort of deity who is approached and the nature of the powers that are dealt with. It is in the myths of Tārā's spiritual origins, which express the manifold and recurring manifestations of her divine essence in the remote ages of the past, that we find a valuable clue to her ritual.

THE SOURCE OF POWER

A beginningless time ago, we are told, there was a worldly realm named Various Lights, in which there appeared a Tathāgata named Sound of Drums, and to him the princess Moon of Wisdom showed great faith and devotion. For a thousand billion years she did reverence to the Buddha and the measureless host of his retinue, the Bodhisattvas and Worthy Ones, and finally she awakened the supreme thought of enlightenment. "The proper thing to do," the monks then said to the princess, "is to make an earnest wish that your body (with which you attend to the teachings) may become that of a man, for surely this desire will be granted." She replied: "Since there is no such thing as a 'man' or a 'woman' (and no such thing as a 'self' or a 'person' or 'awareness') this bondage to male and female is hollow: Oh how worldly fools delude themselves!" And this is the earnest wish she made: "Those who wish to attain supreme enlightenment in a man's body are many, but those who wish to serve the aims of beings in a woman's body are few indeed; therefore may I, until this world is emptied out, serve the aim of beings with nothing but the body of a woman."

Then the princess remained in meditation in the palace for a thousand billion years, and she thereby attained to an acknowledgment that events do not arise; she entered into the meditation called Saving All Beings, and by the power of that meditation she rescued from their worldly minds a thousand billion beings every morning and fixed them in their attainment of acceptance; and she did not eat until she had done so. Every evening she fixed therein the same number of beings, and she thus became famed as Tārā, the Savioress.

Then, in the world era called Vastly Extended, the princess took a vow in the presence of the Tathāgata Amoghasiddhi that she would protect from harm all the sentient beings throughout the numberless realms of the ten directions. She settled into the meditation called Defeating All Māras and thereby fixed in contemplative meditation ten billion billion lords of beings each day, and each night she tamed a thousand billion masters of the Heaven of Power Over the Visions of Others. Thus her name became famed as Quick One and Heroine.

Then, in the world era called Beginningless, a monk named Stainless Light was initiated by the light of great compassion of all the Tathāgatas of the ten directions, and he became the noble Avalokiteśvara. Then, initiated by the great light whose inherent nature was the superior knowledge of all the Tathāgatas of the ten directions, the two lights—of compassion and of understanding—mixed together in the manner of a father and mother and transformed into Tārā; and she, born from the heart of the noble Lord of the World, protects beings from the eight and the sixteen great terrors.[95]

These mythological renewals of Tārā's vows, her creation from initiatory light, symbolize to the Tibetans the source of her divine power, her contact with the ultimate potency of enlightenment, her literal "touching" of omnipotent Emptiness. All their deities are centers of this power, which is impelled into the present by such primordial vows, which is fed by the deities' own meditation, and which is given its final form and direction (in re-creation of its primal genesis) by a ritual. It is, ultimately, this cosmic power that is symbolized by the multitudinous arms and weapons and by the sexual embraces of the highest deities; and it is this power that the practitioner forms "from the realm of Emptiness" by the Process of Generation.

TWO WAYS OF APPROACH

The Tibetans make a broad distinction between two types of ritual approach to the utilization of this divine and primordial power. In a ritual of *evocation*, through the process of self-generation, the practitioner first applies the Process of Generation to himself: he vividly visualizes himself as the deity and grasps the divine pride or ego; he directs the power of the deity into himself and becomes, in effect, the transformer through which the divine power can pass out of the realm of knowledge and into the world of events. Thus he next generates or evokes the same deity (occasionally, a different deity) in front of him by the same Process of Generation—placing the power in the sky or within an object (a flask of pure water, say, or an amulet of protection)—and finally directs it into a ritual function or magical employment; he consciously manipulates and conducts it into an activity, into a magical device, or even, as in the betsowing of initiations, into another person. An ordinary nondivine human body, I was told, simply could not stand the pressure.

Although we note in the myths of her origin how Tārā shares in the basic potency of the divine, how little true personality she has when compared with Hindu or Greek deities, here too the attitude of worship strives to break through the wall of inhuman power, of "otherness," which surrounds her. The Four Maṇḍalas are a ritual of *offering* rather than of evocation: here there is no self-generation, no manipulation of her power through the person of the practitioner. There is no contemplation of the mantra in the practitioner's own heart during self-generation, but rather the effectuation of the mantra in the deity's heart generated "in front": the nexus of power which is the deity is given iconographic form by the ritual Process of Generation and vividly visualized before the practitioner, that the goddess may be approached, her power tapped through her mantra, and the "stream of her heart aroused" with offerings, praises, and prayers.

Yet here, too, the same preparatory requirements are set up for the performance of this ritual as for all others. It is not wholly true to say that "the faithful may appeal to her directly without the intermediary of a lama";[96] rather it is better to say that her power—born of her touching of Emptiness an impelled by her vows of love—may manifest itself spontaneously in answer to the supplication of a devotee, without the demands of conscious manipulation. But when the deity is formed and approached in ritual and her power is applied through the effectuation of her mantra, the performance requires, as we have seen, the presence of monks whose vows are unbroken, who have been duly initiated, and who have gone through the prior ritual service of the goddess. "All the Tantras and all the texts of the great magicians agree," says Yeshe jets'en, "in holding that one must have attained the power to recite the mantra and to perform the mantra rituals by being possessed of yoga—'union'—with the deity: that is, the contemplation of oneself as the holy Tārā."[97]

There is thus never a ritual of offering in isolation from the contemplative preparation of self-generation: an offering is always the delayed second half of an evocation, the first half of which was performed perhaps years before as the prior ritual service of the deity. This fact leads to some semantic level-switching: in a ritual of evocation the self-generation is often called (by analogy with the actual sequence of contemplative training) the "ritual service," and the generation in front is then called the "evocation" proper. This rather involuted terminology may perhaps be clarified by the following table:

<table>
<tr><th>Generation</th><th>Mantra</th><th>Title</th><th colspan="2">Ritual approach</th></tr>
<tr><td>self</td><td>contemplation</td><td>ritual service</td><td>↓</td><td rowspan="2">evocation</td></tr>
<tr><td>in front</td><td>effectuation</td><td>evocation</td><td>offering</td></tr>
</table>

Again we see the paradox of power controlling the functional relationship between the lay and monastic communities, for the necessity of prior ritual service, even for the worship of the deity, limits access to the magical powers of the ritual, which are available only to those able to invest the time required for the contemplative training that alone makes one fit to use them. Thus the monastery acts as a service group— a pool of ritual talent—for the lay community, and suitable recompense in the form of food, tea, and money is given to the monks for any special call upon their professional services. The relationship is reciprocal, however; the lay community demands a proportionate return on its investment in the monastery's support, and lay people are often quite concerned that the monks maintain the moral character necessary for the success of the ritual.

Within the life of the monastic community both ritual approaches play an important role: all the rituals of the afternoon assembly (that is, the prayers to the various protectors) are rituals of offering; all the rituals for the high patron deities in the morning assembly (including the short "hidden treasure" ritual for Tārā) are rituals of evocation. In addition, all the great annual ceremonies of the monastic cult are evocations; for example, the afternoon prayer to the Four-handed Lord is an offering, but his annual ritual is an evocation; and every ritual for the high patron deity Cakrasaṃvara, whether performed daily, monthly, or annually, is an evocation. There are other important and occasional rituals of offering: the offering to the gurus on death anniversaries, the offerings to the sixteen Worthy Ones on the morning of New Years' Day, and the death ritual of the "great liberation."

These two approaches to the deity often symbolize a difference in the practitioner's psychological distance from the deity's power. The rituals of evocation are more clearly soteriological or manipulatory in intent: the practitioner *is* the deity, and gains thereby godlike magical attainments to understand and control reality. The rituals of offering are performed, for the most part, to thank the deity (as a power beyond the practitioner) for favors received, or to pray for future kindness. The distance is most clear in the often quite blatant bribery and coercion of the lower oath-bound protectors; in the case of Tārā, one informant preferred the simile of a mother granting favors to a son who had pleased her.

THE CONTEMPLATIVE PROCESS

In both ritual approaches the divine power must be given form from the womb of Emptiness and directed to a specific locus; the heart and motive power of the ritual are always the contemplation of the deity, whether the practitioner is generating himself as the goddess, evoking her before him, or projecting her into an object. If contemplation is the heart of the ritual, then visualizaton is its living soul. The ability to form a vivid picture of the deity being contemplated in the ritual is the basis for all the uses to which the ritual is put and the foundation of all employment of the deity in her functions, whether to prevent hailstorms or to gain enlightenment: it is the means by which the power of the deity can be directed and the forces in the universe given shape. The ability to control "appearances" is the affirmation of the practitioner's control of reality itself. This point is worth repeating: in a universe where all events dissolve ontologically into Emptiness, the touching of Emptiness in the ritual is the re-creation of the world in actuality; where solid reality is but a fabric of constructions, the deity's ritual gestation and birth are no mere imitation of her primal genesis, but the concrete formation of a symbolically potent reality.

> How have I laboured?
> How have I not laboured
> To bring her soul to birth,
> To give these elements a name and a centre!
> She is beautiful as the sunlight, and as fluid.
> She has no name, and no place.
> How have I laboured to bring her soul into separation;
> To give her a name and her being!
> —Ezra Pound, *Ortus*

Vivid appearance

The final goals of this visualization are in general subsumed under three heads: vivid appearance, pride or ego, and recollection of purity. As one informant put it, the first is a clear mental picture, the second is one's identification with the picture, and the third is the understanding of the meaning of the picture. In one of his texts Tsongk'apa gives clear instructions for achieving the vivid appearance which is the basis for both the others. The practitioner first must contemplate the sequence of formation—the Process of Generation as given in the text of the particular ritual—until the deity is complete; but if the deity has many heads and many hands, the practitioner must begin by concentrating on the main face and the two main hands, leaving the other faces and hands as a uniform vagueness. He should make vivid in a rough way the parts of the deity's body from the top down and from the bottom up; and when he is able to see the deity formed as a whole, he should concentrate upon it one-pointedly, neither too slackly nor too tensely, but in proper moderation.

At first he should visualize only vaguely the parts given in the text which he is not deliberately making vivid, because it is harmful to his concentration to chase after them with his mind; and if the vividness fades, he must nurse it back again until the deity is once more vividly contemplated. As he practices, all the parts grow more and more vivid, until finally he should be able to form a picture of what he is deliberately making vivid and to leave unformed everything else, the picture becoming so vivid that he thinks he could not see it better with his own eyes. In order to concentrate his mind upon this vividness, he must work at it steadily throughout the entire contemplative period, free from drowsiness or distraction.

Once the deity's body has appeared in this rough way, the practitioner must practice in the same way the formation of all the subtle parts, the other faces and hands, the ornaments and so on. After that he must contemplate the deity's consort in the same way; then he adds on the other deities of the retinue; and finally he should be able to settle his mind one-pointedly on a complete and vivid formation of all the rough and subtle parts simultaneously, the entire retinue of the residential palace and all the deities who are its residents.[98]

"He should practice this contemplation from beginning to end," says Tsongk'apa in another text, "his mind not giving in to drowsiness or distraction, with great effort settling his mind one-pointedly on the object he is contemplating: because however long he may yield to drowsiness or distraction, he will gradually reach the point in his practice when, from the beginning to the end of each contemplative period, they will no longer be able to interrupt him."[99] The Longdö lama Ngagwang lozang describes drowsiness and distraction as follows: "There are two sorts of drowsiness and distraction, the coarse and the subtle; and though this designation as such does not appear in the Indian texts, it was asserted by Lozang dragpa [Tsongk'apa] in reply to a question by Lhagsam rabkar. If, he says, when one is preserving an unwavering contemplation, the details of the visualization fade a little, one has been interrupted by 'subtle drowsiness.' If the details disappear but the brightness remains, 'middling drowsiness' has come upon one. And if the brightness disappears, this is 'great drowsiness.' The defining characteristic of drowsiness is the mental fading away, while concentrating one-pointedly, of the Holy One whom the pratitioner is attempting to grasp with mental vividness. . . . Distraction, on the other hand, is a disruption, as when some pleasing image obstructs the Calm of performing the visualization, and one is bothered by things in the category of lust. Here too there are subtle and coarse types. For one's attention to be diverted someplace else while concentrating upon the object of visualization may be considered a 'subtle distraction.' For one's attention to be diverted to the extent that the visualization fades away is 'coarse distraction.' But not all diversions of attention are 'distractions' in the technical sense, because one's attention may also be diverted by hatred."[100]

The ability to achieve single-minded concentration on a vividly appearing picture is the result of long and really rather frustrating practice. We must remember—and this point should be emphasized—that the visualization is performed during a ritual; that is, the practitioner is reciting a text (which is either placed on a small table in front of him or which he has memorized), and the visualization takes place in time with the rhythmically chanted textual description of the evocation. Indeed, a good percentage of any author's corpus consists of precisely these rituals, embellished and refined according to his own contemplative and poetic skills. The reading of the ritual text in the assembly hall often goes at breakneck speed, and the vast majority of monks are unable to visualize that quickly, if indeed they are able to visualize at all. Practice in speed and accuracy came in a monk's periods of solitary contemplation, where the pace might be slowed sufficiently to allow concentration on the process of forming the deity, but there was never a break in the ritual process itself, for the solitary yogin so timed his contemplative periods that they fitted the structure of the ritual as a whole.

Speed and accuracy are both necessary, and both form the standard by which is measured the progress of one's contemplative ability. There are considered to be four states of ability in visualization. As long as a pratitioner is unable to visualize the deity so vividly that it appears to be manifestly there, even in just a rough way, he is classified as a "beginner." He becomes "one to whom a little knowledge has fallen" when he is able to visualize the entire maṇḍala of deities in a rough way and when he is able to "make it manifest in only a minute." This is just a simple visualization, however, compared with those called for in most rituals, which give the process called "deep contemplation of the subtle," here referring to the subtle deities that must be pictured in the various places of one's body, "filling one's whole body with the maṇḍala" to "empower the senses" of the divinity one has become. One of the most detailed of these visualizations—actually rather a contemplative tour de force—is found in a ritual of Guhyasamāja performed at the Tantric College at Trashilhunpo.[101] First the body is visualized as literally a divine mansion, the maṇḍala in which the practitioner (now in divine form) will array the subtle deities:

> Before and behind my body, to the right and left, are the four sides of the maṇḍala; my mouth and nose, anus and penis, are the four gates; the five-colored winds of my five knowledges—the steeds of my constructs—are the five-tiered walls; my tongue-perception is the jeweled border, my intestines the net, my sinews the half net, my portion of semen the half-moons, my eye perception the mirrors, my nose perception the flower garlands, my tongue the bells, my body the yak tails, my ear and body perceptions the flags and silken streamers on the balconies; my calves, thighs, upper and lower arms are the eight pillars, my stomach the flask within the maṇḍala, my ears the vajra-marked half-moons in the intermediate directions; my five aggregates, purified, are the five colors of the maṇḍala; my secret place, navel, heart, and tip of my nose are the four gateways, my eyes the wheels, my mind perception the deer and my nose the flags that decorate the gateways; my mind is the lotus in the middle—and in this way all the parts of my body become the various parts of the divine mansion.

The practitioner then fills this body maṇḍala with the thirty-two subtle deities, visualizing them as quickly as he reads aloud the textual description:

> From the top of my head to the hairline a white OṂ (essence of the aggregate of form) transforms into white Vairocana, adorned on his crown with Akṣobhya, his three faces white, black, and red, holding in his three right hands a wheel, a vajra, and a white lotus, and in his three left hands a bell, a gem, and a sword.
>
> From my hairline to my throat a red ĀḤ (essence of the aggregate of conception) transforms into red Amitābha, adorned on his crown with Akṣobhya, his three faces red, black, and white, holding in his three right hands a lotus, a vajra, and a wheel, and in his three left hands a lotus bell, a gem, and a sword.

From my throat to my breast a blue HŪṂ (essence of the aggregate of perception) transforms into blue Akṣobhya, adorned on his crown with Akṣobhya, his three faces black, white, and red, holding in his three right hands a vajra, a wheel, and a lotus, and in his three left hands a bell, a gem, and a sword.

From my heart to my navel a yellow SVĀ (essence of the aggregate of feeling) transforms into yellow Ratnasambhava, adorned on his crown with Akṣobhya, his three faces yellow, black, and white, holding in his three hands a gem, a vajra, and a wheel, and in his three left hands a bell, a yellow lotus, and a sword.

From my navel to my thighs a green HĀ (essence of the aggregate of motivation) transforms into green Amoghasiddhi, adorned on his crown with Akṣobhya, his three faces green, black, and white, holding in his three right hands a sword, a crossed vajra, and a wheel, and in his three left hands a bell, a green lotus, and a gem.

The visualization continues with the remaining deities: on his navel LAṂ transforms into the goddess Locanā, essence of earth; on his heart MĀṂ transforms into Māmakī, essence of water; on his throat PAṂ transforms into Pāṇḍarā, essence of fire; and on the top of his head TĀṂ transforms into Tārā, essence of wind. On his eyes, ears, nose, tongue, and penis the practitioner visualizes in the same way the five great Bodhisattvas, each arising from his "seed" and thus empowering the five senses of sight, hearing, smell, taste, and touch; and these embrace their five consorts, the Diamond Ladies of forms, sounds, smells, tastes, and tangibles. The eight fierce guardians of the maṇḍala are placed on his hands, arms, knees, mouth, and penis; his joints are Samantabhadra, his sinews are Maitreya, and his mind is Mañjuśrī.

In a ritual evocation of Cakrasaṃvara, written by Pema karpo,[102] the practitioner, after generating himself as the deity and visualizing the entire retinue of the maṇḍala about him, pictures an eight-petaled lotus in his heart on which is a "knowledge being" in the same divine form as himself, just four fingers tall; on the four petals in the four cardinal directions he visualizes the four "inner yoginīs" of the maṇḍala, and in the intermediate directions the four offerings. With the ring finger of his left hand the practitioner touches himself on the twenty-four places of his body, reciting the following syllables and visualizing them in their respective places as fast as he recites them: PUṂ JAṂ OṂ AṂ GOṂ RAṂ DEṂ MĀ KĀṂ OṂ TRIṂ KOṂ KĀṂ LAṂ KĀṂ HIṂ PREṂ GREṂ SAUṂ SUṂ NAṂ SIṂ MAṂ KUṂ. These "seeds" then dissolve into light and "in this divine pavilion of radiance" the syllables transform into the twenty-four deities of the outer circles of the maṇḍala, each visualized separately and completely in the appropriate part of the body, and each part of the body identified with a great site of Tantric pilgrimage. And the yogin further visualizes the female guardians of the gates and intermediate directions of the maṇḍala guarding the bodily orifices of his mouth, nose, penis, anus, left ear, eyes and right ear, "and his whole body is filled with the maṇḍala." Then his "empowered" body is further "armored" with more deities:

OṂ HAḤ ! On the heart of the Lord is Vajrasattva: white, having three heads (white, yellow, red), having six arms (in the three right ones grasping vajra, drum, and head of Brahma, in the three left ones bell, skull bowl, and skull staff).
NAMA HI ! On his forehead is yellow Vairocana.
SO HA HU ! On the top of his head is red Ratnasambhava.
BAU ṢA ṬA HE ! On his two shoulders is black Heruka.
HŪṂ HŪṂ HOḤ ! On his three eyes is blue Amitābha.
PHAṬ HAṂ ! On all his limbs is green Amoghasiddhi. All these have one head and four arms (the first two crossed upon their breasts, holding a bell and, respectively, wheel, jewel, vajra, lotus, and crossed vajra, the remaining two grasping a drum and a skull bowl), are adorned with the accoutrements of a ḍāka, and stand with their right legs stretched out.
OṂ BAṂ ! On the navel of the Mother is Diamond Sow: red, having three heads (red, green, yellow), having six arms (in the three right ones grasping chopper, skull staff, and iron hook, in the three left ones skull bowl, head of Brahma, and noose).
HA YOṂ ! On her heart is blue Lady Slayer-of-Death.
HRIṂ MOṂ ! On her throat is white Lady Infatuation.
HREṂ HRIṂ ! On her hair is yellow Lady Agitation.
HŪṂ HŪṂ ! On her crest is green Lady Terror.
PHAṬ PHAṬ ! On all her limbs is green Caṇḍikā. All these have one head and four arms (in the first two chopper and skull bowl, in the remaining two skull staff and drum), are adorned with the accoutrements of a ḍākiṇī, and stand with their left legs stretched out.

This, again, is visualized as fast as it is read aloud; and when the practitioner is able to visualize in all their detail all these subtle deities which are placed in the body of the rough deity, and when he is able to "make them manifest in only a minute," he has reached the third level of competence and is called "one who has gained a little power in knowledge."

I once asked a highly placed incarnate lama if he could really visualize the subtle deities. He replied that, roughly and in a general way, he could; but he added that the Toden rinpoch'e (the head of all the yogins), with more than fifty years of practice in visualization, could picture these deities in perfect detail and keep track of them all at once. This ability is, by the way, one of the reasons for the high value placed upon having a yogin present at a ritual (another is that a yogin is often a most delightful person to have around anyway): he is one of the few who are able, through long and arduous training, to do the visualizations properly, to impose his contemplative control upon the appearances of reality. An incarnate lama, too, is expected to have spent at least one of his past lives in this constant practice and, in his present life, to have the karmic equivalent of what we would call an innate talent for visualization.

Finally, when the practitioner reaches the fourth and highest level of contemplative ability he is called "one who has gained perfect power in knowledge." He has attained a complete control of appearances; not only is he able to "make manifest in only a minute all the rough and subtle bodies of the deities," but he has also "reached the very limits of his own aim, and he is able, through his contemplation alone, to serve the aim of other beings. . . . He understands the magical attainments, and he is able to accomplish the aims of countless others. . . . If he firmly places himself in Emptiness and then arises therefrom, he is able thereby to empower the appearance of anything he wishes."[103] He is, then, the owner of the universe, for the understands and is able to manipulate the very processes that create the cosmos: he can dissolve reality at will and re-create it as a divine mansion filled with deities; he can produce real effects upon ordinary appearances by the merest projection of a mental event. To know a thing is to own it, and to create it from Emptiness is to know it in its essence.

To gain such contemplative control of reality is the work of many lifetimes. The beginner learns to visualize slowly and gradually. The process is perhaps analogous to learning to play a musical instrument, the student encouraged to play difficult pieces straight through rather than devoting himself only to the most complex passages. Tsongk'apa offers the following encouraging words:[104]

> For how long a time must one contemplate before one can generate deities which appear vividly and distinctly? ... In no text which sets out the length of time one must contemplate does anyone

say that it takes more than a year. Hence, if one who has accepted his vows and pledges, and who knows enough to keep them well, puts forth an uninterrupted effort with great striving, no very great time is necessary for him to complete the vivid appearance of the deities of the maṇḍala. But if one is rubbing sticks of wood together to make a fire, yet does not do it energetically and for a long time, if he stops to take a rest in between times, then the fire will not come: this is the example that Āryaśūra used to show the necessity of working at it continuously.

This constant practice has its inevitable psychological effect. "In general," says Tsongk'apa, "the vivid appearance of *any* abject of perception is gained simply by concentrating upon that object more and more: it is thus the result of nothing but practice. As Rigpe wangch'ug says:

> When one is shaken with wishes, fears and sorrows,
> worried by thieves and dreams,
> then one will see them as if placed before one
> even though they are not there.

This means that one who has lust, for example, may concentrate his attention more and more upon the object of his lust, until he actually sees that object as clearly as if it were in front of him. . . . Thus, too, it is not necessary that one practice upon a proper object to produce its vivid appearance: for if one practice upon *any* object, whether it be perverted or not, its vivid appearance is produced naturally."[105] This awareness of the psychological dangers of uncontrolled visualization is one of the reasons for the erection of preparatory standards and for the constant insistence upon the necessity for preliminary practices, not only because the unprepared practitioner is a danger to himself, with the ever-present possibility of self-induced hallucinatory schizophrenia, but also because he presents a real threat to others, should he happen to achieve any control over reality without being morally prepared to handle his power.

Divine Ego

Not only must the practitioner visualize the deity as vividly as possible, but he must also, in any ritual of evocation (that is, whenever he generates himself as the deity), exchange for his own ordinary ego the ego of the deity, which is the subjective correlative of the exchange of ordinary appearances for the special appearance of the deity and his retinue of the maṇḍala. "In all these practices," says Tsongk'apa, "one should increasingly gain the ability to cut off one's ordinary ego through (1) the vivid appearance of the deity, and (2) the ego of the deity: and for that reason it is not enough just to concentrate on forming the deity's body, but one must also concentrate upon making firm his ego."[106] Thus the Process of Generation, he says, does two special things: it makes one abandon the ordinary appearance of the "residence and its residents," and it makes one abandon one's clinging to the ordinary ego of the "residence and its residents"; that is, the "two maṇḍalas"—the dwelling and its inhabitants—are changed from the ordinary world filled with people into a divine mansion filled with the retinue of the deity, who is the practitioner himself:[107]

> This sort of contemplation—the creation of "special appearances" as the residence and its residents, to nullify "ordinary appearances" and clinging to "ordinary ego"—is not found in the Vehicle of the Perfections, and it is thus a special doctrine of the Vehicle of the Mantra alone. According to this explanation of the Process of Generation—that it consists in the contemplation of the residence as a divine mansion and of its residents as deities—it is (1) by contemplating the "special appearance" of the residence formed as a divine mansion and of its residents formed as deities that one nullifies "ordinary appearances," and it is (2) by contemplating with complete certainly, thinking "I am Akṣobhya" or "I am Vairocana" and so on, that one nullifies one's "ordinary ego." . . . It says in many texts that "one must clear away one's ordinary ego": and thus the contemplation of the ego of the maṇḍalas of residence and residents, as an antidote to one's "ordinary ego," is the most important thing; and the contemplation of the "special appearance" of the residence and residents, to nullify "ordinary appearances," is but a subsidiary of the former.

It is only when one has first turned away from one's ordinary ego, he says, that one may exchange for it the ego of the deity. For example, at the moment the knowledge being descends into one, one casts away one's grasping of one's former essence, whatever it may been, and thinks "I am the deity!" Now this thought is artificial, a "thing of mere words," insofar as one still thinks "I am Akṣobhya, or Vairocana," and so on, as if one were still an ordinary being; it is by the gradual transformation of this artificial thought that one finally gains the special and genuine ego of the deity.[108] Elsewhere, Tsongk'apa describes the actual technique of reaching this complete identification with the deity:[109]

In the practice of "ego," one generates an ego which thinks "I am that deity," and one dwells thereon one-pointedly. If its strength should fade, one should nurse back the strength of the deity's ego as we have described previously [for "vivid appearance," above] and settle oneself therein. Doing it in this way, at first it will be but an artificial thought; but if, after contemplating it . . . the deity's ego becomes firm, he can abandon his mind therein and be able to exchange the ego of a deity for his own ego of an ordinary being, and do so throughout all of the contemplative periods, and even between them.

Of the two things—the vivid appearance of the deity and the ego of the deity—he should visualize each in turn, beginning with the former, and nurse that along. Then, if he can contemplate the "special appearance" of the residence and its residents and bear it continually in mind, if he can cast out from his mind the "ordinary appearances," so that they can no longer arise, and form the "special appearance" alone—then will his mind be purified of "ordinary appearances": and if he can exchange for his own a genuine divine ego, as we have explained above, then will his mind be purified of its clinging to his "ordinary ego." Then, arising from his deep contemplation, whatever "appearances" there may be of the animate or inanimate worlds, he sees them all as the deities and their divine mansion; his deep contemplation becomes both firm and natural, and hence he is counted as having purified, with the Process of Generation, his "ordinary appearance" and his clinging to "ordinary ego." . . .

As Āryadeva says: "If you know that all these various things are the retinue of the maṇḍala, how can you ever be confused?"

And again, Tsongk'apa says: "On these occasions, one must evoke the 'vivid appearance' of the deity, and so one must make him more and more vivid through discriminating contemplation. Here, one first performs the ritual of Generation: then, after the particular residence and its residents have been vividly visualized (but before proceeding to the recitation of the mantra) . . . one should generate as well the ego which thinks 'I am really he'—and both of these must be done. . . . This is not simply bearing in mind such aspects as the body-color, the faces and hands and so on of Vairocana or Akṣobhya, etc., taking those things to be their 'ego': but rather one must visualize oneself as *really* being a Buddha who has obtained all qualities and has exhausted all obscurations. . . . Thus if one gains the ability to root out one's 'ordinary appearances' and clinging to 'ordinary ego,' with the power to exchange them for 'special appearance' and 'special ego' from the beginning of each contemplative period until its end—then after that one must go on to settle one's mind firmly therein, gaining the power to be without any accidental relapse in body or mind. Then it is no longer necessary to do things like continually think 'I am the deity,' for once one has generated a genuine divine ego he is able thereby to cut off his ordinary ego entirely. For example, suppose someone has fallen to a non-human destiny: though his mind is troubled thereby, he does not impose upon his experience the mental construct 'I am a non-human'; but rather, as long as he experiences his karma, the concept 'Once I was a human' simply does not arise."[110]

We may easily see the soteriological thrust of this evocation: the practitioner acquires a divine ego, the total cessation of any merely human personality, accompanied by the actual re-creation of the world as a divine mansion for his dwelling. Even in those rituals of evocation whose intent is manipulatory, wherein the power of the deity is applied to specific, even worldly, ends (as when the practitioner visualizes, say, a person whom he wishes to subjugate as bound naked before him, to be dominated by the mantra), we find the introductory phrase, "Having grasped the ego of the deity . . ." The permanent acquisition of this ego during the lengthy self-generation in the deity's prior ritual service is a prerequisite to following this instruction, and possession of this ego is necessary for the magical manipulation of the divine power before one: to exercise a godlike power over reality, one must indeed be a god. To quote Tsongk'apa one more time:[111]

> When one grasps the maṇḍalas of residence and residents and the ego thereof, then one is able to exchange that ego for one's own, as explained above, as long as there are no accidental relapses. And when one vividly visualizes those two maṇḍalas—visualizing their "vivid appearance" as vividly as one can, and thereby nullifying the "ordinary appearance" of one's True Mind—one effectively nullifies both "ordinary appearances" and clinging to "ordinary ego." But it is insufficient for one merely to be able to nullify those for a little while; it is necessary that this be made quite firm. And when a Diamond Master (who has properly performed his prior ritual service by a method such as this) performs for example a protection ritual against hindering demons . . . he genuinely generates the deity and his ego when he recites "Glorious Vajradhara . . ." If he has not done so, he gains an ego of mere words, and hence it is said that prior ritual service is of the utmost importance.

Recollection of Purity

A practitioner who can thus form, at will, these special appearances and special ego is in conscious control of both his external and internal reality: the world he lives in is one of his own choosing, one that he owns. There is a further contemplative exercise to reinforce the symbolic potency of this new reality, called the "recollection of purity," which is a meditation upon the implicit meaning of the divine image the practitioner has vividly visualized and upon the ontological values of his new identity. In some contemplative rituals the recollection of purity is performed immediately after the vivid appearance and before the exchange of egos, while in others it is performed last of the three. The symbolic interpretations of the deity whom the practitioner has become are often rather farfetched and obviously after the fact; and the same interpretations are often applied to different deities, since Buddhist philosophy is so fond of numerical lists that it can easily provide a meaning for anything that can be enumerated. But the contemplative exercise is an antidote to any reification of the visualized deity; the practitioner is reminded that he has become not a thing but an expression, that his new set of appearances, ontologically just as false or as real as his old set, is at least meaningful symbolically in a way that his old reality, "fabricated and construed," could not have been, and he is provided by its very artificiality with a clue to the source of all appearances and a mechanism for understanding their genesis. Thus it is a recollection of *purity*: the visualization is pure of any construct of reality imposed upon it, just as all the events of his ordinary appearances were pure, could they have been understood as the "Innate Union of appearance and Emptiness." Every alternate reality—ordinary or divine—is meaningful only insofar as it is Empty; otherwise there could be no interpenetration of meaning, and hence there could be no magic.

As an example of this type of meditation, Nāgārjuna gives the following "explanation of the complete purity of the visualization":[112]

> The single face of the Chief Lady is the understanding of all events as a single knowledge. The green color of her body is power in all functions. Her two hands are the understanding of the two truths: her right hand the conventional truth, her left hand the absolute truth. Her right foot stretched out is the abandonment of all the defects of Māra; her left foot drawn back is the understanding of all qualities. Her adornment with all ornaments is the

> completion of the stocks of merit and knowledge. . . . Her right hand in the gift-bestowing gesture is the completion of the Perfection of Charity; her left hand in the protection gesture is the guarding of all beings from terror. Her holding the lotus flower is the giving of joy to all beings. Her being sixteen years of age is the ability to accomplish the aims of all beings. Her throne of the orb of the moon is the possession of Wisdom, and her throne of a varicolored lotus is the possession of an essence of Compassion.

THE CONTEMPLATIVE REALITY

This symbolic reality is rendered even more potent by the process of its creation, the way in which the divine power is given form and directed toward an end. It is the power of the deity which after all is evoked from the realm of Emptiness by the Process of Generation; it is a divine reality the practitioner creates, and into which he gives himself birth.

Even more striking is the assertion that the yogin not only creates his own reality but also imposes it at will upon others, that his ability to control the universe extends also to the appearances perceived by other people: he may make himself appear invisible, or beautiful, to them; he may subjugate or destroy simply by visualizing the effect he wishes to bring about; he may generate a person or a demon into an effigy and destroy it utterly. Here is a present danger in uncontrolled contemplation, and the texts are full of warnings of the dreadful fate of practitioners who misuse their power; but here too the social benefits are clear, for a practitioner may exercise his reality-creating power, for example, to trick a demon into thinking that a "substitute" or "ransom" is—that is, "appears as"—the real object of his malevolence. The yogin can change the weather, remove spiritual hindrances from his followers, and spread virtue among his people. So potent is the visualization of a great yogin that he may appear to his disciples as the very deity whose vivid appearance and ego he has grasped. This happens especially, we are told, during initiations, where the yogin first generates himself as the deity before transmitting the divine power to his followers. In his autobiography, Mila repa gives the following account of his departure from the home of his guru Marpa:[113]

> My guru said to his wife: "Damema, set out the food and the excellent offerings upon the altar. Mila is about to go now, and I have given him my permission."

My Mother laid out the offerings to the gurus and high patron deities, the tormas for the ḍākiṇīs and protectors of the Law, and the excellent feast for my Diamond Brothers. And before the assembly my guru appeared as the high patron deities Hevajra, Cakrasaṃvara, and Guhyasamāja, as their emblems (vajra, bell, wheel, gem, lotus, sword, and so on), as the syllables OṂ ĀḤ HŪṂ, white, red, and blue, as a drop of brilliant light, and finally disappeared altogether.

These many things Marpa showed, and he said: "These things I have formed are called magical transformations of the body. They must never be shown on a spirit of falsehood; but I have shown them now as a parting gift for Mila repa."

Having seen my guru as the Buddha in actuality, I felt immeasurable joy, and I thought that I too must obtain through contemplation magic power such as his. My guru said: "My son, did you see? Did you believe?" And I replied: "I saw, and I could not help but believe; and I thought that I too must do likewise through my contemplation."

He said: "My son, that is good. And now you may go. I have shown you that all events are illusory; so do you experience likewise, adhering to the rocky wastes, the snowy ranges, and the solitary forests. . . . In these places make evocation your foremost aim."

. . . And with tears flowing down he said: "My son, we two shall not meet again in this life. I shall not forget you; do not forget me. If you do as I have said, surely we will meet again in the celestial realms."

The Construction of Reality

This concept—that the yogin's imagination can create not only nonempirical states of mind but also nonempirical states of reality —is so startling to our own presuppositions that we might well examine briefly some of the cultural axioms upon which it is based. Here I propose three models to aid our understanding, based on Western concepts of schizophrenia, surrealism, and alchemy.

It wad Freud who brought into the mainstream of psychological thought the idea of the reality of what philosophers had long called the "imagination," a theory that dominated philosophical thinking until about 1935, that the imagination is a realizing faculty, "images tending of themselves to impose on us and presenting themselves as real"[114]—"real" insofar as they have real effects upon the person, but not "real" as acting in the world. The presumption is always that reality as perceived is somehow hard or solid—a metaphor for "public"—and that the imagination functions only to produce private images. "The mentally ill," one author typically says, "are for the most part people who are living in the realm where ideas have the value of reality."[115] Studies in psychedelic "imagination" have tended to affirm this presumption even while doubting it:[116]

> The perceptual changes were not changes in perception of the external world but rather changes in the quality of internal imagery. *Imagery*, however, is too mild a word for the *S*s experiences, as it connotes something less intense than perception of external qualities, less "real," yet for the *S*s their internal perceptions were in no way less real or less vivid than their ordinary sense-perceptions. They were also much more vivid and real than their usual imagery. Further, the "sensory" qualities of the internal imagery were often *more* vivid than ordinary sense perceptions.

A schizophrenic, it is felt, creates a reality, much as does the yogin, but it is a personal reality of terror and exclusion, unshared and therefore imaginary. R. D. Laing reports how a patient named James evoked a magical universe:[117]

> His "self", as it was only partially real-ized even in and through relationship with others who shared his views, became more and more caught up in, and itself a part of, the world of magic. The objects of phantasy or imagination obey magical laws; they have magical relationships, not real relationships. When the "self" becomes more and more a participant in phantasy relationships, less and less a participant in real relationships, in doing so it loses its own reality. It becomes, like the objects to which it is related, a magical phantom. One implication of this is that, for such a "self," everything and anything becomes possible, unqualified, as even every wish must be sooner or later, by reality, necessity, the conditioned and finite. If this is not so, the "self" can be anyone, be anywhere, and live at any time. With James this was coming to be the case. "In imagination" the conviction was growing and gathering of having phantastic powers.

In a very real sense, it is in this world of magical omnipotence and private freedom that a Tibetan practitioner lives; he is the master of a divine reality created by his own imagination. Even on this level, however, where psychologist and yogin agree on the privacy of the experience, there is a difference. The yogin goes forth to add a reality to his repertoire of awareness; he does not create one universe in frightened retreat from another. For the schizophrenic, says Laing, omnipotence is based on impotence, freedom operates in a vacuum, and activity is without life.

Piece by piece I seem
to re-enter the world: I first begin

a small, fixed dot, I still can see
that old myself, a darkblue thumbtack

pushed into the scenes,
a hard little head protruding

from the pointillist's buzz and bloom.
After a time the dot

begins to ooze. Certain heats
melt it.

Now I was hurriedly

blurring into ranges
of burnt red, burning green,

whole biographies swam up and
swallowed me . . .

Till, wolfed almost to shreds,
I learned to make myself

unappetizing. Scaly as a dried bulb
thrown into a cellar

I used myself, let nothing use me . . .
—Adrienne Rich, *33*

This poem sets forth an experience that is a remarkable parallel, as we shall see, to the Process of Generation; as Tsongk'apa said, the creation of such a reality is "natural" when one is "shaken with wishes, fears and sorrows, worried by thieves and dreams." Here again we see the primary importance of the ritualization of moral attitudes for the Tibetan contemplative: the imagination that evokes a universe belongs to one who is already a Bodhisattva, who has awakened the thought of enlightenment for the benefit of all beings, and who creates his magical reality from a realm that is not only empty and unlabelable but also "wishless." The yogin consciously bases his magical power upon his understanding and hence upon his control of himself and his reality; the schizophrenic's power is based not on control but on chaos:[118]

> . . . when the "centre" fails to hold [writes Laing], neither self-experience nor body-experience can retain identity, integrity, cohesiveness, or vitality, and the individual becomes precipitated into a condition the end result of which we suggested could best be described as a state of "chaotic nonentity."

The yogin, indeed, undergoes a tremendous alteration in "self-experience" and "body-experience"; he alters appearances to gain a divine body and a divine ego, yet he is always under the hold of a controlling "centre." But to the contemplatively unprepared, to those not impelled by the impetus of avowed moral purpose, the very power of the mind over reality is a naked helplessness, as the body disintegrates before the devouring imagination:

> The anchored mind
> screwed into me
> by the sky's
> psycho-lascivious
> thrust
> is the one that imagines
> all temptations
> all desires
> all inhibitions
> —Antonin Artaud, *Artaud le Momo*[119]

In such an altêred state of awareness, perception becomes non-empirical; hard reality softens and dissolves, to become, in Adrienne Rich's words, "trenchant in motion as an eel, solid as a cabbage-head." To many psychologists, this is the result of a confusion of categories:[120]

> One of Bychowski's patients, when asked where her husband was, answered that he was on the wedding picture. Here the realm of reality and the realm of representation are not kept apart. The facility of the schizophrenic in separating the realms of reality and imagination is notoriously impaired. Contrary to so-called normal thinking, which has to keep within the same realm or frame of reference or universe of discourse, the thinking of the schizophrenic is subject to little determining influence from the unitary field.

Here the realms of reality and imagination are axiomatically taken as separate fields, and here the psychologist and the yogin part company. A Tibetan finds it a strange axiom to say that a public reality is necessarily more real than a private one, or even to presume a priori that there is a boundary between the two. Public reality is as amenable to magical control as private reality; the basis for control is ownership, and the foundation of ownership is understanding: to know a thing is to possess it, and to possess it is to be able to manipulate it. "Emptiness" is the magic word that names the essence of the universe; again, as in many magical traditions, to name a thing by its true name—the secret essence of the thing—is to own it, and to understand how public reality evolves from Emptiness into awareness or perception is to be free of its bonds of ordinary causality, to be free, in Buddhist terms, of "being." This public reality is to the yogin experientially and literally a nonreality wherein all events are illusory; it is just as true and just as false as the reality he himself can evoke from Emptiness, in the same way as public nonreality is evoked into awareness by the action of karma. As is said in the *Hevajra Tantra* [II.ii.46-51]:

With the very portion of poison which slays all others
he who knows the essence of poison removes poison . . . .
With the same savage karma which binds all others
he who has the Means is freed from the bonds of being.
The world is bound by passion, and by passion it is freed:
renegade Buddhists do not know this reverse contemplation.

Indeed, the Cartesian dualism that is the psychologists' maxim has not been unchallenged even in the West: it was a disciple of Freud named André Breton who (as Spinoza to Descartes) took the imagination from the realm of the totally subjective and began to break once again the ontological boundaries between the image and the object. In his *First Surrealist Manifesto*[121] Breton wrote: "Perhaps the imagination is on the verge of recovering its rights. If the depths of our minds conceal strange forces capable of augmenting or conquering those on the surface, it is in our greatest interest to capture them." Five years later, in the *Second Surrealist Manifesto*, he again talked of the imagination, the "vital and highest faculty of the mind," as the illuminator and not the falsifier of reality, as the unveiler of hidden zones: "Imagination alone," he writes, "makes me realize what *can be* . . ."[122]

We would give you kingdoms vast and strange
where the mystery in flowers gives itself to those who pluck it
there are new fires of colors never seen
a thousand mysterious phantoms
which we must say are real

—Guillaume Apollinaire, *Calligrammes*[123]

"Reality, then," says Breton's biographer Anna Balakian, "in its dynamic sense proceeding from an interior state, nurtured by what we call imagination, and brought to an exterior existence, . . . is what Breton calls the 'surreal,' in a sense that it has no connection with the *unreal*."[124] And thus, too, the image is no private illusion, but rather may be "real-ized" in the artistic object: "the imaginary," in Breton's definition, "is what tends to become real."[125] And Paul Eluard says:[126] "Images are, images live, and everything becomes image. They were long mistaken for illusions because they were restricted, were made to undergo the test of reality, an insensitive and dead reality."

Thus to Breton, expanding upon Freud and Bergson, the imagination is an omnipotent power that, dwelling within the mental depths, must be brought to the surface through the dream, through free association, through automatic writing, and through madness itself; and the image, once surfaced, is thrust into the reality with all the shock and clash of a dream revelation. Reality to the surrealist becomes, in Eluard's words, "alive, and perpetually moving"; it becomes "nonempirical." Eluard wrote in *The Surrealist Revolution*: "The dream alone entrusts to man all his rights to freedom. Thanks to the dream, the meaning of death is no longer mysterious, and the meaning of life becomes unimportant."[127] Breton's friend Robert Desnos could fall into a state of dreaming at the slightest provocation and produce a rich flow of verbal images for his admiring colleagues. Salvador Dali intentionally cultivated his sense of paranoia, crystallizing "the unbridled force of his mind to contract an infinite number of free associations between objects, and through the representation of these he was to suggest a totally fluid universe shaped according to the artist's private speculations."[128]

It throws a sharp metaphorical light upon the world of the Tibetan yogin to say that he lives in this totally fluid surrealist universe, that his visualization creates a surrealist imaginary landscape projected upon the very fabric of reality; his private realm of freedom and power is indeed an echo of Breton's rhetorical question, "What if everything in the Beyond is actually here, now, in the present, with us?"[129] Ferdinand Alquié might well be describing the Tibetans: "They admit, then, more or less explicitly, the postulates of this conception: identity of sensation and image, proper existence of images, power of actualization inherent in the image."[130]

This provocative surrealist model, however, gives only a limited analogue for the total collapse of the boundary between the public and private universes. What the surrealists call their "magic" indeed increases the repertoire of awareness, adding the imaginary to the objective at the same ontological level. But where the surrealist image is thrust upon a reality already given in experience, the Tibetan yogin sees the complete and absolute interpenetration of the two unitary fields. His image and his object are not superimposed, but rather are primordially one, and this is what makes possible his magical ability to manipulate the universe.

Nevertheless, it was in the Western magical tradition that the surrealists found one of their most fruitful sources of ideas. The omnipotence of the controlled imagination is a central concept in both magic and alchemy, where the boundaries blur even more dramatically, and "the *vis imaginativa* is nearly always present, for it is the fundamental, central force, and the others are usually used only as aids to heightening it or ways of communicating it."[131] From this tradition the concept of the *vera imaginatio* entered into the occult "underground," to surface occasionally in such diverse persons as Aleister Crowley ("the wickedest man in England"), William Butler Yeats, and André Breton himself, who had read the thirteenth-century alchemist Raymond Lulle and was deeply unfluenced by Eliphas Lévi, the 19th-century visionary and magus of "transcendental magic":[132]

> Among the antinomies, the major one that Lévi attacks is the antithesis between spiritual and material; to him it is merely a matter of degree of opacity or of light; "Spiritual and corporeal are simply terms which express the degrees of unity or density in substance." Man has in him the power to transform the opaque into the translucent; Eliphas Lévi defines this power as *imagination*. "To imagine is to see" (*Donner à voir* will reiterate the surrealist!), and to see is to crystallize, to render *diaphane* or "transparent"; that is, imagination is not the creator of illusion, but the illuminator of reality. "Imagination, in effect, is like the soul's eye; therein forms are outlined and preserved; thereby we behold the reflections of the invisible world; it is the glass of visions and the apparatus of magical life."

Lévi is here rendering in its typically materialist terms a concept that had been molded by some of the major figures of the Renaissance. To the magician Giordano Bruno, writes Frances Yates, "this magically animated imagination is the 'sole gate to all internal affections and the link of links.' Bruno's language is excited and obscure as he expounds this, to him, central mystery, the conditioning of the imagination in such a way as to draw into the personality spiritual and demonic forces which will unlock its inner powers."[133]

But this "imagination" of the magus works outwardly as well as inwardly, and these "spiritual and demonic forces" are moved beyond the magician's mind. Sendivogius, whose alchemical work is included in the *Musaeum hermeticum*, writes:

> To cause things hidden in the shadow to appear, and to take away the shadow from them, this is permitted to the intelligent philosopher by God through nature. . . . All these things happen, and the eyes of common men do not see them, but the eyes of the mind and of the imagination perceive them with true and truest vision.

"Matter," says C. G. Jung, "is thus formed by illusion, which is necessarily that of the alchemist. This illusion might well be the *vera imaginatio* possessed of 'informing' power."[134] Note that matter is formed by illusion—a magical and creative power—rather than by hallucination; reality, in the alchemical art, is controlled by the true imagination. Martin Ruland, in his *Lexicon alchemiae*, defines this *imaginatio* as "the star in man, the celestial or supercelestial body," and Jung again comments: "This astounding definition throws quite a special light on the fantasy processes associated with the *opus*. We have to conceive of these processes not as the immaterial phantoms we readily take fantasy-pictures to be, but as something corporeal. . . . The *imaginatio*, or act of imagining, is thus a physical activity that can be fitted into the cycle of material changes, that brings these about."[135]

Alkindi, author of the *Theoria artis magicae*, explains these material effects by supposing that the imagination has "rays" similar to those of the stars and operating in the same way upon reality, to impress on an external object an image conceived in the imagination, where such images have an "actual" existence. Pico della Mirandola, in an indirect attack upon Ficino's "spiritual magic," denies the existence of such rays; he says the only things that can be projected outside a man are the "corporeal spirits," which the soul uses as instruments. But he never questions their power over reality; if some strong desire leads to these spirits being emitted, he says, they may produce an external effect: ". . . . anger may result in fascination [evil eye] and hence a disease. But these effects can be produced only at a very short distance and in suitably receptive material." Daniel Walker (from whose excellent work I have borrowed this discussion) summarizes Pico's attack by saying: "From the weakness of his arguments one can see that his rejection of natural magic is based, not on disbelief in its possibility, but on the feeling that it is somehow threatening to Christianity."[136]

Cornelius Agrippa, perhaps the greatest encyclopedist of Renaissance magic, gives in his *De occulta philosophia* many instances of the magic power of the imagination:[137]

> Our soul causes much through faith: a firm confidence, an intent vigilance, and a resolute devotion . . . lend strength to the Work which we would accomplish. We must, therefore, for every work, for each application to any object, express a powerful desire, flex our imagination, and have the most confident trust and the firmest belief, for this contributes immensely to success.

Agrippa quotes the Muslim philosopher Avicenna as believing that "a man could fell a camel, if he but demanded it with his imagination"; and Marsilio Ficino—leader of the Florentine Academy, translator of Plato, and one of the founders of the Renaissance magical tradition—expressed a similar idea in his *Tractatus de viribus imaginationis*: " . . . through the active imagination a distant rider can be made to fall from his horse and tumble into a well."[138] And again, Fabio Paolini borrowed this Agrippan notion and explained it in Renaissance terminology: "Some people assert that the feelings and conceptions of our souls can by the force of our imagination be rendered volatile and corporeal . . . and will obey us in whatever we want."[139]

This concept of the omnipotence of the imagination occupies a central place even in the writings of those thinkers who attacked the entire magical tradition. Thomas Erastus gives a detailed refutation of "the possibility of producing transitive effects by the power of the imagination conveyed in emissions of spirit." Like Freud he accepts the reality of subjective effects, both psychological ones and the more ordinary psychosomatic ones. But, as he says, "certainly no man in his right mind will think that an image fashioned in the spirit of my fantasy can go out of my brain and get into the head of another man."[140] Yet even so outspoken a critic as Francis Bacon believed in some of the magic of the imagination, and he suggested an experiment to prove it, described by Daniel Walker as follows: "If, for example, you wish to cure a sick gentleman by faith, first pick out one of his servants who is naturally very credulous; while the gentleman is asleep, hand the servant some harmless concoction and tell him that it will cure his master within a certain space of time. The spirits of the servant, made receptive by his complete faith in your medical powers, will be powerfully stamped with the image of this future cure; they will flow out and similarly stamp the spirits of his master, also in a state of receptivity because he is asleep. Thus the cure will be effected." This shows clearly, Walker concludes, that Bacon still believed in at least this ingredient of Ficinian magic, the traditional doctrine of the magical power of the imagination fortified by credulity.[141]

The point to be noted in all these arguments is the materialist presuppositions of the authors; whether they accept or reject the effectiveness of magic, they do not spiritualize the universe so much as render the spirit corporeal. The yogin shares with the Renaissance magus a self-conscious and literate tradition, a sense of system in metaphysics, and a belief in magic, but where the magus breaks the boundary between image and object by hypostatizing the image, the yogin breaks the boundary by dereifying the object, systemically emptying every description of its reference to a real entity. Nāgārjuna applies this process of metaphysical "emptying" to every concept of "real existence"—and hence to every concept of "real nonexistence" wherever it is found; space, time, motion, causality, persons, and events can have existence neither predicated of them nor denied them. Thus public reality—the arising, abiding, and perishing of events—neither exists nor nonexists: it is "like an illusion, a dream, a fairy city in the sky."[142] Vasubandhu, building upon and in many ways systematizing this tradition, says that the "awareness" of this public reality is the "construction of a nonreality": it neither exists in the way it seems, since it is only an appearance where it seems a fact, nor does it nonexist, "since it occurs at least as a phantasy." But then, continues Vasubandhu, why not say that this nonreality simply does not exist? Because beings are bound by it; if it were not real then "there could be neither bondage nor liberation, and we would fall into the error of denying both defilement and purity."[143]

Thus public reality and the divine image, a magical illusion and a dream, have no real existence, but they all occur and have real effects, and hence have no real nonexistence. The Tibetan yogin takes this ontology as his axiom: the public object and the contemplative image coalesce into an "Innate Union of appearance and Emptiness" to which predication is irrelevant. Control of one realm is control of the other; the physical events of the ritual serve as a magical simulacrum for the spiritual path, and the private images of the contemplation govern the appearances of the world. The divine reality and the public nonreality interpenetrate at every point, and both magic and salvation are made possible by the same premise: "There is not the slightest difference between this world and nirvāṇa," says Nāgārjuna. "The limit of nirvāṇa is the limit of the world: not the subtlest something is ever found between them."[144]

The Construction of Nonreality

The Buddhist philosophers in India had long made an axiom of the "softness" of reality and given an ontological status to the omnipotence of the imagination: it devolved upon them to explain not why imagery is private but rather why reality is public. Much of Buddhist "ontological psychology" is an attempt to explain in historical terms why we make a systemic epistemological error in our apprehension of the world, why we attribute to it a solidity that in fact it does not possess. In answering these questions, the philosophers planted many of the seeds that would flower in the Tantric manipulations of reality; they asserted the possibility and provided a model, but the Tantrics built a contemplative technique upon the structures of earlier meditation and gave it a new symbolic potency and the means of magic. "Mysticism has not the patience to wait for God's revelation," wrote Kierkegaard in his journal; if we should ever be forced to attempt a definition of "Tantra," we would say that it is a technique for magically storming the gates of Buddhahood.

In the broadest sense, magic is the manipulation of a distant object through control of a simulacrum that is in some way associated with it, whether by name, resemblance, or attribution. As Anthony Wallace says:[145]

> Simulation, then, is an almost universally used religious device. It supposedly produces an effect that would have been impossible to attain by applying energy directly to the object itself, since the object may be distant in space or time, inaccessible in a supernatural realm, or otherwise invulnerable to natural manipulation.

Perhaps the shortest expression of the magical axiom is found in the celebrated "Emerald Table" or *Tabula smaragdina* ascribed to

Hermes or the Egyptian Thoth; earlier known versions of this expression of alchemical dogma are in Arabic, says Holmyard, and it has been well known since the early Middle Ages in a Latin rendering. Here we read: "True it is, without falsehood, certain and most true: that which is above is like to that which is below, and that which is below is like to that which is above, to accomplish the miracles of one thing."[146] By manipulating events below, the magician can control the course of events above. Francis Yates tells of one ritual based on this axiom:[147]

> We know that Campanella actually practised this magic at Rome in 1628 for Pope Urban VIII who was afraid of some eclipses which his enemies . . . had prophesied would cause his death. Campanella did magic with him to ward off the evil. They sealed a room against the outside air, hung it with white cloths, and burned certain herbs in it. Two lamps (*luminaria*) and five torches were lit, representing the planets, and the signs of the zodiac were imitated in some way "for this is a philosophical procedure, not superstitious as the vulgar think." There was Jovial and Venereal music; stones, plants, colours belonging to the good planets were used, and they drank astrologically distilled liquors.

Campanella tells us that his lights imitate the planets not only in their number but also in their substance, "for both of them are fiery." Again, Daniel Walker gives Campanella's directions for dealing with dangerous comets: "You will not only simulate, within the room, the heavens, with the planets and signs of the zodiac, but you will also add a simulacrum of the comet, made out of aërial, medicated material, so that this will usefully shine for you."[148]

This then is the magical axiom upon which the Tantras are founded, a corollary of their metaphysical axiom. The "effigies" and the "substitutes" of the Tibetan protective rituals are magical simulacra, and the vivid appearance of the visualized image is a simulacrum for both public reality and for the deity himself: to control the image is to control the object. In Tantric soteriology the divine body is a simulacrum for the cosmos; mind, breath, and semen are homologized to one another and to the forces that create and destroy the universe. This is the reason for the lengthy "tables of correspondences" in the Tantric writings: just as a Western astrologer mediates the influence of the planets through manipulation of their corresponding colors, minerals, and plants, the Tantric seeks in the world and in himself as many interconnections as he can find, and the yogin's body is the magical simulacrum not only of the deity he has become but also of truth, bliss, freedom, creation, and dissolution. As the *Hevajra Tantra* says [I.i.12]:

> Great knowledge abides in the body,
> free of all constructs:
> it is the pervader of all things,
> but though abiding in the body it is not born of the body.

The aim of all contemplative manipulation is the power to control the mind, the breath, the universe. Power is the key, and the source of power is the deity; just as the yogin may use his vivid visualization as a simulacrum for events, he uses it as a simulacrum for knowledge. To create and become the deity is to "own" the deity in one's person, to be master even of the deity's enlightenment. And it is, finally, only as a ramification of this divine power—built up through constant contemplative feedback, growing in each contemplative period—that the yogin is able to control the appearances of *all* his realities; he must first be a god to act with the power of a god, for only the deity has the understanding of reality which grants omnipotence.

Here too we see the central place of the mantra in Tantric practice: "visualization and recitation" form an irreducible unity of magical technique, for the mantra too is the divine power, crystallized into its sonic image. Tantra is thus the "quick path" whereon control is synonymous with power; to control the divine appearance, mantra, and ego is to act with the deity's body, speech, and mind, and to control the mind and body is to own the world.

Thus the evolution of reality is of great importance to the Tantric: his contemplation will be its magical reenactment, a simulacrum for the entire world of being; he will dwell in a realm where the world is a divine mansion filled with gods, where effigies are persons, where a lotus is a stage to enlightenment, where a web of colored threads is a gateway to paradise. And the correspondences we see between the philosophical theory and the contemplative evocation form for the yogin himself the magical substratum for this total interpenetration of the human and the divine.

The most authoritative description of the appearance of the world from primordial Emptiness is found in a short text called *On Distinguishing the Extremes from the Middle*,[149] written by Maitreya and/or Asaṅga and commented upon by Asaṅga's half brother

Vasubandhu. Here, the process by which the phenomenal world evolves as perception or awareness from the seeds planted by karma is called *abhūtaparikalpa*—literally, the "construction of a nonreality" or, less literally, the "imposition of false constructs." By this process the constructs of subject and object are imposed upon Emptiness, but the process is itself no more an entity than what it produces: it "has the characteristic of both existing and nonexisting." Asaṅga writes:

> The construction of a nonreality occurs;
> duality is not found therein.
> But Emptiness is found in it,
> and it is found in Emptiness.

To construct a nonreality, says Vasubandhu, is to construe awareness as being bifurcated into a subject and an object, but, when freed from this dualism, the same nonreality is Emptiness. He quotes from Asaṅga's work, *Stage of the Bodhisattva*: "When something does not exist someplace, one sees truly that it is 'empty' with regard to it; and when something remains there, one knows that it is really there."[150] When nonreality is emptied of subject and object, what remains—what is "really there"—is Emptiness. Thus the metaphysical axiom of public reality is reasserted: nonreality exists, since it occurs, but it nonexists as a duality; everything is determined to be neither one-sidedly real nor one-sidedly unreal. And this, says Asaṅga, is the Middle Way.

Given the ontological status of nonreality, karmically impelled awareness hypostatizes the appearance of duality and obscures—"defiles"—the substratum of Emptiness. If the Emptiness of events were not defiled, says Vasubandhu, then all beings would be liberated even without effort; but if events were not Empty—if there were no "purity"—then any undertaking for the sake of liberation would be fruitless, for we would all be bound implacably by the causal chains of nonreality.

Thus awareness takes place, evolving psychologically in eight forms, the first six of which are (1-5) the five sense perceptions and (6) mental perception—the perception of mental events such as dreams and memories, and the faculty of discrimination and attention with regard to the sensory input of the five senses. These may be diagramed as follows:

internal	external	
Awareness	*Sense*	*Field or object*
(1) eye perception	sight	forms
(2) ear perception	hearing	sounds
(3) nose perception	smell	smells
(4) mouth perception	taste	tastes
(5) body perception	touch	tangibles
(6) mental perception ←	mind	mental events

To these six are added (7) the "defiled mind," the mind as defiled by the delusion of self, that is, the false self with which we identify and which seems to lie behind and appraise the processes of mental perception; and (8) the "underlying awareness," the karmic continuum that "contains all seeds" and from which the seeds ripen into awareness and become perceptions in nonreality; as is said in the *Laṅkâvatāra Sūtra* [X.871]:

> All thoughts evolve from the "underlying"
> like waves from the ocean:
> they are all caused by the impressions of karma
> and are born in accord with conditions.

Thus the first seven awarenesses are called "evolutes," since they evolve from the "underlying" and function only to receive the data it supplies them. It is of this underlying awareness in the most general sense—as the source and totality of all perceptual experience—that Asaṅga says: "Awareness arises in the appearance of external objects, living beings, selves, and sense-data." Thus it is nothing but awareness itself that appears externally to be things and persons, and internally to be a self in receipt of sense-data. But "these do not exist with reference to it: and because they nonexist it does not exist either." These appearances are mere projections of duality upon defiled Emptiness: they do not exist with reference to their supposed perception because things and persons, which appear to be "out there," are nothing but awareness itself; they are subjective, and the subject—the self and its sense-data—is illusory. "Because its objects do not exist," says Vasubandhu, "the subject—the awareness—does not exist either." And so Asaṅga concludes: "Thus awareness is demonstrated to be the construction of a nonreality."

In the simplest way, then, nonreality begins from an awareness and evolves as follows:

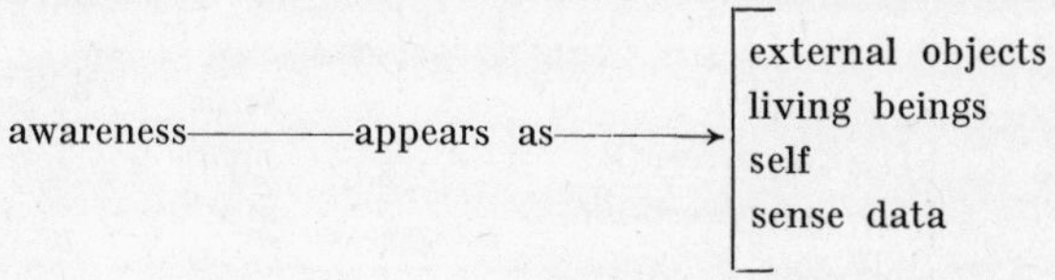

This basic scheme is expanded upon in various ways. According to Vasubandhu, this unqualified awareness, in the construction of its nonreality, simply bifurcates into objects grasped (external objects and living beings) and the subject who grasps them (self and sense-data). He further identifies external objects as the six sense fields, and living beings with the five external senses; the term "self," he says, refers to the mind (both as the internal sense and as defiled), and "sense-data" refers to the six perceptions:

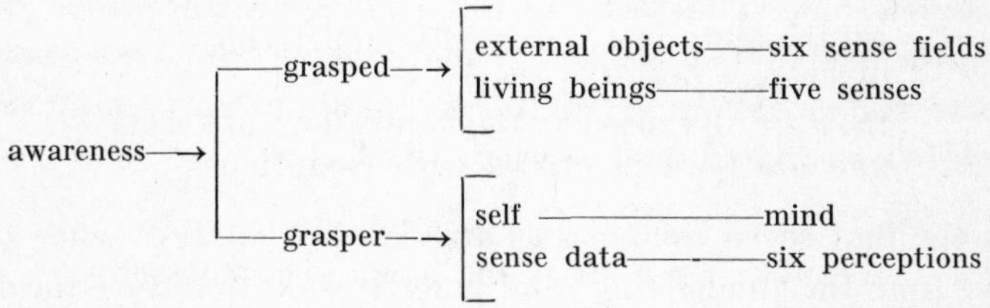

The table of perceptual events (p. 96) thus unfolds from awareness itself, and from this single projection of duality we can then assert that (within the realm of nonreality) a living being with its self comes in contact with an external object and the sense-data it supplies: that is, externally, that a living being (the senses) is in contact with an external object (the sense fields) or, internally, that a self (the mind as perceiver of sensory input and as "false self") is receiving sense-data (perceptions).

An alternative and philosophically more complex scheme is proposed by the commentator Sthiramati. Here it is not just an unqualified awareness that appears in nonreality, but rather all eight awarenesses manifest particular classes of events in the world. Here, too, the defiled mind includes the four defilements of reification of self, delusion of self, pride of self, and love of self (or, sometimes, the six defilements of lust, hatred, pride, ignorance, reification, and doubt). Sthiramati incorporates these into his scheme of the appearances of awareness:

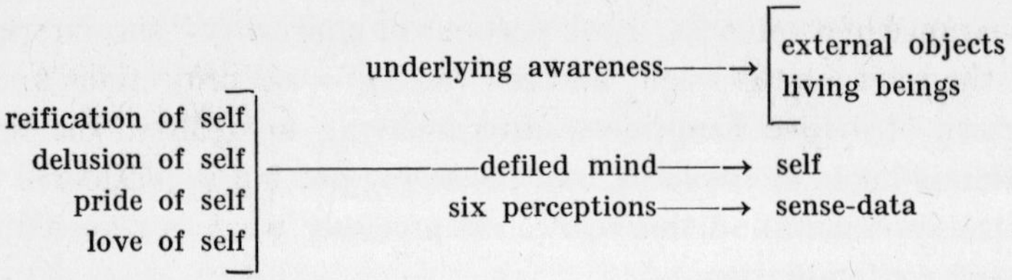

In this scheme it is the underlying awareness that appears externally to be things and persons, or objects grasped; but these, again, have no real existence apart from the fact of their perception by the other seven awarenesses that appear internally to be a self and sense-data, the subject who grasps them. This theory leads to a certain lack of parsimony, for all four appearances arise from their own seeds, which are contained within the underlying awareness; Sthiramati must thus make at least a pedagogical distinction between two sorts of underlying awareness: on one level as one of the eight awarenesses, and on another level as including all eight within itself.

A further elaboration is found in another text by the same author Maitreya and/or Asaṅga, called *Adornment of the Sūtras of the Great Vehicle.* Here we find the following verse [XI.40]:

> The construction of a nonreality
> appears in three kinds and again in three kinds
> characterized as grasped and grasper . . .

Here appearances are expanded to six, as opposed to the four of the first text. This rather casual reference to "three kinds of grasped" and "three kinds of grasper" is commented upon by both Vasubandhu and Sthiramati, who give slightly different terminologies for these six appearances, with Vasubandhu again deriving them from the primary bifurcation of a single awareness and Sthiramati seeing them as manifestations of the eight:

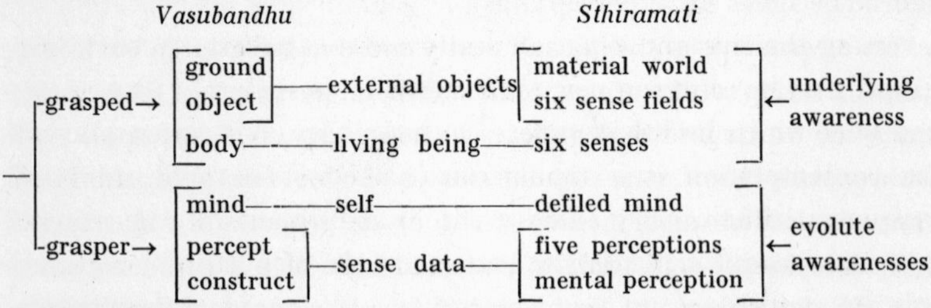

All these elaborations are simply more detailed accounts of the same process: the construction of public nonreality as the dualistic appearance of awareness. Both portions of nonreality—the external and the internal, the "sign" and the "seeing"—are projections upon a screen of defiled Emptiness. In perceiving nonreality, the sign portion is taken as the basis, and the seeing portion is considered to be its expression; and this relation is precisely what is reversed in Tantric contemplation.

The Buddhist Tantras inherited and developed this image of reversal from the preexisting and general yogic cultus; in the Indic vernaculars of their mystic songs, these yogins called their contemplations *ujāna* "going against the current," or *ulṭā* "regressive." Even today, in Bengal, the Bāuls sing of themselves:[151]

> The feeler of feeling, the lover of love,
> his rites and his path are reversed;
> who knows what he will do next?

In this yogic tradition, says Mircea Eliade, contemplation is a complete reversal of human behavior; the yogin subjects himself to petrified immobility, rhythmic breathing and the stoppage of breath, fixing of the flowing mind, the "arrest" and even the "return" of semen: "On every level of human experience, he does the *opposite* of what life demands that he do." This "return," this "regression" implies destruction of the cosmos and hence "emergence from time," entrance into immortality. And immortality, says Eliade, cannot be gained except by arresting manifestation: "The symbolism of the 'opposite' indicates both the post-mortem condition and the condition of divinity. . . . The 'reversal' of normal behavior sets the yogin outside of life."[152]

But here we see the Buddhist Tantric carrying his inherited symbolism into the world of events by the reality of his contemplative image; he reverses the process by which the world appears, and he becomes its master. Thus the yogin begins his evocation by reversing the entropy of karma and dissolving nonreality back into Emptiness; he creates a new reality that he possesses in its essence, and over which he has complete control. The vivid appearance of the contemplation is a simulacrum both for the appearance of awareness in nonreality and for the divine appearance in reality: here the seeing portion is the basis, and the sign portion becomes only its expression. In this new reality—this world of the "Innate Union of appearance and Emptiness"—the yogin is master, and he can control it as he will.

THE PROCESS OF GENERATION

It is into this realm of contemplative reality that the yogin magically manifests the divine power: he controls the unfolding of the divine appearance in reality just as he controls the appearances of events in nonreality, by manipulating the magical simulacrum of his visualization.

Let us say that a great yogin wishes to perform a magical operation in public nonreality, to subjugate, for example, an evil king or a fierce and troublesome demon. He makes an effigy of wax and "generates" it as the person to be subjugated: that is, he dissolves the object contemplatively into Emptiness, and contemplatively recreates it as a visualized image. Into this effigy he then summons the awareness of the victim, in the form of a small syllable A colored bright red: he threads a copper needle with red thread spun by a young maiden, and with this he draws forward the person to be subjugated, "sewing" the syllable into the womb of the effigy; and he "binds" him therein, piercing it with iron hooks of light and fettering it with a brilliant noose. While he is visualizing this he recites the mantra OṂ KURUKULLE HRĪḤ such-and-such a person VAŚAṂ KURU "Subjugate" HOḤ ! ĀKARṢAYA "Sumon" HRĪḤ SVĀHĀ ! The practitioner takes the effigy at dusk and torments it over a fire of khadira wood, holding it over the flames and letting it melt and trickle into them, all the while reciting the mantra. Then he takes the effigy and tramples it underfoot; no sooner does he do so than the victim is subjugated.[153]

There can be no doubt about the magical nature and intent of this operation, but what makes it work is the visualization, which creates the magical link not only between victim and effigy but also between effigy and yogin. It is one thing to play violent games with a wax doll and another to possess the effigy, to control it absolutely. To subjugate the effigy is to subjugate the person, but such power of manipulation belongs only to its true owner. There are thus three basic steps in the contemplative sequence: (1) The effigy is generated as the victim, "known" in essential Emptiness and thus truly pliant to the yogin's control; the wax object becomes but the expression of this contemplative image, and its manipulation but the bodily acting out of a contemplative drama. (2) Into this receptacle created for him is summoned the real victim—his awareness—using as simulacrum the visualized syllable; here is forged the link with public nonreality, and the victim, like the effigy, is converted from inaccessible object to malleable image. (3) Finally these images—the "real-ization" and the coalescence of the two objects—are bound into a unity, an image/object to be manipulated in any way the yogin may wish; this unity of contemplative "appearance and Emptiness" thus exists in two realms simultaneously, to produce its effects in bifurcated nonreality.

The ritual Process of Generation similarly takes the divine power as object, to be controlled in and through its vivid image, and to sanctify this new reality with its appearance; it manifests itself as the blossoming of the seed syllable after the "construed and fabricated" universe is dissolved into Emptiness by the mantra, and it unfolds in four stages:

1) The divine power is given form and shape as the *symbolic being*, the projection upon the ultimate fabric of reality of the practitioner's own visualization; this is, in the words of Tsongk'apa "the body of the deity adorned with faces and hands, whose real nature is as an 'appearance' of one's own mind, a making vivid of one's ordinary ego."[154]

2) It *empowers the senses* of the visualized deity, radiating forth upon it as the power of body, speech, and mind, crystallizing as the syllables OM ĀḤ HŪṂ on head, throat, and heart; in more complex rituals, this may include any of the different sorts of "body maṇḍala," the "deep contemplation of the subtle deities" which fills the body of the visualization—its senses, "aggregates," organs, and orifices—with the entire divine host of the maṇḍala, and may further "put on armor" of still more empowering deities.

3) Into the receptacle thus prepared for it, the divine power descends in actuality from its natural abode of the Dharma realm, compelled by the visualization of its appearance and often greeted with offerings and praise; this is the "real" deity, the *knowledge being*, who is dissolved into the symbolic being with the four hand gestures in figure 14 and the mantra JAḤ HŪṂ BAṂ HOḤ to summon, absorb, bind, and dissolve it therein: and at this very instant the yogin casts off his ordinary ego and grasps the ego of the god. "If one makes the knowledge being enter in," says Tsongk'apa, "his eyes and so on are mixed inseparably with the eyes and so on of the symbolic being, down to their very atoms: and one should firmly visualize their total equality."[155]

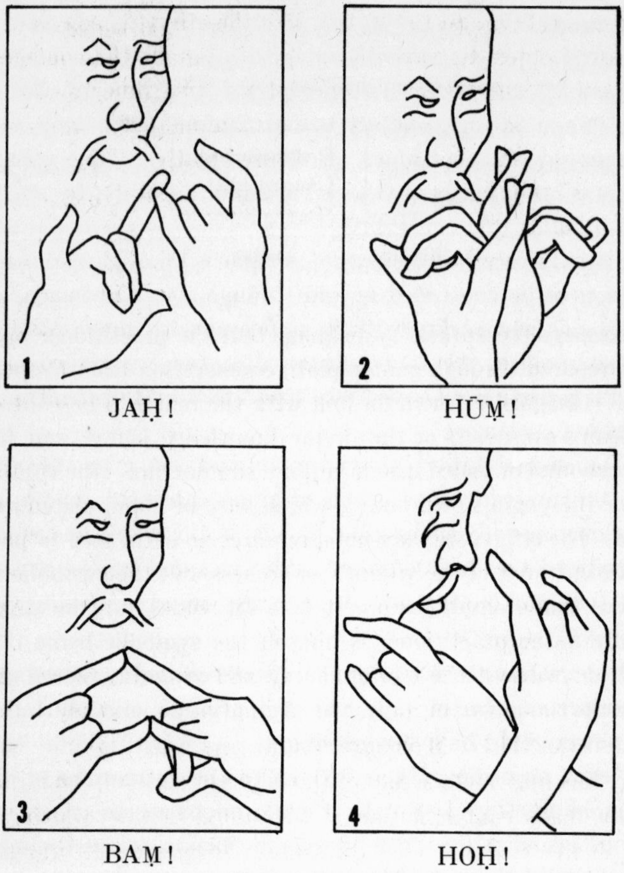

Fig. 14. The mantras and the gestures that (1) summon, (2) absorb, (3) bind, and (4) dissolve the knowledge being.

4) This power is finally "sealed" into a unitary simulacrum by the deity's own ritual initiation by the five families of Buddhas. Again, Tsongk'apa says: "Once the knowledge being has been absorbed, there is the initiation. . . . Here a stream of water whose essence is the thought of enlightenment (in most cases from a flask but occasionally from within a skull-bowl) is said to be bestowed, and with that water of knowledge all defilements and propensities thereto are washed away: therefore the initiatic liquid takes its place upon the head, and so 'seals' the deity."[156]

We may see the structural correspondences between the effigy and the deity below:

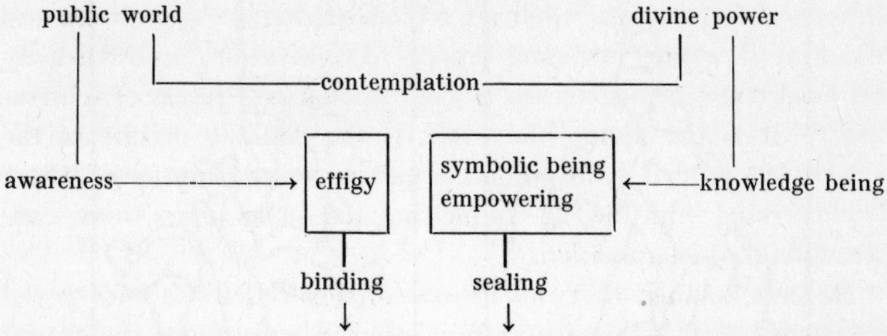

In both cases a "receptacle"—an image that the practitioner possesses—is prepared through contemplative generation from Emptiness; into this is magically drawn the link with the realm to be controlled, the victim's awareness or the divine knowledge being; and finally these are bound or sealed into a unitary simulacrum—the completed effigy or the yogin's own body—which may be manipulated toward any end. The effigy, we may note, requires no extra step to prepare it for the entrance of the victim's awareness, but the symbolic being must be "empowered" before it is a fit vessel for the divinity, especially if the practitioner is himself the symbolic being in self-generation; without the strengthening and armoring of the senses, the simultaneous casting away of ordinary ego and the influx of divine power could be overwhelming.

Now even an ordinary man, driven to the extremities of desire, might mold an effigy and make it work, might coerce events with a fortuitous visualization. But the yogin "firmly grasps the appearance and ego of the deity," and this control guarantees his success; it is the deity himself who manipulates the effigy and links it to the victim. A fallible magic is available to everyone; an unfailing magic belongs only to one who has gone through the prior ritual service and has acquired the power of the god. And it is this same process of feedback—this growing control and power—which allows the yogin gradually to coerce the divine appearance itself with ever greater assurance, to be himself more of a god each time he evokes the god.

It is, after all, only this divine presence that sanctifies the yogin's contemplative reality; we must distinguish the Process of Generation—the evocation of the divine, at whatever locus—from the simple generation of the effigy as the victim, or the mere creation of vivid appearance in lust or hatred. Thus Tenpe nyima[157] says that to know appearances to be without truth is the "illusory

Process of Generation," their miraculous arising as "appearance and Emptiness" is the "profound Process of Generation," and the body of the deity with his consort is the "emanative Process of Generation." It is the divine body that is the defining feature of the entire technique; it is the unique "appearance and Emptiness" which is manifested from the Bliss of melting and which arises from "construction and examination."

He says, further, that this Process of Generation has four special properties that distinguish it from other visualizations: the special property of its ritual is its completeness as a means of generation as found in the Tantras; the special property of its result for the practitioner is his ability to put forth the strength of the mantra; the special property of its nature is its essence of Emptiness and Bliss; and the special property of its function is its completeness in cleansing, perfecting, and ripening.

In other words, this process is a special type of generation whose magical correspondences reverberate far beyond the limited aims of the effigy; it creates a simulacrum of divinity in the yogin's own body, which speaks with the divine power of the mantra, which shares in the Bliss of the Dharma realm, which controls in the very process of its formation both the stages on the path to Buddhahood and the ultimate events of public nonreality: birth, death, and the intermediate state of the *bardo*. The body of the deity, the Bodhisattva Stages, the impelling processes of karma—all these are magically the same, and to control one is to have power over all.

To make clear the four steps of the ritual sequence, I give an example of one of its briefest and simplest forms, part of a little daily ritual for White Tārā written by the Gentle Lord Lodrö t'aye, the Kongtrü rinpoch'e (1813-1899). Here we may see one of the advantages of beginning from the rituals of Tārā, for in their lack of elaboration they provide us with a basic model for the more complex rituals of the monastic cult:[158]

The yoga of generation:

1) OṂ ŚŪNYATĀ-JÑANA-VAJRA-SVABHĀVĀTMAKO 'HAṂ!

> From the sound of HŪṂ, innate prowess of Emptiness,
> a diamond circle of protection. Therein a crystal
> divine mansion. In the middle a white lotus above a moon.
> From TAṂ a white utpala flower marked with TĀṂ.

Light radiates, serves the aim of beings,
is gathered back, and transforms
into myself the noble Tārā, color of the moon,
calm, smiling, sensuous, radiating five-colored light . . .

2) On the three places of my body OṂ ĀḤ HŪṂ. By their light

3) the knowledge being—VAJRASAMĀJAḤ!
JAḤ HŪṂ BAṂ HOḤ!—dissolves inseparably.

4) Again light radiates, inviting the five families.
I pray the initiation deities initiate me!
By this prayer the initiation deities say:
OṂ SARVA-TATHĀGATA-ABHIṢEKATA-SAMAYA-ŚRĪYE
HŪṂ!
"OṂ The glory of the vow of initiation of all the Tathāgatas HŪṂ!"
They initiate me, the water fills my body,
I am adorned on my crest by Amitābha, lord of the family.

This Process of Generation may take place at any locus: the practitioner himself (as here), in front of him, or within an object. The generations that take place in front are perhaps easiest to understand, for the contemplative events unfold before one like images on a movie screen; the closest analogy might be an abstract cinema by Jordan Belson.[159] The constant unfolding and motion of images, too, make of visualization what can only be described as an aesthetic experience, a ballet of light and form charged with meaning and power. The self-generation is rather more difficult to apprehend, as there is not (or should not be) anyone there to watch it; the yogin himself has disappeared in Emptiness, and the images simply occur entirely delocalized. We are used to being at a particular place, and we tend to situate ourselves somewhere in our head, behind our eyes; when the yogin generates himself as the deity, he is no longer there.

But whatever the locus, the visualization is the same. As the practitioner recites the text above, there appears a dance of light, a ballet of images unfolding and moving, which is patterned as follows:

1) From the "realm of Emptiness" there appears a circle of protection and a divine mansion, more or less elaborated according to the ritual. In the midst thereof appears the syllable PAM which transforms into a lotus; upon this is the syllable A which transforms into a flat moon disk, laid down upon the lotus to form a "throne."

Above this appears the syllable TĀM which transforms into Tārā's *emblem*, the lotus flower, marked again with TĀṂ, the *seed* of Tārā, which will blossom into the deity. Thus from the syllable light radiates forth in all directions, making offerings to the Noble Ones and purifying the defilements of the entire world. The light gathers back into the syllable, and at that instant the emblem and seed transform into the *perfected body* of the goddess.

2) Upon the top of Tārā's head appears a white OṂ, the power of body; upon her throat a red ĀḤ, the power of speech; and upon her heart a blue HŪṂ, the power of mind. Again, the different rituals may elaborate upon this in various ways, but finally there appears a green TĀṂ in the center of her heart.

3) From this syllable light radiates forth and summons the knowledge being from its natural abode; it appears in the sky with VAJRASAMĀJAḤ "Diamond gathering!" and dissolves into the deity with JAḤ HŪṂ BAṂ HOḤ!

4) Again light radiates forth from the syllable TĀṂ in her heart, inviting the five Buddhas and their retinue; they pour from their flasks a stream of liquid nectar upon her head, filling her entire body, and the overflowing excess forms on her crown the "sealing" figure of Amitābha.

This basic scheme may be embellished and refined in various ways, extended with incidental verses of offering, praises, and prayer to the diverse deities who appear in the visualization. But the four steps of the Process of Generation, here given so succinctly, are the fundamental sequence of all evocations of the divine, a pattern that is invariable, however much obscured by detail or by compression; as such these steps have received much theoretical attention and have been organized and labeled in various ways.

An early schematization of this process is found in the *Guhyasamāja Tantra*, where it is called the "four limbs of approach and evocation." Later commentators applied this terminology especially to the Father Tantras, and to the rituals of the Guhyasamāja cycle in particular, occasionally disagreeing on particulars of correlation; but with some alternation from the idiosyncrasy of these rituals it is often used to schematize the Process of Generation wherever it is found, and it is applied to the evocations of Tārā (see pp. 445-446). Thus the *Guhyasamāja Tantra* says:[159a]

In all the Tantras of yoga
ever praised by yogins
the ritual of *approach* is first,
near evocation is second,
evocation too is third
and *great evocation* is fourth.

Elsewhere the *Guhyasamāja Tantra* elaborates upon each of these "four limbs," and we read:[160]

1) To apply the meditation of *approach*
one should contemplate the highest enlightenment.

Candrakīrti, in his commentary *The Illumining Lamp*,[161] explains this term as follows: "Approach: it is practiced by those who desire liberation, and so it is called an 'approach' thereto." And Tsongk'a-pa glosses this:[162]

> Hence "approach" is the thought of enlightenment taking Emptiness as its contemplative object: and since one fixes one's mind one-pointedly thereon, the verse calls it a "meditation." Thus "highest enlightenment" is the actual enlightenment which comes about through examining the meaning of the ŚŪNYATĀ mantra: to contemplate this is to "approach." . . . "Approach" is thus considered the generation of the symbolic being.

Next is "empowering the senses" of the visualized deity, and the *Guhyasamāja Tantra* says:

2) In *near evocation*, the highest attainment,
one examines the Diamond Senses.

Here the empowered symbolic being, says Candrakīrti, is the deity called the Ritual Manifestation, the body now "perfect" in power: and Buddhajñāna says:[163]

> "Near" means "close": it means "close to the Great Manifestation," and refers to the first [the symbolic] Lord, who is "near" to the absolute purity of the Great Manifestation.

Empowering the symbolic being brings it near to the knowledge being and prepares it for the entry of the real deity, the Great Manifestation of the divine power in contemplative reality. Thus Tsongk'apa says:

> The "place" to which it is "near" is the completely pure divine body, called the "body of knowledge," the Great Manifestation. What is "near" thereto is the body of the first Lord.

In the verse, he explains, "Diamond" refers to the deities of the maṇḍala, and "Senses" to the "aggregates" and places of the body whereon they are arrayed: these are "examined" because they are placed on the visualized deity "through knowing the causes and effects of arraying the body maṇḍala."

Then the knowledge being is summoned, and the *Guhyasamāja Tantra* says:

> 3) By contemplating the Lord of the mantra
> during *evocation* he is said to be impelled.

The knowledge being is "impelled" into the Ritual Manifestation of the empowered symbolic being: "Evocation," says Tsongk'apa, "is the evocation of the body of the Great Manifestation." Here the "three gates"—the practitioner's body, speech. and mind—become inpeparable from the "three Diamonds"—the Diamond Body, Speech, and Mind of the deity—and the yogin vows to practice as of "one taste" with the god.

And finally the Great Manifestation is "sealed," and the *Guhyasamāja Tantra* says:

> 4) When doing *great evocation*
> the image is the Bearer of the Vajra in his own mantra;
> and visualizing the Lord on one's crown
> one will gain the Diamond of Knowledge.

The "Diamond of knowledge" is the final Diamond of total unity; it is, says Tsonk'apa, "the practitioner possessed of yoga—'union'—with the deity." The great evocation, he says, is sealing with the lord of the family through initiation: "If one contemplates the Great Manifestation, visualizing that one is sealed with the lord of the family, one will gain the magical attainments."

THE SYMBOLIC BEING AND MAGICAL CORRESPONDENCE

Thus the creation of the deity is no random series of syllables and flashes of light, but rather a coherent and meaningful drama whose every element is subordinated to the evocation of divine power in a form both manipulable and symbolically potent, even in the very process of its contemplative unfolding. The variations upon this theme of power tend to center on the malleable image of the symbolic being, on the details of its evocation, and on the magical correspondences in which it participates.

In the cycles of the Father Tantras, the *emblem*, the *seed*, and the *perfected body* of the symbolic being are in themselves often called the "three rites of Diamond" which purify the practitioner's body, speech, and mind. As Jigme ch'öchi wangpo writes:[164]

> By visualizing oneself as manifest in the form of the emblem, such as a five-pointed vajra, one's mind is *cleansed* into the Diamond of Mind. By visualizing that same emblem as marked with such syllables as HŪṂ, one's speech is *perfected* as the Diamond of Speech. By the rite of the radiating and gathering in of light and (having served therewith the aims of oneself and others) its transformation into the divine body, visualized as complete with all ornaments and accoutrements, one's body is *ripened* into the Diamond of Body.

Thus these three rites are a threefold table of correspondences, which fulfills what Tenpe nyima said was the special function of the Process of Generation: to cleanse, to perfect, and to ripen. The rites are magical simulacra for the path of purification which leads to the threefold Diamond of Buddhahood.

These "rites"—emblem, seed, and body—are seen too as simulacra for the processes of birth. Not only is the yogin literally born into his new contemplative reality after "dying" in Emptiness, but also, by his mastery of the Process of Generation, he can control his threefold gestation and birth in the world, and his threefold "fruition" as a Buddha:

> By the first rite, the *bardo*-awareness enters into the mass of red and white in the womb. By the second, the semen, blood and mind are mixed together, and the five states of gestation (foetus and so on) are experienced. By the third, the body assimilates the scattered elements and is completed, and it is born outside.
>
> When purified [by the Process of Generation], at the time of fruition these combine as the causal conditions for the Tathāgata to arise in a Body of Transformation to take others in hand, to dwell in the womb—the vagina—of the Diamond Lady, and to be born forth to show his deeds.

Again, in the cycles of the Mother Tantras, the steps of creating and empowering the senses of the symbolic being are often grouped into a fourfold table of correspondences and called the "four realizations." As it says in the *Hevajra Tantra* [I.iii.2]:

> First, *Emptiness* is the thought of enlightenment,
> second, the *seed* is arisen,
> in the third the *body* is perfected,
> in the fourth the *syllables* are arrayed.

And Jigme chöchi wangpo glosses:

> This sets forth the terminology of the four realizations. "Emptiness is the thought of enlightenment": one possesses the intermediate state between death and rebirth. "The seed is arisen": the awareness of the *gandharva* [the being seeking rebirth] takes its place in the middle of the semen and blood. "The body is perfected": the body is gradually produced by the ten winds. "The syllables are arrayed": having been born, the senses discriminate their objects.

These three- and fourfold tables of correspondences set forth patterns not of mere symbolism but of actual magical powers; the Process of Generation is a reenactment and simulacrum not only for the macrocosmic creation of public nonreality, but also for the microcosmic experience of death, the intermediate state of the *bardo*, and birth in the world. On one level the yogin is gaining simple practice in dying into Emptiness and being reborn in contemplative reality, a rehearsal for the death and rebirth he will experience when his life is over, but on a deeper level this practice means mastery, and this control means power; he "owns" these processes, and they are set forth in these commentaries as the objects of his contemplative image, as the events over which he gains magical control.

Thus when these states are cleansed by their ritual reenactment, they may be ripened into bliss and understanding, and perfected into the knowledges and bodies of Buddhahood; once the yogin has become the deity, he may use the sequence of his own creation as a magical basis for mastering the deity's enlightenment in the Process of Perfection.[165] To the Tibetans a symbol is no abstract counter in an intellectual game, but a key to magical power. Even the symbolic potency of the recollection of purity is a reminder of the power the practitioner wields in the body of the god.

"To tame a rutting elephant drunk on wine," says Jigme ch'öchi wangpo, "one may use a plain elephant hook or a fancy one": the Process of Generation may be more or less elaborated, and its magical correspondences more or less extended, to the limits of numerical analogy. And even in the simplest evocation of the goddess, these correspondences are implicit motifs in the ballet of unfolding images, giving meaning to the bare and unelaborated bones of the recitation.

Perhaps the most important of these tables for the generation of the symbolic being is not found in the rituals of Tārā at all, being used only in the highest rituals of the monastic cult, for the high patron deities and the protecting "Lord of knowledge." Here are what are called the "five realizations," and our understanding of the Process of Generation would be incomplete without some account of them; the magical correspondences worked out by generations of scholars for these five realizations reverberate even in the simpler rituals of Tārā. We must remember, whenever we talk of Tibetan scholasticism, that the dry account book of correspondences is the result of a basically religious search, an attempt to extend the yogin's power to its ultimate bounds, and the yogin who generates the goddess brings to the evocation all the magical analogies of his contemplative career.

"The five realizations," says Tsongk'apa, "are five awakenings: the awakening (1) in Suchness, (2) in the moon, (3) in the seed, (4) in the emblem, and (5) in the perfected body."[166] We may look at an example of this mode of generating the symbolic being as given in a ritual of Guhyasamāja:[167]

1) OṂ ŚŪNYATĀ-JÑĀNA-VAJRA-SVABHĀVÂTMAKO 'HAṂ!

2) Above the central throne is a sun disk arisen from HŪṂ, in the middle of which is a moon disk arisen from OṂ; and above that is a red eight-petaled lotus arisen from ĀḤ, in whose center are the three syllables OṂ ĀḤ HŪṂ, stacked one atop the other. All those mix together and become one complete and perfect moon disk; light radiates forth therefrom, gathers together the entire animate and inanimate world, and dissolves back into the moon. OṂ DHARMA-DHĀTU-SVABHĀVÂTMAKO 'HAṂ! The basis of all animate and inanimate events is nothing but the mind riding upon the winds; that appears as a moon; that is I!

3) Above the moon is a white OṂ, a red ĀḤ, and a blue HŪṂ, sprung from the moon like bubbles appearing from water: light radiates forth therefrom, invites the measureless five families and their retinue, and all dissolve back into the syllables.

4) They immediately transform into a white five-pointed vajra, marked in the middle with OṂ ĀḤ HŪṂ VAJRA-SVABHĀVÂTMAKO 'HAṂ!

5) The vajra and its syllables transform into the Lord.

Or again, in a ritual of Cakrasaṃvara:[168]

1) OṂ ŚŪNYATĀ-JÑĀNA-VAJRA-SVABHĀVÂTMAKO 'HAṂ!

2) Above the central throne, counterclockwise, are the vowels, twice: A Ā I Ī U Ū Ṛ Ṝ Ḷ Ḹ E AI O AU AṂ AḤ, and clockwise the consonants, twice: KA KHA GA GHA NA CA CHA JA JHA ÑA ṬA ṬHA ḌA ḌHA ṆA TA THA DA DHA NA PA PHA BA BHA MA YA RA LA VA ŚA ṢA SA HA KṢA YA RA LA VA ḌA ḌHA. These vowels and consonants transform into a "kissing" sun and moon [that is, a single disk that is half each].

3) In the middle thereof is a HŪṂ like quicksilver and an A like vermilion; light radiates forth therefrom, transforming the world of inanimate objects into a divine mansion, and the world of animate beings into the host of deities of the maṇḍala of Cakrasaṃvara; and it is gathered back in again.

4) The syllables transform into a vajra marked with HŪṂ and a chopper marked with A.

5) All those are mixed into one and transform into the Blessed Cakrasaṃvara . . . and the Mother Diamond Yogin Lady.

The evident differences in detail here derive from the contemplative traditions of individual masters and their schools of commentary upon the basic texts; Tsongk'apa in his *Great Stages of the Mantra Path* devotes much space to a discussion of these ritual variations on the basic theme.[169] But despite differences in detail, the two generations are still structurally identical; and the traditional Buddhist love of the number 5 can here lead to the most elaborate correspondences, and hence to the greatest dissemination of magical power. Thus, for example, the *Hevajra Tantra* correlates the five realizations with the five knowledges of a Buddha [I.viii. 6-8]:

The *moon* is the Mirror-like Knowledge
and the *sun* the Knowledge of Equality;
the *seed* and the *emblem* of the particular deity
are said to be Discriminative Knowledge;
all of them merged into one are Active Knowledge;
and the *perfected body* is the Knowledge of Purity.
The wise man should contemplate these five aspects
in the ritual of which we speak.

The rituals of the high monastic cult differ from those of Tārā in another fundamental way: the high patron deity who is the "chief of the maṇḍala"—called generically the "Heruka" of the ritual, or its "Bearer of the Vajra"—may be generated twice, in a *causal* form and in a *resultant* form. (In the cycles of the Father Tantras the causal deity is often called the "Vajrasattva" and the resultant deity the "Body of Transformation".) Thus, in the evocation above, the Cakrasaṃvara produced through the five realizations is the *causal Heruka*, colored white. The generation continues:

> On a moon at the tops of the heads of both Father and Mother is OṂ, and on a sun at their throats and hearts are ĀḤ and HŪṂ. At the break of their waists is SVĀ, on their sexual organs is ĀḤ, and between their thighs is HĀ.
>
> In the "secret place" of the Father there comes from HŪṂ a white vajra, from BAṂ a red gem [at its tip], and the hole is blocked by a yellow PHAṬ. In the "place of space" of the Mother there comes from ĀḤ a red lotus, from OṂ its white anthers, and the hole is blocked by a yellow PHAṬ.
>
> By the sound of the Bliss of the union of the Father and Mother and by the light from their hearts, there are invited both those whose accomplishment of deity is innate and those beings who had been cleansed into the maṇḍala of Cakrasaṃvara. Entering into union in the sky before me, they all melt into Great Bliss and enter through my mouth; descending the central channel, they pass through the vajra and gem, and fall and mix into the anthers of the Mother. The Father and Mother dissolve into a ball of Bliss which is as if in the form of quicksilver.

In some ritual traditions[170] the Great Bliss of the retinue takes the form of a "syllable of *bardo*-awareness"—either HŪṂ or OṂ ĀḤ HŪṂ—which, again, enters into the Father and passes through his vajra-penis and into the lotus-vagina of the Mother, to be placed between two syllables HOḤ before the deities dissolve; but in any event this "melted deity"—this "ball of Bliss"—is "aroused with song" to create the *resultant Heruka*, colored blue:

> All the Buddhas of the ten directions arouse [the melted deity] with the song OṂ MAHĀSUKHAṂ VAJRASATTVA JAḤ HŪṂ BAṂ HOḤ SURAS TVAṂ DṚṢYA HOḤ ! "OṂ Great Bliss, Vajrasattva JAḤ HŪṂ BAṂ HOḤ ! You are the deity: become visible HOḤ !"—and instantaneously it becomes the Blessed Glorious Cakrasaṃvara, his body colored blue.

And then, after the resultant Heruka is generated, the retinue of the maṇḍala is contemplatively created in the same way:

> In the "secret place" of the Father there comes from HŪṂ a blue vajra, from BAṂ a red gem [at its tip], and the hole is blocked by a yellow PHAṬ. In the "place of space" of the Mother there comes from ĀḤ a red lotus, from OṂ its blue anthers, and the hole is blocked by a yellow PHAṬ.
>
> By the sound of the Bliss of the union of the Father and Mother and by the light from their hearts, there are invited all the Tathāgatas of the ten directions. Entering through the juncture of my eyebrows, they arrive in my heart and melt into lust; descending the central channel, they pass through the gem and fall into the vagina of the Mother, and they assume the roles of the deities who reside in the residential maṇḍala.

The retinue of the maṇḍala radiates out from the Mother's womb, step by step, and they take their proper places in the divine mansion.

This more elaborate generation of the symbolic being has been worked into many of the classic schematizations of the Process of Generation as a whole. Thus we find that the cycles of Yamāntaka talk of "four yogas"; as it is said in the *Tantra of the Black Slayer of Death*:[171]

> First the contemplation is *yoga*,
> second is *further yoga*,
> third is *higher yoga*,
> and fourth is *great yoga*.

And the same text elaborates upon these four:

> The perfected Vajrasattva,
> we maintain, is *yoga*;
> with that as its cause, the divine body
> is known as *further yoga*;
> the complete perfection of all the retinue
> we hold to be *higher yoga*;
> empowering body, speech, and mind,
> the eyes of the deity and so on,
> absorbing the knowledge retinue,
> great offerings and praise,
> is called *great yoga*.

Thus, Tsongk'apa glosses, *yoga* is the meditation of the "Vajrasattva," the "causal Bearer of the Vajra—possessing an essence of Knowledge of Purity—evoked through the five realizations," and *further yoga* is the yoga of the resultant Bearer of the Vajra. *Higher yoga* is the "perfection of the retinue: the Father and Mother enter into union, the retinue of the deities generated in the lotus radiate out and are arrayed each in his own place." And, finally, *great yoga* includes all the remaining acts of the ritual: "empowering body, speech and mind and so on, absorbing the knowledge being, sealing with the initiation, offerings and praise." And he adds:[172]

> All the yogas which are the foundation of the Process of Generation are subsumed under these four yogas: the first two (the evocation of the chief Father-Mother) are considered "little yoga." After that the third yoga (adding the perfect evocation of the retinue of deities) is "middle yoga." And finally evoking oneself as of one taste with the knowledge being, empowering one's eyes and so on, is "great yoga."

In the *Tantra of the Diamond Pavilion*[173] the entire ritual sequence of the Hevajra cycle is arranged under "six limbs," beginning with the generation of the divine mansion from BHRŪṂ, the seed of the Buddha Vairocana, and including the further acts of offering and praise and the "tasting of nectar"—the visualization of the mantra "issuing forth with light from the HŪṂ in one's heart, traversing the vajra path through the central channel, circling through the 'lotus' of the goddess and upward from mouth to mouth."[174] Thus it says:

> Having made perfect the foundation of Buddhahood,
> the substance of the truth of the All-Beneficent,
> having contemplated the five aspects,
> one should do the means of evoking the supreme deity,
> likewise arraying the maṇḍala,
> offerings and praise, nectar, and so on:
> if one contemplates with this sequence,
> we hold it to be the yoga of "six limbs."

Durjayacandra[175] correlates these six limbs with the six families of Buddha spoken of in the Mother Tantras:

> Doing "diamond lust" and contemplating
> the separation of the divine mansion of Buddhahood,
> initiation and the tasting of nectar,
> offerings and praise: contemplate the six limbs.
> What is this six-limbed yoga?
> By it one quickly gains the magical attainments.
> The *palace*: Buddha Vairocana,
> the *initiation*: Akṣobhya Tathāgata,
> *tasting nectar*: Amitābha,
> *praise*: glorious Ratnasambhava,
> *offerings*: Amoghasiddhi's perfect offering,
> *lust*: Vajrasattva.

Thus the first limb is the visualization of the residential maṇḍala; as Indrabodhi says:

> Contemplate the "source of all events,"
> visualize the Buddha placed therein. . . .
> The great Conqueror Vairocana
> is born from the syllable of the Dharma realm;
> he arrays the Buddhas in place.

The first limb, says Tsongk'apa, "is the contemplation of the divine mansion, the place of Buddhahood, arisen from Vairocana: the reason for this is that the body is the residence of the mind: Vairocana, too, is the essence of the 'aggregate of form' of the Tathāgatas, and so he generates their residential divine mansion."[176] The second limb is the actual generation of the deity, here called "diamond lust." The *Diamond Pavilion* says:

> One should contemplate the five aspects,
> first visualizing the person,
> then radiating the circle of ḍākiṇīs.
> The *gandharva* enters
> and falls; they melt; thinking of them
> the goddesses of the quarters arouse it.
> Aroused, they draw in the retinue:
> on the eyes Lady Delusion and so on,
> and the three Diamonds arrayed in the three places.
> This then is "diamond lust":
> knowledge enters in actuality.

Tsongk'apa glosses this as follows:

> In the second limb one generates the causal Father-Mother Bearer of the Vajra through the five realizations, empowers the two "secret places" and performs the pride of lust, produces the goddesses of the retinue and arrays them in place, arouses the melted deity with song, arises therefrom, empowers the eyes and so on and absorbs the knowledge being: there is no one who does not hold that all these are included under the limb of "lust."
>
> Hence all of these—from contemplating the five realizations which generate the deity who resides in the residence, through the perfect generation of the symbolic retinue, empowering and absorbing the knowledge being—is the performance of Vajrasattva, the pride of his lust, and the production of the retinue from oneself: this is the second limb.
>
> The reason for subsuming "lust" under Vajrasattva is because here one emanates the deities of the retinue from the "thought of enlightenment" [the union of vajra and lotus] of the Father and Mother, and therefore the two chief deities must perform "lust": and that is held to be Vajrasattva.

The four remaining limbs are given by Indrabodhi, one in each of the following lines:

> The eight mantra goddesses *initiate*,
> and one should *taste the nectar*;
> the eight goddesses make *offerings*,
> and one should *praise* the conjured retinue.

And Tsongk'apa again identifies each limb with a Buddha.

Similarly, the *Diamond Garland Tantra*,[177] part of the Guhyasamāja cycle, speaks of "three meditations": here *first preparations* includes the preliminary acts and the complete generation of the Father-Mother deity, the *highest king of the maṇḍala* is the deity as radiating the divine retinue from within the womb of the Mother, and the *highest king of the ritual* is the complete maṇḍala employed in serving the aims of all beings.

These three meditations, again, are identified with the three bodies of Buddhahood: in the first preparations, says Tsongk'apa, there is the emanation of the divine to accomplish first one's own aim, so this is considered the Essential Body or Dharma Body; then the first bodies of "form" arise to serve the aim of others through the power of the Essential Body, so the highest king of the maṇḍala is considered the Body of Bliss; and then the divine hosts serve the aim of beings in the ten directions, each one emanating while staying in his own place, so the highest king of the ritual is considered the Body of Transformation.

In the rituals based on the Ārya commentatorial tradition of Nāgārjuna and his followers, however, the first preparations are expanded to include the entire generation through the absorption of the knowledge being, and the two highest kings are together correlated with the initiation of the deity. Candrakīrti's *Illumining Lamp* thus says that the great evocation spoken of in the *Guhyasamāja Tantra* includes both the highest king of the maṇḍala and the highest king of the ritual; it is the "great" evocation because these two highest kings "perform the actions of a Buddha" and accomplish the great aim of others. The first three of the *Guhyasamāja's* four limbs of approach and evocation, then, are all included under first preparations, and they are "subsidiaries of accomplishing one's own aim."

In the commentatorial tradition of Buddhajñāna and his *Evocation Named All-beneficent*, on the other hand, all four of these limbs of approach and evocation are applied separately to the Father, the Mother, and the highest king of the maṇḍala, which are then called the "little," the "middle," and the "great" forms of the four limbs; the rituals of Guhyasamāja based on this school are in consequence sometimes extraordinarily involuted and difficult to follow.

Ritual sequence	*Four limbs*	*Four yogas*	*Three meditations*	*Six limbs*
Emptiness				
Protective circle				
Divine mansion				Vairocana
1) Symbolic being:	Approach		First preparations	
Causal Bearer of the Vajra		Yoga		
Resultant Bearer of the Vajra		Further yoga		
Radiation of the Retinue		Higher yoga	Highest king of the maṇḍala	
2) Empowering the senses	Near evocation			Vajrasattva lust
3) Knowledge being	Evocation			
4) Sealing	Great evocation	Great yoga	Highest king of the ritual	Akṣobhya
Offerings				Amoghasiddhi
Praise				Ratnasambhava
Tasting nectar				Amitābha
Recitation				

Except for these (rather important) complications, the four major classic schemas of the Process of Generation may be easily seen in the accompanying table. And Tsongk'apa concludes his discussion of these systems by saying: "These are the noteworthy classifications of the Process of Generation: if one examines a ritual with these as a basis, one will know whether the main points of this first Process are complete or not."[178]

In all these dry and scholarly analyses we may yet see the hand of magical symbolism. The emotional power of sexual imagery is harnessed to the magic of identity, and we can perceive the direction the correspondences will take: the processes of birth are homologized to the creation of the deity and the achievement of Buddhahood. The body of the yogin contains all these within it, and it is in this high ritual of the monastic cult—with its preliminary pattern of five realizations and its manifold correspondences—that we find the greatest elaboration of magical analogy. There are, indeed, any number of variations upon the basic outline, especially in the generation of the symbolic being; a few schools—notably the Ārya tradition of commentary on the Guhyasamāja cycle—depart sometimes radically from our scheme. But all these variations share the same basic structure and an essential core of magical correspondences, which Tsongk'apa analyzes after a lengthy discussion of individual differences and which he correlates not only with death, birth, and *bardo* but also with the individual events of the path to Buddhahood.

It might be well to review briefly the standard sequence of Bodhisattva Stages over which the Vehicle of the Mantra grants magical control, and which require in the Vehicle of the Perfections three "incalculable eons" to traverse:[179]

1) On the Stage of the "Beginner" the aspirant strives to acquire his stocks of merit and knowledge: this is equivalent to the "Path of Accumulation." This Stage extends from the first thought of enlightenment through the contemplative growth of faith and wisdom, until the experience of "warmth," the first signpost of success in meditation.

2) On the Stage of "Practicing with Conviction" the Bodhisattva cultivates the four "aids to penetration," beginning with the experience of "warmth," through "climax," "acceptance," and finally the "highest event in the world." This is equivalent to the "Path of Preparation," whereon these meditative experiences

overcome and expel the antithesis between subject and object and lead to nondiscriminative knowledge. Then there is the moment of "immediate succession" where the "highest event in the world" is transformed into the supramundane state of the first of the ten basic stages of the Bodhisattva.

3) This "first stage," called "the joyful," is, like the remaining ones, associated with the particular Perfection that is held to characterize it. This is equivalent to the "Path of Vision" where the Bodhisattva for the first time truly "sees" the Four Noble Truths: he sees suffering, its cause, its cessation, and the path to its cessation, and it is this path that he next proceeds to develop.

4) The remaining basic stages are traversed in order. It has taken the Bodhisattva one incalculable eon to reach the first stage and it will take another to reach beyond the seventh; for upon the eighth stage he is no longer liable to reversal since he is bound, in only one more eon, for Buddhahood. These nine remaining basic stages are thus equivalent to the "Path of Development," which culminates in the Diamond-like Contemplation, wherein the Bodhisattva fulfills the Perfections of Meditation and Wisdom and destroys all the residues of defilement in the moment before he achieves enlightenment.

5) Finally, in the moment of "instantaneous realization," the Bodhisattva reaches the Stage of a Buddha, the "Path beyond Learning."

This Bodhisattva Path, and the most important events upon it, are outlined in the accompanying table.

Now suppose, says Tsongk'apa, that someone accumulates the karma that is the cause of his taking birth in a womb, and then dies and reaches the intermediate state of the *bardo*. As a *bardo*-awareness he enters into a mother's womb and stays there until he is born outside, and then he himself takes a wife and begets sons and daughters. Now suppose too that he who has done all these things "makes them into religious objects" and contemplates the Process of Generation in accord with hem.

First he will visualize the field of hosts and accumulate the stocks, which is like accumulating the karma that causes him to be born in this world. Here the acts, such as the "intentional" and "actual" thoughts of enlightenment, are in common with the Vehicle of the Perfections: and this may also be correlated with the Bodhisattva's Path of Accumulation, as it says in Abhayākaragupta's *Clusters of Tradition*:[180]

Thus it is: the Bodhisattva's stage of accumulation is like the state of being in the world, because he accumulates the stocks completely, in accordance with the Law; but here he accumulates only the merit of Charity and so on, whereas before he accumulated both virtue and evil.

Path	*Contemplative events*	*Perfection*	*Stage*
Accumulation	Five aids to liberation: 1. Faith 2. Striving 3. Mindfulness 4. Contemplation 5. Wisdom		Beginner
Preparation	Four aids to penetration: 1. Warmth 2. Climax 3. Acceptance 4. Highest event in the world		Practicing with conviction
	Immediate succession		
Vision		Charity	(1) The joyful
Development		Virtue	(2) The stainless
		Acceptance	(3) The illumining
		Striving	(4) The flaming
		Meditation	(5) The hard-to-conquer
		Wisdom	(6) The face-to-face
		Means	(7) The far-going
		Resolve	(8) The immovable
		Strength	(9) The good-insight
		Knowledge	(10) The cloud of the Law
	Diamond-like contemplation		
	Instantaneous realization		
Beyond learning			Buddha

Next, the contemplation of Emptiness is like death, because when one decides that the "aggregates"—the foundation of clinging to "I" and "mine"—are essenceless, their "appearances" are nullified, and it is like giving up one's worn-out aggregates at the moment of death. And this too may be correlated with the Bodhisattva's Path of Preparation, as Abhayākaragupta says:

> The stage of "practicing with conviction" is like the state where the path of death first becomes visible, because it is inherently a preparatory "aid to penetration." After this, at the end of the preparatory state (like the after-death *bardo* when one's being in the world is cut off), one is in the state of "immediate succession" to the "joyful" stage, as naturally as one instant passes on from the dissolution of the end of the preceding one.

Thus the "highest event in the world," says Tsongk'apa, becomes the "immediate succession" to the first of the ten Bodhisattva stages, just as the *bardo* is preparatory to the state of being in the womb. As it says in the *Adornment of the Sūtras of the Great Vehicle*:[181]

> Then without hindrance
> one quickly touches meditation.

Next the practitioner visualizes the generation of the deity, which is like entering into the womb from the *bardo* and growing therein as an embryo. This too may be correlated with the Bodhisattva's growth through the ten stages, his Paths of Vision and Development, as Abhayākaragupta says:

> After that, as the state of being in the womb follows upon the dissolution of the form (whatever it was) which one had in the state of *bardo*, the state of the ten Bodhisattva stages is to be touched after the dissolution of "immediate succession," because [up to this point] the Bodhisattvas are still possessed of obscuration.

Here, says Tsongk'apa, there are two possibilities: the practitioner may "enter the womb" either with or whitout "melting." Just as a *gandharva* enters the womb wihtout melting, the seed syllable that radiates light has "the nature of the *bardo*-being," placed between two orbs that are semen and blood, the latter "like a sun arisen from many monthly periods of women." Thus, where a text says that a sun is generated from the consonants (as in the ritual of Cakrasaṃvara, above), "the intention is to consider it a 'red moon'"; the entry between these two "moons" of the "syllable symbolizing *bardo*" is like a *bardo*-being entering within the mixed semen and blood of its parents.

Thus, too, the sixteen vowels above the central throne symbolize the "sixteen portions of semen which are the inner places of the body": these are divided into Means and Wisdom, making thirty-two, the number of the bodily "signs of Buddhahood", and for that reason the vowels too are doubled. Abhayākaragupta quotes the following verses:

> The syllable A is at the base of the thumbs,
> the syllable Ā on the calves of the legs,
> the syllable I on the two thighs,
> the syllable Ī on the secret place,
> the syllable U on the base of the navel,
> the syllable Ū on the belly,
> the syllable Ṛ between the breasts,
> the syllable Ṝ on the hands,
> the syllable Ḷ on the neck,
> the syllable Ḹ on the lips,
> the syllable E on the cheeks,
> the syllable AI on the eyes,
> the syllable O on the nase of the ears,
> the syllable AU on the heads,
> the syllables AṂ and AḤ on the crown.
> Let the wise man contemplate in this way:
> he will be placed in the whiteness of fortune
> and turned from the blackness of adversity.

These are the sixteen portions of semen, the thought of enlightenment within the body; they are similarly placed in the *Tantra of the Appearance of Cakrasaṃvara*,[182] and Ratnarakṣita says in his commentary thereon:[183]

> "The left side..." means that the "whiteness of fortune" is taken as the left side of the body, from the thumbs to the head [the order of the verses above], and the "blackness of adversity" enters in on the right side, from the head to the thumbs.

Thus the sixteen portions are divided into thirty-two, according to their position on the left or right side of the body, and the two halves of the body are correlated again with Means and Wisdom, as Ratnarakṣita quotes the *Hevajra Tantra* [I.viii.50]:

> The Blessed One is the form of semen,
> and the Lustful Lady is the Bliss thereof.

Then, again, there are thirty-four consonants above the central throne, from KA to KṢA; and to these are added six more (YA RA

LA VA ḌA ḌHA), making forty, "possessed of menstrual blood." These are divided into Means and Wisdom—Emptiness and Bliss—making eighty, the number of the bodily "secondary signs of Buddhahood," and for that reason the consonants too are doubled.

Of course, not all texts double the vowels and the consonants, nor is there any strong agreement upon which produces the moon and which the "second moon" or "sun."[184] But the basic core of symbolism is clear: the syllable enters between the semen and the blood, and the practitioner enters the womb. Then "from the appropriate seed between the two moons (or the moon and the sun), one contemplates the transformation into the emblem marked with the seed." In many of these rituals this emblem is a five-pronged vajra; as the *Clusters of Traditions* explains in one place, its five prongs are the feet, hands, and head of the embryo, and in another place that its five prongs are the five fingers and toes on each hand and each foot, and the five sense-organs on the head: "anything, in fact," says Tsongk'apa, "classified into a group of five." Hevajra's emblem may be a skull bowl, and that of the Red Slayer of Death a stick: "accordingly we believe that anything which can symbolize the development of the body in the womb is permissible."

On the other hand, if the deity "melts" and is "aroused with song," then the causal Bearer of the Vajra perfected from the five realizations is like the father and mother; from the entry of the *bardo*-being up to but not including the perfection of the deity's body, everything is correlated with the state of being in the womb. Thus the retinue enters into the causal deity and traverses the vajra path; Abhayākaragupta distinguishes two traditions of interpretation: one maintains that this descent through the penis into the womb symbolizes the obscuring with greater degrees of lust in the *bardo* as one descends toward a womb; the other maintains that it serves to symbolize the lust for the Bliss that is the essence of the Means and Wisdom—the semen and blood—which come from the future father and mother.

Again, how does the *bardo*-being enter into the causal deity? Abhayākaragupta says:

> For that same reason the Blessed One expounded intentionally in the Tantras, teaching to some deities that the sentient being—the *gandharva*—enters through the "golden gate," to some that it enters through the mouth, and to some that it enters "in another way."

Thus the *gandharva* may enter through the top of the head (the "golden gate" or the "gate of Vairocana") or through the mouth; or it may enter "in another way," into the vagina of the Mother. These are the three gates through which it enters, says Tsongk'apa, and these are the causes for its entering through them: a *gandharva* enters through the mouth out of a desire to "suck the honey" from one of its parents' lips, and it enters through the gate of Vairocana out of a desire to stroke one of its parents' hair. In both instances it enters through the gate of the father if it has lust for a male, and through that of the mother if it has lust for a female (although some hold that in these cases it enters only through the mother). And the argument is the same for entering into the vagina, either directly or through the Father's penis, for "there is no one way it is done"; it may enter the first through the "lotus" of the Mother, or it may enter into the Father and traverse the vajra path into the womb.

When it enters the womb, however, both Father and Mother "become as if senseless with Bliss"; its entry is the "condition for Father and Mother to melt with great lust," and they remain in the form of a "drop." Then the melted deity is aroused with song: if correlated with the "fruition," this is the practitioner (as Buddha) being aroused to the aim of beings with the Four Immeasurables and arising in a body of form for the sake of his followers; if correlated with the "things to be purified," the four goddesses who arouse the deity with song are the four elements, so it is equivalent to the quickened foetus being "held with earth, amassed with water, ripened with fire, and expanded with air."

If the deity in the particular ritual does not melt and is not aroused with song, then the first four realizations are considered to be the causal deity, and the fifth the resultant deity; when the deity does melt, all five realizations perfect the causal deity, and there the seed syllable (between the two orbs) is not taken as the *bardo*-being.

Thus, finally, the practitioner perfects the body of the chief Father-Mother, which is like being born out from the womb; and the highest king of the maṇḍala—both the Father and Mother producing the male and female deities of the retinue—is like the begetting of sons and daughters (in the original example). As it says in the *Clusters of Tradition*:

> Having grasped the perfected fruit [of his karma = the body], he is born that he may experience all sense objects, for he experiences the objects of all his senses. Then the Body of Transformation in the state of radiating the deities is like the state of begetting sons, and so on.

This too may be correlated with the Bodhisattva's Path beyond Learning, and Abhayākaragupta quotes the *Tantra of Mystic Union*:[184a]

> Thus in the sense of being preparatory
> the ten months are the ten stages:
> they both fall under the rubric of ten stages of beings.

The purport, says Tsongk'apa, is that from entering into the womb until being born outside is correlated with the ten Bodhisattva stages; so those intermediate stages must be classified as the Paths of Vision and Development, and being born as the Path beyond Learning.

Tsongk'apa concludes this lengthy analysis with a summary of its main points, which gives a concise resumé of the magical symbolism outlined above:[185]

> In the Process of Generation, it is necessary to recognize the "thing to be purified" and the "purifier": the method of this recognition is the contemplation of birth, death and *bardo* just as they are: so here we must discuss in addition the actual way in which one "takes birth."
>
> Here, the one who takes birth is the contemplating pratitioner. In what sort of a body does he take birth? He takes birth in the body of the chief Father-Mother, the resultant Bearer of the Vajra. Where does he take birth? Upon the central throne of the divine mansion, in an actual *bardo* arisen from a crossed vajra. By accumulating what sort of karma does he take birth? By his "stocks"—visualizing the special field, making homage and offerings, awakening his thought of enlightenment, taking his vows and so on.
>
> Now it is not proper that he take the "special body" of the deity in that manner without first abandoning his ordinary "aggregates," so he takes it after having nullified his "ordinary appearance" and "ordinary ego" with Emptiness.
>
> But in the trackless interval between giving up his former "ordinary aggregates" until he gains the later "special body" of the deity, he is not born in the divine body: so it is here (after contemplating Emptiness and before perfecting the resultant Bearer of the Vajra) that he must do the yogas of "reposing in Pure Sound" and so on [that is, the contemplation of the "syllable

of the *bardo*-being"]. Here, Śrīphalavajra was once asked: "What is the point of dwelling in the five syllables [the HOḤ OṂ ĀḤ HŪṂ HOḤ in the Mother's womb]? One should take the divine body immediately after contemplating Emptiness, to serve the aim of beings: but here one does not do so." In answer to this contention he said that his evocation was written as an "antidote to the three states," so one must contemplate oneself also as equivalent to a *bardo*-being.

Thus the causal Father-Mother Bearer of the Vajra enter into union, after being perfected from the five realizations: and if one sees them thus (since one has the aspect of a *bardo*-being), one enters into the womb of the Mother. This, too, is clearly stated by Śrīphalavajra:

"He also enters into the glorious Vajrasattva who is enjoying Great Bliss, seeing that all beings enter into his mouth. Desire arises that he himself might possess in actuality those wondrous creatures and sense-objects, and this infallibly results: in this contemplation of the Mother as the 'source of all events,' any being whatever (though possessed of the two obscurations) may attain to Buddhahood by entering into her. Hence let him make his mind firm in this manner: 'Because I should attain to being All-Beneficent, let me enter into this very place'—and in the form of the 'five syllables of the *bardo*-being' he enters like a lamp into the secret lotus of the Mother."

Having granted the necessity of doing as he says, one must learn from the commentaries the exact way in which one enters.

Then he arises through arousing the melted deity with song: we have already explained that this is the occassion of perfectly attaining birth. If one well understands the reasons for this "arousing the melted deity with song," then one will know that it is inadmissible that a Buddha could wish to serve the aim of those he takes in hand only through the Dharma Body without a body of form: it is impossible to effect the aims of sentient beings in "reality" without a body of form, so for that reason a follower of the Great Velicle must consider the part of Means to be the most important.

And having taken birth in that manner, what should one do next? That is shown by what follows in the text: one perfectly generates the deities of the "highest king of the maṇḍala"; and those who have been generated are put to their various employments, that thereby one may serve the aims of beings.

THE PROCESS OF PERFECTION

The Process of Generation is a sequence of contemplative events that produce a divine body; both the body and the events are simulacra for the magical control of a wide range of realities. The extensive correspondences that set forth the manipulable images and their objects are found, as we have noted, only in the high rituals of the monastic cult, where the analogies are applied to basically soteriological ends. Indeed, in many rituals whose intent is magical—whose purpose is the control of aspects of public nonreality rather than divine understanding—the generation may be abbreviated even to the point of being instantaneous. As Tsongk'apa says:[186]

> If the practitioner has no fit followers on any occasion, he simply dwells with the Body of Great Bliss; when they come to him, he "appears" to them in a body of form, so he arouses the melted deity with song that he may act for their benefit; and for the sake of others he does not "melt" but dwells in the ravishing "appearance" of a body produced instantaneously.

In rituals of the soteriological type, however, these correspondences provide the yogin with a range of magical control over the most important events of his mortal and contemplative life, and these analogies form a backdrop of affect even in the simplest evocation, wherever the yogin appears in the body of the god, to whatever end. A diagram of the preceding section will show that these powers of the divine body fall into two main groups:

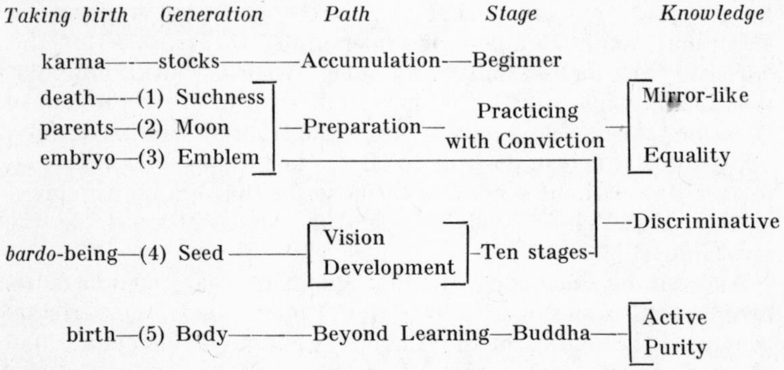

The left-hand column—"taking birth"—is an elaboration of the threefold "birth, death, and *bardo*," the "things to be purified" by the "purifiers," the contemplative events of the generation. This is the same set of magical powers we have seen before in the three rites and the four realizations, here expanded to a fivefold table of correspondences; here too, when these states have been cleansed by the Process of Generation, they may be ripened and perfected into the Stages, the Paths, and the Knowledges. The diagram omits many of the minor correspondences of the generation: the doubled vowels above the central throne, for example, ripen into the thirty-two bodily signs of Buddhahood, and the doubled consonants into the eighty secondary signs. This play of magically potent symbolism may be carried to the limits of ingenuity, restricted only by the received lists of numerical analogies and the authority of the great commentatorial traditions. All these correspondences—the purification of events in the world and their fruition in the divine realms of Buddhahood—are based on the same premise: contemplative events are magical simulacra for all other events, and the yogin's divine body stands between two realities as the "Innate Union of appearance and Emptiness." "We reject the opinion," says Tsongk'apa, "that the 'things to be purified' and the 'purifier' are connected only metaphorically."[187]

This divine body, produced by the Process of Generation and containing in itself and in its own formation the magical correspondences that control both Buddhahood and the world, is called the *mantra body*, for it is this body that exercises the power of divine speech. But this body is yet impure; though it appears and speaks as the god it as yet does not possess the fullness of divine understanding: the mantra body must be purified into the *knowledge body* by immersion in the Clear Light of Emptiness.[187a]

The question is: What does the yogin do with his divinity once he has gained it? A deity generated only in front—as in a ritual of offering—may be asked to depart with the mantra MUḤ! once its "heart has been aroused" with the homage, offerings, and recitation of the mantra for which it was summoned. The practitioner may take empowerment from the deity before him by the "process of gathering in," visualizing that the knowledge being separates and dissolves into his forehead with OṂ ĀḤ HŪṂ; or he may establish the deity in a "basis"—a painting or an image—which is thereby consecrated, visualizing that the knowledge being dissolves into it with SUPRATIṢṬHA "Standing firm!" But though the deity in front may be both requested and coerced by the visualization and recitation to "grant the magical attainments," it is only in the divine body that the practitioner wields the power of attaining the divine enlightenment; the opportunities in self-generation extend beyond the manifest exercise of power in the world, though this is certainly a part of the basic intention (many rituals prescribe that the knowledge being be asked to depart the yogin, who "dwells steadfastly with the ego of the symbolic being" to apply the power of the deity upon public nonreality). But in the most profound of the high rituals, the self-generation ends with the special visualizations of the Process of Perfection, the "gathering in and arising" that plunges the deity into a divine Emptiness and allows the now pure knowledge body to "leap forth" from the Clear Light as the "Innate Union of the Clear Light and Emptiness."

Thus the answer to the question, "What does the yogin do with his divinity?" is simply this: he does anything he wishes. He may control the events of public nonreality with the power of the mantra, or as a Buddha he may immerse himself in a Buddha's Emptiness, controlling his own apprehension through the simulacrum of his divine body. Thus the ritual of Cakrasaṃvara, whose Process of Generation we have reviewed above, concludes its section of self-generation with the following Process of Perfection:[188]

> The vowels and consonants, with five-colored light, radiate forth from my right nostril, bearing on their tips the deities of the three circles of the maṇḍala; they purify the triple world and make it into their own essence; and the entire world—now the same as those ḍākas and yoginīs, innately divine—enters through my left nostril and reaches the level of my navel.
>
> Then from the vowels and from the consonants appears a moon of white and red radiance, and from those ḍākas and yoginīs I see a white and red HŪṂ; and that again becomes the two-armed Blessed One, Father and Mother doing the sport of lust; and by the sound of their experience of Spontaneous Bliss, the symbolic maṇḍala is aroused and satiated with Great Bliss.
>
> From the cremation grounds inward, the entire maṇḍala [including myself in the center] is gathered in due order into the Father and Mother at my navel; and those two again dissolve into light and are retransformed into the moon and its HŪṂ. The moon dissolves into the HŪṂ, the U vowel into the HA, that into the head stroke, that into the crescent, that into the dot, and that dissolves into Pure Sound.
>
> The Pure Sound grows fainter and fainter, until finally I enter into the inconceivability that is free of all objectification.

This is the Process of Perfection in one of its simplest forms, and we shall see a very similar contemplation in the ritual service of Tārā given in chapter iii. But the process is not yet finished, for the practitioner must still arise in the Body of Innate Union, "like a fish leaping from water," that he may serve the aim of beings in a body of form. This arising is instantaneous, and the practitioner dwells in the knowledge body purified by its immersion in the Clear Light.

We should emphasize here the feedback mechanism involved in this contemplation. Both processes begin with the apprehension of Emptiness, and this Emptiness is always the same; it is the apprehension that differs. In the Process of Perfection, Emptiness is approached by the practitioner as deity, and it is apprehended "as it truly is" by a divine understanding. The magical powers of the Process of Generation are here exercised in the coercion of enlightenment itself: the tables of correspondences show the practitioner his control of the Stages and the Paths, his fruition in the Process of Perfection. The yogin manipulates the very steps of his divine generation as simulacra for his ultimate attainment: he can "gather in" his mantra body to the Clear Light because he possesses it in its essence; he can arise from the Clear Light in his knowledge body because of the magical analogies he controls. Thus the Process of Perfection is possible only because the practitioner is a deity, and a deity formed through a series of magically potent contemplative events; thus the Process of Generation is a necessary prerequisite for this final apprehension of the absolute truth. "Yogins who desire the Process of Perfection," one text typically says, "must build upon the foundation of the Process of Generation."[189]

This feedback works through a yogin's entire contemplative career. A beginner in solitary contemplation, no matter how precise his intellectual training, sees Emptiness as a sort of vague blackness, called up to swallow his ordinary awareness and labeled in accordance with the intellectual categories of the monastic college. From the realm of this Emptiness come the first halting visualizations of himself as the deity; yet even these shadowy identifications with the divine grant a magical control (however weak) which brings his final plunge with into Great Emptiness a little closer to true "nonobjectifiability." With this greater apprehension he begins again: each time he is more of a deity, and each time his coercion of the divine understanding becomes more powerful. He moves closer to his "natural flow," wherein he sees that an essence of Clear Light is the basic nature of all events; he sees that he himself, as the deity, is the Innate Union of the Clear Light and Emptiness. And by the time he has spent six months or a year in ritual service, his visualization and understanding reinforce each other: he is the deity because he can create the deity, and he can create the deity because he is the deity.

This rapid increase of understanding—this quick path of Buddhahood—is based upon his magical power, for it is only through the simulacra of the Process of Generation that he can magically manipulate the fruition of the Process of Perfection; out of this spiraling ability comes the power to control all realities, to apply his visualization and recitation upon the public world, to own the universe in his body.

The process of Perfection is generally subsumed under the two headings, "with signs" and "signless." As Tenpe nyima says, quoting the *Oral Teachings of the Lord of Secrets*: "To turn impure appearances into pure appearances, and to contemplate them as the retinue of one's maṇḍala, is the Process of Generation. But these must be understood in the knowledge of Bliss and Emptiness: hence to contemplate the deep contemplation 'with signs' (the channels, winds, and drop) and 'signless' (Suchness) is the Process of Perfection."[190]

The Process of Perfection *with signs* refers to the physical yoga that the Buddhist Tantras share with many Hindu traditions, the control of the "winds" within the "channels" and the manipulation of the "drop" through the central channel to "pierce the vital centers" of the divine body. The *signless* Process of Perfection is the "gathering in" of the body of the god and "arising" therewith from the Clear Light of Emptiness. As Tsongk'apa says:[191]

> Thus if one knows the main points of the technique of bringing forth the channels, winds and drop, and is able to utilize the winds and drop in the yoga which pierces the vital centers, then one is able to produce the deep contemplation of the four joys based upon reversing the evolution of one's bodily elements, and to adorn that contemplation with the Great Bliss and Clear Light, imposing upon it no mental constructs.
>
> But to do nothing else is not the contemplation: rather must one base oneself on those techniques, and then move on to produce the entirely pure view which sets forth the meaning of "essencelessness", because—in other words—even with those two sorts of contemplation one is still unable to cross over from this world. As it says in the *Discourse on the Thought of Enlightenment*:[192]

> Whoever does not know Emptiness
> is no fit basis for freedom:
> deluded, he will be whirled about
> in the six destinies, the prison of this world.

Hence one must enter into the house of meditation and contemplate the meaning of "essencelessness."

From the general Indian yogic cultus the Buddhist Tantras inherited the notion that certain physical manipulations of the body (the raising of the drop of semen through the central channel to the top of the head, the arousing of heat below the navel, and a whole complex of similar exercises) produce experiences of bliss or joy, which are often accompanied by blazing lights and roaring sounds, visual and sonic encounters with a divine state. Dasgupta[193] has written extensively upon these early techniques; but the Buddhists, especially as the Tantras were incorporated into the scholarly framework of the university curriculum, saw these experiences not as ends in themselves but rather as possible magical simulacra within the body for the attainment of the rapture of enlightenment; to the intellectual categories of Emptiness they added the experiential dimensions of Great Bliss and Clear Light, always warning (as above) that bliss or light without Emptiness was simple sensual indulgence.

There have been attempts to correlate this yoga with actual physiology, or to interpret it symbolically, but we must bear in mind that the physical events take place within the body of the god, and the symbolism becomes a set of magical correspondences. If the signless Process of Perfection coerces the divine understanding of Emptiness, then the Process of Perfection with signs coerces the divine experience of the Great Bliss, the divine vision of the Clear Light, the divine hearing of the "unstruck sound" of Emptiness. And this coercion is made through the yogin's manipulation of his divine body, the primary simulacrum for the experience, which in turn becomes the similacrum for the attainment; the divine experience is brought about through possession of the divine body and the attainment of Emptiness is brought about through possession of the divine experience. All these are based upon the Process of Generation, which provides the magical symbolic potency of the manipulable divine image, the primary impetus for the entire branching tree of realization, whose final fruit is a divine body of Innate Union, arisen from Emptiness and possessed of Buddhahood:

Contemplative Reality

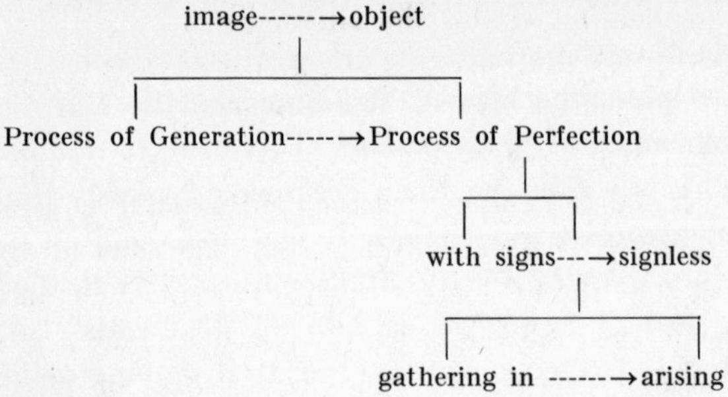

These varied experiences of bliss, light, and sound tumble upon the yogin as he nears the goal, whether they are coerced by manipulation or occur spontaneously in contemplation. Thus we find the texts speaking of "the experience of Light and Emptiness adorned with Bliss," and we read biographical accounts such as the following:[194]

He entered the gate [of initiation] and began to contemplate, and he gained possession of a body of form which was "appearance and Emptiness." He was without outer or inner, above or below, front or rear, before or after; he was unmade, unlimited, undivided; he was without essence in appearance, without bias in Light, without defilement in Bliss; his glow was the Clear Light, his nature the unproduced, his prowess manifold. And in this realm of undefiled Great Bliss he saw the play—the residence and its residents, gods and goddesses, ḍākas and ḍākiṇīs—the subtle and self-sprung understanding, the miraculous knowledge. All events—inner and outer—were the appearance of his mind, occurring as the manifold prowess of his understanding.

From the moment he gained this appearance and Emptiness he penetrated it as the Clear Light, unconstrued, unfathomable, empty of arising, abiding, and perishing; he comprehended the natural pace of his ordinary knowledge as a genuine and innate nature, and whatever appeared as the play of the Dharma Body, Bliss, and Emptiness, the pith of conditioned coproduction. . . .

In this state he purified away subject and object, and he perfected his prowess of great knowledge; as an attainment from this realm of the Clear Light of contemplation, from then on he knew that whatever occured—at the very moment of its appearance—was itself light and itself clarity, unfathomable, unproduced, the nature of Great Bliss, self-sprung, self-erected.

He realized many "gateways to contemplation": the shining of gems, the lamp of gems, the shining of the moon, the lamp of the sun, the seeing of all things. There appeared in his mind endless insights, visions, supernormal powers, and signs of success, such that I cannot write them down, they were so many and so extraordinary.

This cascade of contemplative experiences in the Process of Perfection is the experiential "given" structured by the Tantric texts and their commentators. This process of refinement was both an expansion and a selection, for there occured a typically Buddhist extension of contemplative technique to new areas and an equally typical schematization of the resultant options. Thus the same contemplative technique may be used to different ends: "piercing the vital centers"—the visualization of a HŪṂ moving within the central channel of the divine and "hollow" body—might serve as the image to the object of the "mystic heat" and the "four joys," a gradual approach to the Great Bliss of Emptiness, where the HŪṂ is simulacrum for the drop of semen, itself homologized to the thought of enlightenment. But the HŪṂ might also serve as simulacrum for awareness (the yogin's own or even that of another) and its motion magically control the transference of that awareness through the gates of death, to a different body, or directly to a Pure Land; or the syllable might represent the practitioner's life, and its visualized immobility—called "planting the magic dagger of life in the heart"—grant freedom from death: the same visualization and magical control, but to radically opposite ends.

Again, we find different contemplative exercises and analogies employed for entering into Emptiness: the divine body may be homologized to the "illusory" bodies of the dream, a mirror reflection, the *bardo*, to gain the "Innate Union of appearance and Emptiness," and there are further emphases upon different types of "Innate Union," a choice of the aspects of Emptiness. Emptiness shines with the Clear Light, and its experience is Great Bliss, and in the gradual approach to realization there are different levels of apprehension of Emptiness, of light, and of joy; the path to enlightenment may follow the track of any combination, as long as Emptiness is there.

Thus Virūpa[195] arranges contemplative experience in a sequence of "views" which orders these varied approaches in a hierarchy of Innate Union; he speaks of "appearance and Emptiness"; "Light and Emptiness," "Bliss and Emptiness," and the culminating union of "understanding and Emptiness." But there is also the possibility of choice among these paths to enlightenment, granting always that the final experience includes them all. It is curious, for example, that though Buddhists and Hindus agree on Bliss as an aspect of realization, Buddhism has tended to exclude the sequence of sonic experiences as an approach to the final goal, choosing to emphasize the visual path: the early mystic songs spoke equally of both aspects of contemplative experience, but the Hindu Tantras chose to treat of sound (perhaps a heritage of orthodox Mimāṃsa philosophy) and the Buddhist of light, although there is always an inherited overlap; but the Hindus tend to hear the roaring of enlightenment above its light, and the Buddhists to see its light above its roar.

Indeed, each cycle of Tantric texts has its own technique for immersing the divine body into Emptiness, varying in emphasis upon light and joy and analogical meditation. The well-known set of the "six yogas of Nāropa" is essentially an anthology of these techniques of the Process of Perfection, each presuming a prior Process of Generation, and each traced to its canonical sources and major commentators.[196]

This Tantric notion of "Innate Union" is a central concept de serving more study than is possible here; in chapter iii I examine its integration into ritual and its function in acquiring the divine power. Wayman[197] has given a detailed discussion from the works of Tsongk'apa, based mainly upon the *Guhysamāja* tradition, and Ruegg[198] gives a brilliant summary of the Process of Perfection according to the "five steps" of Nāgārjuna's Ārya tradition.

Perhaps the most important point is the correlation of the Clear Light or of Great Bliss with "Complete Emptiness" as the culmination of a series of realizations; but we must remember that the series of four lights or joys which lead up to this final experience are not different things, but rather serve as "metaphors" for differing levels of awareness of the one "actual" Clear Light or Great Bliss. Similarly, the different levels of realization of the one Emptiness are given different names to correspond to the different apprehensions of its radiance and rapture; we may tabulate the series of realizations as follows, as they are correlated magically with the bodies of Buddhahood and with the four places of the body of the god:

Emptiness	Light	Joy	Body of Transformation	Navel
More Emptiness	Appearance of light	Highest Joy	Dharma Body	Heart
Great Emptiness	Culmination of light	Joy of Cessation	Body of Bliss	Throat
Complete Emptiness	Clear Light	Innate Joy (Great Bliss)	Innate Body	Head

There are both orderings and choices among the possibilities of combination of these experiences, reading the diagram either horizontally or vertically, but here we briefly follow a single path to enlightenment and examine the unfolding of the Clear Light of Emptiness. As Lozang ch'öchi nyima (1732-1802) writes:[199]

> Although the Clear Light and Emptiness are two, they are not separate: Emptiness is the nature of mind, and the Clear Light is found in the shifting interstices of the seeker of Emptiness. Hence when there is the Clear Light there is Emptiness, and from the realm of Emptiness the Clear Light appears of itself. The Clear Light and Emptiness thus occurring are determined to be innately one: thus they are in "Innate Union." And thus arising from the realm wherein one experiences only the absence of mental objects, whatever "appears" occurs as the play of the non-duality of this world and nirvāṇa. Since one experiences this, one understands the entire quality of the mind which is the Innate Union of Light and Emptiness, called "the nature of the genuine mind."

Isolating the elements from the chart above, the gradual unfolding of the light of Emptiness—the growing apprehension of the Clear Light—may be diagramed alternatively, as shown here.

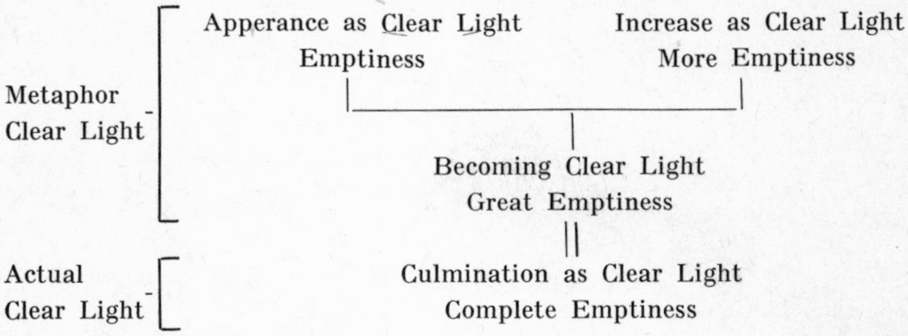

This sequence of development is, as Tsongk'apa has pointed out, a "reversal of evolution," and thus it may work toward the creation of the world of appearances as well as toward its dissolution. The *Abridged Instructions*, an anthology of basic Kajü teachings, contains a section on the Clear Light written by Ngawang zangpo, wherein we find a specifically Tantric scheme of the evolution and devolution of dualistic awareness which parallels the account of the construction of nonreality examined above:[200]

> Someone who has neither been instructed nor has the mindfulness to recognize things as they really are insists upon taking things to be true: thus the first of four stages is that an event *appears as a real thing*.

He then examines this thing, and he decides that it is good or bad, as appropriate: this second stage is that an event *increases as a real thing.*

Through his delusion—not knowing the object neutrally to be Empty form—it becomes, if good, an object of desire which he makes plans to get or, if bad, an object of aversion which he makes plans to avoid: this third stage is that an event *becomes a real thing.*

His joy at getting an object of desire and at no one else getting it involves lust and pride. His chagrin at someone else getting it and at not getting it himself involves hatred and envy. It is through his not knowing the object to be Empty that he tries to get what is good and avoid what is bad—that he has joy or chagrin at whether he or someone else gets it or not—so all of those involve delusion. Thus the five poisons are ever present in a single object of desire, and it is the same for his avoiding or not avoiding an object of aversion. Thus the five poisons are ever present in any object that he first takes to be a real thing; hence he is ever reborn in this world; hence he experiences interminable suffering; hence there occur the intermediate states between the birth and death of appearances which are inversions of the Clear Light: this fourth stage is the way in which an event *culminates as a real thing.*

There is an intimate connection between the Clear Light and these intermediate states which are its inversions, for it is the Clear Light that shines through the "shifting interstices" in the stream of events, any stream of events, macro- or microcosmic, depending solely upon the scope of the context. There are thus intermediate states between two moments in the movement of a single thought, and between the dissolution and recreation of the cosmos; and, in a "medium context," Ngawang zangpo mentions three special *bardo*s—intermediate states—"between the death and birth of an event": the "dream *bardo*" between sleeping and waking, the "waking *bardo*" between two thoughts, and the "*bardo* of dissolution into Emptiness" at the moment of death. This last is also called the "*bardo* of dying" between death and the illusory body-awareness of the "illusory *bardo*" which occurs in turn between death and the next life.

We may note here the level distinctions, the continuous process of subdivision. Since there is an intermediate state between lives, an earlier conception that served as the model for all the other *bardo*s, there is an intermediate state between the moment of actual death and the first intermediate state, and so on (sometimes the foetus in the womb is considered to be in a *bardo* between that last intermediate state and actual birth). Tibetan, not to mention Western, theorists have spent much time and ingenuity in the elucidation, with charts, of these states, but for our purposes the most important thing to bear in mind is that all these intermediate states are the shifting interstices through which one can get a glimpse of the Clear Light. Each *bardo* reveals the Emptiness that lies behind the appearance.

Thus there is a sort of natural awareness of the Clear Light between two thoughts, especially in those instants of great mental tension when there is a break in the otherwise continuous flow of mental events, moments of great anger or rage or of sexual orgasm, or during the change of state from sleeping to waking, or in dreamless sleep—those familiar times when thought slows down or stops for an instant, and one gets a misty glimpse of the light behind the thought. As T. S. Eliot writes:[201]

> Our gaze is submarine, our eyes look upward
> And see the light that fractures through unquiet water.
> We see the light but see not whence it comes.

A brighter and longer Clear Light comes when the causal basis of the physical body is removed by death: this is the "Clear Light of death" which corresponds to the *bardo* of dying. This light is so bright and strong, however, that the average person flees it in panic rather than recognizing it for what it is. The important process of dying has been carefully analyzed, and the removal of the body begins with the dissolution of its component elements:[202]

> First, externally, the dying man vomits undigested food and drink; his warmth diminishes, his head bristles, and he feels that he is falling downward.
>
> Then the five elements dissolve into one another in this manner:
>
> His internal *earth* is flesh and bone; the sign of its dissolution into external earth is that his body grows heavy and falls to the ground, and the internal sign is that he feels that the earth has opened up and he is sinking into it. Because his earth energy dissolves into water, he is unable to maintain his form; his bodily strength slips away and his cognition grows clouded.
>
> His internal *water* is blood and pus, and the sign of its dissolution into external water is that his saliva and mucus trickle and his throat and tongue grow dry. Because his water energy dissolves into fire, his bodily warmth slips away and his cognition is sometimes clear and sometimes darkened.

> His internal *fire* is warmth, and the sign of its dissolution into external fire is that his eyes turn inward and he does not recognize people. Because his fire energy dissolves into air, his warmth contracts.
>
> His internal *wind* is breath; the sign of its dissolution into external wind is that his breath wheezes and his limbs quiver, and the internal sign is that his cognition is distorted, so he thinks he sees cows and so on, and he has quick mirage-like flashes. All his lice leave his body.

The dying man then inverts the pattern by which events originally appeared to him as real things, then increased as real things, became real things, and finally culminated as real things—the very process by which he was first cast into this world. By inverting the process he approaches nearer and nearer to the Clear Light of Death:

> The blood he obtained from his mother goes upward: this is called the "red path," and on this red path his appearances occur. At that time, *appearance* dissolves into *increase*, and the forty mental constructs made from lust are cut off.
>
> The semen he obtained from his father goes downward: this is called the "white path," and on this white path his appearances occur. At that time, *increase* dissolves into *becoming*, and the thirty-three mental constructs made from hatred are cut off.
>
> His breath departs farther and farther away, and all the blood in his body gathers inside his life channel, and the blood mixes into a single drop in the middle of his heart: this is called the "black path," and on this black path he is stricken with panic, he feels as if he were falling into an abyss in the darkness. At that time, *becoming* dissolves into *culmination*, and the seven mental constructs made from delusion are cut off.
>
> Both his eyes open like a cow's, roll upward, and become glazed; external appearances become to him like the setting of the sun. His faculties, memory, and vision are cut off; all appearances become gathered into blackness. Then his breath departs his body to the length of a cubit; internal appearances become to him dark as night. Then the blood in his heart forms two drops; his head bows and his breath departs his body to the length of an arrow. Then the blood in his heart forms three drops; he sighs and his breath departs his body to the length of a fathom.
>
> Forgetting the black path, the breath is cut off outside; the red and white drops meet together in his heart, and then his cognition swoons into the realm of Bliss, his awareness dissolves into the Clear Light, so that he experiences the Innate Joy. The perceptions in the center of his heart dissolve into Reality; the mother dissolves into the son. The breath is cut off inside; the "mind that rides upon the winds" is placed in the central channel.

Now at this point the basic Clear Light appears to all beings, but it is only some few yogins possessed of understanding who can now "have the mother meet the son"—join this basic Clear Light to the "Clear Light of the Path" [which he knows from his contemplations during life] and instantaneously pass upward, to manifest the nonarising Dharma Body and to serve the countless aims of beings with a Body of Bliss and a Body of Transformation. To manifest thus miraculously the three bodies is to be a Buddha.

It is for this reason that there is profit in gaining a human body, and it is very important to experience therewith the counsels of the profound path. The actual Clear Light arises to all beings, but they do not understand it, and they flee from it in terror.

"In the process of rejecting one's ordinary aggregates to acquire a divine body," writes Tsongk'apa, "we have found that it is necessary to contemplate in accord with birth, death and *bardo*. The highest paths of the Process of Perfection too are a practice quite similar to this: so on the occasion of the latter Process as well one awakens in one's stream an understanding of Emptiness which is like the process of death, based on the strength of the yoga of 'channels, winds and drop': and to arise therefrom one must know the ritual of generating a deity 'arisen as a body which is in Innate Union with illusion.'"[203] And thus Ngawang zangpo continues his discourse on the Clear Light, the ontological insight granted by the magical reenactment of the stages of death:

There are thus four stages in the formation of appearances, which are inversions of the developing realization of the Clear Light; but no matter how they occur—in large or small context, persisting for longer or shorter periods of time—the practitioner should apply to them the following instructions, which constitute a method for experiencing the Clear Light alone.

Just after there is formed, in the first moment, an appearance of a male or a female, and so on, as an object of the six sense faculties (which are themselves neutral in terms of deciding whether the object is form or Emptiness, good or bad), he knows that the event is something that is formed unceasingly from his own innate mind; he should remember to abandon any mental construct that imposes "reality" upon it. By holding to this mindfulness the appearance of the perceptual object becomes "uncontrived," without the addition of his own constructs. It thus becomes a "deep contemplation of mindfulness," "knowledge," the Dharma Body, or the Clear Light; at this stage an event *appears as the Clear Light*; it is called the "deep contemplation of Emptiness."

By forming an appearance or thought as the Clear Light, the practitioner does not take it to be or act as if it were either good or bad; at this stage an event *increases as the Clear Light*; it is called the "deep contemplation of More Emptiness."

Because he is free of taking it to be good or bad, he does not, through desire or aversion, try to get it or avoid it; at this stage an event *becomes the Clear Light*; it is called the "deep contemplation of Great Emptiness."

By attempting neither to get it nor to avoid it, he cuts off the happy or miserable feelings which are the result of his getting it or not getting it, avoiding it or not avoiding it, and which are the constructs of the five poisons. He thus cuts off suffering and dwells in the all-absorbing; at this stage an event *culminates as the Clear Light*; it is called the "deep contemplation of Complete Emptiness."

This is the basic experience of the Clear Light of understanding as it is to be performed "in the daytime" [that is, through the waking awareness, the waking *bardo*; the text later gives instructions for its experience "in the night" (the dream *bardo*) and "at the moment of death" (the "*bardo* of dissolution into Emptiness")]. In this method, just described, of entering into contemplative communion with the Clear Light, the practitioner should sit in the posture "precious body of the deity" like Vairocana, his body unmoving, his voice unspeaking, his mind constructing no "reality," entering into uninterrupted contemplative communion like a river falling downward or the flame of a lamp burning upward. But in fact even if the experience were explained a thousand times, there is nothing else for it but the unremitting mindfulness on what is to be experienced.

But having thus experienced, a yogin whose faculties are of the very best forms even his mental constructs themselves as mindfulness. Thus he forms the mindfulness of "recognition": he gains the freedom that occurs simultaneously with appearance. He who becomes firm therein is said to be "in contemplative union even afterward, even when he is doing something else"; he is called "a Buddha in a single lifetime." Thus by his mindfulness of recognition he recognizes each appearance to be neutral Empty form; as soon as it occurs he is freed of it simultaneously, and the four stages of appearance do not occur.

Thus, as it is said, "Understanding the object to be appearance and Emptiness, without truth, the mind becomes Light and Emptiness, without grasping."[204] It is, of course, only the practitioner "whose faculties are of the very best" who could hope to achieve Buddhahood in his lifetime; the main point in the "contemplative communion with the Clear Light," I was informed, is to gain the ability to recognize and embrace the Clear Light of the moment of death, when the hindering presence of the physical body has been removed.

But here again, this rehearsal is a ritual reenactment and hence a magical simulacrum for death: the control of the Clear Light of the Path grants magical access to the actual Clear Light; the son is the simulacrum for the mother. The Process of Perfection grants symbolic power over death and the light that shines through it, and hence control over enlightenment; it is part of the contemplative reality wherein all events become symbols, all symbols become images, and all images become one another.

THE OFFERINGS

We have now traveled some distance through this startling realm of contemplative reality, and we have examined a few of the correspondences that link together in patterns of power and magical control. But in the rituals themselves there is an important subsidiary use of visualization which we have not yet discussed: the creation of offerings (or of goddesses who bear offerings) which are presented to the deity. The deity thus worshiped may be in front of the practitioner, or it may be the practitioner himself, making offerings to the god he has become.

Here again, as in the generation of an effigy, all offerings (including the tormas, which are presented separately) are first dissolved into Emptiness and then contemplatively re-created as "broad and vast"; the offerings are brought under the magical control of the yogin, who renders them a "perfect divine substance" fit for presentation to the god. Various rituals differ in the amount of this preparation of the offerings, but there are three basic steps in the process: (1) their material substance is *cleansed* by the recitation of a fierce mantra, often OṂ AMṚTA-KUṆDALI HANA HANA HŪṂ PHAṬ; (2) they are *purified* into Emptiness with the mantra OṂ SVABHĀVA-ŚUDDHĀḤ SARVA-DHARMĀḤ SVABHĀVA-ŚUDDHO 'HAṂ, then visualized as born from their seeds into perfect divine substance: and (3) they are *empowered* with the mantra OṂ ĀḤ HŪṂ and the special hand gesture called the "flying bird." This process is sometimes called "cleansing, increasing, and kindling" the offerings.

A wide variety of different offerings are visualized in the course of a ritual, and here more than anywhere else we clearly see the ritual interplay of the standard triad of body, speech, and mind, for these contemplative visualizations are inevitably accompanied by the recitation of special mantras and the performance of hand gestures. *Mantras* especially have attracted scholarly attention, and Gonda[205] has written an excellent article on them. As Malinowsky says of spells in general, mantras are "a mode of action and an expression of human will . . . a translation of the urge of human desire into words."[206] But mantras are more than this: they are, as we have seen, the very speech of the god. As Rosen writes:[207]

> However, the effectiveness of curses and blessings, such as those of Balaam, does not depend merely on verbal magic, on the belief that the words uttered are forces let loose in the world for evil or good. Belief in the effectiveness of such utterances is something much more complex. They are regarded as efficacious not only because they are words of power, but because they are held literally to effect what they signify, because they are embodied activity. In short, as Dorothy Emmet has suggested, such verbal acts are in a way "performative utternaces," in which saying is doing.

Thus, for example, a visualization for subjugation is accompanied by a mantra such as OṂ KURUKULLE such-and-such a person VAŚAM ĀNAYA HRĪḤ SVĀHĀ! "OṂ Kurukullā, lead such-and-such a person into my power HRĪḤ SVĀHĀ!" Or the mantra for the dissolution of oneself or of an object into Emptiness is, as we have seen, OṂ SVABHĀVA-ŚUDDHĀḤ SARVA-DHARMĀḤ SVABHĀVA-ŚUDDHO 'HAṂ! "OṂ Pure of essence are all events, pure of essence am I!" One of the most widely used of these mantras of *injunction* is the 100-syllable mantra of Vajrasattva, which the practitioner recites during the preliminary practices of his solitary contemplation, or in the course of a ritual itself (either at the very beginning or before praying to the deity), to purify all his past sins:

> OṂ VAJRASATTVA SAMAYAM ANUPĀLAYA VAJRASATTVA TVENÔPATIṢṬHA DṚḌHO ME BHAVA SUTOṢYO ME BHAVA ANURAKTO ME BHAVA SUPOṢYO ME BHAVA SARVA-SIDDHIM ME PRAYACCHA SARVA-KARMA-SŪCA ME CITTAṂ ŚREYAḤ KURU HŪṂ! HA HA HA HA HOḤ! BHAGAVĀN SARVA-TATHĀGATA-VAJRA MĀ ME MUÑCA VAJRĪ-BHAVA MAHĀSAMAYASATTVA ĀḤ!

> "OṂ Vajrasattva, guard my vows! Vajrasattva, let them be firm! Be steadfast for me, be satisfied, be favorable, be nourished for me! Grant me all the magical attainments! Indicator of all karma: make glorious my mind HŪṂ! HA HA HA HA HOḤ! Blessed One, diamond of all the Tathāgatas: do not forsake me, make me diamond! Great being of the vow ĀḤ!"

In general, the translation into English of such an injunctive mantra used in Tibetan ritual is quite sufficient to show how it is being used, though its stereotyped formulation in sonorous Sanskrit is psychologically more effective. Sometimes, of course, the injunction is not quite clear on the surface, as in the following mantra:

> OṂ NAMO BHAGAVATE PUṢPA-KETU RĀJĀYA TATHĀGATĀYA ARHATE SAMYAKSAMBUDDHĀYA TADYATHĀ PUṢPE PUṢPE MAHĀPUṢPE PUṢPÔDBHAVE PUṢPA-SAMBHAVE PUṢPÂVAKĪRṆE SVĀHĀ!

> "OṂ Homage to the Blessed One, King of the Flowery Banner, Tathāgata, Worthy One, fully enlightened! That is: Flowers, flowers, great flowers! Growing of flowers, birth of flowers, strewing of flowers SVĀHĀ!"

By the power of this mantra, the texts tell us, "as many flowers as there may be, their offering counts for ten million times as many"; the implied injunction is thus made explicit.

But even the untranslatable portions of the mantras—what are here called mantra *particles*—fill well-defined ritual slots and thus function morphemically in the magical utterance: OṂ ĀḤ HŪṂ represent body, speech, and mind, and are used to empower visualized objects and deities; PHAṬ is used as an element of power in fierce mantras; TRI is used to embody or manifest something immaterial into a material object, such as an effigy or torma; JAḤ is used to summon, and MUḤ to dismiss.

Some of these mantra particles serve as seeds for the contemplative generation of an object or deity: BHRŪṂ is the seed visualized in the creation of a divine mansion or any dwelling for the god; the four semivowels YAṂ RAṂ LAṂ VAṂ are the seeds of wind, fire, earth, and water; OṂ HŪṂ TRAṂ HRĪḤ ĀḤ collectively represent the five families of Buddha. Sometimes the derivation of these seeds is relatively transparent: PAṂ is the seed that is visualized as transforming into a lotus (a PAdma), just as TĀṂ is the seed of TĀrā or GAṂ of GAṇapati.

One further functional category of mantra must be distinguished from both injunction and particle: these are stereotyped doctrinal or other *formulas* (even hymns of praise, or the Sanskrit alphabet) used for particular purposes in the ritual and sometimes totally disassociated from their meaning. Included are Tārā's basic mantra, her praises used for protection, the vowels and consonants recited for the empowerment of speech. Thus, for example, the famous verse called the "heart of conditioned coproduction" reads as follows:

YE DHARMĀ HETU-PRABHAVĀ HETUN TEṢĀṂ TATHĀGATO ĀHA / TEṢĀṂ CA YO NIRODHO EVAṂ VĀDĪ MAHĀŚRAMAṆAḤ /

Whatever events arise from a cause,
the Tathāgata has told the cause thereof;
and the great ascetic also
has taught their cessation as well.

This formula is used, as a mantra, for consecration, making firm a deity generated within an object, or fixing a ritual act. Similarly, the following anomolous mantra is used in the offering of tormas:

OṂ A-KĀRO MUKHAṂ SARVA-DHARMĀNĀṂ ĀDY-ANUTPANNATVĀT!

"OṂ The syllable A is first, because of the primordial nonarising of all events!"

The visualization of the offerings is also accompanied by ritual *hand gestures*, as indeed are most of the important acts of the ceremony. For some reason these gestures have not received the scholarly attention that has been lavished upon the mantras, or else they have been confused with the iconographic gestures that serve to identify paintings and images. We may distinguish two functional categories of ritual hand gestures. The first, comparatively few, are *stereotyped gestures* of reverence, threat, welcome, or farewell: the practitioner may join his palms in reverence, hold out his extended palms in a typically Tibetan gesture of good-bye, or cross his arms over his chest to indicate the absorption of the deity within him. The second category includes the ritual hand gestures that accompany the presentation of offerings, and these are explicitly intended as *mimetic representations* of the objects being offered—simulacra that control the transmission of worship to the god, just as the mantras of offering enjoin its acceptance and response.

A wide variety of offerings are visualized in the rituals and thus dispatched to the deity with sound and gesture; these are generally subsumed under the headings of "outer offerings," "inner offerings," and "secret offerings," to which is added in some rituals an "offering of the Truth."

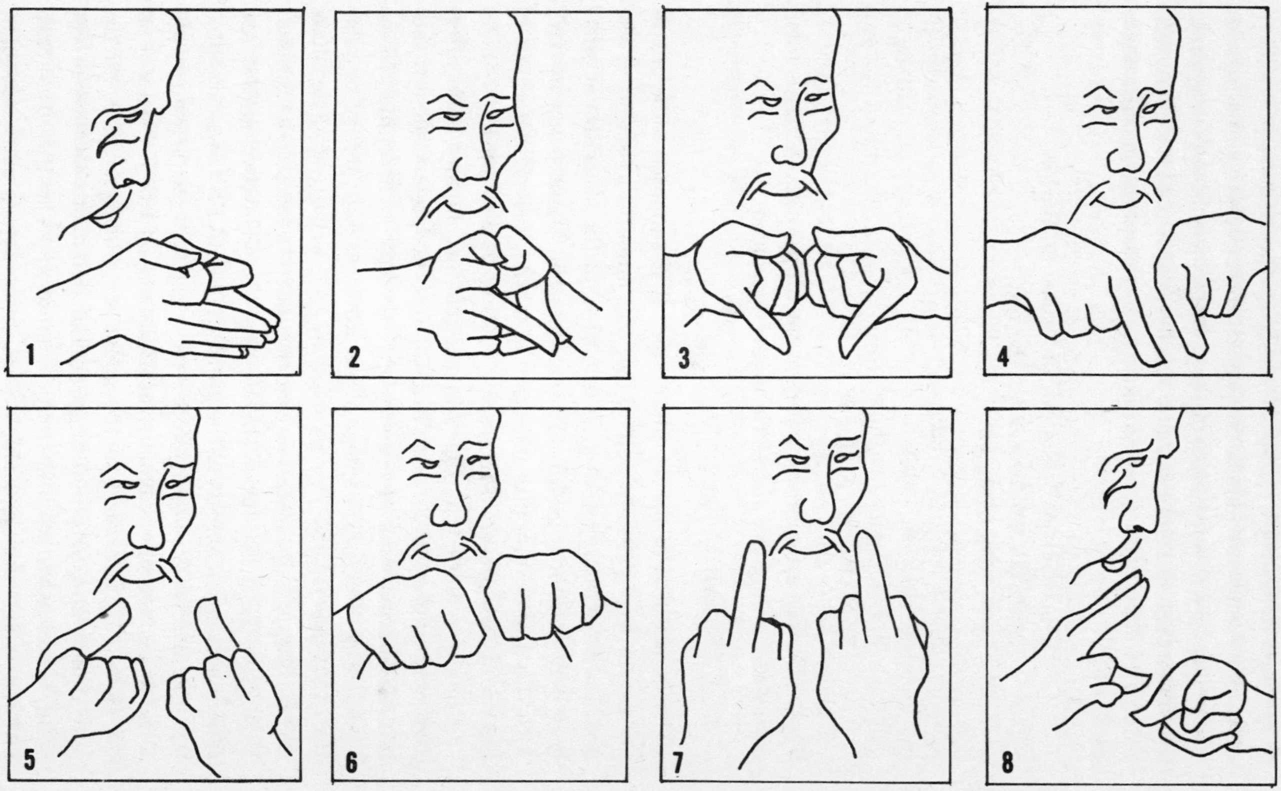

Fig. 15. The outer offerings.

The *outer offerings* are all those things of the external world—animate and inanimate—which are proper to the reception of a royal or divine guest. The most basic of these, whose accompanying gestures are illustrated in figure 15, are the *two waters* and the *five gifts*, listed as follows with their Sanskrit names as given in their mantras:

1) ARGHAṂ "oblation" or "water for the face"
2) PĀDYAṂ "water for the feet"
3) PUṢPE "flowers"
4) DHŪPE "incense"
5) ĀLOKE "lamps"
6) GANDHE "perfume"
7) NAIVEDYE "food"

These offerings are represented upon the altar by seven bowls filled with water and grain; and to these seven is added

8) ŚABDA "music,"

which is not set out on the altar, since it is supposed to be ommipresent in the assembly hall. Here the mimetic intention of the gestures is not so apparent as it is in some of the other sets of offerings; but note how gesture 5 represents the lamps being offered, with the thumbs raised in imitation of a wick rising from a pool of butter, or how gesture 8 represents beating time to music.

We may remark that the mantras that accompany these offerings may appear to a Sanskritist to have undergone some rather bizarre deformations. But many of these may be accounted for as regular early Prakritic analogical assimilations (e.g., dative singular RĀJĀYA for RĀJÑE) or as more or less well-attested Buddhist Hybrid forms (e.g., vocative singular GURU for GURO, present imperative KHĀHI for KHĀDA "eat!"). The two waters are clearly accusative objects of the imperative PRATĪCCHA "accept!" but the five gifts—often offered as a separate sequence—would seem to be feminine singular vocatives (e.g., PUṢPE "O Lady of the flowers!") addressed to the goddesses who emanate from the practitioner and make offerings to the deity, stereotyped in the mantra even when such emanation is not given in the ritual text. ŚABDA seems, anomalously, to be a masculine vocative singular, parallel perhaps to mantras of the form OṂ SUVARṆA-CAKRA PRATĪCCHA "OṂ Golden wheel: accept it!"

The standard pattern of presentation for all these offerings is the recitation (or the chanting, using any one of a number of standard melodies that fit the meter) of a dedicatory verse and then of the Sanskrit mantra, accompanied by the appropriate gesture. Often each gesture is preceded during the course of the verse by a series of prefatory hand motions, which are impossible for me to draw; if the offerings are being made in abbreviated form, with the recitation of the mantra alone, the practitioner makes his gestures flow into each other, perhaps also snapping his fingers after each gesture, like the supple and flowing movements of a manual dance. All these movements vary from sect to sect, even from monastery to monastery, but everywhere, when properly performed, they add a further aesthetic dimension to the sounds of the assembly hall, and provide the individual practitioner with a controlled set of bodily motions to accompany the ballet of his visualization.

For example, the verses and mantras for the offering of the two waters and the five gifts might be recited or sung as follows, each with the appropriate gesture:[208]

1) Lord, it is good that you have come here,
giving us the opportunity for merit;
and when you have accepted our oblation
we pray you remain here.

OṂ GURU-SARVA-TATHĀGATA PRAVARA-SATKĀRA-MAHĀSATKĀRA-MAHĀ-ARGHAṂ PRATĪCCHA HŪṂ SVĀHĀ!

"OṂ Guru and all Tathāgatas: accept this excellent, respectful, most respectful, and great oblation HŪṂ SVĀHĀ!"

2) Just as the Buddha, as soon as he was born,
was bathed by all the gods,
we pray you likewise bathe your body
with this pure divine water.

OṂ GURU-SARVA-TATHĀGATA MAHĀ-PĀDYAṂ PRATĪCCHA HŪṂ SVĀHĀ!

"OṂ Guru and all Tathāgatas: accept this great water for your feet HŪṂ SVĀHĀ!"

This second verse, by the way, is a standard one, used also in "bathing the deity" and in bestowing initiation upon a disciple. And here, too, as in many other rituals, there comes a brief pause between the waters and the gifts to offer the deity a seat:

Out of love for us and for all beings,
with the strength of a magic manifestation,
remain here, Blessed Ones, we pray you,
for as long as we make offering.

OṂ GURU-SARVA-TATHĀGATA PADMAKAMALĀYAS TVAṂ!

"OṂ Guru and all Tathāgatas: a lotus seat for you!"

Next are offered the gifts, and in this standard series the verses and mantras become rather more regularized:

3) Lotus flowers, blue and white,
and red: all sorts of flowers,
all well-colored, well-formed, sweet-smelling,
we offer up to the most precious of incarnations.

OṂ GURU-SARVA-TATHĀGATA PUṢPE PŪJA-MEGHA-SAMUDRA-SPHARAṆA-SAMAYE HUṂ!

"OṂ Guru and all Tathāgatas: flowers: the gathering swelling ocean of clouds of offerings HŪṂ!

4) Aloewood and pine,
the sweetest savors of all the realms:
all the most excellent incense of the world,
we offer up to the most precious of incarnations.

OṂ GURU-SARVA-TATHĀGATA DHŪPE PŪJA-MEGHA-SAMUDRA-SPHARAṆA-SAMAYE HŪṂ!

"OṂ Guru and all Tathāgatas: incense: the gathering swelling ocean of clouds of offerings HŪṂ!"

5) Butter lamps with hearts of oil,
lamps of bamboo and twigs of fruit trees:
all that illuminates the darkness of the world,
we offer up to the most precious of incarnations.

OṂ GURU-SARVA-TATHĀGATA ĀLOKE PŪJA-MEGHA-SAMUDRA-SPHARAṆA-SAMAYE HŪṂ!

"OṂ Guru and all Tathāgatas: lamps: the gathering swelling ocean of clouds of offerings HŪṂ!

6) Camphor, sandalwood, and saffron:
the sweetest-smelling of perfumes, a joy to touch,
both natural and mixed,
we offer up to the most precious of incarnations.

OṂ GURU-SARVA-TATHĀGATA GANDHE PŪJA-MEGHA-SAMUDRA-SPHARAṆA-SAMAYE HŪṂ!

"OṂ Guru and all Tathāgatas: perfumes: the gathering swelling ocean of clouds of offerings HŪṂ"

7) Cooked rice and other pure foods,
prepared with all the countless varieties of cooking,
mixed foods, all of the most excellent flavor,
we offer up to the most excellent of incarnations.

OṂ GURU-SARVA-TATHĀGATA NAIVEDYE PŪJA-MEGHA-SAMUDRA-SPHARAṆA-SAMAYE HŪṂ!

"OṂ Guru and all Tathāgatas: food: the gathering swelling ocean of clouds of offerings HŪṂ!"

8) Great drums, conch shells, clay drums, kettledrums,
cymbals, and tabors, hosts of music:
all the most melodious sounds of the world,
we offer up to the most excellent of incarnations.

OṂ GURU-SARVA-TATHĀGATA ŚABDA PŪJA-MEGHA-SAMUDRA-SPHARAṆA-SAMAYE HŪṂ!

"OṂ Guru and all Tathāgatas: music: the gathering swelling ocean of clouds of offerings HŪṂ!"

Even more pictorial than these are some of the ritual hand gestures that accompany several of the other types of outer offerings. Figure 16, for example, illustrates the gestures that accompany the *seven precious gems of sovereignty*:

1) CAKRA-RATNA "the precious wheel"
2) HASTI-RATNA "the precious elephant"
3) AŚVA-RATNA "the precious horse"
4) MAṆI-RATNA "the precious gem"
5) STRĪ-RATNA "the precious queen"
6) PURUṢA-RATNA "the precious minister"
7) KHAḌGA-RATNA "the precious general" or "sword"

To this list is added

8) UPARATNA "the subsidiary precious things,"

whose gesture is used also to represent the offering called the "space-vast treasury." One of the rituals by Pema karpo, for example, contains the following verses and mantras for the presentation of these offerings:[209]

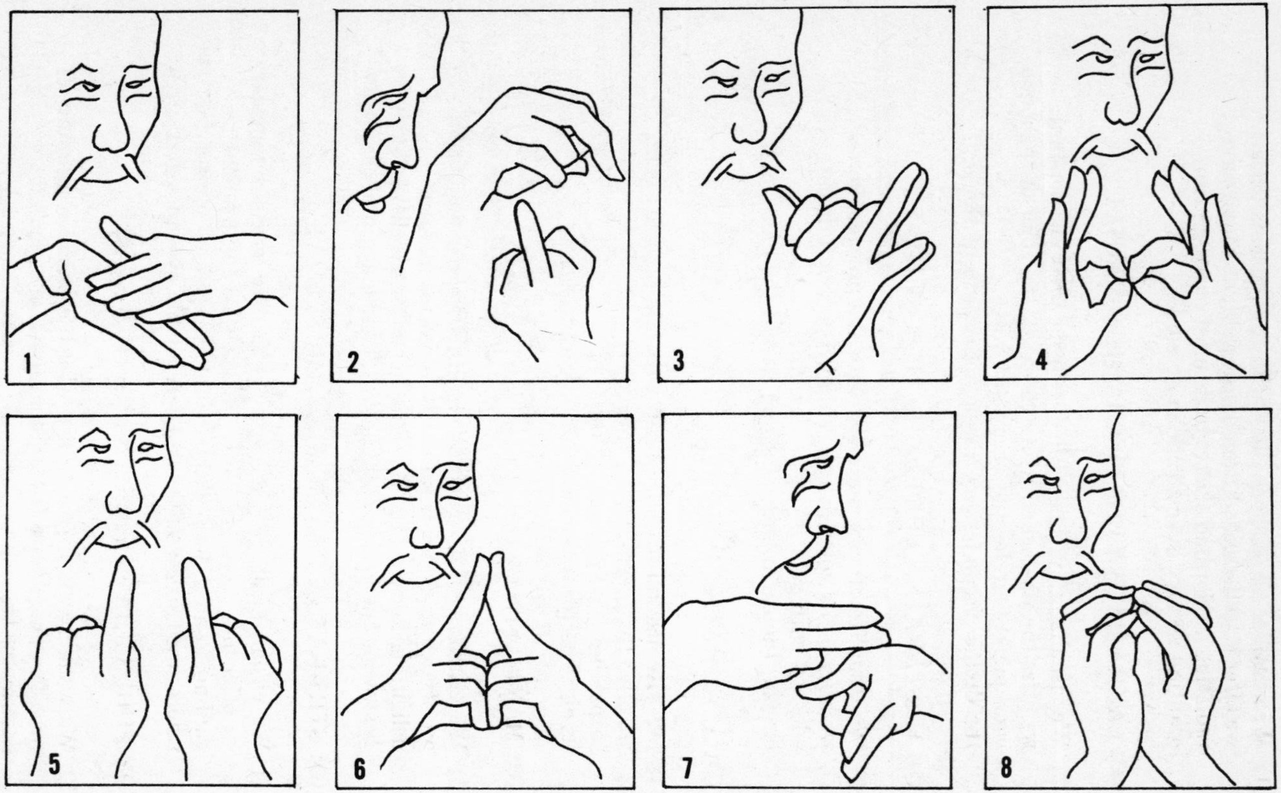

Fig. 16. The precious gems of sovereignty.

1) We visualize all of space filled with the precious wheel;
we offer it, self-created from divine gold, its round nave
radiating a thousand spokes to its most excellent rim,
granting victory over all the most noble.

OṂ CAKRA-RATNA PRATĪCCHA HŪṂ SVĀHĀ!

2) We visualize all of space filled with the precious elephant;
we offer the six-tusked white elephant, the color of the moon,
who quickly circles the ocean-girt earth,
the divine circumference through the path of the sky.

OṂ HASTI-RATNA PRATĪCCHA HŪṂ SVĀHĀ!

3) We visualize all of space filled with the precious horse;
we offer it, its color delightful as a peacock's throat,
adorned with gold, swift as thought,
circling the earth and returning within the morning.

OṂ AŚVA-RATNA PRATĪCCHA HŪṂ SVĀHĀ!

4) We visualize all of space filled with the precious gem;
we offer the green-blazing turquoise,
surpassing the brilliance of the sun,
its eight portions of purity fulfilling all wishes.

OṂ MAṆI-RATNA PRATĪCCHA HŪṂ SVĀHĀ!

5) We visualize all of space filled with the precious queen;
we offer her, as beautiful as an immortal maiden,
delighting body and mind with her most excellent touch,
bestowing the perfume of her skill, knowledge, and eloquence.

OṂ STRĪ-RATNA PRATĪCCHA HŪṂ SVĀHĀ!

6) We visualize all of space filled with the precious minister;
we offer him, his mind like a dagger, wise and prudent,
guiding to all desires with his hidden store of subtlety,
whose words must be heeded, having the eyes of a god.

OṂ PURUṢA-RATNA PRATĪCCHA HŪṂ SVĀHĀ!

7) We visualize all of space filled with the precious general;
we offer him, a hero with the strength of a god;
destroying the enemy, instantly accomplishing
all the aims that move the mind of a champion.

OṂ KHAḌGA-RATNA PRATĪCCHA HŪṂ SVĀHĀ!

8) We visualize all of space filled with soft bedding,
with turquoise knives, with soft hides,
with pleasing garments for the joyful forests,
with strong boots, with divine dwellings.

OṂ UPARATNA PRATĪCCHA HŪṂ SVĀHĀ!

Similarly, as one more example of the kind of thing that may be given as outer offerings to the deity, figure 17 shows the gestures that represent the *eight signs of good fortune*:

1) ŚRĪ-VATSYA "the coiled knot"
2) SUVARṆA-CAKRA "the golden wheel"
3) PADMA-KUÑJARA "the lotus flower"
4) KUNDA-DHVAJA "the banner of victory"
5) SITĀTAPATRA "the white umbrella"
6) NIDHI-GHAṬA "the flask of treasure"
7) ŚAṄKHA-VARTA "the right-handed conch shell"
8) KANAKA-MATSYA "the golden fish"

Pema karpo, in the same ritual,[210] gives the following verses and mantras; we may note here too that these offerings are visualized as carried by the eight goddesses of good fortune—"offering goddesses emanating from one's own heart, bearing aloft inconceivable materials for offering":

1) May there be all good fortune
by offering this holy object of good fortune
(which sets the seal of delight on the heart of the most noble)
by this beautiful maiden,
white as a conch shell, moonlike,
proudly bearing aloft the glorious coiled knot.

OṂ ŚRĪ-VATSYA PRATĪCCHA SVĀHĀ!

2) May there be all good fortune
by offering this holy object of good fortune
(which sets the seal of delight on the heart of the most noble)
by this slender-bodied maiden,
blazing with terrible jasmine light,
gracefully carrying the golden wheel.

OṂ SUVARṆA-CAKRA PRATĪCCHA SVĀHĀ!

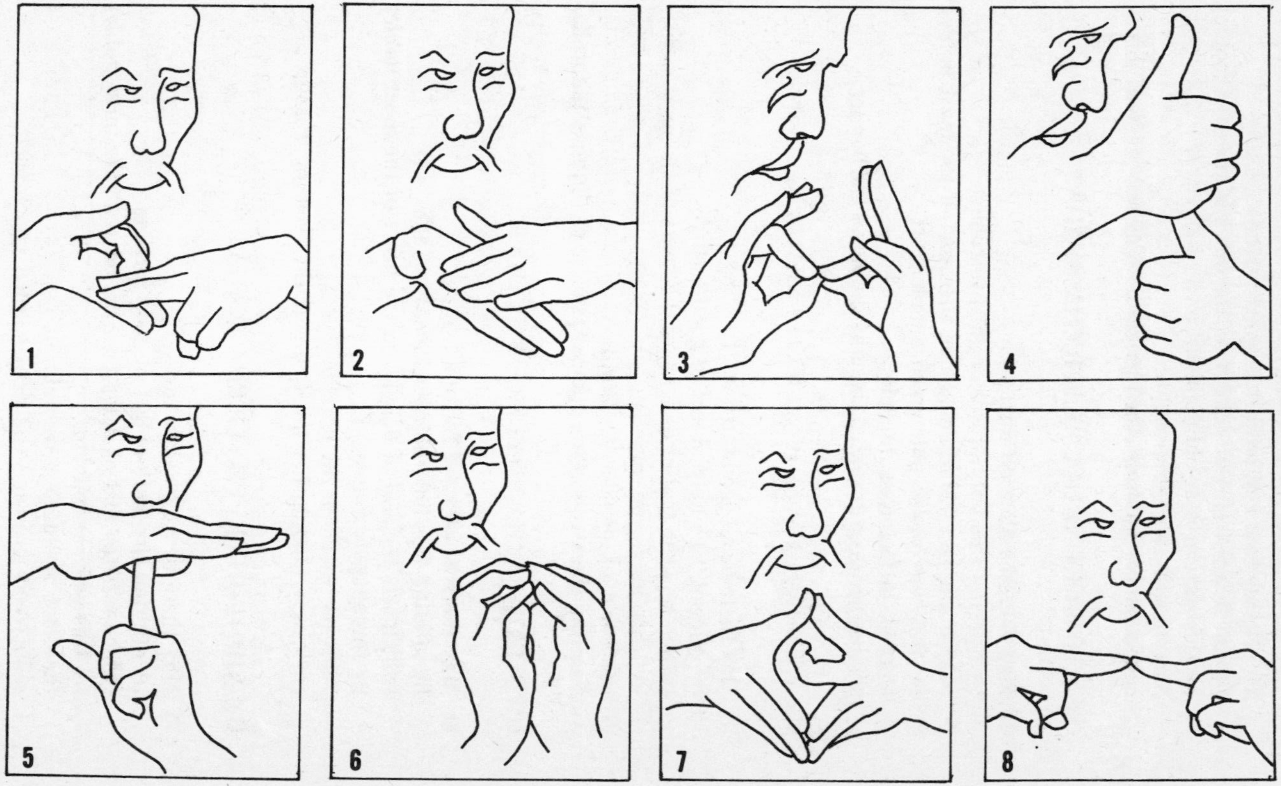

Fig. 17. The signs of good fortune.

3) May there be all good fortune
by offering this holy object of good fortune
(which sets the seal of delight on the heart of the most noble)
by this sixteen-year-old maiden,
blazing with azure-blue light,
coquettishly holding the precious hundred-petaled lotus.

OṂ PADMA-KUÑJARA PRATĪCCHA SVĀHĀ!

4) May there be all good fortune
by offering this holy object of good fortune
(which sets the seal of delight on the heart of the most noble)
by this victorious pale-green maiden,
learned in amorous melody,
singing her deep-throated tones as she raises the banner.

OṂ KUNDA-DHVAJA PRATĪCCHA SVĀHĀ!

5) May there be all good fortune
by offering this holy object of good fortune
(which sets the seal of delight on the heart of the most noble)
by this long-eyed maiden,
the color of powdered vermilion,
shooting the arrow of her glance as she twirls the pearl umbrella.

OṂ SITĀTAPATRA PRATĪCCHA SVĀHĀ!

6) May there be all good fortune
by offering this holy object of good fortune
(which sets the seal of delight on the heart of the most noble)
by this shapely maiden,
white as clouds on the horizon,
enticingly holding her hands about the flask of treasure.

OṂ NIDHI-GHAṬA PRATĪCCHA SVĀHĀ!

7) May there be all good fortune
by offering this holy object of good fortune
(which sets the seal of delight on the heart of the most noble)
by this glorious maiden,
the color of stainless emerald,
seductively grasping the right-handed conch shell.

OṂ ŚAṄKHA-VARTA PRATĪCCHA SVĀHĀ!

8) May there be all good fortune
by offering this holy object of good fortune
(which sets the seal of delight on the heart of the most noble)
by this ravishing maiden,
pleasing as a peacock's neck, her carriage haughty,
flasking like lightening as she holds the golden fish.

OṂ KANAKA-MATSYA PRATĪCCHA SVĀHĀ!

Next, in many rituals there are presented to the deity the *inner offerings*,[211] which most often consist of the *five sense gratifications*:

1) VAJRA-RŪPA "Diamond Forms"
2) VAJRA-ŚABDA "Diamond Sounds"
3) VAJRA-GANDHA "Diamond Smells"
4) VAJRA-RĀSYA "Diamond Tastes"
5) VAJRA-SPARŚA "Diamond Tangibles"

As it says in the *Guhyasamāja Tantra*:[212]

> One should make proper offerings to the Buddhas
> continually with the five sense gratifications:
> and by this fivefold offering
> one will quickly attain to Buddhahood.

Thus these five inner offerings might be presented, for example, with the following verses:[213]

1) The most excellent of forms
in all the worldly realms of the ten directions
(all that pleases the sight of the Conquerors)
are emanated as hosts of the Lady Diamond Form;
and these we offer up to the hosts of glorious gurus.

OṂ GURU-MAṆḌALA-DEVATĀ VAJRA-RŪPA PRATĪCCHA HŪṂ SVĀHĀ!

2) The most excellent of sounds
in all the worldly realms of the ten directions
(all that is melodious to the hearing of the Conquerors)
are emanated as hosts of the Lady Diamond Sound;
and these we offer up to the hosts of glorious gurus.

OṂ GURU-MAṆḌALA-DEVATĀ VAJRA-ŚABDA PRATĪCCHA HŪṂ SVĀHĀ!

3) The most excellent of smells
in all the worldly realms of the ten directions
(all that is blissful to the hearts of the Conquerors)
are emanated as hosts of the Lady Diamond Smell;
and these we offer up to the hosts of glorious gurus.

OṂ GURU-MAṆḌALA-DEVATĀ VAJRA-GANDHA PRATĪC-CHA HŪṂ SVĀHĀ!

4) The most excellent of tastes
in all the worldly realms of the ten directions
(all that is delicious to the tongues of the Conquerors)
are emanated as hosts of the Lady Diamond Taste;
and these we offer up to the hosts of glorious gurus.

OṂ GURU-MAṆḌALA-DEVATĀ VAJRA-RĀSYA PRATĪC-CHA HŪṂ SVĀHĀ!

5) The most excellent of tangibles
in all the worldly realms of the ten directions
(all that is soft to the bodies of the Conquerors)
are emanated as hosts of the Lady Diamond Tangible;
and these we offer up to the hosts of glorious gurus.

OṂ GURU-MAṆḌALA-DEVATĀ VAJRA-SPARŚA PRATĪC-CHA HŪṂ SVĀHĀ!

These five sense gratifications, again, may be identified in the ritual with the *five fleshes* (cow, elephant, horse, dog, and human flesh) or the *five nectars* (urine, execrment, semen, flesh, and blood), and this visualization might be performed as follows:[214]

Next there are before me circles of wind and fire surmounted by three heads, placed on which [as on a tripod] is the syllable A; this transforms into a skull bowl, inside of which are GO [GO "cow"], KU [KUkkura "dog"], NA [NAra "man"], HA [HAstin "elephant"], and DA [DAmya "horse"]; these transform into the five fleshes. And inside it also are VI [VIṭ "excrement"], MU [MUtra "urine"], ŚU [ŚUkra "semen"], MA [MĀṃsa "flesh"], and RA [RAkta "blood"]; these transform into the five nectars. Each is marked with its respective seed and has an OṂ above it, cleansing its impurities.

From an ĀḤ there arises a moon, above which is a HŪṂ, and from that latter there is formed a diamond skull staff which points downward to seal the top.

The wind kindles the fire, and the stream of those substances (boiling together into a single taste, loonking like the surface of

> the rising sun) invites the deities of ḍākas and ḍākiṇīs to the surface of the moon with its diamond skull staff; they enter into union together, and they melt and dissolve into a nectar of knowledge. This falls into the skull bowl, and the offering becomes an inexhaustible ocean of sublime color, taste and smell.

Here there are no representational gestures, but the practitioner usually has a small skull bowl filled with water in front of him; when it is time to offer these inner offerings he uncovers it, holding it in his left hand, and with the ring finger of his right hand he dips into the bowl and flicks a few drops of water, reciting OṂ PAÑCA-AMṚTA-PŪJĀ KHĀHI! "OṂ Eat this offering of the five nectars!"

Next the sixteen *secret offerings* are presented, worshiping the deity with the sixteen goddesses of sensual enjoyment:

1) VAJRA-VĪṆE "Lady of the Diamond Lute"
2) VAJRA-VAṂŚE "Lady of the Diamond Flute"
3) VAJRA-MURAJE "Lady of the Diamond Tabor"
4) VAJRA-MṚDAṂGE "Lady of the Diamond Drum"

5) VAJRA-HĀSYE "Lady of the Diamond Laughter"
6) VAJRA-LĀSYE "Lady of the Diamond Mime"
7) VAJRA-GĪTE "Lady of the Diamond Song"
8) VAJRA-NṚTYE "Lady of the Diamond Dance"

9) VAJRA-PUṢPE "Lady of the Diamond Flowers"
10) VAJRA-DHŪPE "Lady of the Diamond Incense"
11) VAJRA-ĀLOKE "Lady of the Diamond Lamps"
12) VAJRA-GANDHE "Lady of the Diamond Perfume"

13) VAJRA-DARŚE "Lady of Diamond Vision"
14) VAJRA-RĀSYE "Lady of Diamond Taste"
15) VAJRA-SPARŚE "Lady of Diamond Touch"
16) VAJRA-DHARME "Lady of Diamond Mental Events"

We may note, first, that these goddesses fall into groups of four: 1-4 are goddesses of music, 5-8 are goddesses of song and dance, 9-12 are goddesses of offering, and 13-16 are goddesses of the senses. In these groupings, too, the goddesses are sometimes visualized as part of the retinue of the major maṇḍalas given, for example, by Abhayākaragupta;[215] and Pema karpo identifies each group of goddesses with one of the four joys produced by the control of the channels,

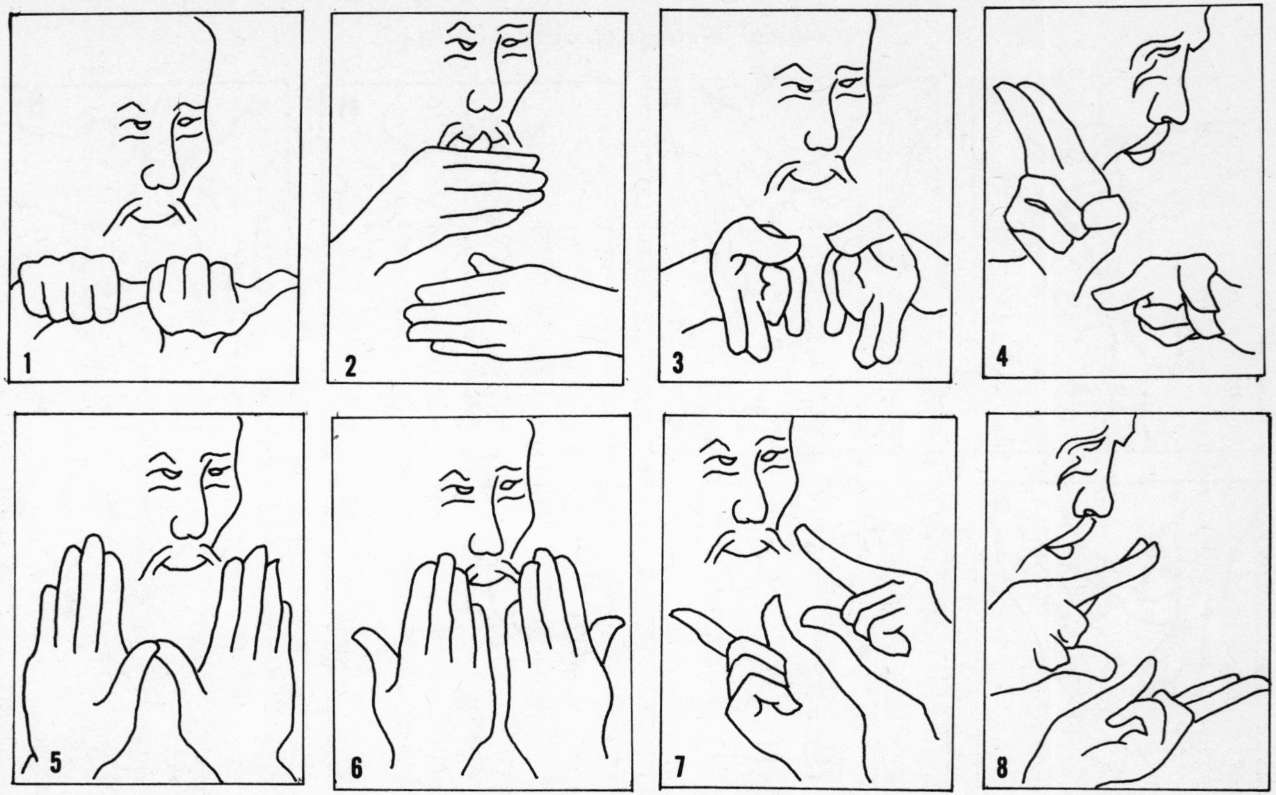

Fig. 18. The secret offerings.

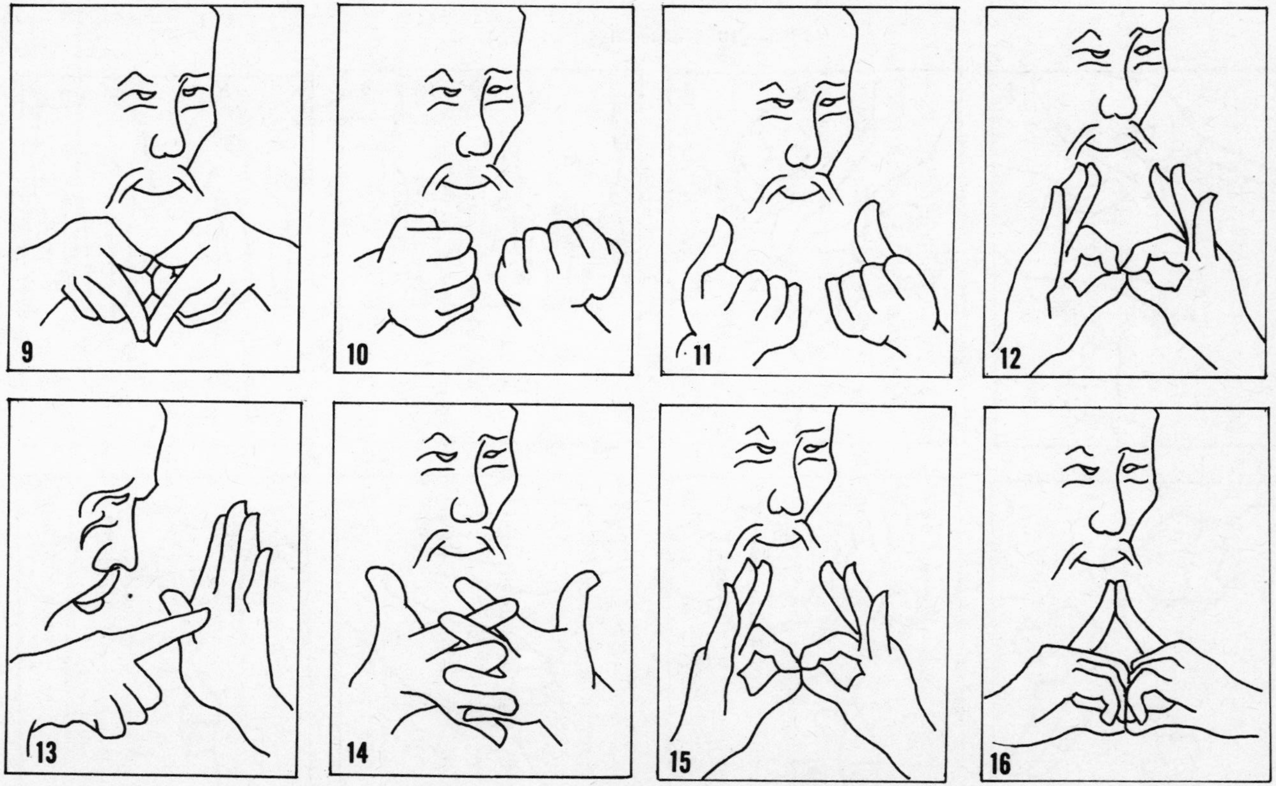

Fig. 19. The secret offerings, continued.

winds, and drop during the Process of Perfection: 1-4 are the "four thoughts of joy," 5-8 are the "four thoughts of highest joy," 9-12 are the "four thoughts of the joy of cessation," and 13-16 are the "four thoughts of innate joy."[216]

We may note in figures 18 and 19 the clearly pictorial intention of the gestures that represent these goddesses. The position of the hands in gesture 1, "Diamond Lute," for example, is clearly that used in the fingering of the South Indian *vīṇā*, as the position in gesture 4, "Diamond Drum," is that used in playing the doubleheaded South Indian *mṛdaṃga*, and that in gesture 2, "Diamond Flute," in fingering a flute played *à bec*; in gesture 7, "Diamond Song," and gesture 8, "Diamond Dance," we see gestures reminiscent of those of the classical Indian theater. Even more abstract notions are represented mimetically: gesture 13, "Diamond Vision," is indicated by the practitioner pointing to his own hand ("like a mirror," one of my informants told me); and gesture 16, "Diamond Mental Events," is indicated by the formation of a triangle with the thumbs and forefingers, in imitation of the triangular shape of the feminine "source of all events" in Tantric contemplation. We may, then, give the following as an example of the verses and mantras that might accompany these gestures in the presentation of the secret offerings of sensual and divine enjoyment:[217]

1) The holy most secret of offerings:
the blue-bodied lady playing the lute,
the beautiful lady with vajra and bell in her hands:
may she delight the Glorious Ones with the highest Bliss!

OṂ ĀḤ VAJRA-VĪṆE HŪṂ!

2) The holy most secret of offerings:
the yellow-bodied lady playing the flute,
the beautiful lady with vajra and bell in her hands:
may she delight the Glorious Ones with the highest Bliss!

OṂ ĀḤ VAJRA-VAṂŚE HŪṂ!

3) . . . the red-bodied lady playing the tabor . . .

OṂ ĀḤ VAJRA-MURAJE HŪṂ!

4) . . . the green-bodied lady playing the drum . . .

OṂ ĀḤ VAJRA-MṚDAṂGE HŪṂ!

5) . . . the laughing red lady, her carriage proud and laughing, holding vajra and bell, making sweet melodious sounds . . .

OṂ ĀḤ VAJRA-HĀSYE HŪṂ!

6) . . . the sensuous blue lady, her carriage proud and sensuous, holding vajra and bell, making sweet melodious sounds . .

OṂ ĀḤ VAJRA-LĀSYE HŪṂ!

7) . . . the singing green lady, her carriage proud and singing . .

OṂ ĀḤ VAJRA-GĪTE HŪṂ!

8) . . . the dancing yellow lady, her carriage proud and sensuous . . .

OṂ ĀḤ VAJRA-NṚTYE HŪṂ!

9) . . . the white-bodied lady with flowers in a lotus vessel, the beautiful lady with skull staff and drum . . .

OṂ ĀḤ VAJRA-PUṢPE HŪṂ!

10) . . . the blue-bodied lady with incense in a lotus vessel, the beautiful lady with skull staff and drum . . .

OṂ ĀḤ VAJRA-DHUPE HŪṂ!

11) . . . the red-bodied lady with a lamp in a lotus vessel . . . .

OṂ ĀḤ VAJRA-ĀLOKE HŪṂ!

12) . . . the green-bodied lady with perfume in a lotus vessel . . .

OṂ ĀḤ VAJRA-GANDHE HŪṂ!

13) . . . the white Lady of Vision with a mirror in a lotus vessel . . .

OṂ ĀḤ VAJRA-DARŚE HŪṂ!

14) . . . the red Lady of Taste with a water-filled conch shell in a lotus vessel . . .

OṂ ĀḤ VĀJRA-RĀSYE HŪṂ!

15) . . . the yellow Lady of Touch with clothing in a lotus vessel . . .

OṂ ĀḤ VAJRA-SPARŚE HŪṂ!

16) The holy most secret of offerings:
the blue Lady of Mental Events with the source of all events in a lotus vessel,
the beautiful lady with skull staff and drum:
may she delight the Glorious Ones with the highest Bliss!

OṂ ĀḤ VAJRA-DHARME HŪṂ!

And, finally, many rituals add to the above three classes an *offering of the Truth*, the highest and culminating gift of Great Bliss itself, which might take the form of verses such as the following:[218]

Emaho! The triple world is filled
with desire for Great Bliss.
Emaho! The peaceful Bliss has come,
spreading manifest enlightenment everywhere.
Emaho! The Great Bliss of Blisses,
the perfect Great Bliss has arisen.
Emaho! It is just like eating something;
appearances are eaten up in Emptiness.
Emaho! Simultaneously there is born a great essence,
the very nature of all events;
let us see beings as like a moon in water,
let us take what we hear to be but an echo,
let us look even upon our minds as like a mirage in the desert.
Thus do we take our food and drink as like space,
odors as like a flower in the sky.
Let our minds pervade like the sun or moon,
be as firmly fixed as mount Meru;
let us dream like the dreaming of a young virgin,
speak designations like an illusory magic show.
All these are simultaneous with the birth of Bliss;
so we are free of our worldly essence, our forms inconceivable.
Homage and praise to the highest path of the Well-gone!
where there ever arise such things.
HŪṂ! Like the sun rising in a cloudless sky,
the sun of knowledge rises in a stainless mind
spreading its illumination, the knowing of all things knowable:
homage to the precious Innate Mind!
Like a river falling in an unbroken stream
contemplative union never ceases in a firm mind;
it grows neither more nor less
but increases the experience of Bliss:

homage to the precious Innate Mind!
As the king among mountains neither trembles nor quakes,
we have gained a firmness unshaken by mental constructs,
the most excellent of fruits, ever steady and unchanging:
homage to the precious Innate Mind!
Emaho! the precious and glorious,
emaho! the precious holy Law,
emaho! the precious Innate Mind:
homage and praise to the thought of enlightenment!

Or this offering of the Truth may make a direct presentation of Great Bliss to the deity:[219]

By union with the Ritual Manifestation,
by visualization of the Knowledge Manifestation,
by coalescence with the Great Manifestation:
we make offering with the Bliss that grows but never changes.

There are other general types of offering that may be made to the various classes of deities. Nebesky-Wojkowitz has fully documented, for example, all the different offerings that may be given to the fierce protective deities;[220] but we may mention here as standard in many rituals the skull bowls that are filled with water to represent *medicine* [= semen] *and blood*, and, of course, all the various types of *tormas* that are presented at the end of the ritual to the four classes of "guest": (1) the major deity, (2) the protectors of the Law, (3) the "lords of the soil," and (4) beings in the six destinies.

The torma for the major deity—the "offering torma" whose shape and decorations vary for each god—may also be grouped together with the medicine and blood to form a separate class of offering —medicine, blood, and torma—which is called *specific* as opposed to the inner, outer, and secret offerings which are considered to be *general*; here too the offering of the Truth is split off to form a third class, called *supreme*. The medicine or symbolic semen—the male element corresponding to the female blood—is also analogized to the five nectars, so that there is a formal resemblance in the two offerings, and the same mantra may be used in both. The following excerpt illustrates how these specific offerings might be presented, for example, to Padmasambhava and the hosts of peaceful and fierce deities who surround him:[221]

Offering the *medicine*:

HŪṂ! This nectar, this distillation
of the hundred sorts of holy thing,

which causes the Fathers and Mothers of the five families,
conditions the five bodies and five knowledges,
occasions the arising of Means and Wisdom from their cause:
this we offer up to the all-beneficent guru
and his hosts of peaceful and fierce deities.
Think of us lovingly with compassion,
grant us power and magical attainment!

OṂ ĀḤ HŪṂ! SARVA-PAÑCA-AMṚTA-KHARAṂ KHĀHI!
Eat, eat all these five nectars!

OṂ ĀḤ HŪṂ! To the mouths of

the gurus of the fivefold lineage,
the gathering of the Three Jewels of the Conquerors,
the hundred families of holy ones, peaceful and fierce,
the holders of the mantra, ḍākas and ḍākiṇīs, Father and Mother,
the hosts of the ḍākiṇīs, highest of mothers,
the divine hosts of Diamond Magic Dagger:

SARVA-PAÑCA-AMṚTA-KHARAṂ KHĀHI! Eat, eat all these five nectars!

To the mouths of

the Three Jewels and Three Basic Ones
of all directions and times,
protectors of the Law, deities of wealth,
lords of hidden treasure:

SARVA-PAÑCA-AMṚTA-KHARAṂ KHĀHI! Eat, eat all these five nectars!

To the mouths of

all the others, the ocean of those worthy of offerings:

SARVA-PAÑCA-AMṚTA-KHARAṂ KHĀHI! Eat, eat all these five nectars!

Accepting the magical attainments:

HŪṂ! The stream of nectar from the union
of the Fathers and Mothers of the five families
in the skull bowl of this realm of the manifest,

this swirling nectar of the five families
possessed of the five knowledges:
grant us now the magical attainments of body, speech, and mind!

KĀYA-SIDDHI OṂ! VĀK-SIDDHI ĀḤ! CITTA-SIDDHI HŪṂ!

Offering the *blood*:

HŪṂ! This blood, which transforms
the five poisons into the five knowledges,
this blood of great passion, passionless, free of passion,
this secret great blood, nondual, free of clinging:
this we offer up to the all-beneficent guru
and his hosts of peaceful and fierce deities.

OṂ ĀḤ HŪṂ! MAHĀ-RAKTA-KHARAṂ KHĀHI! Eat, eat this great blood!

Offering the *torma*:

OṂ ĀḤ HUṂ! In this skull bowl (purity of form)
we set this great torma (purity of feeling),
we surround it with buttons (purity of conception),
we decorate it with ornaments (purity of motivation):
this great torma (purity of awareness)
we offer up to the all-beneficent Dharma Body.
E! In the skull bowl of unimpeded Emptiness
we set this great torma of clear knowledge,
we adorn it with ornaments of continuous compassion
and offer it up to the peaceful Body of Bliss.
OṂ ĀḤ HŪṂ! In the basin (the external inanimate world)
we set the torma (its internal animate beings),
we decorate it with medicine, the fruit of the elixir,
and offer it up to the peaceful and fierce Bodies of Transformation.

OṂ ĀḤ HŪṂ! GURU-DEVA-ḌĀKIṆĪ MAHĀ-BALIṂ TE GṚHṆA KHA KHA KHĀHI KHĀHI!

To you this great torma: take it, eat it, eat it!

THE MAṆḌALA OFFERING

Beyond all the offerings enumerated above there is one further type of offering which, in effect, summarizes them all, and forms the central thematic element in one of the most important and popular of Tārā's rituals. This is the offering of the *maṇḍala* (or *maṇḍalaka*, transliterated into Tibetan rather than translated, to distinguish it from the Tibetan term *chikhor* which translates "maṇḍala of the residence and its residents"). The maṇḍala offering is nothing less than the presentation to the deity of the entire world, visualized in front of the practitioner as a golden realm with Mount Meru and all its continents, a cosmogram filled with "all the entire wealth and glory of men and gods." It is perhaps the highest expression of ritualized devotion: its primary function from its Indian inception[222] has been as a presentation to one's personal guru, serving as a symbol of the complete subordination to him of all one is or has; it is held to be the only "fee" worthy enough to be given to a Master who bestows an initiation, a priceless gift whose price is therefore infinite.

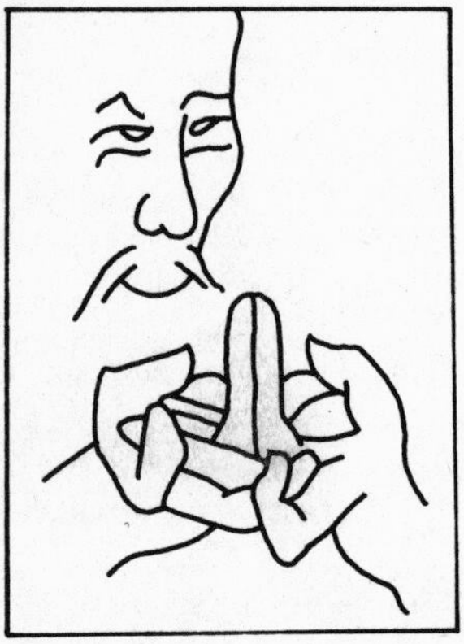

Fig. 20. The maṇḍala gesture.

The ritual hand gesture that accompanies this offering—the maṇḍala gesture—is shown in figure 20: the ring fingers in the center represent Mount Meru in the middle of the world, and the remaining fingers are so joined as to represent the four major continents that surround it. On the altar this offering is represented by a four-tiered tray, often decorated with gold and silver designs and pictures of the offerings supposedly contained therein, filled to overflowing with grain or rice. The flat base of this tray may also be used alone, and sometimes, in place of the gesture, the practitioner holds this base in his left hand and pours out upon it small "piles" of grain from his right hand, each small pile representing one of the thirty-seven offerings traditionally counted as included in the presentation. This ritual has been described by a number of Western scholars,[223] but the following brief visualization shows the standard pattern of the offering:[224]

> OṂ VAJRA-BHŪMI "Diamond foundation" ĀḤ HUṂ! The foundation is pure, greatly strong, founded with gold.
>
> OṂ VAJRA-REKHE "Diamond outline" ĀḤ HŪṂ! In the center is (1) Mount Meru, king of mountains, with HŪṂ in its middle, encircled by the ring of iron mountains.
>
> In the east is (2) Pūrvavideha; in the south is (3) Jambudvīpa; in the west is (4) Aparagodanīya; in the north is (5) Uttarakuru.
>
> Toward the east are (6) Deha and (7) Videha; toward the south are (8) Cāmara and (9) Aparacāmara; toward the west are (10) Śāṭhā and (11) Uttaramantriṇa; toward the north are (12) Kurava and (13) Kaurava.
>
> There is (14) a jewel mountain, (15) a wish-granting tree, (16) a wish-granting cow, and (17) the harvest that comes without ploughing.
>
> There are (18) the precious wheel, (19) the precious gem, (20) the precious queen, (21) the precious minister, (22) the precious elephant, (23) the precious horse, (24) the precious general; and there is (25) the flask of treasure.
>
> There are the eight goddesses: (26) Lady Sensuousness, (27) Lady of Garlands, (28) Lady of Song, (29) Lady of Dance, (30) Lady of Flowers, (31) Lady of Incense, (32) Lady of Lamps, and (33) Lady of Perfumes.
>
> There is (34) the sun and (35) the moon; there is (36) the precious umbrella and (37) the banner of victory in all quarters.
>
> And in the middle there is the entire host of the wealth and glory of men and gods.
>
> With this pure and pleasing field, these clouds of offerings drawn from the ocean of worldly realms that belong to the virtuous hosts of the three times, these enjoyments of my own and others' bodies: with these I make devoted offering to the holy and glorious gurus, my own gracious and personal guru and those of the lineage. . . . .

> I beseech you to accept this with compassion, for the sake of living beings; and, having accepted it, I pray you grant me empowerment.
>
> GURU IDAṂ MAṆḌALAKAṂ NIRYĀTAYĀMI! "Guru, I offer up this maṇḍala!"

The practitioner visualizes all these offerings; he offers up all the virtues, good qualities, and compassionate actions of himself and all beings, whether past, present, or future. He offers up everything that he himself likes or enjoys: food, clothing, palaces, soft beds and warm boots, turquoise knives and coral necklaces, even his own body for the service of the god or guru:

> Tilopa said: "If you want instruction, make a maṇḍala." But Nāropa had no grain, so he made the maṇḍala out of sand; and he sought everywhere, but could find no water for sprinkling. Tilopa asked: "Has your body no blood?" Nāropa let the blood gush from his arteries; and he looked everywhere, but could find no flowers. Tilopa chided him: "Have you no limbs? Cut off your head and put it in the middle of the maṇḍala. Take your arms and legs and arrange them arround it." Nāropa did so, and he offered this maṇḍala to his guru, fainting from loss of blood. When he regained consciousness, Tilopa asked him: "Nāropa, are you happy?" And Nāropa replied:
>
> Happiness is to offer my guru
> this maṇḍala of my own flesh and blood.[225]

THE FOUR MAṆḌALA OFFERING TO TĀRĀ

All the elements discussed so far—the visualizations, the mantras and the hand gestures, the offerings, praises, and prayers—are the building blocks from which a ritual is constructed. A Tibetan ritual is built up on a standard pattern, a set dramatic form; elements may be left out or expanded upon, but the basic structure remains the same. Authors have composed general rituals for a number of purposes, leaving out the name of the deity and his mantra, to allow the individual practitioner to fill these in with his own favorite deity, or with the deity whose basic function most closely matches the particular purpose to which the generalized ritual will be put. It is around these formal structures set out for him that the author of a ritual weaves his own pattern of verse, creating something new on a pattern as fixed as a sonnet; it is upon this written ritual that the practitioner imposes in turn his pattern of music, chanting, gestures, and dance—all as formally patterned as the ritual itself.[226]

Thus the maṇḍala, the offering of the universe, is the basic motif around which the Four Maṇḍala Offering is built, a thematic center that unifies the diverse elements of the ritual (in many ways it is only the language of dramatic criticism which is finally applicable to the description of Tibetan ritual). This ritual is one of the most popular expressions of devotion to Tārā and the most constant form of her worship. It is a ritual of offering rather than of evocation: here the goddess is generated only in front of the assembled practitioners, that she may be approached and the "stream of her heart aroused" with offerings, praises, and prayer. Yet even here the "paradox of power" functions in the recitation of the mantra, that she may not only be aroused with hymns but also coerced to confer her boons. Her very presence before the assembly is a magical image for the divine power, which may be controlled by the practiced yogin; but this power is there to be worshiped, to be requested for protection, and the ritual often includes some of the most moving poetry of Buddhist devotion. The intention is to worship and not to control; but control is in the very nature of the ritual act.

As an example of the popularity of this ritual: Lokesh Chandra has published the catalogue of an anthology (or "cycle") of miscellaneous rituals, prayers, praises, and so on, all devoted to the goddess.[227] Of the 48 different texts included in the anthology, 13—or more than 26 percent—are rituals for offering the Four Maṇḍalas; one of these rituals, the *Wish-granting Ear of Grain* by Jigme wangpo, has been translated twice in modern times into Chinese.[228]

It is not known exactly when the guru's maṇḍala offering was thus expanded and applied to the worship of Tārā. The author of the ritual we shall examine in detail was Ts'ewang norbu (1698-1755), who belonged to the Kat'og branch of the "ancient" Nyingma sect, and who was renowned as scholar, statesman, historian, and discoverer of hidden texts.[229] In the colophon to his ritual he writes that he has heard it said that this offering has a lineage from Guru Padmasambhava, Dampa jagar, and Śākyaśrī—that is, a lineage of the great "ancient" teachers—but that he himself "has never seen a clear example of a Four Maṇḍala ritual which was authentically descended from them." The most famous rituals today, he says, are all descended from Atīśa, from whose lineage three separate streams have flowed: the Kamts'ang (Karma Kajü) school, the Sacha school, and the Nart'ang school.

The lineage of the ritual among the Karma Kajü was founded by the Lord K'achöpa (Zhamarpa II, born 1350),[230] but "though it has a lineage from Atīśa, it is quite different from the other rituals in many ways, and so it is a side stream." The remaining two traditions, however, are "like an underground stream of the ritual, pervading them all up to the present day." The founder of the Sacha tradition was the "Precious Prince"—that is, Dragpa jets'en, whose work on the goddess has been previously noted—and it appears that most of the other writings in this school follow the pattern he established. But the most important tradition is that claimed to have descended from Atīśa to the great monastery of Nart'ang, where the ritual was incorporated into the famous anthology *The Hundred Rites* by the monastery's seventh abbot, Ch'im Namk'adrag (head of Nart'ang 1254-1290).[231] This is the basic text used by Ts'ewang norbu and, indeed, by most authors of Four Maṇḍala rituals.[232]

"Many evocations, rituals of permission, and instructions on the functions of many tutelary deities have been transmitted to us form the great Atīśa, the single glorious deity Dīpaṃkara," writes Yeshe jets'en,[233] "and these were collected together in the work known as *The Hundred Rites of Nart'ang*, in which is contained this ritual of the Four Maṇḍalas for Tārā. In that work it says:

> I bow to the feet of the unequaled guru! In general, it is of the utmost importance for any practitioner who wishes to gain omniscience to protect himself from hindrances. It is said that there are two methods for this: protecting oneself through Means and protecting oneself through Wisdom. Among the many different ways of protecting oneself through Means, there is the Means of praying to the Great Lady, as it is said in her praises [the *Homage to the Twenty-one Tārās*]: 'If one recites twice, three times, seven times . . .' The instructions for this recitation have been written up as the ritual of the Four Maṇḍala Offering."

"Then," continues Yeshe jetsen, "after explaining the way to perform the Four Maṇḍala ritual, it says:

> The lineage for this is as follows: Atīśa gave it to Gönpawa,[234] who gave it to Kampa,[235] who gave it to Lünpawa, who gave it to Ch'umigpa,[236] who gave it to Pedendrö,[237] who gave it to Zhangtönpa; and then it was compiled by the monk Namk'adrag as it was orally transmitted to him from his guru."

"This is to say," he concludes, "that the Four Maṇḍala ritual has a well-founded lineage."

Before performing this ritual, if possible, the practitioners should bathe themselves and cleanse the place and the equipment; if they are unable to do so, the ritual should at least be performed in the morning before any of them has eaten meat or drunk beer.[238] It is most meritorious if this ritual is performed by seven or eight pure monks; if eight monks are unavailable, it is also very potent if performed by four monks; if even those are unavailable, the holy ones of the past have said that it may be performed even by one monk. In general, any act of virtue has greater benefit if performed by those who keep all the vows of the monastic discipline; even if a monk keeps only the most important of these rules—the ten vows of a novice—the benefit of his performance is still greater than that of others. But here especially for the Four Maṇḍala ritual it is not sufficient just to have kept the vows of the monastic discipline, but the practitioners must also have gone through all the necessary initiations and have completed the prior ritual service of the deity.[239]

If this ritual is being performed for the purpose of accumulating merit, says our author after his introductory salutation to the deity, it should be performed especially at the time of the full moon, the new moon, the eighth day, and so on. If it is for cleansing one's obscurations or for clearing away hindrances, it should be performed "as appropriate to the occasion"—that is, after one has committed a sin. And if it is performed as a special provision for gaining a particular desire, it should then be performed on the day immediately preceding the event, or before embarking upon the enterprise. To this Yeshe jets'en adds that the ritual is even more meritorious if peformed on one of the great yearly festivals "when wonders were done by the great compassionate Teacher"—on Buddha's birthday, on the anniversaries of his enlightenment, his first preaching, his descent from the Heaven of the Thirty-three Gods, and so on—or on the holidays that celebrate the birth of the holy ones of the past.[240]

Again, Ts'ewang norbu says simply that the ritual should be performed in a temple or any clean and pleasing place, and to this Yeshe jets'en adds: "According to the Tantras, the texts of the great magicians, and the biographies of the holy ones of the past, it is most beneficial if the ritual is performed in the special places where ḍākas and ḍākiṇīs dwell in person, or in places where there is some special object that has been empowered by a Conqueror; if there is no place like that, it should be performed in a pleasant, clean-surfaced place."[241]

On the altar there is set out a consecrated image of the Holy Lady, if one has it, and also, as available, objects representing the Conqueror's body, speech, and mind (an image, a book, and a small stūpa). The arrangement of the rest of the altar may be seen in plate 2. As Ts'ewang norbu says:

> Arrange four maṇḍalas with seven "piles" on each and draw about each of the four a double fence, a round circle of fragrant flowers. Surround each of them also with the five offerings of butter lamps, food, incense, water, and perfume. Set out flowers in a good vessel, to be scattered at the time of praying, and all the other utensils that will be necessary later on: the offering tormas, the bathing water, and so on.
>
> The place, too, should be made beautiful by an array of decorations on the ceiling and walls: umbrellas or canopies, banners adorned with yak tails, pendants, curtains, and so on, whatever is available. If that much is unavailable, it is sufficient to use just some of the really important things, the maṇḍalas and so on. In general, the more offerings there are the better it is; but otherwise it is all right if they are created by profound contemplation.

Later on in the text, when the ritual reaches the torma offering, he adds that four "round white tormas"—also called "gift tormas" —should be set out in separate vessels in front of the larger offering tormas mentioned above; these gift tormas are those presented to the four classes of "guests" at the end of the ritual. Thus, by referring to plate 2, we can see what he calls the "three rows of tormas, arranged according to size": on the top row are the four offering tormas for the goddess, on the next row the subsidiary food tormas,

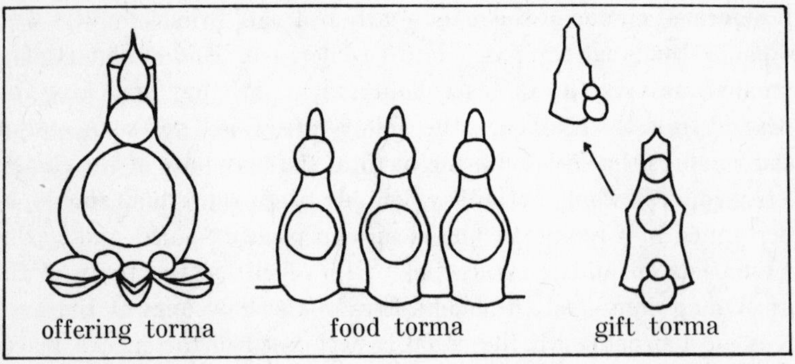

Fig. 21. The tormas for the Four Maṇḍala ritual.

and on the lowest row (nearly hidden by the offering bowls which represent the two waters and five gifts) the gift tormas for the guests.

The day before the actual performance of the ritual is spent in the preparation of the altar—the "arraying of ornaments"—and the hanging of painted scrolls on the walls, the filling of butter lamps, the picking of flowers, and the molding of the tormas. These are made from *zen*—barley flour mixed with water, with perhaps some butter added to give body—and their adornments are made of colored butter, kept cool in a pan of water and shaped with the fingers into the form of flowers, often of the most astonishing delicacy.

As the sponsors of the ritual, we had to pay for all the material necessary for these preparations: the butter for the lamps, the flour for the tormas, the grain for filling the offering bowls, and so on (the cost of the altar shown in plate 2 came to about $3.10). In addition, the sponsor buys the tea that is served throughout the ritual and, since on this occasion the performance lasted all day, lunch for the monastery as well (the food and tea for a monastery of about fifty monks came to about $9.30). Finally, each monk gets paid individually for his professional services; after some discussion with the storekeeper, it was decided that each incarnate lama was to be paid 5 rupees (about 60c), each yogin 3 rupees (about 40c), and each ordinary monk, including the children, 2 rupees (about 27c). These amounts are by no means unreasonable, even by Indian standards, yet the total of more than $20 for the ritual would make a large and perhaps irremediable dent in almost any Tibetan pocket. Aside from our scholarly interest in the performance of the ritual, we felt that our sponsorship would be one means of thanking the monastery and the lay community for their help; no Tibetan could ever think of a better way, in religious or social terms, to spend his money.

The Four Maṇḍalas are the unifying theme in this rather complex ritual of offering; though the goddess is generated only once, in front of the practitioners, the structure of the ritual may easily be obscured by its wealth of detail. A basic outline of the ceremony, as derived from the section headings in the text itself, may be helpful:

1 Preliminaries
- 1.1 Going for refuge, awakening the thought of enlightenment, and contemplating the four immeasurables
- 1.2 Making the cleansing water potent
- 1.3 Therewith empowering the place and the utensils

2 Basics

2.1 Contemplating the field for offerings

2.11 Generating the Chief Lady

2.111 Generating the symbolic being

2.112 Contemplating the syllables

2.113 Inviting the knowledge being

2.114 Sealing with the initiation

2.12 Arraying the general field for offerings

2.2 Making offerings and prayers to them

2.21 Making offerings and prayers to the Three Jewels in general

2.211 Offerings

2.2111 Homage

2.2112 Sevenfold office

2.2113 Awakening the thought of enlightenment

2.2114 Offerings proper

2.2114.1 General offerings

2.2114.2 Maṇḍala

2.2114.3 Flowers

2.212 Prayers

2.22 Offerings and prayers to the Holy Lady in particular

2.221 A recollection that the field of hosts is inherent in Tārā

2.222 Offerings and prayers proper (*repeated three times*)

2.2221 Offerings

2.2221.1 Homage

2.2221.2 General offerings

2.2221.3 Sevenfold office

2.2221.4 Maṇḍala

2.2221.5 Flowers

2.2222 Arousing her heart with her mantra, praises, and prayers

2.2222.1 Arousing her heart with her mantra

2.2222.2 Arousing her heart with praises

2.2222.3 Arousing her heart with prayers

3 Concluding acts

3.1 The filling in of the offerings

3.11 Giving the tormas

3.111 To Tārā
3.112 To the protectors of the Law
3.113 To the lords of the soil
3.114 To beings in the six destinies
3.12 Giving the offering of thanksgiving
3.13 Filling in deficiencies in the performance
3.14 Praying for forbearance toward ritual errors
3.2 The process of gathering in and sealing the ritual
3.21 The process of gathering in or praying to depart
3.22 Sealing the ritual with an earnest wish
3.23 Reciting the verses of good fortune

These section headings (as well as various instructions for the performance of the ritual and miscellaneous discussions of doctrinal points) are given in the text as "notes," distinguished from the parts to be actually recited by being printed in a slightly smaller size (or occasionally, in a manuscript, written in red ink). Sometimes the owner of a ritual text will lightly color over these notes in red so that his eye can easily skip over them when reciting the ritual aloud; and sometimes also he will mark the beginnings of the various sections by pasting small squares of colored paper at the appropriate places in the book.

1 *Preliminaries*

1.1 *Going for refuge, awakening the thought of enlightenment, and contemplating the four immeasurables*

This section begins the actual recitation of the ritual, a moral setting of the contemplative stage which corresponds internally to the empowerment of the utensils, which comes next. As Tsongk'a-pa says: "Then, settling oneself with the body upright and straight, the faculties turned inward away from all the different objects of perception, the neck held like that of a peacock, the breath made to move in and out slowly, the eyes only slightly open and directed at the tip of the nose, the teeth pressed together and the tongue joined to the palate—then one should visualize the entire host of sentient beings and earnestly awaken the thought of enlightenment, thinking: 'Awakening that great compassion which bears the burden of freeing them all from suffering, let me attain supreme enlightenment for their sake.' And one should accumulate one's stock of merit with one's mind dwelling in his vow, that all the virtue which one accomplishes is for the sake of gaining omniscient knowledge, that all the virtue empowered thereby is for the sake of gaining infinite bliss even in this world."[242]

All the monks join their palms together (fig. 22) and recite three times:

Fig. 22. Palms joined in reverence.

> Myself and all beings, as infinite as space, from this time onward until we gain the terrace of enlightenment, go for refuge to our glorious and holy gurus; we go for refuge to the divine hosts of the high patron deities' maṇḍalas; we go for refuge to the perfect blessed Buddhas; we go for refuge to the holy Law; we go for refuge to the Assemblies of the Noble Ones.

Then they "awaken the thought of enlightenment"—no hand gesture—by reciting three times:

> For the sake of all beings may I gain the rank of omniscient Buddha; it is for that reason that I enter into the ritual service and evocation of the holy noble Tārā.

Note how this thought of enlightenment is here placed in a dramatic context, a ritualization of a fundamentally soteriological impulse; and this moral preparation of the assembly—the accumulation of their stock of merit—is expressed again in abbreviated form as the monks once more join their palms and recite three times:

> To the Buddha, the Law, and the highest hosts
> until enlightenment I go for refuge.
> By this my performance of ritual service and evocation
> may I attain Buddhahood for the sake of beings.

Then, finally, putting down the hand gesture, they recite the almost invariable ritual form of the four immeasurables:

> May all beings have Bliss and the cause of Bliss.
> May all beings be freed from suffering and the cause of suffering.
> May all beings be joined with the holy Bliss wherein there is no suffering.
> May all beings dwell in the limitless equanimity that is free of near and far, love and hate.

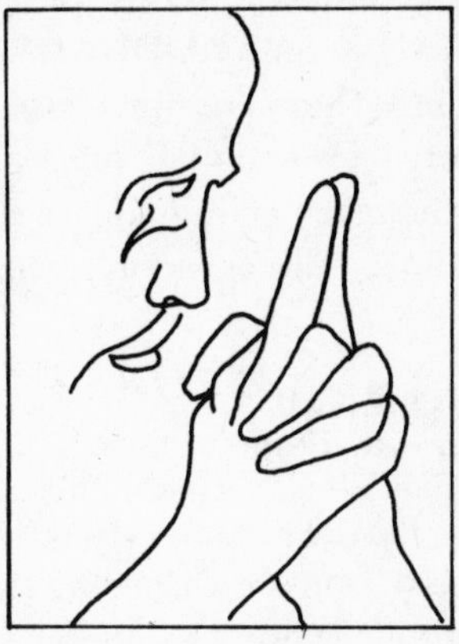

Fig. 23. The diamond-lady-of-the-mind gesture.

1.2 *Making the cleansing water potent*

All the above recitations are performed without a break, recited in a low-pitched, rhythmic, droning chant. Then, these personal preparations completed, the place and the ritual utensils must also be prepared: they are to be cleansed of all hindrances, purified into Emptiness, and contemplatively re-created and empowered. But first the water for the cleansing must be made potent; the monk who is serving the altar, and who will do all the actual work, holds the *kuśa*-grass sprinkler with the gesture called "diamond-lady-of-the-mind" (fig. 23), while the assembly recites the mantra, OṂ AMṚTA HŪṂ PHAṬ ! and visualizes that the water, set out in a large conch shell at one side af the altar, "has become the essence of Swirling Nectar." This mantra is recited 21 or 100 times, at the discretion of the head monk, until the water is magically powerful enough to be used.

1.3 *Therewith empowering the place and the utensils*

The altar server sprinkles the water on the dwelling, the utensils, and the offerings on the altar, which are cleansed with this potent water and with the fierce mantra,

> OṂ VAJRA-AMṚTA-KUṆḌALI HANA HANA HŪṂ PHAṬ!
> "OṂ Diamond Swirling Nectar: kill! kill! HŪṂ PHAṬ!"

Once the dwelling and ritual materials have been cleansed of defilement and hindrance, they are purified of all substance with OṂ SVABHĀVA-ŚUDDHĀḤ SARVA-DHARMĀḤ SVABHĀVA-ŚUDDHO 'HAṂ! Thus they are immersed in Emptiness, and they must be re-created as a divine mansion filled with divine offerings suitable to the gods, and no longer simply bowls of water and grain upon the altar. The assembly recited the visualization of this process:

> From the realm of Emptiness comes BHRŪṂ, arising from which the dwelling becomes a divine mansion, a palace of liberation made of divers precious gems, perfect in all characteristics. In the midst thereof is OṂ, from which come jeweled vessels, broad and great; within them is HŪṂ, which melts into offerings of divine substance: water for oblation, water for the feet, flowers, incense, lamps, perfumes, food, and music, materials whose form is offerings but whose essence is knowledge; and being thus the supreme cause of inhexhaustible great Bliss they pervade the entire realm of space.

These visualized offerings are empowered with their mantras, recited in rapid succession by the monks as they perform the appropriate hand gestures, the motions of their hands flowing into the semblance of a dance:

> OṂ VAJRA-ARGHAṂ SVĀHĀ! OṂ VAJRA-PĀDYAṂ SVĀHĀ! OṂ VAJRA-PUṢPE ĀḤ HŪṂ! OṂ VAJRA-DHŪPE ĀḤ HŪṂ! OṂ VAJRA-ĀLOKE ĀḤ HŪṂ! OṂ VAJRA-GANDHE ĀḤ HŪṂ! OṂ VAJRA-NAIVEDYE ĀḤ HŪṂ! OṂ VAJRA-ŚABDA ĀḤ HŪṂ!

At ŚABDA "music" (as always at the end of this series of offerings) the music that is not represented on the altar is presented in actuality: the head monk rolls the cymbals in a great crash, the monks beat the great drum, blow conches and the long brass trumpets, and the Diamond Master—the high lama who sits at the head of the hall—beats out a rolling tattoo on the *ḍamaru*, while all the rest ring their bells in the long peal and blast called the "peaceful music" of offering. And while the music crashes, almost inaudibly beneath its thunder, the monks "cause the power to descend" by reciting three times:

OṂ VAJRA-DHARMA-RAṆITA PRARAṆITA SAṂPRARAṆITA SARVA-BUDDHA-KṢETRA-PRACALITE PRAJÑĀ-PĀRAMITĀ-NĀDA-SAMBHAVITE VAJRA-DHARMA-HṚDAYĀNI SAṂTOṢIṆI HŪṂ HŪṂ HŪṂ HO HO HO ĀḤ KHAṂ SVĀHĀ!

"OṂ! The sounding of the Diamond Law, the ringing, the resounding, shaking all the Buddha realms, born of the roar of the Perfection of Wisdom, delighting our hearts in the Diamond Law! HŪṂ HŪṂ HŪṂ! HO HO HO! ĀḤ KHAṂ SVĀḤĀ!"

2 *Basics*

When these preparations of the participants, the place, and the materials are completed, the ritual moves into its main portion, which, stripped of its elaboration, consists simply of (1) the visualization of the field to whom the offerings and prayers will be made, and (2) making the offerings and prayers to them.

2.1 *Contemplating the field for offerings*

2.11 *Generating the Chief Lady*

First, then, the Chief Lady of the field is evoked through the Process of Generation; here the Process of Generation takes place in front of the assembly, but the sequence of the visualization is the same as we have examined in detail above, wherever the divine power is made to manifest itself.

2.111 *Generating the symbolic being*

The assembly dissolves everything—all of their construed and fabricated nonreality—into Emptiness, reciting the mantra, OṂ ŚŪNYATĀ-JÑĀNA-VAJRA-SVABHĀVÂTMAKO 'HAṂ! This is the stock of knowledge as opposed to the preceding stock of merit, the actual thought of enlightenment as opposed to the preceding intentional thought of enlightenment; from this omnipotent Emptiness, in a ritual reenactment of Tārā's own primal genesis, they generate the goddess before them—for this is a ritual of offering—by reciting:

It becomes Emptiness. From the realm of Emptiness there is before me an ocean of nectar, in the midst of which is PAṂ, from which there arises the stalk of a lotus, and A, from which there arises a moon. Above the moon is the blue-green syllable TĀṂ, from which there arises a blue-green lotus flower marked with TĀṂ.

From that syllable TĀṂ light radiates forth, making offerings to the Noble Ones and serving the aim of beings.

The light is gathered back in and dissolves in the syllable, and from the transformation thereof arises the holy Tārā: her body is colored blue-green; her peaceful face is smiling; her right hand is in the gift-bestowing gesture; her left hand holds over her heart, with thumb and ring finger, the stalk of a lotus whose flower blossoms into sixteen petals at the level of her ear. She is sixteen years of age; she has an essence of the thirty signs and eighty secondary signs;[243] her manner is charming and sensuous; she is adorned with two swelling breasts. She has a crest of divers jewels, earrings, necklaces, pearl necklaces, amber necklaces, bracelets, girdles, anklets, and a garland of tiny bells; she is made beautiful with many divine flowers. She is dressed in an upper garment of blue silk and lower windings of varicolored silks; her hair is bound on her left side, swirling and hanging down on her right. She is seated in the posture of royal ease, her right foot slightly extended and her left drawn up, and behind her is a halo of an undimmed full moon.

2.112 *Contemplating the syllables*

I visualize a white OṂ on the top of her head, a red ĀḤ on her throat, a blue HŪṂ on her heart, and, on a lotus and a moon, a green syllable TĀṂ in the center of her heart.

2.113 *Inviting the knowledge being*

From that syllable TĀṂ light radiates forth, inviting the knowledge being—who is like the symbolic being already visualized—from the vast field of Potala Mountain, her "natural abode," surrounded by all of Tārā's divine multitudes.

Here the monks pick up their vajras and bells (fig. 24), and the bells are rung as they say, VAJRA-SAMĀJAḤ! "Diamond gathering!" Then, as they recite the following verse (or here sing it to one of the standard melodies that fit its meter), the bells are rung at the end of each line, ending with a great peal of sound as they call out her name:

From the highest place of Potala,
born from the green syllable TĀṂ,
saving beings with the light of the syllable TĀṂ,
Tārā and your retinue: I pray you come!
ĀRYA-TĀRE!

Fig. 24. The bell and vajra.

Then with the four gestures and the mantra JAḤ HŪṂ BAṂ HOḤ! they summon the knowledge being, absorb it, bind it, and dissolve it into the symbolic being, conveying the true power of the deity into the visualization. They join their palms in reverence to the single goddess and say: "Thereby Tārā and her divine hosts dissolve indivisibly into the symbolic being."

2.114 *Sealing with the initiation*

The final step in the Process of Generation is the initiation of the deity, the sealing of its form and its power, and for this purpose the five families of Buddhas are invited: "Once again the light from her heart radiates forth and invites the five Buddhas and their retinue." The Buddhas are welcomed with VAJRA-SAMĀJAḤ! and offerings are made to them with the appropriate gestures and OṂ VAJRA-PUṢPE ĀḤ HŪṂ! . . . VAJRA-DHŪPE . . . ĀLOKE . . . GANDHE . . . NAIVEDYE . . . ŚABDA ĀḤ HŪṂ! This ends, as before, with the crash of the "peaceful music," and the Buddhas are prayed to bestow initiation with OṂ ABHIṢIÑCATU MĀṂ SARVA-TATHĀGATĀḤ! "OṂ Let all the Tathāgatas initiate me!" We may note that this mantra has been taken over unchanged from rituals of self-generation by Tibetan authors innocent of Sanskrit, even though it is here inappropriate to a deity generated in front; but it is in any event the power of the intention crystallized in the magic words which acts as the catalyst for the visualization the monks form, as they recite:

OṂ SARVA-TATHĀGATA-ABHIṢEKATA-SAMAYA-ŚRIYE HŪṂ! "OṂ The glory of the vow of initiation by all the Tathāgatas HŪṂ!"

With this mantra she is bestowed initiation from flasks filled with liquid nectar, which purifies all stains and fills her body, the overflowing excess liquid of forming on her crown an ornament of the guru Amoghasiddhi.

2.12 *Arraying the general field for offerings*

This completes the Process of Generation, with the power of the deity formed, empowered, concretized, and sealed before the assembly. Now, with the Chief Lady vividly visualized, the monks invite the rest of the field for offerings—all the Buddhas and Bodhisattvas—and "array them in the manner of general guests" in the sky before them, by reciting (or singing) the following verses of invitation:

Light radiates from my heart
and from that of the holy Tārā before me:

The gurus, high patron deities, Buddhas, Bodhisattvas, solitary Buddhas, disciples, all the hosts of the Noble Ones, the objects of my offerings VAJRA-SAMĀJAḤ!

You are the lord of all beings,
the deity who irresistibly conquers the Māras and their army,
the Blessed One who knows all things as they are:
I pray you and your retinue, come to this place!

Blessed One, for many inconceivable world eras
you have exercised compassion out of your love for beings
and have fulfilled their hopes and all their earnest wishes;
now is the time for you to serve the aim of beings!

Thus from your miraculous palace of the Dharma realm
send forth all your various magical emanations
that you may save infinite hosts of beings:
I pray you and the lords of your retinue, come!

After this prayer the monks must make sure that no hindering demons have taken advantage of this invitation or have ventured to follow upon the heels of the Buddhas into the cleansed and purified area of the temple; to expel them they recite the fierce mantra OṂ AMṚTA HŪṂ PHAṬ! and wield their vajras in the "three diamond circles," motioning away from the center of the body clockwise at the level of their eyes. Then the guests are given seats:

> OṂ PADMAKAMALĀYAS TVAṂ! The field of hosts, filling the sky before me like powdered sesame seeds on all sides of the Blessed Lady, seat themselves upon the countless precious thrones of lotus and moon which I offer to them.

Then, to aid themselves in the vivid visualization of this field of hosts, the monks join their palms and recite a "recollection of the qualities of the Three Jewels":[244]

> The Blessed Buddha, the Tathāgata, is truly the Worthy One, fully enlightened, perfect in knowledge and conduct, well-gone, knower of the world, leader of men to be tamed, supreme, teacher of gods and men, the Buddha, the Blessed One. The Tathāgata is the sufficient cause of merit, the inexhaustible supply of virtue, adorned with forbearance, the field of the treasures of merit, adorned with the secondary signs, the full-blown flower of the major signs, the proper field of practice, agreeable, delightful to the sight, gladdening those who think of him with devotion, splendid in wisdom, unfailing in strength, teacher of all beings, father of bodhisattvas, king of the noble personages, leader of beings into the city of nirvāṇa, measureless in knowledge, inconceivable in self-reliance, pure in speech, sweet to hear, impossible to cease gazing upon, unequaled in body, unsullied by the Realm of Desire, unstained by the Realm of Form, unhalted by the Realm without Form, freed from suffering, liberated from the aggregates, unpossessed of the fields, controlled in his senses, having cut the knot, liberated from passion, crossed over the stream, perfect in knowledge, dwelling in the knowledge of the Blessed Buddhas of the past, present, and future, not dwelling in nirvāṇa, dwelling at the limits of reality, placed in the stage where he looks upon all beings: such are the qualities of greatness of the Blessed Buddhas.
>
> The holy Law is truly good in the beginning, good in the middle, good in the end, true in its meaning, true in its words, unadulterated, perfect, pure, uncorrupted. The Law of the Blessed One is well-taught, verifiable, sound, immediate, conducive, inviting all to come and see, to be known by each wise man for himself. The monastic rules of the Law taught by the Blessed One are well-proclaimed, conducive to deliverance, leading toward perfect enlightenment, an undivided whole, well-founded, cutting the bonds.

> The Assembly of the Great Vehicle is truly practiced in virtue, practiced in reason, practiced in honesty, practiced in propriety, worthy of reverence, worthy of homage, the glorious field of merit, the great purifier of gifts, the place of offering, the great place of offering wherever they may be.

And, as the author of our ritual adds in a note, "by recollecting these qualities according to the meaning of the recitation, the energy of devotion is awakened."

2.2 *Making offerings and prayers to the field for offerings*
2.21 *Making Offerings and prayers to the Three Jewels in general*

Now that the field of hosts—the Chief Lady and the general guests—have been assembled and vividly visualized, the ritual proceeds to the next section, the offerings and the prayers that are made to them, beginning with the Three Jewels in general. This portion of the ritual incorporates many of the most popular and beautiful works of Buddhist devotion, and we may see, once again, how these set pieces gain in intensity by their dramatic placement within the structure of the ritual: they are no mere flourishes of poetic piety, but expressions of faith set out in the very presence of their object, evoked in reality by the visualization of the assembly.

2.211 *Offerings*
2.2111 *Homage*

The offerings to these guests begin with a homage, whose verses the monks first empower by joining their palms and reciting the following mantra three times:

> OṂ NAMO MAÑJUŚRIYE SVĀHĀ! NAMO UTTAMAŚRIYE SVĀHĀ! NAMAḤ SUŚRIYE SVĀHĀ! "OṂ Homage, sweet glory SVĀḤĀ! Homage, highest glory SVĀHĀ! Homage, splendid glory SVĀHĀ!"

This injunction has the power to increase the merit derived from the recitation of any verse that follows it; and so the monks continue by reciting (or singing) the following verses of homage to the guru and the Three Jewels, repeating each stanza three times:

> The body which is the gathering together of all Buddhas,
> whose inherent nature is the Bearer of the Vajra,
> the root of the Three Jewels:
> homage to the gurus!

The lord possessed of great compassion,
omniscient, the teacher,
the floor of the ocean of merit and qualities:
homage to the Tathāgata!

Pure, the cause of freedom from lust,
saving from evil destinies with its virtue,
alone being the highest truth:
homage to the calming Law!

Themselves saved, showing the saving path,
devoted to the pure doctrine,
having all the qualities of holiness:
homage to the Assembly!

Then there is added a further homage to the Conquerors, their dwelling places and their shrines, while each monk visualizes that he and all beings, whom he emanates from himself in their ordinary bodily forms, as numerous as the dust, prostrate toward them together.

To all those who have incarnated themselves,
the famous perfect Buddhas,
possessed of the thirty-two most excellent signs:
homage to all the Conquerors!
Homage to where the perfect Buddha was born,
to where he touched enlightenment,
turned the wheel of peace
and passed away into reposeful nirvāṇa.
I pay homage, too, to the places
where the Well-gone stayed,
where he arose and walked
and slept like a lion.
I pay homage to his shrines,
above, below, and upon the surface of the earth,
in the directions and intermediate directions,
whether they contain his relics or not.
These are the verses that were taught
by the Conqueror named Hard-to-Serve,
the holy personage who dwells
in the northeastern quarter;
and whoever praises the Tathāgatas
with these four verses
will not fall into an evil destiny
for a hundred billion world eras.

2.2112 *The sevenfold office*

Next the monks recite the sevenfold office taken from the classic text *All-Beneficent's Vow of Conduct*, the last chapter of the *Gaṇḍavyūha Sūtra*. This work sets forth an office implicity consisting of homage, offerings, confession of sins, rejoicing at merit, entreaty to turn the wheel of the Law, prayer not to pass into nirvāṇa, and dedication of merit; but here, as in many rituals, the author of our text does not give the verses to be recited: he merely cites their source, for he makes the valid presumption that every monk knows them by heart. The verses of this devotional work are very important to the Tibetans; they are in general among the most profound and lyric Indian expressions of the attitude of worship, and a copy of the text "has adorned the house altar of every family in the Tibetan-speaking world";[245] Winternitz says that they are one of the "most beautiful expressions of Buddhist piety,"[246] Thus the verses for the sevenfold office are recited as follows:[247]

By the strength of my earnest wish for worthy conduct
I manifest to the minds of all the Conquerors
bodies as the sands of the world bowing before them
and therewith I pay homage to all the Conquerors.
I visualize everything filled with the Conquerors,
as many Buddhas as grains of sand were each grain a beach,
all sitting amidst the sons of the Buddhas,
every single one the Dharma realm.
With all the sounds of the ocean whose portions are melody,
the inexhaustible oceans of praise,
I speak the qualities of all the Conquerors,
I sing the praises of the Well-gone.

With holy flowers, holy garlands,
cymbals, perfumes, most excellent umbrellas,
most excellent lamps, and holy incense
I make offerings to the Conquerors.
With holy clothing, most excellent fragrances,
fine powders piled as high as Mount Meru,
all the most excellent of noble things in special array,
I make offerings to the Conquerors.
I visualize, too, for all the Conquerors
whatever offerings are supreme and vast,
and by the strength of my faith in worthy conduct
I make homage and offerings to all the Conquerors.

Whatever sins I may have committed
under the sway of lust, hatred, delusion,

whether with my body, my speech, or my mind:
I confess them all, every one.

At whatever merit, too, any living being may have,
the Conquerors of the ten directions, the sons of the Buddhas,
the solitary Buddhas, those in training, those beyond training:
I rejoice at it all.

The lamps of the worldly realm of the ten directions,
the successively enlightened Buddhas, attained to detachment:
to all these, to all my lords,
I entreat you, turn the supreme wheel.

With folded hands I pray you
who wish to demonstrate nirvāṇa,
for the benefit and happiness of all beings
remain for world eras numerous as grains of sand.

Whatever little virtue I have acquired
by my homage, offerings, confession,
rejoicing, entreaty, and prayer,
I dedicate to the enlightenment of all.

2.2113 *Awakening the thought of enlightenment*

Then, with the following verses by Śāntarakṣita,[248] they awaken the thought of enlightenment:

Perfect Buddhas and sons of the Conqueror,
you are the witness, the attestor, the measure,
yuors is the power to serve the aims of beings
and the authority of enlightened minds: I pray you hear me!
Just as the Conquerors of the past
and the sons of the Conqueror, the heroes,
dwelling, dwelling on the terrace of enlightenment,
for the benefit and happiness of beings
awakened their hearts to their essence of Emptiness,
their own minds unarisen from the beginning,
the very self of selfless events,
were freed of all substance,
abandoned the aggregates, fields, senses,
renounced subject and object—
in that way I, too, and others like me,
awaken the supreme thought of enlightenment.

2.2114 *The offerings proper*

2.2114.1 *General offerings*

These preliminaries over, the monks make the actual offerings to their guests with the beautiful verses from Śāntideva's *Entering the Practice of Enlightenment*;[249] with the first of these verses, our author adds, "the offerings are augmented into the holy material of enlightenment":

Truly I make these offerings to the ocean of qualities,
to the Tathāgatas and the holy Law,
the three spotless Jewels and the sons of the Buddha,
only that I may grasp the precious thought of enlightenment.

And they continue with the offerings, "contemplating the meaning in their hearts":

However many flowers and fruits there are,
whatever sorts of healing herbs there are,
however many precious things there are in the world:
the clear pleasing waters,
the mountains of precious jewels,
the forests in sweet solitude,
the vines adorned with ornaments of flowers,
the trees whose branches bend with fruit,
and in the realms of the gods, the sweet scents,
the perfumes, wish-granting trees, trees of precious jewels,
the harvest that is gathered without sowing,
and all the ornaments worthy to be offered,
the lakes and ponds adorned with lotus flowers,
resounding with the alluring call of the wild geese:
all these things that belong to no one,
reaching to the very limits of space,
I take with my mind and I offer them
to the Sage, the best of men and his sons.
O holy place of offering, compassionate ones!
Think of me with love, and accept my offerings.
I am but poor and without merit,
I have no other wealth to offer.
O lord who thinks but of the benefit of others!
Accept what you will for my sake.
To the Conqueror and his sons
ever do I offer up all my body:
highest of beings! accept me,
with devotion will I be your slave.
And when you have taken me into your hands
I will fear the world no longer,
I will benefit all beings,
I will pass beyond my former sins
and sin no more hereafter.
In a bathhouse filled with fragrance,
paved with clear shining crystal
and its pleasing pillars ablaze with precious jewels,
there I spread canopies bright with pearls,

I fill the many jeweled pitchers to the brim
with sweet-scented water,
and with songs and music I bathe
the Tathāgatas and their sons.
I cover their bodies with incomparable clothing,
I dress them in pure and scented garments,
I give to them dress of many colors,
holy garments, sweet-smelling,
divers garments, soft and fine,
and with hundreds of most excellent ornaments
I adorn them as Noble Ones,
as All-beneficent, Sweet Voice, Lord of the World.
With the most excellent perfumes,
sweet essence of three thousand worlds,
I anoint the bodies of the Lords of Sages,
that they may blaze with light like gold,
cleansed, refined, purified.
To the Lords of Sages,
most excellent place of offerings,
I offer up the pleasing flowers,
lotus flowers, white and blue,
to weave a garland of all sweet smells.
I offer them also the gathering clouds of smoke,
the pervading sweetness of gladdening incense;
I offer them also the food of the gods,
all the various repasts of food and drink,
I offer them also jeweled lamps,
set out like a string of golden lotuses.
I sweep the ground, moisten it with perfume
and there strew petals of pleasing flowers.
To those whose essence is compassion I offer
a divine mansion filled with the sweet sounds of praise,
its blazing beauty adorned with pearls and precious jewels,
an ornament of infinite space.
Ever do I offer to the Lords of Sages
beautiful jeweled umbrellas, gold-handled,
delighting with their encircled ornaments,
well-formed and comely to the sight.
Let there be here the clouds
that refresh beings from their sufferings;
the hosts of other offerings,
the gladdening sound of music and song!

At this word—it being, in effect, an offering of music—the monks peal forth the sound of their bells, drums, conch shells, trumpets, cymbals, and ḍamaru in the long roll of the peaceful music, and then they continue:

Upon the holy Law and all the Three Jewels,
upon the shrines and the images,
in an unending stream let there fall
a rain of jeweled flowers;
just as Sweet Vioce and the others
have made offerings to the Conquerors,
I too offer to the Tathāgatas
to the Lords and their sons;
I too praise these oceans of qualities
with the ocean whose portions are the sweet sound of praise.
Surely let there be everywhere
the sweet-sounding clouds of their praises!

2.2114.2 *Maṇḍala*

After these general offerings—"offered by reciting the verses or by choosing from among them what one thinks proper"—the first of the four maṇḍalas is offered up to the Buddhas and Bodhisattvas (the remaining three maṇḍalas are presented to Tārā later). The monks make the maṇḍala gesture and recite the mantras and visualization of the offering:

> OṂ VAJRA-BHŪMI ĀḤ HŪṂ! A vast ground of precious gold. OṂ VAJRA-REKHE ĀḤ HŪṂ! The circumference of iron mountains. In the middle HŪṂ, the essence of protection. In the center and the four directions: OṂ HAṂ SUMERAVE NAMAḤ! OṂ YAṂ PŪRVAVIDEHĀYA NAMAḤ! OṂ RAṂ JAMBUDVĪPĀYA NAMAḤ! OṂ LAṂ APARAGODANĪYĀYA NAMAḤ! OṂ VAṂ UTTARAKURAVE NAMAḤ! And from these seeds: Meru, king of mountians; in the east Pūrvavideha; in the south Jambudvīpa; in the west Aparagodanīya; in the north Uttarakuru. To the east and west of mount Meru: OṂ A SŪRYĀYA NAMAḤ! OṂ A CANDRĀYA NAMAḤ! And from these, the sun and moon. All the rest is filled up with all the sublime possessions of gods and men.

This visualized maṇḍala is then offered up with the following standard verse (used also, for example, when offering up the 100,000 maṇḍalas during the preliminary practices):

I visualize this ground as a Buddha realm,
moistened with perfume, strewn with flowers,
adorned with Mount Meru, the four continents, sun and moon;
by my offering it, may all beings practice in this Pure Land!

OṂ ĀRYA-TĀRĀ-GURU-SARVA-BUDDHA-BODHISATTVĀNĀṂ SA-MĀTĀ-PITṚṆĀṂ SÔPASTHĀYIKĀNĀṂ SA-PARI-

VĀRĀṆĀM IDAṂ RATNA-MAṆḌALAKAṂ NIRYĀTAYĀMI!
"OṂ To the noble Tārā, the gurus, all the Buddhas and Bodhisattvas, mothers and fathers, servants and retinue, I offer up this precious maṇḍala!"

And here each monk takes some rice from the pile that the altar server has placed in front of him, and on the last word of the mantra the entire assembly flings the rice into the air. The monks resume the maṇḍala gesture and recite:

From now until I gain the terrace of enlightenment
I offer to you with devotion
for the sake of all beings
the enjoyments of my body and speech,
the substance of my virtue in the three times.
O holy place of offerings
whose eyes look upon everything:
think of me with love,
accept this offering of mine, I pray,
and having accepted, I pray you empower me!

2.2114.3 *Flowers*

Then each monk, again, takes some flowers from the pile in front of him and holds them up in the air as he recites the following mantra seven times:

OṂ NAMO BHAGAVATE PUṢPA-KETU-RĀJĀYA TATHĀGATĀYA ARHATE SAMYAKSAMBUDDHĀYA TADYATHĀ PUṢPE PUṢPE MAHĀPUṢPE PUṢPÔDBHAVE PUṢPA-SAMBHAVE PUṢPÂVAKĪRṆE SVĀHĀ!

"OṂ Homage to the Blessed One, King of the Flowery Banner, Tathāgata, Worthy One, fully enlightened! That is: flowers, flowers, great flowers! Growing of flowers, birth of flowers, strewing of flowers SVĀHĀ!"

These flowers are then offered up to the image of the Buddha, with all the monks throwing their flowers in the direction of the altar; by the power of the above mantra, "as many flowers as there may be, their offering counts for ten million times as many." When the monks offer these flowers thus empowered by the injunction to increase, they recite Śāntarakṣita's "benediction of the thought of enlightenment":[250]

By the empowerment of the Three Jewels,
by the compassion of all the Noble Ones,
by the strength of the Dharma realm,

and by the purity of our intentions and practice,
may every single type of being
(in the triple world, in the five classes, in the four wombs,
in the Realm of Form, in the Realm without Form,
in the Stage of Neither Conception nor Nonconception),
may they quickly leave behind the suffering
of the level of vulgar mental constructs,
may they gain the true and certain understanding
of nirvāṇa, the bliss of the Noble Path,
may all who have attained the Noble Path
gain the most excellent qualities of all the Realms,
may they be immersed in the pure Bliss
of the highest perfect enlightenment!

2.212 *Prayers*

The above benediction concludes the offerings made to the general guests, and the monks proceed to reap the reward of its merit by praying to the assembled hosts. The prayers our author gives in his ritual text are intended for the universal benefit of all beings, but in the course of the ritual there are often added as well any special requests to the deity which may have been made by the sponsor, by one of the monks, or by a member of the lay community. Very often, a lay person who could not afford to sponsor an entire ritual by himself will take advantage of another's patronage (or of the regular and unsponsored monastic rituals) by approaching the head monk before the ceremony or during one of its breaks, clutching perhaps a single rupee in a ceremonial scarf, to ask him to include a special prayer or an earnest wish in his behalf.

At the beginning of this portion of the ritual, the monks first recite the "vowels and consonants," the "heart of conditioned co-production," and the 100-syllable mantra of Vajrasattva; thus they are themselves purified, the preceeding ritual is made firm, and their speech is empowered for the prayer that follows. Then, filling their hands with flowers, they raise them up as they join their palms; one of these flowers is thrown in the air at the end of each stanza of the following prayer (where it says "I pray . . . ," the last Tibetan word of each stanza):

> All the hosts who dwell in the ten directions, who come in the three times, the gurus, the high patron deities, the Buddhas, Bodhisattvas, disciples, solitary Buddhas, ḍākas, yoginīs, ḍākiṇīs, protectors of the Law: whether we be in a human body, whether we be embodied or disembodied, I pray you think of all of us!

You are our holy and glorious lords, masters of inconceivable knowledge of knowing, compassion of loving, power of acting: I pray you empower me, that I may not be led astray in the aims for which I pray, that I may accomplish them from this moment on:

I pray you: spread widely in all directions
the Three Jewels,
the Buddha and his precious teachings,
the three collections:
the Rules, the Discourses, the Philosophy;
let them remain long and undecayed.

I pray you: increase the Assembly of monks,
the receptacle of the teachings;
increase too in all of them
the twelve qualities
of keeping pure their moral conduct,
guarding it as the fruit of their eye.

I pray you: increase our strength of faith
in the thought of enlightenment,
the Great Vehicle, chief of teachings;
augment ever greater and undecayed
friendliness and compassion,
the two highest thoughts of enlightenment.

I pray you: let us keep ever pure and unstained
all the vows of the mantra, foundation of attainment
on the paths of growth and freedom
given in the rituals of the Tantras,
the collection of magical science,
the heart of the teachings.

I pray you: fill up the entire earth
with those who dwell at the gates
of any of the Conqueror's teachings,
with those alone who delight the Noble Ones
in the three studies, who apply themselves
to listening, to thinking, to contemplating.

I pray you: let no hindrance arise
to the holy ones who hold the teachings;
increase their lives and activities,
their advance of the aims of beings;
let them dwell in love and harmony,
ever to hear the sweet sound of the Law.

I pray you: let all the doctrines of the Conqueror's teachings
exchange with one another
their pure individual lineages,
decrease their lust, hatred, jealousy,
be without controversy
to practice the path of highest freedom.

I pray you: let all beings impartially
attain to the great higher destiny
of devotion to the Conqueror's teachings;
let all the massed armies
of humans and nonhumans
make offerings to the teachings of the Buddha.

I pray you: let the humans and nonhumans
who delight in evil,
who are hard to tame,
who deal in black deeds,
helplessly gain a total devotion
to the teachings of the Buddha.

I pray you: let there never arise
in this land
the sorts of doctrines
of unfortunate deluded barbarians;
let all their massed armies
weaken and never advance.

I pray you: let there this instant not be
any who are set in sin,
who transform themselves
into various forms
to harm the best of the Buddha's teachings
or the best of those who hold them.

I pray you: consume especially all the hosts
who corrupt the Conqueror's teachings,
mislead those who hold them,
the deceiving Māras who teach as Law
what is not the Law to mislead those
who in good faith accept their doctrines.

I pray you: weaken those who corrupt
the long and stainless tradition of the Buddhas
with their impure defilements;
let there increase and spread everywhere
those who make perfect
the pure and stainless teachings of the Conqueror.

I pray you: let the teachings of Śākyamuni,
the Vehicles both Great and Small,
remain correct and undecayed
until the time that the Buddha Maitreya
goes to the foot of the Serpent Tree
to show the technique of perfect Buddhahood.

I pray you: cut off diseases of men and cattle;
let there be good harvest and healthy cattle;
pacify this age of contention,
weaken this era of weapons;
let there be bliss the breadth of the land
wherever the Conqueror's teachings dwell.

I pray you: make firm the life and dominion
of the kings who protect the Law;
let their people dwell also
in the law of the ten virtues;
let friends gain the glory of shared joy;
let all the harvests ripen in good season.

I pray you: hold us with compassion,
lead us with the lamp
of the teachings of past Conquerors;
delight us and perfectly fulfill
all the sincere wishes
of those who ride in your most excellent chariot.

I pray you: delight our Master, our guru,
all who have been gracious to us,
from our fathers and mothers of this life;
increase their life,
their merit and knowledge;
accomplish all their desires.

I pray you: cut off our lowly constructs,
increase our faith and wisdom;
all here assembled, Master, disciples, patron,
let us be as happy as we wish,
let us accomplish our desires in accord with the Law,
let us attain all the magical attainments.

I pray you: now that we have aroused
the thoughtful purpose of the Three Jewels
with our pure intentions,
let these prayers for the benefit
of the teachings and of beings
be accomplished unerringly, unhindered.

I pray you: by the strength of offering
the merit thereof to my personal guru,
to the Buddhas and their sons:
increase the life and power of our guru,
that he may accomplish the great aims
of the teachings and of beings.

I pray you: let us ever throughout our future lives
gain good family, clear minds, and lordship in heaven;
let us meet a holy guru
who will teach unerringly the Law;
let us gain the precious gem
of our own and other' aims.

Empower us, thay every single thing we do
serves the Three Jewels
and fulfills the aims of beings,
that we may delight the Conquerors
and quickly attain
the rank of Conqueror, Lord of Beings.

Then, in addition to this "hymn for some of the most important desires in our minds," the monks recite a prose prayer "as is found in the old writings":

I pray you spread the precious teachings of the Buddha; increase in all directions and times, let remain long and undecayed especially the Great Vehicle, whose aim is certain and unerring, and the long and stainless tradition of its diamond heart. Let those who hold the teachings, who have been to us virtuous friends, our fathers, mothers, and Masters who have passed away, accomplish and fulfill ever more greatly their cherished desire for the most excellent enlightenment. Let the Diamond Master who sits before us receive the heartfelt love of those joined to him as disciples. Let no hindrances arise to his life or power, and increase ever more greatly his beneficent qualities of the Path and its Stages. Increase ever more greatly the Assemblies of the ten directions, their harmony, and their deeds of the ten practices of the Law.

I pray you, too, to pacify this entire era of weapons, its harm, disease, famine, and contention throughout the world. Let there never arise the chronic diseases and conditions of death in this lowly body. Free us from the eight and the sixteen great terrors. Let all beings enjoy sublime possessions and happiness, and let them be in accord with the Law of the holy ones.

I pray you especially to increase the power of our glorious holy lord guru———, that he may fulfill all his wishes for the two sublime aims, achieved through the nonduality of his body, speech, and mind with the Lord of Everlasting Life.

> I pray you that through his strength we may be able to purify all the sins and obscurations of ourselves, Master and disciples, and of our patrons and retinue, led by our gracious fathers and mothers of this life: to have our minds think thoughts proper to the Law of the holy ones; to prevent the awakening in our streams even for an instant of any thoughts that are not the Law of the holy ones; to be of benefit to beings with our body, speech, and mind; to awaken in our streams undecaying friendliness and compassion and the thought of enlightenment whose heart is compassion and Emptiness; to attain the wisdom that is without stain and the mantras that are unforgotten; and to hold in our minds the entire Law gathered together in scripture and commentary.
>
> I pray you, in brief, that you let there never arise external or internal obstacles, or conditions averse to the accomplishment of the most excellent enlightenment, whether by us, Master and disciples, or by our relations or retinue. Let us perfect our two stocks, cleanse our two obscurations, and quickly, quickly, become manifest and perfect Buddhas.

Here, if it has been so requested, one of the monks gets up, prostrates three times, and recites in a high-pitched rapid monotone any special requests to the deity, "individual requests to gain virtue for the dead, or life for the living." In our case, we had asked the monks simply to thank the goddess for her past kindness to us and to request her future favor upon us and the community; this request was transmuted in the ritual into a rapid two-minute speech by the monastery's schoolteacher (whose special job in the ritual was to make just such prayers), asking for the happiness of all beings, the long life of K'amtrü rinpich'e, the spread of the Law, and the defeat of the hindering demons. The monks consider it very important that any sponsor of a ritual get his money's worth.

2.22 *Offerings and prayers to the Holy Lady in particular*

2.221 *A recollection that the field of hosts is inherent in Tārā*

This prayer ends the first and most general part of the ritual, the remainder of which is devoted solely to the goddess Tārā. But the monks must first "recollect that the entire field is inherent in the Holy Lady" to whom they will make their offerings and prayers; thus they join their palms in reverence to the gurus, the high patron deities, and the Buddhas, their sons, servants, and disciples whom they had invited previously and who sit "pervading all of space" before the assembly; then they recite (or sing) the following verses:

With devotion I invite
the chief lord of all the Law,
who has the color of refined gold,
more greatly splendid than the sun.
Peaceful, possessed of great compassion,
calm and dwelling in the stage of meditation,
lusting after neither events nor knowledge
but possessed of omnipresent and inexhaustible capacity:
come here ! come here ! pure and peaceful deity,
incarnate sage, omniscient one,
I pray you come to this place of offerings,
into this well-formed image.
Blessed One, it is good that you have come,
giving us the opportunity for merit,
and when you have accepted our offerings
grant us a thought in your heart.
Out of love for us and for all beings,
with the strength of a magic manifestation of yourself,
remain here, Blessed One, I pray you,
for as long as we make offerings to you.
Remain here for the sake of beings,
here united with this image:
I pray you surely grant us life without disease, lordship,
and enlightenment the most excellent of all.

As they recite this prayer, the monks visualize that the vast "field for offerings, all the Three Jewels of the unbounded Dharma realm," gather together and enter indissolubly into the Holy Lady; the assembly makes firm their belief that "the body, speech, mind, qualities, and function of them all become in the goddess a glorious and holy immanence." When they recite the words "united with this image" they should visualize the union actually taking place in the image on the altar, their "concrete support of the visualization;" if no image is available, the field of hosts is to be visualized as entering into the appearance of the goddess they had generated with their visualization.

The ritual text adds in a rather lengthy note that most of the other rituals of offering which have been transmitted from Atīśa here generate and invite the Blessed Lady for the first time, as the principal recipient of the second maṇḍala, but according to the present tradition, the author says, she is generated from the very beginning, though both methods are acceptable. The point is, he says, that the Blessed Lady is here presented with worship at the time of the first set of offerings, since she is then seated at the head of the Three

Jewels in general; and when the three later sets of offerings are presented to the Blessed Lady in particular, they are being presented to the Three Jewels in general as well, since by the above visualization they are made inherent in the goddess. "It is not as if when offering to one the other must stop and wait his turn," he says. "Rather there is just more attention given to the one more important at the time." The author goes on to say in a long poem that "these words are not just a copy from earlier books, nor are they improper, newfangled, and mistaken; rather it has been my intention to impart to the old words the youth of newness."

2.222 *Offerings and prayers* (repeated three times)

Now begins the actual "ritual of offerings, praises, and prayers" to Tārā, and this entire section is repeated three times, thus making up an offering of four maṇḍalas in all.

2.2221 *Offerings*

2.2221.1 *Homage*

As before, the section of offerings to the goddess begins with the recitation of a homage, first empowered by the same mantra (OṂ NAMO MAÑJUŚRIYE SVĀHĀ . . .) and then recited or sung to one of its standard melodies:

Having eyes that flash like lightning,
heroine, TĀRE, TUTTĀRE,
I bow to you, sprung from the corolla
of the lotus of the Buddha's face.
Having a face like the circle
of the full autumm moon,
I pay homage to you, holding a lotus flower
with your gift-bestowing gesture.
From the cage of this world TUTTĀRE!
pacifying defilements with SVĀHĀ!
I bow to you, opening the gate of Brahma
with your inherent OṂ!
I pay homage to Tārā, the mother,
the mother of all,
protecting the entire world
from the eight great terrors.
Gods and demigods bow their crowns
to the lotus of your feet;
I pay homage to Tārā, the mother,
saving from all poverty.

This homage may be abridged, the text adds, by reciting only the mantra that empowers it and repeating just the last verse seven times (this verse is the first stanza of Atīśa's famous *Hymn to Tārā*, discussed above); but in that event the same abbreviated homage must be performed in the next two offering rituals as well. The homage must, in other words, be the same before each presentation.

2.2221.2 *General offerings*

The general offerings for Tārā have already been set out and empowered during the ritual preparations (1.3), but here their strength must be regenerated by the recitation of the "clouds of offerings" mantras and their gestures from ARGHAṂ to ŚABDA (. . . PŪJA-MEGHA-SAMUDRA-SPHARAṆA-SAMAYE HŪṂ!); while ringing their bells for the peaceful music with which the mantra series ends, the monks add beneath the crash and roar:

> OṂ NAMO BHAGAVATE VAJRA-SĀRA-PRAMARDANĀYA TATHĀGATĀYA ARHATE SAMYAKSAMBUDDHĀYA TADYATHĀ VAJRE VAJRE MAHĀ-VAJRE MAHĀ TEJO-VAJRE MAHĀ-BODHI-MAṆḌÔPASAṂKRAMAṆE SARVA-KARMÂ-VARAṆA-VIŚODHANE SVĀHĀ!
>
> "OṂ Homage to the Blessed One, Crushing with Diamond Nature, the Tathāgata, Worthy One, fully enlightened! That is: diamond, diamond, great diamond! Great blazing diamond, aproaching the terrace of great enlightenment, cleansing all obscurations of karma SVĀHĀ!"

And as this power "descends," the monks visualize that the "clouds of offerings radiate like circles of ornaments of the all-beneficent space-vast treasury" and are offered up to the Blessed Lady visualized before them, "whose essence is the Three Jewels who dwell pervading all of space," as they join their palms in reverence and recite (or sing) the following verse:

> I emanate light that arrays the oblations,
> masses of oblations, canopies of oblations;
> and having spread out the various oblations
> I offer it up to the great-souled Conquerors.

And then, with the appropriate gesture, they recite the following mantra:

> OṂ ĀRYA-TĀRĀ-GURU-BUDDHA-BODHISATTVA-SAPARIVĀREBHYO VAJRA-ARGHAṂ PRATĪCCHA PŪJA-MEGHA-SAMUDRA-SPHARAṆA-SAMAYE ĀḤ HŪṂ!

The verse is repeated seven more times, substituting for each ocurrence of the word "oblation," first "water for the feet" and then, similarly, "flowers," "incense," "lamps," "perfumes," "food," and "music"; each offering is accompanied by the above mantra (and the appropriate gesture), substituting therein for the word ARGHAṂ the words PĀDYAM, PUṢPE, DHŪPE, ĀLOKE, GANDHE, NAIVEDYE, and ŚABDA. On the word "music" is the first crash of the cymbals, as the peaceful music is offered up in actuality. These offerings are then filled in by the addition of an abbreviated version, consisting of the recitation (or singing) of the following verses:

> Oblations, water for the feet, flowers,
> incense, lamps, perfumes,
> food, and music:
> as many offerings as might be contained
> in the vast and measurelass ocean,
> that many I set out with devotion,
> that many I offer up;
> masters of compassion!
> having accepted them as you will,
> I pray you serve all the aims of beings.

Then once more the monks recite a series of offering mantras, with the appropriate gestures, beginning with OṂ ĀRYA-TĀRĀ-GURU-BUDDHA-BODHISATTVA-SAPARIVĀREBHYO VAJRA-ARGHAṂ PRATĪCCHA SVĀHĀ! and substituting therein, as before, PĀDYAṂ, PUṢPE, DHŪPE, ĀLOKE, GANDHE, NAIVEDYE, and ŚABDA. Under the rumbling of the peaceful music they recite:

> NAMAḤ SARVA-BUDDHA-BODHISATTVEBHYAḤ OṂ SARVA-VID PŪRA PŪRA AVĀRHEBHYAḤ SVĀHĀ!

> "Homage to all the Buddhas and Bodhisattvas! OṂ Omniscient! Satisfying, satisfying to all those worthy SVĀHĀ!"

This mantra constitutes a final "offering, reverence, and homage with one's head to the feet of all the Tathāgatas."

2.2221.3 *Sevenfold office*

Next, after these general offerings, there is offered up to Tārā the sevenfold office, here quoted from the Four Maṇḍala ritual written by the abbot Ch'im Namk'adrag and included in his *Hundred Rites of Nart'ang*:

I make offerings, I give to the holy blessed mother Tārā and all her hosts of Noble Ones, fathers, mothers, sons, neighbors, and disciples; I fill the depths of space with all that is described in *All-Beneficent's Vow of Conduct*: oblations, water for the feet, flowers, incense, lamps, perfumes, food, music, cymbals, umbrellas, and banners in great measure, all the things set out here in actuality, and all those holy substances of gods and men which have no owner in the worldly realm: the sublime materials of bliss, the clouds of offerings generated by the force of their mantras and the strength of their visualization.

I confess all the sinful and unvirtuous deeds of myself and of all beings, in all the lifetimes we have spun through this world, all our sins and omissions: in brief, all we have done that we should not have done, all we have not done that we should have done.

I rejoice at all the merit of the infinite virtue of the Noble Ones and ordinary people of the three times.

I entreat all the Conquerors of the ten directions to turn the supreme wheel of the Law.

I pray all the Lamps of the World who might wish to demonstrate the technique of passing away into nirvāṇa: do not pass away into nirvāṇa, but serve the aims of the world and long remain.

> Whatever small virtue I may have accumulated
> from my homage, offerings, confession,
> rejoicing, entreaty, and prayer:
> I dedicate it all for the sake of enlightenment.
> Let me be just like those wise men
> whose body, speech, and mind are pure,
> whose conduct is pure, whose realm is pure,
> exemplary in dedicating their merit.

Instead of this prayer, or in addition to it, there may be recited the sevenfold office found at the end of many editions of the *Homages to the Twenty-one Tārās*, here attributed by our author to a "Nun Lakṣmī," the writer of several canonical praises of Avalokiteśvara, but not, as far as I can find, given credit for these verses in the *Tenjur*. Again, this office may be either recited or sung by the monks:

> I pay homage with complete sincerity
> to the holy noble Tārā
> and to all the Conquerors and their sons
> who dwell in the ten directions and the three times.
> I give flowers, incense, lamps, perfumes,
> food, and music,

whether actually set out or emanated by my mind:
I pray the hosts of Noble Ones accept them.
I confess all that I have done
with my mind under the sway of defilement,
the ten unvirtuous acts, the five sins of immediate retribution,
from beginningless time until now.
I rejoice at all the merit
that has been accumulated through virtue in the three times,
by disciples, solitary Buddhas, Bodhisattvas,
and ordinary people.
I entreat you to turn the wheel of the Law
of the Little, Great, and Uncommon Vehicles,
according to the differences of mind
and thought of beings.
I pray you look upon beings
who are sunk in the ocean of suffering;
until this world is emptied out,
let not your compassion pass away into nirvāṇa.
May whatever merit I have accumulated
become a cause of enlightenment for all;
may I have the glory of being the leader
of beings, long and unhindered.

2.2221.4 *Maṇḍala*

Then the second maṇḍala is presented to Tārā with the maṇḍala gesture (see pl. 3):

OṂ VAJRA-BHŪMI ĀḤ HŪṂ! A vast ground of precious gold. OṂ VAJRA-REKHE ĀḤ HŪṂ! The circumference of iron mountains. In the middle HŪṂ, the essence of protection. In the center and the four directions: OṂ HAṂ SUMERAVE NAMAḤ! OṂ YAṂ PŪRVAVIDEHĀYA NAMAḤ! OṂ RAṂ JAMBUDVĪPĀYA NAMAḤ! OṂ LAṂ APARAGODANĪYĀYA NAMAḤ! OṂ VAṂ UTTARAKURAVE NAMAḤ! And from these seeds: Meru, king of mountains; in the east Pūrvavideha; in the south Jambudvīpa; in the west Aparagodanīya; in the north Uttarakuru. To the east and west of Mount Meru: OṂ A SŪRYĀYA NAMAḤ! OṂ A CANDRĀYA NAMAḤ! And from these, the sun and moon. All the rest is filled up with all the sublime possessions of gods and men.

This I give to the field of hosts as infinite as space, the guru holy blessed mother noble Tārā, her sons, servants, and disciples. I pray the great loving one accept it! And having accepted it, I pray you purify the obscurations of all of us, Master and disciples and all connected with us: let us perfect our stocks and quickly gain the holy and most excellent of magical attainments!

OṂ ĀRYA-TĀRĀ-GURU-SARVA-BUDDHA-BODHISATTVĀNĀṂ SA-MĀTĀ-PITṚṆĀṂ SÔPASTHĀYIKĀNĀṂ SA-PARIVĀRĀṆĀM IDAṂ RATNA-MAṆḌALAKAṂ NIRYĀTAYĀMI!

And as before the monks take some rice from the piles before them and on the last word of the mantra fling it into the air as a token of offering. Then, resuming the maṇḍala gesture, they recite:

Born from the ocean of our pure intentions,
full-blown with petals of the continents,
beautiful with the anthers of Mount Meru,
having the color of sunlight and moonlight,
radiating the fragrance of all desired possessions,
pervading all like the circle of the sky:
this most excellent flower of the precious maṇḍala
I offer to the Conquerors and their hosts.

And once again all the monks throw a handful of rice in the air.

The author of the ritual text mentions in another long note that he has derived this version of the maṇḍala with seven piles instead of the usual thirty-seven (there being here only Mount Meru, the four continents, and the sun and moon) from the old writings, which "all agree in speaking of it in that way." Here, however, the visualization itself is not abbreviated, for "the realm of the maṇḍala and the hosts of its possessions must be visualized as greatly expanded and filling the sky." On this basis, he says, the symbolism is as follows: when generating Mount Meru and the sun and moon, there is vividly visualized all the glorious possessions of the gods; when generating the four continents, all the glorious possessions of men, headed by the "seven precious gems of sovereignty"; at the summit of Mount Meru, all the glorious possessions of the demigods; and in the oceans between the continents, all the glorious possessions of the serpent kings. In general, he says, this maṇḍala is offered filled up with the hosts of the sublime and glorious possessions of the entire world, though there is certainly nothing wrong with using instead the expanded version of thirty-seven piles of grain.

2.2221.5 *Flowers*

As before, the monks take some flowers from the piles before them, reciting the mantra that multiplies their offering:

OṂ NAMO BHAGAVATE PUṢPA-KETU-RĀJĀYA TATHĀGATĀYA ARHATE SAMYAKSAMBUDDHĀYA TADYATHĀ PUṢPE PUṢPE MAHĀPUṢPE PUṢPÔDBHAVA PUṢPASAMBHAVE PUṢPĀVAKĪRṆE SVĀHĀ!

Then the flowers are thrown toward the image on the altar, but at this point the benediction is changed to the following one, "found in the old writings," which the monks recite (or sing) as they make their offering:

> Holy blessed compassionate one!
> I pray you, for myself and all infinite beings:
> cleanse our obscurations, perfect our two stocks
> and let us attain perfect Buddhahood!
> Until we attain it, through all our future lives
> I pray you let us gain the highest bliss of gods and men;
> quickly pacify, let there not be
> obstacles to the accomplishment of omniscience,
> evil spirits, hindering demons, diseases, epidemics,
> the various things that make untimely death,
> evil dreams and evil omens,
> the eight great terrors, or any harm.
> I pray you let us all effortlessly attain
> all at once our aims in the augment and increase
> of mundane and supramundane
> sublime happiness and good fortune.
> Let there grow and increase like the waxing moon
> our efforts at evocation, the spread of the holy Law,
> the continual evocation of you,
> and the sight of your most excellent face,
> the precious thought of enlightenment
> which understands the meaning of Emptiness.
> Let us attain a clear prophecy of future Buddhahood
> in the beauteous and joyous maṇḍala of the Conquerors
> where we are born from a beautiful holy lotus:
> let the Conqueror Amitābha say so!
> Let there be the good fortune
> of the Mother who holds the lotus flower,
> the deity I have evoked through all my lives,
> the active power of the Buddhas of the three times,
> the green one-faced, two-handed quick one, the heroine!

2.2222 *Arousing her heart with her mantra, praises, and prayers*
2.2222.1 *Arousing her heart with her mantra*

The foregoing concludes the offerings made to Tārā, and now the ritual proceeds to "arouse the stream of her heart" with the recitation of her mantra, praises, and prayers, that she may fulfill all the desires of the assembly and of its sponsor. Tārā's mantra is here called a *vidyā*, simply in the sense of a mantra for a female deity;[251] but since the word "mantra" has for all practical purposes been naturalized into the English language, we shall continue to use the term, though it is not strictly correct.

The recitation, too, is here an example of the *effectuation of the mantra* in the heart of the deity generated in front, as opposed to the *contemplation of the mantra* in the yogin's own heart during his self-generation; as such, this recitation constitutes the performance of what is called in chapter ii a "ritual function," and this magical control over the stream of her heart requires the completion of the prior ritual service of the deity, which itself presupposes her initiation. There is, indeed, the element of magical coercion here, for the monks had become the goddess in the prior self-generation, in solitary contemplation perhaps years before, and they speak with the very voice of the goddess. To command the deity in this carefully constructed atmosphere of reverent worship is, however, not presumptuous; it is, finally, the goddess who arouses herself, in her own magical speech, out of her own magical intention.

The monks first recite the textual sequence for the visualization of the mantra in Tārā's heart:

> In the Blessed Lady's heart, placed upon a lotus flower and moon, there is the green syllable TĀṂ, around which are the encircling syllables of the Queen of Mantras. The light thereof gathers together and radiates forth, making offerings to the ocean of Conquerors and arousing their hearts. It pacifies all the evil conditions—sins, obscurations, sufferings, diseases, and obstacles—of all beings, represented by a field of visualization consisting of ourselves, Master and disciples, our gracious parents, our patrons, and so on; it augments and increases all their good conditions—life, merit, glory, and knowledge—and I think they attain the magical attainment of the highest enlightenment.
>
> Now let me direct my mind one-pointedly toward the visualization of the Queen of Mantras: OṂ TĀRE TUTTĀRE TURE SVĀHĀ! This is Tārā's basic mantra, the queen of all mantras, which grants all attainments.

In addition to this basic mantra may be attached a number of different "appendixes," according to the particular function the practitioner may wish to accomplish by the recitation. For example, there may be inserted between OṂ TĀRE TUTTĀRE TURE and SVĀHĀ the appendix SARVA———ŚĀNTIṂ-KURU! "Pacify all———!" The blank may be filled in with one of the following: GRAHĀN "evil spirits", VIGHNĀN "hindering demons," VYĀDHĪN "diseases," JVARĀN "fevers," ROGĀN "sicknesses," UPA-

DRAVĀN "injuries," AKĀLAMṚTYŪN "untimely deaths," DUḤ-SVAPNĀN "bad dreams," DURNIMITTĀNI "evil omens," and CITTÂKULĀNI "confusions." For example, to accomplish the function of pacifying an epidemic or fever: OṂ TĀRE TUTTĀRE TURE SARVA-JVARĀN ŚĀNTIṂ-KURU SVĀHĀ! "OṂ TĀRE TUTTĀRE TURE Pacify all fevers SVĀHĀ!"

The above recitations, the author of our text says, are those given in the majority of the old writings; but one may also fill in the above appendix to the basic mantra with ŚATRŪN "enemies," BHAYÔPADRAVĀN "terrors and injuries," YUDDHĀNI "battles," DUṢKṚTĀNI "evil deeds," KṚTYĀ-KĀKORDHĀN "magic and killing curses," and VIṢĀNI "poisons."

Again, one may use the appendix SARVA———RAKṢAM-KURU! "Protect from all———!" In this instance the terms become: GRAHEBHYO "from evil spirits," VIGHNEBHYO "from hindering demons," VYĀDIBHYO "from diseases," JVAREBHYO "from fevers," ROGEBHYO "from sicknesses," UPADRAVEBHYO "from injuries," AKĀLAṂṚTYUBHYO "from untimely deaths," DUḤ-SVAPNEBHYO "from bad dreams," DURNIMITTEBHYO "from evil omens," CITTĀKULEBHYO "from confusions," and similarly ŚATRUBHYO "from enemies," BHAYÂPADRAVEBHYO "from terrors and injuries," YUDDHEBHYO "from battles," DUṢKṚTE-BHYO "from evil deeds," KṚTYĀ-KĀKHORDEBHYO "from magic and killing curses," and VIṢEBHYO "from poisons." For example, to protect from bad dreams: OṂ TĀRE TUTTĀRE TURE SARVA-DUḤSVAPNEBHYO RAKṢAṂ-KURU SVĀHĀ! "OṂ TĀRE TUTTĀRE TURE Protect from all bad dreams SVĀHĀ!"

A mantra for the pacifying of terrors in general is as follows:

> OṂ TĀRE TUTTĀRE TURE SARVA-BHAYA-VIMOCANA RĀJA-CAURA-AGNI-VIṢA-UDAKA-BHAYĀNI PRAŚAMA-YA SVĀHĀ!
>
> "OṂ TĀRE TUTTĀRE TURE Liberation from all terrors: extinguish, extinguish the terrors of kings, thieves, fire, poison, and water SVĀHĀ!"

Or one may recite the basic mantra with an appendix such as:

> OṂ TĀRE TUTTĀRE TURE SARVA-BANDHANA-TĀḌANA-RĀJA-TASKARA-AGNI-UDAKA-VIṢA-ŚASTRĀNI PARIMO-CAKA SVĀHĀ!
>
> "OṂ TĀRE TUTTĀRE Liberating from all bondage, beatings, kings, thieves, fire, poison, water, and weapons SVĀHĀ!"

In this manner, the author says, the basic mantra can be filled in with the name of any sort of thing one may wish to pacify.

Again, to cleanse one's own or another's sins and obscurations, one adds in the same way the appendix SARVA-PĀPAṂ-ĀVARAṆA-VIŚUDDHE! "Cleansing all sins and obscurations!" This should be recited with the addition of the name of the person for whose sake it is being done. To gain wealth, one adds to the basic mantra DHANAṂ ME DEHI! "Give me wealth!" If one wants any special kind of wealth, the name of it should be substituted for DHANAṂ. But best of all, for the increase of life, merit, and knowledge, one adds the most famous of all these appendixes: MAMA ĀYUḤ-PUṆYA-JÑĀNA-PUṢṬIM-KURU! "Increase my life, merit, and knowledge!" If this is being recited for the sake of someone other thon oneself, his name should be substituted for MAMA.

All these present mantras, concludes our author, are the most important ones; after a beginner knows these, their number can be increased.

The text next proceeds to discuss how many times the mantra should be recited. The most excellent holy ones say that at the first and second offerings of the maṇḍala to the Holy Lady (that is, at the second and third maṇḍalas of the ritual) the basic mantra is recited 300 times and with the appropriate appendix 100 times; at the third offering they are recited respectively 800 and 400 times each, thus making a grand total of 2,000 recitations. In some of the other texts, however, the number of times one should recite the mantra is not clear. But we do read in the *Homages to the Twenty-one Tārās* that the basic mantra has a definite sequence of two, three, and seven ("If he recites them clearly two, three, seven times . . ."); hence we follow the count given therein by taking as a base number 100 recitations of the basic mantra and 50 recitations of the mantra with the appendix, so that the grand total in the three offering rituals is 1,800 recitations.

Here our author's mathematics may seem obscure at first, but what he means is that for the recitation after the first maṇḍala to Tārā the base numbers of her mantras are multiplied by two, after the second maṇḍala by three, and after the third maṇḍala by seven. Thus, after the first maṇḍala to Tārā the basic mantra is recited 200 times and with its appendix 100 times: $(100 \times 2) + (50 \times 2) = 300$. After the second maṇḍala the basic mantra is recited 300 times and with its appendix 150 times: $(100 \times 3) + (50 \times 3) = 450$.

After the third maṇḍala the basic mantra is recited 700 times and with its appendix 350 times: $(100 \times 7) + (50 \times 7) = 1{,}050$. And thus the grand total of recitations is $300 + 450 + 1{,}050 = 1{,}800$. In general, however, our author concludes, the more times the mantra is recited the greater is its benefit, and since there is no real certainty about the number, it should be read as much as possible.

At this point in the ritual the assembly hall is filled with the rising and falling drone of the monks reciting the mantra, each monk going at his own pace, until the head monk decides that the requisite number of recitations has been reached; though many monks keep count of their recitations on their rosaries, it is still the head monk who decides how long the recitation shall go on. Then, having thus aroused Tārā's heart with her mantra, visualizing all the while the radiation of healing light from her heart, the monks proceed to "arouse her heart with praise, that they may please the deity and gain her special benefits."

2.2222.2 *Arousing her heart with praises*

The *Homages to the Twenty-one Tārās* is the single most important praise of the goddess in the entire literature, and its Tibetan translation is rendered into a meter unusual in its extreme 8-syllable regularity (x́ x x́ x x́ x x́ x). Its recitation is thus ideally suited to a low and murmurous chanting, a rising and falling hum that lasts as long as one's breath; in every ritual where the goddess is praised at all, almost without exception this is the praise that is used. Thus the monks now visualize that these "praises to the noble Tārā, this King of Tantras," are recited not only by the monks themselves but also by all sentient beings, and that the sound thereof arises even from the very elements. The recitation begins with this introductory verse, called her "praise with the basic mantra":

> OṂ! Homage to the holy and noble Tārā!
> Homage, TĀRE, quick one, heroine,
> removing terror with TUTTĀRE,
> savioress, granting all aims with TURE,
> the syllables SVĀHĀ: to you I bow!

And then the assembly moves directly into the recitation of the twenty-one verses:

> Homage, Tārā, quick one, heroine,
> whose eyes flash like lightning,
> born from the opening corolla
> of the lotus face of the Lord of the triple world.

Homage, Lady whose face is filled
with a hundred autumn moons,
blazing with the laughing beams
of the hosts of a thousand stars.

Homage, Lady whose hand is adorned with a lotus,
a lotus blue and gold,
whose field of practice is charity, striving,
austerity, calm, acceptance, and meditation.

Homage, Lady abiding in infinite victory
in the crown knot of the Tathāgata,
served by the sons of the Conqueror
who have attained every single perfection.

Homage, Lady who fills all quarters of space
with the sounds of TUTTĀRE and HŪṂ,
trampling the seven worlds with her feet,
able to summon all before her.

Homage, Lady worshiped by Indra, Agni, Brahma,
by the Maruts and Viśvêśvara,
honored by hosts of spirits,
of ghosts, celestials, and the walking dead.

Homage, Lady who destroys the magic devices of others
with the sounds of TRAṬ and PHAṬ,
trampling with right foot up and left extended,
blazing with a blazing mass of fire.

Homage, Lady who annihilates the heroes of Māra,
TURE, the terrible lady,
slaying all enemies
by frowning the brows of her lotus face.

Homage, Lady holding her hand over her breast
with a gesture that symbolizes the Three Jewels,
her palms adorned with the universal wheel
radiating a turbulent host of its own beams.

Homage, Lady whose diadem spreads a garland
of shining and happy beams,
subjugating Mārā and the world
with a laughing, mocking TUTTĀRE !

Homage, Lady able to summon before her
all the hosts of protectors of the earth,
saving from all distress by the movement
of her frowning brows and the sound of HŪṂ !

Homage, Lady whose diadem is a crescent moon
blazing with all its ornaments,
ever lit by the beams
of Amitābha in her piled hair.

Homage, Lady placed amidst a garland that blazes
like the fire at the end of the world era,
annihilating the army of the enemy
in her joyous posture of royal ease.

Homage, Lady who strikes the earth with her hand,
who pounds upon it with her feet,
shattering the seven underworlds
with the sound of HŪṂ made by her frowning brows.

Homage, Lady blissful, virtuous, calm,
whose field of practice is calm nirvāṇa,
possessed of SVĀHĀ and OṂ,
destroying great sins.

Homage, Lady who shatters the bodies of enemies
in her joyous posture,
the savioress manifested from HŪṂ
in the mantra arraying the sound of ten syllables.

Homage, Lady who strikes with the feet of TURE,
whose seed is the form of the syllable HŪṂ,
shaking Mount Meru, Mandāra, Kailāśa,
and all the triple world.

Homage, Lady holding the deer-marked moon
in the form of an ocean of gods,
dispelling all poison
with the sound of PHAṬ and twice-spoken TĀRA.

Homage, Lady served by the ruler of hosts of gods,
by the gods and horse-headed celestials,
dispelling contention and bad dreams
with the brilliance of her joyous armor.

Homage, Lady in whose eyes is the brilliant light
of the sun and the full moon,
dispelling terrible fevers
with TUTTĀRE and twice-spoken HARA.

Homage, Lady endowed with the strength of calm
by the array of the three Truths [OṂ ĀḤ HŪṂ],
destroying the hosts of evil spirits, the walking dead,
TURE, most excellent Lady!

This is the praise with the basic mantra,
and these are the twenty-one homages.

After the introductory verse (the "praise with the basic mantra"), the homages are recited twice; then follows a single recitation of the following verses, considered to be part of the basic text, which set forth the benefits of the recitation (the "benefit verses"):

> Reverently recited by an intelligent man,
> by one who has great devotion to the goddess,
> arising at evening or at dawn to remember them,
> they grant complete fearlessness,
> they pacify all sins,
> they destroy all evil destinies.
> Quickly he will be initiated
> by 70 million Buddhas;
> attained the greatness thereof,
> he will proceed to the rank of Buddhahood.
> Even if he has eaten or drunk
> a dreadful poison,
> vegetable or animal,
> by remembering them, it is completely dispelled;
> he completely abandons the hosts of sufferings,
> the afflictions of evil spirits, fevers, and poisons,
> even for other beings as well.
> If he recites them clearly, two, three, seven times,
> by wishing for sons he will gain sons,
> by wishing for wealth he will gain wealth,
> he will gain all that he desires
> and there is no hindrance that can resist him.

And all the monks visualize that the Blessed Lady is pleased with these praises, and that she touches with her gift-bestowing gesture the heads of them all, Master and diciples and those for whose sake the ritual is being performed, granting them holiness.

2.2222.3 *Arousing her heart with prayers*

Finally, then, the monks "arouse the stream of her heart with prayer," praying for their desires and requesting the magical attainments. They fill their hands with the flowers before them and join their palms, and "with a devoted and one-pointed mind" they repeat the prayer made before to the Three Jewels in general (2.212), except that this time, after the first paragraph (which ends ". . . I pray you think of all of us!"), they insert the following lines:

> Holy blessed noble Tārā, with the hosts of fathers, mothers, sons, neighbors, and retinue: I pray you think of all of us!

And as before flowers are scattered at each verse, and a benediction may be recited at the end for the fulfillment of any special prayer or earnest wish.

This concludes the first of the three "rituals of offering and prayer to the holy blessed Lady," and the monks now go back to the beginning (2.222) and repeat the entire ritual again. Here, however, for the third maṇḍala (the second offered to Tārā in particular) the homage at the beginning of the offerings (2.2221.1) is changed to the recitation (or singing) of the following verses:

> Long-eyed mother of the Lord
> of the triple world,
> mother who gives birth
> to all the Buddhas of the three times,
> performing all their functions
> by the strength of your compassion,
> by your knowledge of nonduality,
> by your unwavering power:
> mother of Maitreya
> I pay homage to you.
>
> Performing all functions
> with your green color,
> your youth of sixteen years
> is the vastness of your qualities,
> your smiling face
> is the delight of beings,
> your calming eye
> looks out over the triple world:
> lady of great compassion
> I pay homage to you.
>
> You spread your seat upon a moon
> whose essence is the thought of enlightenment,
> your cross-legged posture
> is unshaken by defilement,
> you sit on a lotus seat
> free of all obscuration,
> your aureole is a full moon
> of inexhaustible Bliss:
> great and inexhaustible Bliss
> I pay homage to you.
>
> You are adorned with the finest garments
> and many precious gems,

your gift-bestowing right hand
grants magical attainment to him who evokes you,
your left hand grasps a lotus flower,
symbol of your stainless purity,
your two hands
are the union of Means and Wisdom:
boundless body of union
I pay homage to you.

The remainder of the second ritual for Tārā is exactly the same as the first, repeating everything over again, save only that here the basic mantra is recited 300 times and with its appendix 150 times; following the same numerical sequence, the *Homages* are here read three times and the benefit verses once.

The fourth maṇḍala (the third "ritual of offering and prayer to Tārā") again goes back to the beginning (2.222), although here, as before, the homage at the start (2.2221.1) is changed to the recitation (or singing) of the following:

Homage to Tārā our mother:
great compassion!

Homage to Tārā our mother:
a thousand hands, a thousand eyes!

Homage to Tārā our mother:
queen of physicians!

Homage to Tārā our mother:
conquering disease like medicine!

Homage to Tārā our mother:
knowing the means of compassion!

Homage to Tārā our mother:
a foundation like the earth!

Homage to Tārā our mother:
cooling like water!

Homage to Tārā our mother:
ripening like fire!

Homage to Tārā our mother:
spreading like wind!

Homage to Tārā our mother:
pervading like space!

In this third ritual for Tārā her basic mantra is recited 700 times and with its appendix 350 times; the *Homages* are read seven times and the benefit verses once.

3 *Concluding acts*

3.1 *The filling in of the offerings*

3.11 *Giving the tormas*

After all four maṇḍalas have been offered, the ritual moves into its concluding acts, which begin with filling in the offerings; the first of these, again, is the presentation of the tormas to the four classes of guests. The most standard list of these consists of (1) the main deity, who represents as well all the gurus, high patron deities, Buddhas, Bodhisattvas, and so on; (2) the protectors of the Law in general; (3) the "lords of the soil," the local spirits who rule over a particular spot—the lands of a village, a mountain pass, or the ford of a river—and whose influence for good or ill can have a profound effect upon the success of the Law in any locality; and (4) the sentient beings in all the six destinies. This list can, of course, vary: sometimes, for example, the latter two classes may be grouped together and offered a single "worldling torma"; very often special "prayer tormas" are offered to the protectors; another torma may be offered to the hindering demons as a bribe not to distrub the ritual, and so on (we shall see examples in the coming chapters). Each of these tormas has its own distinctive shape and decoration; a prospective head monk must know how to make perhaps fifty different types. Thus the presentation of these tormas is by no means a minor part of the ritual, as evidenced by the care given to their decoration and the artistry lavished upon their production. Their offering constitutes as much a ritual function as does the effectuation of the mantra in Tārā's heart and requires as much personal and contemplative preparation.

We have seen that on the altar are three types of torma: here the offering tormas and the food tormas do not play an active part in the ritual, representing simply the general offerings that are made throughout, "effigies" as it were for the contemplative creation of the "divine substances" of the ritual. It is, rather, the gift tormas that are here presented to the guests and, in the case of the last three, actually thrown out the door of the assembly hall to their waiting recipients (the gift torma for Tārā remains on the altar, for she is present there before the assembly).

3.111 *To Tārā*

In presenting the first of these tormas to the goddess, the offering is cleansed by the recitation of the AMṚTA mantra and purified into Emptiness by the recitation of the SVABHĀVA mantra. The monks recite the following visualization:

> From the realm of Emptiness are torma vessels, vast and great, made of precious gems, inside of which are OṂ ĀḤ HŪṂ. These syllables melt and tormas arise therefrom, a great ocean of all that could be desired, sublime in color, odor, taste, and strength.

These visualized tormas are then empowered by reciting OṂ ĀḤ HŪṂ three times, each recitation accompanied by rolling the fingers inward and bringing the hands around to form the special empowering flying-bird gesture (see fig. 25), so named after its spreading, winglike shape. Thus pure and empowered, the tormas are "given to the blessed noble Lady, the gathering into one of the Three Jewels, and to her retinue," by reciting seven times the following mantra:

Fig. 25. The flying-bird gesture.

> NAMAḤ SARVA-BUDDHA-BODHISATTVĀNĀM APRATI-HATA-ŚĀSANĀNĀṂ HE HE BHAGAVATE MAHĀSATTVA-SARVA-BUDDHA-AVALOKITE MÂVILAMBA MÂVILAMBA IDAṂ BALIṂ GṚHṆĀPAYA GṚHNĀPAYA HŪṂ HŪṂ JA JA SARVA-VISAN-CARE SVĀHĀ!
>
> "Homage to all the Buddhas and Bodhisattvas, and to their indestructible doctrine! O Blessed One! great being seen by all the Buddhas! Do not hesitate! do not hesitate! Take! take this torma! HŪṂ HŪṂ! JA JA! Moving about everywhere SVĀHĀ!"

As the monks offer this torma to the goddess, they "visualize that she accepts it": they see her draw up its essence with her narrow tongue, in the shape of a hollow and one-pointed vajra. In addition, they make offerings to her with the mantra series and the gestures of the outer offerings, and they praise her with Atīśa's verse "Gods and demigods bow their crowns . . ." To complete the triad of offerings, praises, and prayers, they pray to her by reciting (or singing) the following standard lines:

> I bow to the Conquerors and their sons,
> by the white light of whose compassion
> the aim of beings is served,
> the refuge and protector of the protectorless.
> May the noble Tārā and her retinue
> accept this torma which we give in offering;
> let us, yogins and retinue,
> attain life without disease, lordship,
> glory, fame, good fortune,
> and all the great increase of our enjoyment:
> grant to us the magical attainment of the functions
> of pacifying, increasing and so on.
> Let the oath-bound guardians protect us,
> be to us friends granting all magical attainments.
> Let us be without untimely death, disease,
> evil spirits, or hindering demons.
> Let us be without bad dreams, evil omens,
> or wicked deeds.
> Let the world be happy: grant good harvest,
> the increase of grain, the increase of the Law.
> Source of all happiness!
> let us accomplish all that we wish.

> I pray you, holy noble Tārā, grant us all the magical attainments, ordinary and most excellent. I pray you be our refuge from all harm, the eight and the sixteen great terrors. I pray you save us from the great ocean of suffering in this world. I pray you pacify all suffering.

Here, too, if the practitioner has any special purpose in mind, he may take advantage of these offerings and praises to "pray fiercely for its accomplishment."

3.112 *To the protectors of the Law*

The second gift torma is then offered to the protectors of the Law in general. As before, it is contemplatively re-created from Emptiness, as the monks recite the AMṚTA and SVABHĀVA mantras and read the textual sequence of its generation, and it is then empowered with OṂ ĀḤ HŪṂ and the flying-bird gesture. Then, with the torma gesture (fig. 26) the monks offer it to the protectors by reciting three times the mantra, OṂ A-KĀRO MUKHAṂ SARVA-DHARMĀNĀM ĀDY-ANUTPANATNVĀT! OṂ ĀḤ HŪṂ PHAṬ SVĀHĀ! And they pray to the protectors:

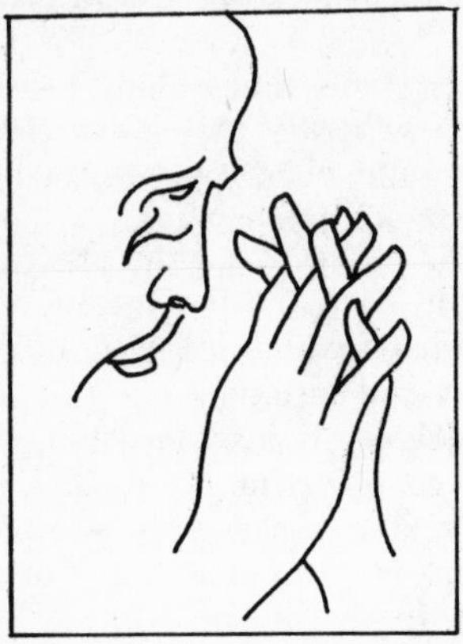

Fig. 26. The torma gesture.

> All the hosts who protect the teachings of the perfect and blessed Buddhas, the ocean of oath-bound outer and inner glorious protectors, their retinue of fathers, mothers, brothers, sisters, and sons, their families and troops: accept this torma! And I pray you, spread the precious teachings of the Buddha, let all beings be happy; raise up the possessions, grant the desires of us all, Master and disciples, our parents and patrons; increase and let us accomplish all the sublime happiness of the certainty of the holy Law!

3.113 *To the lords of the soil*

The third torma is offered to the lords of the soil; it is generated and empowered as before and, as with the protectors, is dedicated to them with the torma gesture and the mantra, OṂ A-KĀRO MUKHAṂ SARVA-DHARMĀNĀM ĀDY-ANUTPANNATVĀT! OṂ ĀḤ HŪṂ PHAṬ SVĀHĀ! But these recipients are not considered so much deities as simply beings who have achieved a potent destiny, to be used for better or worse; thus the torma is further offered them by reciting three times the "burning-mouth" mantra, whose original intention was the magical alleviation of the distress of the "hungry ghosts":

NAMAḤ SARVA-TATHĀGATA-AVALOKITE OṂ SAMBHARA SAMBHARA HŪṂ! "Homage! Seen by all the Tathāgatas! OṂ Maintenance, maintenance HŪṂ!"

Then the assembly makes the following prayer to the lords of the soil:

Homage to the blessed Tathāgata Many Jewels! Homage to the blessed Tathāgata Holy Beauty! Homage to the blessed Tathāgata Abyss of Vast Body! Homage to the blessed Tathāgata Free of All Terror!

To the entire host here assembled, headed by Firm Lady, goddess of the earth, whether they have come here fortuitously or are the inherent dwellers of the place: the lords of the soil, lords of the place, and lords of the village, of this Sahā world system and this continent of Jambudvīpa in general, and in particular of the Snowy Land of Tibet, and especially of this land, this country surrounded by these mountains: to you we give in offering this very great torma! And having accepted it, pacify all the adverse conditions and hindrances of us all, Master and disciples, and all our patrons; be to us virtous friends, let us accomplish all the desires we wish and all our plans in accord with the holy Law.

And then, as ordinary beings who have yet to reach enlightenment, the lords of the soil are given in addition the highest gift of all, the "gift of the Law," in the following words:

Commit no sins
and practice the divine virtues;
the taming of one's own mind
is the teaching of the Buddha.

3.114 *To beings in the six destinies*

The fourth gift torma is then offered to all the infinite numbers of beings in the six destinies, an act of compassion for their hunger and their suffering. It is generated and empowered as before and is dedicated to its recipients by reciting the "blazing-mouth" mantra seven times:

NAMAḤ SARVA-TATHĀGATA-AVALOKITE OṂ SAMBHARA SAMBHARA HŪṂ! "Homage! Seen by all the Tathāgatas! OṂ Maintenance, maintenance HŪṂ!"

Then the monks recite the names of the four merciful Tathāgatas as above:

Homage to the blessed Tathāgata Many Jewels! Homage to the blessed Tathāgata Holy Beauty! Homage to the blessed Tathāgata Abyss of Vast Body! Homage to the blessed Tathāgata Free of All Terror!

And here they add:

> We dedicate and give in offering this vast great torma to all the beings in the six destinies, the five classes and the four birthplaces which comprise the entire triple world. May all beings, their streams satiated with inexhaustible Bliss, quickly have the opportunity to attain the rank of Buddhahood!

And all these beings, too, are given the gift of the Law.

3.12 *Giving the offering of thanksgiving*

The remaining portion of this filling in of the offerings first repeats the general offerings and praises, but here they are presented to the deity as a concluding gesture of thanksgiving. The offering materials are empowered once more with their mantras and gestures, and they are offered up either with the simple series of offering mantras and gestures or with such verses as "Like a vast ocean . . ."—"whichever one wishes," the text says, which means, in effect, at the discretion of the head monk.

Again the goddess is praised either with Atīśa's verse, "Gods and demigods bow their crowns . . . ," or with the *Homages*; and there may even be added a repetition of the sevenfold office which accompanies that text. How extended the offering is, and what texts are used, is decided by the head monk often simply on the spur of the moment, depending upon his mood and other imponderable factors. Therefore the other monks are required to have a vast store of memorized verses, ready to be recited at a moment's notice. The thanksgiving then concludes with a dedication of merit, as the monks join their palms and recite (or sing) the following verses:

> Guru, holy deity Tārā,
> the whole host of Buddhas and Bodhisattvas,
> their fathers, mothers, sons, disciples, neighbors,
> retinue, and servants: think of me!
> May we all, Master and disciples,
> quickly gain the fruit of great enlightenment;
> may the sufferings of all beings, infinite as space,
> quickly be exhausted;
> may we attain the unobstructed strength
> to save the unsaved, rescue the unrescued,
> banish the sighs of the careworn,
> and place all beings in the stage of nirvāṇa.
> May we have the measureless strength
> to study the infinite teachings
> of all the Buddhas of the three times,

to practice enlightenment in great waves.
Thus we dedicate to the fruit of great enlightenment
the hosts of virtue of ourselves and others:
may the holy Tārā ever protect us
unweakened and unerring through all our future lives!

3.13 *Filling in deficiencies in the performance*

The deficiencies in the performance are made up by reciting three times the vowels and consonants, the 100-syllable mantra, and the heart of conditioned coproduction, that the missing speech may be filled in and the ritual itself purified and made firm. The monks end with 108 repetitions of the mantra OṂ VAJRASATTVA HŪṂ!

3.14 *Praying for forbearance toward ritual errors*

The monks recite the following prayer to ask the deity's forbearance toward any mistakes in or omissions from the performance of the ritual:

If something were not at hand, or defiled,
or if we performed or manipulated
with a mind clouded over:
may our Lord be forbearing toward it all!

If our deep contemplation were not vivid because we were under the sway of drowsiness or distraction (defilements of thought common to persons who are just beginners like us), if the utensils were impure, the hosts of offerings too few, our cleanliness incomplete, our mantras unclear, our ritual in error or confused—I pray you noble and compassionate ones be forbearing toward it all, whatever faults we may have committed. I pray you, right now, remove our obscurations, banish our sighs, and let us accomplish unhindered our functions and magical attainments.

3.2 *The process of gathering in and sealing the ritual*

3.21 *The process of gathering in or praying to depart*

The ritual is now drawing to its conclusion, and the invited deities are dismissed. The Process of Perfection is here inapplicable, for its yogic processes and "gathering in and arirsing" in the body of Innate Union can be visualized only in self-generation. But the practitioners may here imbibe the deity's empowerment through the process of gathering in—a designation parallel to "Process of Perfection"—and visualize that the knowledge being dissolves into their foreheads by the recitation of OṂ ĀḤ HUṂ! Similarly they may here establish the deity in the basis upon the altar, visualizing the dissolution of the knowledge being therein, and commanding SUPRATIṢṬHA "Standing firm!" But most commonly the monks simply request the knowledge being to depart to her natural realm with the gesture called, appropriately, "asking to depart"—a typical Tibetan gesture, often used to speed a parting guest (fig. 27)—and the recitation (or singing) of the following verse, snapping their fingers and sounding a peal of music at the mantra:

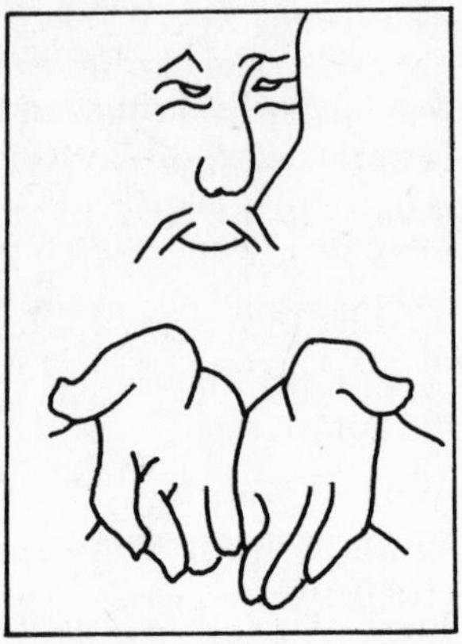

Fig. 27. The asking-to-depart gesture.

OṂ! You have served the aim of all beings:
grant us the concordant magical attainments!
Though you depart to your Buddha country,
I pray that you may return again. OṂ VAJRA MUḤ!

Then the monks request that the "worldlings"—the various local spirits and the beings in the six destinies—depart also to their own place.

3.22 *Sealing the ritual with an earnest wish*

The assembly seals the ritual with the following earnest wish, recited or sung:

By this virtue may all persons
accumulate their stocks of merit and knowledge;
may they attain the two holy things
that are born from merit and knowledge.
May all the Bodhisattvas
succeed in ever thinking of the aims of beings;
may the lords, thinking thereof,
grant blissful possessions to beings;

may they long remain,
receiving, honoring, possessing the teachings,
the one medicine for the suffering of beings,
the source of all bliss.
May our patron be perfected
in the "equalities of giving,"
imposing no construct of "reality" upon the gift,
the one who gives, the one to whom given.
May all our practices be
like the practices performed by Sweet Voice,
for the sake of accomplishing the aims of beings
who stretch to the limits of space in the ten directions.
May there be in this world, in all of existence,
the inexhaustible attainment of merit and knowledge,
an inexhaustible treasury of Means and Wisdom,
of deep contemplation, liberation, all qualities.
May we hold the holy Law of all the Conquerors,
make there appear everywhere the practice of enlightenment;
may we practice in all future eons
the good practice, the perfect practice.

By the empowerment of the truth of the Three Jewels, may it all be accomplished in that way!

3.23 *Reciting the verses of good fortune*

Then the monks recite (or sing) a final benediction, the verses of good fortune:

To the highest holy teacher,
worthy of offerings by gods and men:
homage to the Buddha!
may there now be good fortune!
For all beings, mobile or stationary,
may there now be good fortune!

To the calm and desireless,
worthy of offerings by gods and men:
homage to the Law!
may there now be good fortune!
For all beings, mobile or stationary,
may there now be good fortune!

To the highest holy hosts,
worthy of offerings by gods and men:
homage to the Assembly!
may there now be good fortune!
For all beings, mobile or stationary,
may there now be good fortune!

May whatever ghosts who have here approached,
who yet walk the earth or are in *bardo*,
through all their future lives ever be friendly
and practice the Law both day and night.

By the truth of the Conqueror, victorious over enemies,
speaking the truth, without falsehood;
by that truth, may there now be good fortune!
may they all be freed from the great terrors!

May we all, Master and disciples, our wealthy patron and his retinue, be victorious over all adversity! May there be good fortune!

JAYA JAYA SUJAYA! "Victory, victory, total victory!"

And for the last time the monks "let fall a rain of flowers."

Thus the ritual concludes. The offerings are gathered together and taken away to a clean place to be disposed of, or (since they have been empowered by the mantras recited during the ritual) they may be taken as magical attainments to be passed around and eaten for the absorption of their power.[252]

II

APPLICATION

Protection and Attack

These metaphysics of magicians And necromantic books are heavenly: Lines, circles, scenes, letters and characters: Ay, these are those that Faustus most desires. O, what a world of profit and delight, Of power, of honor, of omnipotence Is promised to the studious artisan! All things that move between the quiet poles Shall be at my command: emperors and kings Are but obeyed in their several provinces Nor can they raise the wind nor rend the clouds; But his dominion that exceeds in this Stretcheth as far as doth the mind of man. A sound magician is a mighty god: Here, Faustus, try thy brains to gain a deity.

—*Christopher Marlowe*, FAUSTUS

THE EIGHT GREAT TERRORS

The idea of an abiding and saving deity slowly gained textual currency in India. In the *Mahābhārata* epic (IV.6 and VI.23) are two "Praises of Durgā"—the Bhīṣmaparvan hymn of Arjuna and the Virāṭaparvan hymn of Yudhiṣṭhira—where new names are coined for the goddess Umā or Pārvatī, who had already appeared briefly in the *Kena-upaniṣad* (III.12 and IV.3); but she is now called Durgā, the "Terrible One," a great protectress who, being prayed to, delivers man from such terrors as captivity, wilderness, great forests, drowning, and harassment by robbers.[1] In the *Lotus Sūtra*, too, Avalokiteśvara saves those who invoke him or utter his name from seven terrors: fire, water, spirits, sword, demons, prison, and thieves; in the verses immediately following the prose section, these terrors become twelve.[2] The cult of Tārā appropriated elements of these lists, and her protective power was early categorized under "eight great terrors," an idea to which the great Indian devotee Candragomin, for example, gave poetic expression in this hymn to the goddess:[3]

Entering upon the road, I see you,
hands and feet reddened with the blood of slain elephants;
upon the road I think of you, a lion trampled beneath your feet,
and thus I pass into the thick-grown impassable forest.

Those who do not stop for an instant on their path of killing,
wandering with the roaring sound of a host of bees
flying at a cheek fragrant with intoxicating liquor:
O Tārā, even they are conquered and bow down before you.

A fire blazing as high as if the firmament
were kindled by the wind's great power
at the dissolution of the world: even that
will be calmed should a city but call out your name.

Entering upon the road linking and bending through mountains,
through ravines and valleys, I see you; and wandering the road
I think of Tārā, greater than the strength of serpents,
and thus is their poison conquered and turned back upon them.

Entering upon the road where robbers
bear aloft their weapons,
I think of them trampled beneath the feet of Tārā,
and with that power I go swiftly and joyfully to my home.

A man wise in daily prayer, bound captive in prison
by all the lords of this earth,
need but think of the feet of Tārā
and instantly bursts his bonds in a hundred pieces.

Though the seas rise clamorously upward
as high as the Abode of Brahma, your body,
the terror of sea monsters, is as a boat in the midst thereof;
by thinking of Tārā I lose all fear.

A vampire, his body brown-haired, dark as collyrium,
bound by his very sinews to hunger and thirst,
delighting in the slaughter of men:
even he is conquered by the thought of your feet.

As part of a recurring Buddhist iconographic process, each of these eight terrors was assigned its own Tārā, and the depiction of the eight Tārās became a popular theme for Indian artists,[4] a tradition continued in Tibet where the painters relished the chance to fill their canvases with delightful drawings of elephants, lions, and threatened caravans. On one Indian image of this goddess, for example, originally from Ratnagiri in Orissa, are depicted miniature scenes of the eight great terrors, in which the person in danger in each instance prays to a miniature replica of the goddess shown above. The eight great terrors depicted in the relief are terror of drowning, of thieves, of lions, of snakes, of fire, of spirits, of captivity, and of elephants.[5] Another representation of the eight terrors is shown in Tucci's *Tibetan Painted Scrolls*:[6] six figures below, and two more on a level with the shoulders of the goddess, signify her forms invoked by devotees to ward off the terrors; the goddess, always with the same gesture, touches with her right hand the head of the man who has run to her for aid. Behind her are the symbols of the terrors: the elephant, the lion, the demon, in the lively folk style common to this theme.

THE PROTECTIVE MANTRA

The surest protection from these inevitable and physical dangers to life—fire and water, wild beasts, and the malignancy of man—is the love and graciousness of Tārā; and her power, too, was soon expanded to the spiritual counterparts of these terrors. We find her guarding her followers from the eight and the sixteen great terrors, the latter including the former and adding doubt, lust, avarice, envy, false views, hatred, delusion, and pride.[7] The simplest cry of her name is, as we shall see, sufficient to gain her protection, but in Tibet the recitation of her mantra is the universal means of gaining safety amidst the snares of life. "If one knows enough to recite her mantra," says Gedündrub, "then, it is said, though one's head be cut off one will live, though one's flesh be hacked to pieces one will live: this is a profound counsel."[8]

"It does not matter whether one is a householder or has left the household life," Doje ch'öpa once said in a speech to his Chinese disciples. "Everyone should practice the recitation of Green Tārā in order to remove all inner and outer hindrances and so become as a pure porcelain vessel. Thus the recitation has consequences that are most great, an evocation that is most quick, and effects that are most keen; just hearing its sound has an inconceivable effect that saves from suffering... Whatever one wants to have, whatever unpleasant thing one wants to be without, she responds to it like an echo. This deity loves and protects the practitioner as if she were the moon accompanying him, never a step away."[9]

We have already seen the wide variety of Tārā's mantras, depending upon the particular appendix and its function [pp. 208-210], but only the short mantra (OṂ TĀRE TUTṬĀRE TURE SVĀHĀ) is actually in common use outside the assembly hall. The long mantra (OṂ TĀRE TUTTĀRE TURE MAMA ĀYUḤ-PUṆYA-JÑĀNA-PUṢṬIM-KURU SVĀHĀ)—which adds the appendix most closely associated with White Tārā—is not very well known among the laity, but they often recite the short one and, indeed, sing it occasionally to a very sweet, slow, rather mournful tune.

THE PROTECTIVE PRAISES

Even more than the mantra, many Tibetans consider the chanting of the Tibetan translation of the *Homages to the Twenty-one Tārās* to be especially meritorious and effective, thus following a common historical pattern of considering a praise in its entirety to be a form of mantra.[10] In the same modern Chinese manual on the Twenty-one Tārās which contains the sermon quoted above, Sun Ching-feng records the words of No-na Hutukhtu, a lama who traveled as far as Hong Kong in the late 1930s, preaching the Tibetan religion: "Now when the world is exploding into war," he said, "we fear that it will not be long before poison gases are killing men. More violently than ever before, disaster descends upon our heads, and we must be prepared; by diligently practicing this recitation, one can be spared from poison gases and calamities and escape from poison. We have special verification for this, for one of our own men has been poisoned three times, yet he gained his life with no illness, for he had in the past fully practiced this recitation . . . It is most certainly fortunate if one is able to recite this entire mantra, these *Homages to the Twenty-one Tārās*; but, if not, then just reciting the mantra of Green Tārā has special efficacy. Moreover, the pains of women are particularly numerous; but if they recite the mantra with a devoted mind, it has an especially wondrous effect."[11]

Everyone in K'am knows this entire hymn, and anyone who might admit that he had not memorized it all is considered to be as laughably foolish as one who had never learned his OṂ MAṆI PADME HUṂ. It is usually chanted in a low monotone, but it may also be sung to its own melody. Families often meet together every day for its recitation, in the morning or evening. A common protection among ordinary people in K'am—for example, in guarding against wolves when traveling from village to village in winter—is to begin the day by offering up a little milk to Tārā and reciting the *Homages* while going about one's morning tasks. A woman visualizes that Tārā has entered into the turquoise ornament she wears on her head; a man will place upon his head a flower, which he later throws away; or the goddess may enter into a ring or any other ornament. She is seen as holding a green ball, inside of which one sits protected for the remainder of the day. Every morning we were awakened by the low and tuneful murmuring of the *Homages* by our cook, as she built up the morning fire; and once, when evil omens arose affecting the life of K'amtrü rinpoch'e (among other things, a rainbow had touched his jeep), a "service" was convened: while the monks and literate lay people read the scriptures, all the others sat outside from morning until evening, spinning their prayer wheels and reciting this hymn.

THE PROTECTIVE MANTRA IN FOLKLORE

No-na Hutukhtu told many stories to illustrate the efficacy of such recitations, or even of the simplest cry of Tārā's name. These were recorded by his disciples both in the Chinese manual and in one privately printed by his followers in Hong Kong.[12] These tales are of great interest, for they seem almost certainly to reiterate parts of an oral hagiographic literature originally circulated in India, the only other source for which known to me is Juwa ch'ödar's biography of his teacher, the Translator of Ch'ag, who brought back from India some of the stories of the goddess he had heard there.[13] Most of No-na Hutukhtu's tales seem to be retellings of standard Indian storytellers' motifs adapted to the cult of Tārā, to celebrate her deeds for the edification of a folk audience, and the stories recall universal folklore themes: the underground vault of treasure, the miraculous conception, the poor peasant who marries the king's daughter. But these folktales have not passed unscathed through the generations of their Tibetan transmission; one tale begins, "Once there was an elephant who seized a girl, wishing to eat her . . ." No Indian would be so unfair to an elephant.

> There was once a man who was fast asleep, when suddenly he was face to face with a host of demons, grasping swords and sticks and coming toward him. This man was greatly frightened, and he called out to Tārā. From beneath his seat there suddenly arose a great wind, which blew and scattered the demon army. Again, there was once a woodcutter carrying a load of firewood on a mountain; he met with a mother lion, who seized him in her mouth and carried him into her cave. The woodcutter, terrified, loudly cried out to Tārā. Suddenly he saw coming a girl, dressed in leaves, who snatched him from the lion's jaws and set him back on the road.
>
> Once there was an elephant who seized a girl, wishing to eat her. The girl cried out to Tārā, and the elephant, bowing his head, awakened compassion in his heart. He knew now that the girl was a disciple of the Buddha and that he had committed sin in no small measure. So he took the girl and lightly placed her upon a rock, knelt to her and paid her homage, thus seeking to expiate his sin. And when he had paid homage to her, he again took her and conveyed her to the ground, where once again he knelt and paid her homage. Then he took her once more and entered into the king's palace, where he set her down and paid her homage as before. The king saw this and was greatly amazed; and he took the girl as his wife.

Once there was a man's enemy who, under cover of night, set a fire to burn his house. Within the house there was only one weak girl; and, as the flames drew near, she loudly cried out to Tārā. Suddenly she saw that there was a green-colored lady standing above the fire; rain fell down like a flood and the fire was extinguished. Again, there was once a girl who had got a necklace of real pearls, five hundred of them. Taking them, she ran away in the night and sat beneath a tree. Up in the leaves there was a snake, who descended and wrapped himself around the girl's body. The girl cried out to Tārā, and the snake was transformed into a jeweled necklace. Sitting there for seven days, the girl became pregnant and later gave birth to a son.

There was once a great merchant who, with five hundred horses and a thousand camels loaded with treasure, was passing through a wilderness. Now at that time there was a robber band of a thousand men who had gathered to kill him and plunder his treasure. They had already killed many merchants, and blood and corpses were scattered about; they even nailed corpses to the trees, hacked at their flesh, and ate them. The merchant, terrified, called on Tārā. Suddenly he saw a numberless host of soldiers, each grasping a sword and a stick, coming out of the sky. The thieves were routed. Again, there was once a robber chief who left his den at night and entered into the king's storehouse. But he drank up the wine in the storehouse and became drunk, so that he was bound and imprisoned. He cried out to Tārā, and suddenly there appeared in the sky a five-colored bird who released him from his fetters and flew away. That night a beautiful girl commanded him to repent of his past sins; and thus he and his whole band of five hundred thieves all became virtuous.

There was once a farmer who was exceedingly poor and who experienced insurmountable hardship. He beseeched Tārā to help him, and suddenly a girl, whose clothing was the leaves of trees placed over her body, instructed him to go eastward and lie down upon a rock. The farmer accordingly went eastward and lay down upon a rock, when all at once he heard the sound of small horse bells and saw a green-colored horse digging in the ground with its hoof. He waited until it left, then he got up and dug into the hole it had made; and in the middle of it there appeared a silver door set with the seven precious stones. He entered in, and it was the palace of the serpent-kings and demons. The farmer thus stayed there, and by the time he got out again the king of his country had changed three times. When he inquired about his family, they had all been dead for a long time. He thus entered a monastery and became a monk. He saw that men and women made offerings to Tārā with incense and flowers; he bought some flowers, scattered them about, and returned. Later, the king of the country heard about these wonders, and he married the farmer to his daughter. When the king died, the farmer ruled the country, and he repaired the 108 buildings of the Tārā temple.

In India, at the time of the Great King Aśoka, there was a very rich elder whom the king hated and whose life he wished to harm. Imperial orders were dispatched to apprehend the elder. The elder was afraid and called out to Tārā. When the guards' feet trod on his doorstep it turned to gold, and the elder presented it to the king. When they put him in jail, jewels fell from the sky like rain, and these too he presented to the king. And when withered trees became laden with fruits and flowers, the king released him and made him a great minister.

Beyond the simple cry of Tārā's name, in these stories the afflicted recite her mantra to gain her protection; and, as the second of the following stories indicates, the more people who recite it and the more often it is recited the more effective it becomes:

There were once five thousand men together in a great ship who went to sea to gather treasure, and they came to a place where there was much red sandalwood. But the serpent-king of the place was displeased; and when the men were returning they suddenly met with a great wind, which seized the boat and blew it about, while the seas ran heavy about them. The men on the ship were all terrified; there were some who cried out to the gods of the sun and the moon, but to no avail. The rigging broke; peril took ten thousand forms. At the very moment of life or death, a man recited the mantra of Tārā; the wind suddenly blew the ship in the opposite direction, and in only one evening conveyed the men on the ship, together with their treasure, back to their home.

Again, there was once in India a novice monk traveling the road who saw beside the path offerings to a heavenly spirit; but he just kicked them aside and passed on. The spirit was enraged and hurled thunder to kill him. The novice monk cried out to Tārā in his fright, and he escaped. He asked five hundred men to recite the mantra of Tārā, and thunder never hurt anyone again.

These stories, beneath the wonders of their folktale trappings, conveyed to their audience the edifying and rather hyperbolic point made above: the simplest cry of suffering to Tārā, the merest mention of her name, or the most perfunctory recitation of her mantra is enough to ensure her protection against all the terrors of this world. But we may note in the last few stories a point to which we shall return: the power of her mantra seems in the process of disengaging itself from the person of the goddess, and it is effective independently of her personal intervention. Indeed, beyond the proven effectiveness of its recitation, her mantra may also simply be written out and hung up, or carved upon a rock, that it may of itself provide continual protection for that place:

> There were once five hundred monks of the Little Vehicle who all saw, every day, a mob of demons in the form of lions and lionesses coming at them from the sky. They were all greatly terrified, madly and wildly frightened, and they all fell prostrate. But among them there was one monk who knew the miraculous virtues of Tārā; he wrote out her mantra and hung it up everywhere in the grove, and immediately the visions stopped.

THE THEME OF THE MIRACULOUS IMAGE

In many of these stories we find that images of Tārā were carved into rock, and tales were told of their miraculous potency:

> A head monk once suffered from the disease called "falling brows." There had already been five monks who had caught the disease, in which the flesh falls off and the brows are stripped, and there was no way to control it. People did not dare to approach him, lest they too catch it. On the road to beg alms, he saw that on a great rock had been carved Tārā's mantra and an image of Tārā (see pl. 4). He knelt down weeping and implored her to save him. From the hand of the stone image there suddenly flowed a liquid that was like medicine. He took it and washed with it, and the disease was cured; and he was adorned with all the signs of a god.

> In India there was once a poor man who was in the very depths of poverty. He saw that upon a rock there was an image of Tārā, and he knelt down and beseeched her. Suddenly the image pointed toward a shrine. He dug where she had indicated, and he found a jar filled with jewels, so that he became very rich. Now this man responded and took to himself seven generations of the poor, so that for seven generations poverty disappeared, and in birth after birth he lived to be a rich old man.

> In the northeast of India was a place where the monks would draw water, and at this place was an image of Tārā carved on a rock. But here lived monks who practiced the Little Vehicle; and when they saw any scriptures of the Great Vehicle they took and burned them. The king was enraged when he heard that they so deeply hated the Tantra that, like enemies, they destroyed its images, and he wished to kill them. He sent men to apprehend

> the monks. The monks quickly knelt before the image of Tārā and begged her to save them. They suddenly heard Tārā say: "Shouldn't you have sought me before you were in trouble? But I'll tell you: kneel down in the water ditch and you may yet be spared." The monks looked down the steps into the water ditch, which was about the size of a bowl, and they thought, "How can we all kneel down there? It would be very difficult." Tārā urged them and said, "Kneel down quickly! The guards are approaching the gate." The monks, greatly startled, crouched their bodies together and went in; and, sure enough, there was no hindrance. Thus the king looked for them, but he couldn't find them, and they were saved.

This theme of the miraculous image seems to have been part of the standard repertoire of the Indian story-teller, from whom it was transmitted to Tibet. Several examples are preserved in the biography of the Translator of Ch'ag, and it is interesting to note that he invariably refers his tales to specific images of the goddess, as if he were repeating the words of an Indian temple guide who was himself repeating the story of a local legend. Thus the traveling translator refers to one such image located in a temple at Vajrâsana:[14]

> In Vajrâsana there was a Tārā temple, in which was a miraculous stone image of the goddess. Originally she had faced toward the outside; but the storekeeper once thought, "Since the offerings are made inside, it is not right that you face the outside." So the image said "All right" and turned her head around to the inside. This image is known as the "Tārā with the turned face," and even today there is a stone image there with its head turned around. And once when Atīśa came to that temple, the door opened for him by itself, and the Tārā with the turned face said to him: "If you wish to pass from the cause, the level of ordinary beings, to the effect, the level of Buddhahood, then you must purify your thought of enlightenment."

Such magical and/or talking images are considered in Tibet to be among the most potent of protections for an individual, a dwelling, or an entire district, and the Tibetans have installed in their temples miraculous images of Tārā, each with its own local story attached to it. Indeed, the native Tibetan temple guidebooks are so full of casual references to talking images of the goddess that one gets the impression that they were not even considered unusual; Hugh Richardson mentions an image of Tārā at Tr'adrug which "was pointed out to me as miraculous and I understood that it had once eaten an offering."[15]

One such image which I have seen was named the "Lady of the Goring Yak." It was a so-called thunderstone image, found already formed within the ground and considered to be a petrified thunderbolt; it was about three inches high, a complete image of Tārā, with the silky sheen and smooth surface typical of such images (see pl. 5). Its present owner, the young Ch'öje jats'o VIII, told me that it had been found about a century ago, buried in the earth in K'am, and had originally been purchased by the sixth incarnation of his lineage. Now this lama was a yogin, who lived in a cave in the hermitage of Drugugön, the monastery of which he was head. Since his cave had no proper shrine room, he handed out his collection of images to various other yogins in the hermitage, that they might be properly enshrined and the proper offerings be made to them. The hermitage, too, could not possess collective property like the monastery, so the yogins would go out begging twice a year, summer and autumn, for their supplies. A man could not travel alone in K'am for fear of wolves and bears, and Dragon Kajü yogins were not allowed to ride horses; so the yogin who had been given the thunderstone image of Tārā lent it to his lay servant for his protection, and they both set out together.

In K'am there are wild yaks, called "eagles," who stand, I was told, five feet high at the shoulder and have their horns pointed forward, and who occasionally become mad and attack travelers. Such a yak charged the two mendicants, and after a chase he caught and gored the servant, but the yak's horns merely bent themselves upon the servant's body. This miracle was attributed, after some discussion, to the magical powers of the image he carried, and as the story spread the image became known as the Lady of the Goring Yak.

After a while the original owner of the image died and was reincarnated as the seventh Ch'öje jats'o, and the thunderstone image found itself involved in the religious politics that periodically afflict Tibet. The image was lent to a monastery of the "ancient" Nyingma sect, named Kajegön and located in the capital of Dragyab, right next to another monastery of the Gelug sect. Indeed, it had been founded by the abbot of the latter monastery, an incarnation called Lord Refuge of Dragyab, who had been fascinated by the "ancient" teachings. The two neighbor monasteries shared the same facilities and officers, differing only in the performance of their rituals in their individual temples; and here the image rested in the amity of these sometimes rival sects.

When the Lord Refuge of Dragyab died, his monastery was taken over, during the minority of his reincarnation, by a regent named Zangmar toden, who was a very different sort of man from the former abbot. Zangmar had originally followed the "ancient" sect (he had been a disciple of the great and famous Drugu Śākyaśrī of Söderk'a) but then had moved to Ch'amdo, where he met and became the disciple of a Gelug lama named Master Refuge P'awang kawa.

Zangmar had fallen under the spell of this new and impressive personality. P'awang kawa was undoubtedly one of the great lamas of the early twentieth century, but he was a man of contradictory passions, and he shows us two different faces when he is recalled by those who knew him. In many ways he was truly a saint; he was sent to Ch'amdo by the central government to represent its interests and administer its Gelug monasteries, and he was sympathetic to the concerns of the K'am people over whom he had been granted jurisdiction, a scholar and an enthusiast for all aspects of Tibetan culture. But many eastern Tibetans remember him with loathing as the great persecutor of the "ancient" sect, devoting himself to the destruction throughout K'am of images of the Precious Guru and the burning of "ancient" books and paintings.

P'awang kawa sent his new disciple back to take charge of the Gelug monastery in Dragyab; Zangmar, with the zeal of the convert, carried with him only his master's sectarianism and implemented only his policy of destruction. He tried to force the monks of Kajegön (who were technically under his authority) to perform the Gelug rituals, and when they obstinately continued to refuse he called in the government police on a trumped-up charge of treason. They raided Kajegön, broke its images, made a fire of its books and paintings, and beat its monks with sticks. The head monk, who carried with him by chance that day our image of Tārā, tried to stop them; while one policeman threatened him with a stick, another shot him in the back.

But the power of the thunderstone had not diminished during its repose: the bullet simply flattened itself upon the old monk's body, just as the yak's horns had bent upon the body of the servant. Everyone present was astonished to see that he was unhurt, and though the looting continued, the miracle most likely prevented the outbreak of real and bloody warfare. Those who knew about the image were further convinced of its power.

After Kajegön had been taken over, all its fittings were sold to Drugugön and the image found its way back to its original home. In the two or three years between the death of the seventh and the birth of the eighth—the present—Ch'öje jats'o, the image was kept by the treasurer of the monastery, who was named Dawa dragpa. He was a man who loved yaks, especially the great white or tawny big-horned yaks called "divine." Once when he went to separate two fighting divine yaks he was gored by both of them as he tried to pull them apart, but once again the image protected its bearer: the horns did not pierce his skin and he received only a few bruises. His escape was considered quite remarkable, for one does not usually survive so lightly a goring by these animals.

When I asked the present Ch'öje jats'o if he had any personal experience with the saving power of this image, he replied that one of his servants had once claimed to have been protected by the image from a bolt of thunder; but my informant qualified the story by remarking that the servant was known to be something of an exaggerator. It seems that there are, indeed, implicit but quite definite criteria for acceptance of a miracle. This does not mean, however, that the age of miraculous images of Tārā is at an end; the Tibetan news magazine *Sheja* reports the following story:[16]

Actual Occurence of a Miracle
Unable to Carry Handbag

> From a Nepalese news report: An English national had paid 400,000 Nepalese rupees [about $4,000] for a magnificent image of the holy Tārā, measuring slightly more than a foot in size. He attempted to take the image [illegally] out of the country, placing it inside the handbag he carried which was not opened for inspection, so that he was able to proceed to the Nepal airfield. But while he was entering the airplane the image began to grow heavier and heavier, until he was completely unable to lift the handbag. This alerted the Nepalese customs officials, who opened and inspected the handbag, found the image, and confiscated it.

THE PROTECTIVE PRAISES IN FOLKLORE

Aside from these stories of miraculous images, Tibet has also preserved a living tradition of folklore which proclaims the efficacy of Tārā's mantra. Many stories are told which compare in format and theme with the Indian stories above, introducing the same motifs and differing only in the wealth of circumstantial detail provided by personal acquaintance and in the replacement of the mantra by the *Homages to the Twenty-one Tārās.*

I was told one such story by two monks in the monastery, Lodrö rabje and Lungten togpa, both of whom came from the village of Norma rowa, ceded to K'amtrü rinpoch'e three hundred years ago by the king of Lhat'og. Forty years ago, they said, there was a man in their village named Ch'ödrub who, at the age of thirty, was supplying horses and yaks for a merchant caravan jointly owned by a Tibetan and a Chinese, plying the main road between Ch'amdo and Dege. Between these two towns is a place called Chornam do-t'ang, and there a thief murdered the Chinese merchant; but the latter's friends in Ch'amdo accused Ch'ödrub not only of the murder but of several others as well. Now Ch'ödrub, my informants agreed, was very honest but not very bright, and he was condemned in court for murder; during the five or six months he was awaiting execution, he recited the *Homages to the Twenty-one Tārās* two hundred times every day. Finally the warden informed him that he was to be killed the next morning, and he cried in despair as his hands were bound behind his back with a long chain ending in a heavy stone.

About one o'clock in the morning, when he could not sleep, he suddenly forgot it was night; there was a little window, for air, near the ceiling in his cell, and although it was the twenty-ninth day of the month he thought he could see moonlight. He looked up and saw, gazing down at him from the window, the form of a girl who was at that time famous in Ch'amdo for her beauty. "Why did she come?" he thought. "That window is small, yet I can see her from the waist up." She was adorned with white roses and pearls, smelling a white rose and smiling. All at once he forgot he was in prison; she pointed to the warden, to show he was asleep; she chewed on the stem of the rose and threw a piece to him. He felt light and happy, and he knew it must be Tārā. She turned away, beckoning him to follow her through the window, and she disappeared. As the light faded he realized that he was unchained. With almost miraculous strength he threw the chain so that the stone hooked over the edge of the window; he climbed out and jumped, and though the window was very high he was unhurt. He left all his clothes behind and ran naked all night.

Toward sunrise he neared Norma rowa and saw two wolves; he thought that if he killed them he could wear their skins. But then he heard inside his head the disgusted snort of a woman ("Hm!" —demonstration by informant), so he had compassion on them and did not kill them.

CONTEMPLATION, EFFECTUATION, APPLICATION

As we review these stories we note again that the mantra has a constant tendency to detach itself from the personality of the goddess and to assume a life and, more important, a power of its own. Once again we see the operation of the paradox of power: Tārā's protection is not only an expression of the benevolence extolled in folklore, but it is also an independent power in the cosmos, set in motion by her primordial vow, which can be tapped and directed by a practitioner who has the capacity to do so. The power of protection can be controlled magically through visualization and recitation, its visual and sonic simulacra.

I was told one protection against what is called being "drenched with defilement"—the demonically inspired half-waking paralysis that accompanies a nightmare, the inability to move or cry out even when one is awake enough to see the objects or people in one's room; or the feeling, when half awake, that something is seated upon one's chest, rendering one incapable of speech or movement—which was originally conceived by the great 15th-century saint and religious innovator T'angtön jepo: one ties a knot in one's sash, reciting the short Tārā mantra twenty-one times and visualizing that the goddess is thus "tied" into the cloth; if the sash, thus empowered, is then laid over one's body while one sleeps, one is completely protected. This protection is an example of the "application" of the mantra, the directing of its protective power into an object that then becomes in itself a protection, just as the power of the goddess can take up residence within a miraculous image. Indeed, we might say that this application of the mantra is the conscious creation of a miraculous object.

All the types and subtypes of protective and aggressive ritual we shall consider in the pages that follow are the frames upon which the practitioner hangs his manipulation of power; grasping the divine appearance and ego, he can effectuate or apply the mantra—the divine power—toward any end he wishes. Visualization and recitation go hand in hand as the basic components of this magic; they are the simulacra, the magical tools of protection, whether applied to public nonreality or to the deity herself.

Gustav Diehl writes of the mantra in South India: "The mantras are instruments. Partly they are without meaning and often they are not understood by him who reads them. They have fixed places in the ritual and varied effects and cannot be interchanged . . . They are all indirect means of achieving something. . . . Formulas (*mantras*), syllables (*bījas*), hold the gods and can be directed; in that way the performer of the rites draws into himself the divine, whereby alone he becomes fit for worshipping."[17]

Thus the mantra can be an instrument of protection, just as an effigy can be an instrument of destruction. In Tibet the mantra is the audible simulacrum of the divine power, and, in the coalescence of image and object, it becomes the divine power itself, manifest and crystallized in a sonic form.

The Gentle Lord Kongtrü rinpoch'e says that "it is in general permissible to apply just the basic 10-syllable mantra to all Tārā's functions." But as we have already seen in chapter i, this basic mantra may be "effectuated" in many different situations by the insertion of the appropriate appendix, and these variations may be used also when the mantra is "applied." Thus Kongtrü rinpoch'e says also:[18]

> One may vary the mantra and the visualization slightly for each of the different functions, but to set about these activities requires a practitioner who has acquired the power to do so by having performed the ritual service . . . the requisite number of times and for the requisite length of time, and who has received the requisite signs of success therein—or at the very least an ordinary person who has recited the basic 10-syllable mantra 10,000,000 times.

In other words, one must first "contemplate the mantra" before one can either "effectuate" or "apply" it. Effectuation and application are two different processes: to *effectuate* the mantra is to arouse the stream of the heart of the deity generated in front; to *apply* the mantra is to direct its power either directly into an object (like the knotted sash, above) or into a deity who is generated within the object. Application of the mantra is called, in the ritual, the *employment* of the divine power, just as the effectuation of the mantra is the ritual *evocation* of the goddess: but before one can evoke or employ this power one must first acquire it through the *contemplation* of the mantra in the prior ritual service of the deity. As it says in the *Mahāvairocana Tantra*:[19]

If one wishes to gain
great waves of knowledge,
the five supernormal perceptions,
or any of the magical attainments
of "holding the mantra"
such as youth or long life:
so long as one does not do the ritual service
one will gain nothing.

The Tibetans are quite serious about the necessity of the massive recitation of the prior ritual service before one can carry out any of the practical uses of the mantra. The Longdö lama Ngawang lozang defines ""ritual service for the requisite length of time" as ritual service for three to six months. "Ritual service for the requisite number of times," he says, depends upon one's previously accumulated merit: one with a great deal of merit need recite the mantra here only 10,000 times; one with medium merit should recite it 100,000 times; and one whose merit is small should recite it 10,000,000 times, Then, and only then, one receives the "requisite signs of success in the ritual service": one sees the face of the deity (either in a dream or in person), and one's body begins to glow from its continual absorption of the knowledge being during the self-generation.

Similarly, Ngawang lozang lists the twelve signs that "one's mind has been made firm in the ritual service," that "one has entered upon the path," and that "one has achieved, with disciplined and blissful mind, the state of one's patron deity." The twelve signs are:[20]

1) One feels little hunger or thirst
2) One is free of illness
3) One's understanding grows excellent
4) One's body begins to glow
5) One's dreams become auspicious
6) One's dreams come true
7) One feels a zestful inclination toward reciting the mantra
8) One feels little fatigue
9) One feels a pleasant warmth
10) One's comprehension of scripture and commentary increases
11) One strives to preserve these qualities
12) One's devotion to the chosen deity grows great

It is difficult to comment upon some of these signs, but Tibetan contemplatives confirm many of them: they report that during contemplation of the mantra they sleep only about four hours a day and awaken with real enthusiasm for continuing the recitation; they eat little but feel great bodily vitality. I was told that some young monks who enter the solitude of the hermitage only reluctantly are equally reluctant to stop reciting at the end of their stay.

This ritual service is performed during the solitary contemplation mentioned in chapter i, and many rituals have an accompanying handbook of instructions upon the requisites of a solitary rather than monastic performance, giving details on the particular visualizations that must be performed during the recitation, the number of times one should recite the particular mantra, and so on (such a ritual service is examined in detail in chap. iii). But always the greatest importance is attached to the accumulation of the proper number of recitations, and these too must be properly performed: one must avoid the "ten faults in the recitation of the mantra," consisting of five "faults" and five "interruptions." The faults are to recite too loudly, too softly, too quickly, or too slowly, or to mumble indistinctly. The interrruptions are to cough, to sneeze, to stumble, to fall asleep, or to have one's mind wander from the recitation. And should one stumble, fall asleep, cough, yawn, sneeze, spit, or break wind, says Ngawang lozang, then one should lay down the rosary with which one has been keeping count of the recitations, bathe oneself, and wash out one's mouth before returning to "count out" the mantra. Moreover, he says, the following numbers of recitations must be subtracted from the total number: for falling asleep, fifteen; for sneezing, ten; for breaking wind, seven; for stumbling, five; for coughing, five; for yawning, three; and for spitting saliva or mucus, ten. If one's mind has wandered in other ways, one must make offerings and recite praises to the deity, mentally confess one's fault and pray for forbearance before one may return to the mantra.[21]

MAGICAL ATTAINMENTS AND FUNCTIONS

The aim of all the preliminary recitation is the capacity to direct the divine power, to evoke and employ it, and to effectuate and apply the mantra that is its sonic form. All the many varieties of this capacity, and all the uses to which it is put, are subsumed by the Tibetans under the rubric of *magical attainments*. This cover term is very widely used in a broad range of contexts, and it is difficult to isolate a semantic nucleus; but a magical attainment is basically an ability, a competence which the practitioner has acquired to perform some act, and, more specifically, it is his ability to perform a *function* of the deity.

This term "function," too, is systematically ambiguous, for it applies both to the deity—White Tārā's main function is to prolong life—and to the practitioner. The ambiguity is resolved in the self-generation that precedes the performance of any function, for there the deity and the practitioner merge into one, and the yogin's ability is the ability of the god. Thus, too, the magical attainments are gained only after the ritual service, for only the ritual service creates this identity of deity and practitioner, to be called upon when needed at any time in the future.

The Tibetans provide no systematic analysis of these functions or of the magical attainments that represent their mastery; the lists they give suffer from the besetting Buddhist fault of overlap and level switching. The Tibetans inherited from the Indian magical tradition a standard list of "eight great magical attainments." As found in the Hindu texts, the magical powers are as follows:[22]

1) To become as tiny as one wishes [to be invisible]
2) To become as light as one wishes [to levitate]
3) To become as large as one wishes
4) To become as heavy as one wishes
5) To transport oneself anywhere
6) To have all one's wishes fulfilled
7) To subjugate anything one wishes
8) To dwell with the delight and power of the god

This same list, as borrowed into Buddhism, was called instead the "eight powers of the Lord" in acknowledgment of their original association with the Hindu god Śiva, and some of the items were subject to variation: Ngawang lozang, for example, takes the terms "large" and "heavy" metaphorically, and he gives those items as "to be worthy of offerings" and "to be master."[23] What the Buddhist tradition considers to be the eight great magical attainments are given by Nāgārjuna as follows:[24]

1) Invincibility with the sword
2) Dominion over the treasure of the underworld
3) Invisibility
4) The elixir of youth
5) The ability to shape oneself into a tiny ball

6) The ability to walk in the sky
7) Swiftness of foot
8) Magical eye ointment

There is some overlap in these two lists of magic powers, especially where they touch upon the universal themes of invisibility, magical flight, and instant transportation. But these traditional abilities were worked into a larger scheme of functions by the Tibetans, where their individuality was subordinated to the structures of the ritual.

The first and most important distinction the Tibetans make is between *ordinary* and *extraordinary* magical attainments: that is, the ability to perform ordinary or extraordinary functions. This latter—the highest possible magical attainment—is enlightenment itself; we may call it the capacity to perform the *soteriological function* of the deity whom the practitioner has become. This is the function associated with the Process of Perfection, wherein the yogin-god of the self-generation "gathers" himself into the divine Emptiness and "arises" again as the deity in public nonreality.

The magical attainment of enlightenment—of whatever degree, from the glimpses of the beginner to actual Buddhahood—is the ability to perform the deity's function of ontological insight and power, and thus it is the foundation for the performance of all the ordinary functions. It is possible only through the prior identity of god and yogin: it is the practitioner's identity with the deity in self-generation which grants the capacity to appropriate magically the divine understanding, the final "real-ization" of Emptiness. As we read in one Tantric text:[25]

> And from then on one will have
> the whole of the magical attainments
> and be delivered from the "self"
> which binds one to this world,
> just as a lotus is untouched
> by the water and mud in which it grows.
> If one touches quicksilver, it breaks in pieces,
> but gathered together it becomes one again;
> if one becomes omniscient
> and touches the quicksilver of attainment,
> one's mind attained to the magical attainments,
> then just as copper becomes alchemical gold,
> the yogin touched with the mantra of attainment
> gains the body of a Buddha.

The practitioner's ability to perform all the ordinary functions, based upon the soteriological function of his primary identity with the deity, is here symbolized by his homologization to the Buddha himself, and his performance of all the acts of the Buddha in the world:

He becomes Lord of the gods,
he becomes Lord of the triple world;
he is born into the family of Buddhas
and turns the wheel of the Law;
he is born,
practices austerities,
performs the practice of enlightenment,
and is conscious of his Buddhahood;
he descends from among the gods,
he creates magical transformations,
turns the wheel of the Law,
passes away into nirvāṇa,
and departs to the burning ground
just as did the Buddha.
Thus he leaves behind his body in the triple world:
the Conqueror, in his Body of Bliss,
departs once more to his Pure Land,
yet his Body of Transformation comes again;
it is by this ritual Process of Perfection
that one is made to enter into the Dharma Body.

This, then, is the extraordinary magical attainment: enlightenment is possible because the practitioner and the deity are one, and this identity is possible because the practitioner and the deity—the object and the image—"neither exist nor nonexist." And so the text continues, expounding this metaphysical axiom of identity:

The Buddhas do not arise
nor do the Buddhas cease,
but the essence of their arising and ceasing
is all of a single taste:
it is the single form of the Dharma realm,
the abandoning of the five obscurations;
they dwell in that same essence,
their form profound and vast and great.
Since there is neither arising nor ceasing
from the beginning there is no "existence":
with no arising they do not cease...
Unarisen they arise:
that they may arise, they do not arise.
Seen from the absolute point of view

> they are thus unarisen from the beginning.
> Similarly when they die they do not die,
> they are deathless and undying;
> they are unfixed, without a place,
> for in such a place no place is necessary.
> If something unarisen were to cease
> then the unarisen would have arisen;
> both arising and ceasing are horns on a rabbit.
> If something existent were to arise
> then the existent would have arisen twice;
> if something nonexistent were to arise
> then there would also arise the son of a barren woman!

This axiomatic allows the total interpenetration of god and yogin, and each is summoned and controlled as the magical simulacrum for the other: to be the deity is to own the image of the deity; to control the image is to control the object and thus to be master of the deity's own enlightenment.

Compared with this soteriological function of the Process of Perfection, the *ordinary* magical attainments present a more chaotic picture. The great Sacha lama Dragpa jets'en, for example, gives the following list of five functions the ritual service has empowered the practitioner to perform:[26]

1) Reciting the mantra to arouse the hearts of all the Tathāgatas
2) Offering up tormas to pacify obstacles
3) Performing the burnt offering to gain quickly the magical attainments
4) Consecrating images and paintings to gain empowerment of body, speech, and mind
5) Performing the miscellaneous functions to take in hand the sort of people who have faith in the ordinary magical attainments

Dragpa jets'en further classifies the ordinary magical attainments into three classes—lower, middle, and upper—and he lists the *lower-class* ordinary magical attainments as the ability to perform the following basic functions: (1) pacifying, (2) increasing, (3) subjugating, and (4) destroying, along with all their subsidiary functions:

> Each of these basic functions has many subsidiary functions. In pacifying, one may pacify a disease, or pacify an evil spirit, or many other things. In increasing, one may increase one's life, or increase one's fortune or enjoyments, and so on. In subjugating,

one may subjugate a king, and so on, or summon him before one, or many other things. And in destroying, one may kill, expel, isolate, petrify, and so on.

These two seemingly disparate lists of functions are related to each other through the process-product ambiguity of the term "function." In English, for example, when someone says "I went to look at the construction," he might mean either that he looked at the process of construction or that he looked at the thing that had been constructed. Similarly, "to perform a function" might mean either to perform a particular ritual technique or to achieve a specific ritual result.

Thus any of the basic functions may be achieved in a variety of ways, and the first list is a sampling of the ritual techniques that may be used. A practitioner who grasps the appearance and the ego of the deity—achieved through the prior ritual service—may direct the divine power he controls toward any end and through any number of these techniques: he may apply the power of the mantra and the strength of his visualization directly upon the appearances of public nonreality, or use the intermediary of a "recipe" or "magical device" (empowered water, say, or an effigy of destruction); or he may evoke the deity before him and effectuate the mantra, arouse the stream of the deity's heart with tormas, or make to the god an appropriate burnt offering.

Similarly, any one technique may be directed toward any number of ends: an amulet may be constructed to protect from thieves, to grant long life, or to destroy an enemy; the practitioner may pacify with a burnt offering in a white circular hearth, increase in a yellow square hearth, subjugate in a red semicircular heart, or destroy in a black triangular hearth. These colors and shapes recur again and again in the rituals as emblems of the four basic functions, however they are achieved; the mandala of Kurukullā, for example, contains a "red semicircular palace of subjugation."

This process-product ambiguity of function may be clarified by the accompanying table. Each technique in the left-hand column may achieve any result in the right-hand column, and each result may be brought about by any technique. If we look just at the process column, we notice that these functions tend to fall into two main types, dependent entirely upon the locus of the ritual action. Thus we may broadly distinguish between a *ritual function* on the one hand, where the deity is evoked in front and offerings are made and the mantra is *effectuated*, and a *magical function* on the other hand, where the deity is either employed directly or generated within an object (a flask of water, or an amulet) and the mantra is *applied*.

function	
process	*product*
effectuation	pacifying
offerings	increasing
burnt offering	subjugating
application	destroying
recipe	protection
magical device	long life
etc.	etc.

Dragpa jets'en continues his account of the larger scheme of functions with what he calls the *middle-class* ordinary magical attainments. Here he lists those universal magic powers of flight and invisbility which are the legacy of the Indian yogic tradition, and which the practitioner may perform at will. There are, he says, three ways in which these powers may be gained: if one's zeal is greatest, one may gain them in this very life; if one's zeal is middling, the conditions will be such that one may gain them in the intermediate states—the *bardo*—after one dies; and if one's zeal is least, one may still gain them in one's next life by one's earnest wish for them in this life.

The middle-class magical attainments, again, may be either *general* or *particular*. Under the first heading Dragpa jets'en seems to include the magical practices of the native Tibetan tradition for which there is no explicit warrant in the Indian texts; the example he gives for this category is the indigenous rite called "the awakened corpse." This ritual is described by Mme David-Neel in perhaps one of the most delightful books on Tibetan magic ever written:[27]

> The celebrant is shut up alone with a corpse in a dark room. To animate the body, he lies on it, mouth to mouth, and while holding it in his arms, he must continually repeat mentally the same magic formula, excluding all other thoughts.
>
> After a certain time the corpse begins to move. It stands up and tries to escape; the sorcerer, firmly clinging to it, prevents it from freeing itself. Now the body struggles more fiercely. It leaps and bounds to extraordinary heights, dragging with it the man who must hold on, keeping his lips upon the mouth of the monster, and continue mentally repeating the magic words.

At last the tongue of the corpse protrudes from its mouth. The critical moment has arrived. The sorcerer seizes the tongue with his teeth and bites it off. The corpse at once collapses.

Failure in controlling the body after having awakened it, means certain death for the sorcerer.

The tongue carefully dried becomes a powerful magic weapon which is treasured by the triumphant magician.

The Tibetan who gave me these details described most vividly the gradual awakening of the corpse: the first conscious look which brightened its glazed eyes and its feeble movements slowly growing in strength until he became unable to prevent the agitation of the jumping monster and needed all his strength to hold it. He described his sensations when he could feel the tongue issuing from the mouth of the corpse and touching his own lips, and realized that the terrible moment had come when, if he failed to conquer it, the horrible being would kill him.

The *particular* middle-class attainments, on the other hand, are specifically the eight great magical attainments as found in the Indian Buddhist texts. Here Dragpa jets'en takes as the source for his list a verse from the fourth chapter of the *Tantra of the Diamond Pavilion*:[28]

Eye ointment, foot ointment,
sword, dominion over the underwold,
magic pill, walking in the sky,
invisibility, alchemy,
holding the mantra, universal sovereignty,
and summoning the holy maiden:
by receiving these a practitioner
gains the diamonds of the magical attainments.

This list differs slightly from that given above, and moreover the verse actually gives eleven items, which Dragpa jets'en must somehow combine into eight. He gives the following glosses:

1) If the practitioner puts the eye ointment upon his eyes, he can see the entire triple world.
2) If he puts the foot ointment upon his feet, his feet become swift.
3) If he puts the sword in his mouth, he can mount into the sky.
4) If he gains dominion over the underworld, he can lift treasure out from underground and give to beings whatever they desire.
5) If he puts the magic pill into his mouth, no one can see him. Like a *nöjin*-spirit he can take whatever form he wishes, and

he can become invisible by making a mark upon his forehead: hence this item includes both invisibility and magical transformations of form.

6) Alchemy comprises three different magical attainments:
a) Alchemy of life: he can make his life last as long as the sun and moon.
b) Alchemy of body: he can make his body eternally be but sixteen years old.
c) Alchemy of enjoyments: he can turn iron and copper into gold.

7) Summoning the holy maiden is the same as evoking the female *nöjin* spirits.

Among the items on the above list, Dragpa jets'en says, the magic pill and invisibility are the same. Thus, if one considers "summoning the female *nöjin* spirits" to be included under the general magical attainments, and if one counts the three sorts of alchemy separately, one arrives at eight items; alternatively, if one includes "summoning the female *nöjin* spirits" among the eight, one may combine the alchemy of life and alchemy of body into one unit, and there too get eight items. The remaining three items in the verse—walking in the sky, holding the mantra, and universal sovereignty—Dragpa jets'en considers to be the *upper-class* ordinary magical attainments, the height of achievement before reaching enlightenment itself. To walk in the sky, he says, is to travel in the air with a "magical emanation" of oneself. To hold the mantra is to be able to prolong one's life with the mantra as long as the sun and the moon shall last. The quality of these two magical attainments is that one's body becomes quite beautiful, appearing as if one were eternally sixteen years old, that whatever enjoyments one wishes come to one from the sky, and that by the strength of one's magical emanations one may travel from Buddha field to Buddha field, to hear the Buddha's Bodies of Transformation preach the holy Law. And finally, to exercise universal sovereignty, he adds almost parenthetically, is to enjoy great fame and renown upon the earth.[29]

These higher magical attainments are generalized abilities that do not depend upon specific ritual techniques for their accomplishment; they are talents that seem to appear spontaneously in the course of contemplation, and they are symbols of the acquisition of comprehensive divine power. As one text says:[30]

Initiated as Tārā by the Buddhas,
one becomes the crown jewel of the Law . . .
when one has attained this precious initiation
one will gain all magical attainments.
So with the ritual that was explained to one,
one should firmly enterprise for half a year,
offering a torma at the three times of the day;
by this mantra, with the ritual
of flour and sugar and so on,
one will attain in a dream the sign;
and once the signs have been shown in one's dream
the magical attainments themselves will follow.

And Nāgārjuna offers this comment:[31]

Contemplating in this way, one should perform the recitation neither too swiftly nor too slowly, neither indistinctly nor in small measure, abandoning the false construction of nonreality . . . . Intent upon one's object, one should contemplate for six months, while the signs of the magical attainments arise: in the first month, one's diseases and other impediments are pacified; in the second month, one gets without asking the most excellent food; in the third, one gets various garments; in the fourth, one continually gets delicacies such as betel of various sorts; in the fifth, one consorts with women adorned with the qualities of beauteous form; and in the sixth month, one consorts with the divine women of the gods.

To Nāgārjuna, "excellent food" and "divine women" not only mean the actual powers of attraction and subjugation (although that is certainly implied), but they also symbolize an intercourse with all the magic powers of delight, mobility, and transformation. We may consider all these higher magical attainments, then, to be the ability to perform what Dragpa jets'en calls "the miscellaneous functions to take in hand the sort of people who have faith in the ordinary magical attainments"; these *general functions* are the control of public nonreality in the most direct and universal manner, as a spontaneous and inherent result of the practitioner's understanding and "ownership." Hence these general functions stand closest to the soteriological function of enlightenment itself; the texts warn of how easily one may be led astray when so close to the goal:[32]

If one gives way to delight,
one's attainment will be meager;
but to one who keeps to the contemplation and recitation
even in dream will be the attainment
of universal sovereignty.

And Nāgārjuna again comments:[33]

> In contemplating the Blessed Lady, most people let themselves be diverted—"damaged"—by the women they obtain thereby..... But if one is not turned away by temptation . . . then one is freed forever from birth, old age, and death; one goes to the Pure Lands of the great magicians and sees the Tathāgatas, and one gains all the stages of the Bodhisattva.

And thus one's magic power and control are made complete by the plunge into the divine Emptiness, the very source of the nonreality of this world.

We may, finally, summarize the relationship between the magical attainments and the functions as in the following diagram.

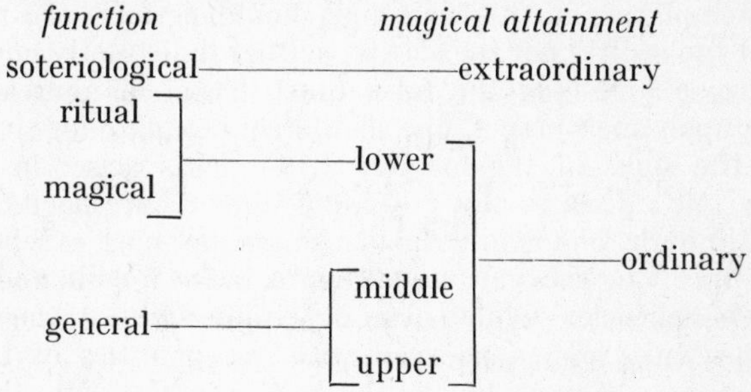

THE STRUCTURE OF FUNCTION

We have already noted how these functions tend to group themselves according to the locus of the "generation" and to the particular mantra ritual that is used therein. The Tibetans themselves distinguish three types of generation: self-generation, generation in front, and generation in the flask. This last generation is the empowering of the water that will be used in an initiation ceremony; the water is rendered potent by the visualization of the deity within the flask and the application of the mantra. Hence—though the Tibetans have no single general rubric for this—the term may well serve for all the times when the deity is generated within an object, since the ritual process is the same. We may thus draw up the following explicit correspondences:

mantra	*generation*	*ritual element*	*function*
contemplation	self	ritual service	soteriological
effectuation	front	evocation	ritual
application	flask (object)	employment	magical

A full-scale ritual may utilize every element in this sequence, or it may emphasize one element over the others. This provides us with a basic typology of Tibetan rituals according to the predominant function found therein.

Ritual type 1: *General function*.—This type class is perhaps furthest from the fully structured ritual of the great monastic assemblies. Here are included all the semiritualized activities of magic power, performed usually in privacy and seclusion, ranging from unstructured feats of levitation and invisibility to the more formally structured rites of "the awakened corpse," "wind running," and alchemy. Here there is no specific administration of the divine power, and the rites are based upon a generalized magical understanding and ability.

Ritual type 2: *Soteriological function*.—This type class is characterized by an emphasis upon the acquisition of power and/or understanding; often the greatest stress is placed on the Process of Perfection, as perhaps best exemplified by the "six yogas of Nāropa." But here too are included those preparatory contemplations of the ritual service where the divine power is acquired through the *contemplation of the mantra* as well as through the final dissolution of the divine appearance and ego into Emptiness.

Ritual type 3: *Ritual function*.—Under this category are all the rituals of offering, where the object of the offerings, divine or demonic, is evoked before the practitioner. If the evocation is divine, this type class includes the *effectuation of the mantra*, but the ritual type is also used in the bribery and coercion of lower spirits and of frankly demonic forces. The offerings may range from simple tormas to burnt offerings to all the complexities of a Four Maṇḍala Offering.

Ritual type 4: *Magical function*.—Here we find perhaps the widest variety of techniques. The practitioner may *apply the mantra* directly upon public nonreality (as in erecting a contemplative "tent of protection" about the person of a patron), or he may use some physical intermediary (as in making potent the cleansing water at the start of a ritual), but in every instance the power is applied to some particular and palpable object, whether it be an amulet of protection, an effigy of destruction, or the visualized heart of some distant person. Many times, too, both techniques are used toward a single end: in an initiation, for example, the recipient is cleansed of obscuration and empowered in body by the master's visualization and application of the mantra directly upon the disciple, and also by the magically potent water that he has generated in the flask.

These ritual types may be depicted as follows:

locus of power	*mantra*	*ritual type*	*examples*
nonreality		general	awakened corpse alchemy
self	contemplation	soteriological	six yogas ritual service
front	effectuation	ritual	burnt offering four maṇḍalas
object	application	magical	initiation thread-cross

These types are the blocks from which rituals are constructed, and the predominant function flavors the entire performance. But we must bear in mind that it is rare to find any one ritual type in total isolation, especially in communal ritual activity; the performance of any function requires the prior ritual service of the deity, and many performances in the ritual and magical type classes begin with a self-generation (no matter how perfunctory) as a symbolic reenactment of the acquisition of the divine power, before it is then directed toward a ritual evocation or magical employment. Thus the paradigm ritual function of the burnt offering is still preceded by a brief self-generation as its "ritual service," and we have noted before that any ritual of offering (even without explicit self-generation) is always the delayed second half of a full-scale evocation. But in all these cases it is the ritual function of approach, offering and effectuation which forms the central motif of the entire ceremony. Again, an initiation, from the recipient's point of view, is a magical function performed upon his person, but the officiating master must perform at least briefly (in private) both the ritual service and the evocation of the deity—the self-generation and the generation in front—before he proceeds to the magical operation that is the focus of the ceremony. Similarly, the thread-cross ritual (to be examined later) begins with a brief ritual service and evocation, but then it emphasizes both a special ritual function of torma offering to various malevolent spirits and the magical function of the thread-cross itself; here it is the combination of motifs which provides the performance with its acknowledged efficacy and its special dramatic flavor.

Thus most communal ritual activity centers upon the ritual of evocation, with the ritual of offering as a specialized and abbreviated version thereof. The full-scale evocation provides the most complete outline of ritual activities, and the particular ritual types may often be seen as selections from this thoroughgoing program or as emphases upon one or another of its portions. It may, then, aid our understanding of what follows if we here reproduce the complete outline of an evocation of Tārā, which forms the skeleton of Kongtrü rinpoch'e's extensive corpus upon the goddess:[34]

1 Preparations: cleaning the assembly hall, erecting the altar, and so on
2 Basics
  2.1 Preliminaries
    2.11 Evoking the cleansing water
    2.12 Expelling hindering demons and erecting a circle of protection
    2.13 Empowering the place and the utensils

We may note briefly that these preliminaries are actually a magical function, utilizing both the device of the cleansing water and the direct imposition upon nonreality of the visualized circle of protection; many rituals add further a preliminary ritual function, wherein the hindering demons are summoned before the assembly and offered a "preliminary torma" as a bribe to depart the sacred precincts: if they do not accept they are then forcibly and magically expelled with the fierce mantra and the "magic mustard seed."

The first part of the ritual begins, consisting, as we have noted, in the following:

mantra	*generation*	*ritual element*	*function*
contemplation——	self—————	ritual service——	soteriological

  2.2 Ritual proper
    2.21 Self-generation
      2.211 Preliminaries
        2.211.1 Ordinary
          2.211.11 Going for refuge
          2.211.12 Awakening the thought of enlightenment
        2.211.2 Extraordinary
          2.211.21 The stock of merit: the sevenfold office
          2.211.22 The stock of knowledge: the ŚŪNYATĀ mantra

2.212 Basics
2.212.1 Process of Generation
2.212.11 The yoga with the deity (self-generation)
2.212.111 Fourfold generation
2.212.112 Offerings and praise
2.212.113 Vivid appearance and firm ego
2.212.12 The yoga with the recitation (contemplation of the mantra)
2.212.121 Visualization of the mantra
2.212.122 Recitation of the mantra
2.212.2 Process of Perfection
2.212.21 With signs
2.212.22 Signless
2.213 Concluding acts
2.213.1 Arising in the body of the deity
2.213.2 Others

When this portion of the ritual outline is subordinated to the evocation that follows, it stops with the practitioners "arising in the body of the deity" after their dissolution into the sources of the power they will evoke. When used as a ritual service in solitary contemplation, however, the secluded yogin will perform the ritual over an entire contemplative period—about four hours—reciting the mantra as much as he can in the time allotted and concluding the whole period with the Process of Perfection. Between these contemplative periods there are many subsidiary concluding acts he can perform, to "fill in" the recitation; the outline provides a sampling of these miscellaneous ritual functions:

2.213.21 Torma offering
2.213.22 Mandala offering
2.213.23 Praise
2.213.24 Circumambulation
2.213.25 Bathing the deity
2.213.26 Prayer
2.213.27 Water offering

The ritual then proceeds to the second part, which is here the structural analogue of the Four Mandala Offering examined in chapter i. It consists, again, in the following:

mantra	*generation*	*ritual element*	*function*
effectuation	front	evocation	ritual

2.22 Generation in front
- 2.221 Generating the chief deity
- 2.222 Inviting the other guests
- 2.223 Accumulating the stocks (generation in front)
- 2.224 Offerings and praise
  - 2.224.1 Empowering the offerings
  - 2.224.2 The two waters and the five gifts
  - 2.224.3 The five sense gratifications
  - 2.224.4 Sensuousness, and so on
  - 2.224.5 The precious gems of severeignty
  - 2.224.6 The signs of good fortune
  - 2.224.7 The substances of good fortune
  - 2.224.8 The maṇḍala
  - 2.224.9 Miscellaneous offerings
  - 2.224.10 Praises
- 2.225 Recitation (effectuation of the mantra)

In special cases—as in the burnt offering—an entirely different sequence may be substituted for that given here, or this same sequence may be used alone as a ritual of offering. In any event, if this evocation is the focus of the ritual, the practitioners then proceed directly to the concluding acts given below. Again, this much of the ritual may simply be a preliminary to the special ritual and/or magical functions to be utilized toward a specific end, such as the appeasement, entrapment, and expulsion of evil spirits, or the initiation of a disciple. This next portion of the ritual then consists in either or both of the following sets of corresponding items:

mantra	*generation*	*ritual element*	*function*
	front	evocation	ritual
application	flask (object)	employment	magical

The ritual outline, not being based upon these specialized performances, gives this portion tersely as follows:

2.23 Generation in the flask

2.24 Torma offering

1. Coating the food tormas with butter.

2. Setting up the altar for the Four Maṇḍala Offering.

3. Offering up the maṇḍala to Tārā.

4. Tārā's mantra and image carved on a great rock. Wayside shrine in Dalhousie, Himachal Pradesh.

5. The Lady of the Goring Yak.

6. The burnt offering.

7. A complex thread-cross used in the large annual evocation of the Four-handed Lord.

8. Winding the five-colored threads on the frame of the thread-cross.

9. Putting butter flowers on the torma; the butter is placed in a pan of water to keep it cool and malleable.

10. The portrait molded of barley lour, in deep relief.

11. Four-tiered Mount Meru and the excellent house, whose roof is being painted with colored butter.

12. Planting shrubbery on the surrounding iron mountains.

13. The portrait complete with house, servants, livestock, and property.

14. The entire structure tied around the outside with thread and set on the altar facing the assembly: note the hundred butter lamps in front.

15. Carrying the thread-cross down the mountain.

16. The multitude tormas.

And finally the outline gives the following concluding acts:

- 2.3 Concluding acts
  - 2.31 Offerings and praise
  - 2.32 Prayer
  - 2.33 Confession of faults in the ritual
  - 2.34 Process of "gathering in" the deity in front
  - 2.35 Dedication of merit
  - 2.36 Earnest wish
  - 2.37 Benediction: "verses of good fortune"

In the pages that follow I give some examples of each ritual type, using as the basic materials the rituals performed for Tārā.

Ritual type 1: General function.—Among the members of this type class are not only the general powers of flight and transformation but also certain standard magical operations whose potency resides in the materials themselves rather than in any contemplative procedure by the practitioner. These operations still require that the practitioner acquire a large amount of generalized power if he is to be succesful in their performance. Here especially are such general functions as alchemy. As an example of this generalized application of ritually acquired power, we may quote from a short alchemical treatise included in the corpus of Kongtrü rinpoch'e, devoted particularly to the alchemy of life, as appropriate to a work on White Tārā:[35]

> It says in the *Tantra of the Red Slayer of Death*:[36] "Mix together *arura* [*Myrobalan arjuna*], *churura* [*Crataegus pinnatifida*], *bhṛṅgarāja* [*Eclipta prostrata*], *piling* [*Piper longum*], pepper, and iron filings with honey and sugar and roll this into pills. By eating these for one month, one will live for three hundred years."
>
> And the Master Kokila, in his *Treatise on the Protection of Life*,[37] gives the following easy recipe: equal parts of butter, honey, and milk mixed in a vessel of oil; add one part barley malt. Decant and eat. Within six months one's nails and teeth will be bright, and one can live for a thousand years; the sign thereof is that one's eyes become sharp and strong.
>
> Grind the dried root of the *nyeshing* [*Polygonatum falcatum*] into a fine powder and mix it with milk; when this "turns," churn it into butter and eat it every morning for twenty-one days, to clear away all diseases from one's body. If one eats this for six years, one will gain life and freedom from the construction of nonreality.
>
> Mix the three fruits—*arura*, *barura* [*Terminalia chebula*], and *churura*—with powdered *bhṛṅgarāja*, butter, and honey, and eat

> it. As the medicine is being digested, eat some rice boiled with milk, and one can live for three hundred years with sharp eyes and no disease.
>
> Rub a syrup of the three fruits into an iron vessel, rinsing it both day and night; mix into this honey and butter, and eat it. Preparing enough for a year, one can live for three hundred years, cleansed of disease, nails and teeth bright, voice as sweet as a cuckoo.
>
> . . . Here, *bhṛṅgarāja* is a medicine whose name means "king bee." It is also called *mārkava*, *keṣarañjana*, and so on [all Indian names for *Eclipta prostrata*]. As a medicine, its distillation turns one's hair black.

The author continues with a lengthy discussion of the various Tibetan translations of the names of Indian medicines, but this brief excerpt should suffice to exemplify the rituals of general function, the semiritualized utilization of the practitioner's comprehensive magical understanding and ability.

Ritual type 2: Soteriological function.—Rituals whose aim is specifically and exclusively soteriological are almost invariably associated with the high patron deities of the monastic cult. We have already seen that the six yogas of Nāropa are derived from the Processes of Perfection found in the different Tantras of the Highest Yoga. Tārā's soteriological function is thus subsumed under her ritual service, and it is examined in detail in chapter iii, where the rituals for the acquisition of her divine power are discussed.

Ritual type 3: Ritual function.—We have already seen that if the deity is generated in front, as for the effectuation of the mantra (or the arousing of the deity's heart), the offering of tormas, or the making of burnt offerings, we may consider this function to be "ritual." We have also noted, however, a number of *minor ritual functions* inserted into the major ritual outline at various places. Here the object of the offering—the "guest"—is not necessarily a divine being, but may well be a demon to be suborned from his malevolence by a torma offering: such is the minor ritual function of the *preliminary torma*, where the hindering demons are expelled and the limits of the sacred area are set or "cut off."

For these fierce purposes, the practitioners visualize themselves as Hayagrīva, the "fierce patron" of the Padma Family of which Tārā is a member, and they offer the preliminary torma as part of the erection of a circle of protection about the place of evocation. The demons are quite frankly bribed to leave the area, and those who obstinately remain are forcibly expelled with the most fearsome threats. Thus the assembly recites:

> Instantaneously I become the highest horse Heruka, fierce and blazing with unbearable brilliance, like the fire at the destruction of the universe.

The preliminary "torma for the hindering demons" is cleansed with OṂ HAYAGRĪVA HŪṂ PHAṬ! and purified into Emptiness with the SVABHĀVA mantra, from whence it is contemplatively recreated:

> From the realm of Emptiness comes BHRŪṂ, and from that a jeweled vessel, vast and broad, within which are OḤ ĀḤ HŪṂ; these melt into light and become a torma, divine in color, smell, taste, and strength.

Then, with their hands in the flying-bird gesture, the practitioners empower this visualized torma by reciting OṂ ĀḤ HŪṂ three times, with HA HO HRĪḤ at the end. The guests are summoned with the iron-hook gesture and OṂ SARVA-BHŪTA ĀKARṢAYA "Summon all demons!" JAḤ! Then the torma is presented to them by reciting three times:

> OṂ SARVA-VIGHNĀN NAMAḤ SARVA-TATHĀGATEBHYO VIŚVA-MUKHEBHYAḤ SARVATHĀ-KHAṂ UDGATE SPHARAṆA IMAṂ GAGANA-KHAṂ GṚHṆA IDAṂ BALIṂ TE SVĀHĀ!

> HŪṂ HRĪḤ! The hosts of evil spirits, hindering demons,
> and ghosts deluded by the appearance of duality:
> let them accept this torma and depart to their own place!

Then this ritual function is supplemented by a magical function, and the demons are expelled by reciting HŪṂ HŪṂ HŪṂ! and the fierce mantra:

> OṂ SUMBHANI SUMBHANI HŪṂ HŪṂ PHAṬ! OṂ GṚHṆA GṚHṆA HUṂ HUṂ PHAṬ! OṂ GṚHṆAPAYA GṚHṆAPAYA HŪṂ HŪṂ PHAṬ! OṂ ĀNAYA HOH! BHAGAVAN-VAJRA HŪṂ HŪṂ PHAṬ!

> "OṂ purifier, purifier HŪṂ HŪṂ PHAṬ! OṂ seize, seize HŪṂ HŪṂ PHAṬ! OṂ grasp, grasp HŪṂ HŪṂ PHAṬ! OṂ lead away HOḤ! Diamond of the Blessed One HŪṂ HŪṂ PHAṬ!

And there is the scattering of magic mustard seed, the burning of *gugü* incense, and the raging sounds of the thighbone trumpet and fierce music. Then there is visualized the circle of protection—"a diamond ground, firm everywhere, with fence, lattice, tent, curtains, and blazing fire of knowledge"—in an evocation that is characteristically terse:

The realm of the Body of the Dharma,
the deific mantra of the knowledge of nonduality:
the self-created essence, the partitioning maṇḍala!
VAJRA RAKṢA RAKṢA "Diamond! protect, protect"
BHRUṂ![38]

We have seen another example of this sort of minor or subsidiary ritual function in the concluding torma offerings of the Four Maṇḍala Offering. The Four Maṇḍala Offering itself is an example of a *major ritual function*, where the focus of the entire ceremony centers upon the evocation of the deity: this is the ritual type properly speaking. Perhaps the most important of these full-scale ritual functions—often performed separately—is the *burnt offering*. Lessing has reported extensively upon this ritual,[39] but here I give just a short example of a burnt offering for Tārā which is included in the corpus of Kongtrü rinpoch'e.[40]

Because Tārā is basically a peaceful deity, the burnt offering achieves only two of the four functions, pacifying and increasing; to evoke Tārā to subjugate or destroy would be out of character for her (but see the rituals of subjugation of Kurukullā, below). The burnt offering may be performed as an addendum to a large ritual of evocation or at the end of a period of ritual service to correct any errors or fill in any omissions (in which case it is a minor ritual function); or the burnt offering may be performed by itself as the most important part of the ritual, as a pure exercise of power in a ritual function toward a specific end, such as the pacifying of one's own sins or of a community's diseases; in this instance the burnt offering is the major ritual function and the ceremony for pacifying should be performed during the fortnight of the waning moon, and that for increasing during the fortnight of the waxing moon (for sound astrological reasons). Such special-purpose burnt offerings may go on for weeks at a time.

The efficacy of this ritual function is given in this verse:

In order to accomplish the various functions,
we shall explain the function of the burnt offering.
It is said: in the mouth of Agni
the burnt offering is very firm;

by the burnt offering are the deities satisfied,
and satisfied they grant the magical attainments.
Every guarantee of the mantra
is fulfilled by the burnt offering.

"Thus," says Kongtrü rinpoch'e, "the deities are made to fulfill the guarantees of the ritual and the mantra and to grant quickly the result that one desires."

The ritual begins with the preparation of the hearth. The monks approach the place where the burnt offering will be performed and say: "I am become the Diamond Fierce HŪṂ Shouter, holding my vajra and bell!" They recite the mantra HŪṂ HŪṂ HŪṂ HŪṂ! seven times and offer a preliminary torma as a bribe for the departure of any hindering demons who might be present, and they expel the obdurate spirits who remain by reciting three times: OṂ ĀḤ HŪṂ! OṂ HANA HANA KRODHA "Kill, kill, fierce one!" HŪṂ! If the burnt offering is being performed on the same spot where a maṇḍala was previously generated, however, this expulsion of evil spirits is unnecessary, because the piece of ground is already pure.

Then there is set out a round table—pacifying is performed in a circular hearth—and it is spread with white sandalwood or some other white substance. Upon the covering are drawn the four "Brahma lines" and the four "corner lines," forming the eight spokes of a wheel. With a marking thread one span long there is drawn from the center a circular line about these spokes, and four fingers beyond the circle are drawn the two circumferences called *muren* and *k'ach'er*; around the latter is drawn another larger circle whose radius is twice the distance from the center to the *muren*, and on this circle, bisecting the angles with a compass, four corners are cut out in the four directions. These corners are connected to form a square, and another square is added two fingers beyond that. Then in the middle is drawn an eight-petaled lotus, with its anthers extending to the *muren*; on the *k'ach'er* is drawn a garland of vajras, and a half-moon with a vajra handle is drawn in each of the four corners. In the center of the lotus is drawn an utpala flower, eight fingers large, marked with a vajra.

All these lines [here: *rekhā* "fences"] are drawn on the white background with unmixed colors. On the first circular line (four fingers inside the two circumferences) is erected a round wall of "sweet-smelling firewood," on which are placed "combustibles" such as kerosene or *tinglo* (small lamps made out of flour) to help the wood catch fire easily. These rather complex instructions may be clarified by figure 28.

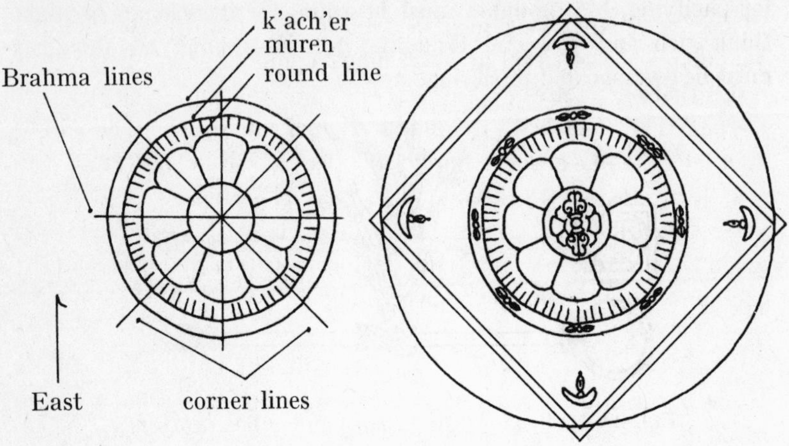

Fig. 28. Drawing the hearth.

On the left of the Diamond Master are placed a large and a small vessel of water, a vessel of cleansing water, the five gifts, a large and a small "round white torma"—for Tārā and Agni respectively—and a *kuśa*-grass sprinkler. On his right are arranged in their proper order the burning materials, such as the melted butter and the *yamshing*, small sticks of wood whose ends are trimmed to resemble lotus flowers. All the materials for the "worldling" Agni are mixed together in one plate, while those for Tārā, the "supramundane deity," are put in separate plates. There is set out a larger quantity of the materials to be used for the particular purpose of the ritual, such as black sesamum for pacifying sins, wheat for pacifying diseases, and so on.

Then, between the Diamond Master and the hearth is placed the *meyö*, a stone carved with pictures of streams, clouds, and mountains and the syllable VAṂ—the "seed" of water—which serves as a protecting wall against possible exposure to "fire poison." Between the Diamond Master and the *meyö* is placed a bell, and in front of that a vajra; between them the two ladles used for pouring liquids and solids into the fire are laid down face to face (see fig. 29), and finally a bundle of *kuśa* grass is added.[41]

From this point on the Diamond Master is technically a Vedic sage, and as such he remains unmoving in his cross-legged posture, wearing his white garments and thinking only the proper thoughts: for pacifying, his thoughts must be calm; for increasing, he must think rich and powerful thoughts; for destroying, his thoughts must be awesone and terrifying.

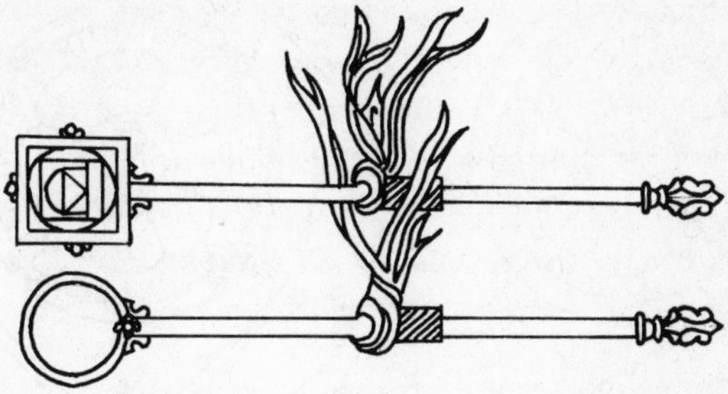

Fig. 29. Ladles for liquids (top) and solids (bottom).

If the burnt offering is being performed in connection with a larger ritual of evocation or offering, by this point in the major ritual outline the self-generation will already have been completed; if the burnt offering is being performed independently, the participants now first go through the self-generation and its contemplation of the mantra, ending with the "gathering in and arising" of the Process of Perfection. Then, arisen from Emptiness in the body of the deity and grasping her ego, they empower the cleansing water and sprinkle it upon the dwelling and the utensils as they recite: OṂ VAJRA-AMṚTA-KUṆḌALI HANA HANA HŪṂ PHAṬ ! OṂ ĀḤ HŪṂ !

They then contemplatively re-create from Emptiness and empower the offerings, and they visualize that all the impurities of the burning materials are cleansed away; the Diamond Master—his bell in his left hand and his vajra in his right, where they will remain throughout the entire ritual—extends his forefinger in the one-pointed-vajra gesture to touch each material in turn, and the participants recite OṂ SVĀHĀ ! three times. The specially trimmed *yamshing* firewood is empowered by reciting three times OṂ ĀḤ SVĀHĀ !, the melted butter by reciting three times OṂ ŚRĪṂ SVĀHĀ !, all the grain by reciting three times OṂ JRIṂ SVĀHĀ !, and all the other materials by reciting three times OṂ KURU KURU SVĀHĀ !

The actual lighting of the fire is accompanied by its contemplative equivalent, the visualization of the fire-god Agni, to whom the first burnt offerings are made. The Diamond Master takes some fire with OṂ ĀḤ HŪṂ (nowadays this is recited while lighting a match) and with it he kindles a lamp, which he sprinkles with cleansing water while reciting the AMṚTA mantra. Then, still reciting the mantra, he circumambulates the hearth and places the lamp inside it, saying OṂ VAJRA JVALA JVALA "Diamond, blaze! blaze!" HŪṂ! The firewood in the hearth is kindled with a fan while reciting HŪṂ HŪṂ! and as the flames begin to blaze the hearth is cleansed with the AMṚTA mantra and purified with the SVABHĀVA mantra; from the Emptiness thereof the fire is contemplatively re-created, evoked in its divine form of the god Agni:

> From the realm of Emptiness is HŪṂ, arising from which is a round white hearth of pacifying, a full cubit deep, encircled with the *muren* and *k'ach'er*, the corners of the table marked with half-moons and vajras, the shape of a full-blown lotus, clear and unobstructed. Inside it, from RAṂ [the seed of fire] is the circle of fire, marked with a RAṂ that in turn transforms into the white Agni of pacifying, holding a rosary in his right hand and a ladle in his left, his crest adorned with Vairocana, surrounded by a garland of white tongues of flame, sitting upon a white gelded he-goat in the cross-legged posture, wearing white clothes and ornaments, his plaited hair bound up on his head.

The knowledge being is then summoned: "From my own heart light radiates forth, inviting from the southeast Agni and all his retinue." The monks beckon the knowledge being by raising their hands in the refuge gesture, their thumbs at the level of their ears, and they invite him with the verse and mantra:

> OṂ! Come here, come here, great element,
> highest Brahman sage of the gods;
> that you may accept this food of clarified butter
> come forward and partake!

> OṂ AGNAYE MAHĀ-TEJAḤ SARVA-KARMA-PRASĀDHAKA MAHĀ-BHŪTA DEVA-ṚṢI-DVIJA-SATVAN GṚHĪTVĀ ĀHUTIṂ ĀHARA ASMIN SAṄNIHITO-BHAVA!

> "OṂ Agni! Great blaze, accomplisher of all rituals, great element, powerful one of the gods, sages, and twice-born! Grasping our sacrifice, take it! Be here close at hand!"

The Diamond Master sprinkles the hearth with the cleansing water and the monks recite the AMṚTA mantra to expel any hindering demons who might have taken advantage of the invitation to intrude upon the sacred precincts. And with JAḤ HŪṂ BAṂ HOḤ! "the knowledge being becomes indissolubly one with the symbolic being."

Then the Diamond Master arranges bundles of *kuśa* grass in the eight directions around the hearth, with their tips pointing to the right, and the monks recite:

> OṂ! This *kuśa* grass, pure and virtuous,
> the most excellent heart of all that springs from the earth,
> is the cleansing substance of the Three Jewels,
> is the cleansing substance of Brahma!

> By this may all demons who would hinder me be pacified, may all misfortunes be pacified! OṂ VAJRASATTVA ĀḤ!

Then, while scattering water with the *kuśa*-grass sprinkler, an oblation is poured from the small vessel of water into a basin, and it is offered with the mantra: OṂ ĀḤ HRIḤ PRAVARA-SATKĀRÂRTHAṂ ARGHAṂ PRATĪCCHA HŪṂ SVĀHĀ! The series of gifts are then presented to Agni, with the proper gestures and the mantras from OṂ VAJRA-PUṢPE ĀḤ HŪṂ through OṂ VAJRA-ŚABDA ĀḤ HŪṂ, and he is praised as follows:

> Lord of the world, son of the most powerful Brahma,
> initiated by ṬAKKI, king of fire-gods,
> burning all defilements with the highest wisdom:
> I bow to Agni, the Seizer!

And he is "bound to his oath" with the mantra:

> OṂ VAJRA-ANALA MAHĀ-BHUTA JVALA JVALA SARVA-BHASMĪ-KURU SARVA-DUṢṬĀN HŪṂ PHAṬ! DṚṢYA JAḤ HŪṂ BAṂ HOḤ SAMAYAS TVAṂ SAMAYA HOḤ!

> "OṂ Diamond fire, great element, burn! burn! reduce to ashes all sins! HŪṂ PHAṬ! Become visible! JAḤ HŪṂ BAṂ HOḤ! Vow your oath HOḤ!"

After the god has thus been bound three times, his offering of liquid butter is poured seven times into the fire with the two ladles (see pl. 6), repeating the same mantra each time, as the practitioners visualize:

> On Agni's heart is HŪṂ, and his tongue is a one-pointed vajra marked with RAṂ. The mouths of the ladles too are marked with HŪṂ.

> OṂ AGNAYE ĀDĪVYA ĀDĪVYA ĀVIŚA ĀVIŚA MAHĀ-SRIYE HAVYA-KAVYA-VAHNĀYA "Agni, shine, shine! approach, approach! Great Glory! Conveyor of offerings and sacrifice!" All my misfortunes, my sins, obscurations, obstacles, diseases, and untimely death ŚĀNTIṂ KURU SVĀHĀ!

Likewise, with the same mantra, the god is offered three times the trimmed *yamshing* firewood, and "as many times as he thinks fit" the Diamond Master burns the offering of all the different burning materials that were mixed together in a single vessel, until he pours a final offering of liquid butter into the fire with OṂ AGNAYE SVĀHĀ! "OṂ! For Agni SVĀHĀ!"

It is the function of the fire-god Agni to convey to the deity the offerings that will be presented to her; thus he was evoked and bound to this function, and he was made offerings which he "ate" with his hollow tongue. This completes the ritual for the worldling Agni, and with confidence that the divine fire will do all that is required, the ritual proceeds to the evocation of the goddess herself in front of the practitioners: "In the center of Agni's vast heart is BHRŪṂ, from which there arises a divine mansion of moon-white crystal," and so on through the generation of the goddess, the visualization of the empowering syllables upon her body, and the invitation of the knowledge being with VAJRA-SAMĀJAḤ!

If, as part of a larger ritual, this knowledge being is already resident in a "residential maṇḍala" (usually in a different place indoors, while the burnt offering is performed outside), a very interesting little ceremony is here used to convey the deity to the vicinity of the hearth. Either the Diamond Master himself or the altar server stands by the maṇḍala and recites the 100-syllable mantra, to purify himself for the transfer of the deity; he shakes the vessel that contains the oblations, so that the deity can hear them, and, swinging the smoking censor, he calls out:

> Residents of the maṇḍala who reside
> in the residence of this maṇḍala of powdered colors:
> I now invite you, I pray you come
> to the maṇḍala in the middle of the hearth!

He takes a flower—visualizing it to be inherently the goddess herself—and touches it to the powdered colors of the maṇḍala, picking up a few grains of powder, all the while reciting the heart of conditioned coproduction (YE DHARMA . . .) to fix the deity in the flower; he places it inside a jeweled vessel, prostrates before it, and carries this knowledge being reverently back to the place of the burnt offering. Here the Process of Generation is completed; the monks recite a praise over the flower, and with JAḤ HŪṂ BAṂ HOḤ it is thrown into the hearth to unite with the symbolic being already generated there. This deity is then sealed with the initiation.

Then, as above for Agni, water is scattered with the *kuśa*-grass sprinkler and an oblation is poured from the large vessel of water into a basin; this same oblation is offered to Tārā by reciting her 10-syllable mantra and the same mantra as given before: OṂ ĀḤ HRIḤ PRAVARA-SATKĀRÂRTHAṂ ARGHAṂ PRATĪCCHA HŪṂ SVĀHĀ! She is offered the same series of gifts, with the proper gestures, from OṂ VAJRA-PUṢPE ĀḤ HŪṂ through OṂ VAJRA-ŚABDA ĀḤ HŪṂ, and the monks recite a praise to the goddess. These offerings and praises may be expanded or abridged as the occassion warrants.

With the deity duly installed in the fire, the ritual proceeds to the burnt offering proper. The monks recite the visualization:

> On the mouths of the two ladels is a vivid syllable HŪṂ,
> and the tongue of the Blessed Lady too
> is marked with the pure syllable TĀṂ;
> it is with this that she accepts
> the nectar of the burning materials.
> OṂ TĀRE TUTTĀRE TURE SVĀHĀ!

Her offering of liquid butter is poured seven times into the fire with the two ladles, repeating each time OṂ AGNAYE SVĀHĀ! and concluding with: "All my misfortunes, my sins, obscurations, obstacles, diseases, and untimely death ŚĀNTIṂ-KURU SVĀHĀ!" Then the individual burning materials are offered up one at a time, and as each is poured into the fire with the ladles, the same mantra as above (for the melted butter) is repeated, substituting for OṂ AGNAYE SVĀHĀ the following:

Burning material	*Mantra*
yamshing firewood	OṂ BODHI-VṚKṢĀYA "for the Bodhi tree" SVĀHĀ!
sesamum	OṂ SARVA-PĀPA-DAHANA-VAJRĀYA "for the diamond that burns all sins" SVĀHĀ!
dūrvā grass	OṂ VAJRA-ĀYUSE "for diamond life" SVĀHĀ!

uncooked rice	OṂ VAJRA-PUṢṬĀYA "for diamond increase" SVĀHĀ !
milk mixed with flour	OṂ VAJRA-SAMPADE "for diamond success" SVĀHĀ !
kuśa grass	OṂ APRATIHATA-VAJRĀYA "for the diamond of nonobstruction" SVĀHĀ !
barley grains	OṂ VAJRA-BĪJĀYAI "for the diamond seed" SVĀHĀ !
husked barley	OṂ VAJRA-MAHĀVEGĀYA "for diamond swift movement" SVĀHĀ !
peas	OṂ VAJRA-MAHĀVALĀYA "for the diamond great vine" SVĀHĀ !
wheat	OṂ VAJRA-GHASMARYAI "for diamond eating" SVĀHĀ !
mustard seed	OṂ SARVA-ARTHA-SIDDHĀYA "for success in all things" SVĀHĀ !

In addition to these, there may also be offered up all the various kinds of food, medicine, grain, precious gems, and fine silks, all of which are placed in the fire with the appropriate "heart" mantra; at the very least the liquid butter and the *yamshing* firewood must be offered.

Each of these substances may be offered hundreds of times, and the ritual itself may last for weeks at a time, the fire never being allowed to die. It is only when all the burning materials for the particular purpose of the ritual have been used up that the burnt offering is concluded. Then, in conclusion, the goddess is offered her torma (the larger of the two round white tormas set out at the beginning of the ritual) and she receives the final offerings, praises, and prayers. Then the monks recite the 100-syllable mantra three times and dismiss the deity with the following words:

> Whatever we have done wrong, or in too small measure,
> with our minds clouded over;
> since you are the refuge of embodied beings,
> Lord ! it is right that you now be forbearing;
> whatever we have done
> because we could not obtain, or did not know,
> or were not able to do:
> it is right that you be forbearing toward it all.
> Grant us the highest magical attainment,
> grant us the fruits of all our deep contemplations,
> and to all beings, too, as you wish,

grant the supreme magical attainment!
Again, that you may depart,
depart to your own place VAJRA MŪḤ!

With this standard closing sequence the monks may visualize that the knowledge being departs to its natural abode and that the symbolic being is gathered in to themselves, or they may gather in both of them to their hearts.

If, however, the knowledge being had previously been brought out from the maṇḍala, it must now be returned in the same way. The Diamond Master, reciting the 10-syllable mantra, makes as if to withdraw the flower from the center of the hearth, bearing the vessel reverently back inside and praying that the deity dwell in the maṇḍala; to the 10-syllable mantra he adds VAJRA-SAMAYAS TVAM! and he recites the visualization:

The invited maṇḍala dissolves
into the maṇḍala of powered colors.

This dismissal concludes the offering to Tārā, the supramundane fire-god, and now Agni too is given a torma, offerings, and praise and asked to depart. With OṂ AGNAYE SVĀHĀ! he is presented a ladleful of melted butter, and he is offered again the oblation and the five gifts with the gestures and mantras from ARGHAṂ through ŚABDA, as before. The monks praise him with the following verses:

Son of Brahma, lord of the world,
king of fire-gods, highest of sages,
emanating a body by the power of compassion
that he may be a refuge to departed spirits,
acting as a sage to accomplish the magic spells,
his light of wisdom burning defilement,
blazing brilliantly as the fire that destroys the world,
possessing supernormal powers, supernatural perceptions,
riding a vehicle emanated by his skillful means,
holding a rosary to count the recitations of the mantra,
bearing a hearth full of a distillation of nectar,
cooling with the nectar of the Law,
celibate, free of the stain of sin,
though dwelling in the world passed into nirvāṇa,
though attained to peace greatly compassionate:
to you I make homage and praise!

Then the fire-god torma—the smaller of the two—is cleansed and purified with the two mantras, and re-created: "From the realm of Emptiness: OṂ ĀḤ HŪṂ, from which there is born a great ocean of nectar." This contemplative torma is empowered with OṂ ĀḤ HŪṂ and HA HOḤ HRĪḤ, the god is addressed with OṂ AGNAYE ĀDĪVYA . . ., and he is given his torma with the mantra A-KĀRO MUKHAṂ . . . as is recited for all worldling tormas, all with the appropriate gestures. Once again he is presented the oblation and the five gifts, and he is "entrusted to his function" with the following words:

> Fire! god who eats what is burned,
> king of sages, lord of spirits:
> to Agni and his retinue
> we make offerings, praises, and homage.
> And having accepted this torma given in offering
> let all of us yogins
> accomplish all that we wish!

Then Agni is given one more oblation as before, and he is prayed for forbearance with the verses "Whatever we have done wrong . . ."

> You have accomplished my own and others' aims;
> depart, eater of what is burned;
> at whatever time you may return
> I will have accomplished all magical attainments!

> OṂ ĀḤ VAJRA MUḤ! The knowledge being departs to his natural abode and the symbolic being dissolves into the blazing fire.

The ritual ends with an earnest wish and a benediction.

After the ritual is finished, the fire is not to be disturbed until it goes out by itself; but if it is absolutely necessary to clean up after the ritual, the following mantra should be repeated 100 times over a mixture of scented water and milk:

> OṂ RURU SPHURU JVALA TIṢṬHA SIDDHA-LOCANI SARVA-ARTHA-SĀDHANI SVĀHĀ!

> "OṂ Roar! flash! blaze! remain! Gazing upon what we have accomplished, accomplishing all aims SVĀHĀ!"

This liquid is then poured into the fire.

The ritual of pacifying may serve as an outline for all four basic types of burnt offering. The burnt offering for increasing, for example, takes place on a square table, and the surface of the hearth is covered with a yellow substance upon which the lines are drawn; in the center of the central lotus is an utpala flower marked with a precious gem, rather than with a vajra. Here the most important burning materials are *dūrvā* grass for the increase of life, barley grains for the increase of merit, and so on; here, too, the posture, clothing, and thoughts of the Diamond Master must be changed to correspond to the intent of the ritual. In the recitation of the visualization, the word "round" must be changed to "square" and the word "white" to "yellow", and in praying for the result of the burnt offering one says: "All my qualities of life, merit, glory, fame, sovereignty, and understanding PUṢṬIṂ-KURU OṂ!" Aside from these changes, the procedure is exactly the same as for pacifying.

Ritual type 4: Magical function.—As we have noted before, a magical function is one in which, after a prior self-generation, the practitioner uses the ego of the deity in the direct control of appearances, the application of the mantra, or the generation of the deity in an object, all commonly subsumed under the heading of *employment* of the deity's power (as opposed to its ritual service or its evocation in front). Compared with the complex equipment and technique required for most ritual functions, the performance of a magical function directly upon public nonreality is often much simpler to carry out, though the creation of an intermediary magical device or recipe may be just as complicated as the intricate actions of the burnt offering. But a magical function by no means requires less personal preparation than does a ritual function, and the texts are stern in their prescription of prior ritual service before one ever attempts to employ the power of the deity through one's own person.

To illustrate the basic patterns of employment and the preparations it requires, I give here a short Tārā ritual written by Dragpa jets'en, divided into two basic parts: the prior *ritual service* and the actual *employment* of the deity's power.[41a]

The first part begins with the practitioner seated in a comfortable position. He has set out the offerings and the tormas, and he has gone through the preliminaries of cleansing and empowering them, as we have seen before. We may note here that the present ritual gives no details on the presentation of these offerings, the praising of the goddess, and so on, for it presumes that the practitioner will be able to fill in the major outline at the proper places; this terseness hides no secrets, but simply presumes a practitioner has attended other rituals.

The practitioner then begins with his accumulation of the stock of merit before the field of hosts. He instantaneously visualizes himself as Tārā, with a TĀṂ in his/her heart above a lotus and a moon.

Varicolored lights radiate forth from that seed and invite into the sky before him his guru and Tārā, surrounded by a retinue of Buddhas and Bodhisattvas. Once again the light from his heart radiates forth, bearing a host of offerings, and these he presents with the gestures and mantras OṂ VAJRA-PUṢPE HŪṂ and so on. He then confesses his sins, rejoices in the virtues of others, dedicates his own merit, goes for refuge, awakens the thought of enlightenment, and offers up his own body. Thus he may perform the seven parts of the sevenfold office separately, or he may recite the short version ("I go for refuge to the Three Jewels . . ."), whichever he prefers. Then he contemplates the Four Immeasurables.

Having thus accumulated his stock of merit, he accumulates his stock of knowledge by reciting the ŚŪNYATĀ mantra and contemplating Emptiness, but by the strength of remembering his thought of enlightenment he thinks: "I should arise from Emptiness in a bodily form, for the sake of sentient beings." So from the realm of Emptiness appears a PAṂ, and from that a lotus; from A there is the orb of a moon, above which is a green TĀṂ; and that syllable transforms into a lotus flower marked with TĀṂ, from which light radiates forth and makes offerings to the Noble Ones. When it has served the aims of sentient beings—when it has purified the entire world—the light is gathered back within the syllable; at that very instant, as it dissolves within the TĀṂ, he visualizes himself as Tārā, her body colored green, her right hand in the refuge gesture which grants fearlessness, holding in her left hand a lotus flower whose petals touch her ear, her hair bound up and swirling down to the right, wearing silken garments, adorned with many jeweled ornaments, in the prime of youth and smiling.

Next the practitioner empowers her limbs: he visualizes upon his/her eyes a white OṂ TĀRE SVĀHĀ, upon her ears a blue OṂ TUTTĀRE SVĀHĀ, on her nose a yellow OṂ TURE SVĀHĀ, on her tongue a red OṂ TU SVĀHĀ, on her heart a blue OṂ RE SVĀHĀ, and on the top of her head a green OṂ TĀREṆI SVĀHĀ, all of them enthroned upon a moon.

His/her senses thus empowered, light radiates forth from the TĀṂ in his/her heart, which invites the knowledge being from Potala, and this dissolves into the visualized deity.

The practitioner invites the deities of initation and prays to them, and they thereby initiate him/her; and he visualizes that Amoghasiddhi becomes an ornament upon his head.

Here again is the standard four-step Process of Generation, and our very difficulty with English pronouns symbolizes the identity of the yogin with the goddess, sealed into unity by the initiation. He proceeds to the recitation of the *ritual service, the contemplation of the mantra* in his own—the deity's—heart.

He visualizes that the TĀṂ above the lotus and moon in his heart is surrounded by the 10-syllable mantra, and with this visualization continually in mind he recites the mantra; the text notes here that he must, for all these practices, be in possession of the ego of the deity.

The ritual service for the requisite number of times is at the very least 300,000 recitations, the middle is 600,000, the best is 1,000,000, and the very best is 1,200,000; though it is said that a practitioner who recites in this way will succeed in the ritual service (i.e., will gain the signs of success), the text recommends that every practitioner recite 1,300,000 times, just to be sure that he will be able to accomplish all the functions. And this, it concludes, is the procedure for the ritual service.

The second part of the ritual is devoted to the magical *employment* of this divine power so laboriously accumulated: its direction by the practitioner's own visualization, and its *application* in its sonic manifestation as the mantra. Thus, for protection—the most important of Tārā's functions—the practitioner generates himself as the deity, following the same yoga he performed during the ritual service; and he visualizes on his/her heart an eight-spoked wheel with nave and rim, colored green, in the center of which he visualizes, between an OṂ and a HĀ, the following appendix: "such-and-such a person RAKṢA RAKṢA!" On the eight spokes he visualizes TĀ RE TU TTĀ RE TU RE SVĀ, and on the rim he visualizes the vowels (A Ā I Ī U Ū . . .) going clockwise and the consoants (KA KHA GA GHA NA . . .) going counterclockwise. The wheel and the syllables thereon radiate forth in the form of blue-green light, and he visualizes that this fills the entire body of the person whom he wishes to protect; if he then recites OṂ TĀRE TUTTĀRE TURE such-and-such a person RAKṢA RAKṢA SVĀHĀ!, that person "will be protected and will cheat death."

The text notes, however, that the Tārā whose specialized function is to cheat death is colored white; and thus for that end—and for others subsumed under the category of pacifying, such as freeing from prison or pacifying a disease and so on—the practitioner visualizes himself as a white Tārā, with a white wheel and syllables, and he recites the desired mantra with the appropriate appendix. If he performs the remainder of the ritual as given above—the radiation of light into the body of the person to be aided, and so on—then he will accomplish that particular function.

For subjugating, the practitioner visualizes himself as the red-colored Holy Lady, with a red wheel, syllables, and light, and he recites the mantra with the appendix: "such-and-such a person VAŚYAṂ-KURU HO!" If the performs the remainder of the ritual as given above, he will perform the function of summoning into his power the person touched by the red light.

For increasing his possessions and so on, the Holy Lady is yellow, with a yellow wheel, syllables, and light, and he recites PUṢṬIṂ-KURU OṂ! at the end of the basic mantra. If he performs the remainder of the ritual as given above, he will accomplish the function of increasing.

There is a special case of increasing, performed for the sake of one who has but feeble wisdom, who is lazy, or who has but little faith, that the qualities of wisdom, energy, and faith may be augmented in him; here the practitioner visualizes the white-colored Holy Lady with a white wheel, in the center of which, between an OṂ and a HĀ, he visualizes: "May the wisdom of such-and-such a person be increased!" The remainder of the ritual is as above, exept that here both the vowels and the consonants are arranged clockwise on the rim. Then if the practitioner radiates white light and recites the mantra with the above appendix for this function, he will accomplish the increase of wisdom, of energy, or of faith.

There are thus, says the text, six different ways of employing the power of the deity one has attained through the prior ritual service (as Kongtrü rinpoch'e said: ". . . changing the mantra and visualization slightly for the various functions"): (1) by changing the color of Tārā, the wheel, and its syllables; (2) by varying the arrangement of the syllables, clockwise and counterclockwise; (3) by visualizing different persons to be the object of the ritual; (4) by radiating light of different colors; (5) by changing the appendix of the mantra recited; and (6) by changing the appendix of the mantra visualized in the center of the wheel. In brief, the text concludes, the practitioner may accomplish any function he wishes by varying the color of the deity and so on.

Here once again we may note the process-product ambiguity of "function": the practitioner is utilizing a single means—visualization and recitation—for the accomplishment of various ends, here arranged under the four basic functions. Each of these product functions determines the color, appendix, and so on of the process function, according to standard correspondences of white with pacifying, yellow with increasing, and red with subjugating.

Thus, too, we find several attempts to group minor and originally independent goddesses as forms of Tārā performing any one of the above specialized functions: for example, the yellow Vasundharā, originally an independent goddess of wealth, is often said to be a form of Tārā performing the function of increasing; the red Kurukullā is even more closely assimilated to Tārā, said to be the goddess in the special red form she takes in performing the function of subjugating. This process of assimilation works in the other direction also, and Tārā has thus dissimilated into two major forms (and many minor ones scattered in the evocation anthologies); it is traditionally held that Vāgīśvarakīrti was inspired to his conception of the death-cheating White Tārā by such canonical passages as the following (found in the *Supreme Tantra of Tārā the Yoginī, Source for All Rituals*:)[42]

> Set the person who is the object of the ritual
> in the middle of an eight-spoked wheel;
> on the eight spokes, eight syllables,
> surrounded by the lords of the city of her mantra.
> By a green wheel one is protected,
> one cheats death with a white one.

And along similar lines, Buddhaguhya[43] says of the color of Green Tārā:

> "Having a green appearance": this means that one gets the color green by mixing white, yellow, and blue, and these colors symbolize, respectively, the functions of pacifying, increasing, and destroying. Uniting all these means the performance of every function.

This then is the basic pattern of the magical function. All the basic ends have been achieved by the visualization of a wheel in the practitioner's heart, his touching its light to the visualized object of the ritual, and his recitation of the appropriate mantra; but Dragpa jets'en notes that these wheels may also be drawn on a sheet of birch bark, using saffron or other appropriate materials, and that if the practitioner evokes this—if he generates the deity within it—it will accomplish the same various functions given above. Thus the author proposes the use of an intermediary magical device which acts continuously and without the further contemplative intervention of the practitioner; to this we may add also the use of an intermediary recipe to which the divine power is applied and which is ingested rather than worn or used. We may thus distinguish three subtypes of this class of magical functions: (*a*) the application of visualization and recitation directly upon the appearances of public nonreality; (*b*) the use of an intermediary recipe; and (*c*) the use of an intermediary magical device. I give examples for each of these subtypes, again using the rituals of Tārā for the basic materials.

Ritual type 4a: *Direct application.*—Aside from the various applications of basic magical principles, it is above all as a goddess of protection that Tārā functions, and it is toward that end that most of the magical rituals employ her power. "Once one has recited her basic mantra 1,000,000 times," says no less an authority than Atīśa himself,[44] "the yogin who dwells in the deep contemplation of Tārā [i.e., who 'holds her ego'] can vary his ritual of recitation, visualizing the name of the person for whom the ritual is performed placed in the middle of the mantra and reciting it as long as he wishes; then he sees that light arises from the seed syllable in his heart and pervades the entire body of that person, and he visualizes that his body is consoled thereby and freed from all harm. This is a protection of pacifying."

Atīśa goes on to explain a similar "protection of averting":

> The yogin possessed of the above ritual visualizes on his own heart a green TĀṂ, quivering with a garland of light; blazing hosts of light arise therefrom, and they enter into the heart of the one to be summoned, his body naked, his hair unbound, shivering and without refuge; and the practitioner visualizes that the light petrifies that person, subdues him, confuses him, and binds him. And whenever he tires of this deep contemplation, he should visualize these syllables about the seed and recite them as the mantra:[45]
>
> NAMO RATNATRAYĀYA NAMA ĀRYÂVALOKITEŚVARĀYA BODHISATTVĀYA MAHĀSATTVĀYA MAHĀKĀRUṆIKĀYA ! TADYATHĀ OṂ TĀRE TUTTĀRE TURE SARVA-DUṢṬĀN PRADUṢṬĀN MAMA KṚTE JAMBHAYA STAMBHAYA MOHAYA BANDHAYA HŪṂ HŪṂ HUṂ PHAṬ PHAṬ PHAṬ ! SARVA-DUṢṬA-STAMBHANI-TĀRE SVĀHĀ !

"Homage to the Three Jewels! Homage to the Noble Avalokiteśvara, Bodhisattva, great being, greatly compassionate! That is: OṂ TĀRE TUTTĀRE TURE all the sins and evils I have done: crush! petrify! confuse! bind! HŪṂ HŪṂ HŪṂ! PHAṬ PHAṬ! Tārā who petrifies all sin SVĀHĀ!"

Another interesting function of this same sort—employing Tārā's power through the imposition of a visualization and the application of a mantra, without the intermediary of any device—was brought to Tibet from India as a corollary of her protective powers and is known as the "binding of thieves." An Indian text translated by Ratnarakṣita gives the short ritual as follows: that there may be no thieves when the practitioner travels the road, it says, he takes with his right hand a fistful of earth from the ground seven paces in front of his doorstep. He then generates himself instantaneously as the Holy Lady, and in the proper manner he goes for refuge and awakens the thought of enlightenment. Then he generates the earth in his hand as Mount Meru—he dissolves it into Emptiness and re-creates it from the syllable LAṂ, the seed of earth—and he generates his left hand as a great ocean, arisen from PAṂ. During this visualization he says: "I now summon before me all thieves who would do me harm!" And he recites the following mantra 108 times, uninterrupted by any human speech: OṂ TĀRE TUTTĀRE TURE ASMĀN APAKĀRA-SARVA-CORA-BANDHA SVĀHĀ! "OṂ TĀRE TUTTĀRE TURE bind all thieves who harm us SVĀHĀ!" Then he visualizes that all the thieves who have been summoned before him are cast into the great ocean, and he transfers the earth from his right hand to his left, that Mount Meru may press down upon them. The earth is wrapped up and thrown away in a safe place, and when the practitioner travels, he goes singing the praises of Tārā.[46]

Kongtrü rinpoch'e gives a short Tibetan version of this ritual: when going out onto the road, the practitioner draws on the ground with his foot the shape of a bow and arrow, and he places his feet thereon so that he stands covering it. He visualizes that they become —once again, from Emptiness—an iron arrow that carries him without delay to the place where he wishes to go, and he recites this mantra 108 times: OṂ TĀRE TUTTĀRE TURE MAMA DHANA "my property": bind all thieves and robbers SVĀHĀ! OṂ TARAṆI TARAṆI MAHĀTARAṆI "Saving, saving, great saving one" SVĀHĀ! If he recites this, the text concludes, it is impossible that there will be any terror on the road.[47]

These rituals for the binding of thieves became very important in Tibet as protections for solitary hermits, and as such they are included in some of the handbooks composed to instruct the practitioner upon the requisites of secluded life. Thus, for example, we read in the text *Dwelling on the Mountains of Desirelessness*:[48]

> A lama named Tsöndrü jats'o
> greatly wished to practice in solitude, but he said:
> "I fear the harm of enemies and thieves,
> when I, weak and alone, practice the Law.
> I need counsel on a protection to avert them."

And this leads us to a story. In Drugugön there was a monk who retired to a cave every evening to practice the ritual of *chö*—"cutting off"—wherein the practitioner offers up his body to be eaten by demons, as an exercise both in compassion toward all hungry beings and in the realization of the Emptiness of his corporeal structure. This can be a terrifying contemplation, as the visualized demons approach and hack the yogin's body to pieces; and it is occasionally the delight of small monks to strip off their clothing, paint themselves in horrid designs, and in general make themselves look as much like demons as possible, and then to sneak up on a practitioner of this ritual and let out sudden bloodcurdling shrieks. In addition to the simple pleasure of scaring someone half out of his wits, this is an attempt to determine exactly how much compassion and Emptiness he has actually realized, at least when confronted with what he takes to be the real thing. Many practitioners have sat as unmoved through such an exhibition as they have through their own visualizations, even to the extent of letting their noses be tweaked by the young "demons".

The small monks of Drugugön attempted to play this trick upon their monk, but he realized that it was only the children out to frighten him, and he determined to teach them a lesson. He quickly recited Tārā's mantra for the binding of thieves, and when the pranksters were thus petrified he whipped them thoroughly with the leather thong of his thighbone trumpet. My informant, who never actually said that he had been among those caught, reported that it felt as if the wind had bound the children, blowing against them form whatever direction they tried to move and rooting them to the spot. The contemplating monk left them to shiver in the cold for an hour before he released them.

Such magical functions as these are again an affirmation of the practitioner's control of the appearances of public nonreality, his ability to impose his vivid visulization upon the world of events and apply to it the divine power of the mantra. "The measure of one's internal power of deep contemplation," says Ngawang lozang, "is the undiluted vividness of whatever one desires to happen. Thus, by visualizing a protective circle one may obstruct the rain; by visualizing stairs of lapis lazuli in the sky one may mount thereon into the intermediate spheres; by visualizing a great river to be adamantine ground one may walk upon it and not sink therein."[49]

Ritual type 4b: *Recipes*.—The protective power of the deity may, moreover, be similarly channeled through the medium of recipes, materials generated as magical substances and then ingested. Perhaps the simplest of these is the water evoked before an initiation, which may be used as a healing medicine. These recipes are different in structure from those given in the alchemical treatises, for here the power resides not so much in the materials themselves as it is injected into them by the visualization and recitation of the practitioner; these materials are then potent independently of any further operation, and they may indeed be stored away and passed down from generation to generation.

Thus, for example, to protect oneself from being poisoned, one may mix together on an auspicious day, such as the third day of the waxing moon, the herb *lagang* [*Cyperus rotundus*], the root of the *ligadur* [*Calosanthes indica*], and the dung of an unweaned calf, making therefrom pills about the size of peas. The practitioner places the pills in a jeweled vessel, generates himself as Tārā, and recites her mantra over them 100,000 times, visualizing the pills evoked from Emptiness as the "nectar of immortality." Whenever he eats one of these magic pills, he should visualize the wheel of the mantra and perform its recitation as above; administered on an empty stomach, each magic pill protects against poison for one month.

To protect oneself against leprosy, one mixes together equal portions of white *gugü* incense [*Styrax benzoin*], petals from a pomegranate tree, the plant *ruta* [*Rosa banksiae*], musk, and arsenic, or of the plant *shudag* [*Angelica anomola*] and asafetida. Over the pills made therefrom, the practitioner recites the mantra with its long-life appendix 100,000 times, and he eats them. In addition, he recites the mantra another 100,000 times over a mixture of musk and his own urine. He smears this mixture with his ring finger over his five limbs, cleansing himself down to his feet. A single application is sufficent to protect from leprosy for six months.[50]

Such magic pills, often called simply *dütsi* "nectar," are an important part of the Tibetan's standard repertoire of protection. A yogin may earn some extra income for his necessities by devoting a certain portion of his contemplative time to their manufacture, and those evoked by great masters are often treasured for years and kept aside for use only in the most extreme emergencies; a box of these *dütsi* pills was one of the most personal going-away presents I received from a friend when I left the community.

Ritual type 4c: *Magical devices.*—The principle of the magical device may be illustrated by the following procedure: the practitioner takes a long white "protective thread" spun by a clever maiden; he cleanses and purifies it into Emptiness with the AMṚTA and SVABHĀVA mantras and, making twenty-one knots in it, he re-creates it with a Tārā at each knot. He changes the appendix after the first eight syllables of the mantra to "Protect the bearer from the terror of thieves and beasts of prey RAKṢA RAKṢA SVĀHĀ !" He recites this 100,000 times, or as often as he can. The deity is thereby absorbed within it, and he consecrates it—he fixes the deity therein—by reciting the heart of conditioned co-production (YE DHARMA . . .). If this thread is then bound upon the person to be protected, it becomes "the highest of protections."[51]

Perhaps the most important of these protective devices is called simply a wheel or a circle—sometimes "protective circle" or "circle carried upon one's person"—since at least the central portion of these devices consists of the same type of wheel that the practitioner visualizes, for example, in the ritual of Dragpa jets'en reviewed above. This circular pattern is drawn or printed on slips of paper or pieces of cloth, often together with a symbolic emblem: there is a drawing of a man with a padlocked mouth on a protection against slander (fig. 30), and one of a chained dog on a protection against dog bite. These are then folded up in a prescribed manner, sealed, and tied with threads of different colors arranged in special patterns.

Kongtrü rinpoch'e describes the following ritual for the manufacture of such a device based upon the power of Tārā. On a piece of clean silk, using saffron for a man and *giwam* (the black concretion

Fig. 30. A protection against gossip and slander: a figure whose lips are locked.

occasionally found in the intestines of animals) for a woman, the practitioner draws an eight-spoked white wheel with a TĀṂ in its center. (The wheel on the silk is actually red or black, but it is visualized as white.) Around that seed syllable, if the device is to be used for purposes of protection, he writes: "OṂ all the misfortunes, diseases, evil spirits, eight terrors, and untimely death of such-and-such a person RAKṢA HĀ!" If it is to be used for purposes of increasing, he writes: "OṂ the life, merit, possessions, fame, and understanding of such-and-such a person PUṢṬIṂ-KURU HĀ!" Thus having inscribed it with the appropriate command, he draws on the eight spokes (clockwise from the front): TĀ RE TU TTĀ RE SVĀ. Outside that, the wheel has seven rims. On the first rim he writes the YE DHARMA mantra. On the second rim he draws a garland of vajras and the seed syllables of the five families of Conquerors in the following manner: OṂ HŪṂ TRAṂ HRIḤ ĀḤ such-and-such a person RAKṢA RAKṢA HŪṂ! On the third rim he writes the vowels and consonants. On the fourth he writes the long mantra of Swirling Nectar:

> NAMAḤ SAMANTA-BUDDHEBHYAḤ! NAMO MAHĀ-VAJRA-KRODHĀYA! MAHĀ-DAṂṢṬRÔTKAṬA-BHAIRAVĀYA! VAJRA-SANDOHA-DARPĀYA! OṂ AMṚTA-KUṆḌALI HŪṂ PHAṬ!
>
> "Homage to all the Buddhas! Homage to him whose wrath is a great diamond, terrible with great furious teeth, whose haughtiness is a massive diamond! OṂ Swirling Nectar HŪṂ PHAṬ!"

On the fifth rim he draws a ring of swords marked with TĀṂ, their blades pointed outward. On the sixth rim he inscribes a ring of HŪṂs. And on the seventh rim he draws a ring of fire and mountains.

He consecrates this by reciting Tārā's mantra and the YE DHARMA mantra. Then he places it inside a jeweled vessel, and for seven days he generates himself as Tārā, evokes her inside the vessel, and makes offerings to her; and he visualizes that Tārā melts and is dissolved into the syllable TĀṂ in the center of the device. Then he folds it up and puts it inside a jeweled container, which a man may carry on his right, a woman on her left, or either may hang around the neck. The text adds that a green circle is mostly used for protection and a white one for increasing life, but that either function may be accomplished by using a white circle.

Kongtrü rinpoch'e describes another such device according to the "old writings." This time the wheel has four rims; in its center the practitioner draws an OṂ facing upward an a HĀ facing downward, and between the two he writes: "The bearer of this RAKṢA RAKṢA KURU!" On the eight spokes he writes the eight syllables as above, and between the spokes he writes, in pairs, the sixteen vowels. Outside that he draws a white lotus and surrounds it with a fence of vajras. He puts this device over the mouth of a flask that is set upon the metal base of an offering maṇḍala, while he visualizes that the wheel stands upon a great river. He evokes the deity therein, consecrates it, and binds it on himself.

"It is clear," concludes the author, "that with these wheels and the appropriate commands, one may accomplish any function: freeing from bonds, increasing one's intelligence, or subjugating."[52] And he quotes the following verses of Nāgārjuna (from the *Evocation of the Greatly Compassionate Tārā, Suitable for All Ritual Visualizations*):[53]

> With these applications one will be protected
> from the king's dungeons and so on;
> through the employment of Tārā
> one will accomplish any of these functions,
> functions of pacifying disease,
> applications of subjugating,
> depending upon the color of the wheel, and so on,
> and the appendix of the mantra
> used as in the preceding ritual. . . .
> If the object of the ritual has but feeble wisdom
> or is lazy or whatever,
> the preceding ritual
> is changed as follows:
> the wheel is just the same as before,
> except that the mantra is arranged thereon clockwise,
> and on the rim, too, one puts the syllables A and so on;
> if one visualizes and recites in that way
> one of weak intellect will become intelligent. . . .
> If one draws the preceding wheel
> on a piece of birch bark, for example,
> and carries it on one's person,
> then just by that one will be protected.

These different types of written protections may also be printed from wooden blocks in the monastic printshops, and such devices are occasionally found listed in the book catalogues along with the texts which might be had from the printery;[54] but these protections, too, had to be printed at special times and the appropriate visualizations and mantras performed over them before they could be used. Thus an ordinary printed protection can be purchased quite cheaply, but one that has been thus empowered, folded up, and tied with multicolored thread immediately becomes more expensive, for the purchaser is paying not so much for the device as for the ritual that has made it potent. And these folded protections must not be opened up, for then their power evaporates and the entire ritual process must be repeated.

There are a great many different types of such protections used in Tibet. Every New Year a high lama will hand out to his followers "knotted protections," similar to the protective thread reviewed above, which are worn around the neck. One may carry with one the relics of a great and famous lama, a small "miraculous image," or the small cones or stamped images called *ts'ats'a*, which are molded of clay or dough mixed with herbs, *dütsi*, relics, or even the ashes of the dead lama, and then empowered as we have seen. In the words of P. H. Pott, "a Tibetan may, in a pinch, exist without either rosary or prayer wheel, but certainly not without an amulet."[55]

A Tibetan carries all these protective devices in a *gau* or charm box, which he usually wears around his neck, but larger and heavier types may be carried at his hip or even strapped to his back; these latter are usually reserved for long journeys. Charm boxes are often of great beauty, ranging from the pearl- and coral-encrusted boxes of the central Tibetan nobility, often six or eight inches across, to the smaller ones of the eastern Tibetans, adorned with perhaps a single coral bead but covered with the delicate metalwork for which these people are famous. Inside the larger types there may be a bewildering variety of devices to protect the bearer from bad dreams and evil omens, dogs and wild beasts, poison, theft, and weapons, or to guarantee the success of his business, the increase of his fortune, or the growth of his herds. Such collections may be passed down in a family, and we have spent an entire afternoon with a proud owner going through a boxful of relics and protections dating back hundreds of years.

Thus, to protect against weapons, the practitioner writes Tārā's 10-syllable mantra in gold on blue paper, followed by: TADYATHĀ YAMATI DHĀVATI DHĀRĀKĪ! KULU RULU ME SVĀHĀ! "Those with sharp blades brandish them, advancing against me! Be to me a kinsman and dash them to pieces SVĀHĀ!" The practitioner performs for this a full consecration of the deity visualized within it, and he binds it upon his head, being careful not to put it on upside down. Then when the time comes that he must enter into battle, he visualizes himself as Tārā and recites the above mantra. One should have no doubt about its effectiveness, the text says, for it operates according to Tārā's vow.[56]

Many such protections are used at the particularly dangerous periods of pregnancy and birth. The practitioner first hangs the following mantra around the neck of a flask:

> OṂ TĀRANI TĀRAYA ! OṂ MOCANI MOCAYA ! OṂ MOKṢANI MOKṢAYA ! JĪVAṂ VARADE SVĀHĀ !

> "OṂ Save me, savioress ! OṂ Liberate me, liberated one ! OṂ Free me, freed one ! You grant the highest gift of life SVĀHĀ !"

He then mixes together the "twenty-five substances of the flask" and pours these into the flask with scented water. He makes offerings and prayers before it and evokes the deity therein; all day he recites OṂ TĀRE SVĀHĀ ! and in the evening he recites the 10-syllable mantra as follows: OṂ TĀRE TUTTĀRE TURE such-and-such a woman MOKṢAYA JĪVAṂ SVĀHĀ !

He continues until he has recited 100,000 times over the water in the flask; then, when midnight has passed, he places the pregnant woman upon a seat of *kuśa* grass, performs the preliminaries of clearing the place of hindering demons and so on, and finally, facing to the east, he washes and anoints her with the water. Similarly, he recites the mantra over some butter and smears this over her body and into her vagina. If he does this, the woman will give birth easily and without fear.

As soon as the child is born the practitioner places upon it one of Tārā's protections. This should be done, the text says, as soon as possible; indeed, I have seen young children and toddlers practically covered with the small leather pouches that contain such devices. Every day both mother and child are anointed with the water that was evoked in the flask, being washed, cleansed, and purified thereby. The practitioner makes offerings to Tārā with a Four Maṇḍala ritual and prays to her for their safety, and he gives tormas to the hindering demons and vengeful ghosts, that they may not harm out of spite the happy mother and the child. Then there is mixed into the mother's milk small amounts of molasses and the drug *manu* [*Aristolochia recurvilabra*?], a bit of sal ammoniac the size of a barley grain, and a bit of musk the size of a pea; this mixture, when given to the infant, guarantees his continued survival.[57]

These prescriptions are textual, and the question arises as to whether such complex and time-consuming rituals are actually performed as given in the texts. The answer is simply that they are; if they are not performed according to this particular text, they are performed according to a similar one, depending upon the preferences of the individual practitioner. Of course, the flourishes and details are sometimes beyond the means of the sponsor; the twenty-five substances of the flask mentioned above—a collective designation that occurs constantly—are given by Ngawang lozang as follows:[58]

1) The five medicines: *tagts'er* [*Potentilla discolor*], *kaṇṭakāra* [*Sambucus racemosa*], *zhenji mit'ubpa* [*Clitoria ternatea*], *utpala* [*Nymphaea caerulea*], and *wanglag* [*Belamcanda chinensis*]
2) The five precious things: gold, silver, pearl, coral, and turquoise
3) The five essences: sesame, salt, butter, molasses, and honey
4) The five grains: husked and unhusked barley, rice, wheat, and peas
5) The five odors: white and red sandalwood, camphor, saffron, and musk

But the family of the woman hire as great a lama as is available or as they can afford (consulting him as to proper procedure just as we might consult an obstetrician), and they provide as much of the material as they can. Although I know through personal experience of cases where such rituals have failed to preserve the lives of a pregnant girl and her unborn child, where prompt Western medical attention might have saved them, I also know of tragedies occurring under the care of obstetricians, where, a Tibetan might add, they might have been saved by the ritual.

Kongtrü rinpoch'e gives two more short rituals under Tārā's function of protection, which I include to show how her power is employed in every conceivable area of life. To free someone from prison, for example, the practitioner makes a maṇḍala not smaller then one cubit in size, smears it with cow dung, and draws thereon with powdered colors an eight-petaled lotus. In its center he draws an iron hook marked with the syllable JAḤ (the mantra "particle" for summoning or drawing forth), and around it he arranges five piles of white flowers. He sets out the offering torma and evokes the deity both in his own person and in front of him; he performs the general offerings, praises, and prayers: and he recites the *Homages* as many times as he can. From a JAḤ in the heart of the self-generated goddess—that is, from his own heart—he visualizes that iron hooks radiate forth and free the person from prison, while he goes through the ritual service, for this particular magical function, of reciting the 10-syllable mantra 10,000 times. Then for one entire night he applies the mantra, reciting it continually and adding on the offerings, praises, and prayers after each 100 recitations. And while dwelling in the deep contemplation of Tārā, he writes out the following appendix to the 10-syllable mantra: OṂ MOCANI MOCAYA ! MOKṢANI MOKṢAYA ! such-and-such a person JĪVAṂ VARADE SVĀHĀ ! He writes this on birch bark, using saffron for a man and *giwam* for a woman, and he binds it upon the head of the person bound in prison. Or—presumably when the prisoner can not be reached—he recites this mantra seven times over some water; and at the three times of the day he scatters seven handfuls in the direction of the jail. In either instance the prisoner will be freed from his bondage; it is even better, the text adds, if the prisoner himself knows the mantra and can recite it continually.

If the practitioner wishes to be victorious in a dispute he first goes through the self-generation; he fills a new flask with sweet-scented water and places therein the following mantra, written on white birch bark with saffron and wrapped up in wax (so it will not get wet): OṂ TĀRE TUTTĀRE TURE such-and-such a person MOKṢAYA JĪVAṂ SVĀHĀ ! He evokes the deity in the flask, following the appropriate text, and makes offerings to her with flowers and sweet scents. By drinking the water, over which he recites the same mantra as many times as he can, he will be victorious in all disputes and debates.[59]

THE DANGERS OF PROTECTIVE POWER

We have thus seen how Tārā's power of protection may be controlled and directed through ritual by a practitioner who is contemplatively prepared to handle it. But the very efficacy of this power makes it occasionally difficult to manipulate save by a real expert, and here we find additional precautionary measures to ensure the safety of the unwary.

Tārā's protective power manifests itself also in the form of a deity named Bhīmadevī, also called the "Blue She-wolf" and depicted as one, with its head turned toward its tail.[60] This is an emanation of Tārā whose special function is the protection of those who practice her rituals and the guarding of the books in which they are recorded. Thus the text of Kongtrü rinpoch'e adds at the end a separate sheet containing the protective mantra of the Blue She-wolf, along with the ritual of its performance; this separate sheet functions also as a magical device in itself to protect the printed work from destruction. I promised the lama who taught me this text that I would not reproduce this mantra, for its potency is so great that he was troubled at the thought of even an inadvertent misapplication on the part of any of my readers. So powerful is this mantra, he said, that anyone who reads it aloud without having had the proper contemplative experience might easily go mad and fly about in the sky, buffeted by the winds. I was permitted to read it, by the way, because this lama knew that I was writing a book about Tārā and that she would therefore protect me, at least until the book was finished.

Similar protections are encountered fairly often, magically bound to various texts. There was one "hidden text" which I was not allowed to read at all, because the enchantment placed thereon was so strong that, had I read it before going through a lengthy ritual process of preparation, wolves would have come and howled at my door, driving me mad, and my library of Tibetan books would have caught fire: ". . . and then," my teacher explained, "you couldn't do any more Tārā."

THE TERROR OF SPIRITS

Yet with all these protections, we have not touched upon what is in Tibet perhaps the greatest terror of all, requiring on occasion the most extreme ritual and magical measures. The standard Indian list of the eight great terrors served merely as a basis for later additions in Tibet, where the category "terror of spirits" was enlarged to receive all the dangerous deities of the native religion, the innumerable malevolent spirits whom the Tibetans consider, along with the human maledictions that often set them in motion, the original cause of almost every calamity.

Fig. 31. A protection to bind malevolent spirits.

In the *Red Annals*, Kunga Doje reports the story that the first to rule the Tibetan people, after they were born from the union of the monkey Bodhisattva and the rock ogress, were the nine *Masang* Brothers.[61] Sumpa k'enpo refers to this passage and glosses the nine brothers as *Nöjin*, *Dü*, *Sinpo*, *Lu*, *Tsen*, *Lha*, *Mu*, *Dre*, and *Gongpo*.[62] These nine "unclean ones" were the native spirits as well as the first rulers of Tibet, and their sovereignty has not diminished with time; so firmly believed in that any attempt to replace them would have been ineffective, they were assimilated with Indian deities and incorporated into a Buddhist cult, which claimed the ritual ability to control their powers as the ultimate agencies of disease and misfortune.

Many attempts were made to classify the bewildering profusion of this native pantheon. The more or less official Buddhist scheme is a list of "eight classes of gods and ogres," which compares in many ways with the more archaic list of the nine *Masang* Brothers given above, but the particular items in the various Buddhist inventories vary considerably. The Longdö lama Ngawang lozang, in his *Enumeration of the Names of the Oath-bound Guardians*, gives the following: "(1) The class of *lha* who are white, (2) the class of *dü* who are black, (2) the class of *tsen* who are red, (4) the class of *za* who are vari-colored, (5) the class of *mu* who are brown, (6) the class of *sinpo* who are eaters of flesh, (7) the class of *jepo* who are lords of treasure and (8) the class of *mamo* who are bringers of disease."[63] But there are also many other lists, as for instance two given in the "Precepts on Gods and Demons" section of the *Five Precepts of Padmasambhava*: (1) *gongpo*, (2) *t'eurang*, (3) *ngayam*, (4) *sadag*, (5) *yülha*, (6) *men*, (7) *tsen*, and (8) *lu*, as well as (1) *sogdag*, (2) *mamo*, (3) *shinje*, (4) *dü*, (5) *nöjin*, (6) *mu*, (7) *dralha*, and (8) *gongpo*.[64]

There is some overlap in these Buddhist lists, but perhaps more discrepancy. The immense literature devoted to all these spirits has been reviewed by Tucci[65] and Nebesky-Wojkowitz;[66] hence in the following pages we give only an outline (with some new material) of the major classes of demon from whose depredations Tārā's relief is sought in her protective rituals.

For our purposes, the most useful classification is an early division—quite independent of Buddhist ideas—into the three classes of *sadag*, *lu*, and *nyen*. We read, for instance, of the "eight classes of gods and ogres, worldlings who dwell above and below in the ten directions: the *zhidag*—lords of the soil—the original inhabitants of the countryside and villages; the *sadag*, *lu*, and *nyen*, with their retinue and servants."[67] Another text asks for protection from "the harms of the evil spirits above: the planets and constellations; the harms of the evil spirits below: the *sadag*, *lu*, and *nyen*; and the harms of the evil spirits upon the surface of the earth: the ghosts, kings, and *tsen*."[68]

It is generally said, reports Tucci, that the *nyen* reside in the space above the earth, the *sadag* upon its surface, and the *lu* in the space beneath it, but the demarcation is by no means rigid.[69] One of my lama informants made the division of *lha* in heaven, *nyen* upon the earth, and *lu* under the ground, giving a picture more closely approximating the Indian scheme (with *lha* identified with the Indian *deva* and *lu* with the Indian *nāga*), and this division is also found in some texts:[70]

> The *lha* above and the *lu* below,
> the *sadag*, *lu*, and *nyen*;
> the eight classes of gods and ogres
> with all their retinue . . .

And too, as we have seen, the *sadag*, *lu*, and *nyen* may be considered, as a group, to live beneath the earth, at lest relative to the celestial phenomena above it and the ghosts that walk its surface.

Indeed, the malignant *nyen* may live anywhere: in the popular but apocryphal "sūtra" *The Eight Appearances in Heaven and Earth*, we read of "the *nyen* Turquoise Blue Dragon with the golden spike, the earth-*nyen* Golden Frog with the turquoise markings, the snow-*nyen* White Lioness with the turquoise mane, the lake-*nyen* Leaping Tadpole with the conch-white sides, and the rock-*nyen* Golden Monkey with the conch-white hair";[71] and the Ladakhi marriage songs published by Francke speak of "the *nyen* of the sun and moon in the blue zenith, the *nyen* of the wind in the high rocks, the harmful *nyen* in the ocean and the roaring *nyen* of running water."[72]

Whereas these *nyen* are nearly always harmful, the *sadag* or "owners of the earth" are neutral but easily offended. They have retained a ritual importance as lords of the ground and the roads, and their permission must be asked before any intrusion upon their territory, to construct a maṇḍala or to cast away an effigy; but judging from the list given, for example, in *The Eight Appearances in Heaven and Earth*—the eighty-one *sadag* in groups of nine according to color, the *sadag* ruling over the eight directions[73]—these deities were traditionally something more than local place spirits. They were originally perhaps the lords of the quarters, but there they have been replaced by the "four great kings" of the Indian tradition; and nowadays even as local spirits they are overshadowed in the popular cult by the lords of the soil and the *tsen*.

The *lu*, on the other hand, are good or bad (see fig. 32) according to individual temperament, although the good ones may be offended and the bad ones propitiated. These *lu* are undisputedly the spirits of the underwold, found in those places where their realm impinges upon ours, such as in springs, wells, and rivers; but Buddhism had

Fig. 32. A peaceful *lu* and a fierce *lu*. From a sketch by Tendzin yongdü.

already incorporated so much of the Indian cult of the *nāgas*, with whom the *lu* are now firmly identified, that it is often difficult to discover how much of their character is original and how much has been imported into their cult.

The more worldly spirits who walk upon the surface of the earth, mentioned in the passage above, are the ghosts, the kings, and the *tsen*. The Tibetan ghosts—called *jungpo*—are identical with our own: they are the vengeful spirits of dead men, impelled by the power of their evil lives or by the violence of a dying thought of hatred. A man murdered or slain in battle is likely to become such a ghost, seeking to vent his dying and spiteful fury not only upon his slayer but upon all men.

Similar are the *jepo* or kings, who often come in the guise of monks or royalty to instigate anger and fighting. Pehar, the great "mundane protector" of the Gelug sect, is often considered to be a king demon who was converted and reformed by Padmasambhava. A monk who performs ritual to gain personal power—using the Process of Generation to gain a godlike potency in this life, but without the ameliorating understanding of either Emptiness or compassion —may become a king demon when he dies. I was told the story of one such monk, whose powers were such that he could cure madness, but who rather used his magic to harm other people; finally, in retaliation, the local populace burned him alive within his house. From then on, wherever his spirit went, they said, anger, fighting, and disease broke out among the people. Nebesky-Wojkowitz tells a similar sort of story concerning the king demon named Drungyig ch'enmo, the "great secretary."[74]

Fig. 33. A *tsen.* From a sketch by Tendzin yongdü.

The *tsen* (fig. 33), says Tucci, were some of the most powerful aboriginal deities of Tibet,[75] but where they have not disappeared they are today reduced to the status of local deities, living primarily in rocks or on mountains: my informants identified the great mountain deity Mach'en pomra (fig. 34) as a "rock-*tsen*." They are red men mounted upon red horses, and where they have been converted

Fig. 34. Mach'en pomra, a mountain deity. From a sketch by Tendzin yongdü.

by some great lama to be "guardians of the teaching" they are occasionally depicted in religious art. Many monasteries live under the protection of such local *tsen*, and they receive their offerings along with the other oath-bound protectors; but travelers in remote places must be careful not to offend them.

A prophecy attributed to Padmasambhava says:[76]

In the evil times, the degenerate era
when the five defilements increase,
here in Tibet the ghosts and *damsi*,
the demons who attack the living,
will hold veritable sway:
by day they will hold sway over all cemeteries,
and by night they will attack the life breath of beings.

Their form is the form of magic kings and queens,
their speech is the speech of brute beasts and wild animals;
and the signs of their demonic diseases are these:
that there come unidentified pestilences,
and sudden delirium and unconsciousness;
some of these are like the diseases
of the planets and constellations,
some are simply death with no warning,
and some are dumbness and trembling of the body;
in many different forms they will come.

These *damsi* are members of the class of *si* demons, an important group of early Tibetan deities whose origin and types are described by Nebesky-Wojkowitz.[77] But in addition to their basic demonic forms, there are mentioned in the texts such *si* as the *si* of disease, the *si* of death, the cemetery *si*, the *si* of adults, the *si* of children, and the *si* of loss. These types of *si* would seem to be, from the description of my informants, the personification of dangerous periods of time in the life of man, and particularly the danger of the recurrence of misfortunes at the same time they originally happened. Thus, I was informed, if a member of one's family died at a particular age, or at a particular time of year, then at that age or at that time of year all the members of the family are susceptible to death at the hands of the *si* of death, whether they be interpreted as actual demons or simply as the tendency of events to recur in cyclic patterns. Similarly, the cemetery *si* threaten at a certain time every year the family of a man whose funeral was performed on that date, and the *si* of loss threaten the recurrence of drought, hailstorm, animal epidemics, and crop failures. Thus, too, we hear of year *si*, month *si*, and day *si*, so that there is a *si* for every day of the year and every year of one's life, and the misfortunes of every date may be repeated in a yearly cycle. It is at these times of extreme danger to life and property that the protective rituals are most urgently needed, and the goddess is prayed to avert the *gumig* (inauspicious years ending in the number nine), the *durmig* (years in whose sign —horse, monkey, pig, etc.—a death has previously occured), and all "the savage dangers of the years, months, days, and times."

In these protective rituals, the "guests" invited to partake of the tormas offered to them differ from the standard pattern, described in chapter i, for here are included specifically all those evil spirits who are the agents of these harms and savage dangers; these guests are here called "the evil spirits: creditors and hindering demons."

"Our guests," says one text, "the lords of the soil of this continent, the six classes of beings, our creditors, especially those who appropriate our life, who steal our life breath, the ghosts who brood evil, sending diseases, evil dreams, evil omens, the eight classes of gods and ogres, malignant, lords of miracles, the creditors of our food, our dwellings, our wealth . . ."[78] These creditors are the spirits of all those to whom we owe a debt, the dead toward whom we did evil whether in this life or in a past life; they are *lench'ag*, literally "those who lust for an answer." They may be either *shak'ön*, who bear "malice toward our flesh," departed spirits impelled against us by the memory of personal injury, or *juk'ön*, who bear "malice toward our substance," impelled by the memory of our crimes against their property.

The other members of this class of guests are the *geg* or "hindering demons," who throw obstacles in the way of our enterprises and thwart all our purposes. Their depredations may range from simple pranks (tripping a traveler on the road) to hindering, as we have seen, the ease of giving birth, from preventing the completion of a building to full-scale demonic interference with the performance of a religious ritual by causing thoughts to wander, tongues to become confused, and hands to slip in the manipulation of the ritual implements. We have seen that in some rituals these hindering demons are offered a special preliminary torma of their own at the beginning rather than at the end of the performance, as part of the erection of a circle of protection around the place of evocation; but here they are considered as agents of calamity to be propitiated by the ritual itself, rather than as obstacles to its performance.

All these classifications, however, do not play a large part in the popular beliefs of the people, who know only that demons dwell in the vast lonely places of their land, that misfortunes come in cycles, that the dead are dangerous, and that one's plans meet inexplicable obstacles. In most protection rituals, it seems that the author simply names as many types of spirit as he can think of, to be sure that any possible malignant power has been included in the invocation. Most common people make no learned distinctions among the various classes of spirits, save only that everyone in K'am, I was informed, knows that if one's horse is unaccountably injured it was done by a *tsen*; indeed, it is thought wise to dismount in lonely places, lest one offend the local *tsen* by riding haughtily past him. As another example, I once described to a lama the symptoms of oxygen starvation at high altitudes—fainting, nausea, swollen hands and feet—and asked him the cause. He replied that he was acquainted with the phenomenon, but that although most people attribute it to a ghost, it is really caused by the local lord of the soil.

KURUKULLĀ AND THE RITUALS OF ATTACK

To deal with these spirits—"the *sadag* dwelling on the mountains, the *lha*, *lu*, and *men* dwelling on the clay peaks, on the shady side of mountains, in the high marshes and the low ravines, the lord *dü* and the lord *tsen* dwelling on the rocky mountains, the *lha* and *lu* dwelling in the rivulets and streams"[79]—requires most stringent measures, often going beyond defense into the darker realms of offense, employing the power of the deity to crush and overwhelm the malig-

Fig. 35. Kurukullā, goddess of subjugation. From an iconographic sketch by Tendzin yongdü.

nant forces that threaten one. Thus, just as there are Tārās to protect one from the constant threat of malevolent powers instigated against one's person, one's property, and one's life, so also may Tārā herself be called upon, in the form of Kurukullā (fig. 35), to subjugate and destroy the evil spirits that work against the Buddhist religion, to bring under one's power a personal enemy, or to bend to one's desires a recalcitrant man or woman.

Kurukullā was most likely an Indian tribal deity incorporated into the Buddhist pantheon, an independent goddess associated with magical domination, and as such we find her mantra already given in the *Hevajra Tantra*. She was gradually assimilated to Tārā as her special form in performing the "red" function of subjugation; she came to Tibet as a deity of power, bringing with her the ritual embodied in her basic Tantra, the *Practices of the Noble Tārā Kurukullā*, translated by Atīśa's own disciple Ts'ütr'im jewa.[80] She was absorbed painlessly into the swelling ranks of the pantheon in Tibet, and her practices took their place in the Tibetan religious experience: she was called upon when building a monastery or when beginning any enterprise, that she might subjugate the human or demonic forces that stood in its way; she was called upon by students before an examination, that she might increase their wisdom; and, within my own experience, she has been called upon by at least one Tibetan refugee group to coerce the Indian government. Tibetan traders seeking profit and Tibetan lovers seeking satisfaction followed upon the ritual tracks established by their Indian predecessors, which had been fixed in her basic texts.

The great magican Ḍombī-heruka sang this hymn to the goddess:[80a]

Homage and praise to her
who serves the aim of beings by understanding,
by unwavering deeds and constant changelessness,
to the one-headed four-armed one,
who is as brilliant as a thousand suns radiating red light.
Homage and praise to her
the goddess arisen from HRĪḤ,
the red-colored four-armed one,
whose hands hold arrow and bow,
who grasps an iron hook.
Homage and praise to her
whose light blazes like the flames that destroy the world,
who is one-headed, three-eyed,
whose hair blazes upward reddish yellow,

who grasps a lotus flower.
Homage and praise to her
who stands in the dancing pose
haughty with furious rage,
who has a diadem of five skulls,
who bears a tiger's skin.
I pay homage to the red one,
baring her fangs, whose body is frightful,
who is adorned with the five signs of ferocity,
whose necklace is half a hundred human heads,
who is the conqueress of Māra.
I pay homage to her
who from the commingling of vowels and consonants
is enlightened, ever delighting in Bliss,
whose diadem is Amitābha,
who is pleased with dancing.
Homage to her
who fixes the eye with bow and arrow,
who subjugates with the lotus flower,
whose iron hook draws forth from the swamp of defilement,
the four-armed enemy of Māra!

There are in Tibet some simple home prescriptions for causing injury which do not depend upon the power of any particular deity and thus may be applied by anyone. A custom practiced by Tibetan men, reports Nebesky-Wojkowitz, is to write the name and age of a person whom one wants to injure together with some harmful mantras on a piece of paper; the paper is then folded and worn inside the boot, under the heel of the person who performs this magic action. Another popular belief claims that the easiest way in which a woman may subjugate a man and gain his love is to burn a cloth stained with her menstrual blood and to mix some of the ashes surreptitiously into the man's food or drink; or she may simply use a drop of her menstrual blood in the same way.[81]

The most powerful rituals of subjugation and destruction, however, remain those wherein the power of the deity is directed through the practitioner's own person and aimed at the object of the ritual, either directly or through the medium of a magical device. This process requires the practitioner to have acquired the requisite powers of visualization and to have gained the capacity of containing within himself, as a fit vessel, the deity's power through the performance of the preliminary ritual service of that deity. This prerequisite in effect limits the availability of destructive power to those who are able to devote at least a minimum amount of time and effort to its acquisition, for the most part professional contemplatives; and the check placed on its misuse is held to be that the prior contemplations themselves, in their inculcation of moral attitudes, limit the greed and hostility of the practitioner.

Many such destructive or coercive rituals are found in Buddhist texts, and even in works held to be the word of the Buddha; and the question arises as to how such acts of enslavement and extermination may be reconciled with the basic Buddhist teachings of nonviolence or with the vows that the practitioner himself has taken. The example most often adduced by my informants was the justifiable homicide of the evil king Langdarma by the monk Peji doje, an act that benefited the king himself by preventing him from accumulating any more evil karma then he already had. They held it to be an act of compassion, also, to use one's contemplative powers to subjugate evil persons or malevolent spirits and convert them to virtue. They did not, however, deny the possibility of using these powers for selfish purposes: we have already seen that a king demon may be the malicious shade of such a worldly and misguided magician.

Indeed, the rituals of destruction avoid the use of the ordinary word "kill" and substitute for it the word "deliver" or "liberate." Thus a prerequisite for these rituals is the contemplative ability not only to destroy the body of the object of the ritual but also to dispatch his "awareness"—which one has thereby freed from corporeal bonds—to a heaven or Pure Land, or even to the Dharma realm itself, that the slain may avoid the eons in hell which might otherwise be his lot, and that he may gain all the spiritual benefits of a fortunate rebirth. "With compassion toward the Māras and their deeds," says Pema karpo, "we wish to liberate them from their wrath."[82] Another ritual says: "With his miraculous visualization . . . he may offer as food to the divine hosts of the maṇḍala the bodies of the enemy evil spirits, and with one fierce PHAṬ! he should liberate their awareness into the great, intrinsically pure Dharma realm, the realm wherein there is neither slain nor slayer."[83] Many other examples may be found, for instance, in the Epic of Gesar, where the hero, in slaying (or liberating) an evil magician, would "conduct his awareness to the Pure Land."[84]

When talking of the "four glances" by which a yogin trained in the proper procedure may overthrow, subjugate, summon, and petrify an enemy, or even an animate object, the *Hevajra Tantra* adds: "Here, actual killing should not be done, for this would be to break one's vows. Let one but renounce deceit and one may do all that should not ordinarily be done; but if one does nothing but evil then one will not gain the magical attainments."[85] In this connection the Longdö lama Ngawang lozang writes:[86]

> The measure of one's attainment in the four glances is as follows: with just a glance to dry up a tree, that its fruit does not ripen, and overthrow it upon the ground; with just a glance to summon downward a rigid upward-growing tree; with just a glance to subjugate and gather before one sweet-smelling flowers from a distance; and with just a glance to petrify the grass, that it does not move even when blown by a fierce wind: these are the magical attainments of the glances. They are also explained as follows: to summon the antelope, to subjugate the buffalo, to overthrow fruit and to petrify an evil person with just a glance.
>
> Now if one attains in such manner the four glances and thereby slays ("liberates") an enemy—even one who is among the ten proper objects of destructive ritual—it is for oneself a grievous sin. But then, one may ask, to what extent may one practice destructive rituals? If the practitioner is not only able to perform the four glances as above and thereby slay ("liberate") an evil person, but is also able to dispatch the victim's awareness into a good embodiment in a heaven, then as long as he is certain of this result he may slay ("liberate") an enemy evil spirit.

He then proceeds to list these "ten proper objects of 'liberation'": (1) those who subvert the teachings of the Buddha; (2) those who blaspheme the Three Jewels; (3) those who rob the goods of the Assembly; (4) those who slander and contemn the Great Vehicle; (5) those who attack the person of a guru; (6) those who slander their Diamond Brothers; (7) those who hinder an evocation; (8) those who have neither love nor compassion; (9) those who break their vows and pledges; and (10) those who hold perverted views about karma and its effects.

The goddess Kurukullā is a most potent deity of subjugation, whose power may be used against such evil persons and malevolent spirits as these listed above, as well as for more mundane and selfish purposes. One visualization, which may stand for all those in ritual type *4a*, wherein a practitioner who has gone through her ritual service may employ Kurukullā directly through his person, is traced back through the lineage of the great magician Anaṅgavajra.[87] It is performed on the first through the fifteenth day of the waxing moon. The practitioner puts on red garments and contemplates himself in the body of the deity; he recites her basic mantra (OṂ KURUKULLE HRĪḤ HŪṂ SVĀHĀ) 10,000 times during each of three or four contemplative periods every day; he gives to the Holy Lady offerings of red garments, red flowers, and maṇḍalas made of red sandalwood; he prays to her that he may subjugate the person who is the object of the ritual; and he performs her burnt offering, following the appropriate text, in the semicircular hearth of subjugation.

When these preliminaries are complete, when he has firmly grasped the vivid appearance and ego of the goddess, the visualization is ready to be performed. Light radiates forth from a HRĪḤ in the practitioner's heart and places the person to be subjugated, naked and with unbound hair, upon a wind maṇḍala arisen from YAṂ: that is, the seed of wind transforms into the round shape symbolic of the air element, and this wind propels forward the person to be subjugated; he is bound around the neck by a noose radiated from the practitioner's—Kurukullā's—lotus flower, drawn forward by an iron hook stuck into his heart, summoned by the stength of the mantra, and laid down helpless upon his back before the practitioner's feet. If the person to be subjugated is male, the text adds, Kurukullā's iron hook is stuck into his heart; if female it is stuck into her vagina.

From the red HRĪḤ upon the sun in the practitioner's heart there springs an eight-petaled lotus whose stalk extends to its corolla from his—Kurukulla's—womb. Upon the eight petals are the eight long vowels—Ā Ī Ū Ṝ Ḹ AI AU ĀḤ—and from these there spring eight fierce red bees. They leave his body through his left nostril together with his breath, and they enter into the person to be subjugated through his right nostril. In the heart of the latter are the eight petals of a red lotus whose stalk extends to its corolla from his navel, and on its petals are the eight short vowels—A I U Ṛ Ḷ E O AḤ—around which the bees cluster and into which they extend their pollen-gathering "sucking tubes."

Then, from the HRĪḤ in the practitioner's heart, red light in the form of iron hooks and HRĪḤs goes out through his right ear, enters the nock of his drawn arrow, and emerges through the arrowhead, streaming into the heart of the person to be subjugated. There the light takes the first syllable of the person's name and returns with it, dissolving with it back into the HRĪḤ in the practitioner's heart. If the person to be subjugated is female, the practitioner thinks that the light strikes into the middle of her vagina, that her menstrual blood trickles down, and that she becomes full of lust.

The bees are then aroused by the practitioner's breath, and they leave the person to be subjugated through the left nostril. The bees return, each one bearing with it one of the vowels from the person to be subjugated; they enter through the practitioner's right nostril and dissolve in the HRĪḤ in his heart.

Once again they leave, this time through his right nostril, and enter into the person to be subjugated through the left nostril; they dissolve into the HRĪḤ in the lotus in his heart, and then once more emerge through the left nostril and enter the practitioner through his right nostril; and when they once again dissolve into his heart, he thinks that the inherent nature of the knowledge of himself and the other are indissolubly one.

Then, from the practitioner's—Kurukullā's—emblem, the arrow, there radiate forth a host of arrows made of red lotus flowers, whose arrowheads pierce the victim in the heart, if male, or in the vagina, if female. Aroused by the sound of the arrows, bees once more leave the person to be subjugated through the left nostril, and they enter and dissolve into the practitioner through his right nostril. And the practitioner visualizes that the awareness of the victim is placed within a net of arrows or a circle of blazing fire; and that person is subjugated, and thereby rendered confused, intoxicated, and senseless.

Then there radiate forth nooses made of red lotus flowers which bind the victim around the throat, and iron hooks made of red lotus flowers which pierce the victim's heart, if male, or vagina, if female. The practitioner thinks that the person is subjugated with his blazing red light; and he recites OṂ KURUKULLE such-and-such a person VAŚAṂ-KURU "Subjugate!" SVĀHĀ! thinking that the mind of the person to be subjugated is filled with delight and lust for him.[88]

This ritual adds that to summon a king, the mantra should be recited 100,000 times, but that ordinarily 10,000 should be sufficient. Another text says: "One should first recite the mantra OṂ KURUKULLE such-and-such a man or woman ĀKARṢAYA 'Summon!' HRĪḤ SVĀHĀ! When the person to be subjugated has thus been summoned, one should recite the same mantra, substituting this time VAŚAM ĀNAYA 'Lead him into my power!' One ordinarily recites 100 times to subjugate hosts of men or women or a king's minister, 10,000 times for the common world, 100,000 times for a king, 700,000 for the daughters of the gods and demigods, and 10,000,000 for divine beasts—garuḍa birds and the elephants that guard the quarters of the world—as well as for ordinary cattle; and by reciting endlessly, attentively, continually, and for a long time, one may subjugate even the entire triple world."[89]

There are many different sorts of mantra practice subsumed under the heading "subjugation." Kongtrü rinpoch'e gives the following technique to be used "when someone is angry at the practitioner or lacks faith in him." The practitioner first awakens his thought of enlightenment and makes offerings, and then he generates himself as the "red-colored Holy Lady." Between her brows he visualizes a red lotus upon which is a TĀṂ surrounded by Tārā's ten-syllable mantra. By its recitation, light radiates forth therefrom, touches the unfaithful one, and summons him forward; and the practitioner visualizes the person to be converted to faith as also being the red-colored Holy Lady, having the mantra between his brows also. Finally the person to be subjugated is dissolved into the nonobjectifiable realm of Emptiness; by doing this over and over again, that person—here by the power of his magically vicarious and saving contact with enlightenment—will become very faithful and devoted to the practitioner.

Another gentle means of conversion is simply to recite the mantra OṂ PADME PADMÂKṢI PADMA-SUBHAGE PHUḤ! PADME PADME AKṢI-PADME SUBHAGE PHUḤ SVĀHĀ! "OṂ Lotus, lotus eyes, lotus enchantment PHUḤ! Lotus, lotus, eyes of lotus, enchantment PHUḤ SVĀHĀ!" This is recited seven times, in front of the person one wishes to subjugate; and no sooner does he see the practitioner reciting it than his anger is calmed and he becomes a devoted follower. If the practitioner washes his face with water over which this mantra has been recited seven times, all persons will delight in his countenance. The practitioner may also recite the following mantra over a piece of *giwam*: NAMO BHAGAVATE! UṢṆĪṢĀYA DHARE DHARANTĪYE SVĀHĀ! "Homage to the Blessed Lady! To the crest, bearing, supporting SVĀHĀ!" If he repeats this 108 times and then makes a mark on his forehead with the *giwam*, anyone who sees him will be delighted. If he recites this mantra seven times over a handful of water and drinks it, he will get food; and if he holds the hem of his garment with his left hand

and recites it twenty-one times, then when he arrives among a multitude of men his words will be influential.[90]

Similarly, just as there are protective circles, one may make for subjugation or destruction magical devices, here again usually designs drawn on paper into which the practitioner directs the power of the deity that he controls. Recommended for the purpose of subjugation are cloths stained with menstrual blood, preferably that of a prostitute, or white birch bark; and in the rituals of Kurukullā the design is drawn thereon with red substances: red sandalwood, saffron, or blood from the practitioner's ring finger, although *giwam* may be used. One such practice is given by Dharmabhadra, that "one who wishes to accomplish the function of the blessed Kurukullā, a yogin who has gone through the prior ritual service of this supreme deity and who has repaired any breaking of his vows with her burnt offering, may easily subjugate a person for the increase of benefit to the teachings and to beings." The ritual is performed on an auspicious day, such as the eighth or fourteenth day of the waxing moon in the constellation Puṣya when it falls on a Thursday. The practitioner faces west, generates himself as the Blessed Lady, and performs the recitation, until he dwells in the deity's vivid appearance and ego. Then he draws an eight-spoked wheel with a nave and a rim: here it is drawn on red silken cloth, birch bark, or paper—whatever is available—with ink made of the mixed juices of saffron and *giwam*, if one is subjugating a man, or with ink made of the mixed juices of red sandalwood and red lac, if one is subjugating a woman.

On the nave of the wheel he draws HRĪḤ and, clockwise around it beginning from the front, the name of the person to be subjugated and VAŚAṂ-KURU HOḤ! Clockwise beginning from the front, with their heads pointed outward, he draws on the eight spokes OṂ KU RU KU LLE HRĪḤ SVĀ HĀ, and on the outer rim the vowels and consonants, ending with SVĀHĀ; he places this device upon a table, with its front facing him, and he sets out the offering bowls in front of it.

The practitioner then recites OṂ VAJRA-GHASMARĪ HŪṂ PHAṬ! (here the equivalent of the AMṚTA mantra) and OṂ SVABHĀVA-ŚUDDHĀḤ . . ., and the wheel that he has drawn becomes Emptiness. Then from the realm of Emptiness is the red syllable HRĪḤ, which transforms into a red wheel with eight spokes, a nave, and a rim, and so on until he has contemplatively re-created the circle and all the syllables thereon. With the light of the HRĪḤ in his heart he invites the circle of knowledge beings from their natural abode, and he makes offerings to them with OṂ JÑĀNA-CAKRA ARGHAṂ . . . ŚABDA PRATĪCCHA SVĀHĀ ! and absorbs them into the device with JAḤ HŪṂ BAṂ HOḤ ! Once again, with the light from the HRĪḤ in his heart, he summons the awareness of the person to be subjugated in the form of a small syllable A colored bright red, and he dissolves this into the syllables of that person's name on the nave of the wheel.

After the practitioner has recited the above ritual, he should make it firm by reciting YE DHARMA . . . 100 times and flinging flowers upon the device; then he should fold it up, according to the particular oral explanation, and tie it round with a red thread spun by a stainless maiden; and he should carry it upon his person so that no one else can see it. Every day he recites the mantra with its appendix: OṂ KURUKULLE HRĪḤ SVĀHĀ such-and-such a person VAŚAṂ-KURU HOḤ ! It is said that by this continual recitation he will subjugate whomever he whishes.[91]

THE LINGAM

In many of these rituals of coercion or destruction a device is made of an effigy to represent the person who is object of the ritual, that the acts performed on the effigy will be visited upon the person it represents, who has been summoned and dissolved into it. This effigy is called a *lingam* (sometimes abbreviated *ling*), and the term refers equally to drawings made on paper or to images molded of various substances, such as wax or, more often, barley flour, butter, and water. These molded effigies, too, may be dressed in pieces of clothing cast off by the person to be subjugated or destroyed, and some of his hair or nail clippings may be embedded in the dough. I have occasionally noted a peculiar and pervasive odor in the home of a Tibetan who had just had his hair cut; he was burning the clipped ends to prevent them from falling into the hands of enemies to be used against him.

We have already examined in chapter i this magical use of an effigy in destructive ritual and the axioms that underlie its efficacy (see pp. 100-103). The text that outlines that ritual, however, also supplies a defensive measure for removing the spell, should a rival cast it upon the practitioner himself. In his case a circle is drawn on a piece of new cloth washed in milk, and thereon is written the name of the practitioner in the mantra: May———be freed from bondage! This device is then consecrated; and the practitioner holds it in his hand as he recites OṂ KURUKULLE HRĪḤ may such-and-such a person be freed from bondage SVĀHĀ! He must then get rid of the device, to cast away the spell; it is recommended that he hide it in the burrow of a weasel—a place where it would not easily be found and destroyed by the caster of the spell—and he will then be freed from the enchantment.[92]

Fig. 36. The lingam effigy in its iron house—the black triangular box—surrounded by the weapons of its destruction; the syllables NṚ TRI on its body cast the demons "down into form" to be "liberated." From a Tibetan wood-block print.

This type of molded effigy is also used as a receptacle for malevolent demons who are to be destroyed; these evil forces are summoned and bound in the lingam, as we have seen before, and then they are slain ("liberated") and their bodies are offered up as food to the deities. In the great masked dances of the monastic cult this lingam is slain by the Black Hat Dancer: it is placed in a black triangular box, which represents the *dharmôdaya*, the primordial and feminine "source of all events," that it may be liberated into the pure Dharma realm, "wherein there is neither slain nor slayer" (see fig. 36).

THE RITUAL OF MULTITUDES

The lingam also plays a central role in the aggressive ritual called "multitudes," an offering to the gods of slain demons within multitudes of tormas, here functioning as a collective effigy. This is a very important and popular part of the monastic ritual cycle, and it finds a place in almost every large annual ceremony.[93] The ritual was originally an Indian one, wherein the participants took the roles of the deities of the maṇḍala and became a "circle of multitudes" with the Diamond Master in the center as the chief deity and his disciples about him as his retinue; visualized as the divine multitudes, they were made offerings by beautiful goddesses, carrying their acting out of divinity even to the extent of ritual intercourse with female partners.[94] But in Tibet the term refers mainly to the magical and protective function of removing demons, and the structure of the ritual, performed at the end of the main ceremony, reiterates the basic pattern of destructive ritual.

Here the multitude tormas are made not only of flour and butter but also of all sorts of delicious food, including even pieces of candy and popcorn from the local Indian cinema, and the tormas are shaped, as one text puts it, "like the breasts of ḍākiṇīs" (see pl. 16).[95] The altar server mixes some nectar into a skull-bowl filled with beer and sprinkles this mixture on the multitudes, while the assembly recites the empowering visualization:

> RAṂ YAṂ KHAṂ! From the seed in my own heart
> vividly visualized as the deity,
> RAṂ YAṂ KHAṂ radiate forth,
> cleansing the substance of the multitudes
> from the stain of holding them to be real;
> by the light of the three syllables it is transformed
> into the nectar of knowledge,
> clouds of offering of sense gratification filling the sky.

As the assembly recites the empowering mantra OṂ ĀḤ HŪṂ with the flying-bird gesure, the altar server covers the multitudes with his left hand on OṂ, with his right hand on ĀḤ and with both hands on HŪṂ, thus cleansing, increasing, and kindling the tormas. Then the guests of the ritual—the deities previously evoked by the assembly—are invited specially to partake of the offering, in this case as follows:

> Three Basic Ones, protectors of the Law,
> deities of wealth, lords of treasure,
> guardians of the world, all the vast numbers
> of deities of the maṇḍala:
> we invite you to these multitudes of knowledge,
> we pray you come!

OṂ ĀḤ HŪṂ! GURU-DEVA-ḌĀKINĪ-DHARMAPĀLA-DHANADEVA-NIDHIPATI-MAṄGALADEVADEVĪ-LOKAPĀLA-SAPARIVĀRA VAJRA-SAMĀJAḤ JAḤ!

And these guests are presented with the *upper multitudes*, the first of the three offerings of the tormas:

> OṂ ĀḤ HŪṂ! The multitudes inherently are a cloud
> of the nectar of knowledge,
> but their form is of goddesses of sense gratification
> filling the sky;
> may the Three Basic Ones
> and the divine hosts of the maṇḍala
> be pleased with these enjoyments
> of great inexhaustible Bliss!

OṂ ĀḤ HŪṂ! GURU-DEVA-ḌĀKINĪ-DHARMAPĀLA-DHANADEVA-NIDHIPATI-MAṄGALADEVADEVĪ-LOKAPĀLA-SAPARIVĀRA SARVA-GAṆA-CAKRA-PŪJA HO!

Next there are the *middle multitudes*, beginning with a long prayer to "satisfy" these guests. The practitioners recite the mantra of the space-vast treasury to increase their offering, and they say,

> HŪṂ HRĪḤ! The great maṇḍala of power
> over the entire world,
> the realm where appearance, sound, and understanding
> are the three Diamonds;
> here, erected upon this worldly base,
> we heap the materials of the multitudes,
> offerings gathered like clouds
> self-sprung on the base of appearance,

the eight gifts and the five sense gratifications,
the signs and substances of good fortune,
the seven precious gems of sovereignty . . .
a lake of blood which is the desirelessness
of the basic and thousand subsidiary lineages,
a torma that is the purity
of the entire animate and inanimate world,
the Great Bliss of the indissolubility
of Means and Wisdom,
pure from the first, miraculously sprung,
a play of the five lights of knowledge,
whose fruit is the manifestation
of the rank of three bodies.

With this we satisfy the guru Prowess of Beneficence:
grant us empowerment, the enjoyment of all our desires!
With this we satisfy the high patron Regent of Conquerors:
grant us the highest and ordinary magical attainments!

and so on through all the myriad deities of the maṇḍala, Kurukullā, the "guardians of the teachings," the "guardians of hidden texts," and the "keepers of the teachings, the five classes of arrogant spirits." And then, to complete the satisfaction of this hosts of divine guests, the practitioners add to the offering a final confession of their sins:

HOḤ! All our sins, obscurations, faults, and downfalls
accumulated from beginningless time,
especially all our falling away, our degeneracy,
from our basic and subsidiary pledges:
all these we confess by offering
these sense gratifications, these multitudes.

And they say SAMAYA-ŚUDDHE "In purity of vow" ĀḤ!

Thus, with all the invited deities satisfied and the practitioners themselves cleansed of impeding sin, the ritual may proceed to its conclusion of ferocity, the final offering of the *lower multitudes*. Here the multitudes become a lingam into which the evil spirits —especially, in this ritual, the demons of loss and poverty—are "summoned and made to enter" and then "liberated and offered as food" to the divine hosts.

I the Lotus Ḍākiṇī instantaneously change my state and become the Lion-faced Ḍākiṇī, very fierce, holding aloft a chopper and skull bowl, my body embraced by the Father, the Black Slayer of Death, who holds a copper-iron wheel.

From E comes an iron house, triangular,
in the depths of which
I vividly visualize those who would harm us,
the *gong* of hunger, the *si* of poverty;
there emanate from me
countless little fierce deities
who helplessly summon and dissolve in the multitudes
all those who would harm us.

This iron house may, in some rituals, actually be represented by a black triangular box painted with dancing skeletons, in which the physical actions of the ritual—planting the magic dagger, chopping with the sword—are performed by the Diamond Master who sits at the head of the assembly.

NAMO! We yogins, by the strength of the truth
of the Three Jewels, the Three Basic Ones,
the guardians of the teachings, the divine hosts:
let all who would harm our life or merit,
our power, might, or life,
our glory, enjoyments, horses, herds,
harvests, or grain,
the *gong* of hunger, the *si* of poverty,
the pursuing demons, the ghosts,
wherever they may dwell in the triple world,
the three earths, the country:
summon them helplessly,
cast them down into form!

Here the practitioners recite the mantra of the Slayer of Death and of the Lion-faced Ḍākiṇi, ending with:

All who would harm us, the *gong* of hunger, the *si* of poverty, the *serag*, the demons of loss, the pursuing demons, the ghosts: TRI! ĀKARṢAYA "Summon!" JAḤ JAḤ!

Thus the demons are embodied—"cast down into form"—with the "mantra particle" TRI! and summoned with JAḤ! And then they are absorbed into the multitudes with JAḤ HŪṂ BAṂ HOḤ!

In the heart of the visualized deity
is a weaponed wheel without a rim,
with countless tips of its spokes
whirling fiercely, cutting to pieces
their awareness, their life and body,
demolishing them to atoms!

And again the practitioners recite the mantra of the Slayer of Death and of the Lion-faced Ḍākiṇī, ending with:

All who would harm us, the *gong* of hunger, the *si* of povery, the *serag*, the demons of loss, the pursuing demons, the ghosts: their CITTA pressed into a package JAḤ ! I incite: MĀRAYA "Slay !" I incite the black spirit bound into the heart of those who would harm us, I incite: enjoy their taste ! MUKTAYA "Liberate !"

As they recite this, the altar server scatters magic mustard seed, and the Master brandishes his magic dagger as the assembly recites:

YA BHYOḤ ! I am the subjugating ḍākiṇī,
the fierce angry Lion-faced,
the Father is Mañjuśrī Slayer of Death;
and the most excellent of our sons
is Diamond Magic Dagger !
He casts down like hail,
he is quick like lightning,
planted in the heart's center
of those to be liberated;
he conquers their six vital juices,
and their life and merit dissolve into me;
out through the magic dagger
is drawn their awareness
and flung to the heart of Padmasambhava,
the depths of all-beneficent intention ĀḤ !

And the practitioners recite VAJRA-KĪLAYA NṚ TRI ! "Diamond Magic Dagger: the person TRI !" I incite: MĀRAYA PHAṬ ! as the Master plants his magic dagger in the hearts of the demons, slaying their bodies and liberating their awareness to the Pure Land of Padmasambhava. Then the Master chops up the multitudes with a magic sword, as the assembly offers up the "corpses" of the evil spirits as food for the gods of the maṇḍala:

The flesh, blood, and bones
of these liberated enemy evil spirits,
these *si* of poverty,
their three poisons purified
into a distillation of the nectar of knowledge:
this we offer up to be eaten
by the divine hosts of the maṇḍala;
accept it with raging delight !
perform your active functions
of subjugating and destroying !

OṂ ĀḤ HŪṂ ! GURU-DEVA-ḌĀKIṆĪ-DHARMAPĀLA-DHANADEVA-NIDHIPATI-MAṄGALADEVADEVĪ-LOKAPĀLA-SAPARIVĀRA the flesh, blood, and bones of all these enemy evil spirits, the *gong* of hunger, the *si* of poverty, the *serag*, the demons of loss, the pursuing demons, the ghosts KHĀHI !

Next, the text says, come "verbal offering and acceptance, the yogins' rejoicing as multitudes of vividly visualized deities, and the making of an earnest wish." Here, says another text of the same ritual, the "Master rejoices in the magical attainments of the Brothers [his sons]." The altar server prostrates to the Master, holding some of the chopped-up multitudes in his two hands held together, and he urges the Master to accept it:

> O Diamond Master, we pray you think of us!
> This our offering of multitudes
> we give with a sincere mind;
> we pray you accept it with compassion
> for the sake of beings.

And the Master replies:

> Ho! Events that appear do not cease,
> events that are Empty do not arise.
> The Great Bliss of the Innate Union
> of appearance and Emptiness!
> Great rejoicing! Alala! Ho!

Thus he accepts the multitudes with the property gesture, and he enjoys it with the special visualization that it is an "internal burnt offering," or that it is an offering to the divine hosts of the maṇḍala with whom his body is united.[96]

Then the *remainder* of this offering of the "lingam corpse" is gathered unstintingly and mixed together in a clean pan with the rest of the multitudes, and it is sprinkled with saliva and "medicine and blood"—from two skull bowls filled with water evoked as blood and semen—as the practitioners empower it with the flying-bird gesture and OṂ ĀḤ HŪṂ recited three times. Then the "guests for the remainder" are summoned with E ARALI HRĪḤ JAḤ!

> BHYO! Hosts of glorious, obedient messengers,
> accept this enjoyment of the remainder;
> in accord with the vows of your past lives
> dispel adversity, increase great strength!

> MAMA HRIṂ HRIṂ! UCCHIṢṬA-BALIṂ TE "To you, the torma of remainder" KHĀHI!

And then the practitioners make the *contract of the multitudes* with the worldly guests who receive this remainder:

> HŪṂ! All gods and demons who were bound to their oaths
> in their past lives, in the first of the world eras,

by the holder of the mantra, the three-lineaged guru:
by the truth of Reality, obey!
It was the Lotus King of Power
who bound to their oaths the oath-bound ḍākiṇīs
in the great cemetery of Silts'il;
in Tibet, at the time of Nyima dzepa,
all the gods and ogres were bound to their oath.
We are the descendants of that holder of the mantra,
you are the families of gods and demons;
in your past lives the Master disciplined you in the teachings,
now we yogins appoint you to your oaths;
accept this adorned torma
and accomplish the active functions entrusted to you!

The altar server rinses a fresh pan with nectar and fills it with the tormas, and the assembly recites the presentation of the remainder to the twelve Tenma Goddesses, native deities who guard the teachings:[97]

HŪṂ! Outside the land of India
are Nepal and Tibet; encircling those lands
in the rocky caverns of the demigods are Fierce Diamond and the Master Vasudhara,
holders of the mantra.
Sitting on thrones that stretch across the entire realm
are the ordered hosts
of the twelve great Tenma
who bestow the nectar of the pledges.
According to their promise and their vow
let them accept this nectar, this offering torma,
and accomplish the active functions
the yogins have entrusted to them!

MAMA LALA LELE TITI TETE KHARAKMA MAMA the sisters HŪṂ BHYO HŪṂ! AMṚTA KHARAṂ KHĀHI!

And the remainder is eaten also by the practitioners and shared with the lay people in the community.[98]

THE THREAD-CROSS

One of the major magical devices used by the Tibetans in their protective rituals is the so-called thread-cross. The basic form of this device is simply two crossed sticks whose ends are connected with colored thread to form, after many windings, a sort of diamond-shaped cobweb. This form may be further elaborated in some rituals to make a complicated structure up to eleven feet high, composed of a number of geometrical objects constructed of sticks and thread in weeks of patient work (see pl. 7). Nebesky-Wojkowitz[99] devotes a short chapter in his monumental book to a general outline of the multitudinous ceremonies involving these devices, wherein he mentions in passing the ritual we are about to consider, and in an article he gives an extensive bibliography of references to the thread-cross;[100] Lessing[101] gives a brief resumé of a thread-cross ritual of Tārā, but, in his words, "the writer had to resign himself to oral information only."

The Tibetans rely heavily upon the effectiveness of the thread-cross ritual, in all its many forms, in dealing with curses, calamities, and malignant spirits. The use of the thread-cross dates back to pre-Buddhist times, when the original conception seems to have been that it functioned as a demon trap: the evil spirits are supposed to get caught in the thread like flies in a cobweb. Such devices are included in the magical practices of the Bön[102] and were used at one time in the ancient Bön funeral rituals;[103] even today, small thread-crosses are placed as traps for demons above the entrance of a house or on top of the roof, and in Ladakh it is customary to protect a monastery and the surrounding area by huge thread-crosses.[104]

A short thread-cross ritual is also often appended to the large annual monastic rituals for the protective deities; but, as we have seen before, the rituals of Tārā are more private affairs, sponsored by lay or monastic devotees rather than by the monastery itself as part of its standard operation. Yet the various types of thread-cross ritual based upon Tārā are not for that reason any the less effective in the eyes of her worshipers: "This ritual is said to have been created by the Lord Nāgārjuna," says Lozang ch'öchi jets'en "who thought lovingly upon the beings of this degenerate era, that curses upon them might be averted, that the harm of false swearers —'those who eat their vows'—might be averted, that evil planets and stars, evil substances, and fierce and spiteful gods and ogres might be averted, that epidemics and loss might be suppressed: in short, that all their calamities might be averted, and all their good fortune increased."[105]

This attribution of Tārā's thread-cross ritual to Nāgārjuna, by the way, is a curious one. Thread-crosses are, indeed, used by a few aboriginal tribes in India, and the introduction of certain types of thread-cross into Tibet is attributed to Padmasambhava;[106] but as far as I can discover, the claim of the Magician Nārārjuna's original authorship of the ritual is a pious fiction, an attempt to align native practice with the great tradition of Indian Buddhism, based upon the fact that the ritual before us contains an evocation of the Twenty-one Tārās according to the iconography associated with Nāgārjuna's name. No such claim of his authorship is made, for example, in the thread-cross ritual of Khadiravaṇī Tārā which the Fifth Dalai Lama, under his secret name of Zahor beṇḍa, "compiled from the old writings,"[107] although this is the very deity with whom Nāgārjuna is canonically associated.[108]

The further association of both these types of thread-cross ritual —that is, of the Twenty-one Tārās and of Khadiravaṇī Tārā—with Atīśa, on the other hand, is more credible, for it is after all entirely possible that he took in hand the native rituals he encountered in Tibet and reworked them into Buddhist forms, transmitting them thus at least orally to his disciples. There seems to be no mention of the thread-cross in his written corpus included in the canon, but the lamas explain this saying that the canon of course excludes the works he wrote in Tibetan rather than in Sanskrit. It was in any event inevitable that the name of Tārā's most famous devotee would be included in the lineage of all her rituals, including even those to whom the goddess herself might originally have been a stranger.

Kongtrü rinpoch'e gives in one text some interesting stories about the use and effectiveness of the thread-cross as a magical device. To illustrate the power of the ritual to avert curses, for instance, he tells of the faithful devotee Ukar, who lived in the country of Jijang; and there too lived a magician named Kulo, who was very skilled in the propitiation of the red and black *shinje* and the red and black *mönpa*, and by the strength thereof he had slain many people. One day Ukar visited Kulo and made him the offerings due a holy man; but he also admonished him with words to the following effect: "Though you may think your magic is swift, the later ripening of your deeds will be heavy." Kulo was enraged at these "wages of his secret sins," and he departed in fury, swearing, "You will not live beyond seven days!" But Ukar performed the thread-cross ritual of Tārā, and after seven days the strength of Kulo turned back upon himself, and he died.

Ukar of Jijang figures again in another story. There was once a Chinese named P'acho, who was being harmed by a king demon. He consulted an astrologer who advised him: "It will help if you perform the ritual of 'transferring the danger' into the corpse of a small boy, and then ship it off to the province of Ü in a cargo of tea," so that the demon would follow after the substitute. P'acho accordingly performed the ritual and shipped the tea (and its pursuing spirit) off to Ü, where in P'enyü it was bought by a native of Ü named Geser. This Geser was also being harmed by a king demon, who had caused him to lose all his horses, mules, and donkeys, and this was a chance for him to see such a demon in person. So Geser asked the demon: "Of whom are you afraid?"

"I am afraid of Ukar of Jijang," the demon replied. "But apart from him, I am not afraid of anybody!"

So Geser decided to trick him, and he said: "How would you like me to kill this Ukar for you? Just show me where he is."

Thus the demon was duped into guiding him, and when they arrived in Jijang, Geser told Ukar his story. So Ukar gave him the thread-cross ritual and its evocation for expelling all kinds of demons, which Geser performed. From then on the harm of the demon was pacified, and his mind was bound to the service of the Law.

Finally the demon managed to return to China, and he went to the place of P'acho. P'acho said to him, "Demon! Where have you been all these years?"

"I went to Ü," the demon said. "At first it was very pleasant, but later it was miserable."

"What frightened you so much that you came back?" asked P'acho.

"I was afraid of Ukar of Jijang; now I am afraid of Geser too! That is why I returned; up to now I have been staying with Geser."

"I too will go to Ü," said P'acho. "Be my guide!"

So they both went to the place of Geser, the demon acting as guide. When P'acho met Geser, he told him his story and gave him excellent gifts, so Geser gave to him the thread-cross ritual for expelling demons and told him how to perform it. So P'acho performed it too, and from then on he was never again harmed by demons.[109]

THE THREAD-CROSS RITUAL

The thread-cross ritual here considered is entitled "Averting Dissension with Tārā, arranged as a ritual visualization and named 'Quickly Showing the Fruit of Truth.'" It was written by Kongtrü rinpoch'e at the hermitage of the great monastery of Pepung. The author gives the lineage of transmission of the ritual as follows: "This ritual was created by the Noble Nāgārjuna, who was prophesied by the Conqueror and who gained all the attainments based on the Tantras of Tārā. He gave it to certain fortunate ones until, proceeding along the unbroken bridge of the lineage, it was taken to Tibet by Atīśa. Now Atīśa, before he died, took it out [secretly] from within his clothing and gave it to the Teacher from the Clan of Drom; he gave it to Ngog of Sangp'u named Legpe sherab[110] who gave it to Neuzurpa[111] and so on in due order through the lineage, until it was personally transmitted to the Teacher of Ja, who wrote many books on it.[112] Later, also, the Regent Dragpa ch'oyang, Zhuch'en and many others wrote texts and handbooks thereon, expanded or abridged according to need; and thus the textual lineage and the lineage of its actual performance continued unimpaired to the present day."

Then, to show the benefits the practitioner may expect to derive from the performance of the ritual, Kongtrü rinpoch'e quotes the following precepts held to be an oral tradition passed down "from the mouth of Nāgārjuna":

> Hereby is pacified the strength
> of mundane and supramundane deities;
> like the wishing gem on the crest of a serpent king
> it grants all one's desires.
> When people trample underfoot
> images, books, and shrines
> and hand one into the power
> of the eight classes of gods and ogres,
> when they cast curses
> with magic weapons, magic substances,
> rolling the magic dagger between their palms,
> when evil omens arise in the land,
> even the strength of all those
> cannot prevail the least bit against one:
> this is the highest recommendation
> that one practice this oneself.

And he quotes another tradition "from the mouth of Atīśa":

> If one is going on a long journey, the performance of this ritual ensures that no evil circumstances will arise: one may avert with this ritual fighting in one's land, the spreading of epidemics and the occurrence of evil omens. Have no doubt about it: though undesired things arise, it is impossible that one not achieve whatever one

> desires by performing this ritual. There is nothing that has greater empowerment or greater strength than this ritual, either for gaining what one desires or averting what one does not desire. So strive greatly herein! Nothing has come to Tibet which is more profound than these books.

In other words, our author glosses, this ritual is profound and powerful in averting curses, drought, evil omens, or bad dreams, fierce and spiteful gods and ogres, the harm and torment of great demons, poxes, epidemics, loss, diseases of livestock, and any harm that might come from evil years, months, days, times, planets, or stars. It is especially effective in averting all evils directed at the practitioner by the counting out of fierce mantras or the swearing of false oaths, the dangers of a long journey or of magical pollution: in short, in averting the strength of all mundane and supramundane spirits and in increasing all good fortune. There is an accumulated weight of evidence for these assertions, he says, in the stories that come from India, Nepal, and Tibet, where practitioners have performed this ritual of such great empowerment and benefit; these stories may be looked up in the old writings.

It was for these reasons that we were advised to sponsor this ritual before leaving the community and returning to America. We had already thanked Tārā—and indirectly the monastery—for our pleasant and productive stay by sponsoring the Four Maṇḍala Offering, and it was felt that it would be prudent to enlist the goddess's further support in averting any demonic influences that might hinder our long journey home. We thus hired ten monks at the previous rate—Toden rinpoch'e, six yogins, and the three monks who lived with them in the hermitage—to perform the ritual on our behalf. They were so delighted with it that they immediately spent several more days performing it for the benefit of K'amtrü rinpoch'e as well.

The preparations this ritual requires are very complex, and for days before its actual performance the assembly hall was filled with activity. Again, for those interested in modern monastic economics, the materials and the construction of the thread-cross, and all the offerings on the altar, came to slightly more than $11, though the tea and food for this smaller group of monks came to only about $3. Thus, as the patron of the ritual, its entire performance cost us just about $18, again not unreasonable but still a very sizable amount nowadays for an individual Tibetan to pay.

1 *Preparations: offerings and substitutes*

The altar is erected—"at an auspicious time, or when it has become necessary"—in a room that, according to the text, has been thoroughly cleaned. On a high covered table there is set out a lotus of twenty petals and a center, either made of powdered colors or painted on cloth. If this is not possible, small piles of grain—one in the middle and five in each of the four directions, twenty-one in all—are arranged on a maṇḍala, that is, the flat metal base of an offering maṇḍala. Above it are placed paintings and images, properly consecrated, either of the Twenty-one Tārās or of Green Tārā alone, depending on what is available; and before it on the altar are laid out the "full garland of the outer offerings" (the seven offering bowls), a washing flask, towels and "clothing" for the goddess, the last represented by the ubiquitous Tibetan ceremonial scarf.

The offering torma, here called the "round torma"—of "clean and pleasing appearance"—is set out in a pure vessel; it is decorated with "ornamental details" of colored flowers made of butter, and it is "surrounded by many *t'ebchu*" (literally "buttons"), small tetrahedrons of dough placed around the base of the torma as an additional food offering.

Upon this altar, where the deities will be evoked during the generation in front, the offerings to the goddess are placed. On a lower table are set out the four tormas for the worldly guests: the *gegtor* for the hindering demons and the *lench'ag torma* for the "creditors," and the *chogdog torma* and the white torma for the lords of the soil. These last are well treated with offerings in the ritual, for it will later be up to them to "clear the road for the thread-cross."

The tormas for the hindering demons and the creditors are both decorated with a special device called a *ch'angbu*, a piece of dough rolled out between the palms and then squeezed in the fist to produce wavy identations; this is said to represent, among other things, the life of the person for whose benefit the ritual is performed, offered along with the torma as a ransom or substitute for his person. The torma for the creditors is decorated in addition with *tinglo*, small cups made of dough: one in the center, filled with offerings and adorned with a dough flower, and one on either side made into butter lamps. Around the base of the torma are placed rows of buttons. The *chogdog torma* is "heaped high with magic pills," these being small spheres of dough set around the base. (See fig. 37.)

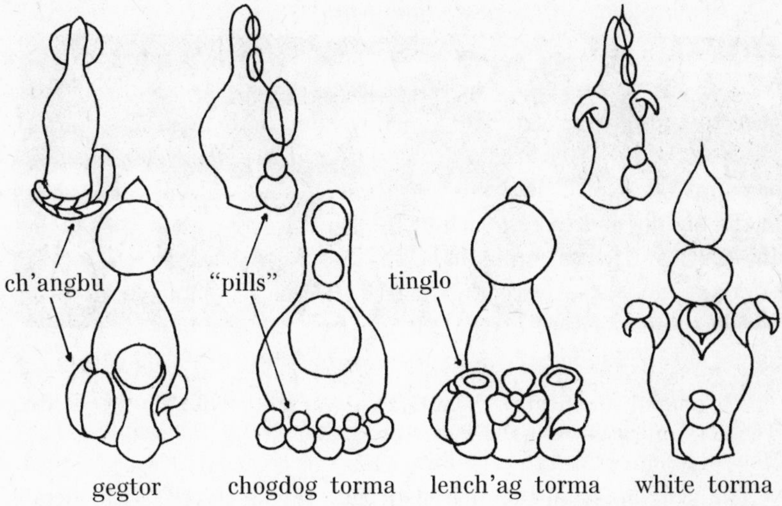

Fig. 37. The tormas for the thread-cross ritual.

There is also set out upon the table an "infusion of various grains," called sometimes a "golden libation," which is offered up to the local protectors in an additional ceremony inserted into the thread-cross ritual. This offering consists of beer or tea in a special long-stemmed goblet, mixed with grain or occasionally with the scrapings from an alloy of the five precious metals.

Then, on another square table, there is erected the thread-cross itself. First there is made a four-tiered "Mount Meru," constructed of earth or of *zen*—barley flour mixed with water—placed upon a supporting wooden framework; on the highest tier a mansion is built of the same materials, "square, with a roof and finial, beautifully colored." In front of the mansion's door is set out the *ngarmi* or "portrait" made of barley flour, a full handspan tall, riding upon a horse and adorned with gold, turquoise, and silken clothing. This portrait, of the most delicate workmanship, functions as a substitute or ransom: it represents the person for whom the ritual is performed, and the evil spirits will be coerced into accepting it as a scapegoat for his person. Thus it is the most important of the many substitutes to be used in the ritual, and the greatest care is observed in its construction.

The remaining substitues represent the household, property, and possessions of the threatened person, for disaster directed at him may fall equally upon his family, his livestock, and his material goods.

Fig. 38. A proof sheet pulled from a *zen par*, a wooden mold for making small substitutes. The block is carved in intaglio, hence the peculiar appearance of the paper print.

Around the horse on the highest tier are placed thirty "little men," either shaped by hand or stamped from the special wood blocks carved for this purpose (fig. 38), and gold dust is scraped onto the dough of which they are made. The second tier is encircled with the "eight foods" and images of the various kinds of birds, similarly made. On the third tier are arranged images of the different kinds of domestic animals (elephants, horses, yaks, cows, oxen, sheep, goats), images of the different kinds of deer (stags, antelopes, elk), and images of the various aquatic creatures (fish, tadpoles, frogs, snakes). And on the fourth and lowest tier are placed eight butter lamps made of dough, one in each of the four cardinal and four intermediate directions.

The entire edifice is surrounded with various grains, various foods, and different kinds of gems and turquoise, with various medicines, small portraits and *ch'angbu*, and with used pieces of clothing and body hair "to act as a substitute" for the sponsor. If evil omens have arisen, such as an owl hooting in the daytime or a raven calling in the night, there is set up also an appropriate image of the omen or the skin of the appropriate animal, if it can be obtained.

Around Mount Meru there are set up the "surrounding iron mountains" which encircle the world and which we have seen before in the maṇḍala offering. This ring of mountains is represented by a low wall of dough into which are inserted the stems of plants and flowers.

The thread-cross proper is here called a "space" or "sky," and three of these are set out behind and on either side of the large portrait on the highest tier, with four more placed in the cardinal directions on the iron mountains. The larger thread-cross, behind the portrait, is made up of five interlocked diamond shapes, and the six remaining smaller ones are simple diamonds. All of them are made of threads of five different colors, forming parallel bands—reading from the center outward—of black, white, red, yellow, green, blue, and white.

In front of the large portrait are placed three *jangbu*, tablets bearing a stylized picture of an arrow or a spindle, to represent male and female respectively. The middle tablet bears a picture of an "excellent house," as a substitute for the threatened dwelling and all it contains. Four more tablets, two arrow-male and two spindle-female, are placed on the iron mountains in the four intermediate directions.

Finally there are placed on the iron mountains six *p'otong* ("male face") on the right and six *motong* ("female face") on the left: these are drawings of men and women, mounted on slender sticks stuck into the soft dough, and offered to the malevolent spirits as substitutes for all the men and women whose lives they threaten (fig. 39). Similarly, three "radiant arrows" and three "radiant spindles"—here the real objects and not representations—are set up, respectively, in front and behind on the iron mountains. Then the entire structure is tied around the outside with thread knotted in front and is set on the altar facing the assembly.

This way of constructing the thread-cross, says the text, is what appears in the commentaries of the ancient texts as the handiwork of the holy ones, and thus it is "of noble origin and descent." But there are, it adds, many different methods, depending upon the type of ritual performed, differences in wealth or intelligence, the various elaborations of the structure and personal innovations in design, so that "there is no one particular way of doing it." We may add that a thorough analysis of these variations may be found in Nebesky-Wojkowitz's brilliant compendium.

The construction of this thread-cross represents a complex coalescence of symbolisms, in which we may distinguish three major elements. First, of course, is the ancient notion of this device as a *demon trap*; as Lessing says, "The assumption that the original lozenge form was suggested by a cobweb (souls and spirits conceived of as flying insects are a folkloristic feature too familiar to need discussion) is very appealing."[113]

Fig. 39. *P'otong* and *motong* offered as substitutes.

Second is the obvious use of a *substitute*, a term Nebesky-Wojkowitz translates as "scapegoat," offered to the malignant spirits as a ransom for the well-being of the person whom they threaten. The use of substitutes is widespread in Tibetan ritual, especially in the complex of ceremonies that center on the idea of cheating or ransoming from death, or ransoming life, another example of an aboriginal Tibetan ritual adapted to a wide range of different Buddhist deities.[114] To illustrate the basic workings of the ransom we may look at a short text on cheating death which is part of the cycle of the *Bardo t'ödrö*, the so-called Tibetan Book of the Dead.[115] "This substitute," it says, "should be as many fingerbreadths tall as the person who is the object of the ritual is years old; the dough may be made black for the *dü* demons, red for the *tsen* and *lutsen* [a cross between a *lu* and a *tsen*], yellow for the *lu* serpents, *nyen*, and *t'eurang*, white for the king demons, green for the female *dü* demons, country gods, and earth ogres, or any combination of colors; mixed into it should be some of the person's own excrement, pieces of clothing, mucus, saliva, tears, hair, fingernails, and so on, and from that the image should be made. It should be adorned with various kinds of colored wool and silk and with many different kinds of feathers from birds of ill omen. In front of each should be set out a torma of the same color, and as many *ch'angbu* as the person is years old, made out of 'effigy' dough. These are all empowered with the six mantras and the six homages [see below], and this verse is recited aloud:

> Carry away! carry away, strong ones!
> desire, lust, and longing,
> memory, grasping, thought, and touch:
> unbind, free, and pacify!"

"Reciting this," the text continues, "the substitute is cast into the middle of a great river. Death is thereby averted for the space of three years. It is said, too, that this should be done three times a year before the signs of death have a chance to arise, and this is much the best thing."

A third and very important major symbolic element is the superimposition upon these native and constantly recurring Tibetan themes of an Indian Buddhist symbolism and contemplative procedure. It is clear that the four-tiered Mount Meru and its surrounding iron mountains represent the same *cosmogram* that is offered to one's guru or to Tārā, here filled with jewels and people and all precious things, offered to appease the spirits. Thus the thread-cross functions in the ritual both as a supreme offering and as an entire visualized universe, symbolically (and hence actually) corresponding to ours in every respect, contemplatively created as an abode for the demons during the course of the ritual. One of my informants rather liked my suggestion of the analogy of a humane animal trap, for the "space" of the thread-cross is the gate of the trap through which the demons enter, attracted by the "bait" of the portrait and all the substitutes, and the five colors of the threads represent all the Buddhist lists of five things—families, elements, aggregates, knowledges—which make up the universe. The portrait is not here an effigy generated as the person to be protected, nor is he "summoned and made to enter" into his ransom, for this would be to hand him over to the demons in actuality. Rather the demons are fooled or cheated by the visualization and recitation of the practitioner into accepting the portrait as a substitute object of malevolence and are coerced into enjoying their prize in the separate dimension created for them. This is one reason for the recommendation that we employ the yogins to perform the ritual for us: it requires highly developed contemplative powers to create an entire world, and indeed the ritual itself presupposes a trained ability in instantaneous generation. The visualization is imposed upon the public nonreality of the evil spirits, who, once they are trapped, can no longer perceive ordinary appearances but are aware only of the appearances of this new universe; yet this new home is after all filled with a paradise of good things—the substitutes—and there is no real lack of humanitarian impulse in their incarceration.

The thread-cross is carried out to a lonely place and left there (in our case it was thrown over a cliff), and the "return of the danger" is blocked and a circle of protection visualized to prevent any escape; here the evil spirits remain until the karma that impelled them to their malevolence is exhausted. Thus the three levels of symbolism converge: the malignant spirits are trapped, offered a substitute object of aggression, and transported to another and contemplatively real dimension through the gate of the space that traps them. All the rest of the ritual is subservient to this aim: the self-generation and generation in front are indeed rather perfunctory, serving merely as introductions to the ritual function of offering the tormas to the goddess and the worldly guests, and to the magical function of visualizing the thread-cross and its substitutes and dispatching them to the spirits (see pls. 8-15).

2 *The ritual*

2.1 *Preliminaries*

The actual performance of the ritual begins with the indispensable preliminary of the rhythmic and droning recitation of one of the monastery's standard prayers to the gurus for empowerment. Then the assembly join their palms and go for refuge:

> Myself and all beings, as infinite as space, from this time onward until we gain the terrace of enlightenment, go for refuge to the

> glorious and holy gurus, go for refuge to the Buddha, go for refuge to the Law, go for refuge to the Assembly, and go for refuge to the hosts of deities of the holy noble Tārā and her retinue.

Then, with no hand gesture, they awaken the thought of enlightenment by reciting three times:

> For the sake of all beings may I gain the rank of omniscient Buddha; it is for that reason that I enter into this contemplation and recitation of the holy noble Tārā.

They then recite three times the short refuges ("To the Buddha, the Law, and the highest hosts . . .") and the Four Immeasurables ("May all beings have Bliss and the cause of Bliss . . ."), just as in the Four Maṇḍala Offering.

2.2 *Basics*

2.21 *Self-generation*

The ritual proceeds immediately to the self-generation without pausing here for the standard preliminary of empowering the offerings, since these will be empowered individually at the time they are presented. Here the practitioners grasp the ego and vivid appearance of the goddess, gaining the power to direct her divine energy. The most important part of the ritual is not the generation of the deity herself, but rather the evocation and employment of her power. This single-minded concentration upon the main point of the ritual leads not only to abbreviation but also to the final departure of the knowledge being, after "ordinary ego" has been cast away through its descent. It is expected that the practitioners, through their ritual srvice and long contemplative training, dwell already in the deep contemplation of Tārā and require only a symbolic ritual generation.

The peculiarities of this self-generation are common to many rituals of the magical type class: it is extremely brief, the steps of the Process of Generation are combined, and the knowledge being is not sealed into the visualized image with the ritual initiation. The ritual insistently focuses forward upon its magical aims; indeed in many magical functions the self-generation is performed instantaneously through "knowledge of one's primordially divine nature," a generation "vividly and perfectly contemplated as a primordial manifestation of the deity, the essence of one's mind, not relying on ritual or verbal recitation."[116] But here the assembly recites:

OṂ SVABHĀVA-ŚUDDHĀḤ SARVA-DHARMĀḤ SVABHĀVA-ŚUDDHO 'HAṂ!

From the realm of Emptiness is an A in my heart, and from that a moon, above which is a green TĀṂ. It fills my body with its light, cleansing my karmically ripened transience together with my sins and obscurations. I myself become the body of Tārā: her body colored green, having one head and two hands, the right in the gift-bestowing gesture and the left holding to her breast the stalk of a blue lotus flower whose petals blossom next to her ear. She sits in the half-crossed posture of royal ease, her right foot extended and her left drawn up; she is adorned with silken garments and ornaments of precious gems.

Light radiates forth from the TĀṂ placed on the moon in my heart and invites the hosts of deities who are the holy noble Tārā's knowledge being VAJRA-SAMĀJAḤ!

As they recite the syllables that gather the hosts of deities in the sky before them, they cross their arms on their breasts and snap their fingers—the assembly gesture—and they mentally perform the offerings with the appropriate gestures, but not reciting the mantras out loud. Then, with the four gestures and JAḤ HŪṂ BAṂ HOḤ . . .,

The knowledge being dissolves indivisibly into me, and I am marked on the top of my head with a white OṂ, on my throat with a red ĀḤ, and on my heart with a blue HŪṂ.

Thus become the deity, and empowered in body, speech, and mind, the practitioners perform the contemplation of the mantra, the brief reenactment of the ritual service and the gathering of power for the specialized divine function they will later perform. "Bearing in mind the vivid appearance of the deity's body," they recite:

Around the edge of the green syllable TĀṂ above the moon in my heart I visualize the encircling 10-syllable mantra: OṂ TĀRE TUTTĀRE TURE SVĀHĀ!

They recite this basic mantra 108 times, and then recite the mantra seven times more with the long appendix noted above in Atīśa's "protection of averting":

I vividly visualize the encircling mantra: NAMO RATNATRAYĀYA! NAMA ĀRYA-AVALOKITEŚVARĀYA BODHISATTVĀYA MAHĀSATTVĀYA MAHĀKĀRUṆIKĀYA! TADYATHĀ OṂ TĀRE TUTTĀRE TURE SARVA-DUṢṬAṂ PRADUṢṬAṂ MAMA KṚTE JAMBHAYA STAMBHAYA MOHAYA BANDHAYA! HŪṂ HŪṂ HŪṂ! PHAṬ PHAṬ PHAṬ! SARVA-DUṢṬA-STAMBHANI-TĀRE SVĀHĀ!

Then the knowledge being is separated once again from the practitioners and placed in the sky before them—"The knowledge being becomes seated before me . . ."—and the assembly presents offerings with the series of gestures and mantras from ARGHAṂ through ŚABDA, ending with the crash of the peaceful music. And they recite the following prayer: "I pray that the holy noble Tārā grant to us and all beings all the highest and ordinary magical attainments!" With the following standard verse—not included in the ritual text proper—they dedicate their merit:

> By this virtue may I quickly
> accomplish as the noble Tārā
> and place every single being
> upon that same stage.

They pray that the knowledge being depart, snapping their fingers with OṂ MUḤ: and "each dwells steadfastly with the ego of the symbolic being."

2.22 *Generation in front*

Thus the assembly is touched by the deity, and they can continue with her symbolic ego and appearance, rendered potent through their prior contemplative experience and their knowledge of innate unity with the goddess. Prepared to direct her power through their symbolic bodies, they generate before them the Twenty-one Tārās, whose names and functions are based on the iconography attributed to Nāgārjuna (see pp. xiii, 470).

OṂ ŚŪNYATĀ-JÑĀNA-VAJRA-SVABHĀVÂTMAKO 'HAṂ!

From the realm of Emptiness is PAṂ, from which comes a multicolored lotus; in the center thereof is A, from which comes the orb of a moon; above that is a green TĀṂ, from which comes a lotus flower marked with TĀṂ, which transforms into the blessed holy noble Tārā, her body colored green, bedecked with various precious ornaments, having one face and two hands, with her right in the gift-bestowing gesture fulfilling the wishes of all beings, with her left grasping a full-blown lotus flower, wearing clothes of beautiful silk, adorned upon her crest by the Conqueror Amoghasiddhi, sitting in a posture of royal ease upon a throne of lotus and moon, in the midst of countless Buddhas and Bodhisattvas.

Around her on the twenty lotus petals. going counterclockwise from the front:

The Tārā swift and heroic, who destroys hindering demons and injuries, her body colored red, holding the red flask that subjugates.

The Tārā white as the autumn moon, who defeats diseases and evil spirits, holding the white flask that pacifies.

The Tārā who increases life and enjoyment, colored yellow, holding the yellow flask that increases.

The Tārā victorious, who grants the highest life, colored yellow, holding the yellow flask of life.

The Tārā crying the sound of HŪṂ, who subjugates and summons with the gesture of wisdom, her body colored red-yellow, holding the red flask that ravishes.

The Tārā victorious over the triple world, who tames ghosts, her body colored red-black, holding the blue flask that confounds ghosts and awakened corpses.

The Tārā defeating others, who averts the magic mantras of others, her body colored black, holding the black flask that averts magic mantras.

The Tārā who defeats *dü* demons and enemies, her body colored red-black, holding the red flask that defeats *dü* demons and enemies.

The Tārā whose gesture symbolizes the Three Jewels, who protects from all terrors, holding the white flask that defeats all terrors.

The Tārā who tames all *dü* demons and obstructions, her body colored red, holding the red flask that defeats *dü* demons.

The Tārā dispelling the suffering of poverty, who grants the magical attainments, her body colored red-yellow like refined gold, holding the yellow flask that dispels poverty.

The Tārā who grants all good fortune, her body the color of gold, holding the white flask of good fortune.

The Tārā who defeats hindering demons and obstacles, her body colored red and blazing like fire, holding the red flask that protects from obstacles.

The Tārā with frowning brows, who destroys hindering demons, her body colored black, holding the dark blue flask that pierces hindering demons, her brows slightly frowning.

The Tārā great and calm, who cleanses sins and obscurations, her body colored white, holding the white flask that cleanses sins and obscurations.

The Tārā victorious over the contentions of others, who increases one's intelligence, her body colored red, holding the red-yellow flask that increases wisdom.

The Tārā pacifying *dü* demons and obscurations, who shakes the triple world, her body colored red-yellow, holding the yellow flask that subdues magic mantras.

The Tārā pacifying the poison of the *lu* serpents, who dispels it, her body colored white, holding the white flask that dispels poison and disease.

The Tārā who dispels bad dreams and suffering, her body colored white, holding the white flask that dispels suffering.

The Tārā who dispels all fevers, her body colored white, holding the white flask that dispels fevers.

The Tārā who fulfills all active functions, her body colored white and radiating varicolored lights, holding the green flask whence come all magical attainments.

All these have one face and two hands: in their right hands, upon the palm of their gift-bestowing gestures, they hold the flasks that accomplish their various active functions, and with their left hands they hold a lotus flower. They are seated with their right feet extended and their left drawn up, on thrones of lotus and moon, adorned with silks and all precious ornaments, radiating forth measureless light, and surrounded on all sides by countless hosts of Buddhas, Bodhisattvas, high patron deities, ḍākiṇīs, and protectors of the Law.

On all their foreheads is OṂ, on their throats ĀḤ, on their hearts HŪṂ; from those light radiates forth, whereupon from Potala the holy noble Twenty-one Tārās, surrounded by countless Buddhas, Bodhisattvas, high patron deities, ḍākiṇīs, and protectors of the Law OṂ VAJRA-SAMĀJAḤ!

Here the assembly has picked up the vajras and bells, and as they recite the mantra they greet the knowledge being with a peal of sound and cross their hands on their breasts in the assembly gesture. The text then says that they should join their palms, but the gesture is actually made only with their right hands, as they sing the following verses to the rhythmic ringing of the bells they hold in their left hands:

You are the lord of all beings,
the deity who irresistibly conquers Mārā and his army,
the Blessed One who knows all things as they are:
I pray you and your retinue, come to this place!
From the highest place of Potala,
born from the green syllable TĀṂ,
adorned upon your crest with Amitābha,
performing the active functions
of the Buddhas of the three times:
for the sake of beings, I pray you come!

And when the knowledge being is seated in the sky before them, the tune of the verses becomes faster, and they sing:

With devotion I invite you
who have the color of refined gold
more greatly splendid than the sun.
Peaceful, possessed of great compassion,
calm and dwelling in the stage of meditation,
lusting after neither events nor knowledge
but possessed of omnipresent and inexhaustible capacity:
come here! come here! pure and peaceful deity,
incarnate sage, omniscient one,
I pray you come to this place of offerings,
into this well-formed image.
Remain here for the sake of beings
here united with this image.
I pray you surely grant us life without disease, lordship,
and enlightenment the most excellent of all.

Thus with a crash of peaceful music they visualize that they have invited all the Buddhas and Bodhisattvas, and to them—in the person of the image on the altar—they proceed to offer a welcoming bath. The altar server reflects the image in a small mirror, and it is upon the reflection of the image that he begins to pour water from the washing flask as the assembly sings:

Because your essence is pure
the bonds of this world have no power over you;
it is in order to cleanse our own obscurations
that we bathe your body with this pure water.

Here the assembly rings their bells, and they continue:

> Just as the Buddha, as soon as he was born,
> was bathed by all the gods,
> I pray you likewise bathe your body
> with this pure divine water.

The altar server removes the feather from the mouth of the washing flask and circles it over the mirror, and the assembly hall reverberates once again to the peaceful music; beneath the roar they recite OṂ HŪṂ TRĀṂ HRĪḤ ĀḤ KĀYA-VIŚODHANA SVĀHĀ ! and the altar server touches the tip of the feather to the center and four directions of the mirror as the seed syllables of the five families of Buddha are said, ending on the word KĀYA-VIŚODHANA "cleansing the body," which represents the bath of all five families at once.

And then the invited Buddhas and Bodhisattvas in the image are offered clothes and ornaments, as the song continues:

> I give to them dress of many colors,
> holy garments, sweet-smelling,
> divers garments, soft and fine,
> and hundreds of most excellent ornaments.

The assembly recites the mantra OṂ VAJRA-VASTRA-ALAṂKĀRA-PŪJA-MEGHA-SAMUDRA-SPHARAṆA-SAMAYA HŪṂ! "OṂ The gathering swelling ocean of clouds of the offering of diamond clothes and ornaments HŪṂ!" as the altar server lays the ceremonial scarf on the altar before the image. And the song goes on:

> Out of love for us and for all beings,
> with the strength of a magic manifestation of yourself,
> remain here, Blessed One, I pray you,
> for as long as we make offerings to you.

The deities are offered a seat with the palms-up gesture—the same as the asking-to-depart gesture—and the mantra OṂ VAJRA-ĀSANA-PADMAKAMALĀYAS TVAṂ! "OṂ A lotus throne to be your diamond seat!" And they are given the offering series of the "five gifts" with the appropriate gestures and the mantras OṂ ĀRYA-TĀRĀ-SAPARIVĀRA PUṢPE PRATĪCCHA SVĀHĀ . . . DHŪPE . . . ĀLOKE . . . GANDHE . . . NAIVEDYE PRATĪCCHA SVĀHĀ!

The goddess is praised by singing "Gods and demigods bow their crowns . . ." ending with the rapid ringing of the bells. Then the assembly forms the full-blown-lotus-flower gesture (fig. 40), and with JAḤ HŪṂ BAṂ HOḤ . . . "the knowledge being mixes indissolubly into the symbolic being."

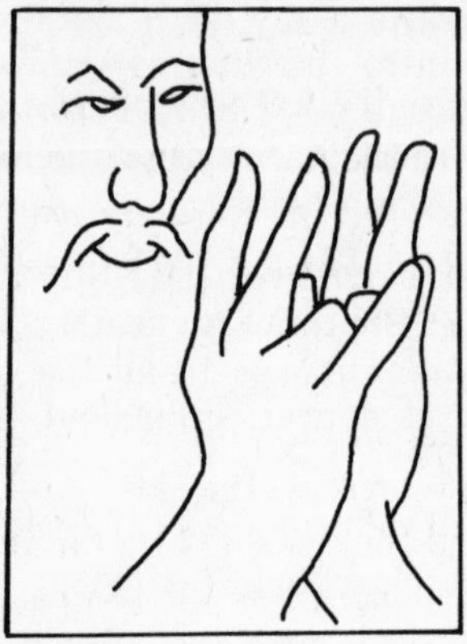

Fig. 40. The full-blown-lotus-flower gesture.

This whole portion of the ritual is sung and recited straight through without pause, as the altar server simultaneously carries out the actions before the altar. And the assembly proceeds immediately to the effectuation of the mantra in the hearts of the deities before them, and they recite the visualization:

> In the hearts of the retinue headed by the Holy Lady generated in front is the green syllable TĀṂ above the orb of a moon, surrounded by the 10-syllable mantra; light radiates forth therefrom, pacifying the misfortunes, the eight and the sixteen great terrors, of myself and others, all beings, and increasing our life, merit, possessions, and anything we might wish for.

And as they visualize the light streaming forth, they recite OṂ TĀRE TUTTĀRE TURE SVĀHĀ 108 times.

2.23 *Offerings, praises, and tormas*

2.231 *Offerings*

The assembly now holds the ego and vivid appearance of the deity and her retinue, and they have generated before them the empowered group of Twenty-one Tārās, whose hearts they have aroused by the recitation of the mantra and whose list of functions contains those they wish to accomplish. The ritual now proceeds to its third phase, the giving of offerings, praises, and tormas, and here the offerings are first empowered:

> By the strength of the empowerment of the Buddhas and Bodhisattvas, by the strength of my merit and my earnest wish, by the strength of the mantra: for the maṇḍala of the retinue of the Buddhas and Bodhisattvas I radiate forth a vast, great, most excellent cloud of offerings, which sets before them all that is in *All-Beneficent's Vow of Conduct*:

> NAMAḤ SARVA-BUDDHA-BODHISATTVĀYA SARVATHĀ-KHAṂ UDGATE SPHARAṆA IMAṂ GAGANA-KHAṂ SAMANTAM SVĀHĀ! "Homage to all the Buddhas and Bodhisattvas! The offerings appear throughout space, dwelling, filling the sky SVĀHĀ!"

The mantra is repeated eight times (for the eight outer offerings), and the offerings are then presented by singing:

> As many oblations as there are
> in the measureless worldly realms:
> that many I set out with reverence
> and offer to the mother of Conquerors.

Then with the appropriate gesture the offering mantra is recited: OṂ ĀRYA-TĀRĀ-SAPARIVĀRA ARGHAṂ PRATĪCCHA PŪJA-MEGHA-SAMUDRA-SPHARAṆA-SAMAYE HŪṂ! And the verse is repeated again (recited this time) for each of the series of gifts, substituting for "oblations" the words "flowers," incense," "lamps," "perfumes," "food," and "music," and similarly replacing ARGHAṂ in the mantra with PUṢPE and so on (note that since these are the gifts, PĀDYAṂ "water for the feet" is left out), ending on ŚABDA with the sounding of the peaceful music. And finally the assembly sings:

> I fill all the realms of the sky
> with storied houses, bathing ponds,
> gardens, the seven precious gems,
> thrones, umbrellas, banners: and these I offer.

> OṂ SARVA-VIŚIṢṬHA-PŪJA-MEGHA-PRASARA-SAMUDRE ĀḤ HŪṂ! "OṂ The swelling torrents of clouds of the offerings of everything remaining ĀḤ HŪṂ!"

2.232 *Praises*

Then the assembly visualizes that the sponsor, the one who is to be protected by the ritual, and all his followers are placed beneath the outstretched right hands—the refuge gesture—of the retinue headed by the Blessed Lady; and they recite her "praise with the basic mantra":

> OṂ! Homage to the holy and noble Tārā!
> Homage, TĀRE, quick one, heroine,
> removing all terrors with TUTTĀRE,
> savioress, granting all aims with TURE,
> the syllables SVĀHĀ: to you I bow!

And they continue to recite the *Homages* from "Homage, Tārā, quick one, heroine . . ." through " . . . These are the twenty-one homages." And once again they make offerings, joining their palms and reciting:

> As many offerings as might be contained
> in the vast and measureless ocean:
> that many I set out with reverence
> and offer to the mother of Conquerors.

And rapidly performing the series of gestures, they say: OṂ ĀRYA-TĀRĀ-SAPARIVĀRA ARGHAṂ PĀDYAṂ PUṢPE DHŪPE ĀLOKE GANDHE NAIVEDYA ŚABDA PRATĪCCHA PŪJA-MEGHA-SAMUDRA-SPHARAṆA-SAMAYE HŪṂ!

This entire procedure is then repeated seven times in all, beginning from the praise with the basic mantra, reciting the *Homages* once, and making the offerings; when this is all finished, the assembly concludes its marathon offerings and praises by reciting the "benefit" verses one time.

2.233 *Tormas*

2.2331 *The offering torma*

In a sense, all this is but preparation for the important ritual function that is now performed, for it is first of all in offering the tormas that the purpose of the rituals is achieved. Thus the first torma—the offering torma on the high altar—is given to the retinue headed by Tārā; and, while the altar server sprinkles water on it, the torma is empowered by the reciting of the visualization:

> From A above the torma is the orb of a moon, upon which is placed a green TĀṂ; light radiates forth therefrom, whereupon it serves the aim of beings and is gathered back in again. As it dissolves into the vessel, the vessel grows vast and broad, and as it dissolves in what the vessel contains, the torma of divine substance becomes nectar.

And this torma is empowered with the flying-bird gesture and OṂ ĀḤ HŪṂ, both repeated three times.

The tongues of the Holy Lady and her retinue generated in front are tubes of light; and therewith they accept the torma and are gladdened.

Seven times the assembly performs the torma gesture, each time reciting OṂ TĀRE TUTTĀRE TURE SVĀHĀ and the A-KĀRO mantra, and then they recite:

I give this torma, given in offering—this torma that is all that could be wished for, the source of all desires, an inexhaustible limitless great ocean of the nectar of knowledge—to my personal guru and the glorious and holy gurus of the lineage, to the twenty-one holy noble Tārās whose essence is compassion, to the high patron deities and their divine hosts of the maṇḍalas of the four classes of Tantra and the nine stages of the Tantric Vehicle, to the Buddhas and Bodhisattvas, to all the hosts of oath-bound guardians and protectors of the Law, outer and inner, who have vowed to protect the teachings and the four turnings of the Wheel of the Law, to the deities of wealth and lords of hidden treasure.

And having accepted it, I pray you pacify all conditions that form outer or inner obstacles. I pray you let us accomplish as we wish in accord with the Law all the aims of ourselves and our retinue. I pray you let there be perfected the two stocks in the streams of ourselves and all beings; let there be cleansed therein the two obscurations, and let us quickly attain the rank of Buddha.

NAMO! By the strength of my visualization,
by the strength of the gifts of the Tathāgatas,
by the strength of the Dharma realm;
let all the aims I have in mind,
all of them, of every sort,
all of them, in this worldly realm
occur without obstruction!

Here there is the crash of the music called "three beats," with the loud clash of cymbals in the rhythm x́ x́ x́ / x/ x́ x́ x́ / x x, as the altar server moves the offering torma before the image. And the assembly recites the first verse of the sevenfold office in the *Homages* ("I pay homage with complete sincerity . . ."), concluding with the mantra OṂ SARVA-TATHĀGATA-KĀYA-VĀK-CITTA-PRAṆĀMENA VAJRA-BANDHANAṂ KAROMI! "OṂ I make the diamond bond by paying homage to the body, speech, and mind of all the Tathāgatas!" Then they recite the second verse of the sevenfold office ("I give flowers, incense, lamps, perfumes . . ."), concluding with the mantras and gestures for the give gifts (OṂ VAJRA-PUṢPE ĀḤ HŪṂ . . . NAIVEDYE ĀḤ HŪṂ) and the mantra for offering the remaining offerings of umbrellas, ponds, banners, and so on (OṂ SARVA-VIŚIṢṬHA-PŪJA-MEGHA-PRASARA-SAMUDRE ĀḤ HŪṂ). Then they recite all the rest of the sevenfold office, from "I confess all that I have done . . ." through ". . . May I have the glory of being the leader . . . ," concluding with a final praise of the goddess, with such verses as "Holy blessed compassionate one . . ."

Then, finally, they join their palms at the level of their heads, and "with an undistracted mind" they recite the prayer that is the entire aim of the ritual, the climax toward which everything up to this point—the generation in front, the offerings, the praises—has been leading:

NAMO ! By the strength of the noble Three Jewels, by the strength of the spell, the mantra, and the vidyā, by the strength of the peaceful and fierce high patron deities, and especially by the strength of the twenty-one noble Tārās whose essence is compassion, by the strength of the oath-bound guardians and protectors of the Law who have vowed to guard and preserve the precious teachings, by the strength of the purity of Reality and of the inexorability of cause and effect in all events, and by the strength, the force, the might of my making vast offerings and expecting nothing in return:

all the evil schemes of harm by *lha* and *lu*, by ghouls, spirits, and flesh-eating demons, by polluters and demons of madness and forgetfulness, by their elders, male and female, by their sons and daughters, by their retinue, male and female, by their servants, by *mamo* demonesses and evil ḍākiṇīs, by all misleading demons, by king demons and demons of death, by *gongpo* and fliers in the sky, by *nyen* and *sadag*, by serpents and ogres and *nöjin*, by all ghosts, by *tsen* and *dü* and hungry spirits, by sages and those who hold the magic spells, by planets, constellations, years, months, days, and times, and by all the evil preparations of all the families of the great evil spirits and hindering demons:

may they be pacified ! may they not be ! nay they not arise ! may they promise to do them no more !

For this reason I give each of them what he desires, and I preach to them the true Law. For all of us—Master, disciples, and sponsors—may human disease, animal disease, bad dreams, evil

> omens, misfortune, maledictions, curses cast with the magic dagger, curses that incite the spirits, unlucky years, unlucky months, unlucky days, unlucky hours, bad harvests, great droughts, blight, frost, hail, thieves, the *si* of disease, the *si* of death, the *si* of adults, the *si* of children, the *si* of youth, the *si* of old age, the cemetery *si*, the *si* of loss, shame, slander, incitations, evil designs, all the hindering and misleading demons, all those who cause untimely death or the decrease of wealth and enjoyment, all those who cause misfortune, all those who harm the body, speech, or mind of us or our retinue, the evil spirits, hindering demons, obstacles, adverse conditions, and all the harms of enemies, demons, and shame:
>
> may they be pacified! may they not be! may they be averted! may they not arise hereafter!

Here the assembly claps their hands loudly three times, the sudden report ringing threateningly in the silent hall after the droning recitation, and they sound a blast of fierce music to drive away all these evil things. Then, as the piercing roar of the music dies down, they perform one further "act of truth" by reciting:

> By the strength of the truth of the Three Jewels and of the empowerment of all the Buddhas and Bodhisattvas, by the great might of the accumulation of the two stocks, by the strength of the purity of essence of the Dharma realm and of the inexorability of cause and effect in all events: may it be accomplished in that way!

2.2332 *The torma for the hindering demons*

The above is the first presentation of offerings, praises, and torma, and the ritual now returns to 2.231 to empower the offerings once again; these offerings are then presented afresh (this time with just the series of mantras and gestures, but ending with the final verse), and the *Homages* are again recited seven times (2.232), concluding with the benefit verses. Then the second torma—the torma for the hindering demons—is empowered as in 2.2331 with the visualization and OṂ ĀḤ HŪṂ, and it is presented by reciting the A-KĀRO mantra seven times, all with the appropriate gestures. And the assembly accompanies the presentation with the following prayer:

> I give this torma, inexhaustible as a space-vast treasury of all sublime desires, agreeable to each individual mind, to the 80,000 families of hindering demons, the fifteen great evil spirits of children, all the families of lords of disease, lords of epidemic, evil spirits, hindering demons and ghosts, to all the sentient beings included among the six destinies of beings, the five classes, the four birthplaces:

> may there arise and increase—in accord with their various wishes—endless enjoyment until this world is emptied out! may they all be freed from their sufferings, and have the opportunity quickly to attain the precious rank of omniscient Buddhahood! may all their enjoyments be inexhaustible as a space-vast treasury! may they be without contention and without injury! may they practice in self-sufficiency!

Then, as before, the assembly recites "NAMO! By the strength of my visualization . . . occur without obstruction!" again ending with the crash of music as the altar server moves the torma for the hindering demons in front of the thread-cross. And the assembly joins their palms at the level of their throats, and they recite once again the prayer "NAMO! By the strength of the noble Three Jewels . . .," interrupting as before with the clapping of their hands and the sound of the fierce music to expel evil, and continuing to ". . . may it be accomplished in that way!" This is the second presentation of offerings, praises, and torma.

2.2333 *The torma for the creditors*

Then again the ritual returns to 2.231 and 2.232, the offerings are empowered and presented, and the *Homages* are recited seven times and the benefit verses once; and the third torma—the torma for the creditors—is empowered as in 2.2331 with the visualization and OṂ ĀḤ HŪṂ, and presented with the A-KĀRO mantra three times, with the appropriate gestures. And this presentation is accompanied by the following prayer:

> I give this torma, given in offering—this torma sublime in form, sound, odor, taste, and touch, an inexhaustible enjoyment agreeable to each individual mind—to our creditors, to those who own malice toward our flesh, because we (Master and disciples, our retinue of supporters) have acted from our beginningless lives in this world to this very day under the sway of the three poisons of defilement, the five poisons: our creditors of poverty, because we robbed and stole from them; our creditors of disease and life, because we beat and tortured them; our creditors of a shortened life, because we killed them, murdered them, cut them to pieces; all our creditors of the past, whose high houses we cast down, whose low countries we conquered, whose men or horses we slew. All who are in the families of harmful ghosts, evil spirits, hindering demons, and creditors:
>
> may they be satisfied! may they be content! may all the creditors we have gathered through our beginningless lives be cleansed away! may our debt be canceled! may all we have injured in

> body or mind be pacified! may they be freed from their evil thoughts, ideas of harm, and spitefulness! may they have benefit and peace and the thought of enlightenment! may they have the opportunity quickly to attain the precious rank of omniscient Buddhahood! may all their enjoyments be inexhaustible as a space-vast treasury! they may be without contention and without injury! may they practice in self-sufficiency!

Then, as before, the assembly recites "NAMO! By the strength of my visualization . . ."and then fills the hall with music as the altar server moves the torma for the creditors in front of the thread-cross. And the assembly joins their palms at the level of their breasts, and they recite once again the prayer "NAMO! By the strength of the noble Three Jewels . . . ," clapping their hands and sounding the fierce music, and ending with " . . . may it be accomplished in that way!" This is the third presentation of offerings, praises, and torma.

2.2334 *The white torma*

This concludes the offerings and prayers whose function it is to avert the evil spirits and calamities that threaten the patron, but there is yet one more ritual function to be performed: the fourth torma—the white torma—is presented to the lords of the soil that they may "clear the road for the thread-cross." Here, too, there may be presented the "golden libation," and the ceremony may be expanded by the addition of any of the numerous white torma rituals which are composed and printed separately. But in the abridged presentation of our text, the white torma is empowered with the visualization and OṂ ĀḤ HŪṂ (as in 2.2331) and presented by reciting the A-KĀRO mantra three times, with the appropriate gestures; then the lords of the soil are given the gift of the Law with the words "Commit no sins . . ." (p. 221), and the assembly recites:

> I give this vast, great torma, given in offering, to the inherent dwellers of the place, the lords of the place, the lords of the soil, the lords of the land, the lords of the village. May you spread the Buddha's teachings, and let virtue become great in the world! May you pacify the adverse conditions and obstructions of us all, Master and diciples, our sponsor and his retinue, may you be to us a friend, that we may accomplish our plans as we wish in accord with the Law!

And the tormas for the lords of the soil are carried outside the assembly hall and thrown down the road in the direction the thread-cross will be carried.

2.24 *Dispatching the substitutes*

2.241 *Empowering*

This much of the ritual had occupied the entire morning, and the assembly now dispersed to eat the lunch we had provided for them. The afternoon portion of the ritual then began with added prayers and torma offerings to the fierce and potent monastic protectors, the "four-handed Lord" and the glorious Goddess "Smoke-eater." Then the assembly returned to the text for the climax of the entire protective ritual, the creation of the "appearance" of the thread-cross and of its substitutes, and the presentation of these to the evil spirits.

If the torma offering and its accompanying prayer constitute a ritual function, this portion of the ritual is a magical function in the sense I have defined the term: it is a ceremonial application of visualization and recitation, an employment of the divine power. Here, then, the thread-cross is first empowered with what are called the "six mantras and six gestures," a standard series used especially in the contemplative generation from Emptiness of ransoms or substitutes (see fig. 41).

2.2411 *The purity of the Dharma realm*

For the first of these six steps in the process of creating the appearance of the thread-cross, the altar server sprinkles the thread-cross with pure water as the assembly recites:

> From the white syllable A of the gesture
> whose essence is the blessed Śākyamuni
> light radiates forth, cleansing the substance of the torma
> of the stain of holding it to be real: it becomes Empty.

The assembly binds the purity-of-the-Dharma-realm gesture and recites the corresponding mantra: OṂ SVABHĀVA-ŚUDDHĀḤ SARVA-DHARMĀḤ SVABHĀVA-ŚUDDHO 'HAṂ! This is repeated three times, unbinding the gestures and snapping the fingers after each recitation. Then the assembly continues:

> By the truth of the gesture,
> of the mantra, and of the deep contemplation
> of the purity of the Dharma realm,
> may the substance of the torma be purified
> of its ugliness, dirt, pollution, and faults,
> of the stain of clinging to labels!

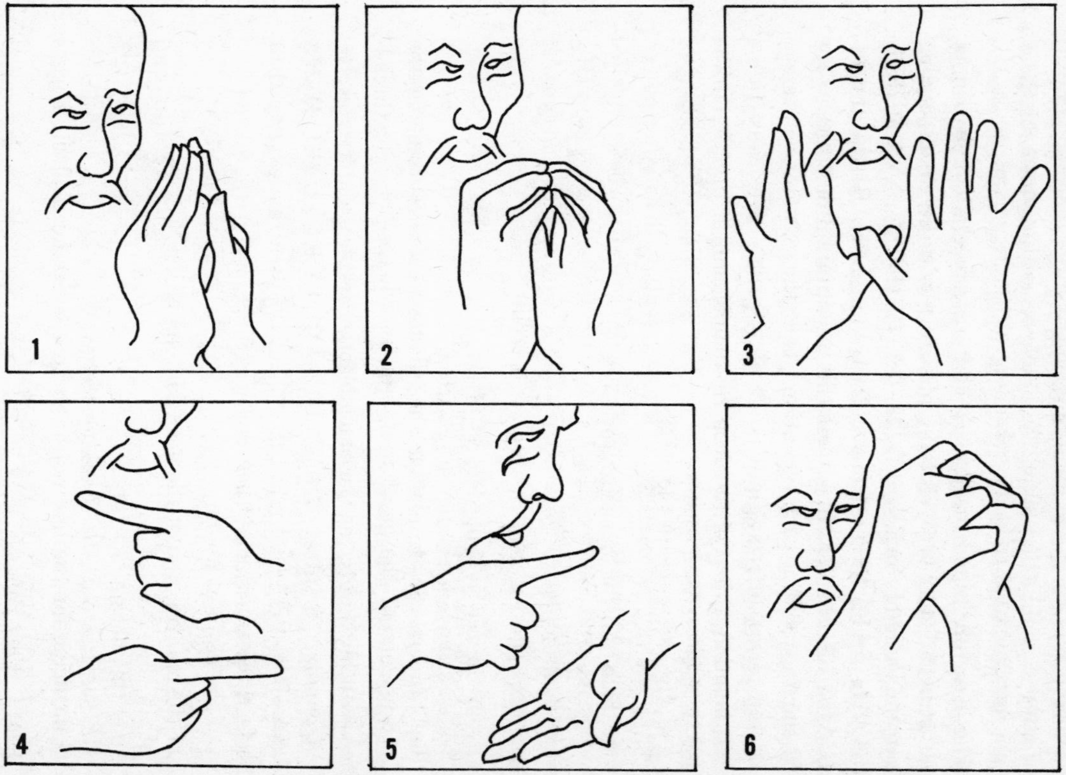

Fig. 41. The six gestures that generate the substitutes.

2.2412 *The space-vast treasury*

Then the second step of the process is recited:

From the blue syllable KHAṂ of the gesture
whose essence is the blessed Vairocana
light radiates forth, making the substance of the torma
an inexhaustible treasury pervading all the realms of space.

The assembly binds the jeweled-casket gesture and moves it in a circle between their eyebrows, as they recite the corresponding mantra: NAMAḤ SARVA-TATHĀGATEBHYO VIŚVA-MUKH-EBHYAḤ SARVATHĀ-KHAṂ UDGATE SPHARAṆA IMAṂ GAGANA-KHAṂ SVĀHĀ! Again this is repeated three times, snapping the fingers after each recitation. Then the assembly continues:

By the truth of the gesture,
of the mantra, and of the deep contemplation
of the space-vast treasury,
may the substance of the torma
grow great and fill the sky,
inexhaustible for an entire world era!

2.2413 *Swirling Nectar*

Then the third step of the process is recited:

From the red syllable HRĪḤ of the gesture
whose essence is the blessed Swirling Nectar
light radiates forth, making the substance of the torma
the essence of the great nectar of knowledge.

The assembly binds the Swirling Nectar gesture and recites the corresponding mantra: OṂ VAJRA-AMṚTA-KUṆḌALI HANA HANA HŪṂ PHAṬ! Again they repeat the mantra and snap their fingers three times, and they continue:

By the truth of the gesture,
of the mantra, and of the deep contemplation
of Swirling Nectar,
may this become nectar,
the substance of the five knowledges,
a medicine for the five poisons whose substance is death!

2.2414 *Vast potency*

Then the fourth step of the process is recited:

From the yellow syllable TRĀṂ of the gesture
whose essence is the blessed Ratnasambhava
light radiates forth, making the substances of the torma
the five sense gratifications according to each one's desires.

The assembly binds the vast-potency gesture, their right hands pointing toward the thread-cross and their left hands over their hearts, and they recite the corresponding mantra: NAMAḤ SARVA-TATHĀGATA-AVALOKITE OṂ SAMBHARA SAMBHARA HŪṂ! Again they unbind the gesture and snap their fingers after each of the three recitations, and they continue:

> By the truth of the gesture,
> of the mantra, and of the deep contemplation
> of vast potency,
> may there fall a rain
> of the various sense gratifications,
> satisfying the fields of the senses!

2.2415 *The comet of knowledge*

Then the fifth step of the process is recited:

> From the green syllable HA of the gesture
> whose essence is the blessed Amoghasiddhi
> light radiates forth, eliminating contention
> according to the better or worse karma of each.

The assembly binds the comet-of-knowledge gesture, their left hands in the gift-bestowing gesture as if they were holding up a vessel, and they recite the corresponding mantra:

OṂ JÑĀNA-AVALOKITE SAMANTA-SPHARAṆA-RAŚMI-BHAVA-SAMAYA-MAHĀMAṆI DURU DURU HṚDAYA-JVA-LANI HŪṂ! "OṂ Looking down with knowledge! Great gem, gathering of splendor spreading everywhere! Burn, burn, blazing heart HŪṂ!"

Again they repeat the mantra and snap their fingers three times, and they continue:

> By the truth of the gesture,
> of the mantra, and of the deep contemplation
> of the comet of knowledge,
> may there be no contention
> among winners and losers,
> may they be happy and all their hopes fulfilled!

2.2416 *Universal sovereignty*

And, finally, the sixth step in this process of creation and empowerment is recited to summon the guests:

> From the red syllable JAḤ of the gesture
> whose essence is the blessed Bearer of the Vajra
> light radiates forth, subjugating the guests
> and accomplishing any active function we desire.

The assembly binds the universal-sovereignty gesture to symbolize this control and summoning of the spirits, moving it in a circle at the tops of their heads as they recite the corresponding mantra:

> NAMAḤ SAMANTA-BUDDHĀNĀṂ GRAHÊŚVARA-PRABHĀ-JYOTENA MAHĀSAMAYE SVĀHĀ! "Homage to all the Buddhas! By the blazing light of the master over the evil spirits, a great assembly SVĀHĀ!"

And again this is repeated three times, snapping the fingers after each recitation. And they continue:

> By the truth of the gesture,
> of the mantra, and of the deep contemplation
> of universal sovereignty,
> may we subjugate all the families of guests
> that they may be friends to accomplish
> whatever we entrust to them!

And then they empower the entire structure once more "by the strength of truth," as they recite:

> NAMO! By the strength of my visualization,
> by the strength of the gifts of the Tathāgatas,
> by the strength of the Dharma realm,
> that we may entice our guests and creditors
> and give benefit to all beings,
> let all the aims I have in mind,
> all of them, of every sort,
> all of them, in this worldly realm
> occur without obstruction!

2.242 *Presentation*

The assembly here performs an extra and separate special visualization before presenting the thread-cross and its substitutes to the spirits. While the altar server sprinkles the "excellent house" on top of Mount Meru, the assembly cleanses it with the AMṚTA mantra and purifies it with the SVABHĀVA mantra, and then they re-create it as follows:

> I visualize before me a four-tiered Mount Meru made of precious gems, the house in the middle, encircled by the surrounding iron mountains; and upon the tiers of Mount Meru are inexhaustible enjoyments of the five sense gratifications, substances agreeable to the pleasure of each one of our guests, pervading all the earth and sky and space between.

Then they present this doubly visualized and empowered creation by reciting again the SAMBHARA mantra seven times—the burning-mouth mantra that "maintains" the hungry ghosts—and then continuing:

> Homage to the blessed Tathāgata Many Jewels! Homage to the blessed Tathāgata Holy Beauty! Homage to the blessed Tathāgata Abyss of Vast Body! Homage to the blessed Tathāgata Free of All Terror!
>
> Through the strength of this mantra and the empowerment of reciting your names, O Tathāgatas, and paying homage to you, by the strength of our performing this great vast thread-cross and torma with no hope of personal profit:
>
> may all the families of guests be satisfied and gladdened! may we accomplish as we wish in accord with the Law all the aims we have in mind for ourselves and others!

Then, for the purpose of dispatching the thread-cross and expelling the evil spirits, the assembly instantaneously generates themselves as the fierce high patron deity—Hayagrīva, the fierce horse-headed patron of the Padma Family:

> Instantaneously I become the Blessed Lotus Lord, his body colored red, having one face and two hands, with his right hand brandishing in the sky a cudgel of khadira wood and his left hand in the threatening gesture upon his breast. His three round eyes gape and stare, his mouth bares four fangs; his eyebrows and beard are red-yellow, blazing like the fire at the end of time; his hair is pale yellow, bristling upward, and on his crest is a green horse head, whinnying. He is adorned with the eight great serpent-kings, his lower garment is a tiger skin, he stands with his right foot drawn in and his left stretched out, in the center of a mass of blazing fire of knowledge: my body is unrivaled in majesty, to burn spiteful bringers of harm and all sins and obscurations,
>
> Tārā and her retinue generated before me are there as mediators; as I present the substitutes and speak the words to avert the evil spirits, they perform their active functions, that all the guests obey, and the active function is quickly accomplished.

Then the assembly sounds forth the complex cymbal rolls of the "inviting music," and as the roar of the instruments dies down the great drum begins its steady and syncopated rhythm, and they sing the following verses to an archaic and moving melody which recalls the oldest streams of Tibetan music:

HŪṂ! Listen and think of me! all of you hear me!
All the gurus of the lineage, my personal guru:
today I pray you avert!
All the divine hosts of the high patron deities:
today I pray you avert!
All the holy noble Tārās:
today I pray you avert!
Everything that is evil,
avert it quickly! make it not be!
Oath-bound guardians and protectors of the Law:
here perform the function entrusted to you!
Take this thread-cross, the tormas,
the substitutes given in offering,
bear them away and do no harm!
The eight classes of gods and ogres in the world:
listen to my voice, I who hold the mantra,
do not listen to the instigations of others:
you great evil spirits and hindering demons,
pacify your evil schemes!
The tormas that you want,
these many substitutes for life and wealth,
things of the mountain passes,
things of the valleys,
all your desires,
the beautiful turreted house,
the beautiful great swift stallion,
the great mounted portrait of grain,
bearing ornaments of gold and turquoise,
the beautiful ornaments *silili*!
wearing clothes of silk *lhubselhub*!
wise in speech, his face clear and broad,
riding a horse beneath him *zhungsezhung*!
wearing a hat on his head *pururu*!
wise in all the arts of play,
the little boots of turquoise *zululu*!
the girdle of gold *tr'ululu*!
his body adorned with "space," tablets, images,
the "male face" and "female face,"
speaking with human speech,
the arrows, the cloth, all your desires,
we offer to you as a substitute
for the owner of this fee!
There the many beautiful treasures,
the food of nine flavors, of ten sweetnesses,
his retinue of servants, the thirty little men,
the medicine, the incense, the bright lamps,
we give to you in offering!
Accept this with a willing mind

and avert, turn back the strength
of the magicians
who roll the magic dagger between their palms,
who fling white mustard seed as magic,
who cast their magic weapons,
who prepare for destructive magic!

Here there roars forth the music of the three beats, and the rhythm of the song changes slightly as the drum again picks up its insistent beat:

The black Bön who beat the magic drum,
who hold the whirring blue-red slingshot,
who cause the sin of strife:
avert them!
Those who practice the sorcery of fierce mantras,
who incite the ferocity of the eight classes:
avert them! turn back their strength!
All the protectors of the Law,
the gods and demons:
some follow on the track of our property,
some come as executioners of eaters of oaths,
some are incited to ferocity by magicians,
some wish to teach us how deeds bring results,
some send fevers and pestilences
or send the bad years when no rain falls
or send the frost and hail;
creditors pursuing their debt,
following on the track of relatives and friends,
serpents who send leprosy,
harmful spirits, creditors, gods and demons,
eaters of flesh and blood and breath,
eaters of our fruits and harvests,
eaters of polluted mucus,
gods of the elements, owners of the earth,
the twelve animals of the cycle of years,
the eight trigrams,
the nine numbers of the magic square:
may they all be pleased with these substitutes!
pacify your harm and evil!
We entrust our creditors:
wipe clean our debts!
let our enjoyments increase!
I pray you avert the maledictions
that incite the evil spirits!

Now the beat of the drum grows faster as the song nears its climax:

Let us attain the aims we desire!
Preach the holy Law
with the strength of compassion;

you too wander lost in this world,
awaken now the thought of enlightenment!
Arise as an example in your own person,
inflict no harm on others,
aspire to the path of freedom,
the cleansing of obscuration!
Look upon your stream:
ungrasping, unmoving,
your innate mind
is the self-absorption of the Dharma Body!
Pacify your fevers and pestilences
in the inner realm of Emptiness and compassion.
Let the years be good, send the rain in season!
Let us all, yogins and our retinue,
avert the vindictive enemies of the past,
the barbarous enemies of the present,
the foreign enemies mobilized against us,
avert the eighty-one sudden calamities,
avert the 360 afflictions,
avert the 440 diseases,
avert the 80,000 hindering demons.
I pray you avert them all, every one:
the deceit of the upper *dü*,
the awakening of the *damsi*,
the lower *dü*, the mother-ancestors,
the demons who follow behind,
the demons who bring shame to a mother and her son,
vindictive enemies and hurtful hindering demons:
I pray you avert them!
Avert evil years, months, days, and times,
I pray you avert all demons of decay,
I pray you avert all demons of hunger,
I pray you avert malice to our sons,
I pray you avert evil spirits of our children,
I pray you avert evil spirits of our cattle!
Do not send gossip and slander,
pacify the battle array of others,
make good our means of battle,
pacify our enemies, thieves and robbers,
dispel our confusion and darkness,
pacify all epidemics,
of one day or two, of three or seven,
avert terror and persecution!
This moment I pray you avert
all the families of savage evil;
I pray you let us be virtuous,
I pray you spread the Law,
I pray you pacify contention,

I pray you let us live a hundred years,
I pray you let us see a hundred Teachers!
Grant us the firm mountain of good fortune
and the sunlit sky of merit;
grant us, full and unshaken, the magical attainments!

Here once again the music of three beats is sounded, and the steady beat of the drum begins again as the assembly returns to the beginning of the song and sings it through in its entirety twice more. Then the thread-cross is finally dispatched or "sent on its way," and there may be inserted an additional offering of a white torma and golden libation for the lords of the soil, just to be certain that the "road is cleared."

2.25 *Averting with the strength of truth*

Thus, as the thread-cross is lifted into the air, they recite once again the prayer that expresses the central theme of the ritual: they "avert with the strength of truth," keeping firm the ego of the patron deity—with Tārā and her retinue again as mediators—and reciting "NAMO! By the strength of the noble Three Jewels . . ." through ". . . may they not arise hereafter!" And to this they add:

The magicians who roll the magic dagger between their palms, who fling white mustard seed as a magic substance, who perform destructive magic with magic weapons: avert them! turn back their strength upon them!

The black Bön who beat the great drum, who fling the whirring blue-red slingshot, who beat upon pots, who practice the sorcery of fierce mantras, who incite the ferocity of the eight classes: avert them! turn back their strength upon them!

The protectors of the Law, the gods and demons, who follow on the track of our property, who come as executioners of eaters of oaths, who have been incited to ferocity by magicians, who wish to teach us how in truth our deeds bring results, who send fevers and pestilences, who send the great drought when no rain falls, who send the years of bad harvest, frost, and hail, creditors pursuing their debt, following on the tracks of relatives and friends, who send the diseases of the serpent-kings, leprosy and scabies: avert them! turn back their strength upon them!

Those who steal our flesh, our blood, our life's breath, seeking the chance for harm, furious-minded, the savage dangers of the years, months, days, times, the eight trigrams and the nine numbers of the magic square, weakening our life-power or our life-object, exhausting our body, our fortune, our fate: avert them all, I pray you!

The pestilences that spread like fire, the evil omens that cover like darkness, the evil signs we see in dreams: avert them all, I pray you!

The 440 families of disease, the 80,000 families of hindering demons: avert them all, I pray you!

The harms of the eighty-one sudden calamities: avert them all, I pray you!

The fifteen great evil spirits of children, the harms of the upper *dü* and king demons, the harms of the lower *dü* and demonesses, the harms of the *damlog* and *damsi*, the father-ancestors, the demons who follow behind, the demons who bring shame to a mother and her son, the inauspicious years that end in the number nine, the inauspicious years when a death has occured, the evil directions, the slaying *dü*, the vicious enemies, the harmful ones: avert them all, I pray you!

The evil dangers of years, months, days, and times, the demons of decay, the *si* of decay, the *si* of poverty, the *serag*, the misleading demons, the *gongpo*, the loss of cattle: avert them all, I pray you!

The ambush upon our prosperity, the raid upon our dominion, the wars, the thieves, the afflictions: avert them all, I pray you!

The darkening and clouding of our memory, the sending of gossip and slander, the evil omens of the day and the bad dreams of the night: avert them all, I pray you!

The shameful conditions of this life, the demons who hinder the accomplishment of the holy Law, the adverse conditions and obstacles that harm us on the path hereafter: avert them all, I pray you!

In brief, anything that arises to us as any sort of bad fortune, the enemies, the harms, the evil thoughts, the savage plans, the spread of evil, the planting of the magic dagger, the leading into perverted views: turn them back this moment! avert them!

For us and for our retinue, I pray you increase—like the waxing moon, miraculously, effortlessly—all the infinite qualities of good!

Here there crashes forth the roll of the cymbals and the fierce music, and beneath its roar the assembly recites the fierce mantras: MĀRAYA MĀRAYA HŪṂ PHAṬ HŪṂ PHAṬ! or OṂ SUMBHANI SUMBHA HŪṂ HŪṂ PHAṬ! OṂ GṚHṆA GṚHṆA HŪṂ HŪṂ PHAṬ! OṂ GṚHṆĀPAYA GṚHṆĀPAYA HŪṂ HŪṂ PHAṬ! OṂ ĀNAYA HOḤ BHAGAVAN VAJRA HŪṂ HŪṂ PHAṬ!

As the music and the mantras reverberate through the hall, a group of willing monks and lay people carry the thread-cross, the tormas that were placed before it, and the substitutes it contains outside the assembly hall to the place where it will be thrown away, shouting fierce cries that the "gate for the 'transferring of danger' may be opened": the thread-cross may be thrown over a cliff (as in our case) or left at a crossroads; it may be carried in the direction of the disease or curse or demon that is to be averted; to cause rain to fall in a great drought it may be thrown into a stream or left on the shore of a lake. And while the thread-cross is thus being dispatched, the assembly enters for a moment into the nonobjectifiable, the realm wherein there is neither one who averts nor that which is averted; then they perform their final act of truth by reciting once again:

> By the strength of the truth of the Three Jewels and of the empowerment of all the Buddhas and Bodhisattvas, by the great might of the accumulation of the two stocks, by the strength of the purity of essence of the Dharma realm and of the inexorability of cause and effect in all events: may it be accomplished in that way!

And then, as a final guarantee of security, they "block the return of the danger" by reciting the visualization:

> Emanated from the fierce deity of knowledge is a *garuḍa* bird, blazing blue-black, his face turned gazing away, blocking the return of the ghosts, and they may never be free to follow us back.

And they erect the circle of protection:

> OṂ VAJRA RAKṢA RAKṢA HŪṂ PHAṬ! There is a diamond ground, fence, lattice, tent, and canopy: firm and strong, a pavilion of weapons pointing outward, blazing with the fire of knowledge, the sound of fierce mantras swirling like dust, that it could not be moved even by the wind at the end of the world.
>
> I visualize that within this protective circle all of us, the person to be protected and his retinue, are sheltered beneath the gestures of refuge of Tārā and her retinue, generated before us; thus are we victorious over all misfortune, all hindering demons and obstacles.

3 *Concluding acts*

After the end of the main body of the ritual, the assembly performs the various concluding acts: they once again empower the offerings (as in 2.231) and present them with the full complement of verses, mantras, and gestures, they recite the *Homages* with the benefit verses, ending with the sevenfold office, and they make a final prayer:

OṂ! May it be accomplished! Holy compassionate one,
by the strength of our ritual service
and evocation of the Noble Lady,
our offerings, praises, and prayer:
from this day onward until we gain enlightenment,
Noble Lady, may we never be separated from you.
Let there increase life without illness, power and enjoyment,
let there be no obstacle to the attaining of enlightenment!
Let us perfect the qualities of the stages and the path
and attain omniscient perfect Buddhahood,
to accomplish at once the aims of ourselves and others.

They make up the deficiencies in the performance by reciting the 100-syllable mantra three times, and they pray for the deity's forbearance toward any errors in or omissions from the ritual:

If something were not at hand, or defiled,
or if we performed or manipulated
with a mind clouded over:
may our lord be forbearing toward it all!

If our deep contemplation was not vivid because we were under the sway of the defiled thoughts of ordinary people, if we were under the sway of drowsiness or distraction, if the utensils lacked power, the substances for offering too few or impure, our cleanliness incomplete, if we were unable to follow the ritual—I pray you noble and compassionate ones be forbearing toward all the faults we have committed. I pray you, right now, empower us that our obscurations may arise no more.

And they conclude with an earnest wish:

By this merit may all beings
be like the holy Tārā;
and may we too, by accomplishing this deep contemplation,
gain Buddhahood for the sake of beings.

Then, if there is no basis or support—that is, a painting or image—for the generation in front, the assembly forms the asking-to-depart gesture; and they pray that the knowledge being leave, with the verse and mantra "OṂ! You have served the aim of all beings . . . . OṂ VAJRA MUḤ!" and they gather in the symbolic being to themselves with OṂ ĀḤ HŪṂ! But when there is a "basis," and especially an image, they establish the knowledge being therein:

"Let the invited knowledge being be established in the basis, and I pray that it grant to all beings, headed by our patron, all the highest and ordinary magical attainments." And as they fling grain upon the image, they guard the three gates of its body, speech, and mind: "It becomes marked on the top of its head with OṂ, on its throat with ĀḤ, and on its heart with HŪṂ." They recite the final benediction, the verses of good fortune, and "let fall a rain of flowers."

As a final word, let us quote what our author says in the colophon to his ritual: "In general, just by bearing in mind the name of the holy Tārā one is preserved from all terrors and averts all obstacles; especially is she the supreme deity and single protector of those who follow the Great Vehicle, the hereditary deity of the Snowy Land of Tibet, the swiftest empowerment in these degenerate times. Thus if one strives in this, rather than in the trifling rituals of transferring the danger which are associated with the doctrines of the Bön, then will one easily accomplish hereafter the great aims of oneself and others."[117]

III

ACQUISITION

Initiation and Ritual Service

I am not resigned to the shutting
away of loving hearts in the
hard ground.
So it is, and so it will be, for
so it has been, time out of
mind:
Into the darkness they go, the
wise and the lovely.
Crowned with lilies and with
laurel they go; but I am not
resigned.

. . . Down, down, down into the
darkness of the grave
Gently they go, the beautiful,
the tender, the kind;
Quietly they go, the intelligent,
the witty, the brave.
I know. But I don't approve.
And I am not resigned.

—*Edna St. Vincent Millay,*
DIRGE WITHOUT MUSIC

THE POWER OF LIFE

We have seen in chapter ii the various ways in which the divine power can be directed and used, once it has been acquired by the practitioner. And the axiom of acquisition is this: a power must always be received first from some holy person who possesses it. Thus the primary transmission of power is inevitably a magical operation performed upon the recipient by his Master; the power of contemplation is acquired first through another and then through oneself as the deity, for the initiation must empower the young contemplative as a fit vessel for the divinity he achieves in the ritual service. "The initiation is the basis of the magical attainments," says Tsongk'apa. "If one does not have it, then however much one may persevere upon the path it is impossible to gain the special magical attainments."[1]

The ability to live long is also a power, a magical attainment whose transmission and acquisition are structurally the same as those of any other power. But its transmission is not limited to those who are setting out upon the path of contemplation; the lives of great lamas are filled with requests to bestow the power of long life upon their followers, both monk and lay. We are now in a position to understand the means of this magical transmission, but we should first investigate the notion of "long life" in Tibetan culture and examine the signs that prophesy its loss.

THE VALUE OF LIFE

We have already noted that it was Vāgīśvarakīrti[2] who conceived White Tārā in the specialized function of cheating death. Though she was thus linked to one particular function from the beginning, her activities were soon expanded to cover the entire range of pacifying, increasing, and subjugating, toward all of which ends her

Fig. 42. White Tārā. From an iconographic sketch by Tendzin yongdü.

rituals may be used. But all commentators are agreed that it is primarily as a goddess of life that she is called upon; among the boons for which the Tibetans pray their deities, or the magical attainments they hope to gain from contemplation, perhaps none is more frequent, next to enlightenment itself, than length of life.

> Now that I have obtained the jewel of human birth on this path of despair and hope, the many births of this beginningless world, let me cling fast to the benefits of what is hard to obtain, whatever the causes and conditions, and bind myself to the Law whose aim is certain and whose counsel is unerring.

> The world of animate and inanimate objects is conditioned, and its substance is impermanence: if death is certain, when will I be without death? If the time of death should appear now, nothing would be of any use; thus let me put forth striving and disgust at the world, for in this life there is no time to spare.[3]

Human life, to the Tibetans, is not only precarious—threatened on all sides and easily terminated by their harsh environment or the malevolent actions of men or spirits—but also infinitely precious, for it is only in this human body that progress can be made toward the ultimate goal of Buddhahood. Thus the hard-won human condition, with its opportunity to hear the holy Law, is called the life of "quietude and benefit":[4]

> We must strive to avoid birth in this world, whose sufferings are hard to endure, but the only basis for achieving this end is our human body. And since we have but this one chance which is hard to obtain, we should single-mindedly yearn to get the utmost use of it, come what may . . . .
>
> If one is born in the three evil destinies—hell beings, hungry ghosts, or animals—then one's burden of suffering is so fierce and one's body is so very vile that this condition is adverse to the Law. And the gods of the Realm of Desire are so avid for sense gratification that their minds are inattentive and their sorrows are few; the gods of the Realm of Form or the Realm without Form are for the most part continually so intoxicated with deep contemplation that these conditions too are adverse to the Law.
>
> If one is born in a worldly realm where a Buddha has not come, or in a place empty of Buddhas; or if one is born in a barbarian border country where, though a Buddha has come, the Law has not spread; or if one is born in a place where the Law has spread, yet one holds perverted views that there are no former lives, no karma and its effects, and no Three Jewels; or if one is born so stupid that one does not understand what should be accepted or rejected, so that one has no idea what to begin or avoid—all these make up the eight adverse conditions. Thus the three evil destinies and the long-lived gods are the nonhuman adverse conditions, and the remaining four are the human adverse conditions. . . . To be free of all these eight adverse conditions is called *quietude*. . . .
>
> The ten items under *benefit* include first the five personal benefits: . . . to have gained a human body; to have been born in a place where the Law has spread, particularly the Middle Country; to be complete in all five sense faculties, so that one is able to know what should be accepted or rejected; not to have committed the five sins of immediate retribution or to have incited their commission; and to have faith in the teachings of the Buddha. . . . These five are the prerequisite conditions for practicing the Law which are part of one's own stream, and hence they are called

personal benefits. These five personal benefits, further, have the same import as the quietude that is the opposite of the eight adverse conditions.

The five environmental benefits are as follows: . . . the advent in the world of a Buddha; his preaching the Holy Law; the continuance and stability of its doctrines; the existence of many others who believe in the doctrine; and the existence of many who are willing to provide, out of the kindness of their hearts, the requisites of food, clothing, and so on to those who practice the Law. This last item is also interpreted as "love of others," that is, the existence of virtuous friends who, out of love, lead others to the Law. These five are the prerequisite conditions for practicing the Law which are part of the streams of others, and hence they are called enviromental benefits. . . .

Here, quietude is the essential thing, and the benefits are special items thereof. Thus a body like ours, complete with all eighteen items of quietude and benefit, is exceedingly difficult to obtain; hence we should single-mindedly concentrate on the necessity of using this opportunity to strive in the Law.

Thus we see that human life—especially in Tibet, where the doctrine flourished and the environmental benefits were great—is considered a unique concatenation of opportunities whose loss should not be taken lightly. This goes even beyond the fact that they

. . . do not love the fluttering breath,
The obscene shudder of the finished act—
What the doe feels when the ultimate fact
Tears at her bowels with its jaws.
—Archibald MacLeish, *Hypocrite Auteur*

But death to the Tibetans represents most of all a loss of opportunity, a chance for spiritual advancement and the accumulation of merit which may not be repeated for millions of years, in addition to the keenly felt loss of the simple pleasures of this life. It is interesting to note that the earliest Indian medical texts give exactly the same reasons for the nobility of a physician who preserves human life. "There is no greater gift," says Caraka, "than the gift of life."[5] The *Aṣṭâṅgahṛdaya* says: "Life is to be desired, for thereon depends the performance of duty and the attainment of success and happiness."[6] And in another chapter of his *Saṃhitā*, Caraka says:[7]

There are three goals, considered to be of benefit in this world and the next, for which one should strive: these are the goal of life, the goal of wealth, and otherworldly goals. Among these goals, one should obtain as foremost of all the goal of life. Why is that? Because when life is lost, all is lost.

THE SIGNS OF DEATH

The Tibetans are constantly aware of the fragility of man's hold on life, and this awareness has led to the formulation of an entire science of death, the interpretation of signs of the decay of life, and the creation of rituals to deal with its causes. This is not morbid, but simply the exercise of reasonable forethought, and indeed these same topics were included in the curriculum of ancient Indian medicine; we read in Arunadatta's *Sarvâṇgasundara* commentary on Vāgbhāṭa's *Aṣṭâṇghṛdaya* that the science of medicine consists not only of a knowledge of the body and of chemistry but also of the interpretation of omens and the signs of approaching death.[8] The Tibetans know, as good Buddhists, that their term of life inevitably comes to an end; the great terror lies in untimely death, the snatching away of life before its appointed end, a tragedy of waste, an "auto wreck":

> Already old, the question Who shall die?
> Becomes unspoken Who is innocent?
> For death in war is done by hands;
> Suicide has cause and stillbirth, logic.
> But this invites the occult mind,
> Cancels our physics with a sneer,
> And spatters all we knew of denouement
> Across the expedient and wicked stones.
> —Karl Shapiro, *Auto Wreck*

Thus the search for causes extends beyond the range of the simply inevitable, and all the texts that deal with death seek the signs of its approach as well as the means of avoiding it. The basic Indian texts for the cult of White Tārā, Vāgīśvarakīrti's cycle on *Cheating Death*, contain an entire chapter devoted to the signs of approaching dissolution and decay of life. Among the works included in the cycle of the *Bardo t'ödrö*—the so-called Tibetan Book of the Dead—there is an entire text devoted to the subject. Therein we read:[9]

> Alas! This feeble and illusory lump of form!
> Created from causes and conditioned things,
> like a windblown lamp, it cannot be permanent;
> there is nothing that cannot be a cause of death,
> there is never a time when there is no death.
> Always, death is certain, so strive in virtue.
> There are two conditions for the death of a human being:
> untimely death and death when life is exhausted.

If one offers a substitute for untimely and sudden death
it can be averted;
but death when life is exhausted
is like a lamp whose oil is used up:
there is no way to avert it with a substitute
so one should prepare to depart.

Another text gives a slightly differing account:[10]

There are three conditions for untimely death: the exhaustion of one's life, of one's karma, or of one's merit. If one's life is exhausted, one should be cured through a long-life ritual. If one's karma is exhausted, one should be cured through the recitation of a ransom for one's life. If one's merit is exhausted, one should be cured through the giving of offerings [to accumulate more merit]. The following are some of the conditions for the decay of life which may be cured by these means:

Broken vows, distracted mind, quarrels and panic,
being destroyed by demons incited to fierce anger,
breaking one's vows of body, speech, or mind,
dwelling in evil places:
these are when life decays,
panting with fear under the sway of hindering demons.

In any event, the *Bardo t'ödrö* text continues, the signs of death are of the utmost importance. It divides these signs into six classes: (1) external, (2) internal, (3) secret, (4) distant, (5) near, and (6) miscellaneous. Here are a few samples from each category.[11]

The external signs are the signs of death which appear on the body, for "before this body, composed of the four elements, is destroyed, there occur certain premonitory omens." Thus, if one loses one's appetite, if one's sense faculties become unclear, if one is consumed by burning pain in body, speech, or mind, if one's thoughts become unsteady or sad, if one's dreams are disturbed, or if the color of one's flesh fades—all these are omens that impediments to life have arisen.

There are also omens that give warning of inevitable death: if one's fingernails and toenails become bloodless and lusterless, one will die in nine months; if one's eyes become clouded over, one will die in five months; if the hair on the nape of one's neck grows upward instead of downward, one will die in three months. The text gives a long list of such signs: if one urinates, defecates, and sneezes simultaneously, it says, this is a sign of death; if one's urine falls in two forks, if one's excrement is loose and flowing, if one urinates and defecates during sexual orgasm, if one becomes pale or hoarse, if one no longer perceives or misjudges the perception of forms, sounds, smells, tastes, and tangibles—"these are signs that one has been delivered into the hands of the Lord of Death."

When one presses one's eyes with one's fingers, luminous circles appear, and these too can be interpreted as pointing to the time one will die: if they do not appear at the bottom of the left eye, one will die after six months; if they do not appear at the top, one will die after three months; if they do not appear on the side of the nose, one will die after one month; if they do not appear at the side of the ear, one will die after two months. Similarly for the right eye: if the luminous circles do not appear at the bottom, one will die after ten days; if they do not appear at the top, one will die after five days; if they do not appear at the side of the ear, one will die after three days; if they do not appear at the side of the nose, one will die after two days, "even if one is not sick." A similar interpretation is made of the buzzing sound heard when the ears are stopped up with the fingers.

Finally, there are external signs that are basically emotional: if one is fierce and angry, if one feels terror and panic wherever one may be, if one loses one's faith and devotion, if one hates holy personages, if one is unhappy wherever one may be and wishes to go elsewhere, if one wishes to avoid the company of people who are in accord with the Law, if one delights in the distractions and amusements of this world, if one feels great lust, hatred, pride, or jealousy—"these are signs that one has been placed in the hands of the Lord of Death."

Second, there are two different types of internal signs of approaching death, discovered through the interpretation of breathing and through the interpretation of dreams. Thus, for instance, one should take a full day and night as one unit of time and determine the basic pattern of one's breath: on the first day of the month, beginning at daybreak, one should sit upright, observing the "seven points of posture," and note the motion of one's breath from within. Say, for example, that it moves through the left nostril only for a period of three days and then on the fourth shifts to the right nostril for three days, and so on alternately for three "units" through each nostril. One should keep a careful count of the period for which it maintains this sequence, for it is the breaking of one's basic pattern which serves as the sign: if it departs from this steady alternation within a month and a half, one will die after six months;

if it departs from its rhythm within a month, terrible adversities will come; if it departs within two weeks, a fierce fever will come; if it breaks its pattern after only a few days, there will be slander and calumny. If one's breath does not shift nostrils at all within ten days, then as soon as it does shift one will die; if it moves through one's mouth and both nostrils simultaneously, one will die in half a day; if its movement through one's nose is blocked and it moves only through one's mouth, it is said that one will die immediately.

The interpretation of dreams has a long and honorable history in both India and Tibet,[12] and many works deal with the subject. Here are just a few examples of dreams that are potents of death. Dreams between evening and midnight, our text says, are uncertain in meaning; but if toward morning, before one gets up, one dreams that one is riding a cat or a red-faced white monkey, going farther and farther toward the east, this is a sign that one is being slain by king demons. Similarly, if one dreams that one is riding a tiger, a fox, or a corpse, a buffalo, pig, camel, or donkey, going farther and farther toward the south, this is a sign that one has been placed in the hands of the Lord of Death.

Furthermore, it is a sign of death to dream that one is eating things unclean to eat, that one is wearing clothes of black goat's hair and falling downward, that one is ensnared in a trap or bound with iron chains, or that one keeps copulating in the form of a black woman or animal. If one dreams that one is disemboweled by a fierce black woman, that a black man with an iron staff approaches and tells one to depart, that one is naked with one's hair and beard shaved off, that one keeps falling asleep in a terrifying cemetery, that one has grown old and is carrying a heavy burden, that in sudden darkness the sun and moon fall down upon the plain, that one is falling upside down into a pit, that one is dancing together with a host of ogres—all these are inauspicious dreams; yet if one is not sick at the time then death is not certain, and with the proper ritual one may be freed from it. If, however, one dreams these continually, then death will come within a year.

Again, if one dreams that the sun and moon are eclipsed—"eaten by Rāhu"—or that they fall down upon the plain, or that they set over and over again, this means that one's father, mother, or Master may die; and if he is sick at the time then it is said that his death is inevitable. These, then, are the internal signs of death: to perform a ransom from these, the text adds, is rather more difficult.

The text then explains the secret signs of death. When the external and internal signs of death appear, it says, they may be averted by performing again and again the ritual for cheating death; but if these signs are not averted thereby, then the secret signs of death must be interpreted. One first awakens the thought of enlightenment, goes for refuge, and prays; then on the morning of the first day of the month the "falling of the drop" is interpreted as follows: if it happens that a man's semen is black or a woman's menstrual blood white, then he or she will die within two months; if a man's semen is red, he will die within six months. But if the semen is white and undeteriorated, on the other hand, then it is permissible to eat it: while it is still warm, he should inhale it through his nose. This, the text says, is a ritual for cheating death.

Furthermore, if the semen is ejaculated without any feeling, or if within it there are scattered drops like quicksilver the size of sesame seeds, it is said that he is well on his way to death. If a woman's menstrual blood does not stop its flow, and at the time too she dreams that she is gathering red flowers, then she will die. Again, if a man's semen trickles in a stream even when he is not engaged in sexual intercourse, it is said that he will die within four months. If there suddenly appears a black mole at the tip of the glans penis—"the gem of the vajra"—where there was none before, if one is defiled by lust and fornicates uninterruptedly, if one thinks of nothing but women, if one breaks one's vows—not only are these signs of death, but they are also signs that one will later fall into the Diamond Hell. If one does not devote oneself to a full measure of confession of one's sins, one will ever taste the sufferings of hell; one should confess them and cheat this secret death, but this death is harder to cheat than the two preceding ones.

The signs of distant death, the text says, are the signs of a death that is yet a year or a month away, and these signs are discovered through the interpretation of one's shadow projected optically into the sky. The interpreter makes offerings and prayers, and then he goes to a solitary place; then, in the morning or afternoon of the first day of month, or at evening or dawn on the fifteenth day of the month, when the sky is clear and there is no cold wind, he finds a comfortable place and sits there naked, praying fiercely and reciting a hundred times the mantra OṂ ĀYUṢE SAṂHĀRAKÊŚVARE HŪṂ PHAṬ! Then he gets up, still naked, pays homage seven times to the gods of the directions. and stretches out his four limbs away from his body, holding in one hand a rosary or some other emblem. On the heart of the shadow that he thus casts he draws the syllable A, and he stares at that A unblinkingly with both eyes, assiduously observing its shape until tears of fatigue well up in both his eyes; then he looks into the center of the cloudless sky, whereupon he sees an optical afterimage of his own form.

If this afterimage is a pale whitish yellow, with no deformity in its head or body, it is an auspicious sign that he will not die. If he cannot see his form in the sky at all, he should try it again, this time sitting cross-legged with his hands flat on his lap; if the afterimage still does not appear, there is nothing the matter: it has been blocked by clouds in the sky or by cold wind, and he should try again later when the sky is clear.

There are three parts to the interpretation of this afterimage: its completeness, its shape, and its color.

Its completeness indicates, first of all, the number of years he has left to live: if the emblem in his hand is missing, this is called the "disjunction from the deity of durability," and he will die after seven years; if the right hand is missing, he will die after five years; if the left hand is missing, after three years; if the right leg is missing below the knee, after two years; if the entire right leg is missing, after one year. Again, its completeness indicates the number of months he has left to live: if the right part of the head is missing, he will die after nine months; if the left part of the head is missing, after seven months; if everything above the neck is missing, after five months; if the neck is missing also, after three months; if the upper trunk is missing, after two months; and if the lower trunk is missing, after one month. And again, its completeness indicates the number of days he has left to live: if the right part of the body is missing, he will die after twenty-nine days; if the left part is missing, after twenty-one days.

Second, the shape of the afterimage may be interpreted as follows: if it is square, he will die after five months; if it is round, after four months; if it is semicircular, after three months—but these may be averted by a ritual of cheating death. If it is triangular, he will die after one month; if it is shaped like a burial mound, after two weeks; if it is pointed at the top, after ten days—and this death may not be averted.

Third, the color of the afterimage may be interpreted; if its color is white, fading away from the center, it is a sign that he is being enjoyed by the *lu* serpents, the king demons, and the demigods; if it is black, fading off from the right, it is a sign that he is being consumed by the *dü* demons and the *mamo* demonesses; if it is red, fading off from the left, it is a sign that he is being consumed by the *tsen* and the five personal gods, and so on.

Whereas these signs arise when a person is well and thus present many possibilities for cheating them, the signs of near death, the text says, are the signs of death which occur when the person has become sick. Here the text enters more or less into the technical realm of medical diagnosis, of which I give a few examples. If the patient's gums grow grimy and black, this is called the "gathering of the *dü* demons of the four elements," and he will die after nine days. If the patient's nostrils contract and grow flat, this is called the "blockage of the gate of breath," and he will die after nine days. If his limbs stretch out and contract again and again, this is called "hastening up the mountain of the elements," and he will die after five days. If his upper and lower orifices become blocked, this is called "cutting off the path of the elements," and he will succumb by noon of the third day.

Whenever these signs of death appear, it is as if the patient's time had been inevitably fixed, so all the rituals for cheating death should be well performed three times each. If one does so, an untimely death may yet be averted; but if these rituals do not succeed, though one put forth one's best efforts and perseverance, then the patient's measure of life has come to its term and he will surely die.

Last of all are the miscellaneous signs of death, which apply whether one is sick or not. Thus, for example, if one cannot see the tip of one's nose with one's eyes, then one will die after five months; if one cannot see the tip of one's tongue, then even if one is not sick one will die after three days. If, when one looks at one's face in a polished mirror, one cannot see one's left eye, one will die after seven months; if one breathes on the palm of one's hand but one's breath feels icy, one will die after ten days.

If when bathing the water does not cling to one's chest, or if the water on one's chest does not dry at all, one will die; death approaches if one snaps one's fingers but no sound comes, if one leaves no footprints on soft earth, if one casts no shadow. If one's image reflected in water or in a mirror has its head cut off or lacks its limbs, this too is a sign of death. If one's penis is swollen yet is not erect, if one coughs up phlegm without sneezing, if one cannot perceive the smell of a dying lamp—these are all signs of inevitable death.

Furthermore, if one's cognition is muddy and darkened, if one's appetite comes and goes, if one cannot feel content with the religious acts one has performed, if one does not want to stay in one place but always wishes to go, if one is depressed with fatigue but cannot fall asleep, if one grows thin and pale and acts clumsily, if one remembers one's former kindred and wishes to see them again, if one thinks that one will die and wishes to commit suicide, if one wants to wander alone with no friends, if one's former disposition changes to sloth and faintheartedness, if one's dreams are disturbed and evil, if one beomes dejected or full of fierce hatred, if the five poisons of the defilements increase and one behaves impiously, if what one says is unclear and irrational, if one's semen is infirm and always trickling—these are signs that one is near death.

These signs of death are a surprising amalgam of folklore, traditional medicine, and sometimes acute psychological insight; even more, they are symbols of the tenuousness of life even as they reaffirm life's meaning: they are part of the magical connections that web the cosmos and enclose the body of the lay person as well as the body of the yogin. "The many forms of prediction," writes Robert Ekvall, "are all manifestations of an effort to extend comprehension . . . If it were assumed that events were not subject to the rules of a universal order but are capriciously accidental, there could be no divination, no forecast, and no prognosis. Thus, the existence of divination is a confession of faith in an ordered universe." And he continues:[13]

> As thus defined and placed in the conceptual world of the Tibetans, the universality of divination in the Tibetan pattern of behavior is unquestionable . . . . Accepted and practiced in some way by every Tibetan, it has a part in influencing or guiding his decisions or plans. Not all Tibetans I have known have equal faith in its value—their comments are very frequently tinged with skepticism and are sometimes disparaging and even denunciatory—but everyone I have consulted has stated flatly that every Tibetan must have had repeated recourse to divination throughout his life, either as practitioner, client, or both.

These, then, are the signs of warning, a projection of comprehension into the future, the obverse of the "magical axiom," and an admission of the precariousness of the human situation; they may appear spontaneously, be deliberately sought in ritual, or be part of a basically medical diagnosis. Whenever they occur—and often when they do not—a Tibetan turns to White Tārā for the prolongation of his life, and in her initiation into life he seeks to absorb her divine and sustaining power.

THE INITIATION INTO LIFE

The basic preliminary initiation of White Tārā—the "permission" to practice her rituals, the indispensable prerequisite to her ritual service, her evocation and employment—is sometimes referred to rather loosely as an "initiation into life" because it is held to include her specialized function of prolonging the recipients' lives through removing their "diseases, sins, obscurations, and untimely death" and empowering their body, speech, and mind. But an initiation into life, properly speaking, is rather a special case of this initiation: it adds the performance by the Master of a magical operation of ritual type 4*b*, the transference of power from "life substances" he has previously evoked (just as in the case of the magic pills and nectar considered in chapter ii). The power the Master magically transmits to his disciples is the power of long life, and not the power of contemplation; and when a delegation of lay people approach a high lama to request his performance of this ritual—and the life of any high lama is a constant succession of such requests—they have in mind not so much his bestowing of authorization and capacity for their future practice as the exercise of his magical powers to prolong their lives.

Tara rinpoch'e is such a high lama, a young but quite learned Gelug who has earned the informal title "lama of the roadworkers." The refugees from Tibet who first came to India found no employment open to them except on the Himalayan road gangs, repairing the annual ravages of the heavy winter snowslides. This lama traveled and lived among them, granting them the encouragement of his presence and the benefits of his rituals in the cure of disease and the alleviation of distress.

When Tara rinpoch'e visited Dalhousie, his many followers requested that he perform for them an initiation into life. The local nunnery made available its facilities, for the nuns wished the ritual especially for the benefit of a group of young Tibetan schoolgirls who were about to take the vows of novices. The workers climbed up the long path to the top of the hill where the nunnery looked out

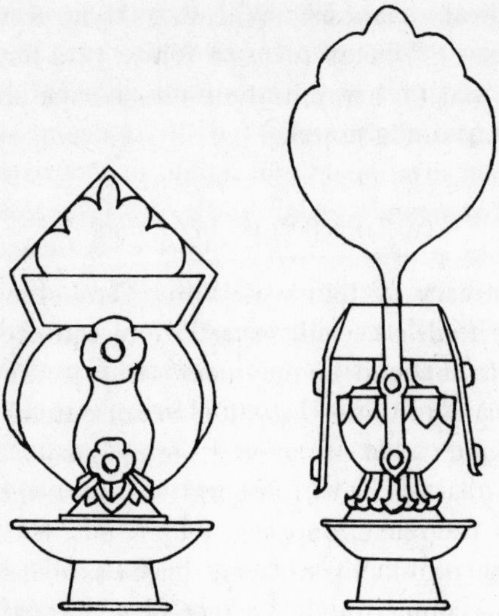

Fig. 43. A metal initiation torma (left) and a flask of life (right).

over the valley, and they packed themselves into a tight and overflowing crowd in the room set aside for the ritual. In the front were lined up the young girls who were the occasion for the initiation, their hair carefully brushed back, wearing their blue and white government school uniforms. The crowd of lay people filled the room, its porch, and a good portion of the mountainside, the somber cloaks of the men contrasting with the rich colors of the women's blouses, with an occasional flash of silver or coral from an amulet box, some of the men still grimed and dusty from the nearby road camps, some in their best clothes, their hair oiled and plaited with red tassels.

The altar was set up beneath a painting of Tārā hung on the wall. In its center was the metal base of an offering maṇḍala, upon which an eight-petaled lotus was drawn with grains of colored rice—a peculiarly Gelug technique. In the center of the lotus was placed the "life torma" in which the Master generates the deity, so that her protective power is available to the recipients in tangible form. Here Tara rinpoch'e used simply the usual offering torma for this purpose, made of dough and adorned with flowers of colored butter. But often there is used a special metal "initiation torma," which is thus portable and may be taken with the lama on his journeys, for bestowing initiations along the way. It is designed so that one face shows the angular outline of a torma for a fierce deity and the obverse the smooth curves of a torma for a peaceful deity, delicately molded in gold and silver and set with coral and turquoise to represent the flower ornaments. Or again, in this ritual, the goddess may be generated in the special "flask of life," a vase-shaped flask such as Amitāyus is depicted as holding, with four silver pendants hanging from its rim (perhaps reflecting the Indian theme of the full vase which overflows with bounty) and a leaf-shaped top (see fig. 43). The choice depends upon individual preference and upon what is available, save only that an offering torma so used has the advantage of being edible.

Thus there are said to be three aspects of a torma: as an *offering* it is presented to the deity; as an *evocation* the deity is generated within it, and the power thereof may be transmitted to a recipient through physical contact; and as a *substance of magical attainment* it may be eaten by the participants at the end of a ritual, to absorb the empowerment it contains.

On top of the life torma was placed a small painting, called a *tsakali*, of White Tārā. To the right of the maṇḍala was set out "in a crystal or silver bowl" the "nectar of life," made from milk mixed with sugar; and to its left the "pills of life," made from "life substances" of healing herbs and potions, and the relics of departed saints. In front of the maṇḍala was a "round white torma"—that is, another offering torma—and the seven offering bowls containing the two waters and the five gifts.

Finally, on a small table behind which the lama was to sit, were set out his vajra and bell, the rice or grain he would scatter over the heads of the assembly, and the working flask in which he would empower the cleansing water. The entire effect was rather Spartan compared with the luxuriance of offerings and implements I was used to; it is generally true that Gelug altars are simpler than those of the Kajü.

In this initiation into life, with its use of magical devices and recipes (in addition to the nectar and pills, different rituals may use the "beer of life," the "silken arrow," and so on), we see an essential similarity with the thread-cross ritual described in chapter ii: it is an employment of powers already acquired by the Master, the evocation of life substances and the control of the "appearances" of his disciples. The power of long life is bestowed by the magic of the initiating lama rather than appropriated by the capacity of the disciple. And thus the lama prepares himself ahead of time, either alone in the assembly hall before the others are called in or, in the present instance, in a private room from which he emerges when the crowd has assembled. His preparations closely follow those of any employment of the deity's power: he first generates himself as the deity and recites her mantra, gathering within himself the potency that will be transmitted to the recipients, and then he generates the deity before him as the ritual objectification of her power. Hence the ritual text itself is divided into three parts: the self-generation, the generation in front, and the actual bestowing of the initiation into life. Here we will follow our lama through his private preparations, that we may see the process by which the initiation functions.

1 *Self-generation*

As always, the self-generation begins with the "going for refuge": the Master joins his palms and visualizes the "field of refuge" surrounded by an array of all beings, and he recites three times:

> I and beings—all sentient beings as infinite as space—from this time until we attain the terrace of enlightenment, go for refuge to the glorious and holy gurus; we go for refuge to the perfect blessed Buddhas; we go for refuge to the holy teachings; we go for refuge to the noble community of monks.

Then he prays to them once:

> I prostrate myself and go for refuge to the guru and the precious Three Jewels. I pray you: empower my stream!

And then, three times, he awakens the thought of enlightenment:

> It is for the sake of all beings that I should attain the rank of perfect Buddhahood, and it is for that reason that I shall experience this visualization and recitation of the life-bestowing Cintācakra [White Tārā].

And the practitioner invites before him the field of hosts:

> I myself instantaneously become the Holy Lady, and on my heart, above the circle of a moon, is a white syllable TĀṂ. Light radiates forth therefrom and, in the sky before me, the holy Cintācakra, surrounded by the hosts of gurus in the lineage of the "life teaching," Buddhas and Bodhisattvas VAJRA-SAMĀJAḤ!

He praises them with the mantra NAMO GURUBHYAḤ! NAMA ĀRYA-TĀRĀ-SAPARIVĀREBHYAḤ! and he makes offerings to them with OṂ GURU-ĀRYA-TĀRĀ-SAPARIVĀRA ARGHAṂ . . . ŚABDA PRATĪCCHA SVĀHĀ! and the appropriate gestures. Three times he confesses himself with "I go for refuge to the Three Jewels . . ." and he contemplates the Four Immeasurables with "May all beings have Bliss . . ."

With these preparations finished and his stock of merit accumulated, he proceeds to the self-generation, which again begins with the accumulation of his stock of knowledge in Emptiness and the re-creation of himself therefrom as the goddess, the empowering of the body, speech, and mind of this symbolic being, its absorption of the knowledge being and its sealing with the initiation by the five families of Buddhas:

> OṂ SVABHĀVA-ŚUDDHĀḤ SARVA-DHARMĀḤ SVABHĀVA-ŚUDDHO 'HAṂ!

> All becomes Emptiness. From the realm of Emptiness is PAṂ and from that a lotus; from A is the circle of a moon, above which my own innate mind is a white syllable TĀṂ. Light radiates forth therefrom, makes offerings to the Noble Ones, serves the aim of beings, and is gathered back in, whereupon my mind the syllable is transformed, and I myself become the holy Cintācakra: her body is colored white as an autumn moon, clear as a stainless crystal gem, radiating light; she has one face, two hands, three eyes; she has the youth of sixteen years; her right hand makes the gift-bestowing gesture, and with the thumb and ring finger of her left hand she holds over her heart the stalk of a lotus flower, its petals on the level of her ear, her gesture symbolizing the Buddhas of the three times, a division into three from a single root, taking the form of an open flower in the middle, a fruit on the right, and a new shoot on the left; her hair is dark blue, bound up at the back of her neck with long tresses hanging down; her breasts are full; she is adorned with divers precious ornaments; her blouse is of varicolored silk, and her lower robes are of red silk; the palms of her hands and the soles of her feet each have an eye, making up the seven eyes of knowledge; she sits straight and firm upon the circle of the moon, her legs crossed in the diamond posture.

> On the top of her head is a white OṂ; on her throat is a red ĀḤ; on her heart, above the circle of a moon, is a white syllable TĀṂ marked with a blue HŪṂ.

> From the seed in her heart light radiates forth and, from her natural abode, the holy Cintācakra, surrounded by hosts of Buddhas and Bodhisattvas OṂ VAJRA-SAMĀJAḤ! And with JAḤ HŪṂ BAṂ HOH they become one with the symbolic being.

Having fully formed himself as the goddess, sealed in her identity and holding her ego, he makes offerings and praises to her. He cleanses the offerings with the AMṚTA mantra and purifies them with the SVABHĀVA mantra, and from the Emptiness thus evoked he proceeds to re-create them:

> From the realm of Emptiness comes BHRŪṂ, and from that I generate jeweled vessels, vast and broad, inside of which is OṂ: this melts into light and becomes oblations . . . and music, made of divine substance, clear, unimpeded, as infinite as space, with all the qualities of inexhaustible Bliss.

He empowers the offerings with the mantras OṂ ARGHAṂ ĀḤ HŪṂ . . . ŚABDA ĀḤ HŪṂ ! and the appropriate gestures, and he visualizes: "They are offered by offering goddesses emanated from my own heart," while he recites the offering mantras OṂ ĀRYA-TĀRĀ-SAPARIVĀRA ARGHAṂ PRATĪCCHA SVĀHĀ ! and so on through ŚABDA, again with the appropriate gestures; and then he praises the goddess with the following verse:

> Homage to you who grant any desired magical attainment,
> deathless life, knowledge, and merit,
> to anyone who makes devoted offering to your lotus feet
> and simply recites your TĀRE mantra.

It is important to bear in mind that in the visualization the practitioner is making these offerings and praises to himself or, more accurately, to the goddess in his own person. The goddess is the only one "there," for the practitioner has been dissolved in Emptiness, save only that the goddess is generated from his own "innate mind" in the form of her seed syllable. Thus at this point, the text says, the practitioner should direct his attention to his—the deity's—body, which is an "inseparable union of appearance and Emptiness," and for as long as he can he should remain absorbed or in "communion"—even, by semantic extension, in "intercourse"—therewith.

The realizations that arise therefrom concerning the nature of events are, for the practiced contemplative, a reconfirmation of previous ontological insight, a deepening of awareness of the nature of appearances. With this preparation he is ready to control and manipulate these appearances in the visualizations he now begins, building up his own reserves of power for transmission to his disciples in the initiation later.

On the heart of myself—vividly visualized as the noble White Tārā—is a white eight-spoked wheel, with a nave and three rims. On its nave, above a moon, is my own mind as a white syllable TĀṂ, surrounded by the appendix [MAMA ĀYUḤ . . .] inserted between OṂ and HĀ. On the eight spokes are the eight syllables TĀ RE TU TTĀ RE TU RE SVĀ. Clockwise on the innermost rim are the vowels, counterclockwise on the middle rim are the consonants, and counterclockwise on the outermost rim is the heart of conditioned coproduction [YE DHARMA . . .]. The seed and all the syllables thus arrayed blaze with the brilliant radiance of light whose essence is the nectar of immortality.

On the top of my head is the lord of the family, the Conqueror Amitāyus: his body is colored red; he has one face; upon his two hands, held in the meditation gesture, he holds a golden flask filled with a stream of the nectar of immortal life; he is adorned with silks and precious ornaments; he sits with his legs crossed in the diamond posture. On his heart he is marked with the syllable HRĪḤ, from which red light radiates forth in the ten directions like iron hooks, and these gather together and summon—in the form of varicolored and multiform nectar with its light—all my life which has been stolen or ravished away by men or spirits, which has been scattered or dispersed; it gathers and summons a distillation of the five elements, the life and merit of all beings, the luster and brilliance of the triple world, and all the empowerment of body, speech, and mind of the gurus, the Conquerors, and their sons.

All these dissolve into the flask in his hands, and from their dissolving it overflows with wavelets of white nectar, which enter into me through the hole of Brahma in the top of my head; it in turn dissolves into the wheel in my heart, with its seed and garland of the mantra; from this there falls a stream of nectar which fills up the entire inside of my body and washes its entire outside, so that it cleanses and makes pure all the sins, obscurations, diseases, and impediments to life which I have accumulated from beginningless time; it restores my life and merit and renews the vows and pledges I have broken, and I gain the magical attainment of deathless life.

This sequence is visualized as it is recited; and then, maintaining this visualization, the practitioner recites the mantra OṂ TĀRE TUTTĀRE TURE MAMA ĀYUḤ-PUṆYA-JÑĀNA-PUṢṬIṂ-KURU SVĀHĀ ! This is the "contemplation of the mantra" in self-generation. He then proceeds to erect a series of visualized "pavilions," each one homologized to a "basic function" and its color:

> Once again, from the wheel of the mantra in my heart, there radiates forth a host of white light, which fills the entire inside of my body, pacifying all my diseases, sins, obscurations, and impediments to life. The light radiates outward through the pores of my body, surrounding my body with a pavilion of white light, such that I accomplish all the functions of pacifying.
>
> Again, there radiates forth a host of yellow light, which fills my body, increasing my life and merit, and the wisdom that comes of hearing, thinking, and contemplating. The light radiates outward, surrounding the white pavilion with a pavilion of yellow light, such that I accomplish all the functions of increasing.
>
> Agzain, there radiates forth a host of red light, granting me the strength to subjugate the triple world. The light radiates outward, surrounding the yellow pavilion with a pavilion of red light, such that I accomplish all the functions of subjugation.
>
> Again, there radiates forth a host of blue light, granting me the strength to accomplish all the functions of destroying. The light radiates outward, surrounding the red pavilion with a pavilion of blue light, such that I accomplish all the fierce functions.
>
> Again, there radiates forth a host of green light, granting me the power to accomplish all the vast numbers of functions. The light radiates outward, surrounding the blue pavilion with a pavilion of green light, such that I accomplish all the vast numbers of functions.
>
> Again, there radiates forth a host of vermilion light, making firm my ability in all the functions and magical attainments. The light radiates outward, surrounding the green pavilion with a pavilion of vermilion light, making all the pavilions firm.
>
> Then all six pavilions of light cohere into a single piece, whose shape and openings correspond to those of my body, solid and hard, unable to be shaken even by the wind that dissolves the world, and all the space between the surface of my body and the pavilion is filled with flowers of the blue lotus, quivering with their filaments and their new and supple shoots.

Then, if he whishes, he may further surround himself with a circle of protection:

> Again, from the wheel of the mantra in my heart, there radiates forth infinite light in the ten directions; and this becomes, outside the six combined lights, a surrounding circle of protection, without interstice in any direction, a diamond ground with fence, tent, and canopy.

Here, the text adds, beginning from the vivid visualization—the communion with the deity's "union of appearance and Emptiness"—up through the visualization of the six pavilions and the circle of protection, the practitioner should recite the mantra, with the proper focus of attention and control of his breath, as it is given in the appropriate handbook. We shall see how this is done when we consider the ritual service, which gives details on these subjects. But we may note how the Master is building up his stores of power, coercing into himself with visualization and recitation the "luster and brilliance of the triple world" and surrounding himself with his own magical attainments. And finally, as we have seen before, he recites the 100-syllable mantra, fills in the omissions, and makes offerings and praises. He concludes by dedicating the merit he has gained through the self-generation:

> By this virtue may I quickly
> attain to Cintācakra,
> and may every single being
> be placed on that same stage.

2 *Generation in front*

The second part of the ritual is the generation of the goddess in front, here meaning within the life torma; the torma becomes the goddess, and this unitary simulacrum of the divine power is approached ritually in this section and then employed magically in the initiation. Thus the evocation of the torma is a magical function, like the employment of the life substances which follows; but the emphasis here is upon arousing the stream of her heart with offerings, praises, recitation, and the offering torma, so that these ritual functions "flavor" the practitioner's approach to the goddess.

The Master begins with the ritual empowerment of the cleansing water in the working flask, and he recites the visualization as follows:

> Inside the working flask, upon a sun throne, is the syllable HŪṂ, surrounded by the AMṚTA mantra; light radiates forth therefrom, inviting in the form of light all the potency and empowerment of all the Buddhas and Bodhisattvas in the ten directions, and this light dissolves into the syllable HŪṂ and its mantra garland. From that there falls a stream of nectar which dissolves into the water in the flask.

The Master then recites OṂ VAJRA-AMṚTA-KUṆḌALI HANA HANA HŪṂ PHAṬ! and he visualizes: "The syllable HŪṂ with its mantra garland melts into light and dissolves into the water in the flask." Next he uses this potent water from the working flask to sprinkle the life torma, cleansing it with the AMṚTA mantra; with the SVABHĀVA mantra he purifies it into Emptiness, re-creating it as the goddess herself: "From the realm of Emptiness, upon a throne of lotus and moon before me, is a white syllalbe TĀṂ, which transforms into the holy noble Tārā Cintācakra, indissolubly one with the torma." This generation of the deity within the torma continues as given above in the self-generation, down through the sealing by initiation. The practitioner then makes offerings as before to this Tārā/torma, presenting either the simple series of mantras and gestures or the appropriate verses, as he wishes; and he praises her with the following verse:

> Noble Lady, by hearing nothing more than your name
> the Lord of Death, Māra and his army are defeated;
> homage to the feet of Cintācakra
> who grants the highest magical attainment of deathless life!

The practitioner next arouses her heart by the recitation of her mantra—here with the specific object in view of engaging her consideration for the diciples whom he will initiate—accompanied by the following visualization, that the divine power may be concentrated within the torma:

> In the heart of the Holy Lady generated before me is a white eight-spoked wheel with a nave and three rims. On its nave, above a moon, is a white syllable TĀṂ, surrounded by the appendix between OṂ and HĀ. On the eight spokes are the eight syllables TĀ RE TU TTĀ RE TU RE SVĀ. Clockwise on the innermost rim are the vowels, counterclockwise on the middle rim are the consonants, and counterclockwise on the outermost rim is the heart of conditioned coproduction. All these, thus arrayed, broadcast the inherent sound of the mantra, and they let fall as it were a rain of the nectar of life.
>
> From the syllable HRĪḤ in the heart of the lord of the family, Amitāyus upon her head, there radiates forth infinite light in the ten directions, which gathers together, in the form of nectar with its light, all the life and merit of my disciples which has been stolen by men or spirits, which has been scattered or dispersed. It gathers a distillation of the five elements, the life and merit of all beings, and all the empowerment of body, speech, and mind of the gurus, the Conquerors and their sons.

> All these dissolve into the flask in the hands of the lord of the family of the Holy Lady before me, and into the wheel of life in his heart; and they become a blazing light, the sublime strength that conquers death.

And he recites, as many times as possible, OṂ TĀRE TUTTĀRE TURE Increase the life, merit, and knowledge of my disciples SVĀHĀ!

Having thus prepared the life torma for his disciples, generating it for them as the goddess and arousing her heart on their behalf, he proceeds to evoke—to re-create from Emptiness and to empower ritually—the nectar of life and the pills of life. Thus he cleanses and purifies these life substances with the two mantras as above, and he visualizes:

> From the realm of Emptiness is BHRŪṂ, and from that jeweled vessels, vast, broad, and great, inside of which are OṂ ĀḤ HŪṂ. These melt and becomes nectar of life and pills of life, in the form of different potions and pills made of nectar, made of various elixirs and medicines as antidotes to the 440 families of disease. From the seed in my own heart, light radiates forth, summoning all the potency and distillation of the mundane and supramundane, which dissolves into the nectar and pills of life.

Maintaining this visualization he has recited, he says the three syllables of empowerment—OṂ ĀḤ HŪṂ—with the flying-bird gesture, and he repeats as much as possible the same mantra as above ("Increase the life . . ."), finally making the empowerment firm with the 100-syllable mantra. And he concludes this generation of the deity in front by offering up a torma to the goddess, a standard finish, as we have seen, to this portion of a full ritual. He cleanses and purifies the offering torma with the two mantras, and he re-creates it from Emptiness with the following visualization:

> From the realm of Emptiness is BHRŪṂ, and from that jeweled vessels, vast, broad, and great, inside of which are OṂ ĀḤ HŪṂ. These melt and become a torma made of divine substance, clear and unimpeded, a great ocean of the nectar of inexhaustible knowledge.

He recites OṂ ĀḤ HŪṂ with the flying-bird gesture three times to empower the offering, and he visualizes: "The tongue of the Holy Lady generated before me is a hollow tube of light; and with that she draws out and consumes all the distillation of the torma." The practitioner is thus, in effect, offering a torma to a torma, save only that the latter is the deity in front; and he offers the torma by reciting three or seven times OṂ ĀRYA-TĀRĀ-SAPARIVĀRA IDAṂ BALIṂ TE KHA KHA KHĀHI KHĀHI! He makes the final offerings to her with ARGHAṂ and so on; he praises her with "Lady Tārā, saving from this world . . ."; and he prays to her for the sake of his disciples.

3. *The initiation into life*

3.1 *Preliminaries*

Though all the equipment for these contemplations was set out in the shrine room with the assembling lay people, the private ritual was performed in a separate room; the lama entered to find his disciples "having bathed, prostrated themselves three times and seated in rows." Flowers are passed around, and the Master offers the preliminary tormas to the hindering demons, erects a circle of protection, and tells the recipients to visualize him vividly as being Cintācakra as they offer him a maṇḍala as their "fee" for this initiation into life. These preliminaries are examined more closely in the next ritual.

Every initiation, too, commences with an explanation of the initiation, as the disciples, now protected from all evil influence, are given a lesson in the Law, perhaps an extemporaneous talk on the beneficence of Tārā or the meaning of her initiation, or a short sermon on the proper uses of the long life she grants. In this case Tara rinpoch'e addressed his remarks to the young schoolgirls: it is not enough simply to gain long life, he told them, but we must endow this life with the qualities of religous practice; and especially as nuns, he said, we must ignore sectarian differences, and be not just a Nyingma or Gelug, Kajü or Sacha, but rather a Buddhist.

Many lamas do not give such speeches, but every initiation text includes at least a brief outline of the lineage that is being transmitted to the recipients. Tara rinpoch'e concluded his remarks with the following speech from the ritual text:

> O yes! It is truly necessary that we not waste this opportunity, obtained but this once, this human body of "quietude and benefit," but rather we must get the utmost use of it; getting the utmost use of it means to hear, to think about, and to contemplate the perfect, complete, and unerring heart of the teachings of the Conqueror, to fulfill the aims of ourselves and others.

But to do so, it is of great importance at the very outset to extend our life-spans, basing ourselves particularly upon the deities of long life; and so holy Tārā appears to us in the form of a goddess, though she is a generalized function of all the Buddhas. The Holy Lady herself said to the Teacher of Drom, the King of the Law: "I will protect your followers," thus making a vow to protect like her own sons especially those in the lineage—those who "hold all the biographies"—of the Kadam.

The main source for these teachings is the text *Cheating Death* by Vāgīśvarakīrti; but, in addition to that, instructions appended thereto have been given by Tārā herself. Thus they were taught to Amoghavajra, who wrote many evocations and taught them to the Translator of Bari,[14] who in turn rendered them into Tibetan and taught them to the lama Lenagpa. And he in turn evoked her for six years, until he clearly saw her face, and she taught him the Law, and he taught it to the Precious Drepa, under the following circumstances:

When Drepa was studying [as opposed to contemplating], he showed the lines on his palm to a yogin who said he was from the area of Ladakh. "Master," the yogin said, "the rest of your work in the Law had best be *real*; you cannot live longer than three more years."

Considering this together with the many signs that had also appeared in his dreams, Drepa decided to postpone his study and devote his life to contemplation: "It will be well if for the rest of this life I get the real experience of the Law, whether it be but for a year or however long I have left; I must seek out a virtuous friend to teach me these special instructions."

On the road to Ü, he met the Lama Lenagpa before the Fort of Nyemozhu, and he told him his story. "I have a special method," said Lenagpa, "which clears away obstacles from the path of attaining enlightenment: so, teacher, let your heart rejoice!"

He gave Drepa the evocation of Tārā along with all its instructions, and he added: "Now go nowhere else, but stay where you are and contemplate."

In that district was a place called the Valley of the Fort of Lunglag, and on the high ground thereof he evoked Tārā one-pointedly. After only a month had passed, he clearly saw the Holy Lady's face, and she told him: "You will live to be sixty years old and be of benefit to beings."

Later, when he had reached sixty years of age, he prayed to the Holy Lady, and she said: "Erect an image of me, and you will live another ten years." Thus, it is said, he set up a painting.

When he turned seventy, he prayed again, and again she said: "Erect another image, and you will live ten years." Thus, it is said, he set up a metal statue. Both these images are reputed to have great empowerment, and it is said that the painting may be found in Radreng Monastery even to this very day.

When he turned eighty, he prayed again to the Holy Lady, and she said: "Now if you erect an image of me, you will be able to live for many more years." So he set one up in front of his dwelling to the north, and it is said that he lived to be ninety-five years old.

If one prays to this goddess, she grants not only long life but also the greater and greater increase of one's wisdom; this is found in the biographies of Gedündrub and of many other holy men of the past. The initiation into life of such a deity, the blessed Cintācakra, is a special counsel based upon instructions transmitted orally in solitary places: it was passed along from ear to ear in an extraordinary lineage of teachers, a stream of tradition which is the stamp of an initiation into life of the Kings of Magicians, until it reached, as an unbroken flow of empowerment, my own gracious guru.

And so you must be firm in the faith of your belief, and recite after me this prayer, that you may ask for this profound initiation into life.

And the Master recites the following verse three times, pausing after each line so that the disciples may repeat it:

I pray the glorious guru, who is the essence
of all the Buddhas of the three times,
to grant me the profound initiation into life
of Cintācakra.

He then leads the disciples in their going for refuge and the awakening of their thoughts of enlightenment, as the preparation for "establishing the ground" of the initiation:

Next, you must visualize as follows: All beings, filling up the sky before you, are no one but your own gracious mothers; you awaken an unbearably powerful compassion toward these mothers, who are stricken with many sufferings as they dwell in this world. You think, "Quickly, quickly I must certainly gain the rank of perfect Buddhahood for the sake of all beings; it is for that reason that I ask for this profound initiation into life."

You wish this fiercely, and, from that state, you visualize that this very place where you are has no longer its ordinary appearance, but is in actuality a divine mansion made of the Holy Lady's own brightness, like the array of the Pure Land of Happiness in the west.

Visualize, too, that your guru does not have his ordinary appearance, but is in actuality the holy Cintācakra seated here, and that this life torma before you is also the holy Cintācakra: her body is colored white as a new moon; she has one face and two hands, the right making the gift-bestowing gesture, and the left holding the stalk of a lotus flower with the refuge gesture; she has

> jeweled ornaments and silken garments; she has the seven eyes of wisdom, and she sits in the cross-legged diamond posture; her head is adorned with the lord of the family, the Conqueror Amitāyus, and her face radiates forth light in the ten directions.
>
> Above her head are the gurus in the lineage of the "life teaching," one on top of the other; and all around her are the hosts of high patron deities, Buddhas, Bodhisattvas, ḍākas, ḍākiṇīs, protectors and guardians of the Law, gathered together like clouds.
>
> When you have got them vividly visualized, you first—before their eyes—go for refuge to the Three Jewels, confess your sins and rejoice in the virtues of others, and you think, "I must gain the rank of Buddhahood for the sake of all beings, and it is for that reason that I take upon myself the vows of a Bodhisattva, that until I gain enlightenment I will study according to the infinite practices of a son of the Conqueror"—by that means taking upon yourselves the vow of a Bodhisattva. So repeat after me:
>
> I go for refuge to the Three Jewels . . . .

This verse is repeated three times, again pausing after each line.

The "ground" for the initiation is the disciple himself, visualized as the goddess in self-generation; an ordinary human body could not withstand the influx of divine power which prolongs its life. Thus the Master next "establishes the ground" for the initiation, leading the recipients in their visualization:

> Next, in order to establish the ground for the initiation into life you must generate yourselves as the deity; so as I recite the words of the ritual, you must visualize yourselves arising from the realm of Emptiness in the body of White Tārā, mother of the Conquerors.

He sprinkles the disciples with water from the working flask, cleansing them of hindering demons with the AMṚTA mantra, and purifying them into Emptiness with the SVABHĀVA mantra, and he recites the text for the Process of Generation: "From the realm of Emptiness, on a throne of lotus and moon, the disciples become the holy Cintācakra . . . marked with a blue HŪṂ." Here, of course, the Master fills in the gap in the text with the appropriate sequence of contemplative events, leading the disciples through the first two steps of the self-generation that he himself had performed earlier; and he simultaneously performs all the visualizations in which he leads the recipients, visualizing his disciples unfolding from Emptiness as the empowered symbolic being, applying for their benefit his own control of the appearances of reality. Thus this creation of the ground is structurally a magical function performed by the Master upon the recipients, for it is basically his control that achieves their generation: it is little expected that the lay disciples have any control of reality.

3.2 *The initiation proper*

Once the ground has been established and the recipients have been vividly visualized as the deity, empowered in the three places and with the deity generated before them in the person of the Master and the life torma, the ritual proceeds to the initiation into life which, the Master informs them, is here divided into four parts: (1) initiation through the life torma; (2) initiation through the nectar of life; (3) initiation through the pills of life; and (4) the increasing of life.

3.21 *Initiation through the life torma*

In the initiation through the life torma, he says, there are again three parts: (1) summoning the scattered; (2) healing the degenerate; and (3) absorbing life.

3.211 *Summoning the scattered*

Thus the Master continues:

> First, then, is summoning the life that has been scattered. Because of your fierce devotion and love for your guru, you vividly visualize the guru as the holy Cintācakra, from whose heart light radiates forth, touching the heart of the holy Cintācakra generated in front of you as the life torma and arousing the stream of her heart.
>
> From the syllable HRĪḤ in the heart and from the flask in the hands of the lord of the family Amitāyus, light radiates forth in the shape of iron hooks, pervading the triple world and gathering together—as iron is drawn forth by a lodestone—all your life and merit that have been robbed or stolen, carried off or scattered by the Lord of Death, by the *dü*, *tsen*, *mamo*, or king demons, or any other nonhuman evil spirit, hindering demon or ghost who would hurt or harm you, summoning it back in the form of flasks filled with deathless life, skull bowls and alms bowls filled with nectar.
>
> And it dissolves into the wheel of life in the heart and in all the parts of the body of the holy Cintācakra who is placed before you. Visualize that from all those parts of her body there falls a measureless stream of nectar colored red and white, which enters into you through the hole of Brahma in the tops of your heads, just

> exactly filling up the entire inside of your bodies, cleansing away your sins, obscurations, diseases, and impediments to life, healing the scattering and dissolution of your lives, and granting you the magical attainment of deathless life.

The Master also visualizes this as he recites it: he holds up the life torma in his right hand, his vajra tucked between his thumb and forefinger (in all initiations, the Master always holds his vajra in his right hand throughout the entire ritual, whatever else he may be handling), and he rings his bell with his left hand, reciting the 10-syllable mantra with its appendix as many times as possible. Then he recites the following invocation:

> Let this be to these fortunate sons an initiation into life, let it be for them a magical attainment, let it be for them an emblem of unchanging life, let it be for them a diamond of unwavering, let it be a royal banner of never-diminishing life, let it be an attainment of the mantra of life without death!

And he recites the first benediction:

> Like the wishing jewel atop a royal banner
> it is the crest ornament of the supreme deity,
> the highest endeavor a practitioner could wish for:
> may the unequaled supreme guru grant us good fortune!

And the Master scatters flowers—rice or grain if it is winter and no flowers are available—over the heads of the assembly, and he says: "Thereby is summoned the life that has been scattered."

3.212 *Healing the degenerate*

The second part of the initiation through the life torma—healing the degenerate—is again divided into three parts: (1) healing the degeneration of life; (2) healing the degeneration of strength and merit; and (3) healing the degeneration of vows and pledges.

3.2121 *Healing the degeneration of life*

The Master says:

> Among the three sections of this second part—healing the degenerate—we shall here heal the degeneration of your lives.

> Once again from the flask in the hands of Amitāyus, lord of the family of the Holy Lady before you, measureless light radiates forth in the shape of iron hooks, summoning the measureless elements of the worldly realm:

all the strength that is a distillation of the element earth in the form of yellow light and nectar, having the color of melted gold;

all the distillation of the element water in the form of white light and nectar, having the color of milk;

all the distillation of the element fire in the form of red light and nectar, having the color of vermilion, whose essence is warmth;

all the distillation of the element air in the form of green light and nectar, having the color of emerald;

and all the distillation of the element space in the form of blue light and nectar, having the color of melted indigo.

Visualize that these dissolve into the body and the wheel of life of the Holy Lady; from her in turn there falls a stream of the nectar of deathless life, which enters into you through the tops of your heads, filling up the entire inside of your bodies, cleansing away your sins, obscurations, diseases, and impediments to life, healing the degeneration of your life and of the five elements that make up your body, granting you possession of a sublime, dazzlingly brilliant body and the mantra of life without death.

The Master again holds up the life torma in his right hand, with his vajra as always tucked behind his thumb, and recites the mantra while ringing his bell, following it with the same invocation: "Let this be to these fortunate sons an initiation into life . . ." And he recites the second benediction:

Living to a hundred years, seeing a hundred Teachers,
the sublime happiness of long life without disease,
setting out in the highest Vehicle:
may there now be that good fortune!

3.2122 *Healing the degeneration of strength and merit*

Next the Master leads his disciples in healing the degeneration of their strength and merit, with a visualization identical in structure with the one that healed the degeneration of their lives:

Now that we have thus healed the degeneration of life, we shall here heal the degeneration of your strength and merit.

As before, from the flask in the hands of Amitāyus, lord of the family of the Holy Lady before you, infinite light radiates forth, gathering together helplessly, in the form of light and nectar, the glory and strength of Brahma and Indra and all the other powerful gods, the blazing brilliance of the sun, moon, planets, and stars,

> the empowerment of all the special gurus and masters, the understanding of the magicians and yogins, the great knowledge of the wise men and scholars, the merit and sovereignty of the universal monarchs and all their puissant ministers, the knowledge of deathless life of all who possess the mantra of life without death, the strength of their mantras and deep contemplations which conquer death—all the sublime qualities of happiness and glory in the world, the eight signs of good fortune, the eight substances of good fortune, the seven precious gems of sovereignty.
>
> Visualize that these dissolve into the wheel of life in the heart of the Holy Lady before you: and from her in turn there falls a stream of the nectar of deathless life, which enters into you through the tops of your heads, filling up the entire inside of your bodies, cleansing away your sins, obscurations, diseases, and impediments to life, healing the degeneration of your strength and merit, granting you all the qualities of happiness and glory, and giving you possession of the magical attainment of deathless life.

And again the Master lifts the torma before the assembly, recites the mantra and the evocation, and recites the third benediction: "Merit increasing until it is as high as the king of mountains . . ."

3.2123 *Healing the degeneration of vows and pledges*

The Master once more leads the recipients, healing the degeneration of their vows and pledges, with a visualization again identical in structure:

> Now that we have thus healed the degeneration of strength and merit, we shall here heal the degeneration of your vows and pledges, and prolong your lives through the ritual of "permission" of body, speech, and mind.
>
> Because of your fierce devotion and love for your guru, light radiates forth from the guru's heart, which touches the heart of the Holy Lady generated before you and thereby arouses the stream of her heart. From the syllable TĀṂ in her heart, light radiates forth and invites the empowerment of body, speech, and mind of all the gurus, high patron deities, Buddhas and Bodhisattvas, ḍākas and ḍākiṇīs, protectors and guardians of the Law in the ten directions, and especially of White Tārā Cintācakra, mother of the Conquerors who dwell in all the Pure Lands, and of the gurus in the lineage of the life teaching of the Conqueror Amitāyus and others—all in the form of the bodies of the Buddhas and Bodhisattvas, in the form of their mantras, syllables, emblems, and seeds, and in the form of the nectar of deathless life and its light, colored white, red, and blue.
>
> Visualize that these dissolve into the three places of the body of the Holy Lady before you; and from their dissolving there

> falls in turn three streams of the nectar of life—white, red, and blue, from head, throat, and heart—which dissolve into the tops of your heads, throats, and hearts, filling up the entire inside of your bodies, cleansing away all the sins, obscurations, and broken vows of your body, speech, and mind, your murders and so on from beginningless time in this world, granting you empowerment of body, speech, and mind, and granting you the magical attainment of deathless life, because your "three gates" have become the essence of the "three Diamonds."

And the Master again recites the mantra, holding up the life torma and ringing his bell as before, following it with the same invocation and reciting the fourth benediction:

> May there be good fortune of body: an unchanging mass.
> May there be good fortune of speech: the sixty sweet sounds.
> May there be good fortune of mind: no confusion, free of extremes.
> May there be the good fortune of the body, speech, and mind of the Conqueror!

3.213 *Absorbing life*

This final step in a series of strengthenings leads to a climax—the disciples' bodies fortified to the point where they can endure a massive transfer of divine energy—wherein they absorb the deity herself in the "absorption of life," the ultimate moment of this torma initiation and the final employment of the deity generated in the torma by the Master:

> Vividly visualize the guru as the Holy Lady, by the light of whose heart there is invited over each of your heads the Holy Lady Cintācakra generated before you, surrounded by the Conquerors and their sons. When I pray to them seated there, from all the parts of the bodies of the gurus of the lineage and of the Holy Lady there falls a measureless stream of the nectar of deathless life, which enters into you through the hole of Brahma in the tops of your heads, filling up the entire inside of your bodies; and thereby all the sins, obscurations, and diseases you have accumulated from beginningless time and, especially, all the sins, obscurations, and impediments to life which shorten your lives—all emerge black and thick through the gates of your sense organs and through all the pores of your bodies in the form of smoke and soot; they are cleansed away, and your bodies become pure as polished crystal, increasing and expanding all your qualities of life, merit, and understanding.
>
> Then, finally, when I say JAḤ HŪṂ BAṂ HOḤ! visualize that the gurus of the lineage who are above you and all the surrounding

> vast numbers of peaceful and fierce deities dissolve into the Holy Lady; from her body there separates a second one like it, which melts into the essence of the nectar of deathless life and dissolves into you through the tops of your heads; and thereby your body, speech, and mind become inseparably of a single taste with the body, speech, and mind of the holy Cintācakra, granting you all the highest and ordinary magical attainments, including the mantra of life without death.

Then the Master, having given these instructions, places the torma on the head of each recipient, that the power of the deity generated therein may pass by contact through the hole of Brahma, and he recites the prayer to the lineage of gurus from whom he himself has obtained the transmission of the initiation:

> May the holy, blessed, and glorious gurus in the lineage, in the ten directions and the three times, empower you! May Cintācakra, mother of the Conquerors, empower you! May the unequaled great Drepa empower you! May Gampopa Daö zhönnu empower you! May P'amo drupa Doje jepo empower you! May the great magician Lechi doje empower you! May the lotus-holding Gedündrub empower you! May the great scholar Norzang jats'o empower you! May the Conqueror's regent Gedün jats'o empower you!. . .

and so on through a list of the Dalai and Pench'en Lamas, the lineage of the Gelug, until finally, ". . . May my own gracious personal guru Jampa tendzin tr'inle jats'o pezangpo empower you!"

This prayer is filled in differently, of course, for each Master. The Master continues to pray, while he and his disciples perform the visualization he has given:

> Divine hosts of the blessed White Tārā Cintācakra, yours is the inconceivable mastery of the knowledge of understanding, the compassion of loving, the active power of doing, the strength of protecting: so pacify the illness of these disciples' bodies, the sufferings of their minds, their despair at impediments and lust, the harm of hindering demons, evil spirits, and ghosts, above, below, and on the surface of the earth, their terror of untimely death. Protect and preserve them, I pray you, from all those; increase all their qualities of life, merit, glory, enjoyment, and understanding. In short, empower them, that they may gain right now all the highest and ordinary magical attainments!

Then as before the Master recites the mantra and its appendix, and at the end of the recitation he dissolves the deity into the disciples with JAḤ HŪṂ BAṂ HOḤ! Then, to make the divine power firm within the disciples, he touches each one's head with his vajra—first horizontally, then vertically, making a vajra cross to seal the deity —saying each time SUPRATIṢṬHA! "Be very firm!" This is here equivalent to the absorption of the knowledge being in the Process of Generation, where the recipients were established as the ground of initiation by visualizing themselves as the empowered symbolic being. Here the real deity—the life torma—is dissolved into them and sealed, not with the initiation of the five families, but rather by the Master's vajra cross. And the Master says: "Thereby is bestowed the initiation through the life torma."

3.22 *Initiation through the nectar of life*

The ritual then proceeds to the next major division of the initiation, the nectar of life. Whereas the initiation through the life torma consisted in the visualization and recitation of ritual type 4*a* and the magical device of ritual type 4*c*, this privately evoked nectar is a magical recipe of ritual type 4*b*; it is in this use of recipes that the initiation into life proper expands upon the outline of the ordinary initiation of the goddess. Thus the Master explains:

> Second, we shall here bestow intitiation based upon the nectar of life. This is a special holy substance formed from the "cleansing, understanding, and kindling" of the five external nectars [the cleansing, purifying, and re-creation of the substance of the nectar]. Visualize that by drinking it the entire inside of your bodies will be filled with the nectar of the thought of enlightenment, curing all the degeneration in the strength of your "channels, winds, and drop," pervading your body and mind with Bliss, freeing you from all impediments to life, and granting you the mantra of life without death.
>
> With this nectar of deathless life, this holy material
> which is the essence of the five unchanging knowledges,
> I bestow initiation upon you, my fortunate sons.
> May you gain the magical attainment of life without death!

The Master recites the basic mantra while a spoonful of nectar is poured into the right palm of each disciple; as the recipients drink he says: "Thereby is bestowed the initiation through the nectar of life."

3.23 *Initiation through the pills of life*

The Master then proceeds to the magical pills of life:

> Third, we shall here bestow initiation based upon the pills of life. This pill is a distillation of deathless life, a gathering of all the

distillations of this world and nirvāṇa, the essence of the 404 sorts of medicine. Visualize that by eating it, it cleanses you of all 404 families of disease, increasing the seven bodily constituents of life, freeing you from any condition leading to untimely death, and granting you the magical attainment of life without death.

This is the distillation that gathers the quintessence
of glorious foods that make firm
your good fortune and life. Eat it now, my sons.
Eat this, for the mother of Conquerors, bestower of life,
will free you from all disease
when this food is served. Have no doubt.

And again he recites the basic mantra as the pills are passed out to the disciples. As each of the recipients takes one pill and eats it, he says: "Thereby is bestowed the initiation through the pills of life."

3.24 *The increasing of life*

Finally there is the last part of the ritual, the verses of good fortune for the increasing of life:

Fourth, we shall here recite the invocation of good fortune for the increase of life. Visualize that in the sky above you is Cintācakra, mother of the Conquerors, surrounded by the gurus in the lineage of this teaching, by Buddhas, Bodhisattvas, ḍākas, ḍākiṇīs, protectors and guardians of the Law, and by the gods and men who are possessed of this mantra, and that in order to increase your life they let fall upon you a rain of flowers at the same time as does your Master, letting music sound and with sweet song singing this benediction:

By the strength of charity is the Buddha noble,
for the lion of men understands the strength of charity;
entering the city of compassion
he roars forth the sound of the strength of charity.
Let there be the perfection of charity and the increase of life!

This verse is repeated six times; inserting in the appropriate places "virtue," "striving," "acceptance," "meditation," and "wisdom," and summing up by repeating a seventh time, saying "By the strength of the six perfections . . ." After each verse the Master scatters flowers (or rice) over the heads of the assembly.

O yes! In this way you have obtained the profound initiation into life. Rejoice and be happy! And vow that from this day forward you will take Cintācakra, mother of the Conquerors, as your patron deity, and that you will duly preserve your vows and pledges, both general and particular, as you repeat after me:

> Whatever has been preached by the Lord,
> that we will do.

This is repeated three times, and the Master concludes:

> Since you have been given this empowerment as passed down by the holy gurus, this profound initiation into life through the holy noble White Tārā Cintācakra according to the school of extraordinary lineage, I now ask you to offer up a maṇḍala as a fee of thanksgiving.

And they repeat after him the words of the offering.[15]

THE POWER OF CONTEMPLATION

This ritual sets forth very clearly the magical transmission of a power, here the power of long life; it is gathered by the Master and passed on by his visualization and recitation, a magical function imposing upon the "appearances" of the recipients and employing the power of the deity. Indeed, strictly speaking, the recipient need not even be present, save to drink the nectar and eat the pills, any more than, say, a prisoner to be magically freed from prison need be present at the ritual performed on his behalf. The active participation of the disciple, however, while not materially aiding the efficacy of the performance (except when the recipient is himself a contemplative), involves his own conscious absorption of power, a support for the Master's visualization, and a base for the physical contact of the devices and recipes. Thus the initiation, like any magical function, is the precise opposite of the Catholic doctrine of ex opere operato: the sacraments are effective independent of the spiritual state of the priest who performs them, but the Tibetan initiation depends almost exclusively upon the contemplative capacities of the bestowing lama.

It is the same when the power to be transmitted is the power to contemplate the deity, the primary authorization for the performance of the ritual service, the initiation in the strict sense of the word. We have already noted in chapter i the great importance attached to the entire concept of this initiation in the life of any practitioner. But we should note here especially that the term "initiation" in Tibet comprises both more and less than the merely esoteric connotations that have been given it by Western writers, no doubt influenced by lingering memories of Greek mystery cults and by the self-conscious coteries of modern occult enthusiasts. The primary signification of "initiation" in Tibet is as a guarantor of lineage—of authenticity of doctrinal transmission—and as a preliminary and proper authorization of practice; only secondarily is it considered as a means in itself to genuine realization. It is only the very highest type of personage, contemplatively prepared over many lifetimes, the Tibetans say, who can receive from an initiation the ontological insights it is capable of giving. But this in no way limits the usefulness of the ritual, for where the divine power is transmitted as part of the authorization to evoke the deity—where the recipient is empowered as a fit vessel to contain the deity—it is bestowed, as we have seen, by the vivid visualization of the initiating Master rather than appropriated by the capacity of the disciple.

TYPES OF INITIATION

There are said to be five different modes of this transmission of lineage and authority. The first of these is called the "thought lineage of the Conquerors," the transmission directly from mind to mind without physical intermediary, a revelatory inspiration of a doctrine or a practice. The second is the "sign lineage of the 'holders of the mantra,'" the transmission without speech by the use of manual signs and gestures. The third is the "ear-whispered lineage of humankind," the oral transmission from ear to ear, a lineage of revelation passed on by a Master only to his chief disciples; it is this transmission of authority which forms the lineage of gurus of any particular sect, who communicate from generation to generation of Masters—as from Marpa to Mila to Gampopa—their special doctrines and contemplative revelations. A fourth is the "entrusted lineage of the ḍākiṇīs", the transmission especially of a hidden text composed by the Precious Guru Padmasambhava and entrusted to the guardianship of a ḍākiṇī, who might hold the text for, say, five hundred years before passing it on to a "revealer of hidden texts," and thus the gap between the original promulgation and its discovery does not "break the bridge" of its lineage.

For present purposes the most important of these transmissions of lineage and authority is the fifth mode, called the "lineage of initiation, textual transmission, and instruction." Of the three items included in this enumeration, the most fundamental is the *textual transmission*. It is the means of transmitting a text, a ritual, or even a mantra to guarantee its lineage; before one is permitted to read a text, recite a mantra, or even learn the alphabet, one must hear it in its entirety, read out loud by a teacher who had himself similarly heard it from his teacher. Thus the transmission of the text stretches in an unbroken line back to its author or to the Buddha himself, who first recited it to his disciples. It is not enough just to get the printed text, even when it is given by one's Master; to be part of its lineage, and thus to be permitted its study and practice, it must actually be heard.

Included under this rubric, too, is the *textual transmission of a teaching*, which is the special transmission of a philosophical text from a Master to a student who has read and understood it and who is judged to be capable of teaching it. Whereas the textual transmission is the simple authorization to read a text or perform the ritual it contains, the textual transmission of a teaching is the permission received from one's teacher to transmit the text to others.

Second, an *instruction* is basically the transmission of a technique of performance. An instruction often accompanies a particular text or ritual as a set of subsidiary suggestions, helpful hints for the more effective performance of the ceremony, outlining perhaps special visualizations or offerings for particular purposes and different variations that may be performed. It often includes advice on the erection of the altar, or on how to regulate the contemplative periods. The term here includes also the techniques for improving a visualization which are transmitted from one's Master in informal session; for example, the visualized deity may seem "wobbly," so the Master may suggest visualizing a larger lotus throne to make the seat more stable.

Included under this category is every sort of technique, and those techniques that are basic to a ritual performance (rather than subsidiary advice) are collectively called *teachings* rather than instructions proper. Thus, for example, the transmission in an informal session with the head monk of how to make the tormas, perform the hand gestures, or sing the chants of a ritual or contemplation is technically a teaching; this does form a true lineage, for the style of singing can vary considerably from monastery to monastery, and the decorations on the tormas may have been passed down from an earlier Master in a particular sect. More often, however, the term "teaching" implies the more formal transmission from one's Master of a contemplative technique, such as the proper visualizations to accompany the recitation of a ritual, the meaning of the various acts performed therein, or even the correct yogic postures and breathing exercises.

A special subsidiary of this is the *deep teaching* that deals particularly with contemplative problems; here, in formal consultation with one's Master (offering him a maṇḍala and so on), one receives permission to change the actual content of a received contemplation to alleviate any special difficulties one may have in performing it. Occasionally too, a very difficult text will be accompanied by its own deep teaching, which is given as an appendix wherein the author outlines a range of permissible variation. Thus a teaching tells how to perform a ritual, expanding upon the outline recitation of the ritual text; an instruction gives advice as to how the visualization may be better performed or adapted to special purposes; and a deep teaching changes the visualization itself to suit the individual practitioner.

Third, *initiation* includes a wide range of different rituals. In its strictest sense it refers to the *great initiation* that is received only for the high patron deities of the Tantras (Guhyasamāja, Cakrasaṃvara, Hevajra, and so on), or occasionally (there seems to be some disagreement between the Karma and the Dragon Kajü about this) for the fierce patrons and the "Lord of knowledge." This great initiation is received in a private and very formal session with one's Master, who is visualized to be the deity himself (and may indeed appear as the deity to his disciple), and it consists of the well-known fourfold sequence of flask initiation, secret initiation, initiation into the knowledge of wisdom, and the "fourth" initiation.[16] The Dragon Kajü, for instance, have four special "golden initiations" for the lineage of gurus, the Diamond Sow, Cakrasaṃvara, and the Four-handed Lord; these are most difficult to obtain and correspondingly precious. The "ancient" Nyingma ritual of "evoking the heart of the guru" is considered to be the equivalent of a great initiation.

Every great monastic ritual of evocation, whether for the high patron deities or for the Lord of knowledge, includes as an integral part of the ceremony another sort of initiation, which is received not from one's Master in the form of the deity but rather from the deity himself generated in the maṇḍala on the altar in front of the practitioner, whether evoked in solitary contemplation or in the assembly hall with the other monks. The empowerment of this initiation may be passed along to lay people waiting outside the assembly hall, by touching them on the head with the flask, crown, vajra, bell, and so on, which are used as part of the initiation ritual inside. This initiation is called a *self-entering* or an *evocation initiation*. The first term implies a contemplative rather than an actual physical entering into the maṇḍala, for no one would ever step on or into a maṇḍala made of powdered colors, for obvious reasons.

There is some difference in the usage of these two terms between the Gelug and the Kajü sects. The Gelug, following the usage of Tsonk'apa's *Great Stages of the Mantra Path*, take the term "self-entering" as meaning the initiation received from the deity when the yogin is either practicing alone in solitary contemplation or when he is preparing himself in private to bestow a great initiation upon a disciple; and they consider an "evocation initiation" as meaning the initiation from the deity with the assembled monks during a large monastic ritual. The Kajü, on the other hand, subsume both these solitary and collective initiations under "self-entering"; they use the term "evocation initiation" to refer to the transmission of empowerment to nonparticipants, lay people who gather outside the hall to receive the purifying touch of the divine implements. It is convenient, in any event, to use the single term "self-entering" as a general designation for initiation from the visualized deity in front, as opposed to the great initiation received from one's Master in the form of the deity.

Whereas these initiations are limited to the high patron deities and the high protectors of the Law, the initiation for all other deities, including Tārā, is called a ritual of *permission* or *authorization*. Thus, for example, it is impossible to receive an initiation of Avalokiteśvara in any strict sense; rather one receives permission to practice his rituals and to contemplate his mantra in the ritual service. But the Tibetans themselves often use the term "initiation" to refer indiscriminately to both permission and initiation proper: if one is told that a high lama is giving an "Avalokiteśvara initiation" in the next monastery, and let's all go, it is presumed one knows that this is not a great initiation.

On its most basic level, permission is simply the empowerment of one's body, speech, and mind (and often also one's qualities and functions); indeed, the Sacha term for "permission" is simply "empowerment," and we have seen—in "healing the degeneration of vows and pledges"—that an empowerment of body, speech, and mind is termed a "permission." In other words, the permission consists essentially in making the recipient's body, speech, and mind pure and strong enough to practice the rituals of the particular deity, to visualize his body, recite his mantra, and contemplate his meditation—to gain all the magical powers that accrue to the self-generation; and the empowerment of function is the prerequisite permission to evoke and employ the deity's power and to effectuate and apply his mantra. But the empowerment thus bestowed by the initiating lama is of benefit even beyond its authorization to practice, and many Tibetans avidly collect initiations (with the intensity with which many Westerners collect stamps), seeking not only the rare and ultimately precious great initiations but also the empowering permissions of as many deities as possible. "There are three Vehicles," says one text,[17] "the Vehicle of the Disciples, the Vehicle of the Solitary Buddhas, and the Great Vehicle; this ritual is the Great Vehicle. Therein also are two: the maturing initiation and the liberating path; this ritual is the initiation. Therein also are three: the maturing initiation which includes the four preliminary initiations [the great initiation], the ritual of permission of body, speech, and mind, and the simple empowerment of the deity gathered in at the end of the ritual; this is the ritual of permission."

To this permission there is often added what is called a *torma initiation*, where the Master (to use an informant's metaphor) "introduces" the deity to the recipient; here the deity is generated in a torma, the Master prays the deity's favor for his disciple, and the deity is aborbed by contact into the recipient's body, now rendered a fit vessel to contain this power through the preceding ritual of permission. The structure here is exactly the same as that we have seen in the "initiation through the life torma," and again there may be used either the usual offering torma made of dough or the special metal initiation torma. Thus the power to contemplate the deity is transmitted through the primary magical means of the Master's visualization and recitation in the ritual of permission, and to this there may be added the further magical device of the torma, in its second and third aspects—as an evocation and as a substance of magical attainment.

THE VOWS AND PLEDGES

In the course of his career a practitioner has made two types of vow: the vows of the monastic discipline and the vows of a Bodhisattva. But before he is bestowed any full-scale initiation he must make a third vow—either in private session with his Master or as part of the ritual text itself—as a "holder of the mantra." He binds himself with a fearsome oath to guard this Tantric vow and the pledges that accompany it:[18]

> When the disciple enters the maṇḍala, the Master should speak these words: "You must not speak this highest secret of all the Tathāgatas before anyone who has not entered the maṇḍala. If your vows are broken, if you do not guard them, then when you die you will most surely fall into hell." And then the pledges should be given:
>
> Not forsaking the Three Jewels . . .
>
> and so on, as it is given in full in the Tantras. And the disciple swears an oath:
>
> I take this great pledge, this King of the Law;
> should I ever break it
> I pray the Buddhas and Bodhisattvas,
> all who protect the highest practice of the mantra,
> pluck out from me
> my heart and blood!
> You who guard the teachings of the Law:
> do not spurn me!

Thus, as Tsongk'apa says, "one stakes one's life on the vows and pledges, and it is necessary to keep them."[19] Indeed, in some rituals the monks will here drink a mixture of nectar, magic pills, and beer which has been empowered with OṂ ĀḤ HUṂ, and they will recite: "This is your water of hell, and if I depart from my pledges let it consume me! But if I keep my pledges, may this diamond water of nectar grant me the magical attainments!"[20]

Usually, the vows the disciple here takes include those common to both Tantra and the Great Vehicle, as well as those peculiar to the Tantra. One initiation text begins the vows with the following most general and basic Buddhist precepts:[21]

> You must not kill living beings,
> or speak what is not true;
> you must not take what is not given,
> or consort with the wives of others.
> Abandon all sins:
> the three sins of the body,
> the four sins of speech,

and the three sins of the mind.
You must ever give the four gifts:
the Law, material possessions,
friendliness, and fearlessness—
if without them yourself, then by rituals of meditation.
You must ever resort to
the four methods of conversion.
You must never revile those who have been perfected,
those with strengths, those with powers,
women, or any living being.

Beyond these are the peculiarly Tantric vows, generally subsumed under the headings of the fourteen "basic downfalls" and the eight "gross transgressions"; the vow to avoid all these is considered general to the five families of Buddhas. The Longdö lama Ngawang lozang lists the basic downfalls of the Tantric practitioner as follows:[22]

1) to slander one's guru
2) to transgress the ordinances of the Well-gone One
3) to be angry at one's Diamond Brothers
4) to abandon friendliness
5) to give up one's thought of enlightenment
6) to disparage the tenets of other sects
7) to tell the secrets
8) to be contemptuous of one's [enlightened] essence
9) to slander Emptiness
10) to be friendly toward evil persons
11) not to contemplate Emptiness
12) to argue with others
13) to be shaken from one's pledges
14) to slander women, who are the source of wisdom

Similarly, he lists the gross transgressions as follows:

1) to get things on the strength of one's wisdom
2) to get things on the strength of one's nectar
3) to give away secrets to the uninitiated
4) to dispute in an assembly
5) to preach perverted views to the faithful
6) to dwell among those of the Little Vehicle
7) to pride oneself on one's yoga
8) to teach the Law to the unfaithful

The basic intentional thrust of these vows is clear: the yogin should keep his own counsel, avoid falling into intellectual or spiritual pride, and devote himself to contemplation.

The recipient next takes the ancillary pledges, considered to be individual to each of the five families. Ngawang lozang lists these as follows: (1) the pledge of Vairocana: to be faithful to the Three Jewels and the Three Disciplines; (2) the pledge of Akṣobhya: to be faithful to the vajra, the bell, the hand gesture, and the Master; (3) the pledge of Ratnasambhava: to give material possessions, fearlessness, friendliness, and the Law; (4) the pledge of Amitābha: to be faithful to the higher and lower Tantras and to the Three Vehicles; and (5) the pledge of Amoghasiddhi: to strive in the inner and outer offerings and in one's vows. Thus the Master might say to his disciple:[23]

The Buddha, the Law, the Assembly:
to the Three Jewels you have gone for refuge.
Let this be your firm pledge
of the pure Buddha family.

The wise man should cling to
the vajra, the bell, the hand gesture,
for the vajra is the thought of enlightenment
and wisdom is the bell.

He should also cling to his Master,
for this guru is the equal of all Buddhas.
Take this vow as your pledge
of the pure Vajra family.

For the highest and great Ratna family
three times each day and night
you should ever give the four gifts:
material possessions, fearlessness,
friendliness, and the Law.

You should cling to the holy Law,
the Three Vehicles: outer, inner, secret.
Take this vow as your pledge
of the pure Padma family.

For the highest and great Karma family
take all the vows
and keep them truly:
be fit for the rites of offering.

And finally the recipient takes the ancillary pledges for the particular deity whose initiation he is to receive. Thus one text gives the following pledges which must be kept by one who practices the rituals of Tārā:[24]

In particular you must never take
a woman whose name is Tārā,
for she is the residence of the mantra practice.
In the walled towns and villages,
in the country districts,
you should ever pay homage to Tārā,
especially at the sides of a door,
at crossroads, beside a wall,
or where three roads cross,
praising her and making great offerings there.
You should station yourself at those places
and evoke her mantra.
Whenever you as a yogin see any woman
whose name is Tārā,
pale red in color, beautiful-eyed,
with devotion
pay her homage with your mind.
The practitioner should take to himself
the pāṇḍu flower,
and likewise the karavīra,
and never should he tread
on any other red flower.

The recipient of the authorization to perform Tārā's rituals thus pledges himself to bear her ever in his mind and to evoke her especially at the places that symbolize the boundary between this world and the divine. Every woman whose name is Tārā (and it is a common name in both India and Tibet) becomes to him a symbol of the goddess, and every red flower reminds him of her red Lotus family. And thus the text continues:

When all the vows have thus been given,
with water placed in the flasks,
divine water, clean and pure,
with water of the mantra
the disciple should be purified.

This, then, is the initiation proper, and to it we now turn.

THE RITUAL OF PERMISSION

The permission of white Tārā as given in the corpus of Kongtrü rinpoch'e is preparatory authorization which, in the text's own words, "makes one a fit vessel for her practice." Thus this ritual is the necessary preliminary to the ritual service of the goddess; without the strengthening of this initiation, no ordinary human body could contain her power, no ordinary human speech could recite her mantra, and no ordinary human mind could contemplate the Emptiness that is her essence. The recipients of this permission are not only authorized to enter upon the particular ritual service whose textual transmission they receive, but they are also now rendered capable of its performance through the magic of the Master. The structure of this transmision of contemplative power is the same as that for the transmission of the power of life: here the guru's magic is directed into the persons of his disciples, and his own visualization and recitation make his followers fit to acquire the deity's power on their own.

1 *Preparations*

In giving the permission that makes one a fit vessel for her practice, there are two parts: the preparations and the ritual itself. Thus the Diamond Master—who has reached the limits of the ritual service and evocation of this deity and has obtained the signs of success therein—should, when he wishes to bless his disciples, set out on the altar at an auspicious time the same items mentioned for evocation and offering [the generation in front].

Thus the assembly hall is cleaned and swept out, and the main altar is erected; it is adorned with the ritual utensils, a consecrated painting of the Holy Lady, and the bases of the body, speech, and mind of the Three Jewels: an image as representative of body, a book as representative of speech, and a stūpa as representative of mind as made manifest in the relics of a holy person.

In front of the altar is a clean, covered table for the materials of the initiation. In its center is placed the metal base of an offering maṇḍala; drawn on that with white powder is an eight-petaled lotus, in the center of which is arranged a pile of rice; above that on a raised stand is reverently placed an image of the Holy Lady. In front of the maṇḍala is a round white offering torma with four lotus petals and ornamental details of flowers made of colored butter; since the altar is here being set up to include a torma initiation, a similar offering torma, with the same ornamental details, is placed behind the maṇḍala as well.

For the permission proper there are set out two flasks—"having all the proper characteristics, unflawed by splits or cracks"—which are two-thirds filled with "water fetched from a waterfall by a pure youth or maiden, mixed with sweet perfume and the 'twenty-five substances of the flask.'" The *chief flask* is tied around the neck with a white ceremonial scarf, and on top of it is placed a small conch shell, inside of which is a tiny "mantra vajra"; this flask is placed to the right of the maṇḍala. (If there is no image of Tārā, or if there is being performed only the "generation in the flask," this chief flask is placed on top of the maṇḍala.) The *working flask* is tied around the neck with a green scarf and placed to the left of the maṇḍala. (See fig. 44).

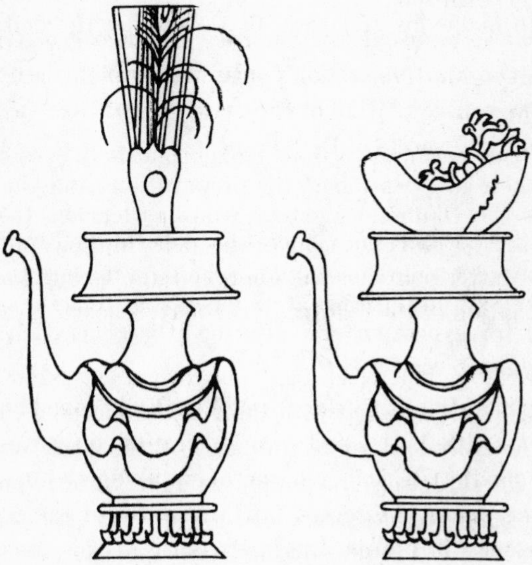

Fig. 44. The working flask (left) and the chief flask (right).

There are also set out ornaments of silk and precious gems placed in a silver pot and a small painting—the *tsakali*—of Tārā's emblem, the white lotus; these will be used in the permission rituals of "ornaments" and "emblem". And there is poured out food and drink, represented on the main altar by the food tormas, and in front of everything are placed the seven offering bowls containing the two waters and the five gifts.

On a table in front of the Diamond Master are placed his vajra and bell, a vessel filled with flowers, a white conch shell filled with scented water, a *kuśa*-grass sprinkler, grain for tossing upon the heads of the recipients, and mixed incense. On a small table to one side are set two white preliminary tormas and an offering maṇḍala to represent the fee given to the Master by his disciples.[25]

2 *The ritual*

The ritual itself begins with the Diamond Master, alone and in private, performing the three generations: self-generation, generation in front, and generation in the flask. The sequence follows the pattern for all rituals of evocation, and it may be briefly outlined as follows:

2.1 *Self-generation*

Beginning with the usual preliminaries of empowering the cleansing water and so on, this section continues through the Process of Generation, the contemplation of the mantra, and the "gathering in and arising" of the Process of Perfection.

2.2 *Generation in front*

Here, again, the Process of Generation is performed in front, and the Diamond Master performs the abbreviated offerings and praises and the effectuation of the mantra in the deity's heart.

2.3 *Generation in the flask*

This third generation is the focus of all that has gone before; as in the thread-cross ritual, the first two generations prepare the Diamond Master for the magical function of applying the mantra, but here the divine power is directed into the water of the flask, with which the Master will bestow the initiation upon his disciples. As the *Hevajra Tantra* says [II.iii.12]:

> One is bathed, one is sprinkled [*sicyate*],
> and therefore it is called "initiation" [*seka*].

And K'edrubje Geleg pezangpo says:[26] "By initiation with water, if one contemplates the path based thereon, one is able to wash away the defilements which block the way to Buddhahood." Thus the generation in the flask is the equivalent of the evocation of the life torma and life substances of the initiation into life: all these are magical devices and/or recipes for the transmission of power. The initiation into life combined the generation in front with the evocation of the divine torma, so that the mantra was effectuated therein; in our ritual of permission the evocation and then the employment are kept separate, so the mantra is applied to the divine water. But the axioms and structure of both rituals are the same: the individual authors of ritual texts create variations on a dramatic theme, even for the same ritual. A practitioner's enjoyment of a ritual—his liking for one text over another—is in no small measure an aesthetic decision.

In most instances there are two flasks used to contain this magically potent and divine water of initiation: the flask that is actually used in the ritual is called, appropriately, the "working flask," while the flask in which the deity is originally generated—in exactly the same way as she is generated into, say, an amulet of protection or a life torma—is called the "victorious flask" or, more often in conversation than in the texts, the "chief flask."

As we have seen, the flasks are filled with sweet-scented water, and on top of the chief flask is placed a small conch shell, in which there is some water and the miniature mantra vajra: a five-colored "mantra thread" is tied around the vajra, the other end of which will be held over the Master's heart as he recites the mantra, that its power may be transmitted along the thread and applied to the water in the flask.

Then the *chief flask* is cleansed and purified with the two mantras, and the Master visualizes as he recites:

> From the realm of Emptiness is PAṂ; from that, a varicolored lotus; from A a moon, and upon that throne is BHRŪṂ, and from that a jeweled white flask, its belly broad, its neck long, its spout suspended, clear and unimpeded, completely perfect in all characteristics, a piece of divine cloth tied around its neck and its mouth adorned with a wishing tree. It is filled inside with water of the "five times five" [the twenty-five substances of the flask] and of nectar, and in the middle is PAṂ; from that, a white lotus . . .

And the Master continues through the standard steps of the fourfold Process of Generation, concluding with the initiation of the goddess. He "fills in" the offerings—replacing water that has evaporated from the bowls and so on—and he empowers the offerings as we have seen before, generating them from Emptiness and reciting OṂ ĀḤ HŪṂ with the flying-bird gesture. He recites:

> This oblation, of holy and divine substance,
> arisen through conditioned coproduction,
> I offer to the Noble Lady and her retinue;
> I pray she accept it for the sake of beings.

OṂ SARVA-TATHĀGATA-ĀRYA-TĀRĀ-SAPARIVĀRA ARGHAṂ PRATĪCCHA PŪJA-MEGHA-SAMUDRA-SPHARAṆA-SAMAYE ĀḤ HŪṂ!

He repeats the verse and the mantra, substituting the proper words, for all the offerings up to ŚABDA, and having thus made the offerings to the goddess he has evoked in the flask, he praises her with the hymn composed by Vāgīśvarakīrti himself:

Lady whose eyes flash like lightning,
heroine, TĀRE, TUTTĀRE,
born from the corolla of the lotus
of the Buddha's face: to you I bow.
Lady whose face is like the circle
of the full autumn moon,
lady who grasps a lotus flower
with the gift-bestowing gesture,
homage to you!
From the cage of this world TUTTĀRE!
Pacifying defilements with SVĀHĀ!
With OṂ by your very essence
opening the gate of Brahma: to you I bow.
Protecting the entire world
from the eight great terrors,
Blessed Lady, mother of all,
homage to Tārā, the mother!

The Master then recites the mantra, holding one end of the mantra thread to his heart, beginning with the recitation of his visualization:

From the mantra garland in my own heart [visualized during the preceding self-generation] there radiates forth an unbroken outpouring of white light, which travels along the mantra thread and touches the wheel and syllables in the heart of the deity in the flask, so that it arouses the stream of her heart. From that wheel light radiates forth and invites as an essence of nectar all the empowerment of the knowledge of all the Buddhas and all the life and merit of all animate beings and inanimate objects. This dissolves into the heart of the deity in the flask, so that there falls a stream of the nectar of knowledge from the wheel and its syllables and all parts of her body, and the flask is filled with it completely.

Maintaining this visualization, he recites the ten-syllable mantra and its appendix for long life (MAMA ĀYUḤ . . .). If he has any special use in mind, the text adds, such as a function of pacifying, he may change the visualization and insert the appropriate appendix.

And he concludes by performing the slightly abbreviated offerings, praises, and prayers.

Then, reciting OṂ VAJRA-ARGHAṂ ĀḤ HŪṂ! he takes the conch shell—not removing the mantra vajra or the mantra thread—and pours the water therefrom into the flask, "as if it were an oblation." While ringing his bell, he recites the 100-syllable mantra three times:

> The Blessed Lady and the wheel in her heart melt into an essence of the nectar of knowledge, which becomes indissolubly one with the water of the symbolic flask [i.e., the visualized flask, the analogue of the symbolic being].

He visualizes that the flask is covered with a "diamond net," and he protects it with OṂ ĀḤ HŪṂ!

Except for some specific differences (the conch shell and the mantra thread, for instance), this generation is structurally identical with the evocation of the various magic and protective devices described in chapter ii; indeed, this water may now be used in a large number of different ways, depending upon the mantra that has been applied to it. "The gurus of the past maintained," says one text,[27] "that the mantra garland travels along the mantra thread and dissolves into the heart of the deity inside the flask, so that the nectar falls from the wheel and its mantra, mixing with the water in the flask. One may then, for example, wash a sick person with the water from the flask or, leaving a little leftover water in the conch shell on top of the chief flask, wash with that, and stop the ritual right there."

If the flasks are to be used in an initiation, however, it is further necessary to generate the *working flask.* Most of the permission rituals of Tārā specify the evocation therein of Hayagrīva, the fierce high patron deity of the Padma Family; but our text gives the more general evocation of Swirling Nectar. With his mantra (OṂ VAJRA-AMṚTA-KUṆḌALI HANA HANA HŪṂ PHAṬ!) the working flask is cleansed, and with the SVABHĀVA mantra it is purified:

> From the realm of Emptiness, upon a lotus and sun in the middle of the working flask, is HŪṂ, and from that there arises Swirling Nectar, his body colored blue-green, in his right hand a vajra club and his lift hand in the threatening gesture, with all the appurtenances of a fierce deity.

Again the Master recites the AMṚTA mantra, and he makes offerings with OṂ VAJRA-ARGHAṂ and so on. He praises the deity with this verse:

> Blessed Nectar, I join my palms in reverence
> and do homage and praise to the blessed great fierce one
> who knows the anger that annihilates the four Māras
> by the strength of raising his thought of enlightenment
> up to the top of his head.
>
> The fierce deity Swirling Nectar melts into light, and every single atom of water becomes a host of fierce deities.[28]

The same basic structure is used in the texts that generate Hayagrīva in the working flask, but in this case the flask is cleansed with his mantra OṂ VAJRA-KRODHA-HAYAGRĪVA HULU HULU HŪṂ PHAṬ! and then purified into Emptiness with the SVABHĀVA mantra. His generation, as follows, may be compared with that of Swirling Nectar:

> From the realm of Emptiness, upon a lotus and sun in the middle of the working flask, is a red HRĪḤ [the seed syllable of the Lotus Family] upon a throne of the four Māras, which transforms into Hayagrīva, the king of the fierce deities, his body colored red, one-faced, two-handed. With his right hand he brandishes a stick, and his left hand makes the threatening gesture. The red-yellow hair on the crown of his head bristles upward, and there protrudes from its midst a green horse head whose fierce muzzle screams and whinnies, subjugating the triple world. His head, body, and limbs are adorned with all the appurtenances of a fierce deity, with snakes and dried skulls and tiger skin. He wears clothes of the flayed skin of the king of death. No one is able to harm him; he is short and thick, his belly hangs down, he stands with his feet in the "flinging" posture in the midst of light and unequaled brilliance.
>
> In his heart, above the circle of a sun, is HRĪḤ, its edge surrounded by the garland of his mantra, annihilating all who would cause harm; and nectar falls from the mantra garland, mixing with the water in the flask, which becomes sublime in color and in strength.

Again the Master recites the mantra OṂ VAJRA-KRODHA-HAYAGRĪVA HULU HULU HŪṂ PHAṬ! and he makes offerings with OṂ VAJRA-ARGHAṂ PRATĪCCHA SVĀHĀ and so on. He praises the deity with this verse:

> Body of the highest horse, born from HRĪḤ,
> burning defilements with light like that of the sun,
> hero who conquers all four Māras:
> homage to Hayagrīva!

And then the deity is "entrusted to his function":

> May Nayagrīva, king of fierce deities, perform his function of averting obstacles and hindering demons![29]

3 *The initiation*

When both flasks have been generated, the disciples (who have been waiting outside until the Master completed the above private rituals) wash themselves with the empowered water from the working flask, reciting "Just as when the Buddha was born . . ." They rinse out their mouths and take off their shoes at the side of the door, prostrate three times, and seat themselves in rows before the Master.

3.1 *Preliminaries*

3.11 *The preliminary torma and circle of protection*

The first step in the initiation proper is the establishment of an area of sacred ground, freed of all harmful influence by bribing the hindering demons to depart and expelling the obstinate spirits who remain. The Master sprinkles cleansing water on the preliminary tormas with his *kuśa*-grass sprinkler held in the diamond-lady-of-the-mind gesture, as he cleanses them with the AMṚTA mantra and purifies them with the SVABHĀVA mantra:

> From the realm of Emptiness is OṂ, and from the OṂ jeweled vessels, vast and broad, inside of which is OṂ. From the melting thereof arise tormas of divine substance, an ocean of nectar, the five sense gratifications.

He empowers these visualized tormas with OṂ ĀḤ HŪṂ and the flying-bird gesture, repeated three times; and he summons the guests with the iron-hook gesture and SARVA-BHŪTA ĀKARṢAYA JAḤ! Then, holding his vajra in his open palm, he says three times: OṂ SARVA-BHŪTA-SAPARIVĀRA NAMAḤ TATHĀGATE-BHYOḤ VIŚVAMUKHEBHYAḤ SARVATHĀ-KHAṂ UDGATE SPHARAṆA IMAṂ GAGANA-KHAṂ GṚHṆÊDAṂ BALY-ĀDI SVĀHĀ! Then, with the sword-striking gesture, he presents the demons with the tormas by reciting the A-KĀRO mantra three times; and then, with his right hand in the fearless gesture holding his vajra, and his left hand ringing the bell, he recites:

To whatever *lha* or *lu* there are,
nöjin, *sinpo*, or any others,
I give this torma for the sake of our mantra practice:
I pray you accept it!
And having accepted this torma given in offering
let us all, yogins and retinue,
accomplish all that we wish!

And the preliminary tormas are thrown out the door of the assembly hall to the spirits gathered and waiting to receive them.[30] Then the Master expels all the remaining demons by saying:

> By the empowerment of the truth of the holy and glorious gurus, my own reverend guru and those of the lineage, the truth of the teachings of the Buddha, the Law and the Assembly, of the mantras, vidyās, spells, heart mantras, and hand gestures, of Reality and of Suchness, the truth of the inexorability of cause and effect in karmic things, the truth of the Protectors and their retinue who guard the Diamond Law, and the Great Truth:
>
> may all evil spirits and hindering demons, who would create obstacles to the accomplishment for these Diamond Disciples of the permission of the blessed White Tārā Cintācakra, who would disturb their reading or, especially, who would harm their body, speech, or mind, or who would kill them: may they not remain here! May they go elsewhere! And by the blazing fire of the Diamond of Knowledge, may the heads of all those who do not depart crack into a hundred pieces!

He recites the fierce OṂ SUMBHANI mantra while the fierce music sounds in the assembly hall; the demons are expelled by the flinging of magic mustard seed and the smoke of *gugü* incense, while he visualizes: "The hindering demons are expelled by many hosts of fierce deities who radiate forth from my own heart." Then, about the sacred precincts cleared of demons, he erects a circle of protection:

> The fierce deities dissolve back into me. From the seed in my heart [remaining from the previous self-generation] light radiates forth in the ten directions, and there arises therefrom a circle of protection, vast and broad, a diamond ground, with fence, lattice, tent, canopy, and blazing fire of knowledge, firm everywhere. OṂ VAJRA-RAKṢA HŪṂ HŪṂ HŪṂ PHAṬ SVĀHĀ!

3.12 *The lesson in the Law*

The disciples are now given their explanation of the initiation, here rather more detailed than the one we have seen before, it being expected that the recipients of a "permission" are to proceed upon the path of contemplation and require a more extensive analysis of their lineage:[31]

> We should be placed in the rank of the holy Tārā, who pacifies the impediments to life which are the condition of all beings, as infinite as space, and who is ultimately the essence of deathless life and knowledge. It is to that end that you should awaken the thought of enlightenment, deeply desiring the profound permission of the supreme deity Cintācakra, and pay the most clear and continual attention to the Law as it is taught in the scriptures and Tantras. So listen carefully.
>
> Now the Tantras wherein the holy White Tārā is expounded are as follows: in the *Tantra of Tārā the Yoginī, Source for All Rituals*[32] it says:
>
> Set the person who is the object of the ritual
> in the middle of an eight-spoked wheel;
> on the eight spokes, eight syllables,
> surrounded by the lords of the city of her mantra.
> By a green wheel one is protected;
> one cheats death with a white one.
>
> In the *Tantra of the Four Sites of Pilgrimage*,[33] at the end of its explanation of the evocation of Green Tārā, it says:
>
> On a wheel that is an eight-petaled lotus
> surrounded by an outside rim,
> in the middle, above, and below,
> should be placed the whole recitation,
> the rim encircled with the vowels:
> thus one should contemplate the white wheel.
>
> Now Tāranātha and Tenpe nyinje [Situ VIII, 1700-1775] and his disciples all assert that these are the sources for White Tārā. Earlier scholars in Tibet, on the other hand, maintained that her cult was based on the *Basic Ritual of Tārā*[34] and other of the Practical Tantras in the Lotus family. But in that work (as well as in others of the same group, such as the *Tantra Which is the Source for All the Functions of Tārā*[35]) the description of and the teachings about Cintācakra are different from those given in the works quoted above, even though it does explain her mantras in general and her four basic functions in particular.
>
> Now the commentaries in which she is found are as follows: The master Vāgīśvarakīrti, blessed in person by the holy Tārā herself, extraced from various scriptures and Tantras his *Cheating Death*,[36] a clear and extended evocation of the White Tārā Cintācakra.
>
> Here in Tibet, five traditions have come down to us based upon the redaction of that work by the one called "Scholar Chief Disciple." These are the school of Ngog, the school of Atīśa, the school of Bari, the school of Nyen, and the school of Nachi rinch'en.

> Among these, the most distinguished is the school of Atīśa: both he and his own teacher, Dharmakīrti of the Golden Isles, continually saw the face of the Holy Lady, and upon them was bestowed the tradition. This was the earliest of the traditonal streams of her schools to come to this country; and, descending from him right up to our own times, it has been an unboken lineage of those who have gained the two sorts of magical attainment in general, and the magical attainment of bodily life in particular.
>
> Again, among the many streams of tradition into which this split, the one that has the brilliance of empowerment is the stream of tradition of the Karma Kajü, who follow the school of Gampopa [1079-1153], for not only did Gampopa himself gather together the rivers of counsel of all the traditional schools, both earlier and later, beginning with the school of Ngog, but this tradition is also mixed together with the lineage of those counsels given personally by the Holy Lady to the Great Magician Karma Bakṣi [Karmapa II, 1206-1283] and the Lord of the Law Röpe doje [Karmapa IV, 1340-1383]. And in later times, too, the Omniscient Chöchi jungne [i.e., Situ VIII Tenpe nyinje, 1700-1775] was also empowered with certainly and blessed by the Holy Lady.[37]

We have already seen how the Geshe Drepa received the Bari lineage from Lenagpa, when he had been frightened from his scholarly complacency by the prediction of the palmist from Ladakh; but many texts report that Drepa received also the Atīśa lineage, which had passed from Jewe jungne, Atīśa's chief disciple, to the Chenngawa Ts'ütr'imbar.[38] Thus there are stories that Drepa approached the Chenngawa about the "many signs that had appeared in his dreams": he had dreamed that the circle of the sun rose in the west and set in the east. When he told this dream to the Chenngawa, the latter said: "This dream is very bad. It is well known that the sun sinking into a valley is a sign of death. But I will give you this evocation of Cintācakra, a profound method by which it is impossible that you not avert death, even if your limbs have been scattered."[39]

Drepa thus passed both the Bari and Atīśa lineages on to Gampopa, who found himself, like his teacher, in danger of untimely death. It seems that when Gampopa was just 42 years old he was practicing evocation one-pointedly in a solitary cave in the mountains, when all at once a ḍākiṇī prophesied that he would die after only three more years. So he set out to wander with no fixed abode, cultivating his contemplative skill in homeless travel, until he heard of the great fame of the Geshe Drepa; he came into Drepa's presence and asked to be taught the Law.

"You are an especially holy person," the Geshe told him, "and you will augment the aims of beings."

"I will not have time to serve the aim of beings," Gampopa said. "A ḍākiṇī has predicted that I have left but three years of life."

"Not quite," the Geshe replied. "I have a special teaching that is effective even if your grave is dug, even if there come hosts of signs of death, and I will give it to you."

So the Geshe gave him the evocation of White Tārā Cintācakra, along with the ritual of permission to practice it; and because Gampopa truly experienced it in his mind, he averted all the obstacles to his bodily life and lived until he was eighty years old, augmenting the aims of beings.[40]

Thus the Kajü claim through Gampopa at least three lineages of White Tārā: Tārā to Dharmakīrti to Atīśa and his disciples to Chenngawa to Drepa; Tārā to Vāgīśvarakīrti to Amoghavajra to Bari to Lenagpa to Drepa; and Atīśa to Nejorpa to Nyugrumpa. All of these were "collected" by Gampopa.[41] And Gampopa passed these teachings on to Lord Düsum ch'enpa [Karmapa I, 1110-1193], who gave them to Rech'enpa, who gave them to Bomdragpa, who gave them to Karma Bakṣi [Karmapa II, 1206-1283], who gave them to Ojenpa, who gave them to Rangjung doje [Karmapa III, 1284-1339], who gave them to Yungtönpa, who gave them to Röpe doje [Karmapa IV, 1340-1383], "and so on through the lineage."[42]

Meanwhile the Master is continuing to address his disciples:

> The traditional practice is to perform Tārā's daily rituals according to the Practical Tantras. The source of this tradition is that when Atīśa came to Tibet he was enjoined by the Tibetans from teaching the Tantras of the Highest Yoga; thus was established the tradition of evoking Tārā in a manner agreeable to the Common Vehicle. But we know that Atīśa had a ritual of her evocation based on the Tantras of the Highest Yoga which was included in his *Hayagrīva and the Fourfold Retinue of Dog-faced Ḍākiṇīs*:[43] and this ritual was given already in the canonical *Tantra of Tārā the Yoginī, Source for All Rituals*, though legend has it that this was a personal revelation—a "face-seeing"—of Atīśa.

Then, whether the Master has been reading the above or has been giving his own extemporaneous lecture on the Law, he continues in the following words:

> Now these instructions, which have come down to us from such an especially distinguished stream of tradition as this, are of many

different sorts, writings and handbooks both long and short; but the best of those we have at the present time is as stated in the hidden prophecy discovered by the Rigdzin Zhigpo lingpa:

> He will be named "Īśvara" and bear the Black Hat,
> conquering savage Māra
> and preserving the teachings of the Buddha;
> just seeing his face will shut the doors of evil destiny.

This prophecy refers to Wangch'ug doje [Karmapa IX, 1556-1603], the ninth Black Hat incarnation of the Lord of the World, who was taught personally by the noble Tārā and other supreme deities. He collected together many evocations, old and new, and he wrote two anthologies: the *Jeweled Garland of Ritual Visualizations* and the *Ritual of Permission: Knowing One, Liberated in All*.[44] Here we shall perform the ritual of permission of the noble Tārā Cintācakra according to this school.

3.13 *The offering of the maṇḍala*

But now I have done all that is proper for a Master to do, and you, my disciples, must do your part: I ask you to offer up a maṇḍala.

The disciples proceed to do so, following a separate text, although the recitation of this part is so well known that it is often unnecessary for it to be read, even the lay people saying it by heart. When they have offered up their fee for this initiation—and the fee for anything as precious as an initiation is inevitably infinite, the offering up of the whole world in the form of a maṇḍala—the Master continues:

Now, in the presence of your guru, who is indistinguishable from Cintācakra herself, you must repeat after me the following prayer, that you may ask for this profound permission:

> Through the graciousness of my glorious guru
> and of all the Buddhas of the three times,
> I pray that I may be given
> the permission of Cintācakra.

This is repeated three times, the Master pausing after each line so that the assembled disciples can repeat it. Then he once again continues:

In order that you, my disciples, may purify your streams, you should now, before your guru who is inseparable from the patron deity, recite after me the following sevenfold office, the preliminary awakening of the thought of enlightenment:

> I go for refuge to the Three Jewels . . .
> . . . and may I attain Buddhahood for the benefit of beings.

Again this is repeated three times, with a pause after each line.

3.14 *The ground for permission*

To establish the ground for the ritual, the Master leads the assembled recipients step by step through the self-generation, and through their visualization of the bestowing deity before them, and of the Master himself as the deity. He begins by saying: "Now, in order to establish the ground for this permission, you should all perform the following visualization." He sprinkles them with water from the working flask, cleanses them with the OṂ VAJRA-KRODHA mantra, purifies them into Emptiness with the SVABHĀVA mantra, and recites for them the Process of Generation:

> Visualize that from the realm of Emptiness there is, instantaneously, a circle of protection, a diamond ground with fence, tent, fire, and mountains; and in the middle thereof—in the place where each of you is sitting—is PAṂ, and from that a white lotus. . . Upon that, each of your own innate minds is a white TĀṂ . . . and from its transformation you yourselves become the noble Tārā . . . marked on the heart with a blue HŪṂ.

Here the Master again fills in the text with the appropriate contemplations, simultaneously visualizing his disciples' generation as the empowered goddess, that his own control of appearances may make up for any lack in the contemplative ability of the recipients.

> Thus, you who will receive this initiation have generated yourselves as the patron deity, the noble Tārā, and now you must vividly visualize the bestower of the initiation; there is set out in front of you an image in the middle of a maṇḍala to serve as a support for your visualization during this generation in front.
>
> That image, together with the torma that is also set out ["if there is going to be a torma initiation," the text adds in a note], instantaneously becomes a circle of protection, a diamond ground with fence, tent, fire, and mountains, in the middle of which, on a throne of white lotus and moon, is the noble Tārā . . . marked in the heart with a blue HŪṂ.
>
> You must also forcefully and vividly visualize that the Master too is Cintācakra in person; and from the Master's heart and from all parts of his body there radiate forth hosts of multicolored lights, which touch the goddess generated in front. From the heart and from all parts of the body of the goddess generated in front there radiate forth hosts of multicolored lights, which enter

into you through your foreheads; they pervade the entire inside and outside of your bodies, and by dissolving into you they pacify all your sins and obscurations, all your broken vows, lusts, diseases, impediments, all your misfortunes.

There comes the blessed Lady Cintācakra, surrounded by hosts of Buddhas and Bodhisattvas neither great nor small but infinite. And, in the form of light, all the empowerment and magical attainments of the body, speech, mind, qualities, and functions of the Three Highest Jewels and the Three Basic Ones who dwell in the vast numbers of Buddha fields in the ten directions—all of it dissolves within you, that your body, speech, and mind become inseparable from the body, speech, and mind of the blessed Cintācakra.

From the realm of thought which arises through this descent of the knowledge being, there is your own genuine mind; relax therein, and into this realm of Great Bliss and the Clear Light enter unhesitatingly as long as it lasts.

While the disciples thus earnestly contemplate, the altar server waves the smoke of sweet-smelling incense; to the drawn-out playing of the "gentle music"—the ringing of the Master's bell—the Master recites the basic 10-syllable mantra, adding on at its end: ĀVEŚAYA ĀVEŚAYA "Enter, enter" A A ! OṂ ĀḤ HŪṂ ! JAḤ HŪṂ BAṂ HOḤ ! repeated over and over again. Then, to make the knowledge being firm within the disciples, he makes a vajra cross on each disciple's head, saying each time TIṢṬHA VAJRA ! "Be firm, O Diamond !" If there are too many people for this to be done at all conveniently, he may, however, say it only once, flinging a handful of rice or grain over the heads of the assembly, instead of touching them individually. When the ground has thus been established—each of the disciples sealed by the Master in possession of the knowledge being, the disciple and deity bound into a unity by the vajra cross—the Master continues:

Now that we have thus finished establishing the ground for this permission, you should repeat after me this prayer, that you may ask for the five individual permissions—body, speech, mind, qualities, and functions—included within the permission proper:

May the master of the body, speech, and mind
of all the Buddhas of the three times
bestow upon me the permission
of the body, speech, and mind of Cintācakra.

This prayer is repeated three times, and then the actual ritual of permission begins.

3.2 *The permission*

3.21 *The permission of body*

We may note that the self-generated goddess has not yet been sealed by the initiation of the five families, but rather by the Master's vajra cross: this essential fourth step of the Process of Generation is here taken as the permission of body, the final actualization of the disciples' divinity and thus the authorization to contemplate themselves in the body of the goddess.

> Since you have thus prayed, light radiates forth from the HŪṂs in the heart of your Master, of the goddess in front, and of yourselves, inviting from their natural abode, each from his own abode, the five families of Father and Mother initiation deities and their retinues.

The entire assembly greets these initiation deities with offerings of ARGHAṂ and so on, reciting the mantras and performing the gestures together; and then the Master says:

> I pray that you bestow initiation upon these disciples!

> And because of my prayer, there come five families like themselves, Father and Mother, holding in their hands flasks filled with streams of the nectar of knowledge. Visualize that they bestow initiation upon you.

During this recitation the chief flask and the working flask are brought from the altar and placed before the Master. Here he holds up the chief flask in his right hand, his vajra (as always in an initiation) tucked between his thumb and forefinger; and he places the flask upon the disciples' heads (if there are too many people present he just holds it up in the air) as he recites:

> I give the great diamond of initiation,
> paid homage by the triple world,
> the source of the three secrets,
> the body, speech, and mind of all the Buddhas.

> OṂ SARVA-TATHĀGATA-KALĀŚA-GUHYA-PRAJÑĀJNĀNA-CATUR-ABHIṢEKATA-SAMAYA-ŚRĪYE HŪṂ!

> "OṂ The glory of the vow of initiation—the flask initiation, the secret initiation, the initiation of the knowledge of wisdom, the fourth initiation—of all the Tathāgatas HŪṂ!"

Here he touches the flask to the disciples' heads, throats, hearts, and navels, each place of the body corresponding to one of the four initiations (but again, if there are too many people, he simply walks down the rows as he recites the mantra, touching the flask briefly to the top of each one's head); and he pours out water from the chief flask into each of the recipient's hands, and each one drinks the water which is the goddess.

> Since you have thus been bestowed initiation, the stream of nectar from the flasks of the initiation deities fills the entire inside of your bodies; all the sins and obscurations of your body, speech, and mind are cleansed, and especially all the diseases, sins, obscurations, and untimely death which hurt or harm your body. You attain the four initiations; the remainder of the nectar overflows the top of your head, and you are thereby adorned upon your crown with an emanation of Amitābha, lord of the family. The initiation deities also, in the same manner as did the knowledge being, dissolve inseparably into you, and you contemplate with certain knowledge: "I am in truth the noble Tārā!"

And the Master recites the first benediction:

> Sublime as a mountain of gold,
> lord of the triple world,
> who has abandoned the three defilements,
> the Buddha whose eyes are like petals
> of a full-blown lotus:
> this is the first good fortune
> of the virtue of the world!

The Master rings his bell and scatters rice over the heads of the assembly:

> Thereby are cleansed all the sins and obscurations accumulated through your body, and are pacified all the misfortunes, diseases, hindering demons, and impediments which hurt or harm your body.
>
> This is the initiation that you may contemplate the body of Cintācakra through your own body; you now have the opportunity to manifest the Diamond of Body, and the fruit thereof is that you will gain a Body of Transformation adorned with the signs and secondary signs of a Buddha.
>
> This is the permission of body.

3.22 *The permission of speech*

The second permission is that of speech, and the Master bestows upon the recipients the authorization and the capacity to recite the mantra of the goddess:

Visualize that in your hearts, upon a lotus and moon, is a white eight-spoked wheel, in the center of which is a white syllable TĀṂ. Encircling the edge is OṂ MAMA ĀYUḤ-PUṆYA-JÑĀ-NA-PUṢṬIṂ-KURU HĀ, and on the eight spokes are TĀ RE TU TTĀ RE TU RE SVĀ. The syllables of the mantra are white, standing upright and facing inward, and have the form of blazing white light.

You should visualize the same thing in the hearts of the Master and of the goddess in front; and from those there radiate forth two garlands of mantras and light, of the same color, departing through their mouths and entering into you through your mouths. These dissolve into your hearts, and you should think that thereby you attain all the empowerment and magical attainments of the speech of the blessed Cintācakra, and of all the Conquerors who dwell in the ten directions and the three times. And while you are visualizing that, repeat after me the mantra.

The disciples then repeat after the Master the 10-syllable mantra seven times and the mantra with its long-life appendix three times. If there is only one person receiving the initiation, both the Master and the recipient hold the same rosary, counting off the recitations together as the disciple repeats the mantra. If there are many people present, actual practice varies from Master to Master: some lamas put the rosary in a bowl and walk down the rows, touching it to the recipients' throats; the present Karmapa simply holds the rosary himself as he recites.

Visualizing that each one of you gives to the Master a garland of flowers, recite after me:

I have grasped the Blessed One,
and I pray her look after me!

This is repeated three times, and the recipient gives a flower to the Master, or the assembly throws flowers (or rice) in the Master's direction. He continues: "Visualize that the garland of the mantra in your hearts becomes a garland of flowers, and that this is bound upon your heads." While reciting this the Master rings his bell, and he in turn touches the recipient upon the head with a flower, or flings flowers (or rice) over the heads of the assembly.

Blessed One, this has been bestowed upon them.
I pray you look after them,
I pray you grant them the magical attainments of the mantra,
I pray you make perfect their functions,
I pray you make firm their virtuous conduct.

May there enter into the streams of these holders of the mantra all the empowerment and strength of the Blessed Cintācakra!

And the Master recites the seond benediction:

The unwavering excellence which he taught,
famed in the triple world,
worshiped by gods and men,
the holiness of the Law,
source of happiness through all our lives:
this is the second food fortune
of the virtue of the world!

The Master again rings his bell and scatters rice over the heads of the assembly:

Thereby are cleansed all the sins and obscurations accumulated through your speech, and are pacified all the misfortunes, diseases, hindering demons, and impediments which hurt or harm your speech.

This is the initiation that you may recite the mantra of noble Tārā through your own speech; you now have the opportunity to manifest the Diamond of Speech, and the fruit thereof is that you will gain a Body of Bliss which has the sixty sorts of sweet speech.

This is the permission of speech.

3.23 *The permission of mind*

The third permission is that of mind, and the Master bestows upon the recipients the authorization and the capacity to enter into deep contemplative union with the goddess.

Vividly visualize the Master as the blessed Cintācakra, on whose heart is the seed syllable with its garland of the mantra. Light radiates forth therefrom, and there falls upon you a rain—in the form of white lotus flowers, Tārā's emblem—of all the strength, the knowledge of nonduality of mind, the empowerment and the magical attainments of the gurus, high patron deities, Buddhas, Bodhisattvas, ḍākas, ḍākiṇīs, protectors and guardians of the Law, who dwell in all the vast numbers of Buddha fields in the ten directions.

This dissolves into your hearts, and because of it light radiates forth from the seed therein, arousing the stream of the heart of the goddess in front. And from the goddess in front—just as one lamp is ignited from another—there comes a vivid and perfect body of the holy Cintācakra, which enters into you through the tops of your heads. It dissolves into your hearts, and you gain thereby the empowerment and magical attainments of her mind; you become of a single taste with the mind of the holy Tārā, and in this realm of thought you cease all your fabrications of the three times, you enter into deep comtemplation in the realm of the all-absorbing, the genuine and innate inseparability of light, knowledge, and Emptiness.

The Master touches each recipient's head with the image from the altar—that is, with Tārā herself, generated in front—and recites the mantra, adding at its end OṂ ĀḤ HŪṂ VAJRA-SAMAYAS TVAṂ! And the Master recites the third benediction:

The holy Assembly, possessed of the Law,
field of good fortune,
place of worship of men, gods, and demigods,
most excellent of hosts,
rich in modesty, knowledge, and glory:
this is the third good fortune
of the virtue of the world!

The Master again rings his bell and scatters rice over the heads of the assembly:

Thereby are cleased all the sins and obscurations accumulated through your mind, and are pacified all the misfortunes, diseases, hindering demons, and impediments which hurt or harm your mind.

This is the initiation that you may contemplate the deep contemplation of holy Tārā through your own mind; you now have the opportunity to manifest the Diamond of Mind, and the fruit thereof is that you will gain a Dharma Body which knows all things as they are.

This is the permission of mind.

Sometimes a Master—for instance, the present Jamyang ch'entse—will take a short break here for a minute or two, that he himself may contemplate the goddess before continuing.

3.24 *The permission of qualities*

The fourth permission is that of the deity's qualities, and the Master bestows upon the recipients the authorization and the capacity to perform the physical yoga of the Process of Perfection, the "permission of the ornaments":

Vividly visualizing yourselves as the deity, you are bestowed with her ornaments; hence you should think that you gain the magical attainments of the qualities of this deity and of all the Buddhas, in the form of actual ornaments that symbolize the adornment of your streams with these qualities.

Here the Master is brought the bowl of ornaments from the altar, and he tolds it up in his right hand (along with his vajra, as always) as he recites:

These are the holy Tārā's
ornaments of silk and precious gems;
if you wear them always
you will be a fit vessel for all the qualities
of the Innate Union of Means and Wisdom
and of all the Buddhas of the three times
until finally you yourselves gain Buddhahood.

OṂ ALAṂKĀRA-RATNA-PAṬA-KĀYABHĀSA-ABHIŚIÑCA HUṂ!

And the Master recites the fourth benediction:

Pacifying the 80,000 families of hindering demons,
freeing us from harm and misfortune,
granting us bounty and sublimity:
may there now be that good fortune!

The Master again rings his bell and scatters rice over the heads of the assembly:

Thereby are cleansed all the obscurations of deep contemplation which you have accumulated, and are pacified all the misfortunes, diseases, hindering demons, and impediments which hurt or harm your "channels, winds, and drop."

This is the initiation that you may accomplish the infinite qualities of the path through "piercing the vital centers" in your channels, winds, and drop; you now have the opportunity to manifest the Diamond of Knowledge, and the fruit thereof is that you will gain a Body of Great Bliss endowed with the qualities of purity and perfection.

This is the permission of qualities.

3.25 *The permission of function*

The fifth permission is that of function, and the Master bestows upon the recipients the authorization and the capacity to perform all the deity's basic and subsidiary functions—indeed, to be "Diamond Masters" themselves through the power of the goddess.

From the forehead of your guru, now inseparable from the goddess in front, there radiates forth the white light of pacifying, from his throat the red light of subjugating, from his heart the blue light of destroying, from his navel the yellow light of increasing, and from his secret place the green light of miscellaneous functions.

These lights invite all the magical attainments of these four functions in the form of five-colored light, which dissolves into the five places of your bodies. From these there radiate forth the five different-colored lights, which purify the diseases, sins, and obscurations of all beings, yourself and others, which increase their life, merit, and knowledge, which subjugate the two sorts of magical attainment, which annihilate the four Māras, and which accomplish all the vast numbers of functions.

The lights are once again gathered back in, bringing with them the empowerment of the Conquerors and their sons; they are absorbed back into you, and you should think: "I am the essence of the perfect active function of the vast numbers of Conquerors!"

May you accomplish all the vast numbers of functions of a Diamond Master, conferring blessings upon your own disciples!

Then the Master touches his vajra and bell to the recipients' hands, crossing his wrists so that his varja touches the disciples' right hands and his bell their left hands (that is, so they are received in the correct position), and he recites:

> Empower this pair into diamond,
> this great vajra and great bell:
> you are now become a Diamond Master.
> Gather hosts of disciples!
> May you accomplish all the functions.

Here the Master is brought the small painting of Tārā's white lotus from the altar, for just as her ornaments symbolized her qualities, her emblem symbolizes her functions. The Master holds up the painting and thus bestows the "permission of the emblem":

> This is the holy Tārā's emblem,
> the white lotus flower;
> if you bear it always
> you will have the power to perform all functions
> of the Innate Union of Means and Wisdom
> and of all the Buddhas of the three times
> until finally you yourselves gain Buddhahood.

OṂ KĀYA-VĀK-CITTA SARVA-ŚĀNTIṂ-KURU PUṢṬIṂ-KURU VAŚAṂ-KURU MĀRAYA VIŚVA-KARMA-ABHIŚIÑCA HŪṂ!

"OṂ Body, speech, and mind: the initiation of all functions: pacify! increase! subjugate! slay! HŪṂ!"

The Master touches the small painting to the recipients' hands, and he recites the fifth benediction: "Pacifying all misfortunes, whatever the condition . . ." Then the Master again rings his bell and scatters rice over the heads of the assembly:

> Thereby are cleansed all the sins and obscurations accumulated equally through your body, speech, and mind, and are pacified all the misfortunes, diseases, hindering demons, and impediments which hurt or harm those three gates equally.
>
> This is the initiation that you may accomplish the vast numbers of functions; you now have the opportunity to manifest the Diamond of Pervasion, and the fruit thereof is that you will gain an Essential Body, having the power—as your pervasive and permanent essence—to accomplish the active functions of a Buddha.
>
> This is the permission of function.

3.3 *The torma initiation*

Beyond these five permissions and their magical bestowal of contemplative power upon the recipients, the Master may if he wishes continue with a torma initiation, to infuse the total power of the deity into the disciples now rendered fit to receive it. There is no real tradition, says the text, concerning the bestowing of a torma initiation based on White Tārā; the author says he will follow the present-day practices of the Karma Kajü as set forth in the treatises of the "Lord Ninth"—that is, the ninth Black Hat Wangch'ug doje. Thus the Master says to his disciples:

> You have now gained a vivid visualization of yourselves as the holy Tārā with the three syllables—OṂ ĀḤ HUṂ—on the three places of your bodies.
>
> Now this torma before you has three aspects: but here we are concerned with it as being in the form of a torma yet having an essence vividly visualized as being the blessed Cintācakra in person. On its upper portion are all the gurus of the Kajü; on its middle portion are all the hosts of the high patron deities; on its lower portion are the hosts of protectors and guardians of the Law—all of them gathered like clouds.
>
> They enter into you through the tops of your heads, and you must visualize one-pointedly, fervently, that they give to you all their empowerment and magical attainments, just as I describe when I recite the following prayer:
>
> Holy blessed Cintācakra, Master Vāgīśvarakīrti . . . [and so on, the text says, giving the names of the lineage of the Kajü gurus, the hosts of the ocean of great magicians] and my own guru [inserting his name]: the high patron deities, the divine hosts of the four classes of Tantra, and the protectors who guard the Diamond Law— I pray that you bestow the empowerment of body, speech,

mind, qualities, and function upon these Diamond Disciples. I pray that you pacify their diseases, hindering demons, and impediments, that you increase all their life, glory, and merit, that you subjugate for them all mundane and supramundane magical attainments, that you annihilate for them all the savage Māras and bringers of harm, in short that you bestow upon them unimpededly all mundane and supramundane magical attainments.

I give the great initiation of the torma,
the empowerment of the body, speech, and mind
of all the Buddhas,
the source of the two sorts of magical attainment.

OṂ ĀḤ HUṂ! BALIṂ KĀYA-VĀK-CITTA-ABHIŚIÑCA MĀṂ! JAḤ HUṂ BAṂ HOḤ!

The Master touches the torma in which the deity was generated to the head of each recipient, and he seals that initiation—absorbed into the disciple with his JAḤ HŪṂ BAṂ HOḤ!—by touching the top of each disciple's head with his vajra or, if there are too many people, by scattering rice over the assembly. The Master then erects a circle of protection around the initiated disciples, reciting "By the truth of the Conquerors and their sons . . ." and the mantra OṂ VAJRA-RAKṢA HŪṂ! He scatters rice over the heads of the assembly and says:

The torma, vividly visualized as the deity, melts into light and dissolves into you; and you must visualize that thereby your body, speech, and mind become inseparable from the body, speech, and mind of the supreme deity.

Thus the disciples absorb the goddess herself, generated in front, and the Master gives to each of the recipients a piece of the torma to eat, as a substance of magical attainment, as they recite three times the following pledge: "Whatever has been preached by the Lord, that we will do." Then, following the general pattern of the concluding acts, they offer up a maṇḍala in thanksgiving, and offer up all their bodily enjoyments; and they dedicate all the merit accruing to them from their participation in the ritual with the following verse, a standard one used after many initiations:

With this merit may we attain all-seeing,
and may we defeat our enemy, our moral failing;
may we rescue beings from the ocean of this world
whose clashing waves are birth, old age, and death.[45]

THE RITUAL SERVICE

We have now examined two different rituals included by the Tibetans under the rubric of initiation, and we have pointed out their structural similarities: both rituals require the Master to be himself possessed of the power he bestows, and both include a preliminary consolidation of this power in self-generation and its preparatory propitiation in front. The actual transmission of this power —whether it be permission of speech or healing the degenerate—is magical, and each section of the rituals consists of a visualization, a recitation, and a sealing benediction.

But we may see, too, certain specific differences between the rituals which directly result from the difference of intention. The initiation into life is an end in itself, a bestowing of the magical attainment of longevity, and the major aim of the recipients is fulfilled by their increase of life; hence we find the use of devices and recipes that function more or less independently of the spiritual state of the disciples. The permission, on the other hand, is ideally but a preparation for further practice, though it does indeed cleanse the impediments to life of those who receive it; hence there is a stronger emphasis upon the participation of the recipients, as they themselves recite the mantra, put on the ornaments, and radiate the lights that perform their functions.

Thus the ritual of permission is aimed at the creation of a fit vessel for the practice of the particular deity, to contain the divine power that the disciple will next accumulate by himself in the ritual service; he is strengthened not only to increase his life, but also to bear the pressures of the divinity he will achieve. Thus he is rehearsed in the steps of yoga and given power over them by the Master's magical transmission.

> His guiding purpose, though it was supernatural, was not impossible. He wanted to dream a man; he wanted to dream him down to the last detail and project him into the world of reality. This mystical aim had taxed the whole range of his mind. . . He realized that, though he may penetrate all the riddles of the higher and lower orders, the task of shaping the senseless and dizzying stuff of dreams is the hardest that a man can attempt—much harder than weaving a rope of sand or coining the faceless wind.
>
> —Jorge Luis Borges, *The Circular Ruins*

Now that he is authorized to do so, the contemplative will create himself as the goddess; he will purify himself for this task with the preliminary practices and in the ritual service he will *be* the deity and will contemplate her mantra, that he may truly possess the simulacrum of her body, speech, and mind. Again, Borges talks of the difficulty of "real-izing" this dream of divinity:

> . . . And so, as I sleep, some dream beguiles me, and suddenly I know I am dreaming. Then I think: This is a dream, a pure diversion of my will; and now that I have unlimited power, I am going to cause a tiger.
>
> Oh, incompetence! Never can my dreams engender the wild beast I long for. The tiger indeed appears, but stuffed or flimsy, or with impure variations of shape, or of an implausible size, or all too fleeting, or with a touch of the dog or the bird.
>
> —Jorge Luis Borges, *Dreamtigers*

To prepare himself for the demands of this dream, the practitioner requires all the resources he can muster, even beyond the magical empowerment he received from his Master. Thus, after arousing himself with the "common" preliminaries, he again purifies and empowers himself with the four uncommon contemplations: (1) the visualization and recitation of Vajrasattva which cleanse his stream; (2) the going for refuge and awakening the thought of enlightenment which elevate him from wrong and lowly paths; (3) the maṇḍala offering which perfects his stocks; and (4) the yoga with his gurus which quickly introduces empowerment into him.

The ritual service here examined is considered to be a "life teaching" in the sense that it sets forth a technique for achieving long life; that is, since it is based on the accumulation of the power of White Tārā, it may be used simply for that acquisition of divinity as an end in itself, or it may be performed to a specific end such as the alleviation of an illness. We shall see how the ritual varies in these cases when we look at its accompanying instructions—its subsidiary advice—given in the ritual handbook. But here we are interested in the ritual as a soteriological function, the acquisition of power through the contemplation of the mantra and the gaining of the divine understanding through the Process of Perfection; and we shall follow the young practitioner through his preliminary practices as given in the text, which slightly alters their usual contemplative content to accommodate them to White Tārā rather than to the lineage of a particular sect.

THE PRELIMINARY PRACTICES

Visualization and Recitation of Vajrasattva

At daybreak, before hearing the sound of crows, the practitioner arises and bathes. Sitting in the cross-legged posture on a comfortable seat, he exhales sharply three times, visualizing that this action clears away his sins, obscurations, and impediments to life.

On the top of his head—he is in his "ordinary appearance"—sits Vajrasattva on a throne of lotus and moon, inseparably one with the practitioner's own guru: his body is colored white; he has one head and two hands, holding in his right hand a vajra over his heart and in his left hand a bell at his side; he is adorned with all ornaments, the signs and secondary signs of a Buddha. In his heart is the 100-syllable mantra, arranged like the beads of a pearl rosary.

In the practitioner's own heart, on a throne of lotus and moon, sits the Blessed Lady, also inseparably one with his own guru, and in her heart is the syllable TĀṂ.

While he is visualizing this, the practitioner's mind should be filled with repentance for the sins he has done; with fierce devotion to his guru, inseparably one with the patron deity, he prays:

> Lord ! By the darkness of ignorance
> I am fallen and degenerate from my vows.
> O chief of the Bearers of the Vajra,
> I go for refuge to the chief of beings
> whose very essence is great compassion.

> I confess, I repent all the degeneration of my vows, major and minor, all the sins, obscurations, faults, and downfalls of myself and all beings; I do not conceal them, I do not hide them ! I pray you make me cleansed and pure !

Because the practitioner thus prays, the guru Vajrasattva smiles: he melts into light, enters through the top of the practitioner's head, and dissolves into the White Tārā in his heart. Then, by the practitioner's recitation and devotion the stream of her heart is aroused, and a stream of white light which is nectar flows forth from the syllable TĀṂ in the Blessed Lady's heart. This fills the inside of her body, and the nectar falls like a stream of milk from the ring finger of her right hand held out in the gift-bestowing gesture; it fills the inside of the practitioner's body, and all his sins, obscurations, diseases, untimely death, and degeneration of his vows—all issue forth from the pores of his body like husks washed away with water. He visualizes that his body becomes without obscuration inside or out, and he recites the 10-syllable mantra and Vajrasattva's 100-syllable mantra, one after the other, as much as he can.

Finally, when he has thus prayed for his desire, confessed, and been purified, the Blessed Lady melts into light and dissolves into him; and he visualizes that thereupon he himself becomes the Blessed Lady in actuality, and the three components of the visualization—the cleanser, the cleansed, and the act of cleansing—are placed, with no mental constructs imposed upon them, in the realm of Reality.

If this ritual service is being divided into contemplative periods—so that this contemplation is performed during the whole of one such period—then, at this point, the practitioner should perform the dedication of his merit; this dedication is appended to each of the contemplations that follow, that is, at the end of each contemplative period.

This contemplation of Vajrasattva, the author also adds, may be abbreviated, as for instance when it is performed as a daily ritual. In this case the practitioner—again in his ordinary appearance—visualizes a white syllable TĀṂ above a moon in his heart, encircled around its edge with the 100-syllable mantra "like a pearl rosary." From this there comes a moonlike light, filling his body and cleansing his diseases, sins, and obscurations, his deeds and their ripening, his whole "pile of flesh and blood"; and he visualizes that his body becomes the essence of light. Then, after reciting the 10-syllable and 100-syllable mantras, he prays as above, except that he says, "Goddess! . . . from my vows" and "May my guru Tārā . . ." Thereupon the syllable and its throne melt into light and dissolve into him, and the sins to be cleansed away are seen to have been the pure nonobjectifiable Dharma realm from the very beginning, and he enters into communion therewith.

If we refer back to our previous discussion of these preliminaries we see that the visualization and recitation are here placed out of the normal sequence. To this criticism of his arrangement, the author says:

> This contemplation of Vajrasattva is, if one follows the general stages of the teaching, performed *after* going for refuge and awakening the thought of enlightenment. But although it is not necessary to follow exactly the order given here, the tradition of the old writings, as a matter of fact, does put Vajrasattva in this

place. For example, if food is placed in an impure vessel, it is as if it were wasted; since the visualizations of the path do not arise for one who has obscurations—and since there is no difficulty in the way of the deep contemplation of the two Processes if at the outset one *does* cleanse the vessel's obscurations, faults, and downfalls—this contemplation is of the utmost importance as the first thing to be done, because it is the equivalent of washing the vessel.

The Going for Refuge and
Awakening the Thought of Enlightenment

The second part of the preliminaries is going for refuge and awakening the thought of enlightenment before the field of hosts. The practitioner visualizes in the sky before him a lotus of four spreading petals, with sublime stalk, branches, leaves, and fruit. In the center of the lotus sits he whose form is the Lord Amitābha, whose person is the gathering into one of all the gurus, and whose essence is the inseparability of the Blessed Lady and the practitioner's own guru. The practitioner visualizes that seated upon the front petal is the noble Tārā, the gathering into one of all the patron deities; seated to the right is the Powerful One of the Śākyas, the gathering into one of all the Buddhas; seated upon the back petal is the Great Mother Prajñāpāramitā herself, the holy Law inherent in all Three Jewels; and seated to the left is Avalokiteśvara, the gathering into one of all the Assembly. And all around and in the spaces between, like a gathering of clouds, there are ḍākas, ḍākiṇīs, protectors and guardians of the Law.

If the practitioner wishes, he may here perform the offerings, praises, and prayers, but ordinarily it is not necessary.

He visualizes himself at the head of a crowd of all sentient beings, all "old mothers," and he thinks of how they experience suffering; from the depths of his heart he thinks, "I pray that you preserve us from these sufferings!" He visualizes that all these beings, with himself leading them, go for refuge with devotion of body, speech, and mind, and they recite together in a whisper—with the hushed sound *diriri*—"Myself and all beings . . ." and "To the Buddha, the Law, and the highest hosts . . ." up to the requisite number of recitations.

Then the practitioner awakens his thought of enlightenment, taking as the object of his visualization all sentient beings, of number such as to fill the sky. He awakens his intentional thought of enlightenment, joining it to the following vow, thinking: "There is not one of these who, from beginningless time, has not been my father or mother. I feel compassion for them, since though they wish for happiness they eternally wander unliberated in the unendurable ocean of suffering in this world; and I vow that I will place them all, not excepting even one, in the rank of deathless, permanent, holy, perfect Buddhahood."

Then the practitioner awakens as well his actual thought of enlightenment, taking the following vow, thinking: "For that reason, may they have long life in this human condition, may they be without disease, and may their impediments be pacified; especially, may my guru's bodily life be made firm, and may there be happiness and joy for beings! Thus, that I may quickly and easily gain the rank of the noble Tārā, mother of all the Conquerors constant in the three times, I set out upon the Processes of Generation and Perfection of the blessed lady Cintācakra, striving with great diligence until I reach the end, and I will not quit until I attain to this patron deity, even though it cost my life."

The practitioner then recites out loud a few times such verses as "For the sake of all beings . . ." Finally, the "field of refuge" melts into light and dissolves into the guru as Amitābha in the center of the lotus; and he in turn melts into light and dissolves into the practitioner, who thereupon thinks that the empowerment of the Three Jewels and of the guru enters into his stream.

By accomplishing this, the author says, surely the practitioner will gain all the qualities and magical attainments; if there is no break in his faith and belief, this is a perfect instruction to fulfill quickly all his aims.

The Maṇḍala Offering

The practitioner next offers up the maṇḍala. He first cleanses and purifies (with the two mantras) the maṇḍala that he will evoke (it is not necessary to sprinkle it with cleansing water, the text adds in a note) to re-create from Emptiness the contemplative counterpart of the physical object he holds in his hands.

He first visualizes a protection against hindering demons with HŪṂ! flinging if he wishes a small pile of grain. Then with OṂ VAJRA-BHŪMI ĀḤ HŪṂ he visualizes the evocation of a ground of gold, upon which are Mount Meru, the four continents, the subsidiary continents, and all the requisites of offering; and upon the mountain and the continents is a throne of lotus and moon. He anoints the maṇḍala with the "five products of the cow" and with sweet-scented water, reciting OṂ VAJRA-REKHE ĀḤ HŪṂ and visualizing that all the spaces between the continents are filled with scented water having the eight features of delight, and that the whole is surrounded on the outside by a ring of iron mountains.

The practitioner vividly visualizes a TĀṂ on the throne in the center and, in the four directions, TĀṂ, MUṂ, A, and HRĪḤ. He vividly visualizes himself as Cintācakra, and above a moon in his heart is a white TĀṂ. Light radiates forth therefrom, and therewith he invites—with OṂ VAJRA-SAMĀJAḤ and the diamond-assembly gesture—his own guru, having the form of Amitābha and surrounded by the hosts of the gurus of the lineage, into the upper portion of the sky before him, and into its lower portion the holy noble White Tārā with all the hosts of Buddhas and Bodhisattvas.

On the maṇḍala itself he arranges in the center and in the four directions piles of white flowers, according to the Indian method, or, according to the Tibetan technique, if flowers are unavailable, piles of grain; while doing so he recites PADMA-KAMALĀYAS TVAṂ! Thereby the knowledge beings enter into their respective "seeds" on the thrones, and these seeds transform themselves as follows: the practitioner visualizes from TĀṂ the guru Tārā above Mount Meru, adorned upon her crown with Amitābha, surrounded by the gurus of the lineage; from TĀṂ on the eastern continent of Pūrvavideha hundreds of Tārās surrounded by the high patron deities of the four and six classes of Tantra; from MUṂ on the southern continent of Jambudvīpa, Śākyamuni surrounded by the Buddhas of the three times; from A on the western continent of Aparagodanīya the Great Mother Prajñāpāramitā surrounded by books of the holy Law; and from HRĪḤ on the northern continent of Uttarakuru, Avalokiteśvara surrounded by the Assemblies of the Great and Little Vehicles. And in the spaces between, like a gathering of clouds, there are ḍākas, ḍākiṇīs, protectors and guardians of the Law.

He then places the maṇḍala on a high table in front of him, and, if he has them, he should place before it the seven offering bowls that represent the "outer offerings." He visualizes that he emanates bodies, of himself and of all beings, numerous as the dust of the field, and that they all prostrate together to the guru, as the practitioner recites NAMO GURUBHYAḤ . . . , and then turn toward the high patron deity and her retinue as he recites NAMA ĀRYA-TĀRĀ . . . And he adds the verses "By whose graciousness . . . ."

He visualizes that many offering goddesses emanate from the light in his heart, adorned with ornaments, smiling and sublimely beautiful, who make many offerings while he recites the mantras ARGHAṂ and so on, with their respective gestures and the following visualizations: white offering goddesses pour from gold and lapis lazuli vases a stream of water having the eight features of delight; red goddesses wash the deities' feet with pure water and soap made of the five nectars, the five medicinal fruits, and so on; white goddesses scatter over their heads ravishingly beautiful flowers, mind-sprung lotuses and wild flowers; brown goddesses offer to their noses sweet-smelling incense, both natural and mixed; pale red goddesses arrange in their path of vision those things that illuminate all the worlds in the ten directions, all sorts of jewels, suns, moons, and lamps; green goddesses take from conch-shell bowls sweet-smelling perfumes of camphor, saffron, and sandalwood, which they scatter, anoint, and dab upon all parts of their bodies, their hearts, and so on; red goddesses offer to their tongues hundred-flavored food fit for a goddess, mixed, "transformed" (that is, curds, liquor, etc.), and "natural" (that is, fruits, grains, etc.); blue goddesses please the field of hosts with inexhaustible Bliss, playing in the path of their hearing all sorts of divine music, cymbals, flutes, viols, and drums. Then the practitioner visualizes that all the goddesses dissolve back into the seed in his heart.

The practitioner then summarizes the above sequence: in order that he may make "vivid and perfect" the remainder of the sevenfold office, he recites "Blessed Lady . . ." and emanates all the other offerings as well, a cloud of the offerings of *All-Beneficent's Vow of Conduct*, all the substances of bodily enjoyment and virtue of the three times, and he offers it all without hesitation. And he says:

> I confess with shame and repentance all the sins that have been committed by me or others, whether inherently vicious or proscribed by ordinance, or which I have led others to commit; and from now on I vow to commit them no more, though it cost my life.
>
> I rejoice with heartfelt happiness at all the virtue that has been performed, all the qualities of the Law in accord with complete enlightenment within this world or nirvāṇa.
>
> I entreat you, just as the great Brahma prayed the Blessed One again and again, to turn unceasingly the wheel of the supreme Law of the highest Vehicle.

> I pray that you remain until this world is emptied out, never waning but constant, firm, and tangible, only showing forth the bodily form of the guru Blessed Lady.
>
> I dedicate all the roots of my virtue of the three times, that I may attain the rank of the holy Tārā, the essence of the Perfection of Wisdom and the mother of the Conquerors.
>
> I earnestly wish that by the virtue of these I may be blessed through all my future lives and be accompanied always by the holy Cintācakra, until I arrive at the farther shore of the ocean of the practice of enlightenment.

And the practitioner then directs his mind toward the deities of the field of hosts and recites as many times as he can the 10-syllable mantra with its appendix.

Then the practitioner dusts the "piles" off the maṇḍala, and he performs the actual offering of the maṇḍala to the field of hosts as he sets out fresh piles of flowers or grain "wet with sweet-smelling water or water mixed with precious substances." Here, the author says, it is generally considered proper that the maṇḍala be presented with the full complement of thirty-seven piles; but according to the opinion of the "Lord Ninth," he says, one makes the offering by repeating the "five-piled maṇḍala" given when the field was first generated before the practitioner. This part of the offering then concludes with the miscellaneous offerings presented with the verse, "The wish-granting tree . . ."

The author reminds the practitioner that the external form of the maṇḍala he is presenting—Mount Meru with the four continents—is inseparably one with the internal aggregates and senses; and as the practitioner offers each individual item—each possessing a "measureless array of adornment"—he should bear in mind its proper symbolism, such as that Mount Meru is the vajra, the essence of all the Buddha fields of the five families of Conqueror. And finally it is by the offering of his own appearance or luminosity—which is the actual Clear Light—for their enjoyment that the deities reach to the very heights of satisfaction; visualizing this he prays to the guru Cintācakra for his desires.

When the practitioner has thus offered up the maṇḍala, he gathers together the piles of flowers or grain from its surface and places them upon his head, visualizing at the same time that the field of hosts melts into light, enters into him through the top of his head, and dissolves into him. Thereby he becomes inseparably one with their "bodies of fruition" which have perfected both the stocks.

Here, the author says, he has put together an expanded ritual of invitation, offering of seats, and verses for the sevenfold office of homage, offerings, and so on. This method is clearly set forth in the White Tārā ritual of the Lord Ninth. But here too, he says, he is expounding a complete life teaching which is designed to be performed—literally "experienced"—during a series of separate contemplative periods. In other instances the practitioner may follow the evocation as ordinarily given, presenting to the field of hosts invited into the sky only a brief and unadorned sevenfold office and maṇḍala offering, it not being necessary here to generate the field into the maṇḍala that is evoked.

The Yoga with the Gurus

The final preliminary is the yoga with the gurus. The practitioner vividly visualizes on top of his head a jeweled throne supported by eight lions. Upon it is a white eight-petaled lotus, in the center of which is the blessed Cintācakra, inseparably one with his own guru: her body is colored white as an automn moon, perfectly adorned with ornaments, and marked in the three places with the three syllables, and upon a moon on her heart is a wheel with the seed and the garland of the mantra. From those syllables light radiates forth, inviting individually the Three Jewels and the gurus of the lineage; these dissolve into the guru Tārā, who becomes the gathering into one of the Three Jewels. The practitioner awakens a knowledge of absolute certainty that she is

> The ocean of the Three Jewels in actuality
> who grants just by thinking of her
> all the highest and ordinary magical attainments
> like a wish-granting gem.

It is said that here he may, if he wishes, perform offerings and praise; but then he should pray to the lineage according to the text given separately, and this prayer for empowerment he should then recite once. In addition, he may if he wishes perform a prayer service; this is not given specially in the ritual texts, the author says, but according to the general practices of the precious Kajü the practitioner recites the fourfold "Mothers, filling all of space . . ." And then, as ordinarily given, he should recite "with the fierce strength of faith and devotion" the text called the "sevenfold refuge" as many times as he thinks proper, taking refuge in the guru, in the Three Jewels, and in the Three Basic Ones. And finally he should join his palms and pray for his desire to the guru Cintā-cakra.

After all these optional prayers to the gurus in the person of the goddess above his head, the practitioner performs the actual yoga, the taking of empowerment called "the four initiations on the occassion of the path." From the forehead of the deity—his guru and the Blessed Lady inseparably one—there comes the white nectar and light of body; from her throat the red nectar and light of speech; from her heart the blue nectar and light of mind; and from her navel the yellow nectar and light of knowledge. These enter into the same four places of the practitioner; they fill his entire bidy, purify his four obscurations, grant him the four initiations, and through this entering into him of the empowerment of body, speech, mind, and knowledge he has the opportunity to manifest the four bodies of a Buddha. The guru Tārā melts into light and dissolves into him, and, thereby visualizing their inseparability, he enters communion with the Inherent, with her Innate Bliss, Light, and Emptiness.

As before, this performance—this "experience"—may be abbreviated in those cases where an entire contemplative period cannot be devoted to it. As described above, the field of hosts is invited, and they are presented with homage, offerings, and so on, and the maṇḍala offering; then the entire retinue of the field of hosts dissolves into the Chief Lady, and that deity—the guru and the Blessed Lady inseparably one—moves over to the top of the practitioner's head and is seated upon a throne of lotus and moon. While visualizing the deity above his head, the practitioner prays and so on, and then the guru Blessed Lady melts into light and dissolves into him; he visualizes that thereby his three gates and the guru's three secrets become inseparably one. By doing nothing more than this, the author says, he actually completes all four initiations.

THE RITUAL SERVICE IN SELF-GENERATION

1 *Preliminaries*

After these preliminary practices have been completed, the ritual service proper begins with the accumulation of the two stocks, the "relative" stock of merit (= the intentional thought of enlightenment) and the "absolute" stock of knowledge (= the actual thought of enlightenment). In general, the author says, the performance of the maṇḍala offering and so on, described above, is an accumulation of the stocks, but there it was simply a means to awaken the precious thought of enlightenment. There are, actually, two sorts of thought of enlightenment for the accomplishment of Buddhahood, both of which are causal conditions without which it cannot occur; thus he is here separating them into two visualizations.

1.1 *The stock of merit*

For the first of these the practitioner contemplates the four immeasurables. He thinks: "May all beings, fathers and mothers as infinite as space, not only be possessed of Bliss, whether temporary or permanent, but may they also practice in the realm of the sublime virtue which is its cause!"—this is the "immeasurable contemplation" of Friendliness. And similarly he thinks: ". . . but may they also enter into the realm of abandoning suffering and the wickedness that is the cause of suffering!"—this is the immeasurable contemplation of Compassion. And he thinks ". . . but may they also never be separated from the holy Bliss: not simply the bliss appropriate to their condition, but freedom from suffering forever!"—this is the immeasurable contemplation of Sympathetic Joy. And he thinks: ". . . but may they also attain an even-mindedness like that of a seafarer in a foreign land, free of conceptions of enemy or friend, near or far, my side or his side!"—this is the immeasurable contemplation of Equanimity. And as he earnestly bears in mind their meaning, he slowly recites them aloud. The author comments:

> By contemplating nothing more than these, the practitioner will be reborn in the Heaven of Brahma; and if in addition their contemplation is joined to an omniscient mind, they become a cause for the attainment of ultimate Brahmahood, the rank of perfect Buddha. Hence they are called the "four abodes of Brahma."
>
> Here too one sets out with the intention of placing in continual Bliss all beings, infinite in number, every single being individually and not those of the present time or life. Hence they are also called the "four immeasurables."

1.2 *The stock of knowledge*

The second stock is that of knowledge, and here again the author comments:

> This is to be placed in Emptiness, according to the analysis made thereof in such lines as the "four great proofs"; here one must avoid the extremes, for it is absolutely necessary to contemplate Emptiness without imposing any mental constructs thereon.

These four great proofs are found in the introductory stanza of Nāgārjuna's *Basic Verses on the Middle Way*, wherein he says that all events (1) neither arise nor cease, (2) are neither destroyed nor permanent, (3) are neither one nor many, and (4) neither arrive nor depart. The author continues:

> Here we do not mean "Emptiness" simply in the sense that nothing is brought about through any nature of its own, for this ineffectiveness is relative, a designation for a conjunction like that in an illusion, wherein a perception is connected to what is but a mental appearance. But rather we mean the highest of all the enumerations of Emptiness—to commune in all things from the absolute point of view, with a perception free of all fabrication.
>
> Now when a beginner thinks about this, placing himself in the Inherent through mental constructs imposed upon his basic nature, he must make it vivid to himself with words; thus we recite the ŚUNYATĀ mantra. The meaning of this mantra is as follows:
>
> SUNYATĀ is Emptiness, the fact that there are no events other than mind itself, subsumed under the categories of subject and object; whether it be the inanimate world, the animate beings it contains, or one's own body on the one hand, or the mind that perceives those things on the other, they are not brought about by anything inherent to them, but are Empty from the beginning.
>
> JÑĀNA is knowledge, but this is not an empty receptacle like space, a mere recorder of impressions, but rather a perception of the formation of all things from the absolute point of view.
>
> VAJRA is diamond, for it is what is meant as the essence of the permanent, the firm, the peaceful, the auspicious.
>
> SVABHĀVA is essence, the fact that the diamond of knowledge is the basic nature of all events, that is, that they have it as their essence.
>
> ĀTMAKA is oneself; since the diamond of knowledge is true as a basic nature, it is oneself from the absolute point of view.
>
> AHAṂ is I; such is the essence of one's innate mind, so one must grasp the ego that knows it to be such.
>
> "Emptiness" thus means the ultimate rejection of relative fabrications; and by stock of knowledge we mean the diamond of the knowledge of the absolute truth. And when the practitioner understands that, he should enter into contemplation as firmly as possible, in the realm of his own True Nature.

2 *Basics*

From the realm of Emptiness thus evoked by the recitation of the mantra, the practitioner proceeds to the main body of the ritual service. Here there are two sections: the Process of Generation and the Process of Perfection.

2.1 *The Process of Generation*

Here again there are two parts: the "yoga with the deity" and the "yoga with the recitation"—that is, the self-generation and the contemplation of the mantra.

2.11 *The yoga with the deity*

2.111 *The fourfold generation*

2.1111 *The limb of approach*

From the realm of that same Emptiness, the sound of HUṂ radiates forth and fills all of space, an appearance of the innate mind unfalsified by labeling constructs. And from this there comes a diamond ground below; resting thereon a surrounding diamond fence; a diamond pavilion above with a diamond finial; diamond draperies around the inside of the fence and tent; a dangling trellis outside, an interlaced lattice of arrows with their feathered ends touching the pavilion and their diamond tips pointing outward; and a blazing fire surrounding it in all directions. All this is colored white and is vast and broad; even the fiery wind at the end of the world era would be unable to shake it —why even mention hindering or misleading demons?

In the middle thereof is a white BHRŪṂ, the seed syllable of Vairocana, and this transforms into a divine mansion, made solely of crystal and jewels; it is square, with four gates and archways and an infinite variety of ornaments and offerings.

In the middle thereof is a white syllable PAṂ, from which there comes the sort of lotus called "padma": white, with broad leaves and petals, and a stiff hard stem of jewels. Above its anthers is a white A, from which there comes the orb of a moon, full and stainless, free of impurity.

Upon that throne, by the power of my earlier earnest wish and great compassion, my innate mind becomes a white syllable TĀṂ, with the long vowel, crescent, and dot; and this transforms into a white lotus flower, with leaves and stem, marked with a white TĀṂ. From that an inconceivable radiation of white light pours forth, unimpeded through all the worlds in the ten directions; it makes offerings to the Conquerors and their sons, it dispels the eight and the sixteen great terrors of all beings, their untimely death, and so on, cleanses their twofold obscuration and their propensity thereto, and raises them to the rank of noble Tārā. Then the light is gathered back in again and dissolves into the lotus flower and the syllable TĀṂ.

The TĀṂ transforms, and I myself become the noble Tārā (and so on, contemplating the formation of the goddess according to the standard visualization), having the aureole of a moon.

This vivid visualization of her perfected body is the limb of approach.

2.1112 *The limb of near evocation*

On her forehead is a white OṂ, on her throat is a red ĀḤ, and on the lower part of her heart is a blue HUṂ; these are inherently the Diamonds of the Body, Speech, and Mind of all the Buddhas. In the center of her heart, on a white lotus and moon, is a white syllable TĀṂ.

This vivid contemplation is the limb of near evocation.

2.1113 *The limb of evocation*

From that syllable TĀṂ light radiates forth, and therewith I invite, with VAJRA-SAMĀJAḤ and the diamond-assembly gesture, the knowledge being, from the Dharma realm, from Potala, and so on. I seat them upon thrones of lotus and moon in the sky before me, and I make them offerings with goddesses I emanate from myself. And with JAḤ JŪṂ HOḤ! they dissolve into me, the symbolic being, and become inseparably one with me.

Visualizing that they will never leave me until I attain enlightenment is the limb of evocation.

2.1114 *The limb of great evocation*

Once again, light from the seed TĀṂ in my heart invites the five families of initiation deities, Bodhisattvas, and fierce deities, Father and Mother. As before, I make offering to them with offerings; and because I pray for initiation, the five families think kindly of me, the Bodhisattvas make offerings and recite benedictions, and the fierce deities, male and female, expel the hindering demons. The five Mothers [Locanā and so on] hold up jeweled flasks filled with liquid nectar and, reciting the mantra and the verse, initiate me; thereupon my whole body is filled with the water from the flasks, the impurities of my three gates are purified, and the overflow of water ornaments my crown in the form of a Body of Transformation of Amitāyus, lord of the family, red, holding an alms bowl in his meditation gesture.

And visualizing that the meditation deities also dissolve into me is the limb of great evocation.

2.112 *Offerings and praise*

Then the practitioner performs the offerings and praise to the deity he has thus generated; goddesses emanate from a realm like that "wherein practice the gods of the Heaven of Enjoyment of Magical Creations"; they make offering to him with all the varieties of offering spoken of before, and they praise him with a hundred sorts of sweet sound. And after he visualizes and recites this worship paid to the goddess in his person, he gathers the offering goddesses also into himself.

2.113 *Vivid appearance, firmness of ego, and recollection of purity*

2.1131 *Vivid appearance*

The author says: "Having thus finished generating himself as the deity by contemplating these four limbs, along with the offerings and praise, the practitioner must apply himself one-pointedly to vivid appearance. This is the most basic part of the first stage, the Process of Generation; the simple recitation of the mantra is but a subsidiary. Now a beginner should make his visualization vivid step by step; once he has achieved a little vivid appearance, all at once everything will become vivid. Thus at the beginning we shall vividly visualize each separate part of her body." And he proceeds to give a list of the deity's bodily qualities, which the practitioner must concentrate on visualizing one at a time:

> The color of her body is white as an autumn moon, as clear as a crystal gem, radiating forth an unbearably bright five-colored light for a long distance.
>
> Her eyes and earlobes are long, and the whites and blacks of her eyes are sharply differentiated; she is beautiful with eyelashes like those of the finest cow, and with eyebrows slightly curved.
>
> The sweet smell of lotuses diffuses from her nose and mouth; the line of her lips is pure and red.
>
> Her forty teeth are a fine-textured garland; her tongue is fine and soft.
>
> Her hair is black as bees or onyx, bound up at the top of her head, the rest falling to the right and left.
>
> Her neck is round and has three folds.
>
> Her fingers are like the filaments of a lotus, thin and soft, wondrously beautiful.
>
> Just by seeing her sensuous manner—one can't have enough of looking at it—she gives inexhaustible bliss.
>
> With her smiling and passionate manner like a sixteen-year-old girl, her firm round breasts, the slimness of her waist, and her "secret lotus" curved high as the back of a tortoise on the broad fullness beneath, she ravishes away the steadiness of the triple world.
>
> On her head are three eyes, including one on her forehead, and four more on the palms of her hands and the soles of her feet: in all, seven beautiful and smiling eyes of knowledge.
>
> Her right hand is in the gift-bestowing gesture, stretched out above her knee; with her left hand by her heart, the ring finger and thumb joined, the rest extended, she holds the stem of a white lotus, with leaves and sublime color and smell, whose petals bloom at the level of her ear.

As an ornament on her crown she wears human and divine gems, their light radiating far off, placed in a garland of open golden lotuses around her hair; her ear ornaments are jeweled earrings, round and bordered with gems; the throat ornaments upon her beautiful neck are a string of pearls reaching to her breast and a necklace circling to below her navel; she wears bracelets on her upper arms and on her wrists, the same shape but different in size; and her anklets encircle her feet.

All these are clusters of three jewels beautifully bound into a three-strand garland of gems, bedecked with many fine hanging strings of jewels; her golden girdle is a belt holding the settings of gems, and small silver bells tinkle at the ends of its hanging nets and strings of jewels.

Her upper garment is white silk with golden threads; her lower garment is varicolored silk, like a rainbow. Her sash has the color of sapphire, and her whole body, above and below, is tantalizingly adorned with many divine flowers, placed in rows both long and short.

She sits with her body straight upon a throne of lotus and moon, her two feet crossed in the diamond posture; behind her back is the full orb of the moon, radiating cool beams of light far off, bright and stainless.

On her head is the lord of the family; on the three places of her body are the three syllables; on her heart is the wish-granting wheel; her throne is a lotus and moon.

The divine mansion is of crystal; around the outside is the circle of protection.

"Thus he should vividly visualize," says the author, "concentrating in sequence from the inside to the outside; then, turning about, he should vividly visualize the circle of protection, the divine mansion, the throne, the parts of her body, and so on, from the outside to the inside. He should especially grasp one-pointedly any part or aspect that may become especially vivid, and thereby increse the vivid appearance in general. As he practices these general aspects, he should contemplate for a long time on the essencelessness of her appearance as like a reflection in a mirror, the undilutedness of her vividness as like a rainbow, and her pervasiveness as like a moon in water; thus he will at the very least make her vivid as a mental object, next best as if she were really present, and best of all even more vivid than that. And if this vivid appearance becomes firm—continuous—he will gain without impediment all the functions and magical attainments that have been spoken of."

2.1132 *Firmness of ego*

Next the practitioner makes firm his possession of the ego of the goddess. Whether or not the parts of her body are vivid, he should cast aside the conception that clings to his ordinary ego, and he should think: "I am in actuality the blessed Cintācakra, essence of the Perfection of Wisdom, mother who gives birth to the Conquerors and their sons; I possess all her body, speech, mind, qualities, and active functions!" By ever cherishing the ego that thus conceives itself, during all the contemplative periods and between all the contemplative periods, all the empowerments arise therefrom.

2.1133 *Recollection of purity*

Finally the practitioner performs the recollection of purity. "Though the deity's body has been amalgamated with his ordinary body," the author says, "it is not as if this were truly substantial; rather, all the resultant qualities are displayed as aspects of her form." And he gives the following meditation on this theme:

> The white color of her body is the abandonment of the two obscurations and the propensity thereto. The radiation of five-colored light is the impartial arising of prowess in the five knowledges. The single face is the one taste of Suchness. The two hands are the Innate Union of the two truths. The two feet are the dwelling in neither extreme of this world or nirvāṇa. The seven eyes gaze upon Reality—the way it truly is—through the three gates of deliverance, and they set out in compassion toward all events, as many as there may be, through the four immeasurables. The right hand is the gift-bestowing of the two sorts of magical attainment. The joining of the thumb and ring finger of the left hand is the Innate Union of Means and Wisdom, and the stretching out of the remaining fingers is a symbol of the Three Jewels. The holding of a white lotus flower is the vastness of the qualities of understanding and liberation, and the casting down of what should be abandoned. The binding of her hair into one is the binding of all fabrications in the Dharma realm. Her manner of charm and sensuousness is being the mother who gives birth to all the Conquerors and uninterrupted compassion for beings. The ornaments of varied silk and precious gems is the mastery of infinite qualities and deeds. The body sitting straight is the unwavering from the diamond-like deep contemplation. The diamond posture is being untouched by defilements. Her family is symbolized by Amitābha, and the moon behind her is the increase of inaxhaustible Bliss. The moon is all the portions of the absolute thought of enlightenment. The white lotus is the entering into this world with the relative thought of enlightenment, yet being

> unstained by the dirt of this world. And the throne made of both of these is the constant dwelling in both thoughts of enlightenment.

"By knowing how these things are formed as her aspects," the author concludes, "he will be protected from imposing any labeling constructs upon the brilliant deity."

2.12 *The yoga with the recitation*

The second major part of the Process of Generation is the yoga with the recitation; once the young monk in solitary contemplation has achieved at least a modicum of vivid appearance and ego in his yoga with the deity, he will be spending most of his remaining ritual service in this contemplation of the mantra.

2.121 *Visualizing the wheel*

The recitation begins with the practitioner vividly visualizing himself as White Tārā; right in the middle of his heart he visualizes an eight-petaled white lotus, with the disk of a moon laid down flat upon it. Above this "throne" is an eight-spoked white wheel of the Law with one rim, in the center of which is a white TĀṂ. When he performs the basic part of the recitation—the 10-syllable mantra—he should visualize an OṂ floating like a bird over the drop or point on top of the TĀṂ, and a HĀ below it, all three within the center of the wheel, with the eight remaining syllables arrayed on the eight spokes. But if he is adding the appendix to the mantra, he should visualize the TĀṂ in the center of the wheel surrounded by OṂ MAMA ĀYUḤ-PUṆYA-JÑĀNA-PUṢṬIṂ-KURU HĀ clockwise from the front, with TĀ RE TU TTĀ RE TU RE SVĀ facing inward on the eight spokes beginning from the front. All these syllables, too, are like pearl beads, white and radiating their own light, unwavering firmly fixed in position. And he should visualize them with assurance, concentrating upon them one-pointedly, just as he did for the vivid appearance.

2.122 *Reciting the mantra*

2.1221 *The settling recitation*

There are three different types of recitation which the practitioner now proceeds to perform. The first of these is called the "settling recitation," a sort of introductory practice just to get into the rhythm of the mantra. He lets his breath settle into its usual cadence, while he silently visualizes with one-pointed attention that the wheel and its syllables themselves whisper the mantra with the hushed sound of *silili*—"this is the application of settling the mind."

2.1222 *The diamond recitation*

Next is the "diamond recitation," which begins the movement of the visualized mantra. The practitioner exhales forcibly three times, visualizing that he thus dispels his sins and obscurations, his propensity thereto, and all the impediments to his life. Then with his breathing only very soft or medium, he silently visualizes that when he exhales light radiates forth from the TĀṂ in his heart, that when he inhales the light is gathered back therein, and that when his breath is quiet, he concentrates upon the syllable TĀṂ itself. He should perform this visualization about a hundred times.

2.1223 *The verbal recitation with radiation and gathering in*

The practitioner then settles down to the real verbal recitation, with "radiation and gathering in:"

> If one tires of these contemplations, or has attained vivid appearance in them, then should be performed the verbal recitation, joining to it the gathering in and absorption of the stream of life.

The practitioner holds an empowered rosary made of the wood of the bodhi tree or other material suitable to the particular function, and he recites aloud, avoiding the eight faults of going too fast, stumbling, and so on. From the wheel and its syllable comes white light, which fills the entire inside of the practitioner's body, cleansing his sins, obscurations, diseases, untimely death, and especially all the life-shortening obscurations of his past karma, such as killing or taking away the basis of another's livelihood.

Then the light radiates forth outside and is gathered back in as nectar, all the distillation and juice of the inanimate world, a firmness garnered as the four elements: earth, water, fire, and air. He visualizes that this dissolves into his body and the wheel in his heart, and thereby it becomes the strength of his body and the prop of his mind, granting him a life of diamond, strong and firm.

Once again the light radiates forth, and it gathers together harmlessly a distillation of the life and merit of beings, a "distillation of mobility" from those who hold the mantra of life, from gods and sages, from wise men and scholars, from universal monarchs, guardians of the directions, and the eight classes of gods and ogres.

He visualizes that this dissolves into his body and the wheel in his heart, and thereby it becomes the strength of his body and the prop of his mind, granting him a life of diamond, strong and firm.

And once again the light radiates forth, making offerings to all the Three Jewels and the Three Basic Ones, and arousing their thoughtful purpose, so that the empowerment of their body, speech, and mind, their potent qualities of knowledge and love, and especially all their magical attainments of deathless life and knowledge—all are gathered back in as light. This dissolves into him, and thereby he visualizes that he blazes with a dazzling brilliance, and he gains the magical attainment of a life of diamond.

And the practitioner recites: for the ritual service the 10-syllable mantra is the most important thing, but during an evocation or employment the mantra with the appendix is the most important. When the mantra is recited with its life appendix, the practitioner with the force of his devotion arouses the stream of the heart of the lord of the family on top of his head; the light from his heart gathers in as nectar all the distillation of this world and nirvāṇa, which enters into the alms bowl in his hands; it melts and boils, and a stream of nectar enters downward into the practitioner through his hole of Brahma, and the practitioner visualizes that his entire body becomes like a crystal flask filled with milk.

Finally, at the end of the contemplative period, when the practitioner has recited the mantra with its visualization as many times as possible, he should make up any deficiencies in his performance with the 100-syllable mantra, and make the ritual firm with YE DHARMA . . . and so on, adding these on in accordance with general practice. And, as is proper, says the author, he should then set out upon the concluding Process of Perfection, which brings the contemplative period to its close.

2.2 *The Process of Perfection*

2.21 *With signs*

The Process of Perfection "with signs" here used is called "planting the magic dagger of life in one's heart," one of the standard operations of physical yoga which did not find its way into such contemplative collectanea as the "six yogas of Nāropa"; but it is discussed by Tsongk'apa[46] and analogues are found in the Hindu Tantras.[47] The practitioner as Cintācakra vividly visualizes the inside of his body as completely empty and hollow. His body is like a tent of white silk or a flask of white crystal, and upright in the middle thereof is the "life channel," the *avadhūtī* like a firmly planted pillar of crystal, its upper point just not touching the top of his head, and its lower point just not touching his "secret place". It is blocked at its upper point by a white drop having the essence of Bliss, and at its lower point by a red drop having the essence of Warmth. And the practitioner visualizes that in the middle thereof, inside the channel at the level of his heart, is a white syllable TĀṂ, which is his own mind, the mind that rides upon the steeds of the winds within his body, radiating light and now firmly fixed in place.

When this is vivid, he exhales and holds his breath in the "flask," deep in his lungs, so that his stomach protrudes like the belly of a jar. He visualizes that the central channel is filled with the blue-red "wind of life" coming from the TĀṂ, so that it presses upon his "life"—the TĀṂ—and it cannot move either upward or downward in the central channel, for its departure in either direction is death. And he concentrates one-pointedly thereon.

2.22 *Signless*

Then, finally, the practitioner performs the signless Process of Perfection, the gathering in of the body of the deity. Light radiates forth from the seed in his heart, turning into light all the appearances of this world which had become the maṇḍala of noble Tārā; that light—the entire world—dissolves into the circle of protection, the circle of protection dissolves into the divine mansion, and the divine mansion melts into light and dissolves into the practitioner. He himself, along with his throne, is gathered together from above downward and from below upward, and he dissolves into the wheel in his heart. The wheel dissolves into the syllables, those into the syllable TĀṂ, the subjoined long vowel into the TA, the TA into the crescent, the crescent into the drop, and the drop into Pure Sound, as fine as the tip of a hair, which grows fainter and fainter until it finally disappears into nonobjectifiability. And the practitioner enters into deep contemplative union with the Clear Light, which is by its very essence Great Emptiness, the realm wherein every single aspect of the objective world and its subjective perceiver are perfect, pure as space.

In that realm of his basic nature he does not discriminate the past, he pays no mind to the future, he imposes no mental constructs upon the present, and he in no way objectifies this world, or nirvāṇa, or anything else; and herein he settles himself, his natural flow now genuine and relaxed, neither too tense nor too slack, not grasping any "is" or "isn't," not objectifying, not imposing mental constructs, free of distinctions of contemplator and contemplated.

Should any mental construct suddenly arise, the practitioner should neither dam it up nor stretch it out, but rather cut it off entirely; settled into this natural state, he views all events with discriminative wisdom, and he sees that the basic nature of all events is an essence—the Clear Light—which is pure from the beginning; he sees that all events are the Innate Union of the Clear Light and Emptiness. His perception of this is inseparably one with a realm unstained by any fabrication of an appearance of duality—"true" or "false," "is" or "isn't"—and thus there arises to him universally the "knowledge born simultaneously": simultaneously with his perception of every single event that appears, he knows it to be the Innate Union of the Clear Light and Emptiness. And our author links this contemplation with the standards Buddhist notions of Insight and Calm:

> To see in the manner of not seeing; to see with a knowledge individually and distinctly aware of each event as free of arising, abiding, or ceasing, a knowledge clear, bright, and all-pervading as the center of a spotless sky, free of all extremes and labels; to settle into one's genuine and natural flow, contemplating to no specific end and forming no concepts; thus vividly to see Reality, passed beyond labeling fabrications—this is "Insight."
>
> To be firmly stilled all at once within one's natural flow, free of any clinging therein to contemplator and contemplated—this is "Calm."
>
> "Calm" is when one's construction of nonreality is pacified of itself, when one is firmly stilled in one's inherent nonimposition of mental constructs; and "Insight" is its instrinic manifestation of understanding, decisive and cognizant yet free of fabrication—know that the Innate Union of these two is the supreme and supramundane conjunction of Calm and Insight.
>
> This is thus the necessary foundation for all future practice of evocation and recitation, and when this communion is mixed with an evocation and a recitation during the main part of a ritual, that becomes a yoga of Innate Union.

3 *Concluding acts*

3.1 *Arising in the body of Innate Union*

But the ritual service is not yet completed, for the practitioner must arise from his communion in the body of the deity, for only then can he serve the aim of beings and apply through ritual and magical functions his control over the appearances of public nonreality whose nature he now—ideally—truly understands. Thus instantaneously, "like a fish leaping from the water," he perfects from that realm of the Clear Light the body of Cintācakra in all its aspects, visualizing it vividly to be like an illusion, its essence freed of all truth or falsehood, upon the top of its head OṂ, upon its throat ĀḤ, and upon its heart HŪṂ, white, red, and blue. These syllables are inherently the three Diamonds, which prevent any impediment from entering through the three gates—and the practitioner should arise into the path of the great metaphysical doctrine of the Process of Perfection, knowing that all events subsumed under the categories of appearance, of sound, and of understanding are from the absolute point of view not brought about through any essence, knowing thus too that the body, the speech, and the mind of the Holy Lady are pure in essence, that her appearance is but an illusion.

But here, also, White Tārā's specialized function of prolonging life is not ignored: the above method of "arising in the body of Innate Union" is general to all deities, and the author of our ritual service provides an alternative technique, which may also be practiced separately as a magical function, but here applied to "arising in the body of the deity." Thus, from the realm of Emptiness brought about through the Process of Perfection there appears in a single instant a white spherical pavilion, having eight ribs, one in each of the eight directions, and two more above and below, making ten in all. The sharp points of their tips rotate clockwise just fast enough so that they are blurred; and in the middle of its round center, upon a throne of lotus and moon, is the practitioner himself, instantaneously arisen as the holy Cintācakra, with all her ornaments, the lord of the family upon her head, and the wheel and its syllables in her heart.

Inside the lower part of the upper spoke—the part nearest the outside surface of the pavilion and farthest from the tip of the spoke—is an OṂ, and inside the upper part of the lower spoke is a HĀ, and inside the empty holes at the bases of the spokes in the eight directions are TĀ RE TU TTĀ RE TU RE SVĀ, clockwise from the front. All these syllables blaze with white-colored light; and the practitioner visualizes that this sphere with its syllables is solid and firm, without joints, not to be passed even by the icy wind at the end of the world era. And he remains in this contemplation for a long time.

Here the practitioner is forming a circle of protection, which may be applied for the benefit of others besides himself: thus he should visualize, all inside the pavilion with him, his gurus in the upper part, other persons whom he wishes to protect—"high and low in due order"—to the right and left, and animals and so on below him; and when he proceeds to the radiation and absorption of light, he should visualize that it also radiates from and dissolves back into these beings to be protected.

Then the practitioner begins a visualization such as we have outlined once before, as the Master preparing for the initiation into life gathered the power of life he would pass on to his disciples:

> From the wheel and its syllables in my heart there radiates forth white light like moon drops, filling my body and dispelling all my sins, obscurations, diseases, hindering demons, impediments, and terror of timely and untimely death. Once again light radiates forth, cleansing the impurities of the animate and inanimate worlds, making the inanimate world into a Pure Land and raising all the animate beings it contains to the rank of Tārā. It makes offerings to the Conquerors and their sons, and it invites in the form of white light the knowledge of my inseparability from their body, speech, and mind.
>
> This light is gathered back in and fills my body, dissolving into the wheel and its syllables in my heart; and thus I accomplish the function of pacifying, and I blaze with a brilliant light.
>
> The overflowing light reaches a full fathom outside the spherical pavilion, and circling into a sphere it forms a pavilion of light, solid and firm, without joints, not to be passed even by the wind at the end of the world era. And I visualize that the empty space between the two pavilions is filled with full-blown blue lotus flowers. Here I enter into contemplation . . . .

And here too, if the erection of the circle of protection is the main thing, the practitioner recites the 10-syllable mantra. All the details of the above visualization, the text adds, should be read into the ones that follow:

> Once again, yellow light like refined gold radiates forth, fills my body, dispels death, and increases my life, merit, glory, power, enjoyments, fame, understanding, and wisdom. Once again light radiates outward . . . in the form of yellow light . . . and thus I accomplish the function of increasing. The overflowing light reaches a full fathom outside the white pavilion and circling into a sphere . . . And I visualize that the empty space between the two pavilions is filled with blue lotus flowers. . . .

> Red light like ruby . . . subjugates all the knowledge, love, and power of the mobile and immobile in this world and in nirvāṇa. . . . The red light dissolves into me . . . and thus I accomplish the function of subjugation. . . . It forms a pavilion of red light outside the other two pavilions of light. . . .
>
> Iron-blue light like the early morning sky . . . cuts down all misfortunes, the five poisons, enemies, hindering demons, imepdiments, misleading demons, and so on . . . The blue light dissolves into me . . . and thus I accomplish the function of destroying . . . It forms a pavilion of blue light outside the other three pavilions of light. . . .
>
> Green light like emerald . . . accomplishes all at once all the highest and ordinary magical attainments . . . The green light dissolves into me . . . and thus I accomplish all the miscellaneous functions. . . . It forms a pavilion of green light outside the other four pavilions of light. . . .
>
> Dark-blue light like sapphire. . . makes firm and unimpaired all the functions and magical attainments. . . The dark-blue light dissolves into me . . . and thus I will never be terrified or defeated by anything, and all the empowerments and functions I have accomplished are made firm. . . It forms a pavilion of dark-blue light outside the other five pavilions of light. . . .

The practitioner performs this entire series of six protective pavilions, including all the details given in the first white light of pacifying, and he should vividly visualize each point thus expanded upon.

> All these things are like an illusion, a moon in water, a mirage, a fancy, a reflection in a mirror, free from "true" or "false," having no essence in their appearance, inherently the Perfection of Wisdom—thus the practitioner enters into contemplation, an Innate Union which, like a moon in water, neither yearns after Great Bliss nor clings to the Clear Light.

When the practitioner tires of this contemplation, he should recite the 10-syllable mantra as often as he can, moving only the tip of his tongue. All external and internal sound and all the movements of his breath are now heard to be in their very essence the sound of Tārā's mantra; this sound is like an echo, sound and Emptiness, free from "true" or "false," and in this realm the practitioner relaxes his cognition of the mantra. And finally, as above, he gathers himself into the Clear Light and arises therefrom in the body of Innate Union.[48]

3.2 *The acts between contemplative periods*

Once this part of the ritual is finished, the practitioner can spend his spare time in the "acts between contemplative periods," the ritual functions that fill in his period of solitary contemplation between his sessions of visualization and recitation. "Without being separated from that deep contemplation of himself in the deity's body of Innate Union," says our author, "he should exert himself between the contemplative periods in all the 'virtuous acts' he is able to perform, both general and particular, such as offering tormas, offering maṇḍalas, praising, circumambulating, bathing the deity, praying for his desires, making the water offering, giving gifts, and so on. By thus practicing—experiencing—he will accomplish in just a year or a month whatever aim he has in mind, whatever condition of life, intelligence, or wealth he desires, or any ultimate magical attainment such as the knowledge of Bliss and Emptiness."[49]

THE INSTRUCTIONS ON THE RITUAL SERVICE

The author of our text gives quite detailed instructions, subsidiary advice on the exact manner in which the solitary contemplation of the ritual service should be carried out (see fig. 45). This information is embodied in a chapter of his text called the "handbook" or, perhaps, the "instruction manual," which begins by describing how to make the painting of the deity which will serve as a symbolic support during the ritual visualization.

A point to be noted in this connection, by the way, is that some lamas advise against the use of a painting as a support for these visualizations, giving as a reason that the practitioner may then too easily and all unknowingly visualize the painting rather than the deity herself, and it is considered that he should not become dependent upon such externals; indeed, the contemplative image would then be a simulacrum for the painting and not the goddess, and the magical coercion of the divine power would be ineffective. On the other hand, the painting may serve a purely significatory function, being placed above the altar as a representation of the deity's body, in conjunction with the book representing her speech, and a small stūpa containing the relics of a revered master or teacher in one's lineage to represent her mind.

In any event, the instructions say, the painting should be made on the eighth day or the full-moon day of any of the four *rawa* months—months that begin a new season. The artist should be one who "keeps the vows above those of a lay devotee": he should be bathed and in a state of purity, with all lapses in his vows cleansed away,

Fig. 45. Solitary contemplation: a yogin in meditative posture, shoulders thrown back, elbows turned in, and arms locked on the thighs. From a Tibetan wood-block print.

eating only the three "white foods" while he paints, and he should finish the painting, including its consecration, in a single day; his fee for this is "anything he asks for." This is a feat whose difficulty, even if the painting is a small one, may be appreciated by considering that the average Tibetan painting may take three months to complete; I have seen an artist making such a one-day painting for a sick lama, painting furiously while his food and tea (no Tibetan can work without tea, whatever the handbooks may say) were brought to him by anxious monks.

A painting thus finished in a single day on the eighth or fifteenth of the month is considered "special," but it may be painted through the six days between those dates, or even, if all else is impossible, between the first and the fifteenth days; but the basic idea would seem to be that the painting must be made in phase with the increasing moon, capturing its increase, as it were, at its height, and completing the painting either on the day of the full moon or halfway thereto, when the moon's power of increase is at its most potent.

The practitioner who will consecrate the painting for use in the ritual service first performs the visualization and recitation of the self-generation, and he "bathes" the painting—actually he pours the water upon the painting's reflection in a mirror—with water from a flask over which the 10-syllable mantra has been recited. He then generates the painting with the complete fourfold Process of Generation, and he "opens its eyes" by painting them in; and he recites the basic mantra followed by the heart of conditioned coproduction to make the consecration firm, offering up flowers after each recitation, offering clothing in the form of the ceremonial scarf, and then performing the sevenfold office and the recitation. A special image completed in a single day requires no other ritual than this, which may be even further abbreviated, according to some texts, to the bathing, the recitation of the heart of conditioned coproduction, and the offerings, or simply to the offering up of flowers or grain. Some lamas will simply recite the mantra a few times and scatter some rice upon the painting, generating the divine power therein instantaneously. A statue is consecrated in the same way.

The actual performance of the ritual service should begin when the planets and stars are auspicious, and on a day, such as the eighth, when the moon is waxing in one of the four *rawa* months. The painting, rice maṇḍala, offering torma, and so on should be set out facing south, and, since here the chief thing is to accomplish the function of increasing, the practitioner himself should face to the north, the direction in which the sun moves as the days grow longer.

If one consults the *Tantra of Tārā the Yoginī*, the author says, it would seem that little importance is attached to daily purity and so on; but, according to the long-established tradition of Atīśa, it is best if the practitioner washes the dwelling, the utensils, and himself with bathing water over which has been recited the "conquering" mantra, if he gives up meat and beer and so on while he is practicing the ritual service, and if in short he keeps himself in a condition of bodily purity. He should avoid garlic and onions, which pollute the strength of his speech, and beer and drugs, which produce drowsiness; he should avoid anything that might cause contamination or distraction, and he should wash himself again and again with water over which the mantra has been recited. In this connection, the text recommends the ritual of Bhavabhadra[50] for the practitioner to cleanse away any lapses in his vows. And before beginning the ritual, he should first determine by an examination of omens, such as his dreams of the night before, whether or not he will have the "luck"—the good karma—to succeed in it.

As a "connection" for the increase of life, merit, and understanding, the practitioner should establish the beginning of the contemplative period in the morning, when the sun rises. If he would practice—experience—according to the full life teaching, he must do all the expanded preliminary practices, the visualization and recitation of Vajrasattva, and so on. But for the ordinary ritual service it is presumed that he has done all the preliminaries previously, whether according to this text or another; so now he should offer a preliminary torma to the hindering demons and erect outside his door a small pile of white stones as a marker of the "limits" of his retreat, indicating the area outside which he vows not to go; he appoints the Four Great Kings, or Swirling Nectar, to stand guard over the place; with magic mustard seed, with *gugü* incense, and with fierce mantras he expels the demons who remain; and he visualizes a firm surrounding circle of protection which he will not gather in until the very end of his ritual service, visualizing it again and again as the days go by.

The practitioner evokes the cleansing water and empowers therewith the place and the utensils. He begins from the "going for refuge" and the "thought of enlightenment," doing them earnestly a number of times; and, accumulating his stocks of merit and knowledge, he first performs the self-generation up through the offerings and praise.

He should work slowly and carefully through this generation, and then concentrate especially upon the exercises of vivid appearance, firmness of ego, and recollection of purity which follow, for it is only after he has achieved at least some slight vivid appearance of the deity's body and of her divine mansion with its throne that he proceeds to visualize vividly the wishing wheel in her heart, and until this vividly appears he should contemplate upon it one-pointedly, performing a calm verbal recitation.

The school of instructions followed by our text holds that the practitioner first visualizes an eight-spoked wheel, in the center of which is TĀṂ; above the drop or point on top of that syllable is an OṂ "like a flying bird," beneath its subjoined long vowel is a HĀ inside the nave of the wheel, and the eight remaining syllables are on the eight spokes. When the life appendix is added on, the visualization for the recitation is augmented accordingly.

There is also, the text says, a visualization according to the school of Bari, whose transmission has been lost, wherein Tārā's emblem as a three-pointed flower and a wheel of five rims are surrounded by the vowels and consonants, the heart of conditioned coproduction, a ring of vajras, fire, and mountains, each on one of the rims.

There is no direct descent, either, of the school of Atīśa, but its instructions are not only clearly found in the Indian texts that were his sources and in the writings of many scholars learned in the original texts, but they also occur in the oral tradition of the gurus.

The sixth Red Hat Karmapa Ch'öchi wangch'ug (1584-1638) said that during the settling recitation the wheel and its syllables rotate to the right and to the left, but this text is also lost, and the opinion is not held by anyone else; hence our author maintains that during this part of the recitation the wheel and its syllables should be quite firm and unmoving, the white portions blazing with light, and the practitioner should contemplate it with his body held erect. These are the most important things.

Thus visualizing, there arises the correct vivid appearance of the wheel and its mantra garland, and the practitioner should then perform first the settling recitation and then the diamond recitation for an appropriate length of time, before proceeding—as the primary activity of the contemplative period—to the verbal recitation of the 10-syllable mantra, with radiation and absorption of light. At the end of the contemplative period, it is all right for him to recite the mantra with the appendix perhaps a hundred times or so, but at this point it is by no means absolutely necessary.

At the end of the contemplative period he may perform for a little while both Processes of Perfection with signs as given in the text—that is, the circle of protection and the magic dagger of life—or he may visualize the circle of protection (doing its recitation perhaps a thousand times) at the end of the morning and evening contemplative periods, and visualize planting the magic dagger of life either at the end of the noon and afternoon contemplative periods or, indeed, whenever it is most convenient.

At the end of each contemplative period he should also complete the gathering in and arising of the signless Process of Perfection; he should dedicate his merit and then offer up a torma "with no hope of personal profit therefrom." In other words, each of the four contemplative periods of the day should be so timed as to allow the practitioner to run through the ritual completely.

It is not necessary, however, to perform every single one of the other functions to be done between contemplative periods, the maṇḍala offerings and so on, "without hope of personal profit"; but each one of these individually is necessary and is of great benefit, so the practitioner should certainly fit them into his schedule.

Thus, the text concludes, the contents of a contemplative period should proceed from the going for refuge and the thought of enlightenment through to the completion of offering the concluding torma, and the practitioner should do nothing else until he has completed the requisite number of recitations of the 10-syllable mantra in the ritual service, whether it be the highest number, the middle, or the least.

We have mentioned before that this ritual is a life teaching as well as a ritual service; in general, our author says, we find in the texts and expanded histories that by this much alone the practitioner gains all the highest and ordinary magical attainments. But since the chief thing on this occassion is the gaining of life, the practitioner should, after having finished the requisite amount of ritual service for this function, recite the mantra with its life appendix while performing the following visualization.

The light from the heart of Amitābha on top of the practitioner's head gathers together as nectar a distillation of this world and nirvāṇa. This nectar flows into the alms bowl Amitābha holds in his hands, and from it there flows a stream of melted and boiling nectar down into the practitioner through his hole of Brahma, filling up his entire body.

According to the school of Atīśa, on the other hand, the chief visualizations for the prolonging of life are the following five: radiation and absorption, recitation, diamond recitation, circle of protection, and planting the magic dagger of life. Hence it has long been held that one may complete simultaneously all the ends of the self-generation, the visualizations therein granting the highest attainment as well as the prolongation of life; so it is also all right for the practitioner, during the contemplation of the mantra in the ritual service, to recite the mantra with its appendix a little bit at the beginning and end of each contemplative period. in addition to reciting just the 10-syllable mantra during its main portion.

A practitioner who has previously finished the ritual service and evocation for his own benefit may also turn the above recitation into a service for his guru, visualizing that the light clears away impediments of his guru's body, speech, mind, qualities, and functions, and that it gathers together the empowerment of Tārā, of the Three Jewels, and of the Three Basic Ones, the magical attainments, especially that of life without death, and a distillation of the animate and inanimate: this dissolves into the guru, increasing his bodily life and his ability to function for the infinite good of beings. If it is his own guru, the practitioner visualizes him seated on the top of his head; if it is for another, he visualizes that the light dissolves into him wherever he may be. Similarly, substituting any appropriate name for the MAMA in the appendix to the mantra, its recitation may be applied also to any other person.

Here, where the recitation is directed mainly toward gaining life, it is best if the practitioner performs an expanded ritual offering at the end of all four contemplative periods; it is middling if he does so at the end of the morning and evening contemplative periods; and he must certainly do so at least at the end of the morning contemplative period, just offering a torma at the conclusion of the rest.

The rosary with which the practitioner keeps count should be made of conch shell, crystal, or gold—that is, white or yellow colors—consistent with the function of pacifying or increasing. The Lord Ninth and others hold that it should be empowered according to the Practical Tantras by reciting over it seven times OṂ VASUMATI-ŚRIYE SVĀHĀ and OṂ VAJRA-ACCHINTĀYA SVĀHĀ!

At the end of the contemplative period the practitioner may, if he wishes, make up any deficiencies in the recitation by reciting the vowels and consonants, the 100-syllable mantra, and the heart of conditioned coproduction; this is not very important, though it certainly does no harm.

Always and in all practices, he must visualize himself as the Holy Lady, bearing in mind that his appearance is the deity, that his speech is her mantra, and that his memory and mental constructs are her knowledge—that everything is an untrue illusion, a play of Reality.

The practitioner empowers his food and drink into nectar with the three syllables OṂ ĀḤ HŪṂ, and he eats it as if it were an offering to the deity whom he vividly visualizes himself to be; he empowers his clothing and seat also into "ornaments of self-luminous knowledge" with the three syllables, and thus he enjoys them.

When he goes to sleep he places his mind in Emptiness, as at the signless Process of Perfection; or, having gathered himself in as far as the life—the TĀṂ—in his heart, he places his mind in that syllable; or, vividly visualizing himself as the patron deity, he concentrates on the syllable TĀṂ blazing with light in his heart—and thus he falls asleep, using whichever of these contemplations he likes. And when he awakens, he visualizes that his patron deity arrives in the sky and arouses him with the sound of the 10-syllable mantra.

In considering the proper measure of the ritual service, three things are taken into account: the length of time, the signs of success, and the number of recitations. As for the requisite length of time, our author quotes Vāgiśvarakīrti:

> With one-pointed mind
> contemplate six months with firm certainty;
> recite with an unwavering mind
> the 10-syllable mantra.

And the "Chief Disciple Scholar" said:

> For that purpose, for the space of six months
> contemplate the wheel in Tārā's heart;
> thereby one gains all the magical attainments
> and one is undefiled by the stain of death.

These excerpts represent the tradition of the expanded ritual service; to recite for three months is middle, and for one month is least, but even then to recite as much as one is able has measureless benefits. Finally, if one breaks one's solitude even after only seven days, the Great Omniscient said, as long as one recites with devotion and energy one will still be able to avert untimely death; and the Lord Ninth said that if one counts out the recitation unceasingly, not even stopping to sleep, then one may succeed in seven days at best; and if one completes more than that number of recitations or exceeds that length of time, one will assuredly see the deity's face and accomplish all the vast numbers of functions.

Second, although the signs proper are the actual accomplishment of the functions and magical attainments, there may occur beforehand an omen that the practitioner has succeeded, or a beginner may gain in his thoughts or dreams a sign that he has been empowered by the Holy Lady, that he is now in possession of the ability of the mantra. The Master Sahajalalita[51] says: "What occur in one's dreams are signs of future practice: a beginner learns in his dream by the strength of the mantra whether or not he will succeed by reciting more." Thus signs of success are to dream that the gurus of former times are pleased, that women wearing beautiful clothes prophesy and offer garlands and silk and the three white foods, that one wears beautiful white clothing and ornaments, that the sun and moon rise, that music plays, that one meets the deity's emblem or shrine or person, that one is liberated from terror, and so on; and according to the oral tradition ascribed to Drepa the special signs are that "if one dreams of flowers or *ts'ats'a*, then death and impediments are averted."

We may here depart from our handbook for a moment to report an actual dream that served as a sign of success. When one of my informants was sick, he performed this ritual as a life teaching, and one night he and three other monks all had the same dream. He was traveling as he used to in K'am, with a retinue of thirty or forty people, his horse all decorated and his banner of rank held up on a pole. They were crossing a pass on the face of a steep cliff overlooking a terrifying valley filled with rushing and roaring clouds, booming noise and darkness, and the path was overhung by the mountain above. All at once the land beneath their feet started slipping away, and the poles holding the banners melted and bent like soft wax candles. His retinue slipped and fell with the landslide inexorably into the fearsome valley below; and the cliff on the other side of the valley fell down upon them and buried them. My informant dreamed that he alone was left, and across the rubble of the fallen cliff there blew upon him a dense fog, which he knew to be a deadly poison. Through all this he clung to a white rock, which grew larger and larger, and which was all that prevented him from falling into the abyss; and now, though fierce winds threatened to dislodge him and cast him into the deadly fog, the white rock grew large and protected him until he woke up. From that moment on he began to get well.

Finally, the handbook talks of the requisite number of recitations in the ritual service, and our author quotes Candragomin: "Reciting 300,000 or 600,000 or 1,000,000 times, one accomplishes all functions." And Vāgīśvarakīrti said: "The count for the syllables of the mantra is 100,000." Thus the basic measure of ritual service is 100,000 recitations; but it is also held that in this "age of contention" one should recite four times as much. Drubch'en rinpoch'e said: "It is said that if one recites the 10-syllable mantra 10,000,000 times, one's qualities will equal those of the noble Tārā herself." That is to say, if one completes 10,000,000 recitations, one will have the power to accomplish all functions and magical attainments. The oral tradition ascribed to the Chenngawa, however, holds that if the practitioner devotes himself to a ritual service of 100,000 recitations he will be unharmed by any impediments; since she is a deity of active function, it is quick and easy to succeed in her ritual service. And since there is a great deal of evidence for this position in the expanded commentaries upon the various histories of Tārā, our author concludes, we may place our belief therein.[52]

Notes

I PREFACE

[1] Ferdinand Diederich Lessing, *Yung-ho-kung: An Iconography of the Lamaist Cathedral in Peking*, Reports from the Scientific Expedition to the Northwestern Provinces of China under the Leadership of Dr. Sven Hedin, XVIII (Stockholm, 1942).

[2] David L. Snellgrove, *Buddhist Himalaya: Travels and Studies in Quest of the Origins and Nature of Tibetan Religion* (New York: Philosophical Library, 1957).

[3] René de Nebesky-Wojkowitz, *Oracles and Demons of Tibet: The Cult and Iconography of the Tibetan Protective Deities* ('S-Gravenhage: Mouton, 1956).

[4] Lessing, *Yung-ho-kung*, p. 139.

[5] Giuseppe Tucci, *Tibetan Painted Scrolls* (Rome: Libraria dello Stato, 1949), II, 387 ff.

[6] Hirananda Shastri, *The Origin and Cult of Tārā*, Memoirs of the Archaeological Survey of India, XX (Calcutta, 1925).

[7] L. Austine Waddell, "The Indian Buddhist Cult of Avalokita and His Consort Tārā 'the Saviouress,' Illustrated from the Remains in Magadha," *Journal of the Royal Asiatic Society* (1894), pp. 63 ff.; Godefroy de Blonay, *Matériaux pour servir à l'histoire de la déesse buddhique Tārā* (Paris: Librairie Émile Bouillon, 1895); Satis Chandra Vidyabhusana, *Bauddha-stotra-saṁgrahaḥ, or a Collection of Buddhist Hymns*, Vol I: *Sragdharā-stotram, or a Hymn to Tārā in Sragdharā Metre, by Bhikṣu Sarvajña Mitra of Kāśmīra* (Calcutta: Asiatic Society of Bengal, 1908); M. Lalou, "Mañjuśrīmūlakalpa et Tārāmūlakalpa," *Harvard Journal of Asiatic Studies* I (1936), 327-349; Alex Wayman, "The Twenty-one Praises of Tārā, a Syncretism of Śaivism and Buddhism," *Journal of the Bihar Research Society* (1959).

[8] D. C. Sircar, ed., *The Śakti Cult and Tārā* (Calcutta: University of Calcutta, 1967).

[9] For example, see Cintāmaṇirāja, *Sita-tārā-sādhana*, P. 4158, vol. 80, 232.1.1-232.2.3, Rgyud-'grel DU 34b-35a.

[10] On this lineage see pp. 11-12, 387-388, 417-418, above.

[11] The school of Sūryagupta depicts all twenty-one deities as completely different in posture, color, mood, and emblem. See Sūryagupta, *Tārādevī-stotra-ekaviṃśatika-sādhana-nāma*, P. 2557, vol. 59, 51.2.6-53.1.1, Rgyud-'grel LA 7b-12a; *Rje-btsun-ma 'phags-ma sgrol-ma'i*

sgrub-thabs nyi-shu-rtsa-gcig-pa'i las-kyi yan-lag dang bcas-pa mdor-bsdus-pa zhes bya-ba (no Sanskrit), P. 2558, vol. 59, 53.1.1-59.5.4, Rgyud-'grel LA 12a-29a; *Tārā-sādhanôpadeśa-krama*, P. 2559, vol. 59, 59.5.4-60.2.8, Rgyud-'grel LA 29a-30a; *Bhagavatī-tārādevy-ekaviṃśati-stotrôpāyikā*, P. 2560, vol. 59, 60.2.8.-64.4.7, Rgyud-'grel LA 30a-41a; *Devītārâikaviṃśati-stotra-viśuddha-cuḍāmaṇi-nāma*, P. 2561, vol. 59, 64.4.7-66.3.5, Rgyud-'grel LA 41a-45b. On the lineages proceeding from these texts, see 'Gos lo-tsā-ba Gzhon-nu-dpal, *Bod-kyi yul-du chos-dang chos-smra-ba ji-ltar byung-ba'i rim-pa deb-ther sngon-po* PHA, George N. Roerich, trans., *The Blue Annals*, Royal Asiatic Society of Bengal Monograph Series, VII (Calcutta, 1949, 1953), II, 1050 ff. I have seen only one ritual wherein the goddesses were visualized in this manner: Rnam-rgyal-rgyal-mtshan, *Mi-tra brgya-rtsa'i nang-gi grub-chen nyi-ma sbas-pa'i lugs-kyi sgrol-ma nyi-shu rtsa-gcig-gi mngon-par rtogs-pa* [blockprint, 16 folios, Yung-dgon (Yung-ho-kung, Peking) edition], which attributes the transmission to the great Mitra-yogin. For illustrations of this series, see *Rin-'byung snar-thang brgya-rtsa rdor-phreng bcas-nas gsungs-pa'i bris-sku mthong-ba don-ldan*, Lokesh Chandra, ed., *A New Tibeto-Mongol Pantheon* (Delhi: International Academy of Indian Culture, 1961 —), IX, 92-100; and Rol-pa'i rdo-rje [Lcang-skya I], *Chu Fo P'u-sa Sheng Hsiang Tsan*, Walter Eugene Clark, ed., *Two Lamaistic Pantheons* (New York: Paragon Book Reprint Corp., 1965), II, 276-283. This artistic tradition seems to have been the one most extensively studied in the West; see, for example, Giuseppe Tucci, *Indo-Tibetica* (Rome: Reale Academie d'Italie, 1936), II, pt. 2, pp. 156-161; and Siegbert Hummel, *Lamaistische Studien* (Leipzig: Otto Harrassowitz, 1959), pp. 89-111.

The artistic school associated with the name of Nāgārjuna depicts the twenty-one goddesses all as ordinary Tārās, but of different colors and each holding a different-colored flask in her outstretched hand; see pp. 333-335, above. See also, for example, Ngag-dbang blo-bzang chos-ldan dpal-bzang-po [Lcang-skya II], *Sgrol-ma nyer-gcig-gi sgrub-thabs las-tshogs mu-tig phreng-ba zhes bya-ba*, P. 6334, vol. 164, 143.5.2.-145.2.7. in *Collected Works* JA 24a-27b. This Nāgārjuna tradition is also often attributed to Atīśa; see Tucci, *Tibetan Painted Scrolls*, II, 388; see also, for example, Blo-bzang chos-kyi rgyal-mtshan [Paṇ-chen bla-ma I], *Jo-bo-rje'i lugs-kyi sgrol-ma nyer-gcig-gi sgrub-thabs las-tshogs dngos-grub rnam-gnyis-kyi bang-mdzod zhes bya-ba* [block print, 11 folios, Bkra-shis lhun-po edition] in *Collected Works* GA.

Finally, the Rnying-ma-pa [*Klong-chen snying-thig*] tradition depicts all the Tārās as the same, but in different colors and each holding an individual emblem on top of the lotus in her left hand rather than a flask in the right. See Thub-bstan bshad-grub rgya-mtsho, *Sgrol-ma phyag-'tshal nyer-gcig rgyud-kyi 'grel-chung phan-bde'i gter-bum mchog-sbyin zhes bya-ba* [block print, 12 folios, no edition given], where this iconography is traced back to 'Jigs-med gling-pa (1729-1798) and thence to the "Great Long"—Klong-chen rab-'byams-pa—himself (1308-1363).

CHAPTER I: WORSHIP

[1] *Rgyal-po bka'i thang-yig*, in *Pad-ma bka'-thang sde-lnga* [block print, 281 folios, Sde-dge edition], fol. 18a, trans. in David L. Snellgrove, *Buddhist Himalaya: Travels and Studies in Quest of the Origins and Nature of Tibetan Religion* (New York: Philosophical Library, 1957), p. 129, and in Giuseppe Tucci, *Tibetan Painted Scrolls* (Rome: Libraria dello Stato, 1949), II, 732.

[2] Kun-dga' rdo-rje, *'Tshal-pa kun-dga' rdo-rjes mdzad pa'i hu-lan deb-ther* [*Deb-ther dmar-po*] (Gangtok, Sikkim: Namgyal Institute of Tibetology, 1961), fol, 15b. See also Ye-shes dpal-'byor [Sum-pa mkhan-po], *'Phags-yul rgya-nag chen-po bod-dang sog-yul-du dam-pa'i chos byung-tshul dpag-bsam ljon-bzang zhes bya-ba*, Sarat Chandra Das, ed., *Pag Sam Jon Zang* (Calcutta: Presidency Jail Press, 1908), p. 149; and *Blon-po bka'i thang-yig*, in *Pad-ma bka'-thang sde-lnga*, fol. 4a. Cf. the discussion and translation in Snellgrove, *Buddhist Himalaya*, pp. 122 ff.

[3] See 'Gos lo-tsā-ba Gzhon-nu-dpal, *Bod-kyi yul-du chos-dang chos-smra-ba ji-ltar byung-ba'i rim-pa deb-ther sngon-po*, George N. Roerich, trans., *The Blue Annals*, Royal Asiatic Society of Bengal Monograph Series, VII (Calcutta, 1949, 1953), p. vi.

[4] Ye-shes dpal-'byor, *Dpag-bsam ljon-bzang*, p. 149.

[5] Roerich, *Blue Annals*, p. ix. But see also the complete discussion in Bunkyo Aoki, *Study on Early Tibetan Chronicles* (Tokyo: Nippon Gakujutsu Shinkokai, 1955), pp. 27 ff.

[6] Kun-dga' rdo-rje, *Deb-ther dmar-po*, fol. 16b; Bu-ston Rin-chen-grub, *Bde-bar gshegs-pa'i bstan-pa'i gsal-byed chos-kyi 'byung-gnas gsung-rab rin-po-che'i mdzod ces bya-ba*, in *Collected Works* YA [block print, 212 folios, Lhasa edition], fol. 138b, E. Obermiller, trans., *History of Buddhism by Bu-ston* (Heidelberg: Otto Harrassowitz, 1931, 1932), II, 184; Ye-shes dpal-'byor, *Dpag-bsam ljon-bzang*, p. 168; Bsod-nams rgyal-mtshan, *Rgyal-rabs chos-'byung sel-ba'i me-long*, B. I. Kuznetsov, ed. (Leiden: E. J. Brill, 1966), chap. xi-xiii and *passim; Ladvags rgyal-rabs*, A. H. Francke, ed. and trans., *Antiquities of Indian Tibet* (Calcutta: Archaeological Survey of India, 1926), II, 31; Ngag-dbang blo-bzang rgya-mtsho [Dalai Lama V], *Gangs-can yul-gyi sa-la spyod-pa'i mtho-ris-kyi rgyal-blon gtso-bor brjod-pa'i deb-ther rdzogs-ldan gzhon-nu'i dga'-ston dpyid-kyi rgyal-mo'i glu-dbyangs zhes bya-ba*, Kalsang Lhundup, ed., *The History of Tibet by Fifth Dalai Lama* (Varanasi: privately printed, 1967), pp. 34, 39.

[7] 'Jam-dbyangs mkhyen-brtse'i dbang-po, *Dbus-gtsang-gi gnas-rten rags-rim-gyi mtshan-byang mdor-bsdus dad-pa'i sa-bon zhes bya-ba*, Alfonsa Ferrari, ed. and trans., *Mkhyen brtse's Guide to the Holy Places of Central Tibet* (Rome: Istituto Italiano per il Medio ed Estremo Oriente, 1958), pp. 3, 40, 87 n. 42.

[8] Ngag-dbang blo-bzang rgya-mtsho [Dalai Lama V], *Lha-ldan sprul-pa'i gtsug-lag khang-gi dkar-chag shel-dkar me-long zhes bya-ba* [block

print, 23 folios, Dga'-ldan edition], fol. 18a, Albert Grünwedel, ed. and trans., *Die Tempel von Lhasa* (Heidelberg: Sitzungsberichte der Heidelberger Akademie der Wissenschaften, 1919), p. 67.

[9] See the sources given in note 6 above, as well as Jacques Bacot, "Le mariage chinois du roi tibétain Sroṅ bcan sgam po (Extrait du *Maṇi bka' 'bum*)," *Mélanges chinois et bouddhiques*, III (1933-34), 1-61.

[10] See Luciano Petech, *A Study on the Chronicles of Ladakh*, supplement to *Indian Historical Quarterly*, XIII and XV (Calcutta, 1939), p. 50. See also Giuseppe Tucci, "The Wives of Sroṅ btsan sgam po," *OriensExtremus*, IX (1962), 121-126. In this article, noted only after my text was written, Tucci is very skeptical about the existence of Khri-btsun, and he adds some sources not then available to me; but he comes to the same conclusion about the iconographization of the king, and I am pleased to have this speculation confirmed by so eminent a scholar.

[11] J. F. Scheltema, *Monumental Java* (London, 1912), pp. 181 f. See also Hirananda Shastri, *The Origin and Cult of Tārā*, Memoirs of the Archaeological Survey of India, XX (Calcutta, 1925), pp. 8, 12.

[12] Subandhu, *Vasavadattā*, Louis H. Gray, ed. and trans. (New York: Columbia University Press, 1913), p. 172.

[13] *Ibid.*, p. 146.

[14] See Sukumari Bhattacharji, *The Indian Theogony* (Cambridge Cambridge University Press, 1970), pp. 155 f.

[15] For discussion of and further references on Subandhu's date, see S. N. Dasgupta and S. K. Dey, *A History of Sanskrit Literature* (Calcutta: University of Calcutta, 1962), I, 217-219.

[16] Hsüan-tsang, *Ta-t'ang hsi-yü-chi* (Nanking: Chinese Buddhist Association, 1957), VIII, 11a-b, Samuel Beal, trans., *Travels of Hiouen-Thsang* (Calcutta: Susil Gupta, 1957), p. 335. See also Thomas Watters, trans., *On Yuan Chwang's Travels in India* (Delhi: Munshiram Manohar Lal, 1961), p. 105.

[17] Hsüan-tsang, *Ta-t'ang hsi-yü-chi*, IX, 19b-20a; Beal, *Travels of Hiouen-Thsang*, p. 388; Watters, *On Yuan Chwang's Travels in India*, p. 171.

[18] Smin-grol No-mon-han [Bla-ma Btsan-po], *'Dzam-gling chen-po'i rgyas-bshad snod-bcud kun-gsal me-long zhes bya-ba*, Turrell V. Wylie, ed. and trans., *The Geography of Tibet According to the 'Dzam-gling-rgyas-bshad* (Rome: Istituto Italiano per il Medio ed Estreme Oriente, 1962), pp. 41, 101.

[19] Pad-ma dkar-po, *Chos-'byung bstan-pa'i pad-ma rgyas-pa'i nyin-byed ces bya-ba*, Lokesh Chandra, ed., *Tibetan Chronicle of Padma Dkar-po.* (Delhi: International Academy of Indian Culture, 1968), fol. 158b.

[20] Albert Grünwedel, *Mythologie du Buddhisme au Tibet et en Mongolie*, trans. from German by Ivan Goldschmidt (Leipzig: F. A. Brockhaus, 1900), p. 146.

[21] L. Austine Waddell, *The Buddhism of Tibet, or Lamaism* (Cambridge: W. Heffer and Sons, 1939), p. 23. Waddell adds, in a note,

that "E. Schlagintweit transposes the forms of the two princesses, and most subsequent writers repeat his confusion."

22 Jacques Bacot, *Introduction à l'histoire du Tibet* (Paris: Société Asiatique, 1962), p. 13.

23 Hisashi Sato, *Kodai Chibetto Shi-kenkyū* (Kyoto: Tōyōshi-kenkyū-kai, 1958), p. 288.

24 Kun-dga' rdo-rje, *Deb-ther dmar-po*, fol. 16b; Ye-shes dpal-'byor, *Dpag-bsam ljon-bzang*, p. 168; *La-dvags rgyal-rabs*, p. 31; Ngag-dbang blo-bzang rgya-mtsho, *Bod-kyi deb-ther dpyid-kyi rgyal-mo'i gludbyangs*, pp. 34, 39; Pad-ma dkar-po, *'Brug-pa'i chos-'byung*, fols. 158b ff.

25 Ariane MacDonald, *Le Maṇḍala du Mañjuśrīmūlakalpa.* (Paris: Adrien-Maisonneuve, 1962), p. 108.

26 Taishō 848, XX, 7a3 ff.

27 Ryūjin Tajima, *Les deux grands maṇḍalas et la doctrine de l'esotérisme Shingon* (Tokyo, 1955), p. 87.

28 See, for example, *Sādhanamālā*, Benoytosh Bhattacharyya, ed. (Baroda: Oriental Institute, 1925, 1928), pp. 38 ff., 74 ff., etc.

29 For a discussion of these dates and for further references, see Alaka Chattopadhyaya, *Atīśa and Tibet*, Indian Studies, Past and Present (Calcutta, 1967), pp. 212 ff.

30 Dpal-brtsegs and Nam-mkha'i snying-po, *Pho-brang stod-thang ldan-dkar-gyi bstan-bcos 'gyur-ro tshog-gi dkar-chag*, P. 5851, vol. 154, 143.2.5-152.5.8, Mdo-'grel JO 352a-373a.

31 Marcelle Lalou, "Les textes bouddhiques au temps du roi Khri-sroṅ-lde-bcan," *Journal Asiatique*, 241 (1953), p. 313-353.

32 *Ārya-avalokiteśvaramātā-nāma-dhāraṇī*, P. 389, vol. 8, 148.5.4-149.3.5, Rgyud TSA 56b-58a; *Tārā-devī-nāmâṣṭaśataka*, P. 392, vol. 8, 156.5.6-158.1.8, Rgyud TSA 76b-79b; Candragomin, *Āryâṣṭa-mahâbhayôttārā-tārā-stava*, P. 4873, vol. 86, 126.1.1-126.2.6, Rgyud-'grel ZU 184b-185a.

33 See Chattopadhyaya, *Atīśa and Tibet*, pp. 250 ff.; Aoki, *Early Tibetan Chronicles*, pp. 48 ff.

34 Bu-ston, *Chos-'byung chen-mo*, fol. 145a, Obermiller, trans., *History of Buddhism by Bu-ston*, II, 197.

35 See Chattopadhyaya, *Atīśa and Tibet*, pp. 266 ff.; Aoki, *Early Tibetan Chronicles*, pp. 60 ff.; Roerich's introduction to 'Gos lo-tsā-ba, *Deb-ther sngon-po*, pp. xiii ff.

36 See Chattopadhyaya, *Atīśa and Tibet*, p. 311. This book provides an excellent summary of standard sources on the life of Atīśa.

37 Ye-shes dpal-'byor, *Dpag-bsam ljon-bzang*, p. 183.

38 'Gos lo-tsā-ba, *Deb-ther sngon-po* CA, fol. 1a, Roerich, trans., *Blue Annals*, pp. 241-242.

39 Ye-shes dpal-'byor, *Dpag-bsam ljon-bzang*, p. 184.

40 The temple is the famous Sgrol-ma lha-khang. See Bla-ma Btsan-po, *'Dzam-gling rgyas-bshad*, Wylie, ed. and trans., *Geography of Tibet*, pp. 20-21, 76, 147 n. 300. On the construction of the temple see 'Gos lo-tsā-ba, *Deb-ther sngon-po* CA, fol. 10a, Roerich, trans., *Blue Annals*, p. 263.

[41] Dipaṃkaraśrījñāna, *Ārya-tārā-stotra*, P. 4511, vol. 81, 94.5.5-95. 2.1, Rgyud-'grel DU 425a-b; Dipaṃkaraśrījñāna, *Rje-btsun sgrol-ma'i sgrub-thabs* (no Sanskrit), P. 4508, vol. 81, 90.4.5-91.5.7, Rgyud-'grel DU 414b-417b; Dipaṃkaraśrījñāna, '*Jigs-pa brgyad-las skyob-pa* (no Sanskrit), P. 4510, vol. 81, 94.4.2-94.5.5, Rgyud-'grel DU 424b-425a; Dipaṃkaraśrījñāna, *Ārya-tārā-sādhana*, P. 4512, vol. 81, 95.2.1-95.5.5, Rgyud-'grel DU 426a-427b.

[42] Candragomin, *Ārya-aṣṭabhaya-trāta-nāma-tārā-sādhana*, P. 4494, vol. 81, 74.1.1-74.5.4, Rgyud-'grel DU 373a-375a, and *Ārya-tārādevī-stotra-muktikā-mālā-nāma*, P. 4869, vol. 86, 123.4.6-124.4.8, Rgyud-'grel ZU 178-181a; anonymous, *Sgrol-ma dkon-mchog gsum-la bstod-pa* (no Sanskrit), P. 2567, vol. 59, 72.5.8-73.1.5, Rgyud-'grel LA 61b-62a; Vāgīśvarakīrti, *'Chi-ba bslu-ba'i bsdus-don* (no Sanskrit), P. 4806, vol. 86,19.2.2-19.5.7, Rgyud-'grel ZHU 146a-147b, *'Chi-bslu'i bsdus-don* (no Sanskrit), P. 4807, vol. 86, 19.5.7-21.2.1, Rgyud-'grel ZHU 147b-150b, and *Mṛtyu-vañcanôpadeśa*, P. 4808, vol. 86, 21.2.1-30.4.1, Rgyud-'grel ZHU 151a-174a (= P. 2620, vol. 59, 103.5.2-110.3.8, Rgyud-'grel LA 139a-155b, but the latter without the interlinear notes and three folios of charts given in the former).

[43] [Karma] Tshe-dbang kun-khyab, *Yi-dam zhi-ba dang khro-bo'i tshogs-kyi sgrub-thabs nor-bu'i phreng-ba'i lo-rgyus chos-bshad rab-'byams* [block print, 87 folios, 'Og-min mtshur-mdo'i chos-grva edition], fol. 22a ff.

[44] 'Gos lo-tsā-ba, *Deb-ther sngon-po*, Roerich, trans., *Blue Annals*, pp. 843-844, 455-456. For a discussion of the extent to which this injunction was really applied, see also Chattopadhyaya, *Atīśa and Tibet*, pp. 350 ff.

[45] Tucci, *Tibetan Painted Scrolls*, I, 128-131, 163-164.

[46] Tshe-dbang kun-khyab, *Yi-dam tshogs-kyi lo-rgyus*, fol. 22b. Tāranātha wrote a short history of Tārā's cult, entitled *Sgrol-ma'i rgyud-kyi 'byung-khungs gsal-bar byed-pa'i lo-rgyus gser-'phreng*, which is unfortunately not available to me. See A. I. Vostrikov, *Tibetan Historical Literature*, Indian Studies, Past and Present (Calcutta, 1970), p. 178.

[47] *Bcom-ldan 'das-ma sgrol-ma yang-dag-par rdzogs-pa'i sangs-rgyas bstod-pa gsungs-pa*, P. 77, vol. 3, 154.2.3-154.4.7, Rgyud CA 45a-46b. This text is also called *Sgrol-ma-la phyag-'tshal nyi-shu-rtsa gcig-gis bstod-pa phan-yon dang bcas-pa*, and variations thereof; there are innumerable Tibetan editions. For the Sanskrit text, see Godefroy de Blonay, *Matériaux pour servir à l'histoir de la déesse buddhique Tārā* (Paris: Librairie Émile Bouillon, 1895), pp. 58 ff.; Alex Wayman, "The Twenty-one Praises of Tārā, a Syncretism of Saivism and Buddhism," *Journal of the Bihar Research Society* (1959). For Mongolian, see Lokesh Chandra, ed., *Hymns to Tārā* (Delhi: International Academy of Indian Culture, n.d.). There are two Chinese translations in the Taishō collection, 1108a and b, XX, 478b12-486a6, the former by the Han-lin scholar An-tsang of the Yüan Dynasty, the latter anonymous. There seem to be several modern Chinese trans-

lations, of which we may mention that of Sun Ching-feng in his anthology, *Ta-jih ju-lai tsan-tʻan erh-shih-i tsun tu-mu ching* (K'ai-feng: Pei-hsing Street Niao-chi-wen Publishing Office, 1939).

Although all the other canonical scriptures on Tārā are included in the Kriyā Tantra section of the *Bka'-'gyur*, this text is considered an Anuttarayoga Tantra, mainly because Sūryagupta's commentaries upon it use Anuttarayoga terminology; see Dge-legs dpal-bzang-po [Mkhas-grub-rje], *Rgyud-sde spyi'i rnam-par gzhag-pa rgyas-par brjod*, Ferdinand Lessing and Alex Wayman, eds. and trans., *Mkhas grub rje's Fundamentals of the Buddhist Tantras* (The Hague: Mouton, 1968), pp. 128-129, and Alex Wayman, "Analysis of the Tantric Section of the Kanjur Correlated to Tanjur Exegesis," in Lokesh Chandra, ed., *Indo-Asian Studies* (Delhi: International Academy of Indian Culture, 1962), I, 120. The *Bstan-'gyur* Rgyud-'grel LA groups together [P. 2555-2623, 1a-183a] the miscellaneous works taken to be commentary upon this scripture, including the above-mentioned works of Sūryagupta as well as a varied collection of evocations, praises, offerings, etc.

[48] Grags-pa rgyal-mtshan, *Bstod-pa'i rnam-bshad gsal-ba'i 'od-zer*, in *Sa-skya bka'-'bum* NYA, fol. 189b, Bsod-nams rgya-mtsho, ed., *The Complete Works of the Great Masters of the Sa Skya Sect of the Tibetan Buddhism* (Tokyo: Toyo Bunko, 1968), IV, 94.2. On Gnyan lo-tsā-ba, see 'Gos lo-tsā-ba, *Deb-ther sngon-po* KHA, fol. 4b, and CA, fol. 24a, Roerich, trans., *Blue Annals*, pp. 71, and 293; Bu-ston, *Chos-'byung chen-mo*, fol. 154b, Obermiller, trans., *History of Buddhism by Bu-ston*, II, 219.

[49] 'Gos lo-tsā-ba, *Deb-ther sngon-po* KHA, fol. 5b, Roerich, trans., *Blue Annals*, p. 73.

[50] 'Jam-dbyangs mkhyen-brtse, *Dbus-gtsang-gi gnas-rten*, Ferrari, ed. and trans., *Mkhyen brtse's Guide*, pp. 22, 63, 149 n. 490. See also Bu-ston, *Chos-'byung chen-mo*, fol. 155a, Obermiller, trans., *History of Buddhism by Bu-ston*, II, 219; 'Gos lo-tsā-ba, *Deb-ther sngon-po* NGA, fol. 4a, Roerich, trans., *Blue Annals*, p. 211.

[51] These dates are given in 'Gos lo-tsā-ba, *Deb-ther sngon-po* NGA, fol. 4a, Roerich, trans., *Blue Annals*, p. 211. See also Tucci, *Tibetan Painted Scrolls*, I, 101, and Giuseppe Tucci, *Indo-Tibetica* (Rome: Reale Academie d'Italie, 1932-1941), IV, p. 1, p. 72, this latter giving Sa-skya-pa genealogical tables.

[52] These works are found in the *Sa-skya bka'-'bum* NYA, fols. 136a-197b, Bsod-nams rgya-mtsho, ed., *Complete Works of the Sa Skya Sect*, IV, 67.3.1-98.2.6. They include commentaries on the *Homages to the Twenty-one Tārās*, some based on the Indian commentaries of Sūryagupta, many of which had already been translated into Tibetan by Mal-gyo Blo-gros grags-pa (on whom see Bu-ston, *Chos-'byung chen-mo*, fol. 155b, Obermiller, trans., *History of Buddhism by Bu-ston*, II, 220). Also included are a "four maṇḍala offering" and a "sixfold evocation" [sgrub-thabs yan-lag drug-pa], i.e., for subjugating, offering gtor-mas, drawing a "protective circle," binding thieves, gain-

ing ritual "permission," and reciting her hundred names. We may thus see that all the various functions of Tārā had been established in Tibet by this time.

[53] *Sarvatathāgatamātanitārevisvakarmabhava-tantra-nāma*, P. 390, vol. 8, 149.3.5-155.5.8, Rgyud TSA 58a-74a. Cal Chos-kyi bzang-po was a contemporary of the great Kha-che paṇ-chen Śākyaśrībhadra. See Bu-ston, *Chos-'byung chen-mo*, fols. 155n-156a, Obermiller, trans., *History of Buddhism by Bu-ston*, II, 222-223. On the dates of this latter paṇḍit, see 'Gos lo-tsā-ba, *Deb-ther sngon-po* BA, fols. 1b-11a, Roerich, trans., *Blue Annals*, pp. 1063-1071, and Tucci, *Tibetan Painted Scrolls*, I, 335-336. This text, which Chos-kyi bzang-po translated with Dharmaśrīmitra, is the closest thing we have to a complete textbook on the practice of Tārā's cult, although it gives every appearance of being late and synthetic. Mkhas-grub-rje, *Rgyud-sde spyi'i rnam-gzhag*, Lessing and Wayman, eds. and trans., *Fundamentals of the Buddhist Tantras*, p. 126, along with other scholars, considers it to be the "most important Tantra of the Mother of this [Padma] Family." He also notes that it contains, in its third chapter, a transliteration into Tibetan script of the Sanskrit text of the *Homages to the Twenty-one Tārās*, given as a single long mantra; it was this clue that led Wayman to his Sanskrit edition.

It would be difficult to erect any real chronology for the translations of the canonical scriptures on Tārā which are grouped with this text in the Kriyā Tantra section of the *Bka'-'gyur*, since the catalogue gives very little information as to who translated them. These texts are:

Ārya-avalokiteśvaramātā-nāma-dhāraṇī, P. 389, vol. 8, 156.5.8-149.3.5, Rgyud TSA 56b-58a, trans. and rev. Jinamitra, Dānaśīla, and Ye-shes-sde; these translators worked under Khri-srong lde-btsan and were among those who helped compile the *Mahāvyutpatti* under Ral-pa-can (see Bu-ston, *Chos-'byung chen-mo*, fol. 145a, Obermiller, trans., *History of Buddhism by Bu-ston*, II, 197); their translation is listed in the eighth-century catalogue of Dpal-brtsegs and Nam-mkha'i snying-po. There is a Chinese translation by Fa-hsien, Taishō 1117. This text consists of a variation on Avalokiteśvara's "expanded" mantra, but it seems never to have become particulary popular in Tibet.

Sarvatathāgatamātānitārevisvakarmabhava-tantra-nāma, P. 390, vol. 8, 149.3.5-155.5.8, Rgyud TSA 58a-74a, trans. Dharmaśrīmitra and Chos-kyi bzang-po (see above).

Ārya-tārābhaṭṭārikā-nāma-aṣṭaśataka, P. 391, vol. 8, 155.5.8-156.5.6, Rgyud TSA 74a-76b, and *Tārā-devī-nāmâṣṭaśataka*, P. 392, vol. 8, 156.5.6-158.1.8, Rgyud TSA 76b-79b, no translators given. These are two different texts; the latter version seems to be the one listed in the eighth-century catalogue. There are two Chinese translations of the prologue with transliterations of the 108 names: Taishō 1105 by Fa-hsien (= P.392), and 1106 by T'ien-hsi-tsai (= P. 391); Taishō 1107 translates the Sanskrit text in its entirety. The Sanskrit was published in Blonay, *Matériaux*, pp. 48-53, with a French translation, pp. 54-57; there is an English translation in Edward Conze, ed., *Buddhist Texts through the Ages* (New York: Harper Torchbooks, 1964), pp. 196 ff.

'Phags-ma sgrol-ma'i gzungs (no Sanskrit), P. 393, vol. 8, 158.1.8-158.2.1, Rgyud TSA 79b-80a, no translator given; this text gives the most familiar of Tārā's expanded mantras.

Ārya-tārā-svapratijñā-nāma-dhāraṇī, P. 394, vol. 8, 158.2.1-158.2.7, Rgyud TSA 80a, no translator given.

Ārya-tārā-aṣṭaghoratāraṇī-sūtra, P. 395, vol. 8, 158.2.7-159.1.6, Rgyud TSA 80a-84a, no translator given; this sūtra incorporates the mantra of P. 393, but gives in addition the story of its preaching and a eulogy of its many benefits.

Ārya-aṣṭamahābhayatāraṇī-nāma-dhāraṇī, P. 396, vol. 8, 159.1.6-159.2.8, Rgyud TSA 84a-b, no translator given, is a mantra, different from both P.393 and P.394, which saves from a most unusual list of the eight great terrors. Neither this mantra nor that of P.394 ever became particularly popular.

Ūrdhvajaṭā-mahākalpa-mahābodhisattvavikurvaṇapaṭalavisarā bhagavatī-āryatārāmūlakalpa-nāma, P.469, vol. 10, 201.1.1-vol.11, 61.1.5, Rgyud ZA 1a-332a, translated by Rin-chen-grub [Bu-ston] and Bsod-nams-grub. This was supposedly translated from a text of Atīśa, an attribution doubted by M. Lalou ("Mañjuśrīmūlakalpa et Tārāmūlakalpa," *Harvard Journal of Asiatic Studies*, I [1936], 330); the text in fact is largely a copy or adaptation of the *Mañjuśrīmūlakalpa*, a third of which has been inserted into it, or of another text from which both derived. But the translation itself is certainly late (Bu-ston lived from 1290 to 1364), though the text is so long and so full of a number of things that later authors rather liked to quote it.

[54] Life and dates of Tsongk'apa are given in David L. Snellgrove and H. E. Richardson, *A Cultural History of Tibet* (New York: Frederick A. Praeger, 1968), pp. 180-182.

[55] Dates are given in Luciano Petech, "The Dalai-lamas and Regents of Tibet: A Chronological Study," *T'oung Pao*, XLVII (1946), 3-5, pp. 368-394.

[56] Ye-shes rgyal-mtshan, *Sgrol-ma maṇḍal bzhi-pa'i cho-ga'i lag-len-dang ngag-gi gnad gsal-bar bkod-pa'i bdud-rtsi'i bum-bzang zhes bya-ba* [block print, 16 folios, Tshe-mchog-gling edition], in *Collected Works* THA, fol. 13b.

[57] *Ku-ru-ku-lle'i man-ngag* (no Sanskrit), P. 4713, vol. 82, 192.3.6, Rgyud-'grel PHU 220b. Grags-pa rgyal-mtshan wrote the *Ku-ru-ku-lle'i sgrub-thabs*, in *Sa-skya bka'-'bum* NYA, fols. 110b-112b, Bsod-nams rgya-mtsho, ed., *Complete Works of the Sa Skya Sect*, IV, 55.2.6-56.2.5.

[58] Snellgrove and Richardson, *Cultural History of Tibet*, p. 135.

[59] E. Gene Smith's introduction to Pad-ma dkar-po, *'Brug-pa'i chos-'byung*, Lokesh Chandra, ed., *Tibetan Chronicle*, p. 2.

[60] Pad-ma dkar-po, *'Brug-pa'i chos-'byung*, Lokesh Chandra, ed., *Tibetan Chronicle*, fol. 290a-b.

[61] *Ibid.*, fol. 290b.

[62] Snellgrove, *Buddhist Himalaya*, p. 220.

[63] Ngag-dbang kun-dga' bstan-'dzin [Khams-sprul rin-po-che III], *Phyag-chen sngon-'gro'i bsgom-rim gsal-'debs ngag-'don rgyas-spel dngos-gzhi'i rtsa-tho-dang bcas-pa zab-don rgya-mtsho'i lam-tshang* [blockprint, 25 folios, Dpal phun-tshogs chos-'khor gling edition].

[64] Tsong-kha-pa, *Zab-lam nā-ro'i chos-drug-gi sgo-nas 'khrid-pa'i rim-pa yid-ches gsum-ldan*, P. 6202, vol. 160, 208.4.2-209.2.3, in *Collected Works* TSHA 81a-82b.

[65] See, for example, *'Phags-pa bzang-po spyod-pa'i smon-lam-gyi rgyal-po* [*Āryabhadracaripraṇidhānarāja*], Sunitikumar Pathak, ed. (Gangtok, Sikkim: Namgyal Institute of Tibetology, 1961), pp. 5-9. See also Rol-pa'i rdo-rje [Lcang-skya I], *'Phags-pa bzang-po spyod-pa'i smon-lam-gyi rnam-par bshad-pa kun-tu bzang-po'i dgongs-pa gsal-bar byed-pa'i rgyan zhes bya-ba*, Lokesh Chandra, ed. (Gangtok, Sikkim: Namgyal Institute of Tibetology, 1963), pp. 26-30. There have been innumerable commentaries on this text; Kun-dga' grags-pa rgyal-mtshan, *'Phags-pa bzang-po spyod-pa'i tshig-don-gyi 'grel-pa legs-bshad kun-las btus-pa* [block print, 35 folios, no edition given], fol. 33b, mentions his sources in particular as lo-tsā-ba Ye-shes-sde, Jo-nang rje-btsun Tāranātha, Mkhan-chen Chos-dpal rgya-mtsho, and Lcang-skya Rol-pa'i rdo-rje (he himself was a disciple of 'Jam-dbyangs mkhyen-brtse'i dbang po).

[66] For slightly varying contents or arrangements see, for example, Mkhas-grub-rje, *Rgyud-sde spyi'i rnam-gzhag*, Lessing and Wayman, eds. and trans., *Fundamentals of the Buddhist Tantras*, pp. 178-186; Tsong-kha-pa, *Rgyal-ba khyab-bdag-rdo-rje-'chang chen-po'i lam-gyi rim-pa gsang-ba kun-gyi gnad rnam-par phye ba zhes bya-ba* [*Sngags-rim chen-po*], P. 6210, vol. 161, 77.4.6-79.1.2, in *Collected Works* DZA 58b-62a; Pad-ma dkar-po, *Snyan-rgyud yid-bzhin nor-bu'i bskyed-pa'i rim-pa rgyas-pa 'dod-pa'i re-skong zhes bya-ba* [mechanical type, 19 and 33 folios, Phun-gling edition], fol. 6a; Rnam-rgyal rgyal-mtshan, *Mitra brgya-rtsa'i nang-gi grub-chen-nyi-ma sbas-pa'i lugs-kyi sgrol-ma nyi-shu rtsa gcig-gi mngon-par rtogs-pa* [block print, 16 folios, Yung-dgon (Yung-ho-kung, Peking) edition], fol. 5a-b. This theme has served as a basis for poetic expansion; for example, see 'Jam-dbyangs mkhyen-brtse'i dbang-po, *Yan-lag bdun-pa'i tshigs-su bcad-pa lam-rim-gyi smon-lam dang bcas-pa phan-bde'i sprin-gyi rol-ma zhes bya-ba* [block print, 11 folios, no edition given].

[67] 'Jam-dbyangs mkhyen-brtse'i dbang-po, *Rgyud-sde bzhi-dang rjes-su 'brel-ba'i rje-btsun sgrol-ma'i sgrub-thabs rgyun-khyer snying-por dril-ba* [manuscript (dbu-med), 9 folios], fols. 5a-6a. Also in the anthology is *Sgrol-ma dkar-sngon-gyi bstod-pa dang gzungs-bcas*, in many editions, which also contains, in addition to this and some anonymous works, the *Rje-btsun bcom-ldan 'das-ma seng-ldeng nags-kyi sgrol-ma-la bstod-pa mkhas-pa'i gtsug-rgyan zhes bya-ba*, by Dge-'dun-grub [Dalai Lama I]. Although this office is not the word of the Buddha, it is in many rituals considered an almost integral part of the basic

text; see, for example, the "hidden text" [gter-ma] which was edited by "Guṇa," i.e., Yon-tan rgya-mtsho [Kong-sprul rin-po-che], *Dgongs-gter sgrol-ma'i zab-tig-las / maṇḍal cho-ga tshogs-gnyis snying-po zhes bya-ba,* in many editions. There is also a Chinese version in Taishō 1108b, 483b28-c12, and in Sun ching-feng, *Ta-jih ju-lai tsan-t'an erh-shih-i tsun tu-mu ching,* 13b-14b.

[68] Anupamarakṣita, "Tārā-sādhanam," in *Sādhanamālā,* Benoytosh Bhattacharyya, ed., I, 201-204 (= P. 4313, vol. 80, 292.5.6-293.5.1, Rgyud-'grel DU 186b-189a). See also Benoytosh Bhattacharyya, *The Indian Buddhist Iconography* (Calcutta: K. L. Mukhopadhyaya, 1958), pp. 20-22, and Edward Conze, *Buddhist Meditation* (New York: Harper Torchbooks, 1969), pp. 133-136.

[69] Tsong-kha-pa, *Sngags-rim chen-po,* P. 6210, vol. 161, 193.5.2-5, in *Collected Works* WA 129a.

[70] *Ibid.*, 193.5.6-194.3.2, in *Collected Works* WA 129a-130b.

[71] Buddhajñāna, *Samantabhadra-nāma-sādhana,* P. 2718, vol. 65, 15.4.3-19.2.5, Rgyud-'grel TI 33b-42b.

[72] Vaidyapāda, *Caturaṅga-sādhanopāyikā-samantabhadrā-nāma-ṭīka,* P. 2735, vol. 65, 178.3.8-201.3.6, Rgyud-'grel TI 440b-498a.

[73] Nāgārjuna, *Bodhicitta-vivaraṇa,* P. 2665, vol. 61, 285.2.7-287.3.2, Rgyud-'grel GI 42b-48a.

[74] Śrīphalavajra, *Samantabhadra-sādhana-vṛtti,* P. 2730, vol. 65, 69.3.6-91.5.3, Rgyud-'grel TI 168a-224a.

[75]. *Ārya-subāhu-paripṛcchā-nāma-tantra,* P. 428, vol. 9, 33.5.6-42.5.4, Rgyud TSHA 179b-202a.

[76] Tsong-kha-pa, *Sngags-rim chen-po,* P. 6210, vol. 161, 83.5.2-5, in *Collected Works* DZA 74a.

[77] *Susiddhikara-mahātantra-sādhanopāyika-paṭala,* P. 431, vol. 9, 54.1.8-75.5.7, Rgyud TSHA 230a-284b.

[78] Tsong-kha-pa, *Sngags-rim chen-po,* P. 6210, vol. 161, 73.1.1-4, in *Collected Works* DZA 47a.

[79] Ngag-dbang blo-bzang [Klong-rdol bla-ma], *Gsang-sngags rig-pa 'dzin-pa'i sde-snod-las byung-ba'i ming-gi rnam-grangs,* in *Collected Works,* Ven. Dalama, ed., *Tibetan Buddhist Studies of Klong-rdol bla-ma Ngag-dbang-blo-bzang* (Laxmanpuri, Mussoorie: privately printed, 1963-1964), I, 57.

[80] Rje Lha-khab 'Jig-rten blos-btang, *Mtshams sgrub-byed-skabs thun mgo-mjug-tu 'don-rgyu gsol-'debs* [mechanical type, 3 folios, Phun-gling edition].

[81] This arrangement is found, for instance, at the beginning of the well-known hidden text *Gsol-'debs le'u-bdun-ma,* in many editions; the table was originally drawn up for me by the artist Bstan-'dzin yongs-'dul.

[82] 'Gos lo-tsā-ba, *Deb-ther sngon-po GA,* fol. 3a, Roerich, trans., *Blue Annals,* p. 106. See also René de Nebesky-Wojkowitz, *Oracles and Demons of Tibet: The Cult and Iconography of the Tibetan Protective Deities* ('s-Gravenhage: Mouton, 1956), p. 320, and Li An-che,

"Rñiṅ ma pa: The Early Form of Lamaism," *Journal of the Royal Asiatic Society* (1948), p. 147.

The iconography of the protective deities is given in Nebesky-Wojkowitz, *Oracles and Demons of Tibet*, chaps. ii, iii, where are translated the descriptions in Blo-bzang bstan-pa'i nyi-ma [Paṇ-chen rinpo-che IV], *Yi-dam rgya-mtsho'i rin-chen 'byung-gnas-kyi lhan-thabs rin-'byung don-gsal*, which is itself a supplement [lhan-thabs] to Tāranātha, *Yi-dam rgya-mtsho'i sgrub-thabs rin-chen 'byung-gnas*, both these works being among the most important of native Tibetan evocation anthologies; see Tucci, *Tibetan Painted Scrolls* I, 310; F. A. Peters, "The Rin-Ḥbyuṅ," *Journal of the Royal Asiatic Society*, IX (1943), 1-36; and Lokesh Chandra, "The Rin-lhan and Rin-'byuṅ," *Oriens Extremis*, VIII.2 (1962). The Paṇ-chen's *Rin-lhan*—along with the *Snar-thang brgya-rtsa* and Abhayākaragupta's *Vajrâvalī-nāma-maṇḍala-sādhana* (see Lokesh Chandra, "Maṇḍalas of a Tibetan Collectaneum," *Asiatishe Forschungen* [1966]) — was illustrated by Mongolian artists under the title of *Rin-'byung snar-thang brgya-rtsa rdor-'phreng bcas-nas gsungs-pa'i bris-sku mthong-ba don-ldan*, Lokesh Chandra, ed., *A New Tibeto-Mongol Pantheon* (Delhi: International Academy of Indian Culture, 1961 —), vols. VIII, IX; the protective deities are pictured at IX, 113-135. As we have noted before, however, all these anthologies attempt to be exhaustive rather than selective; often they give no clue as to what traditions are in actual use. Thus, for information concerning these sectarian differences in the traditions of the high patron deities and protectors, I am grateful once again to Bstan-'dzin yongs-'dul. On the annual rituals for these deities, see also Li An-che, "The Bkah-brgyud Sect of Lamaism," *Journal of the American Oriental Society*, LXIX (1949), 59.

83 *Vajrakīlaya-mūlatantra-khaṇḍa*, P. 78, vol. 3, 154.4.8-155.3.8, Rgyud CA 46a-48a; Nāgārjuna, *Piṇḍīkṛta-sādhana*, L. de la Vallée Poussin, ed., *Études et textes tantriques: Pañcakrama* (Louvain: J.-B. Istas, 1896), pp. 1 ff. (= P. 2662, vol. 61, 267.1.1-273.1.6, Rgyud-'grel GI 1-12a).

84 Herbert Guenther, *Tibetan Buddhism without Mystification* (Leiden: E. J. Brill, 1966), p. 103.

85 Snellgrove, *Buddhist Himalaya*, p. 175.

86 Fosco Maraini, *Secret Tibet* (New York: Grove Press, 1960), pp. 52-53.

87 The text recited is the above-mentioned *Dgongs-gter sgrol-ma'i zab-tig-las / maṇḍal cho-ga tshogs-gnyis snying-po*, ed. Kong-sprul rinpo-che.

There are generally considered to be four types of hidden text: those found buried in the earth [sa-gter], those found in lakes or rivers [mtsho-gter], those fallen from the sky [gnam-gter], and those that are inspired in meditation [dgongs-gter]. The *zab-tig*—"deep and weighty" — in the title indicates a special subclass of this last category: "Because these 'deep and weighty books' are the quintessence of profundity," says the text, "it is not necessary for them to have a lot of detail."

[88] See Ferdinand Lessing, "'Wu-liang-shou': A Comparative Study of Tibetan and Chinese Longevity Rites," in *Studies Presented to Hu Shih on His Sixty-fifth Birthday*, Bulletin of the Institute of History and Philology, Academia Sinica, XXVIII (Taipei, 1957), for a description of this maṇḍala and its ritual in Tibet.

[89] This triad consists of Amitāyus in the center, with White Tārā on his right and Uṣṇīṣavijayā on his left. It is extremely popular with artists and authors.

[90] This text is given a garbled and practically unintelligible translation in Marion H. Duncan, *Harvest Festival Dramas of Tibet* (Hong Kong: Orient Publishing Co., 1955), pp. 175 ff.; a much better one, though without the prologue, is in R. Cunningham, "Nangsal Obum," *Journal of the West China Border Research Society*, XII.A (1940), 35-75. The text is summarized in Waddell, *Lamaism*, pp. 553 ff., and a variant version is given in Jacques Bacot, *Trois mystères tibétains* (Paris, 1921). The text from which I copied the present version was a block print with the cover title *Rigs-bzang-gi mkha'-'gro-ma snang-sa 'od-'bum-gyi rnam-thar*, but since the last several folios were missing (a not unusual circumstance, because the outside pages are the most exposed to damage), I have no idea of its provenance.

[91] See 'Jam-dbyangs mkhyen-brtse, *Dbus-gtsang-gi gnas-rten*, Ferrari, ed. and trans., *Mkhyen-brtse's Guide*, pp. 2 f., 39 f., 85 f. The image of Tārā on the middle story of this temple is the one that may or may not have been brought by Khri-btsun from Nepal.

[92] 'Jam-dpal nor-bu Pad-ma dbang-gi rgyal-po, *Rje-btsun 'phags-ma sgrol-ma dkar-mo tshe-sbyin-ma-la bstod-cing gsol-ba 'debs-pa 'chi-bdag gdong-bzlog ces bya-ba* [manuscript (dbu-med), 3 folios], fol. 3a.

[93] Ngag-dbang blo-bzang rgya-mtsho [Dalai Lama V], *Rje-btsun sgrol-ma-la bstod-cing gsol-ba 'debs-pa'i tshigs-su bcad-pa*, in *Phyogs-bcu bde-gshegs byang-sems slob mi-slob-kyi dge-'dun dang bcas-pa'i bstod-tshogs dngos-grub rgya-mtsho'i gter-mdzod*, in *Collected Works* [block print, 21 volumes, 'Bras-spungs edition], BA, fols. 17b-18a.

[94] Blo-bzang bstan-pa'i rgyal-mtshan, *Rje-btsun sgrol-ma'i gdung-'bod* [manuscript (dbu-can) 8 folios].

[95] Tshe-dbang kun-khyab, *Yi-dam tshogs-kyi lo-rgyus*, fols. 21b-23a.

[96] Alice Getty, *The Gods of Northern Buddhism* (Rutland, Vt.: Charles E. Tuttle, 1962), p. 120.

[97] Ye-shes rgyal-mtshan, *Sgrol-ma maṇḍal bzhi-pa'i cho-ga*, fol. 3a.

[98] Tsong-kha-pa, *Zab-lam nā-ro'i chos-drug*, P. 6202, vol. 160, 212.1.1-8, in *Collected Works* TSHA 89b.

[99] Tsong-kha-pa, *Sngags-rim chen-po*, P. 6210, vol. 161, 186.3.5-7, in *Collected Works* WA 110b.

[100] Klong-rdol bla-ma, *Gsang-sngags ming-gi rnam-grangs*, Ven. Dalama, ed., *Tibetan Buddhist Studies*, I, 69.

[101] *Dpal gsang-ba 'dus-pa'i bla-brgyud gsol-'debs dang bdag-bskyed ngag-'don bkra-shis lhun-po rgyud-pa grva-tshang-gi 'don-rgyun* (Kalimpong: Bod-yig me-long par-khang, n.d.), fols. 24a ff.

[102] Pad-ma dkar-po, *Snyan-rgyud yid-bzhin nor-bu bskyed-rim*, fols. 12b ff.

[103] This discussion of the four states [gnas-skabs] of contemplative ability is found in Tsong-kha-pa, *Sngags-rim chen-po*, P. 6210, vol. 161, 184.4.7-186.2.2, in *Collected Works* WA 106a-110a. The quoted passage is found at 186.1.6-186.2.2, WA 109b-110a.

[104] Tsong-kha-pa, *Sngags-rim chen-po*, P. 6210, vol. 161, 187.1.7-187.2.3, in *Collected Works* WA 112a-b.

[105] *Ibid.*, 186.2.6-186.3.2, in *Collected Works* WA 110a-b.

[106] *Ibid.*, 76.4.1-2, in *Collected Works* DZA 56a.

[107] *Ibid.*, 184.2.3-184.3.3, in *Collected Works* WA 105a-b.

[108] *Ibid.*, 184.4.2-4, in *Collected Works* WA 106a.

[109] Tsong-kha-pa, *Zab-lam nā-ro'i chos-drug*, P. 6202, vol. 160, 212.1.8-212.2.8, in *Collected Works* TSHA 89b-90a.

[110] Tsong-kha-pa, *Sngags-rim chen-po*, P. 6210, vol. 161, 186.5.6-187.1.7, in *Collected Works* WA 111b-112a.

[111] *Ibid.*, 184.3.5-184.4.2, in *Collected Works* WA 105b-106a.

[112] Nāgārjuna, *Tārā-sādhana*, P. 2555, vol. 59, 47.1.1-50.5.7, Rgyud-'grel LA 1a-6b.

[113] Gtsang-smyon He-ru-ka, *Rnal-'byor-gyi dbang-phyug chen-po rje-btsun mi-la-ras-pa'i rnam-thar thar-pa dang thams-cad mkhyen-pa'i lam-ston zhes bya-ba*, J. W. De Jong, ed., *Mi la ras pa'i rnam thar* ('S-Gravenhage: Mouton, 1959), pp. 102-103.

[114] Ferdinand Alquié, *The Philosophy of Surrealism* (Ann Arbor: University of Michigan Press, 1969), p. 126.

[115] Anton T. Boisen, *The Exploration of the Inner World* (New York: Harper Torchbooks, 1962), pp. 193-194.

[116] Charles T. Tart, "Psychedelic Experiences Associated with a Novel Hypnotic Procedure, Mutual Hypnosis," in Charles T. Tart, ed., *Altered States of Consciousness* (New York: John Wiley and Sons, 1969), p. 305.

[117] R. D. Laing, *The Divided Self* (Baltimore: Penguin Books, 1965), p. 141.

[118] *Ibid*, p. 162.

[119] Translated in Naomi Greene, *Antonin Artaud: Poet without Words* (New York: Simon and Schuster, 1970), p. 173.

[120] Andras Angyal, "Disturbances of Thinking in Schizophrenia," in J. S. Kasanin, ed., *Language and Thought in Schizophrenia* (New York: Norton, 1944), p. 119.

[121] André Breton, "Le Manifeste du Surréalisme," trans. in Patrick Waldberg, *Surrealism* (New York: McGraw-Hill, 1971), p. 66.

[122] André Breton, "Le Second Manifeste du Surréalisme," quoted and trans. in Anna Balakian, *André Breton: Magus of Surrealism* (New York: Oxford University Press, 1971), p. 89.

[123] Guillaume Apollinaire, "La Jolie Rousse," quoted in Anna Balakian, *The Literary Origins of Surrealism* (New York University Press, 1947), p. 106 (my translation).

[124] Balakian, *André Breton*, p. 89.

[125] André Breton, "Il y aura une fois," in *Le Revolver à cheveux blancs*, quoted and trans. in Alquié, *Philosophy of Surrealism*, p. 126.

[126] Paul Eluard, "Poetry's Evidence," trans. Samuel Beckett in *This Quarter*, V. 1 (1932), 146, quoted in Paul C. Ray, *The Surrealist Movement in England* (Ithaca: Cornell University Press, 1971), p. 49.

[127] Paul Eluard, J.-A. Boiffard, and R. Vitrac, editorial in *La Révolution Surréaliste*, I (Dec. 1924), trans. in Waldberg, *Surrealism*, p. 47.

[128] Anna Balakian, *Surrealism: The Road to the Absolute* (New York: Dutton Paperback, 1959), pp. 127, 130.

[129] Quoted in Paul Carroll, *The Poem in its Skin* (New York: Follett Press, 1968), p. 12.

[130] Alquié, *Philosophy of Surrealism*, p. 127.

[131] Daniel P. Walker, *Spiritual and Demonic Magic from Ficino to Campanella* (London: Warburg Institute, 1958), p. 76.

[132] Balakian, *André Breton*, p. 37.

[133] Frances A. Yates, *Giordano Bruno and the Hermetic Tradition* (New York: Vintage Books, 1969), p. 266.

[134] The quotation and the comment are both in Carl G. Jung, *Psychology and Alchemy* (London: Routledge and Kegan Paul, 1953), pp. 239, 241.

[135] Quotation and comment are in *ibid.*, pp. 265-266.

[136] Walker, *Spiritual and Demonic Magic*, pp. 149 f.

[137] Agrippa von Nettesheim, *De occulta philosophia*, Auswahl, Einführung, und Kommentar von Willy Schrödter (Remagen: Otto Reichl Verlag, 1967), p. 94.

[138] Quoted by Schrödter in *ibid*, p. 88. For background I have also used Charles G. Nauert, *Agrippa and the Crisis of Renaissance Thought* (Urbana: University of Illinois Press, 1965), and Paul Oskar Kristeller, *Eight Philosophers of the Italian Renaissance* (Stanford: Stanford University Press, 1964).

[139] Walker, *Spiritual and Demonic Magic*, p. 136.

[140] *Ibid*, p. 159.

[141] *Ibid*, p. 200.

[142] Nāgārjuna, *Mūlamadhyamakakārikā*, Kenneth K. Inada, ed. and trans. (Tokyo: Hokuseido Press, 1970), p. 70 (= VII.34).

[143] Vasubandhu, *Madhyāntavibhāga-bhāṣya*, Gadjin M. Nagao, ed. (Tokyo: Suzuki Research Foundation, 1964), p. 19 (= I.4).

[144] Nāgārjuna, *Mūlamadhyamakakārikā*, Inada, ed. and trans., p. 158 (= XXV.19-20).

[145] Anthony F. C. Wallace, *Religion: An Anthropological View* (New York: Random House, 1966), p. 60.

[146] E. J. Holmyard, *Alchemy* (Baltimore: Penguin Books, 1957), p. 97.

[147] Yates, *Giordano Bruno*, p. 375.

[148] Walker, *Spiritual and Demonic Magic*, p. 223.

[149] Vasubandhu, *Madhyāntavibhāga-bhāṣya*, Gadjin M. Nagao, ed.; Sthiramati, *Madhyāntavibhāga-ṭīkā*, S. Yamaguchi, ed. (Tokyo : Suzuki Research Foundation, 1966). Whatever I may understand of these

texts I owe to the kindly teachings of Professor Gadjin Nagao, one of the finest scholars and gentlemen it has ever been my great good fortune to know, and to whom I am more grateful than can possibly be expressed in a footnote; any insights are his, and all errors are mine.

150 Asaṅga, *Bodhisattvabhūmi*, U. Wogihara, ed. (Tokyo, 1930-1936), p. 47. The other texts quoted in this section are *Laṅkâvatārasūtra*, P. L. Vaidya, ed. (Darbhanga: Mithila Institute, 1963), and Asaṅga, *Mahāyānasūtrâlaṁkāra*, Sylvain Levi, ed. (Paris, 1907).

151 Text in Shashibhusan Dasgupta, *Obscure Religious Cults* (Calcutta: K. L. Mukhopdhyaya, 1962, p. 163 (my translation).

152 Mircea Eliade, *Yoga: Immortality and Freedom* (New York: Pantheon Books, 1958), pp. 270, 318, 362.

153 Amoghavajra, *Kurukulle'i las-sbyor-gyi man-ngag*, P. 4711, vol. 82, 191.2.3-192.1.1, Rgyud-'grel PHU 217b-219b.

154 Tsong-kha-pa, *Sngags-rim chen-po*, P. 6210, vol. 161, 199.1.4-5, in *Collected Works* WA 142a.

155 *Ibid.*, 199.2.5, in *Collected Works* WA 142b.

156 *Ibid.*, 199.2.8-199.3.2, in *Collected Works* WA 142b-143a.

157 Bstan-pa'i nyi-ma, *Bskyed-rim-gyi zin-bris cho-ga spyi-'gros-ltar bkod-pa man-ngag kun-btus zhes bya-ba* [stencil, 102 folios, no edition given], fols. 17ạ ff.

158 Yon-tan rgya-mtsho Blo-gros mtha'-yas ['Jam-mgon Kong-sprul rin-po-che], *Rje-btsun yid-bzhin 'khor-lo'i rgyun-gyi rnal-'byor khyer-bde 'chi-med grub-pa zhes bya-ba* [block print, 8 folios, Rum-dgon chos-sgar edition], fols. 3a-4a.

159 See Gene Youngblood, "The Cosmic Cinema of Jordan Belson," in *Expanded Cinema* (New York: Dutton, 1970).

159 *Guhyasamāja Tantra*, Benoytosh Bhattacharyya, ed., Gaekwad's Oriental Series 53 (Baroda, 1967), p. 162.

160 *Ibid.*, p. 58.

161 Candrakīrti, *Pradīpôddyotana-nāma-ṭīkā*, P. 2650, vol. 60, 23.1.1-117.3.7, Rgyud-'grel SA 1-233a.

162 Tsong-kha-pa, *Sngags-rim chen-po*, P. 6210, vol. 161, 189.3.6-7, in *Collected Works* WA 118a, and 190.2.1, in *Collected Works* WA 120a.

163 Buddhajñana, *Samantabhadra-nāma-sādhana*, P. 2718, vol. 65, 15.4.3-19.2.5, Rgyud-'grel TI 33b-42b.

164 A-bu hral-po [Dpal-sprul O-rgyan 'Jigs-med chos-kyi dbang-po], *Klong-chen snying-gi thig-le-las bskyed-rim lha-khrid 'og-min bgrod-pa'i them-skas* [mechanical type, 43 folios, Phun-gling edition], fols. 5a ff.

165 See *Ibid.*, fols. 5b-8a.

166 Tsong-kha-pa, *Sngags-rim chen-po*, P. 6210, vol. 161, 195.5.6-7, in *Collected Works* WA 134a.

167 *Dpal gsang-ba 'dus-pa'i bla-brgyud gsol-'debs dang bdag-bskyed ngag-'don bkra-shis lhun-po rgyud-pa grva-tshang-gi 'don-rgyun* (Kalimpong: Bod-yig me-long par-khang, n.d.), fol. 23a.

168 Pad-ma dkar-po, *Snyan-rgyud yid-bzhin nor-bu'i bskyed-pa'i rim-pa rgyas-pa 'dod-pa'i re-skong zhes bya-ba* [mechanical type, 19 and 33 folios, Phun-gling edition], fols. 9a ff.

[169] Tsong-kha-pa, *Sngags-rim chen-po*, P. 6210, vol. 161, 193.1.3-201.4.1, in *Collected Works* WA 127a-148b.

[170] *Ibid.*, 197.1.1-3, in *Collected Works* WA 137a.

[171] *Śrī-raktayamāri-tantrarāja-nāma*, P. 109, vol. 4, 177.5.1-190.4.3, Rgyud JA 159a-191a.

[172] Tsong-kha-pa, *Sngags-rim chen-po*, P. 6210, vol. 161, 190.2.6-190.3.8, in *Collected Works* WA 120a-b.

[173] *Ārya-ḍākiṇī-vajrapañjara-nāma-mahātantrarāja-kalpa-nāma*, P. 11, vol. 1, 223.1.6-238.5.4, Rgyud KA 262a-301b.

[174] Pad-ma dkar-po, *Snyan-rgyud yid-bzhin nor-bu bskyed-rim*, fol. 16b.

[175] Durjayacandra, *Suparigraha-nāma-maṇḍalôpāyikā-vidhi*, P. 2369, vol. 56, 142.2.4-154.1.4, Rgyud-'grel ZHA 150a-179b, and *Ṣaḍaṅga-nāma-sādhana*, P. 2368, vol. 56, 140.3.8-142.2.4, Rgyud-'grel ZHA 145b-150a.

[176] Tsong-kha-pa, *Sngags-rim chen-po*, P. 6210, vol. 161, 190.4.7-8, in *Collected Works* WA 121a.

[177] *Śrī-vajramālā-abhidhāna-mahāyogatantra-sarvatantrahṛdayara-hasya-vibhaṅga*, P. 82, vol. 3, 203.2.1-231.4.2, Rgyud CA 167b-238b.

[178] Tsong-kha-pa, *Sngags-rim chen-po*, P. 6210, vol. 161, 191.4.1-2, in *Collected Works* WA 123b. My entire discussion has been based on this section of Tsong-kha-pa's work, and I give him full credit for its impressive scholarship. My job has here been basically that of a translator; I have tried to track down the sources of the quotations and references I have borrowed from him, and it is to be expected that I have not always been succesful. All errors in attribution are therefore mine rather than his.

[179] This outline in the main follows the *Abhisamayâlaṅkāra*, F. Th. Stcherbatsky and E. Obermiller, ed., Biblioteca Buddhica, 23 (Leningrad, 1929), and Edward Conze, trans. (Rome: Istituto Italiano per il Medio ed Estremo Oriente, 1954), and the chart given in Edward Conze, "Marginal Notes to the Abhisamayālaṅkara," in Kshitis Roy, ed., *Liebenthal Festschrift* (*Sino-Indian Studies*, V.3-4 [1957]), as well as the excellent summary in Richard Robinson, *The Buddhist Religion* (Belmont: Dickenson Publishing Co., 1970), pp. 54-58.

[180] Abhayākaragupta, *Śrī-sampuṭa-tantarāja-ṭīkā-āmnāya-mañjarī-nāma*, P. 2328, vol. 55, 105.1.1-250.5.8, Rgyud-'grel TSHA 1-357a.

[181] Asaṅga, *Mahāyānasūtrâlaṁkāra*, Sylvain Levi, ed.

[182] *Śrī-mahāsaṃvarôdaya-tantrarāja-nāma*, P. 20, vol. 2, 202.3.8-221.5.7, Rgyud GA 136b-184a.

[183] Ratnarakṣita, *Śrī-saṃavrôdaya-mahātantrarājasya padminī-nāma-pañikā*, P. 2137, vol. 51, 71.1.1-119.2.6, Rgyud-'grel NA 1-117b.

[184] Tsong-kha-pa, *Sngags-rim chen-po*, P. 6210, vol. 161, 196.1.4-7, in *Collected Works* WA 134b: "This is not very clear in the texts. We find that Ratnākaraśānti in his commentary sets forth a tradition of other scholars who do not hold that they should be doubled: in our own tradition they are doubled, and Śrīdhara says the same. In the Mother Tantras, the evocations of Kambala and Luipāda et al say they are to

be doubled; in Ratnākaraśānti's evocation of the Father-Mother Hevajra they are said to be generated from the vowels and consonants without doubling; and in Ḍombipa's evocation of Nairātmya and in Durjayacandra's evocation of Hevajra it is not clear whether they are doubled or not. . . . The tradition of Buddhajñāna says that the moon is generated from the consonants; according to Śrīdhara and Loipa it is rather the sun which is thus generated, and this is found in most evocations of the Father-Mother Hevajra and in Kambala's evocation of the thirteen deities of Saṃvara." And so on.

[184a] *Saṃpuṭa-nāma-mahātantra*, P. 26, vol. 2, 245.5.2-280.2.5, Rgyud GA 244a-330a.

[185] Tsong-kha-pa, *Sngags-rim chen-po*, P. 6210, vol. 161, 198.3.3-199.1.2, in *Collected Works* WA 140b-142a. Again my discussion has been based upon Tsong-kha-pa's awesome scholarship (for an example of which see note 184 above) in this section of his work and the ones preceding.

[186] *Ibid.*, 197.2.4-6, in *Collected Works* WA 137b.

[187] *Ibid.*, 198.5.3-4, in *Collected Works* WA 141b.

[187a] *Ibid*, 207.2.8 ff., in *Collected Works* WA 162b, quoting from Buddhajñāna, *Mukti-tilaka-nāma*, P. 2722, vol. 65, 24.4.5-27.3.2, Rgyud-'grel TI 56a-63a. See Mkhas-grub-rje, *Rgyud-sde spyi'i rnam-gzhag*, Wayman's note 26 on p. 37.

[188] Pad-ma dkar-po, *Snyan-rgyud yid-bzhin nor-bu'i bskyed-rim*, fol. 17a.

[189] Quoted in Bstan-pa'i nyi-ma, *Bskyed-rim zin-bris*, fol. 17a.

[190] *Ibid.*

[191] Tsong-kha-pa, *Sngags-rim chen-po*, P. 6210, vol. 161, 220.2.8-220.3.4, in *Collected Works* WA 195a-b.

[192] Nāgārjuna, *Bodhicitta-vivaraṇa*, P. 2665, vol. 61, 285.2.7-287.3.2, Rgyud-'grel GI 42b-48a.

[193] Dasgupta, *Obscure Religious Cults*, esp. pp. 87-109.

[194] Rin-chen rnam-rgyal, *Chos-rje thams-cad mkhyen-pa bu-ston lo-tsā-ba'i rnam-par thar-pa snyim-pa'i me-tog ces bya-ba*, fols. 11b4-12a3, D. S. Ruegg, ed. and trans., *The Life of Bu Ston Rin Po Che* (Rome: Istituto Italiano per il Medio ed Estremo Oriente, 1966). My translation of this passage should be compared with that of Ruegg, pp. 82 ff., who has done exhaustive research on many of its Tantric technical terms.

[195] Ruegg, *Life of Bu Ston*, note 2 on pp. 58 ff.

[196] See Tillopa, *Ṣaḍdharmôpadeśa*, P. 4630, vol. 82, 34.4.2-35.1.1, Rgyud-'grel PU 134b-135b, and Ngag-dbang blo-bzang [Klong-rdol bla-ma], *Nā-ro chos-drug-gi sa-bcad zin-bris* in *Collected Works* NGA, Ven. Dalama, ed., *Tibetan Buddhist Studies*, I, 119 ff., for a brief outline of these attributions.

[197] Alex Wayman, "Notes on the Sanskrit Term *Jñana*", *Journal of the American Oriental Society*, 75 (1955), 253.

[198] Ruegg, *Life of Bu Ston*, note 1 on pp. 101 ff. It is worth noting that one of Ruegg's masterly footnotes is often worth an entire book

by another scholar; this particular note goes on for five pages, and it is the best summary of the subject I have yet seen.

[199] Thu'u-bkvan Blo-bzang chos-kyi nyi-ma, *Grub-mtha' thams-cad-kyi khungs-dang 'dod-tshul ston-pa legs-bshad shel-gyi me-long zhes bya-ba* (Varanasi: Chhos je lama, 1963), pp. 136 f. Quoted and translated also in Ruegg, *Life of Bu Ston*, p. 59, from which my reference is borrowed.

[200] Ngag-dbang bzang-po, *'Od-gsal gdams-ngag*, in *Gdams-ngag thor-bu bkod-pa* [no further information on this text, because my informant simply copied out the relevant folios], fols. 121, 122.

[201] Quoted in Genesius Jones, *Approach to the Purpose* (London: Hodder and Stoughton, 1964), p. 90.

[202] Grub-thob Karma-gling-pa, *'Chi-ltas mtshan-ma rang-grol*, fol. 12b.

[203] Tsong-kha-pa, *Sngags-rim chen-po*, P. 6210, vol. 161, 198.5.6-199.1.2, in *Collected Works* WA 141b-142a.

[204] Text quoted in Ruegg, *Life of Bu Ston*, p. 58 (my translation).

[205] Jan Gonda, "The Indian Mantra," *Oriens*, XVI (1963), 244-297.

[206] Quoted in Raymond Firth, *Human Types* (New York: Mentor Books, 1958), p. 128.

[207] George Rosen, *Madness in Society* (New York: Harper Torchbooks, 1969), pp. 45-46.

[208] Gling-ras-pa, *Dpal-ldan bla-ma'i mchod-pa'i cho-ga yon-tan kun-'byung lhan-thabs dbang-chog dang bcas-pa* (with supplement [lhan-thabs] and initiation ritual [dbang-chog] by Pad-ma dkar-po) [block print, 33 and 4 folios, He-mi rgod-tshang sgrub-sde edition, reissued by Phun-gling], fols. 8b-11a.

[209] Pad-ma dkar-po, *Snyan-rgyud yid-bzhin nor-bu bskyed-rim*, II, fols. 2a-3a.

[210] *Ibid.*, fol. 3a-b.

[211] Tārā does not often receive these inner and secret offerings, which are usually reserved for the powerful deities of the monastic cult, but they are occasionally presented to her. See Rnam-rgyal rgyal-mtshan, *Mi-tra bryga-rtsa'i nang-gi grub-chen nyi-ma sbas-pa'i lugs-kyi sgrol-ma nyi-shu rtsa-gcig-gi mngon-par rtogs-pa.*

[212] Quoted in Gling-ras-pa, *Bla-ma mchod-pa yon-tan kun-'byung*, fol. 16a, *Guhyasamāja Tantra*, Benoytosh Bhattacharyya, ed., p. 24.

[213] Gling-ras-pa, *Bla-ma mchod-pa yon-tan kun-'byung*, fol. 16a-b.

[214] Pad-ma dkar-po, *Snyan-rgyud yid-bzhin nor-bu bskyed-rim*, fol. 15a-b.

[215] Abhayākaragupta, *Niṣpannayogâvalī*, Benoytosh Bhattacharyya, ed. Gaekwad's Oriental Series, 109 (Baroda, 1949). See, for example, *Śrī-saṃpuṭa-tantrôkta-vajrasattva-maṇḍala*, p. 10. Sometimes only one or two groups out of these sixteen goddesses will appear in the maṇḍala. For example, in the Saptadaśâtmakahevajra-mandala are Vaṃśā, Vīnā, Mukundā (for Mṛgaṃdā), Murajā; in the Vajrâmṛta-maṇḍala are Puṣpā, Dhūpā, Dīpā (for Ālokā), Gandhā, Vaṃśā, Vīnā, Mukundā, Murajā; in the Yogâmbara-maṇḍala are Lā-

syā, Gandhā, Vīṇā, Puṣpā, Gītā, Dhūpā, Nṛtyā, Dīpā, etc. An alternate group for 5-8, the goddesses of song and dance, consists of Lāsyā, Mālā, Gītā, and Nṛtyā (in, e.g., the Dharmadhātuvāgīśvaramaṇḍala, the Durgatipariśodhanamaṇḍala, the Pañcaḍākamaṇḍala, etc.), and these then are often grouped with 9-12, the goddesses of offerings, in the retinues of various deities, e.g., of Mañjuśrī (Dharmaśaṅkhasamādhisādhana, *Sādhanamālā* # 81) or of Prajnāpāramitā (Kanakavarṇaprajñāpāramitāsādhana, *Sādhanamālā* # 152, Ācārya-asaṅgasya Prajñāpāramitāsādhana, *Sādhanamālā* # 159), etc.

216 Pad-ma dkar-po, *Snyan-rgyud yid-bzhin nor-bu bskeyd-rim*, fol. 15a.

217 Gling-ras-pa, *Bla-ma mchod-pa yon-tan kun-'byung*, fols. 17b-18b.

218 *Ibid.*, fols. 19a-20a.

219 Pad-ma dkar-po, *Snyan-rgyud yid-bzhin nor-bu bskyed-rim*, II, fol. 5b.

220 Nebesky-Wojkowitz, *Oracles and Demons of Tibet*, chap. xviii.

221 'Ja'-tshon snying-po [gter-ston], *Zab-chos nges-don snying-po'i sgo-nas rang-dang gzhan-gyi don mchog-tu sgrub-pa'i lam-rim 'khor-ba'i mun-gzhom kun-bzang thugs-rje'i snang-mdzod zhes bya-ba* [block print, 170 folios, no edition given], fols. 55b-57a.

222 See, for example, the following canonical works: Jayasena, *Maṇḍala-vidhi-ratnamarakata*, P. 2234, vol. 52, 129.4.8-130.1.8, Rgyud'grel PHA 48b-49b: "Since it is from pleasing one's guru that all magical attainments arise, I will explain the maṇḍala offering to the guru"; Niṣkalaṅkavajra, *Maṇḍala-vidhi*, P. 2796, vol. 67, 66.2.4-66.4.1, Rgyud-'grel PI 70a-71a; Kamalarakṣita, *Maṇḍala-vidhi-nāma*, P. 2797, vol. 67, 66.4.1-66.5.6, Rgyud-'grel PI 71a-b; anonymous, *Bla-ma'i maṇḍal yi-dam-gyi cho-ga* (no Sanskrit), P. 2972, vol. 68, 7.1.5-7.3.2, Rgyud-'grel PHI 195a-196a; Kamalaśrī, *Maṇḍala-vidhi-nāma*, P. 3163, vol. 69, 185.2.1-185.3.7, Rgyud-'grel TSI 282b-283a; Kambala, *Maṇḍala-vidhi*, P. 4580, vol. 81, 240.3.6-240.5.5, Rgyud-'grel NU 330b-331b; Buddhaguhya, *Maṇḍala-kriyā-vidhi*, P. 4581, vol. 81, 240.5.5-241.1.3, Rgyud-'grel NU 331b-332a; Guhyajetāri, *Maṇḍala-vidhi*, P. 4582, vol. 81, 241.1.3-241.1.7, Rgyud-'grel NU 332a-b; Ratnākaragupta, *Maṇḍala-vidhi*, P. 4583, vol. 81, 241.2.7-241.4.3, Rgyud-'grel NU 332b-333b; anonymous, *Maṇḍala-vidhi*, P. 4586, vol. 81, 246.3.2-246.4.3, Rgyud-'grel NU 345b-346a; Ratnākaraśānti, *Maṇḍala-vidhi-nāma*, P. 5087, vol. 87, 167.1.7-167.4.2, Rgyud-'grel RU 142a-143b; Ratnākaraśānti, *Maṇḍal-gyi cho-ga* (no Sanskrit), P. 5088, vol. 87, 167.4.2-169.5.4, Rgyud-'grel RU 143b-149a, which gives a legendary account of the invention of the ritual. Note also P. 5439 (= P. 4581), P. 5440 (= P. 5482), P. 5441 (= P. 4583), P. 5442 (= P. 2796), and P. 5443 (= P. 4580), which are gathered together under the title *Maṇḍal bya-ba'i cho-ga* in vol. 103, 249.3.4-250.5.2, Dbu-ma GI 163a-166b. Most of the above texts are quite short (a folio or less) and all of them are quite similar.

223 There is an extensive bibliography in Johannes Schubert, "Das Reis-maṇḍala: Ein tibetischer Ritualtext Herausgegeben, übersetzt,

und erläutert," *Asiatica: Festschrift Friedrich Weller* (Leipzig: Otto Harrassowitz, 1954). More recently published are F. D. Lessing, "Notes on the Thanksgiving Offering," *Central Asiatic Journal*, II.1 (1956), 58-71, and Erik Haarh, "Contributions to the Study of Maṇḍala and Mudrā," *Acta Orientalia* (Soc. Orient. Danica Norvegica Svecica), XXIII (1959), 57-91. See also Ferdinand Lessing, *Yung-ho-kung: An Iconography of the Lamaist Cathedral in Peking*, Reports from the Scientic Expedition to the Northwestern Provinces of China under the Leadership of Dr. Sven Hedin, XVIII (Stockholm, 1942), 105-106.

224 Kun-dga' bstan-'dzin, *Phyag-chen sngon-'gro*, fols. 8b-9b.

225 Rin-chen rnam-rgyal, *Mkhas-grub mnyam-med dpal-ldan nā-ro-pa'i rnam-par thar-pa dri-med legs-bshad bde-chen 'brug-sgra*, Herbert Guenther, trans., *The Life and Teaching of Nāropa* (Oxford: Clarendon Press, 1963); my text is adapted from pp. 82-83.

226 Thus, for example, the anonymous *Tshe-g.yang 'gugs-pa'i phrin-las khrigs-su bsdebs-pa tshe-bsod 'dod-dgu'i dpal-ster zhes bya-ba* [block print, 15 folios, no edition given] begins by saying simply, "Set out the offering torma for the particular deity as whom one will generate oneself." Many Rnying-ma rituals, such as this, perform the self-generation (= ritual service) for one deity and the generation in front (= evocation) for another; here one first generates oneself as one's own personal deity and then generates O-rgyan Tshe-dpag-med in front to be "employed." Pad-ma dkar-po, too, wrote an outline ritual for the "permission" of twenty-two different deities, leaving blanks in the appropriate places for the insertion of the name and mantra (for example: "Thus obtaining the permission of body, speech, and mind of the particular deity . . ."): *Rjes-su gnang-ba nyi-shu-rtsa gnyis-kyi chog-chings lo-rgyus zab-rgyas tshang-spros phreng-ba bkod-pa tshogs-gsung rigs-gcig* [manuscript (dbu-can), 25 folios]. Thus, too, such works as Tsong-kha-pa's *Sngags-rim chen-po* are basically extended ritual outlines of the same sort, although this format may be obscured by philosophical digression.

227 Lokesh Chandra, *Materials for a History of Tibetan Literature* (Delhi: International Academy of Indian Culture, 1963), III, 727-728, comprising #s 17189-17236.

228 'Jigs-med dbang-po, *Maṇḍal bzhi-pa'i cho-ga dpag-bsam snye-ma*. See Lung lien-fang, trans., *Tu-mu szu man-ch'a i ju-i sui* (no edition given; 1948), and Yen-ting, trans., *Lü tu-mu szu man-ta ju-i sui i-kuei: Pao Wu-wei tzu-tsai ta-shih tsao* (no edition given; 1946).

229 Dates and biographical summary are in H. E. Richardson, "A New Inscription of Khri Srong Lde Brtsan," *Journal of the Royal Asiatic Society* (1964), pp. 1 ff.

230 'Gos lo-tsā-ba, *Deb-ther sngon-po* GA fol. 23a, Roerich, trans., *Blue Annals*, p. 151. Mkha'-spyod-pa was the second "red hat" [zhva dmar-pa] Karma-pa. See H. E. Richardson, "The Karma-pa Sect: A Historical Note," *Journal of the Royal Asiatic Society* (1958), pp. 139-164, and *ibid.* (1959), pp. 1-18, esp. the chart on p. 18.

[231] 'Gos lo-tsā-ba, *Deb-ther sngon-po* CA, fol. 19a, Roerich, trans., *Blue Annals*, pp. 282-283, gives the following sequence: Gtum-ston Blo-gros grags-pa founded Snar-thang in 1153 [chu-mo-bya] and was its abbot for 14 years, and his successors were Rdo-ston Shes-rab-grags (20 years), Zhang-bstun Rdo-rje-'od (8 years), Gro-ston Bdud-rtsi-grags (39 years), Zhang-ston Chos-kyi bla-ma (10 years), Sangs-rgyas sgom-pa Seng-ge-skyabs (10 years), and finally Mchims Nam-mkha'-grags (36 years).

[232] For example, see Dharmabhadra, *Sgrol-ma maṇḍal bzhi-pa'i cho-ga mdor-bsdus* [block print, 6 folios, Dngul-chu edition], in *Collected Works* KHA, fol. 4b.

[233] Ye-shes rgyal-mtshan, *Sgrol-ma maṇḍal bzhi-pa'i cho-ga*, fol. 2b.

[234] On Dgon-pa-ba, see 'Gos lo-tsā-ba, *Deb-ther sngon-po* CA, fols. 8a, 20a, 31a, 35a. Roerich, trans., *Blue Annals*, pp. 258, 284, 311-312, 320-321, etc.

[235] On Kam-pa, see 'Gos lo-tsā-ba, *Deb-ther sngon-po* CA, fols. 28b, 34a, 35a, Roerich, trans., *Blue Annals*, pp. 305, 318, 320.

[236] Chu-mig-pa was abbot of Gsang-phu, 1223-1241. See 'Gos lo-tsā-ba, *Deb-ther sngon-po* GA, fol. 42a, CHA, fol. 1a, Roerich, trans., *Blue Annals*, pp. 195, 329.

[237] If he is the same person, this Dpal-ldan-gros would seem to have been an astrologer among his other attainments (see 'Gos lo-tsā-ba, *Deb-ther sngon-po* KHA, fol. 9a, Roerich, trans., *Blue Annals*, p. 81). It is uncertain who was the Zhang-ston-pa mentioned next, for there were many teachers with that appellation, but it is likely that he was the Zhang-ston Chos-kyi bla-ma, abbot of Snar-thang, mentioned in note 231 above.

[238] Kong-sprul rin-po-che [gter-ston], *Dgongs-gter sgrol-ma'i zab-tig-las maṇḍal cho-ga tshogs-gnyis-snying-po*, fol. 2a.

[239] Ye-shes rgyal-mtshan, *Sgrol-ma maṇḍal bzhi-pa'i cho-ga*, fol. 3a.

[240] *Ibid.*, fol. 3b.

[241] *Ibid.*

[242] Tsong-kha-pa, *Sngags-rim chen-po*, P. 6210, vol. 161, 75.2.4-8, in *Collected Works* DZA 52b.

[243] Out of the thirty-two signs [lakṣaṇa] of a great person, Tārā definitely lacks at least one: the "sexual organs withdrawn into a sheath" [kaśôpagatavastiguhya]. It is not clear which is the other sign she lacks; my informants suggested the short-cut hair "curling to the right" [ekâikaromapradakṣiṇâvarta]. On these signs see also Alex Wayman, "Contributions Regarding the Thirty-two Characteristics of the Great Person," in Kshitis Roy ed., *Liebenthal Festschrift* (*Sino-Indian Studies*, V.3-4 [1957] 243-260).

[244] On these, see Buddhaghosa, *Visuddhimagga*, Henry Clarke Warren, ed. (Cambridge: Harvard University Press, 1950), chap. vii, and Conze, *Buddhist Meditation*, pp. 45-52. Partially parallel lists of epithets are in *Mahāvyutpatti*, XIX, 350-443, Sūtrânta-uddhṛtāni tathāgata-mahātmya-nāmāni; XLVIII, 1075-1126, Śrāvaka-guṇāḥ; and LXIII, 1280-1307, Dharma-paryāyaḥ.

245 Lokesh Chandra's introduction to Rol-pa'i rdo-rje, *'Phags-pa bzang-po spyod-pa'i smon-lam-gyi rnam-par bshad-pa kun-tu bzang-po'i dgongs-pa gsal-bar byed-pa'i rgyan*, p. i.

246 M. Winternitz, *History of Indian Literature* (Calcutta, 1933) II, 326.

247 For text and commentaries, see note 65, above.

248 Śāntarakṣita, *Śrī-vajradhara-saṃgīta-bhagava-stotra-ṭīka* P. 2052, vol. 46, 110.3.5-113.2.4, Bstod-tshogs KA 270b-277b.

249 For Sanskrit, see Śāntideva, *Bodhicaryâvatāra*, Vidhushekhara Bhattacharyya, ed. (Calcutta: The Asiatic Society, Bibliotheca Indica, 1960), pp. 12-19. Also, with the pañjikā of Prajñākaramati, P. L. Vaidya, ed. (Darbhanga: Mithila Institute of Postgraduate Studies and Research in Sanskrit Learning, 1960), pp. 22 ff. Perhaps the best translation is Louis de la Vallée Poussin, trans., *Introduction à la pratique des futurs bouddhas* (Paris, 1907), pp. 8 ff.

250 Śāntarakṣita, *Śrī-vadjradhara-saṃgīta-bhagava-stotra-ṭīka*, P. 2052, vol. 46, 110.3.5-113.2.4, Bstod-tshogs KA 270b-277b. I am not sure of this reference in the ritual nor of that at note 248.

251 See Mkhas-grub-rje, *Rgyud-sde spyi'i rnam-gzhag*, Lessing and Wayman, ed. and trans., *Fundamentals of the Buddhist Tantras*, p. 116, Wayman's note 18, quoting from Padmavajra, *Tantrârthâvatāra-vyākhyāna*, P. 3325, vol. 70, 73.4.7-188.5.8, Rgyud-'grel TSHI 98b-383a.

252 Kaḥ-thog Tshe-dbang nor-bu [Dpa'-bo Don-grub rdo-rje], *'Phags-ma sgrol-ma-la gsol-gdab mchod-pa maṇḍal bzhi-par grags-pa'i cho-ga 'dod-don yid-bzhin grub-pa'i ljon-shing* [block print, 28 folios, being a reissue, with added postface by Karma-pa XVI (Rang-byung rig-pa'i rdo-rje), of the original Dpal-spungs edition carved at the orders of the Si-tu Bstan-pa'i nyin-byed].

CHAPTER II: APPLICATION

1 See H. D. Bhattacharyya, "Minor Religious Sects," in R. C. Majumdar, ed., *The History and Culture of the Indian People* (Bombay: Bharatiya Vidya Bhavan, 1951), II, 467; Jitendra Nath Banerjea, *The Development of Hindu Iconography* (Calcutta: University of Calcutta, 1956), pp. 491 ff.

2 *Saddharmapuṇḍarīka Sūtra*, U. Wogihara and C. Tsuchida, ed. (Tokyo: Seigo-kenkyūkai, 1935), III, 362 ff.

3 Candragomin, *Āryâṣṭamahābhāyôttārā-tārā-stava*, P. 4873, vol. 86, 121.1.1-121.2.6, Rgyud-'grel ZU 184b-185a.

4 See Debala Mitra, "Aṣṭamahābhaya-tārā," *Journal of the Asiatic Society* (Bengal), XXIII (1957), 19-25.

5 *Ibid.*, pp. 19 f.

6 Giuseppe Tucci, *Tibetan Painted Scrolls* (Rome: Librario dello Stato, 1949), Tanka 44, pl. 78, discussed in II, 403 f.

[7] Giuseppe Tucci, *Indo-Tibetica* (Rome: Reale Academie d'Italie, 1932-1941), III, pt. 2, pp. 161-162.

[8] Dge-'dun-grub [Dalai Lama I], *Sgrol-ma dkar-mo'i tshe-sgrub-kyi sgo-nas tshe-bsring-ba*, in *Rje thams-cad mkhyen-pa dge-'dun grub-pa dpal-bzang-po'i gsung thor-bu sna-tshogs* [block print, 123 folios, Lhasa edition], fol. 29a, in *Collected Works* CA.

[9] Chang Hsin-jo, *Fu-lu to-chieh chüeh-pa shang-shih shih*, in Sun Ching-feng, *Ta-jih ju-lai tsan-t'an erh-shih-i tsun tu-mu ching*, p. 29a-b.

[10] This was often true of Chinese transliterations; for example, see the following reconstructions of the *Bhagavatyā ārya-tārāya daṇḍaka-stotra*: Chou Ta-fu," Three Buddhist Hymns Restored into Sanskrit from Chinese Transliterations of the Tenth Century A.D., " *Sino-Indian Studies*, I.2 (1954), and Sakai Shinten, "Sanshu no bongo-san ni tsuite," in *Nakano kyōju koki kinen rombunshū* (Koyasan: Koyasan University, 1960), p. 165.

[11] Sun Ching-feng, *Erh-shih-i tsun tu-mi mu-chou kung-tê lu: chin-kang shang-shih no-na hu-t'u-k'o-t'u fu-shou*, in Sun Ching-feng, *Ta-jih ju-lai tsan-t'an erh-shih-i tsun tu-mu ching*, p. 15a-b.

[12] No-na Hutukhtu, *Tu-mu sheng-chi chi*, in Sun Ching-feng, *Ta-jih ju-lai tsan-t'an erh-shih-i tsun tu-mu ching*, pp. 24a-29a; and No-na Hutukhtu, *Sheng chiu-tu fo-mu sheng-chi ts'o-yao*, in Wu Jun-chiang, ed., *Sheng chiu-tu fo-mu yu-ch'ih fa* (Hong Kong: Hsiang-chiang no-na ching-shê, 1964), pp. 22a-25b.

[13] Ju-ba chos-dar, *Chag lo-tsā-ba'i rnam-thar 'ju-ba chos-dar-gyis mdzad-pa ngo-mtshar-can bla-ma'i gsungs dri-ma med-pa bsgrigs-pa zhes bya ba*, G. Roerich, ed. and trans., *Biography of Dharmasvāmin* (Patna: K. P. Jayaswal Research Institute, 1959).

[14] 'Ju-ba chos-dar, *Chag lo-tsā-ba'i rnam-thar*, fol. 21a, Roerich, ed. and trans., *Biography of Dharmasvāmin*, pp. 19, 75.

[15] 'Jam-dbyangs mkhyen-brtse'i dbang-po, *Dbus-gtsang-gi gnas-rten rags-rim-gyi mtshan-byang mdor-bsdus dad-pa'i sa-bon zhes bya-ba*, Alfonsa Ferrari, ed. and trans., *Mkhyen-brtse's Guide to the Holy Places of Central Tibet* (Rome: Istituto Italiano per il Medio ed Estremo Oriente, 1958), p. 125 n. 240. This same text speaks of talking and miraculous images at 'Bras-spungs (p. 42), Glang-thang (p. 39), etc.

[16] *Shes-bya* (Oct. 1968), p. 19.

[17] Carl Gustav Diehl, *Instrument and Purpose: Studies on Rites and Rituals in South India* (Lund: C. W. K. Gleerup, 1956), pp. 94, 100. See also Agehananda Bharati, *The Tantric Tradition* (London: Rider, 1965), chap. 5, "On Mantra," esp. pp. 110-111, where Diehl is cited as here. Bharati's discussion of mantras in Indian religiosity is quite excellent.

[18] Yon-tan rgya-mtsho Blo-gros mtha'-yas ['Jam-mgon Kong-sprul rin-po-che], *Rje-btsun yid-bzhin 'khor-lo'i rjes-su gnang-ba dang bsnyen-sgrub-las gsum gsal-bar byed-pa'i yi-ge zla-ba 'dod-'jo bya-ba* [block print, 55 folios, Dpal-spungs edition], fols. 38b, 36a.

[19] Quoted Tsong-kha-pa, *Sngags-rim chen-po*, P. 6210, vol. 160, 72.5.8-73.1.1, in *Collected Works* DZA 46b-47a.

[20] Ngag-dbang blo-bzang [Klong-rdol bla-ma], *Gsang-sngags rig-pa 'dzin-pa'i sde-snod-las byung-ba'i ming-gi rnam-grangs*, in *Collected Works*, Ven. Dalama, ed., *Tibetan Buddhist Studies of Klong-rdol bla-ma Ngag-dbang-blo-bzang* (Laxmanpuri, Mussoorie: privately printed, 1963-1964), I, 71-72.

[21] *Ibid.*, I, 65.

[22] See Alain Danielou, *Yoga: The Method of Re-integration* (New York: University Books, 1949), pp. 137 ff., 143 ff. See also Patañjali, *Yoga Sūtras*, III, 44, in Rām Śaṃkar Bhaṭṭācārya, ed., *Pātañjala-yogadarśanam Vācaspati-kṛta-ṭīkâyuta-Vyāsa-bhāṣya-sametam* (Vārāṇasi: Bhāratīya Vidyā Prakāśan, 1963), pp. 145 ff.

[23] Ngag-dbang blo-bzang [Klong-rdol bla-ma], *Gsang-sngags rig-pa 'dzin-pa'i sde-snod-las byung-ba'i ming-gi rnam-grangs*, in *Collected Works*, Ven. Dalama, ed., *Tibetan Buddhist Studies*, I, 72.

[24] Nāgārjuna, *Muktakena tārā-kalpôdbhava-kurukullā-sādhana*, P. 4384, vol. 81, 25.3.4-26.2.5, Rgyud-'grel DU 251b-253b [= *Sādhana-mālā*, Benoytosh Bhattacharyya, ed., Gaekwad's Oriental Series, 26, 41 (Baroda: Oriental Institute, 1925, 1928), #172, II, 347]. See also Wayman's note 13 in Dge-legs dpal-bzang-po [Mkhas-grub-rje], *Rgyud-sde spyi'i rnam-par gzhag-pa rgyas-par brjod*, Ferdinand Lessing and Alex Wayman, eds. and trans., *Mkhas grub rje's Fundamentals of the Buddhist Tantras* (The Hague: Mouton, 1968), p. 220, for a discussion of the list from some works of Tsong-kha-pa. Yet another variant listing is in Ngag-dbang blo-bzang [Klong-rdol bla-ma], *Gsang-sngags rig-pa 'dzin-pa'i sde-snod-las byung-ba'i ming-gi rnam-grangs*, in *Collected Works*, Ven. Dalama, ed., *Tibetan Buddhist Studies*, I, 70.

[25] *Ārya-tārā-kurukulle-kalpa*, P. 76, vol. 3, 148.2.5-154.2.2, Rgyud CA 30a-45b.

[26] Grags-pa rgyal-mtshan, *Rgyud-kyi mngon-par rtogs-pa rin-po-che'i ljon-shing*, in *Sa-skya bka'-'bum* CHA, fols. 102b, 107a-109b, Bsod-nams rgya-mtsho, ed., *Complete Works of the Great Masters of the Sa Skya Sect of the Tibetan Buddhism* (Tokyo: Tokyo, Bunko, 168), III, 50, 54-55. See also Grags-pa rgyal-mtshan, *Rgyud-sde spyi'i rnam-gzhag dang rgyud-kyi mngon-par rtogs-pa'i stong-thun sa-bcad*, in *Sa-skya bka'-'bum* CHA, fols. 157a-159a, Bsod-nams rgya-mtsho, ed., *Complete Works of the Sa Skya Sect*, III, 78-79.

[27] Alexandra David-Neel, *Magic and Mystery in Tibet* (New York: University Books, 1958), pp. 134 ff.

[28] *Ārya-ḍākiṇī-vajrapañjara-mahātantrarāja-kalpa-nāma*, P. 11, vol 1, 223.1.6-238.5.5, Rgyud KA 262a-301b.

[29] Grags-pa rgyal-mtshan, *Rgyud-kyi mngon-rtogs*, in *Sa-skya bka'-'bum* CHA, fol. 109b, Bsod-nams rgya-mtsho, ed., *Complete Works of the Sa Skya Sect*, III, 55.

[30] *Ārya-tārā-kurukulle-kalpa*, P. 76, vol. 3, 148.2.5-154.2.2, Rgyud CA 30a-45b.

[31] Nāgārjuna, *Muktakena Tārā-kalpôdbhava-kurukullā-sādhana*, P. 4384, vol. 81, 25.3.4-26.2.5, Rgyud-'grel DU 251b-253b [= *Sādhana-mālā*, Bhattacharyya, ed., #172, II, 347].

[32] *Ārya-tārā-kurukulle-kalpa*, P. 76, vol. 3, 148.2.5-154.2.2, Rgyud CA 30a-45b.

[33] Nāgārjuna, *Muktakena Tārā-kalpôdbhava-kurukulle-sādhana*, P. 4384, vol. 81, 25.3.4-26.2.5, Rgyud-'grel DU 251b-253b [= Sādhanamālā, Bhattacharyya, ed., #172, II, 347].

[34] Kong-sprul rin-po-che, *Rje-btsun yid-bzhin 'khor-lo'i zla-ba édod-'jo*, passim.

[35] *Ibid.*, fol. 46b. For identification of names of medicinal plants, I have relied mainly upon Franz Hübotter, *Chinesisch-Tibetische Pharmakologie und Rezeptur* (Ulm-Donau: Karl G. Haug Verlag, 1957), but to all the Latin names it might be well to add *var. cum grano salis.*

[36] *Śrī-raktayamāri-tantra*, P. 109, vol. 4, 177.5.1-190.4.3, Rgyud JA 159a-191a.

[37] Kokila, *Āyuḥ-parirakṣa-nāma*, P. 3262, vol. 69, 214.2.4-214.4.5, Rgyud-'grel TSHI 60a-61a.

[38] 'Jam-dpal nor-bu Pad-ma dbang-rgyal, *Rtsa-gsum nor-bu dbang-gi rgyal-po'i sgrub-thabs 'dod-dgu'i char-'bebs khams-gsum dbang-sdud ces bya-ba* [manuscript (dbu-can), 33 folios], fol. 3a-b.

[39] Ferdinand Lessing, *Yung-ho-kung: An iconography of the Lamaist Cathedral in Peking*, Reports from the Scientific Expedition to the Northwestern Provinces of China under the Leadership of Dr. Sven Hedin, XVIII (Stockholm, 1942); pp. 150-161.

[40] Kong-sprul rin-po-che, *Rje-btsun yid-bzhin 'khor-lo'i zla-ba 'dod-'jo*, fols. 30a-35b.

[41] This account may be compared, for example, with the following: Dbyangs-can grub-pa'i rdo-rje, *Rje-btsun-ma yid-bzhin 'khor-lo-la brten-pa'i zhi-ba'i sbyin-sreg mdor-bsdus bya-tshul zag-med-bdud-rtsi'i gru-char zhes bya-ba* [block print, 12 folios, Dngul-chu edition], in *Collected Works* KHA, fols. 1b-3a.

[41a] Grags-pa rgyal-mtshan, *Sgrol-ma'i chos-skor-las spyi'i sgrub-thabs*, in *Sa-skya bka'-'bum* NYA, fols. 139a-141a, Bsod-nams rgya-mtsho, ed., *Complete Works of the Sa Skya Sect*, vol. 4, 69.1.4-70.1.4. Similarly, see Bu-ston Rin-chen-grub, *Sgrol-ma btson-'don-gyi cho-ga*, in *Collected Works* JA, Lokesh Chandra, ed., *Collected Works of Bu-ston* (Delhi: International Academy of Indian Culture, 1967), VII, 763-768.

[42] *Samājaparamârthasarvakarmôdaya-nāma-tārāyoginī-uttaratantra-rāja*, Tohoku University Catalogue of the Sde-dge Canon Number 449 (not in Peking edition), Rgyud CA 295a-309a. Quoted by Kong-sprul rin-po-che, *Rje-btsun yid-bzhin 'khor-lo'i zla-ba 'dod-'jo*, fol. 2a.

[43] Buddhaguhya, *Vairocanâbhisambodhivikurvitâdhiṣṭhāna-mahātantra-bhāṣya*, P. 3487, vol. 77, 110.5.8-215.1.3, Rgyud-'grel NGU 76b-337a. I am grateful to Professor Alex Wayman for this reference.

[44] Śrī Dipaṃkarajñāna, *Ārya-tārā-sādhana*, P. 4512, vol. 81, 95.2.1-95.5.5, Rgyud-'grel DU 426a-427b.

[45] This is the long mantra from the canonical *'Phags-ma sgrol-ma'i gzungs* (no Sanskrit), P. 393, vol. 8, 158.1.8-158.2.1, Rgyud TSA 79b-80a.

[46] Anonymous, *Cora-bandha*, P. 4513, vol. 81, 95.5.5.-96.1.4, Rgyud-'grel DU 427b-428a.

[47] Kong-sprul rin-po-che, *Rje-btsun yid-bzhin 'khor-lo'i zla-ba 'dod-'jo*, fol. 39b.

[48] Mkhas-grub Rāga-asya, *Chags-med ri-chos* [block print, 298 folios, no edition (first and last folios sewn in cloth binding)], fol. 124a.

[49] Ngag-dbang blo-zang [Klong-rdol bla-ma], *Gsang-sngags rig-pa 'dzin-pa'i sde-snod-las byung-ba'i ming-gi rnam-grangs*, in *Collected Works*, Ven. Dalama, ed., *Tibetan Buddhist Studies*, I, 70.

[50] Kong-sprul rin-po-che, *Rje-btsun yid-bzhin 'khor-lo'i zla-ba 'dod-'jo*, fol. 39a-b.

[51] *Ibid.*, fol. 38b.

[52] *Ibid.*, fols. 36a-37a.

[53] Nāgārjuna, *Mahākāruṇikâryatārā-sādhana-sāmānyâbhisamayanāma*, P. 2556, vol. 59, 51.2.1-6, Rgyud-'grel LA 7b.

[54] See, for example, Lokesh Chandra, "Tibetan Buddhist Texts Printed by the Mdzod-dge-sgar-gsar Monastery," *Indo-Iranian Journal*, VII (1963-64), 306.

[55] P. H. Pott, *Introduction to the Tibetan Collection of the Natonal Museum of Ethnology, Leiden* (Leiden: E. J. Brill, 1951), p. 121.

[56] Kong-sprul rin-po-che, *Rje-btsun yid-bzhin 'khor-lo'i zla-ba 'dod-'jo*, fol. 40a.

[57] *Ibid.*, fol. 44b.

[58] Ngag-dbang blo-bzang [Klong-rdol bla-ma], *Gsang-sngags rig-pa 'dzin-pa'i sde-snod-las byung-ba'i ming-gi rnam-grangs*, in *Collected Works*, Ven. Dalama, ed., *Tibetan Buddhist Studies*, I, 83.

[59] Kong-sprul rin-po-che, *Rje-btsun yid-bzhin 'khor-lo'i zla-ba 'dod-'jo*, fol. 40b.

[60] Kong-sprul rin-po-che, *Sgrol-ma sprul-pa lce-sbyang sngon-mo'i srung-ba* [block print, 1 folio (bse-ru), Dpal-spungs edition (addendum to *Rje-btsun yid-bzhin 'khor-lo'i zla-ba 'dod-'jo*)].

[61] Kun-dga' rdo-rje, *Deb-ther dmar-po*, fol. 15b.

[62] Ye-shes dpal-'byor, *Dpag-bsam ljon-bzang*, p. 148.

[63] Ngag-dbang blo-zang [Klong-rdol bla-ma], *Bstan-srung dam-can rgya-mtsho'i ming-gi rnam-grangs*, in *Collected Works*, Ven. Dalama, ed., *Tibetan Buddhist Studies*, II, 362. This is a very famous list, quoted for instance in Tucci, *Tibetan Painted Scrolls*, II, 717, and in René de Nebesky-Wojkowitz, *Oracles and Demons of Tibet: the Cult and Iconography of the Tibetan Protective Deities* ('S-Gravenhage: Mouton, 1956), p. 299.

[64] *Lha-'dre bka'i thang-yig* in *Pad-ma bka'-thang sde-lnga* [block print, 281 folios, Sde-dge edition], fol. 37a.

[65] Tucci, *Tibetan Painted Scrolls*, II, 717-730.

[66] Nebesky-Wojkowitz, *Oracles and Demons*, esp. pp. 257-317 and *passim*.

[67] Yon-tan rgya-mtsho Blo-gros mtha'-yas ['Jam-mgon Kong-sprul rin-po-che], *Bka' 'khor-lo bar-pa'i yang-bcud shes-rab snying-po'i mdo-la brten-pa'i bdud-zlog bar-chad kun-sel lag-len bltas-chog-tu bkod-*

pa rnam-thar stobs-bskyed zhes bya-ba [block print, 21 folios, "Guṇa-śāstra" books, Bum-thang bkra-shis chos-gling edition] fol. 16b.

[68] Anonymous, *Dpal phyag-na rdo-rje 'byung-po 'dul-byed-kyi sgrub-thabs* [block print, 10 folios, no edition given], fol. 8a.

[69] Tucci, *Tibetan Painted Scrolls*, II, 721.

[70] Anonymous, *Dang-po bgegs-la gtor-ma byin-pa* [manuscript (dbu-can), 2 folios, a separable insert for Rnying-ma-pa rituals], fol. 1b.

[71] Anonymous, *'Phags-pa gnam-sa snang-brygad ces bya-ba theg-pa chen-po'i mdo* (rgya-nag skad-du ā-rya pa-ra yang rgyad-rta) [block print, 19 folios, no edition given], fol. 5b. For a discussion of this text, see Tucci, *Tibetan Painted Scrolls*, II, 723 and n. 29.

[72] August Hermann Francke, "The Ladaki Pre-Buddhist Marriage Ritual," *Indian Antiquary*, XXX (1901), 131-149.

[73] *'Phags-pa gnam-sa snang-brgyad*, fol. 13b.

[74] Nebesky-Wojkowitz, *Oracles and Demons*, pp. 233-234.

[75] Tucci, *Tibetan Painted Scrolls*, II, 718.

[76] Anonymous, *Gsang-bdag dregs-pa 'dul-byed las-tshogs dam-sri'i glud-mdos zhes bya-ba* [manuscript (dbu-can), 5 folios], fol. 1b.

[77] Nebesky-Wojkowitz, *Oracles and Demons*, pp. 300-303.

[78] Anonymous, *Rig-'dzin srog-sgrub-las ri-bo bsang-mchod* [block print, 4 folios, Khams-sgar phun-gling edition], fol. 1b.

[79] *'Phags-pa gnang-sa snang-brgyad*, fol. 14b.

[80] *Ārya-tārā-kurukulle-kalpa*, P. 76, vol. 3, 148.2.5-154.2.2, Rgyud CA 30a-45b. On the background and adventures of Tshul-khrims rygal-ba, see Bu-ston Rin-chen-grub, *Bde-bar gshegs-pa'i bstan-pa'i gsal-byed chos-kyi 'byung-gnas gsung-rab rin-po-che'i mdzod ces bya-ba*, in *Collected Works* YA [block print, 212 folios, Lhasa edition], fols. 152b ff., E. Obermiller, trans., *History of Buddhism by Bu-ston* (Heidelberg: Otto Harrassowitz, 1931, 1932), II, 212 ff.; 'Gos lo-tsā-ba Gzhon-nu-dpal, *Bod-kyi yul-du chos-dang chos-smra-ba ji-ltar byung-ba'i rim-pa deb-ther sngon-po* CA, fols. 3a ff., George Roerich, trans., *The Blue Annals*, Royal Asiatic Society of Bengal Monograph Series, VII (Calcutta, 1949, 1953), pp. 247 ff.; Pad-ma dkar-po, *Chos-'byung bstan-pa'i pad-ma rgyas-pa'i nyin-byed ces bya-ba*, Lokesh Chandra, ed., *Tibetan Chronicle of Padma Dkar-po* (Delhi: International Academy of Indian Culture, 1968), fols. 174a ff. See also David Snellgrove, *Buddhist Himalaya: Travels and Studies in Quest of the Origins and Nature of Tibetan Religion* (New York: Philosophical Library, 1957), p. 120; and Helmut Hoffman, "Die Qarluq in der Tibetischer Literatur," *Oriens*, III (1950), 190 ff.

[80a] Ḍombī-heruka, *Ārya-tārā-kurukullā-stotra*, P. 2448, vol. 57, 51. 4.3-51.5.1, Rgyud-grel ZA 123b-124a.

[81] Nebesky-Wojkowitz, *Oracles and Demons*, pp. 483, 500.

[82] Pad-ma dkar-po, *Bdud-kyi g.yul-las rab-tu rgyal-bar byed-pa'i dam-can rgya-mtsho'i mchod-sprin* [block print, 34 folios (part of *Sku-gsung-thugs snying-po'i dngos-grub sgrub-pa'i cho-ga bdud-kyi g.yul-las rab-tu rgyal-ba zhes bya-ba*), Phun-gling edition], fol. 29b.

[83] 'Ja'-tshon snying-po, *Zab-chos nges-don snying-po'i sgo-nas rang-dang gzhan-gyi don mchog-tu sgrub-pa'i lam-rim 'khor-ba'i mun-gzhom kun-bzang thugs-rje'i snang-mdzod ces bya-ba*, fol. 118b.

[84] See R. A. Stein, "Le liṅga des danses masquées lamaïques et la théorie des âmes," in Kshitis Roy, ed., *Liebenthal Festschrift* (*Sino-Indian Studies* V.3-4 (1957), p. 220, and R. A. Stein, *L'épopée tibétaine de Gesar dans sa version lamaïque de Ling*, Annales du Musée Guimet, Bibliothèque d'Études, LXI (Paris, 1956), II, 39b.

[85] *Hevajra Tantra*, David Snellgrove, ed. (London: Oxford University Press, 1959), I.xi.6-7 (= II, 43).

[86] Ngag-dbang blo-bzang [Klong-rdol bla-ma], *Gsang-sngags rig-pa 'dzin-pa'i sde-snod-las byung-ba'i ming-gi rnam-grangs*, in *Collected Works*, Ven. Dalama, ed., *Tibetan Buddhist Studies*, I, 70.

[87] Anonymous, *Ārya-śrīmatī-kurukullā-sādhana*, P. 4387, vol. 81, 26.3.5-26.5.5, Rgyud-'grel DU 254a-255a [= *Sādhanamālā*, Bhattacharyya, ed., #178, II, 356]. On this as well as other Siddhas, see Toni Schmid, *The Eighty-five Siddhas*, Reports from the Scientific Expedition to the Nortwestern Provinces of China under the Leadership of Dr. Sven Hedin, XLII (Stockholm, 1958), p. 58.

[88] Amoghavajra, *Kurukulle'i las-sbyor-gyi man-ngag* (no Sanskrit), P. 4711, vol. 82, 191.2.3-192.1.1, Rgyud-'grel PHU 217b-2119b.

[89] Anonymous, *Ārya-śrīmatī-kurukullā-sādhana*, P. 4387, vol. 81, 26.5.2-5, Rgyud-'grel DU 255a [= *Sādhanamālā*. Bhattacharyya, ed., #178, II, 357].

[90] Kong-sprul rin-po-che, *Rje-btsun yid-bzhin 'khor-lo'i zla-ba 'dod-'jo*, fol. 43b.

[91] Dharmabhadra, *Bcom-ldan 'das-ma kurukulle'i 'khor-lo'i las-tshogs* [block print, 3 folios, in "Dngul-chu" books], in *Collected Works* CA

[92] Amoghavajra, *Kurukulle'i las-sbyor-gyi man-ngag*, P. 4711, vol. 82, 191.2.3-192.1.1, Rgyud-'grel PHU 217b-219b.

[93] For an excellent description of some aspects of this ritual, see Stein, "Le liṅga des danses masquées," in Roy, ed., *Liebenthal Festschrift.*

[94] On this ritual, see Bu-ston Rin-chen-grub, *Tshogs-'khor dang dpa'-bo'i ston-mo'i cho-ga'i lag-len bde-chen rnam-rol zhes bya-ba*, in *Collected Works*, Lokesh Chandra, ed., *The Collected Works of Bu-ston*, VII, 769 ff.

[95] Blo-bzang ye-shes, *Rje-btsun sgrol-ma'i sgo-nas tshogs-mchod 'bul-tshul* [block print, 4 folios, Rva-sgreng edition], fol. 1b.

[96] 'Ja'-tshon snying-po, *Zab-chos nges-don snying-po'i sgo-nas rang-dang gzhan-gyi don mchog-tu sgrub-pa'i lam-rim 'khor-ba'i mun-gzhom kun-bzang thugs-rje'i snang-mdzod ces bya-ba*, fol. 119a.

[97] On these Bstan-ma, see Nebesky-Wojkowitz, *Oracles and Demons*, pp. 181-198.

[98] 'Jam-dpal nor-bu Pad-ma dbang-rgyal, *Rtsa-gsum nor-bu dbang-gi rgyal-po'i sgrub-thabs 'dod-dgu'i char-'bebs khams-gsum dbang-sdud ces bya-ba* [manuscript (dbu-can), 33 folios], fols. 23a ff.

[99] Nebesky-Wojkowitz, *Oracles and Demons*, pp. 369-397.

[100] René de Nebesky-Wojkowitz and Geoffrey Gorer, "The Use of Thread-Crosses in Lepcha Lamaist Ceremonies," *Eastern Anthropologist*, IV.1 (1950), 65-87.

[101] Lessing, *Yung-ho-kung*, pp. 148-149.

[102] See *'Dus-pa rin-po-che dri-ma med-pa gzi-brjid rab-tu 'bar-ba'i mdo*, David L. Snellgrove, ed., and trans., *The Nine Ways of Bon* (London: Oxford University Press, 1967), pp. 76, 78, 84; Tucci, *Tibetan Painted Scrolls*, II, 715 f.

[103] M. Lalou, "Rituel Bon-po des funérailles royales," *Journa Asiatique*, 241 (1953), 13 f.

[104] Nebesky-Wojkowitz, *Oracles and Demons*, p. 370.

[105] Blo-bzang chos-kyi rgyal-mtshan [Paṇ-chen bla-ma I], *Sgrol-ma g.yul-zlog ji-ltar bya-ba'i cho-ga dgra-las rnam-rgyal zhes bya-ba* [block print, 8 folios, Bkra-shis lhun-po edition], in *Bkra-shis lhun-po'i rgyud-pa grva-tshang-gi rig-sngags 'chang-ba-rnams-kyi 'don-cha'i rim-pa*, fol. 1b.

[106] Nebesky-Wojkowitz, *Oracles and Demons*, pp. 369 f.; *Pad-ma bka'i thang-yig*, G. Ch. Toussaint, trans., *Le Dict de Padma* (Paris: Lèroux, 1933), p. 360.

[107] Ngag-dbang blo-bzang rgya-mtsho [Dalai Lama V], *Rje-btsun seng-ldeng nags sgrol-la brten-pa'i mdos-chog mthong-bas don-sgrub zhes bya-ba* [block print, 18 folios, 'Bras-spungs edition], in *Collected Works* (Pt. II: "Secret Books") NGA, fol. 17a.

[108] Nāgārjuna, *Khadiravaṇī-tārā-sādhana*, P. 4487, vol. 81, 64.4.4-65.2.3, Rgyud-'grel DU 349b-351a.

[109] Kong-sprul rin-po-che, *Sher-snying bdud-zlog*, fols. 2a ff.

[110] 'Gos lo-tsā-ba, *Deb-ther sngon-po* CA, fol. 37a-b, Roerich, trans., *Blue Annals*, pp. 324-325. Gsang-phu-ba Rngog Legs-pa'i shes-rab came from Yar-'brog and settled in Dbus in 1045; he was a disciple of 'Brom-ston. His birth and death dates are unknown.

[111] 'Gos lo tsā-ba, *Deb-ther sngon-po* CA, fols. 31a-32b, Roerich, trans., *Blue Annals*, pp. 311-314. Sne'u-zur-pa was the chief disciple of Dgon-pa-ba; he was born in 1042 and died in 1118.

[112] Two teachers of Rgya are mentioned in *Pad-ma bka'i thang-yig*, Toussaint, trans., *Le Dict de Padma*, pp. 376, 377: Rgya lo-tsā-ba Rdo-rje bzang-po and Rgya Zhang-khrom, both of them "revealers of hidden texts" [gter-ston]. See Tucci, *Tibetan Painted Scrolls*, I, 258.

[113] Lessing, *Yung-ho-kung*, p. 148.

[114] See F. D. Lessing, "Calling the Soul: A Lamaist Ritual," *Semitic and Oriental Studies*, University of California Publications in Semitic Philology, XI (1951), 263-284. Compare the items set out in the *Slob-dpon pad-mas madzad-pa'i bla-bslu bla-khyer bslu-byed zhes bya-ba* [manuscript (dbu-can), 8 folios], fol. 1b, with which the life is "ransomed from the hands of the lha," etc.

[115] Grub-thob Karma-gling-pa [gter-ston], *Rdzogs-pa chen-po'i lo-rgyus mdo-byang po-ti smug-chung-las 'chi-bslu zab-mo* (in other editions called also *Zab-chos zhi-khro dgongs-pa rang-grol-las 'chi-bslu*

'jigs-pa rang-grol zhes bya-ba) [block print, 9 folios, no edition given], fol. 4a.

116 A-bu hral-po [Dpal-sprul O-rgyan 'Jigs-med chos-kyi dbang-po], *Klong-chen snying-gi thig-le-las bskyed-rim lha-lkhrid 'og-min bgrod-pa'i them-skas* [mechanical type, 43 folios, Phun-gling edition], fol. 2b.

117 Yon-tan rgya-mtsho Blo-gros mtha'-yas ['Jam-mgon Kong-sprul rin-po-che], *Dpal-mgon 'phags-pa klu-sgrub zhal-snga-nas brgyud-pa'i sgrol-ma g.yul-bzlog bltas-chog-tu bkod-pa bden-'bras myur-ston ces bya-ba* [block print, 20 folios, "Guṇaśāstra" books, Bum-thang bkra-shis chos-gling edition].

CHAPTER III: ACQUISITION

1 Tsong-kha-pa, *Zab-lam nā-ro'i chos-drug*, P.6202, vol. 160, 209.4.6-7, in *Collected Works* TSHA 83b.

2 On the life of Vāgīśvarakīrti, see Tāranātha, *Dam-pa'i chos rin-po-che 'phags-pa'i yul-du ji-ltar dar-ba'i tshul gsal-bar ston-pa dgos-'dod kun-'byung zhes bya-ba*, Anton Schiefner, trans., *Tāranāthas Geschichte des Buddhismus in Indien* (St. Petersburg: Kaiserlichen Akademie der Wissenschaften, 1869), pp. 235 ff.

3 Kun-dga' bstan-'dzin, *Phyag-chen sngon-'gro*, fol. 2b.

4 Sangs-rgyas bstan-'dzin, *Thun-mong-gi sngon-'gro'i chos-bshad rin-chen them-skas zhes bya-ba* [block print, 44 folios, O-rgyan smin-grol-gling edition], fol. 3a.

5 *Caraka Saṃhitā* VI.1.4.61, in *The Caraka Saṃhitā of Agniveśa* (Varanasi: Chowkhamba Vidya Bhawan, 1962), II, 63.

6 *Aṣṭāṅgahṛdaya* I.1.2, in *Aṣṭāṅgahṛdayam* (Varanasi: Chowkhamba Sanskrit Series Office, 1962), p. 2.

7 *Caraka Saṃhitā* I.11.1.3-4, in *The Caraka Saṃhitā of Agniveśa*, I, 207-208.

8 Arunadatta, *Sarvāṅgasundara*, quoted in C. Dwaraknath, *The Fundamental Principles of Āyurveda* (Mysore: Governments Ayurvedic College, n.d.), III, 7.

9 Grub-thob Karma-gling-pa [gter-ston], *Zab-chos zhi-khro dgongs-pa rang-grol-las 'chi-ltas mtshan-ma rang-grol zhes bya-ba* [block print, 16 folios, no edition given], fol. 1b.

10 Karma Tshe-dbang kun-khyab, *Yi-dam tshogs-kyi lo-rgyus*, fol. 83a.

11 Grub-thob Karma-gling-pa, *'Chi-ltas mtshan-ma rang-grol*, fol. 1b.

12 For analysis and bibliography, see Alex Wayman, "Significance of Dreams in India and Tibet," *History of Religions*, VII.1 (1967), 1-12.

13 Robert B. Ekvall, *Religious Observances in Tibet: Patterns and Function* (Chicago: University of Chicago Press, 1964), pp. 255 f.

14 On this transmission, see 'Gos lo-tsā-ba Gzhon-nu-dpal, *Bod-kyi yul-du chos-dang chos-smra-ba ji-ltar byung-ba'i rim-pa deb-ther sngon-*

po, George N. Roerich, trans., *The Blue Annals*, Royal Asiatic Society of Bengal Monograph Series, VII (Calcutta, 1949, 1953), II, 1020.

[15] Ngag-dbang Gsung-rab mthu-thob, *Rje-bstun-ma yid-bzhin 'khor-lo'i sgo-nas tshe-dbang bskur-tshul bla-ma dam-pa'i man-ngag 'chi-med bdud-rtsi'i chu-rgyun zhes bya-ba* [block print, 23 folios, no edition given (last folio torn)].

[16] On these, see *Hevajra Tantra*, David Snellgrove, ed. and trans. (London: Oxford University Press, 1959), I, 131f., and index under "consecration(s)"; Dge-legs dpal bzang-po [Mkhas-grub-rje], *Rgyud-sde spyi'i rnam-par gzhag-pa rgyas-par brjod*, Ferdinand Lessing and Alex Wayman, eds. and trans., *Mkhas grub rje's Fundamentals of the Buddhist Tantras* (The Hague: Mouton, 1968), index under "initiation." See also, for example, S. Dasgupta, *An Introduction to Tāntric Buddhism* (Calcutta: University of Calcutta), pp. 159-161.

[17] Pad-ma dkar-po, *Rjes-su gnang-ba nyi-shu-rtsa gnyis-kyi chog-chings lo-rgyus zab-rgyas tshang-spros phreng-ba bkod-pa tshogs-gsung rigs-gcig*, fols. 8b-9a.

[18] *Ārya-tārā-kurukulle-kalpa*, P. 76, vol. 3, 148.3.5-145.2.2, Rgyud CA 30a-45b.

[19] Tsong-kha-pa, *Sngags-rim chen-po*, P. 6210, vol. 161, 175.4.2, in *Collected Works* WA 83b.

[20] Pad-ma dkar-po, *Snyan-rgyud yid-bzhin nor-bu bskyed-rim*, II, fol. 15a.

[21] *Ārya-tārā-kurukulle-kalpa*, P. 76, vol. 3, 148.3.5-154.2.2, Rgyud CA 30a-45b.

[22] Ngag-dbang blo-bzang [Klong-rdol bla-ma], *Gsang-sngags rig-pa 'dzin-pa'i sde-snod-las byung-ba'i ming-gi rnam-grangs*, in *Collected Works*, Ven. Dalama, ed., *Tibetan Buddhist Studies of Klong-rdol bla-ma Ngag-dbang-blo-bzang* (Laxmanpuri, Mussoorie: privately printed, 1963-1964), I, 62. This list may be compared with that of Aśvaghosa, following Tsong-kha-pa's comments thereon, given in Wayman's note 14 in Mkhas-grub-rje, *Rgyud-sde spyi'i rnam-gzhag*, Lessing and Wayman, eds. and trans., *Fundamentals of the Buddhist Tantras*, pp. 328-329.

[23] Pad-ma dkar-po, *Snyan-rgyud yid-bzhin nor-bu bskyed-rim*, II, fol. 15b.

[24] *Ārya-tārā-kurukulle-kalpa*, P. 76, vol. 3, 148.3.5-154.2.2, Rgyud CA 30a-45b.

[25] On the altar see also Kong-sprul rin-po-che, *Rje-btsun yid-bzhin 'khor-lo'i zla-ba 'dod-'jo*, fols. 20a f.

[26] Mkhas-grub-rje, *Rgyud-sde spyi'i rnam-gzhag*, Lessing and Wayman, eds. and trans., *Fundamentals of the Buddhist Tantras*, p. 315.

[27] Chos-kyi don-grub Dkon-mchog yan-lag [Zhva-dmar-pa V], rev. by Rgyal-dbang Theg-mchog rdo-rje [Karma-pa XIV], *'Phags-ma sgrol-dkar-gyi cho-ga dngos-grub kun-stsol zhes bya-ba* [block print, 24 folios (?), no edition given (last folio missing)], fol. 13b.

[28] Kong-sprul rin-po-che, *Rje-btsun yid-bzhin 'khor-lo'i zla-ba 'dod-'jo*, fol. 26b.

[29] Dkon-mchog yan-lag [Zhva-dmar-pa V], *'Phags-ma sgrol-dkar-gyi cho-ga dngos-grub kun-stsol,* fol. 14a.

[30] Kong-sprul rin-po-che, *Rje-btsun yid-bzhin 'khor-lo'i zla-ba 'dod-'jo,* fol. 21a

[31] *Ibid.*, fol. 2a.

[32] *Samājaparamârthasarvakarmôdaya-nāma-tārāyoginī-uttaratantra-rāja,* Tohoku University Catalogue of the Sde-dge Canon Number 449 (not in Peking edition), Rgyud CA 295a-309a.

[33] *Śrī-caturpītha-mahāyoginī-tantrarāja-nāma,* P. 67, vol. 3, 69.1.8-89.1.2, Rgyud NGA 167a-217a.

[34] *Ūrdhvajaṭā-mahākalpa-mahābodhisattva-virkurvaṇa-paṭala-visarā bhagavatī-ārya-tārā-mūlakalpa-nāma,* P. 469, vol. 10, 201.1.1-Vol. 11, 61.1.5, Rgyud ZA 1a-332a.

[35] *Sarva-tathāgata-mahānitārā-viśvakarmabhava-tantra-nāma,* P. 390, vol. 8, 149.3.5-155.5.8, Rgyud TSA 58a-74a.

[36] Vāgīśvarakīrti, *Mṛtyuvañcanôpadeśa,* P. 4808, vol. 86, 21.2.1-30.4.1, Rgyud-'grel ZHU 151a-174a.

[37] For names and dates, see H. E. Richardson, "The Karma-pa Sect: A Historical Note," *Journal of the Royal Asiatic Society* (1958), pp. 139-164; (1959), pp. 1-18.

[38] See 'Gos lo-tsā-ba, *Deb-ther sngon-po* CA, fols. 10b, 15a, 34a, etc., Roerich, trans., *Blue Annals,* pp. 263, 273, 318, etc.

[39] Karma Tshe-dbang kun-khyab, *Yi-dam tshogs-kyi lo-rgyus,* fol. 19b. The text then continues to give the same story of Sgre-pa's prophecy from the palmist and his eventual meeting with Sle-nag-pa.

[40] Karma Tshe-dbang kun-khyab, *Yi-dam tshogs-kyi lo-rgyus,* fol. 20b.

[41] Dkon-mchog yan-lag [Zhva-dmar-pa V], *'Phags-ma sgrol-dkar-gyi cho-ga dngos-grub kun-stsol,* fol. 14b.

[42] Karma Tshe-dbang kun-khyab, *Yi-dam tshogs-kyi lo-rgyus,* fol. 20b. On these masters of the Karma Bka'-brgyud, see also 'Gos lo-tsā-ba, *Deb-ther sngon-po* NYA 38b ff., Roerich, trans., *Blue Annals,* pp. 492 ff.

[43] See 'Gos lo-tsā-ba, *Deb-ther sngon-po* CA 9a, Roerich, trans., *Blue Annals,* p. 260.

[44] These two texts are given in their abbreviated titles as *Mngon-rtogs rin-chen phreng-ba* and *Rjes-gnang gcig-shes kun-grol.* I have not been able to locate a copy of either text. Again, for all Karma-pa identifications and dates, see Richardson, "The Karma-pa Sect," esp. the chart in pt. 2, p. 18.

[45] Kong-sprul rin-po-che, *Rje-btsun yid-bzhin 'khor-lo'i zla-ba 'dod-jo,* fols. 3a ff.

[46] Tsong-kha-pa, *Sngags-rim chen-po,* P. 6210, vol. 161, 218.5.8-219.1.6, in *Collected Works* WA 191b-192a. Here the visualization for "cheating death" is derived from the Cakrasaṃvara cycle.

[47] See, for example, the interesting account in Paul Brunton, *A Search in Secret India* (New York: Samuel Weiser, 1970), pp. 76-94.

[48] Tsong-kha-pa, *Sngags-rim chen-po*, P. 6210, vol. 161, 205.2.3-221.2.7, in *Collected Works* WA 157b-200a, gives a complete and very neatly arranged summary of the Process of Perfection according to the various Tantric textual cycles.

[49] Yon-tan rgya-mtsho Blo-gros mtha'-yas ['Jam-mgon Kong-sprul rin-po-che], *Dge-ba-can-ma yid-bzhin 'khor-lo'i tshe-khird dpal-ldan mar-me-mdzad-kyi lugs gtsang-la ma-'dres-pa bdud-rtsi'i za-ma-tog ces bya-ba* [block print, 20 folios, Dpal-spungs edition].

[50] Bhavabhadra, *Ārya-tārā-maṇḍalâvatāra-kṛtyā-nāma*, P. 4497, vol. 81, 75.4.6-86.3.5, Rgyud-grel DU 377a-404b.

[51] Sahajalalita, *Samantamukhapraveśaraśmi-vimalôṣṇīṣa-prabhāsa-sarvatathāgata-hṛdaya-samaya-vilokita-nāma-dhāraṇī-vṛtti*, P. 3512, vol. 78, 180.2.7-203.5.8, Rgyud-'grel CHU 285a-344a.

[52] Kong-sprul rin-po-che, *Rje-btsun yid-bzhin 'khor-lo'i zla-ba 'dod-'jo*, fols. 48a ff.

Bibliography

Non-Tibetan Sources

Abhayākaragupta. *Niṣpannayogâvalī.* Benoytosh Bhattacharyya, ed. Gaekwad's Oriental Series, 109. Baroda, 1949.

Agehananda Bharati. *The Tantric Tradition.* London: Rider, 1965.

Agrippa von Nettesheim. *De occulta philosophia.* Auswahl, Einführung, und Kommentar von Willy Schrödter. Remagen: Otto Reichl Verlag, 1967.

Alquié, Ferdinand. *The Philosophy of Surrealism.* Ann Arbor: University of Michigan Press, 1969.

Angyal, Andras. "Disturbances of Thinking in Schizophrenia." In J. S. Kasanin, ed., *Language and Thought in Schizophrenia.* New York: Norton, 1944.

Aoki, Bunkyo. *Study on Early Tibetan Chronicles.* Tokyo: Nippon Gakujutsu Shinkokai, 1955.

Āryabhadracaripraṇidhānarāja. Sunitikumar Pathak, ed. Gangtok, Sikkim: Namgyal Institute of Tibetology, 1961.

Asaṅga. *Abhisamayâlaṅkāra.* F. Th. Stcherbatsky and E. Obermiller, eds. Biblioteca Buddhica, 23. Leningrad, 1929. Edward Conze, trans. Rome: Istituto Italiano per il Medio ed Estremo Oriente, 1954.

———. *Bodhisattvabhūmi.* U. Wogihara, ed. Tokyo, 1930-1936.

———. *Mahāyānasūtrâlaṅkāra.* Sylvain Levi, ed. Paris, 1907.

Bacot, Jacques. *Introduction à l'histoire du Tibet.* Paris: Société Asiatique, 1962.

———. "Le mariage chinois du roi tibétan Sroṅ bcan sgam po (Extrait du *Maṇi bka' 'bum*)," *Mélanges chinois et bouddhiques,* III (1933-34), 1-61.

———. *Trois mystères tibétaines.* Paris, 1921.

Balakian, Anna. *André Breton: Magus of Surrealism.* New York: Oxford University Press, 1971.

———. *The Literary Origins of Surrealism.* New York: New York University Press, 1947.

———. *Surrealism: The Road to the Absolute.* New York: Dutton Paperback, 1959.

Banerjea, Jitendra Nath. *The Developmnet of Hindu Iconography.* Calcutta: University of Calcutta, 1956.

Bhattacharji, Sukumari. *The Indian Theogony.* Cambridge: Cambridge University Press, 1970.

Bhattacharyya, Benoytosh. *The Indian Buddhist Iconography.* Calcutta: K. L. Mukhopadhyay, 1958.

Bhattacharyya, H. D. "Minor Religious Sects." In R. C. Majumdar, ed., *The History and Culture of the Indian People.* Bombay: Bharatiya Vidya Bhavan, 1951. II, 463-475.

Blonay, Godefroy de. *Matériaux pour servir à l'histoire de la déesse buddhique Tārā.* Paris: Librairie Émile Bouillon, 1895.

Boisen, Anton T. *The Exploration of the Inner World.* New York: Harper Torchbooks, 1962.

Brunton, Paul. *A Search in Secret India.* New York: Samuel Weiser, 1970.

Buddhaghosa. *Visuddhimagga.* Henry Clarke Warren, ed. Cambridge: Harvard University Press, 1950.

Caraka Saṃhitā of Agniveśa. Varanasi: Chowkhamba Vidya Bhawan, 1962.

Carroll, Paul. *The Poem in Its Skin.* New York: Follett Press, 1968.

Chandra, Lokesh. "Maṇḍalas of a Tibetan Collectaneum," *Asiatische Forschungen* (1966).

———. *Materials for a History of Tibetan Literature.* Delhi: International Academy of Indian Culture, 1963.

———. "The Rin-lhan and Rin-'byuṅ", *Oriens Extremis,* VIII.2 (1962).

———. "Tibetan Buddhist Texts Printed by the Mdzod-dge-sgar-gsar Monastery," *Indo-Iranian Journal,* VII (1963-64).

———, ed. *Hymns to Tārā.* Delhi: International Academy of Indian Culture, n.d.

Chang Hsin-jo. *Fu-lu to-chieh chüeh-pa shang-shih shih.* In Sun Ching-feng, *Ta-jih ju-lai tsan-t'an erh-shih-i tsun tu-mu ching.* Pp. 29a-b.

Chattopadhyaya, Alaka. *Atīśa and Tibet.* Indian Studies, Past and Present. Calcutta, 1967.

Chou Ta-fu. "Three Buddhist Hymns Restored into Sanskrit from Chinese Transliterations of the Tenth Century A. D.," *Sino-Indian Studies,* I.2 (1954).

Conze, Edward. *Buddhist Meditation.* New York: Harper Torchbooks, 1969.

———. "Marginal Notes to the Abhisamayālaṅkāra." In Kshitis Roy, ed., *Liebenthal Festschrift. Sino-Indian Studies,* V.3-4 (1957).

———, ed. *Buddhist Texts through the Ages.* New York: Harper Torchbooks, 1964.

Cunningham, R. "Nangsal Obum," *Journal of the West China Border Research Society,* XII.A (1940), 35-75.

Danielou, Alain. *Yoga: The Method of Re-integration.* New York: University Books, 1949.

Dasgupta, Shashibhusan. *An Introduction to Tāntric Buddhism* Calcutta: University of Calcutta, 1958.

———. *Obscure Religious Cults.* Calcutta: K. L. Mukhopadhyay, 1962.

Dasgupta, S. N., and S. K. Dey. *A History of Sanskrit Literature.* Calcutta: University of Calcutta, 1962.

David-Neel, Alexandra. *Magic and Mystery in Tibet.* New York: University Books, 1958.
Diehl, Carl Gustav. *Instrument and Purpose: Studies on Rites and Rituals in South India.* Lund: C. W. K. Gleerup, 1956.
Duncan, Marion H. *Harvest Festival Dramas of Tibet.* Hong Kong: Orient Publishing Co., 1955.
Dwaraknath, C. *The Fundamental Principles of Āyurveda.* Mysore: Government Ayurvedic College, n.d.
Ekvall, Robert B. *Religious Observances in Tibet: Patterns and Function.* Chicago: University of Chicago Press, 1964.
Eliade, Mircea. *Yoga: Immortality and Freedom.* New York: Pantheon Books, 1958.
Firth, Raymond. *Human Types.* New York: Mentor Books, 1958.
Francke, August Hermann. "The Ladaki Pre-Buddhist Marriage Ritual," *Indian Antiquary*, XXX (1901), 131-149.
Getty, Alice. *The Gods of Northern Buddhism.* Rutland, Vt.: Charles E. Tuttle, 1962.
Gonda, Jan. "The Indian Mantra," *Oriens*, XVI (1963), 244-297.
Greene, Naomi. *Antonin Artaud: Poet without Words.* New York: Simon and Schuster, 1970.
Grünwedel, Albert. *Mythologie du Buddhisme au Tibet et en Mongolie.* Trans. from German by Ivan Goldschmidt. Leipzig: F. A. Brockhaus, 1900.
Guenther, Herbert. *Tibetan Buddhism without Mystification.* Leiden: E. J. Brill, 1966.
Guhyasamāja Tantra. Benoytosh Bhattacharyya, ed. Gaekwad's Oriental Series, 53. Baroda, 1967.
Haarh, Erik. "Contributions to the Study of Maṇḍala and Mudrā," *Acta Orientalia* (Soc. Orient. Danica Norvegica Svecica), XXIII (1959), 57-91.
Hackin, Joseph, ed. *Formulaire Sanskrit-Tibétaine.* Paris: Paul Geuthner, 1924.
Hevajra Tantra. David Snellgrove, ed. London: Oxford University Press, 1959.
Hoffman, Helmut. "Die Qarluq in der Tibetischer Literatur," *Oriens*, III (1950).
———. *The Religions of Tibet.* New York: Macmillan, 1961.
Holmyard. E. J. *Alchemy.* Baltimore: Penguin Books, 1957.
Hsüan-Tsang. *Ta-t'ang hsi-yü-chi.*
Nanking: Chinese Buddhist Association, 1957. Samuel Beal, trans. *Travels of Hiouen-Thsang.* Calcutta: Susil Gupta, 1957. Thomas Watters, trans. *On Yuan Chwang's Travels in India.* Delhi: Munshiram Manohar Lal, 1961.
Hübotter, Franz. *Chinesisch-Tibetische Pharmakologie und Rezeptur.* Ulm-Donau: Karl F. Haug Verlag, 1957.
Hummel, Siegbert. *Lamaistische Studien.* Leipzig: Otto Harrassowitz, 1959.

Jones, Genesius. *Approach to the Purpose.* London: Hodder and Stoughton, 1964.

Jung, Carl G. *Psychology and Alchemy.* London: Routledge and Kegan Paul, 1953.

Kristeller, Paul Oskar. *Eight Philosophers of the Italian Renaissance.* Stanford: Stanford University Press, 1964.

Laing, R. D. *The Divided Self.* Baltimore: Penguin Books, 1965.

Lalou, M. "Mañjuśrīmūlakalpa et Tārāmūlakalpa," *Harvard Journal of Asiatic Studies,* I (1936), 327-349.

———. "Les textes bouddhiques au temps du roi Khri-sroṅ-lde-bcan," *Journal Asiatique,* 241 (1953), 313-353.

———. "Rituel Bon-po des funérailles royales," *Journal Asiatique,* 241 (1953), 13 ff.

Laṅkâvatāra Sūtra. P. L. Vaidya, ed. Darbhanga: Mithila Institute, 1963.

Lessing, Ferdinand. "Calling the Soul: A Lamaist Ritual," *Semitic and Oriental Studies,* University of California Publications in Semitic Philology, XI (1951), 263-284.

———. "Notes on the Thanksgiving Offering," *Central Asiatic Journal,* II.1 (1956), 58-71.

———"'Wu-liang-shou': A Comparative Study of Tibetan and Chinese Longevity Rites." In *Studies Presented to Hu Shih on His Sixty-fifth Birthday.* Bulletin of the Institute of History and Philology, Academia Sinica, XXVIII. Taipei, 1957.

———. *Yung-ho-kung: An Iconography of the Lamaist Cathedral in Peking.* Reports from the Scientific Expedition to the Northwestern Provinces of China under the Leadership of Dr. Sven Hedin, XVIII. Stockholm, 1942.

Li An-che. "The Bkah-brgyud Sect of Lamaism," *Journal of the American Oriental Society,* LXIX (1949), 59.

———. "Rñiṅ ma pa: The Early From of Lamaism," *Journal of the Royal Asiatic Society* (1948), pp. 147 ff.

Lung lien-fan, trans. *Tu-mu szu man-ch'a i ju-i sui,* 1948.

MacDonald, Ariane. *Le Maṇḍala du Mañjuśrīmūlakalpa.* Paris: Adrien-Maisonneuve, 1962.

Maraini, Fosco. *Secret Tibet.* New York: Grove Press, 1960.

Miller, Roy Andrew. "The Independent Status of the Lhasa Dialect within Central Tibetan," *Orbis,* 4 (1955), 49-55.

Mitra, Debala. "Aṣṭamahābhaya-tārā," *Journal of the Asiatic Society* (Bengal), XXIII (1957), 19-25.

Nāgārjuna. *Mūlamadhyamakakārikā.* Kenneth K. Inada, ed. and trans. Tokyo: Hokuseido Press, 1970.

Nauert, Charles G. *Agrippa and the Crisis of Renaissance Thought.* Urbana: University of Illinois Press, 1965.

Nebesky-Wojkowitz, René de. *Oracles and Demons of Tibet: The Cult and Iconography of the Tibetan Protective Deities.* 'S-Gravenhage: Mouton, 1956.

Nebesky-Wojkowitz, René de, and Geoffrey Gorer. "The Use of Thread-crosses in Lepcha Lamaist Ceremonies," *Eastern Anthropologist*, IV.1 (1950), 65-87.

No-na Hutukhtu. *Sheng chiu-tu fo-mu shengchi ts'o-yao*. In Wu Junchiang, ed., *Sheng chiu-tu fo-mu yu-ch'ih fa*, 22a-25b.

———. *Tu-mu sheng-chi chi*. In Sun Chingfeng, *Ta-jih ju-lai tsan-t'an erh-shih-i tsun tu-mu ching*, 24a-29a.

Patañjali. *Yoga Sūtras*. In Rām Śaṃkar Bhaṭṭācārya, ed., *Pātañjala-yogadarśanam Vacaspati-kṛta-ṭīkâyuta- Vyāsa-bhāṣya-sametam*. Vārāṇasi: Bhāratīya Vidyā Prakāśan, 1963.

Petech, Luciano. "The Dalai-lamas and Regents of Tibet: A Chronological Study," *T'oung Pao*, XLVII.3-5 (1946), 368-394.

———. *A Study on the Chronicles of Ladakh*. Supplement to *Indian Historical Quarterly*, XIII and XV. Calcutta, 1939

Peters, F. A. "The Rin-Ḥbyuṅ," *Journal of the Royal Asiatic Society* LX (1943), 1-36.

Pott, P. H. *Introduction to the Tibetan Collection of the National Museum of Ethnology, Leiden*. Leiden: E. J. Brill, 1951.

Poussin, Louis de la Vallée. *Introduction à la pratique des futurs bouddhas*. Paris, 1907.

Ray, Paul C. *The Surrealist Movement in England*. Ithaca: Cornell University Press, 1971.

Richardson, H. E. "The Karma-pa Sect: A Historical Note," *Journal of the Royal Asiatic Society* (1958), pp. 139-164; (1959), pp. 1-18.

———. "A New Inscription of Khri Srong Lde Brtsan," *Journal of the Royal Asiatic Society* (1964), pp. 1 ff.

Robinson, Richard H. *The Buddhist Religion*. Belmont: Dickenson Publishing Co., 1970.

Rosen, George. *Madness in Society*. New York: Harper Torchbooks, 1969.

Saddharmapuṇḍarīka Sūtra. U. Wogihara and C. Tsuchida, eds. Tokyo: Seigo-kenkyūkai, 1935.

Sādhanamālā. Benoytosh Bhattacharyya, ed. Gaekwad's Oriental Series, 26, 41. Baroka: Oriental Institute, 1925, 1928.

Sakai Shinten. "Sanshu no bongo-san ni tsuite. In *Nakano kyōju koki kinen rombunshu*. Koyasan: Koyasan University, 1960.

Śāntiveda. *Bodhicaryâvatāra*. Vidhushekhara Bhattacharyya, ed. Calcutta: Bibliotheca Indica, 1960. P. L. Vaidya, ed. Darbhanga: Mithila Institute of Post-Graduate Studies and Research in Sanskrit Learning, 1960.

Sato Hisashi. *Kodai Chibetto Shi-kenkyū*. Kyoto: Tōyōshi-kenkyūkai, 1958.

Scheltema, J. F. *Monumental Java*. London, 1912.

Schmid, Toni. *The Eighty-five Siddhas.* Reports from the Scientific Expedition to the Northwestern Provinces of China under the Leadership of Dr. Sven Hedin, XLII. Stockholm, 1958.

Schubert, Johannes. "Das Reis-maṇḍala: Ein tibetischer Ritualtext herausgegeben, übersetzt, und erläutert," *Asiatica: Festschrift Friedrich Weller.* Leipzig: Otto Harrassowitz, 1954.

Shastri, Hirananda. *The Origin and Cult of Tārā.* Memoirs of the Archaeological Survey of India, XX. Calcutta, 1925.

Sircar, D. C., ed. *The Śakti Cult and Tārā.* Calcutta: University of Calcutta, 1967.

Snellgrove, David L. *Buddhist Himalaya: Travels and Studies in Quest of the Origins and Nature of Tibetan Religion.* New York: Philosophical Library, 1957.

Snellgrove, David L., and H. E. Richardson. *A Cultural History of Tibet.* New York: Frederick A. Praeger, 1958.

Stein, R. A. *L'épopée tibétaine de Gesar dans sa version lamaïque de Ling.* Annales du Musée Guimet, Bibliothèque d'Études, LXI. Paris, 1956.

———. "Le liṅga des danses masquées lamaïques et la théorie des âmes." In Kshitis Roy, ed. *Liebenthal Festschrift. Sino-Indian Studies,* V. 3-4 (1957).

Sthiramati. *Madhyānta-vibhāga-ṭīkā.* S. Yamaguchi, ed. Tokyo: Suzuki Research Foundation, 1966.

Subandhu. *Vasavadattā.* Louis H. Gray, ed. and trans. New York: Columbia University Press, 1913.

Sun Ching-feng. *Erh-shih-i tsun tu-mu mi-chou kung-tê lu: ching-kang shang-shih no-na hu-t'u-ko-t'u fu-shou.* In Sun Ching-feng, *Ta-jih ju-lai tsan-t'an erh-shih-i tsun tu-mu ching,* 15a-b.———. *Ta-jih ju-lai tsan-t'an erh-shihyi tsun tu-mu ching.* K'ai-feng: Pei-hsing Street Niao-chi-wen Publishing Office, 1939.

Tajima, Ryūjin. *Les deux grands maṇḍalas et la doctrine de l'esoterisme Shingon.* Tokyo, 1955.

Tart, Charles T. "Psychedelic Experiences Associated with a Novel Hypnotic Procedure, Mutual Hypnosis." In Charles T. Tart, ed. *Altered States of Consciousness.* New York: John Wiley and Sons, 1969.

Tucci, Giuseppe. *Indo-Tibetica.* Rome: Reale Academie d'Italie, 1932-1941.

———. *Tibetan Painted Scrolls.* Rome: Libraria dello Stato, 1949.

———. "The Wives of Sroṅ btsan sgam po," *Oriens Extremis,* IX (1962), 121-126.

Vāgbhāṭa. *Aṣṭāṅgahṛdaya.* Varanasi: Chowkhamba Sanskrit Series Office, 1962.

Vasubandhu. *Madhyānta-vibhāga-bhāṣya.* Gadjin M. Nagao, ed. Tokyo: Suzuki Research Foundation, 1964.

Vidyabhusana, Satis Chandra. *Bauddha-stotra-saṁgrahaḥ, or a Collection of Buddhist Hymns.* Vol. I: *Sragdharā-stotram, or a Hymn to Tārā in Sragdharā Metre, by Bhikṣu Sorvajña Mitra of Kāśmīra.* Calcutta: Asiatic Society of Bengal, 1908.

Waddell, L. Austine. *The Buddhism of Tibet, or Lamaism.* Cambridge: W. Heffer and Sons, 1939.

———. "The Indian Buddhist Cult of Avalokita and His Consort Tārā 'the Saviouress,' Illustrated from the Remains in Magadha," *Journal of the Royal Asiatic Society* (1894), pp. 63 ff.

Waldberg, Patrick. *Surrealism.* New York: McGraw-Hill, 1971.

Walker, Daniel P. *Spiritual and Demonic Magic from Ficino to Campanella.* London: Warburg Institute, 1958.

Wallace, Anthony F. C. *Religion: An Anthropological View.* New York: Random House, 1966.

Wayman, Alex. "Analysis of the Tantric Section of the Kanjur Correlated to Tanjur Exegesis." In Lokesh Chandra, ed., *Indo-Asian Studies.* Delhi: International Academy of Indian Culture, 1962, I, 120 ff.

———. "Contributions Regarding the Thirty-two Characteristics of the Great Person," In Kshitis Roy, ed., *Liebenthal Festschrift. Sino-Indian Studies,* V.3-4 (1957), 243-260.

———. "Notes on the Sanskrit Term Jñāna," *Journal of the American Oriental Society,* 75 (1955).

———. "Significance of Dreams in India and Tibet," *History of Religions,* VII.1 (1967), 1-12.

———"The Twenty-one Praises of Tārā, a Syncretism of Śaivism and Buddhism," *Journal of the Bihar Research Society* (1959).

Winternitz, M. *History of Indian Literature,* Calcutta, 1933.

Wu Jun-chiang, ed.*Sheng chiu-tu fo-mu yu-ch'ih fa.* Hong Kong: Hsiang-chiang no-na ching-shê, 1964.

Yates, Frances A. *Giordano Bruno and the Hermetic Tradition.* New York: Vintage Books, 1969.

Yen-ting ———, trans. *Lü tu-mu szu man-ta ju-i sui i-kuei Pao Wu-wei tzu-tsai ta-shih tsao.* 1946.

Youngblood, Gene. *Expanded Cinema.* New York: Dutton, 1970.

Tibetan Sources

Bka'-'gyur

Ārya-avalokiteśvaramātā-nāma-dhāraṇī, P. 389, vol. 8, 146.5.8-149.3.5, Rgyud TSA 56b-58a.

Ārya-aṣṭamabhâbhayatāraṇī-nāma-dhāraṇī, P. 396, vol. 8, 159.1.6-159.2.8, Rgyud TSA 84a-b.

Ārya-ḍākiṇī-vajrapañjara-nāma-mahātantrarāja-kalpa-nāma, P. 11, vol. 1, 223.1.6-238.5.4, Rgyud KA 262a-301b.

Ārya-tārā-aṣṭaghoratāraṇī-sūtra, P. 395, vol. 8, 158.2.7-159.1.6, Rgyud TSA 80a-84a.
Ārya-tārā-kurukulle-kalpa, P. 76, vol. 3, 148.3.5-154.2.2, Rgyud CA 30a-45b.
Ārya-tārā-bhaṭṭārikā-nāma-aṣṭaśataka, P. 391, vol. 8, 155.5.8-156.5.6, Rgyud TSA 74a-76b.
Ārya-tārā-svapratijñā-nāma-dhāraṇī, P. 394, vol. 8, 158.2.1-158.2.7, Rgyud TSA 80a.
Ārya-subāhu-paripṛcchā-nāma-tantra, P. 428, vol. 9, 33.5.6-42.5.4, Rgyud TSHA 179b-202a.
Ūrdhavajaṭā-mahākalpa-mahābodhisattvavikurvaṇapaṭalavisarā bhagavatī-āryatārāmūlakalpa-nāma, P. 469, vol. 10, 201.1.1-vol. 11, 61.1.5, Rgyud ZA 1a-332a.
Bcom-ldan 'das-ma sgrol-ma yang-dag-par rdzogs-pa'i sangs-rgyas bstod-pa gsungs-pa, P. 77, vol. 3, 154.2.3-154.4.7, Rgyud CA 45a-46b.
Tārā-devī-nāmâṣṭaśataka, P. 392, vol. 8, 156.5.6-158.1.8, Rgyud TSA 76b-79b.
'Phags-ma sgrol-ma'i gzungs, P. 393, vol. 8, 158.1.8-158.2.1, Rgyud TSA 79b-80a.
Vajrakīlaya-mūlatantra-khaṇḍa, P. 78, vol. 3, 154.4.8-155.3.8, Rgyud CA 46a-48a.
Śrī-caturpīṭha-mahāyoginī-tantra-rāja-nāma, P. 67, vol. 3, 69.1.8-89.1.2, Rgyud NGA 167a-217a.
Śrī-mahāsaṃvarôdaya-tantrarāja-nāma, P. 20, vol. 2, 202.3.8-221.5.7, Rgyud GA 135b-184a.
Śrī-raktayamāri-tantra, P. 109, vol. 4, 177.5.1-190.4.3, Rgyud JA 159a-191a.
Śrī-vajramālā-abhidhāna-mahāyogatantra-sarvatantrahṛdayarahasya-vibhaṅga, P. 82, vol. 3, 203.2.1-231.4.2, Rgyud CA 167b-238b.
Samājaparamârthasarvakarmôdaya-nāma-tārāyoginī-uttaratantrarāja, T. 449 (not in Peking ed.), Rgyud CA 295a-309a.
Sampuṭa-nāma-mahātantra, P. 26, vol. 2, 245.5.2-280.2.5, Rgyud GA 244a-330a.
Sarvatathāgatamātānitārevīśvakarmabhava-tantra-nāma, P. 390, vol. 8, 149.3.5-155.5.8, Rgyud TSA 58a-74a.
Susiddhikara-mahātantra-sādhanôpāyika-paṭala, P.431, vol. 9, 54.1.8-73.5.3, Rgyud TSHA 230a-284b.

Bstan-'gyur

Anupamarakṣita. *Tārā-sādhana*, P. 4313, vol. 80, 292.5.6-293.5.1, Rgyud-'grel DU 186b-189a [= *Sādhanamālā* I.201-204].
Abhayākaragupta. *Śrī-sampuṭa-tantrarāja-ṭīkā-āmnyāyamañjarī-nāma*, P. 2328, vol. 55, 105.1.1-250.5.8, Rgyud-'grel TSHA 1-357a.
Amoghavajra. *Kurukulle'i las-sbyor-gyi man-ngag*, P. 4711, vol. 82, 191.2.3-192.1.1, Rgyud-'grel PHU 217b-219b.

Ārya-śrīmatī-kurukullā-sādhana, P. 4387, vol. 81, 26.3.5-26.5.5, Rgyud-'grel DU 254a-255a [=*Sādhanamālā* II.356].

Kamalarakṣita. *Maṇḍala-vidhi-nāma*, P. 2797, vol. 67, 66.4.1-66.5.6, Rgyud-'grel PI 71a-b.

Kamalaśrī. *Maṇḍala-vidhi-nāma*, P. 3163, vol. 69, 185.2.1-185.3.6, Rgyud-'grel TSI 282b-283a.

Kambala. *Maṇḍala-vidhi*, P. 4580, vol. 81, 240.3.6-240.5.5, Rgyud-'grel NU 330b-331b.

Kurukulle'i man-ngag, P. 4713, vol. 82, 192.3.6, Rgyud-'grel PHU 220b.

Kokila. *Āyuḥ-parirakṣa-nāma*, P. 3262, vol. 69, 214.2.4-214.4.5, Rgyud-'grel TSHI 60a-61a.

Guhyajetāri. *Maṇḍala-vidhi*, P. 4582, vol. 81, 241.1.3-241.1.7, Rgyud-'grel NU 332a-b.

Sgrol-ma dkon-mchog gsum-la bstod-pa, P. 2567, vol. 59, 72.5.8-73.1.4, Rgyud-'grel LA 61b-62a.

Candrakīrti, *Pradīpôddyotana-nāma-ṭīkā*, P. 2650, vol. 60, 23.1.1-117. 3.7, Rgyud-'grel SA 1-233a.

Candragomin. *Ārya-aṣṭabhaya-trāta-nāma-tārā-sādhana*, P. 4494, vol. 81, 74.1.1-74.5.4, Rgyud-'grel DU 373a-375a.

———. *Ārya-aṣṭamahābhayôttārā-tārā-stava*, P. 4873, vol. 86, 121.1.1-126.2.6, Rgyud-'grel ZU 184b-185a.

———. *Ārya-tārādevī-stotra-muktikāmālā-nāma*, P. 4869, vol. 86, 123.4.6-124.4.8, Rgyud-'grel ZU 178b-181a.

Cintāmaṇirāja. *Sita-tārā-sādhana*, P.4158, vol. 80, 232.1.1-232.2.3, Rgyud-'grel DU 34b-35a.

Cora-bandha, P. 4513, vol. 81, 95.5.5-96.1.4, Rgyud-'grel DU 427b-428a.

Jayasena. *Maṇḍala-vidhi-ratnamarakata*, P. 2234, vol. 52, 129.4.8-130.1.8, Rgyud-'grel PHA 48b-49b.

Ḍombī-heruka. *Ārya-tārā-kurukullā-stotra*, P. 2448, vol. 57, 51.4.3-51.5.1, Rgyud-'grel ZA 123b-124a.

Tillopa, *Ṣaḍdharmôpadeśa*, P. 4630, vol. 82, 34.4.2-35.1.1, Rgyud-'grel PU 134b-135b.

Dīpaṃkaraśrījñāna. *Ārya-tārā-sādhana*, P. 4512, vol. 81, 95.2.1-95.5. 5, Rgyud-'grel DU 426a-427b.

———. *Ārya-tārā-stotra*, P. 4511, vol. 81, 94.5.5-95.2.1, Rgyud-'grel DU 425a-b.

———. *'Jigs-pa brgyad-las skyob-pa*, P. 4510, vol. 81, 94.4.2-94.5.5, Rgyud-'grel DU 424b-425a.

———. *Rje-btsun sgrol-ma'i sgrub-thabs*, P. 4508, vol. 81, 90-4.5-91.5. 7, Rgyud-'grel DU 414b-417b.

Durjayacandra. *Ṣaḍaṅga-nāma-sādhana*, P. 2368, vol. 56, 140.3.8-142.2.4, Rgyud-'grel ZHA 145b-150a.

———. *Suparigraha-nāma-maṇḍalôpāyikā-vidhi*, P. 2369, vol. 56, 142. 2.4-154.1.4, Rgyud-'grel ZHA 150a-179b.

Nāgārjuna. *Tārā-sādhana*, P. 2555, vol. 59, 47.1.1-50.5.7, Rgyud-'grel LA 1a-6b.

———. *Piṇḍīkṛta-sādhana*, P.2662, vol. 61, 267.1.1-273.1.6, Rgyud-'grel GI 1-12a [L. de la Vallée Poussin, ed., *Études et textes tantriques: Pañcakrama*. Louvain: J.-B. Istas, 1896].

———. *Bodhicitta-vivaraṇa*, P. 2665, vol. 61, 285.2.7-287.3.2, Rgyud-'grel GI 42b-48a.

———. *Mahākāruṇikâryatārā-sādhana-sāmānyâbhisamaya-nāma*, P. 2556, vol. 59, 50.5.7-51.2.6, Rgyud-'grel LA 6b-7b.

———. *Muktakena tārā-kalpôdbhava-kurukullā-sādhana*, P. 4384, vol. 81, 25.3.4-26.2.5, Rgyud-'grel DU 251b-253b [= *Sādhanamālā* II.347].

Niṣkalaṅkavajra. *Maṇḍala-vidhi*, P. 2796, vol. 67, 66.2.4-66.4.1, Rgyud-'grel PI 70a-71a.

Padmavajra. *Tantrârthâvatāra-vyākhyāna*, P. 3325, vol. 70, 73.4.7-188.5.8, Rgyud-'grel TSHI 98b-383a.

Dpal-brtsegs and Nam-mkha'i snying-po. *Pho-brang stod-thang ldan-dkar-gyi bka'-dang bstan-bcos 'gyur-ro tshog-gi dkar-chag*, P. 5851, vol. 154, 143.2.5-152.5.8, Mdo-'grel JO 352a-373a.

Buddhaguhya. *Maṇḍala-kriyā-vidhi*, P. 4581, vol. 81, 240.5.5-241.1.3, Rgyud-'grel NU 331b-332a.

———. *Vairocanâbhisambodhivikurvitâdhiṣṭhāna-mahātantra-bhāṣya*, P. 3487, vol. 77, 110.5.8-215.1.3, Rgyud-'grel NGU 76b-337a.

Buddhajñāna. *Mukti-tilaka-nāma*, P. 2722, vol. 65, 24.4.5-27.3.2, Rgyud-'grel TI 56a-63a.

———. *Samantabhadra-nāma-sādhana*, P. 2718, vol. 65, 15.4.3-19.2.5, Rgyud-'grel TI 33b-42b.

Bla-ma'i maṇḍal yi-dam-gyi cho-ga, P. 2972, vol. 68, 7.1.5-7.3.2, Rgyud-'grel PHI 195a-196a.

Bhavabhadra. *Ārya-tārā-maṇḍalâvatāra-kṛtyā-nāma*, P. 4497, vol. 81, 75.4.6-86.3.5, Rgyud-'grel DU 377a-404b.

Maṇḍala-vidhi, P. 4586, vol. 81, 246.3.2-246.4.3, Rgyud-'grel NU 345b-346a.

Mātaṅgipa. *Kurukullā-sādhana*, P. 4712, vol. 82, 192.1.1-192.2.4, Rgyud-'grel PHU 219b-220a.

Ratnarakṣita. *Śrī-saṃvarôdaya-mathātantrarājasya padminī-nāma-pañjikā*, P. 2137, vol. 51, 71.1.1-119.2.6, Rgyud-'grel NA 1a-117b.

Ratnākaragupta. *Maṇḍala-vidhi*, P. 4583, vol. 81, 241.2.7-241.4.3, Rgyud-'grel NU 332b-333b.

Ratnākaraśānti. *Maṇḍala-vidhi-nāma*, P. 5087, vol. 87, 167.1.7-167.4.2, Rgyud-'grel RU 142a-143b.

———. *Maṇḍal-gyi cho-ga*, P. 5088, vol. 87, 167.4.2-169.5.4, Rgyud-'grel RU 143b-149a.

Vāgīśvarakīrti. *'Chi-ba bslu-ba'i bsdus-don*, P. 4806, vol. 86, 19.2.2-19.5.7, Rgyud-'grel ZHU 146a-147b.

———. *'Chi-bslu'i bsdus-don*, P. 4807, vol. 86, 19.5.7-21.2.1, Rgyud-'grel ZHU 147b-150b.

———. *Mṛtyu-vañcanôpadeśa*, P. 4808, vol. 86, 21.2.1-30.4.1, Rgyud-'grel ZHU 151-174a [= P. 2620, vol. 59, 103.5.2-110.3.8, Rgyud-'grel LA 139a-155b].

Vaidyapāda. *Caturaṅga-sādhanôpāyikā-samantabhadrā-nāma-ṭīkā*, P. 2735, vol. 65, 178.3.8-201.3.6, Rgyud-'grel TI 440b-498a.

Śāntarakṣita. *Śrī-vajradhara-saṃgīta-bhagava-stotra-ṭīkā*, P. 2052, vol. 46, 110.3.5-113.2.4, Bstod-tshogs KA 270b-277b.

Śrīphalavajra. *Samantabhadra-sādhana-vṛtti*, P. 2730, vol. 65, 69.3.6-91.5.3, Rgyud-'grel TI 168a-224a.

Sahajalalita. *Samantamukhapraveśaraśmi-vimalôṣṇīṣa-prabhāsa-sarvatathāgata-hṛdayasamayavilokita-nāma-dhāraṇī-vṛtti*, P. 3512, vol. 78, 180.2.7-203.5.8, Rgyud-'grel CHU 285a-344a.

Sūryagupta. *Rje-btsun-ma 'phags-ma sgrol-ma'i sgrub-thabs nyi-shu rtsa-gcig-pa'i las-kyi yan-lag-dang bcas-pa mdor-bsdus-pa zhes bya-ba*, P. 2558, vol. 59, 53.1.1-59.5.4, Rgyud-'grel LA 12a-29a.

———. *Tārādevī-stotra-ekaviṃśatika-sādhana-nāma*, P. 2557, vol. 59, 51.2.6-53.1.1, Rgyud-'grel LA 7a-12b.

———. *Tārā-sādhanôpadeśa-krama*, P. 2559, vol. 59, 59.5.4-60.2.8, Rgyud-'grel LA 29a-30a.

———. *Devītāraikaviṃśati-stotra-viśuddha-cuḍāmaṇi-nāma*, P. 2561, vol. 59, 64.4.7-66.3.5, Rgyud-'grel LA 41a-45b.

———. *Bhagavatī-tārādevy-ekaviṃśati-stotrôpāyika*, P. 2560, vol. 59, 60.2.8-64.4.7, Rgyud-'grel LA 30a-41a.

Noncanonical Texts

[Grub-thob] Karma-gling-pa [gter-ston]. *Rdzogs-pa chen-po'i lo-rgyus mdo-byang po-ti smug-chung-las 'chi-bslu zab-mo* (in other editions called also *Zab-chos zhi-khro dgongs-pa rang-grol-las 'chi-bslu 'jigs-pa rang-grol zhes bya-ba*) [block print, 9 folios, no edition given].

———. *Zab-chos zhi-khro dgongs-pa rang-grol-las 'chi-ltas mtshan-ma rang-grol zhes bya-ba* [block print, 16 folios, no edition given].

Kun-dga' grags-pa rgyal-mtshan. *'Phags-pa bzang-po spyod-pa'i tshig-don-gyi 'grel-pa legs-bshad kun-las btus-pa* [block print, 35 folios, no edition given].

Kun-dga' rdo-rje. *'Tshal-pa kun-dga' rdo-tjes mdzad-pa'i hu-lan deb-ther* [*Deb-ther dmar-po*]. Gangtok, Sikkim: Namgyal Institute of Tibetology, 1961.

Grags-pa rgyal-mtshan. *Kurukulle'i sgrub-thabs*. In *Sa-skya bka'-'bum* NYA, fols. 110a-112b. Bsod-nams rgya-mtsho, ed., *Complete Works of the Great Masters of the Sa Skya Sect of the Tibetan Buddhism*. Tokyo: Toyo Bunko, 1968. IV, 55.2.6-56.2.5.

———. *Rgyud-kyi mngon-par rtogs-pa rin-po-che'i ljon-shing*. In *Sa-skya bka'-'bum* CHA, fols. 1a-139a. Bsod-nams rgya-mtsho, ed., *Complete Works of the Sa Skya Sect*, III, 1.1.1-70.2.1.

———. *Rgyud-sde spyi'i rnam-gzhag-dang rgyud-kyi mngon-par rtogs-pa'i stong-thun sa-bcad*. In *Sa-skya bka'-'bum* CHA, fols. 140a-162a. Bsod-nams rgya-mtsho, ed. *Complete Works of the Sa Skya Sect*. III, 70.2.1-81.3.1.

———. *Sgrol-ma'i chos-skor las-spyi'i sgrub-thabs.* In *Sa-skya bka'-'bum* NYA, fols. 139a-141a. Bsod-nams rgya-mtsho, ed., *Complete Works of the Sa Skya Sect.* IV, 69.1.4-70.1.4.

———. *Bstod-pa'i rnam-bshad gsal-ba'i 'od-zer.* In *Sa-skya bka'-'bum* NYA, fols. 185b-189b. Bsod-nams rgya-mtsho, ed., *Complete Works of the Sa Skya Sect.* IV, 92.2.3-94.2.2.

Gling-ras-pa. *Dpal-ldan bla-ma'i mchod-pa'i cho-ga yon-tan kun-'byung lhan-thabs dbang-chog-dang bcas-pa* (with supplement and initiation ritual by Pad-ma dkar-po) [block print, 33 and 4 folios, He-mi rgod-tshang sgrub-sde edition, reissued by Phun-gling].

'Gos lo-tsā-ba Gzhon-nu-dpal. *Bod-kyi yul-du chos-dang chos-smra-ba ji-ltar byung-ba'i rim-pa deb-ther sngon-po.* George N. Roerich, trans., *The Blue Annals.* Royal Asiatic Society of Bengal Monograph Series, VII. Calcutta, 1949, 1953.

Dge-'dun-grub [Dalai Lama I]. *Sgrol-ma dkar-mo'i tshe-sgrub-kyi sgo-nas tshe-bsring-ba.* In *Rje thams-cad mkhyen-pa dge-'dun grub-pa dpal-bzang-po'i gsung thor-bu sna-tshogs* [block print, 123 folios, Lhasa edition], fol. 29a, in *Collected Works* CA.

———. *Rje-btsun bcom-ldan 'das-ma seng-ldeng nags-kyi sgrol-ma-la bstod-pa mkhas-pa'i gtsug-rgyan zhes bya-ba.* In *Sgrol-ma dkar-sngon-gyi bstod-pa-dang gzungs-bcas* [many editions].

Dge-'dun rgya-mtsho [Dalai Lama II]. *Rje-btsun-ma gsang-sgrub-kyi bstod-pa.* In *Sangs-rgyas-dang byang-sems-kyi bstod-pa* [block print, 34 folios, Lhasa edition], fols. 29a-30a, in *Collected Works* NGA.

Dge-legs dpal-bzang-po [Mkhas-grub-rje]. *Rgyud-sde spyi'i rnam-par gzhag-pa rgyas-par brjod.* Ferdinand Lessing and Alex Wayman, eds. and trans., *Mkhas grub rje's Fundamentals of the Buddhist Tantras.* The Hague: Mouton, 1968.

Rgyal-po bka'i thang-yig. In *Pad-ma bka'-thang sde-lnga* [block print, 281 folios, Sde-dge edition].

Ngag-dbang kun-dga' bstan-'dzin [Khams-sprul rin-po-che III]. *Phyag-chen sngon-'gro'i bsgom-rim gsal-'debs ngag-'don rgyas-spel dngos-gzhi'i rtsa-tho-dang bcas-pa zab-don rgya-mtsho'i lam-tshang* [block print, 25 folios, Dpal phun-tshogs chos-'khor gling edition].

Ngag-dbang blo-bzang [Klong-rdol bla-ma]. *Bstan-srung dam-can rgya-mtsho'i ming-gi rnam-grangs.* In *Collected Works.* Ven. Dalama, ed., *Tibetan Buddhist Studies of Klong-rdol bla-ma Ngag-dbang-blo-bzang.* Laxmanpuri, Mussoorie: privately printed, 1963-1964. II, 362-390.

———. *Nā-ro chos-drug-gi sa-bcad zin-bris.* In *Collected Works.* Ven. Dalama, ed., *Tibetan Buddhist Studies.* I, 119-123.

———. *Gsang-sngags rig-pa 'dzin-pa'i sde-snod-las byung-ba'i ming-gi rnam-grangs.* In *Collected Works.* Ven. Dalama, ed., *Tibetan Buddhist Studies.* I, 48-94.

Ngag-dbang blo-bzang rgya-mtsho [Dalai Lama V]. *Gsangs-can yul-gyi sa-la spyod-pa'i mtho-ris-kyi rgyal-blon gtso-bor brjod-pa'i deb-ther rdzogs-ldan gzhon-nu'i dga'-ston dpyid-kyi rgyal-mo'i glu-dbyangs zhes bya-ba.* Kalsang Lhundup, ed., *The History of Tibet by Fifth Dalai Lama.* Varanasi: privately printed, 1967.

———. *Rje-btsun sgrol-ma-la bstod-cing gsol-ba 'debs-pa'i tshigs-su bcad-pa.* In *Phyogs-bcu bde-gshegs byang-sems slob mi-slob-kyi dge-'dun-dang bcas-pa'i bstod-tshogs dngos-grub rgya-mtsho'i gter-mdzod* [block print, 26 folios, 'Bras-spungs edition], fols. 17b-18b, in *Collected Works* BA.

———. *Rje-btsun seng-ldeng nags sgrol-la brten-pa'i mdos-chog mthong-bas don-sgrub zhes bya-ba* [block print, 18 folios, 'Bras-spungs edition]. In *Collected Works* (Pt. II: "Secret Books") NGA.

———. *Lha-ldan sprul-pa'i gtsug-lag khang-gi dkar-chag shel-dkar me-long zhes bya-ba* [block print, 23 folios, Dga'-ldan edition]. Albert Grünwedel, ed. and trans., *Die Tempel von Lhasa.* Heidelberg: Sitzungsberichte der Heidelberger Akademie der Wissenschaften, 1919.

Ngag-dbang blo-bzang chos-ldan dpal-bzang-po [Lcang-skya II]. *Sgrol-ma nyer-gcig-gi-sgrub-thabs las-tshogs mu-tig phreng-ba zhes bya-ba*, P. 6334, vol. 164, 143.5.2-145.27, in *Collected Works* JA 24a-27b.

Ngag-dbang bzang-po. *'Od-gsal gdams-ngag.* In *Gdams-gnag thor-bu bkod-pa* [no further information].

Ngag-dbang Gsung-rab mthu-thob. *Rje-btsun-ma yid-bzhin 'khor-lo'i sgo-nas tshe-dbang-bskur-tshul bla-ma dam-pa'i man-ngag 'chi-med bdud-rtsi'i chu-rgyun zhes bya-ba* [block print, 23 folios, no edition given (last folio torn)].

Chos-kyi don-grub Dkon-mchog yan-lag [Zhva-dmar-pa V], rev. Rgyal-dbang Theg-mchog rdo-rje [Karma-pa XIV]. *'Phags-ma sgrol-dkar-gyi cho-ga dngos-grub kun-stsol zhes bya-ba* [block print, 24 folios(?), no edition given (last folio missing)].

'Jam-dpal nor-bu Pad-ma dbang-gi rgyal-po. *Rje-btsun 'phags-ma sgrol-ma dkar-mo tshe-sbyin-ma-la bstod-cing gsol-ba 'debs-pa 'chi-bdag gdong-bzlog ces bya-ba* [manuscript (dbu-med), 3 folios].

———. *Rtsa-gsum nor-bu dbang-gi rgyal-po'i sgrub-thabs 'dod-dgu'i char-'bebs khams-gsum dbang-sdud ces bya-ba* [manuscript (dbu-can), 33 folios].

'Jam-dbyangs mkhyen-brtse'i dbang-po. *Rgyud-sde bzhi-dang rjes-su 'brel-ba'i rje-btsun sgrol-ma sgrub-thabs rgyun-khyer snying-por dril-ba* [manuscript (dbu-med), 9 folios].

———. *Dbus-gtsang-gi gnas-rten rags-rim-gyi mtshan-byang mdor-bsdus dad-pa'i sa-bon zhes bya-ba.* Alfonsa Ferrari, ed. and trans., *Mkhyen Brtse's Guide to the Holy Places of Central Tibet.* Rome: Istituto Italiano per il Medio ed Estremo Oriente, 1958.

———. *Yan-lag bdun-pa'i tshigs-su bcad-pa lam-rim-gyi smon-lam-dang bcas-pa phan-bde'i sprin-gyi rol-ma zhes bya-ba* [block print, 11 folios, no edition given].

'Ja'-tshon snying-po [gter-ston]. *Zab-chos nges-don snying-po'i sgo-nas rang-dang gzhan-gyi don mchog-tu sgrub-pa'i lam-rim 'khor-ba'i mun-gzhom kun-bzang thugs-rje'i snang-mdzod ces bya-ba* [block print, 170 folios, no edition given].

'Ju-ba chos-dar. *Chag lo-tsā-ba'i rnam-thar 'ju-ba chos-dar-gyis mdzad-pa ngo-mtshar-can bla-ma'i gsungs dri-ma med-pa bsgrigs-pa zhes bya-ba.* G. Roerich, ed. and trans., *Biography of Dharmasvāmin.* Patna: K. P. Jayaswal Research Institute, 1959.

Tāranātha. *Dam-pa'i chos rin-po-che 'phags-pa'i yul-du ji-ltar dar-ba'i tshul gsal-bar ston-pa dgos-'dod kun-'byung zhes bya-ba.* Anton Schiefner, trans., *Tāranāthas Geschichte des Buddhismus in Indien.* St. Petersburg: Kaiserlichen Akademie der Wissenschaften, 1869.

Bstan-pa'i nyi-ma. *Bskyed-rim-gyi zin-bris cho-ga spyi-'gros-ltar bkod-pa man-ngag kun-btus zhes bya-ba* [stencil, 102 folios, no edition given]

Thub-bstan bshad-grub rgya-mtsho. *Sgrol-ma phyag-'tshal nyer-gcig rgyud-kyi 'grel-chung phan-bde'i gter-bum mchog-sbyin zhes bya-ba* [block print, 12 folios, no edition given].

Thu'u-bkvan Blo-bzang chos-kyi nyi-ma. *Grub-mtha'i thams-cad-kyi khungs-dang 'dod-tshul ston-pa legs-bshad shel-gyi me-long zhes bya-ba.* Varanasi: Chhos je lama, 1963.

Dang-po bgegs-la gtor-ma byin-pa [manuscript (dbu-can), 2 folios, separable insert for Rnying-ma-pa rituals].

'Dus-pa rin-po-che dri-ma med-pa gzi-brjid rab-tu 'bar-ba'i mdo. David Snellgrove, ed. and trans., *The Nine Ways of Bon.* London: Oxford University Press, 1967.

Dharmabhadra. *Sgrol-ma maṇḍal bzhi-pa'i cho-ga mdor-bsdus* [block print, 6 folios, Dngul-chu edition], in *Collected Works* KHA.

———. *Bcom-ldan 'das-ma kurukulle'i khor-lo'i las-tshogs* [block print, 3 folios, Dngul-chu edition] in *Collected Works* CA.

Rnam-rgyal rgyal-mtshan. *Mi-tra brgya-rtsa'i grub-chen nyi-ma sbas-pa'i lugs-kyi sgrol-ma nyi-shu rtsa-gcig-gi mngon-par rtogs-pa* [block print, 16 folios, Yung-dgon (Yung-ho-kung, Peking) edition].

Pad-ma dkar-po. *Chos-'byung bstan-pa'i pad-ma rgyas-pa'i nyin-byed ces bya-ba.* Lokesh Chandra, ed., *Tibetan Chronicle of Padma Dkar-po.* Delhi: International Academy of Indian Culture, 1968.

———. *Rjes-su gnang-ba nyi-shu rtsa-gnyis-kyi chog-chings lo-rgyus zab-rgyas tshang-spros phreng-ba bkod-pa tshogs-gsung rigs-gcig* [manuscript (dbu-can), 25 folios].

———. *Snyan-rgyud yid-bzhin nor-bu'i bskyed-pa'i rim-pa rgyas-pa 'dod-pa'i re-skong zhes bya-ba* [mechanical type, 19 and 33 folios, Phun-gling edition].

———. *Bdud-kyi g.yul-las rab-tu rgyal-bar byed-pa'i dam-can rgya-mtsho'i mchod-sprin* [block print, 34 folios (part of *Sku-gsung-thugs snying-po'i dngos-grub sgrub-pa'i cho-ga bdud-kyi g.yul-las rab-tu rgyal-ba zhes bya-ba*), Phun-gling edition].

Pad-ma bka'i thang-yig. G. Ch. Toussaint, trans., *Le Dict de Padma.* Paris: Léroux, 1933.

Dpal phyag-na rdo-rje 'byung-po 'dul-byed-kyi sgrub-thabs [block print, 10 folios, no edition given].

Dpal gsang-ba 'dus-pa'i bla-brgyud gsol-'debs-dang bdag-bskyed ngag-'don bkra-shis lhun-po rgyud-pa grva-tshang-gi 'don-rgyun. Kalimpong: Bod-yig me-long par-khang, n.d.

'Phags-pa gnam-sa snang-brgyad ces bya-ba theg-pa chen-po'i mdo (rgya nag skad du ā rya pa ra yang rgyad rta) [block print, 19 folios, no edition given].

Bu-ston Rin-chen-grub. *Sgrol-ma btson-'don-gyi cho-ga,* in *Collected Works* JA. Lokesh Chandra, ed., *Collected Works of Bu-ston.* Delhi: International Academy of Indian Culture, 1967, VII, 763-768.

———. *Bde-bar gshegs-pa'i bstan-pa'i gsal-byed chos-kyi 'byung-gnas gsung-rab rin-po-che'i mdzod ces bya-ba,* in *Collected Works* YA [block print, 212 folios, Lhasa edition]. E. Obermiller, trans., *History of Buddhism by Bu-ston.* Heidelberg: Otto Harrassowitz, 1931, 1932.

———. *Tshogs-'khor-dang dpa'-bo'i ston-mo'i cho-ga'i lag-len bde-chen rnam-rol zhes bya-ba,* in *Collected Works* JA. Lokesh Chandra, ed., *Collected Works of Bu-ston.* VII, 769 ff.

Blo-bzang chos-kyi rgyal-mtshan [Paṇ-chen bla-ma I]. *Sgrol-ma g.yul-zlog ji-ltar bya-ba'i cho-ga dgra-las rnam-rgyal zhes bya-ba* [block print, 8 folios, Bkra-shis lhun-po edition], in *Bkra-shis lhun-po'i rgyud-pa grva-tshang-gi rig-sngags 'chang-ba-rnams-kyi 'don-cha'i rim-pa.*

———. *Jo-bo-rje'i lugs-kyi sgrol-ma nyer-gcig-gi sgrub-thabs las-tshogs dngos-grub rnam-gnyis-kyi bang-mdzod zhes bya-ba* [block print, 11 folios, Bkra-shis lhun-po edition], in *Collected Works* GA.

Blo-bzang bstan-pa'i rgyal-mtshan. *Rje-btsun sgrol-ma'i gdung-'bod* [manuscript (dbu-can), 8 folios].

Blo-bzang ye-shes. *Rje-btsun sgrol-ma'i sgo-nas tshogs-mchod 'bul-tshul* [block print, 4 folios, Rva-sgreng edition].

Blon-po bka'i thang-yig. In *Pad-ma bka'-thang sde-lnga* [block print, 281 folios, Sde-dge edition].

Dbyangs-can grub-pa'i rdo-rje. *Rje-btsun-ma yid-bzhin 'khor-lo-la brten-pa'i zhi-ba'i sbyin-sreg mdor-bsdus bya-tshul zag-med bdud-rtsi'i gru-char zhes bya-ba* [block print, 12 folios, Dngul-chu edition].

Smin-grol No-mon-han [Bla-ma Btsan-po]. *'Dzam-gling chen-po'i rgyas-bshad snod-bcud kun-gsal me-long zhes bya-ba.* Turrell V. Wylie, ed. and trans., *The Geography of Tibet According to the 'Dzam-gling-rgyas-bshad.* Rome: Istuto per il Medio ed Estremo Oriente, 1962.

Tsong-kha-pa Blo-bzang grags-pa. *Rgyal-ba khyab-bdag rdo-rje-'chang chen-po'i lam-gyi rim-pa gsang-ba kun-gyi gnad rnam-par phye-ba zhes bya-ba* [*Snags-rim chen-po*], P. 6210, vol. 161, 53.1.1-226.5.8, in *Collected Works* DZA 1a-WA 210a.

———. *Zab-lam nā-ro'i chos-drug-gi sgo-nas 'khrid-pa'i rim-pa yid-ches gsum-ldan,* P.6202, vol. 160, 208.3.3-vol. 161, 13.2.8, in *Collected Works* TSHA 80b-106b.

Gtsang-smyon He-ru-ka. *Rnal-'byor-gyi dbang-phug chen-po rje-btsun mi-la-ras-pa'i rnam-thar thar-pa-dang thams-cad mkhyen-pa'i lam-ston zhes bya-ba.* J. W. De Jong, ed., *Mi la ras pa'i rnam thar.* 'S-Gravenhage: Mouton, 1959.

[Karma] Tshe-dbang kun-khyab. *Yi-dam zhi-ba-dang khro-bo'i tshogs-kyi sgrub-thabs nor-bu'i phreng-ba'i lo-rgyus chos-bshad rab-'byams* [block print, 87 folios, 'Og-min mtshur-mdo'i chos-grva edition].

[Kaḥ-thog] Tshe-dbang nor-bu [Dpa'-bo Don-grub rdo-rje]. *'Phags-ma sgrol-ma-la gsol-gdab-mchod-pa maṇḍal bzhi-par grags-pa'i cho-ga 'dod-don yid-bzhin 'grub-pa'i ljon-shing* [block print, 28 folios, reissue, with added postface by Karma-pa XVI (Rang-byung rig-pa'i rdo-rje), of original Dpal-spungs edition carved at the orders of the Si-tu Bstan-pa'i nyin-byed].

Tshe-g.yang 'gugs-pa'i phrin-las khrigs-su bsdebs-pa tshe-bsod 'dod-dgu'i dpal-ster zhes bya-ba [block print, 15 folios, no edition given].

Ye-shes rgyal-mtshan. *Sgrol-ma maṇḍal bzhi-pa'i cho-ga'i lag-len-dang ngag-gi gnad gsal-bar bkod-pa'i bdud-rtsi'i bum-bzang zhes bya-ba* [block print, 16 folios, Tshe-mchog-gling-edition].

Ye-shes dpal-'byor [Sum-pa mkhan-po]. *'Phags-yul rgya-nag chen-po bod-dang sog-yul-du dam-pa'i chos byung-tshul dpag-bsam ljon-shing zhes bya-ba.* Sarat Chandra Das, ed., *Pag Sam Jon Zang.* Calcutta: Presidency Jail Press, 1908.

Yon-tan rgya-mtsho Blo-gros mtha'-yas ['Jam-mgon Kong-sprul rin-po-che]. *Bka' 'khor-lo bar-pa'i yang-bcud shes-rab snying-po'i mdo-la brten pa'i bdud-zlog bar-chad kun-sel lag-len bltas-chog-tu bkod-pa rnam-thar stobs-bskyed zhes bya-ba* [block print, 21 folios, "Gunaśastra" books, Bum-thang Bkra-shis chos-gling edition].

———. *Dge-ba can-ma yid-bzhin 'khor-lo'i tshe-khrid dpal-ldan mar-me mdzad-kyi lugs gtsang-la ma-'dres-pa bdud-rtsi'i za-ma-tog ces bya-ba* [block print, 20 folios, Dpal-spungs edition].

———. [gter-ston]. *Dgongs-gter sgrol-ma'i zab-tig-las maṇḍal cho-ga tshogs-gnyis snying-po zhes bya-ba* [many editions].

———. *Sgrol-ma'i sprul-pa lce-sbyang sngon-mo'i srung-ba* [block print, 1 folio (bse-ru), Dpal-spungs edition].

———. *Rje-btsun yid-bzhin 'khor-lo'i rgyun-gyi rnal-'byor khyer-bde 'chi-med grub-pa zhes bya-ba* [block print, 8 folios, Rum-dgon chos-sgar edition].

———. *Rje-btsun yid-bzhin 'khor-lo'i rjes-su gnang-ba-dang bsnyen-sgrub-las gsum gsal-bar byed-pa'i yi-ge zla-ba 'dod-'jo zhes bya-ba* [block print, 55 folios, Dpal-spungs edition].

———. *Dpal-mgon 'phags-pa klu-sgrub zhal-snga-nas brgyud-pa'i sgrol-ma g.yul-bzlog bltas-chog-tu bkod-pa bden-'bras myur-ston ces bya-ba* [block print, 20 folios, "Guṇaśastra" books, Bum-thang Bkra-shis chos-gling edition].

Rāga-asya [Karma Chags-med]. *Chags-med ri-chos* [block print, 298 folios, no edition given (first and last folios sewn in cloth binding)].

Rig-'dzin srog-sgrub-las ri-bo bsang-mchod [block print, 4 folios, Khams-sgar Phun-gling edition].

Rigs-bzang-gi mkha'-'gro-ma snang-sa 'od-'bum-gyi rnam-thar [no further information; final folios missing].

Rin-chen rnam-rgyal. *Mkhas-grub mnyam-med dpal-ldan nā-ro-pa'i rnam-par thar-pa dri-med legs-bshad bde-chen 'brug-sgra.* Herbert Guenther, trans., *The Life and Teachings of Nāropa.* Oxford: Clarendon Press, 1963.

———. *Chos-rje thams-cad mkhyen-pa bu-ston lo-tsā-ba'i rnam-par thar-pa snyim-pa'i me-tog ces bya-ba.* D. S. Ruegg, ed. and trans., *The Life of Bu Ston Rin Po Che.* Rome: Istituto Italiano per il Medio ed Estremo Oriente, 1966.

Rin-'byung snar-thang brgya-rtsa rdor-phreng bcas-nas gsungs-pa'i bris-sku mthong-ba don-ldan. Lokesh Chandra, ed., *A New Tibeto-Mongol Pantheon.* Delhi: International Academy of Indian Culture, 1961——, vol. IX.

Rol-pa'i rdo-rje [Lcang-skya I]. *Chu fo p'u-sa sheng hsiang tsan.* Walter Eugene Clark, ed., *Two Lamaistic Pantheons.* New York: Paragon Book Reprint Corp., 1965.

———. *'Phags-pa bzang-po spyod-pa'i smon-lam-gyi rnam-par bshad-pa kun-tu bzang-po'i dgongs-pa gsal-bar byed-pa'i rgyan zhes bya-ba.* Lokesh Chandra, ed. Gangtok, Sikkim: Namgyal Institute of Tibetology, 1963.

La-dvags rgyal-rabs. A. H. Francke, ed. and trans., *Antiquities of Indian Tibet.* Calcutta: Archaeological Survey of India, 1926. Vol. II.

Sangs-rgyas bstan-'dzin. *Thun-mong-gi sngon-'gro'i chos-bshad rin-chen them-skas zhes bya-ba* [block print, 44 folios, O-rgyan Smin-grol-gling edition].

Slob-dpon pad-mas mdzad-pa'i bla-bslu bla-khyer bslu-byed zhes bya-ba [manuscript (dbu-can), 8 folios].

Gsang-bdag dregs-pa 'dul-byed las-tshogs dam-sri'i glud-mdos bya-ba [manuscript (dbu-can), 5 folios].

Gsol-'debs le'u bdun-ma [many editions].

Bsod-nams rgyal-mtshan. *Rgyal-rabs chos-'byung sel-ba'i me-long.* B. I. Kuznetsov, ed. Leiden: E. J. Brill, 1966.

Lha-khab 'Jig-rten blos-btang. *Mtshams sgrub-byed-skabs thun mgo-mjug-tu 'don-rgyu gsol-'debs* [mechanical type, 3 folios, Phun-gling edition).

Lha-'dre bka'-thang. In *Pad-ma bka'-thang sde-lnga* [block print, 281 folios, Sde-dge edition].

A-bu hral-po [Dpal-sprul O-rgyan 'Jigs-med chos-kyi dbang-po]. *Klong-chen snying-gi thig-le-las bskyed-rim lha-khrid 'og-min bgrod-pa'i them-skas* [mechanical type, 43 folios, Phun-gling edition].

Index

(NOTE: *Subentries are arranged under the main headings according to a progression of related ideas.*)

Abhayākaragupta, 120, 122, 123, 124, 126, 159
Abodes of Brahma [tshangs-pa'i gnas]. *See* Immeasurables, four
Abyss of Vast Body [sku-byams-klas], 221, 351
Ach'e lhamo [a-che lha-mo], 56
Agni [me-lha], 212, 261, 266, 268, 269, 270, 271, 273, 274
Agrippa, Cornelius, 90
Akṣobhya [mi-bskyod-pa], 4, 42, 72, 73, 77, 115, 118; pledge of, 406
Akṣobhyavajra [mi-bskyod rdo-rje], 53
Alchemy [bcud-kyis len-pa], 252, 257, 261-262
Alkindi, 89
Alquié, Ferdinand, 87
Amdo [a-mdo] district, 57
Amitābha ['od-dpag-med], 42, 44, 72, 74, 105, 106, 115, 118, 207, 303, 336, 424, 438, 449, 463; pledge of, 406
Amitāyus [tshe-dpag-med], 55, 198, 377, 381, 384, 389, 390, 391, 392, 393, 446
Amoghasiddhi [don-yod grub-pa], 42, 65, 73, 74, 115, 118, 184, 226, 333, 349; pledge of, 406
Amoghavajra, 387, 419
Aṃśuvarman, 5
Anaṅgavajra, 305
Ancient. *See* Nyingma
Anupamarksita, 31, 34
Appearance [snang-ba]: control over, 69, 81, 100; ordinary, 78, 126; of the deity, 69-76, 103, 447-448, 461, 462; at death, 140; as a real thing [dngos-por snang-ba], 137, 140; as the Clear Light ['od-gsal-du snang-ba], 141; and Emptiness [snang-stong], 80, 92, 101, 129, 135, 380. *See also* Vivid appearance; Visualization; Innate Union
Appendix [spel-tshig], 208-210, 211, 216, 217, 231, 243; to bind thieves, 281; for childbirth, 289; to gain victory in disputes, 291; to free from prison, 291; long-life, 231, 395, 412, 440, 452, 463, 464. *See also* Mantra
Apollinaire, Guillaume, 86
Arousing the heart [thugs-rgyud bskul-pa], 64, 67, 129, 207-217, 249; with praises, 211-214; with prayer, 214-217; with the mantra, 207-211, 384. *See also* Offering, ritual of; Function, ritual
Arousing with song [glus-bskul], 113, 124, 125, 127, 128
Arrogant spirits [dregs-pa], 314
Artaud, Antonin, 85
Arunadatta, 367
Arura [a-ru-ra], 261
Ārya tradition ['phags-lugs] of the *Guhyasamāja Tantra*, 117, 119, 136
Āryadeva, 78
Āryaśūra, 76
Asaṅga, 29, 94, 95, 96, 98
Aśvaghoṣa, 28

Atīśa, xiii, 3, 11, 12, 13, 14, 15, 28, 29, 171, 172, 200, 202, 219, 222, 280, 302, 320, 322, 332, 417, 418, 419, 460, 462, 463
Avalokiteśvara [spyan-ras-gzigs], 4, 8, 10, 12, 63, 65, 90, 204, 229, 281, 402, 436, 438
Awakened corpse [ro-langs], 251, 256, 257
Awareness [rnam-shes]: evolution of, 94-99; summoned magically, 100, 310; transfer of, 135; sent to Pure Land, 304, 316. *See also* Effigy; Lingam

Bacon, Francis, 90, 91
Bacot, Jacques, 9
Balakian, Anna, 87
Bardo [bar-do]: *bardo*-awareness, 113; *bardo*-being, 122, 124, 125; syllable of, 113, 127. *See also* Intermediate state; *Gandharva*
Bardo t'ödrö [bar-do thos-grol], 328-329, 367, 368
Bari, Translator of [ba-ri lo-tsā-ba], 13, 387, 417, 418, 419, 462
Barura [ba-ru-ra], 261
Basic downfalls [rtsa-ltung], 405
Basic nature [gnas-lugs], 131, 453. *See also* Process of Perfection
Basic Ones, Three [rtsa-gsum], 38
Basis [rten]: of body [sku-rten], speech [gsung-rten] and mind [thugs-rten], 408, 458; painting or image as, 358; knowledge being installed in, 223-224; as symbolic support [dam-tshig-gi rten], 458
Bathing [khrus-gsol]: the deity, 149, 336-337; an image, 460
Bāuls, 99
Bearer of the Vajra [rdo-rje 'dzin-pa], 124, 126, 127, 186, 349; of the ritual, 113, 114
Becoming [thob-pa]: at death, 140; a real thing [dngos-por thob-pa], 138, 140; the Clear Light ['od-gsal-du thob-pa], 142
Belson, Jordan, 105
Benediction [shis-brjod], 207, 225, 359, 391, 392, 393, 394, 424, 426, 427, 428, 429. *See also* Verses of good fortune
Bergson, Henri, 87
Bhavabhadra, 461
Bhīmadevī, 292
Bhṛkuṭī [khro-gnyer can-ma], 9, 10
Binding of thieves [chom-rkun bcing-ba], 281-282
Black Master of Life [tshe-bdag nag-po]. *See* Yamāntaka
Black Poison-faced [dug-gdong nag-po]. *See* Yamāntaka
Blue She-wolf [lce-sbyang sngon-mo], 292
Body: as magical simulacrum, 94; illusory [sgyu-ma'i sku], 135; knowledge [ye-shes sku], 129, 130; mantra [sngags-kyi sku], 129; of the god [lha'i sku], 132, 133, 267, 453; of Innate Union [zung-'jug-gi sku], 130-131, 133, 141, 380, 454-457; of Transformation [sprul-pa'i sku] of the ritual, 113; maṇḍala in, 72-74, 101, 108. *See also* Subtle deities
Bomdragpa [sbom-brag-pa], 419
Bön [bon], 353, 355, 359; thread-cross used by, 319
Bongpa trüku ['brong-pa sprul-sku], 21-22
Borges, Jorge Luis, 432, 433
Breton, André, 86, 87, 88
Bruno, Giordano, 88, 89
Buddhaguhya, 279
Buddhajñāna, 107, 117, 118
Buddhakapāla [sangs-rgyas thod-pa], 41. *See also* High patron deities
Burnt offering [sbyin-sreg]: as ritual function, 257, 264; to fill in [kha-skong] the ritual service, 264; ritual of, 260, 264-275. *See also* Hearth
Butön [bu-ston], 9, 52
Buttons [theb-kyu], 324. *See also* Torma

Cakrasamvara [bde-mchog, 'khor-lo sdom-pa], 41, 42, 47, 53, 54, 68, 82,

122; Process of Generation, 112-114; Process of Perfection, 130; great initiation, 401; golden initiation, 401. *See also* High patron deities
Calm [zhi-gnas], 28, 29, 454
Campanella, Tommaso, 93
Candragomin, 12, 229, 467
Candrakīrti, 107, 117
Caraka, 366
Caturpīṭha [gdan-bzhi], 41. *See also* High patron deities
Causal deity [rgyu'i lha], 113, 114, 124, 125, 127. *See also* Resultant deity; Heruka
Ceremonial scarf [kha-btags], 194, 460; offered as clothing, 324, 337
Ch'ag, Translator of [chag lo-tsā-ba], 233, 237
Ch'amdo [chab-mdo] district, 22, 239, 341
Chandra, Lokesh, 171
Ch'angbu [chang-bu], 324, 326, 329. *See also* Torma
Ch'emch'og [che-mchog], 42, 44. *See also* High Patron deities
Chenngawa Tsütr'imbar [spyan-snga-ba tshul-khrims-'bar], 418, 419, 467
Chief Disciple Scholar [paṇḍita thu-bo], 417, 465
Chik'or [dkyil-'khor]. *See* Maṇḍala
Ch'im Namk'adrag [mchims nam-mkha'-grags], 172, 203
Chö [gcod]. *See* Cutting off
Ch'öchi jungne [chos-kyi 'byung-gnas]. *See* Tenpe nyinje
Ch'öchi wangch'ug [chos-kyi dbang-phyug, zhva-dmar karma-pa VI], 462
Ch'öchi zangpo [chos-kyi bzang-po], 13
Ch'ödrub [chos-grub], 241
Ch'öje jats'o [chos-rgyal rgya-mtsho], xv, 238-240
Chornam dot'ang [gcor-gnam mdo-thang] village, 241
Ch'umigpa [chu-mig-pa], 172
Churura [skyu-ru-ra], 261
Cintācakra [yid-bzhin 'khor-lo]. *See* Tārā
Cintāmaṇirāja, xiii
Circle of protection [srung-gi 'khor-lo], 105, 264, 431, 464; as magical function, 258; to prevent return of the danger, 357; erection of, 415-416, 456-457; around area of solitary contemplation, 461; at end of contemplative period, 463
Cleansing [bsangs] with the AMṚTA mantra, 143, 180, 380; the gift torma, 218, 219, 220, 221; the dwelling, 180; the excellent house, 350; the maṇḍala, 437; the multitude tormas, 313; the preliminary torma, 267, 415; the chief flask, 411; the disciples, 389, 421; the nectar and pills of life, 385; the offering torma, 385; the life torma, 384. *See also* Purifying; Empowering; Offering; Mantra
Cleansing water [bsangs-chu], 179, 377, 383; as magical device, 258
Clear Light ['od-gsal], 132-135, 137-143, 422, 457; of death ['chi-ba'i 'od-gsal], 139, 140; of the path [lam-gyi 'od-gsal], 141, 143; metaphor [dpe 'od-gsal], 136, 137; actual [don-gyi 'od-gsal], 136, 137, 141, 143; offered up as luminosity [rang-snang], 440; immersion in, 130-131, 142, 453, 454; and Emptiness [gsal-stong], 130, 133, 134, 135, 137, 454. *See also* Innate Union
— appearance as ['od-gsal-du snang-ba], 136, 141; increasing as ['od-gsal-du mched-pa], 137, 142; becoming ['od-gsal-du thob-pa], 137, 142; culmination as ['od-gsal-du nye-bar thob-pa], 137, 142
Conch shell [dung-chos], in the initiation, 409, 411, 413
Connection [rten-'brel], astrological, 461
Consecration [rab-gnas], 129, 233-234, 359, 460
Construction of nonreality [yang-dag

ma-yin-pa'i kun-tu rtog-pa], 91, 92, 95-99
Contemplation [sgom-pa]: training in, 25-27, 36-38; moral basis of, 27-36; magically transmitted, 398, 408; reality of, 81-99; solitary [mtshams], 25-27, 36-38, 245, 458, 459, 461
— states [gnas-skabs] of: beginner [las dang-po-pa], 71; one to whom a little knowledge has fallen [ye-shes cung-zad babs-pa], 71-72; one who has gained a little power in knowledge [ye-shes-la cung-zad dbang-thob-pa], 72-74; one who has gained perfect power in knowledge [ye-shes-la yang-dag-par dbang-thob-pa], 75
Contemplative period [thun], 259, 435; begins at sunrise, 461; contents of, 463; offerings at end of, 463; acts between [thun-mtshams bya-ba], 259, 457, 458, 463
Contemplative union [mnyam-par bzhag-pa], 380, 453, 454; with the Clear Light, 142; even afterward or when doing something else [mnyam-rjes 'dres-pa], 142; authorization to perform, 426
Cotton-clad brothers [ras-pa mched], 26
Creditors [lan-chags], 300, 324, 344, 353, 355; with malice toward our flesh [sha-'khon], 300; with malice toward our substance [rgyu-'khon], 300
Crowley, Aleister, 88
Culmination [nye-bar thob-pa]: as a real thing [dngos-por nye-bar thob-pa], 138, 140; at death, 140; as the Clear Light ['od-gsal-du nye-bar thob-pa], 142
Cutting off [gcod], 47, 282

Dagger, magic [phur-pa]: slaying demons with, 315; rolling between the palms [phur-pa sgril-ba], 45, 353, 355; of life [tshe-phur], 135, 452-453
Ḍāka [mkha'-'gro, dpa'-bo], 45, 74
Ḍākiṇī [mkha'-'gro-ma], 45-47, 74, 82; as keepers of hidden texts, 399; evil, 342; yoginī as, 47
— Vajravārāhī, the Diamond Sow [rdo-rje phag-mo], 46, 401; Vajrayoginī [rdo-rje rnal-byor-ma], 46; Lion-faced [seng-ge gdong-ma], 47, 314-316; Yeshe ts'oje [ye-shes mtsho-rgyal], 47; Nāro k'achöma, [nā-ro mkha'-spyod-ma], 47; Machig labdrön [ma-gcig slab-sgron], 47
Dalai Lama, 14, 59, 395; secret name of, 320
Damchen doje legpa [dam-can rdo-rje legs-pa]. *See* Protectors of the Law
Damema [bdag-med-ma], 81
Damlog [dam-log], 356
Dampa jagar [dam-pa rgya-gar], 171
Dampa sangje [dam-pa sangs-rgyas], 47
Damsi [dam-sri], 298, 299, 354, 356
Daṇḍin, 7
Danger: transferring [gto], 321, 357, 359; blocking the return of [gto-yas-kyi rjes phyi-bcad], 330, 357
Daö zhönnu [zla-'od gzhon-nu]. *See* Gampopa
Darmadra [dar-ma-grags]. *See* Nyen, Translator of
Dasgupta, Shashibhusan, 133
David-Neel, Alexandra, 251
Dawa dragpa [zla-ba grags-pa], 240
Day painting [nyin-thang], 459-460
Death: untimely [dus-min 'chi-ba], 367; Clear Light of ['chi-ba'i 'od-gsal], 139, 140, 141; signs of, 367-375; process of, 139-141; and the Process of Perfection, 139-143
Dege [sde-dge] district, 22, 241
Demigod [lha-min], 373
Denkar [ldan-dkar] palace, 10
Desnos, Robert, 87
Deva, identified with *lha*, 295
Device, magical ['khrul-'khor], 250, 280, 284-291, 413; destructive, 309; thread-cross as, 318

Dharmabhadra, 309
Dharmakīrti, 418, 419
Diamond Magic Dagger [rdo-rje phur-pa], 42, 44-45, 316. *See also* High patron deities
Diamond Prince [rdo-rje gzhon-nu], 44. *See also* High patron deities
Diamond Sow [rdo-rje phag-mo]. *See* Ḍākiṇī
Diamond Terrifier [rdo-rje 'jigs-byed]. *See* Yamāntaka
Diehl, Gustav, 243
Dīpaṃkaraśrījñāna. *See* Atīśa
Doctrines, eight [bka'-brgyad]: five families of supramundane deities ['jig-rten-las 'das-pa'i sde-lnga], 44; Mañjuśrī the deity of body ['jam-dpal sku-lha], 44; Amitābha the deity of speech [pad-ma gsung-lha], 44; Yangdag the deity of mind [yang-dag thugs-lha], 44; Ch'emch og the deity of quality [che-mchog yon-tan lha], 44; P'urpa the deity of function [phur-pa phrin-las lha], 44, 45; three classes of the mundane families ['jig-rten-pa'i rigs-kyi sde-gsum], 44; deities to bring down visitations of the *mamo* [ma-mo rbod-gtong lha], 44; deities of fierce mantras and maledictions [dmod-pa drag-sngags lha], 44; deities of worldly offerings and praise ['jig-rten mchod-bstod lha], 44
Doje ch'öpa [rdo-rje chos-pa], 231
Doje p'urpa [rdo-rje phur-pa], 42, 44-45. *See also* High patron deities
Ḍombi-Heruka, 302
Dragpa ch'oyang [grags-pa mchog-dbyangs], 322
Dragpa jets'en [grags-pa rgyal-mtshan], 13, 14, 172, 249, 251, 252, 253, 254, 275, 279, 284
Dragyab [drag-yab] district, 238, 239; Lord Refuge of [drag-yab skyabs-mgon], 238, 239
Dralha [drag-lha], 294
Dre ['dre], 293
Drenched with defilement [grib-gnon], 242
Drepa [sgre-pa], 387, 395, 418, 419, 466
Drime künden, Legend of [dri-med kun-ldan-gyi gtam-rgyud], 56
Drom, Teacher of ['brom-ston]. *See* Jewe jungne
Drubch'en rinpoch'e [grub-chen rin-po-che], 467
Drug ['brug]. *See* Kajü, Dragon
Drugu [gru-gu] district, xv; Śākyaśrī of, 239
Drugugön [gru-gu-dgon] monastery, 238, 240
Drungyig ch'enmo [drung-yig chen-mo], 297
Dü [bdud], 293, 294, 301, 329, 334, 335, 342, 354, 356, 373, 390
Durgā, 229
Durjayacandra, 115
Durmig [dur-mig]. *See* Year
Düsum ch'enpa [dus-gsum mkhyen-pa, zhva-nag karma-pa I], 419
Dütsi [bdud-rtsi]. *See* Nectar
Dzomo [mdzo-mo]. *See* Yak

Earnest wish [smon-lam], 224, 358
Effigy, 100-104; generation of, 100; as device of destruction, 310; as receptacle for demons, 312. *See also* Lingam; Multitudes
Ego [nga-rgyal], 36, 76-79, 103, 126, 130, 449, 461. *See also* Vivid appearance; Recollection of purity
Ekajaṭā [e-ka-dza-ti]. *See* Glorious Goddess
Ekvall, Robert, 374
Eliade, Mircea, 99
Eliot, T. S., 139
Eluard, Paul, 87
Employment [las-la sbyar-ba]: of the deity, 64, 243, 245, 255-261, 275, 277, 378; of the life torma, 394; of life substances, 383; as a magical function, 251
Empowering [byin-gyis rlab-pa]: the senses [skye-mched byin-rlab], 72, 101, 107; the offerings with OM

ĀḤ HŪṂ, 143, 380; the gift torma, 218, 220, 221; the preliminary torma, 263, 415; the multitude tormas, 313; the offering torma, 341; the life torma, 385; the chief flask, 411. *See also* Cleansing; Purifying; Offering; Mantra

Emptiness [stong-pa-nyid]: in the ritual, 33-36; in the Process of Perfection, 132-135; and appearance [snang-stong], 101, 135, 380; and Great Bliss [bde-stong], 133, 134, 135; and the Clear Light [gsal-stong], 130, 133, 134, 135, 137, 454. *See also* Innate Union

— stages of: Emptiness [stong-pa], 136, 141; More Emptiness [shin-tu stong-pa], 137, 142; Great Emptiness [stong-pa chen-po], 137, 142, 453; Complete Emptiness [thams-cad stong-pa], 137, 142

Erastus, Thomas, 90

Ernst, Max, 24

Evil spirits [gdon], description of, 292-301

Evocation [sgrub-pa]: ritual of, 66-68, 171, 255-261, 267; of the deity, 67, 243, 245; as a ritual function, 250; of the torma, 383; of the nectar and pills, 385; of the heart of the guru [gu-ru thugs-sgrub], 401; initiation [sgrub-dbang], 402. *See also* Offering, ritual of

Excellent house [khang-bzang], 327, 350

Female face [mo-tong], 327, 328, 352

Ficino, Marsilio, 89, 90

Field: of hosts [tshogs-zhing], 27, 30, 185, 199, 378, 440, 441, 442; for offerings [mchod-zhing], 184; of refuge [skyabs-zhing], 378, 437

Fire-god [me-lha]. *See* Agni

Fire poison [me dug], 266

Five Bodies [sku-lnga]. *See* Protectors of the Law

Flask [bum-pa]: working [las-bum], 377, 383, 389, 409, 410, 411, 413, 414, 423, 460; chief [gtso-bum], 409, 411-413, 423; victorious [rnam-rgyal bum-pa, rnam-bum], 411; of life [tshe-bum], 377; symbolic [dam-tshig-gi bum-pa], 413; twenty-five substances of, 289, 290, 409, 411; water [bum-chu] as a magical device, 413

Francke, August, 295

Free of All Terror ['jigs-pa thams-cad-dang bral-ba], 221, 351

Freud, Sigmund, 82, 86, 87, 90

Function [las, las-tshogs]: structure of, 255-261; ambiguity in, 246, 279; and magical attainments, 245-255; specialized, 277-278; authorization to perform, 428; associated with shape and color, 250; use of mantra and visualization in, 231, 250, 278, 279; use of recipes in, 250; use of magical devices in, 250; entrusting to [phrin-las bcol-ba], 274; of Kurukullā, 302

— general, 254, 255, 256, 261; soteriological, 247-249, 255-261, 262; ritual, 208, 251, 255-261, 262-275, 340; magical, 251, 255-261, 275-280, 302, 346

— basic [rtsa-ba'i las]: pacifying [zhi-ba], increasing [rgyas-pa], subjugating [dbang-'dus], destroying [drag-shul, mngon-spyod], 249; subsidiary [yan-lag las], 249-250; visualized as pavilions, 381-382

Gampopa [sgam-po-pa], 15, 39, 395, 399, 418, 419

Gandharva, 116, 124, 125. *See also* *Bardo*-being; Intermediate state

Gau [ga'u], 288

Gedündrub [dge-'dun-grub], 14, 231, 388, 395

Gedün jats'o [dge-'dun rgya-mtsho], 395

Geg [bgegs]. *See* Hindering demons

Gegtor [bgegs-gtor]. *See* Torma, for the hindering demons

Geleg namje [dge-legs rnam-rgyal], xv

Gelug [dge-lugs], xiv, 14, 41, 44, 49, 52, 53, 54, 238, 239, 375, 386; rituals of, 38-54; lineage of, 395; protectors of, 296; initiations of, 402; style of altar, 376-377

Generation: in front [mdun-bskyed], 67, 129, 255-261, 333, 383, 410; in the flask [bum-bskyed], 255-261, 410-415; within an object, 225, 251; of the symbolic being, 108-127; of the substitutes, 349-350; of the hearth, 271; of the life torma, 383-386; of the effigy, 100; of Guhyasamāja, 111; of Cakrasamvara, 112-113; of Tārā, 104-105. *See also* Process of Generation; Self-generation

Gesar [ge-sar], 304; Royal Anecdotes of [gling-rje ge-sar-gyi rgyal-po'i sgrung], 56

Geser [dge-ser], 321

Geshe [dge-bshes], 20

Gesture [phyag-rgya]: stereotyped, 146; mimetic, 146; for the offerings, 146-164; to absorb the knowledge being, 101-102

— asking-to-depart [gshegs-gsol-rgya], 224, 337, 358; assembly [bsdu-ba'i phyag-rgya], 332, 336; diamond-lady-of-the-mind [sems-ma rdo-rje-ma'i phyag-rgya], 179, 415; flying-bird [bya-lding rgya], 218, 220, 221, 263, 313, 341, 385, 411, 415; full-blown-lotus-flower [ut-pal kha-bye-ba'i phyag-rgya], 338; iron-hook [lcags-kyu'i rgya], 263, 415; maṇḍala [maṇḍal-rgya], 168, 192-193, 206; one-pointed-vajra [rdo-rje rtse-gcig-pa'i phyag-rgya], 267; palms joined [thal-mo sbyar], 178, 183, 330, 336, 342, 344, 345; palms-up [lag-zad phyag-rgya], 337; refuge [skyabs-sbyin-gyi phyag-rgya], 268; sword-striking [ral-gri 'debs-pa'i rgya], 415; three diamond circles [rdo-rje 'khor-gsum], 185; torma [gtor-rgya], 220, 221, 341

— for the substitutes: purity of the Dharma realm [chos-dbying rnam-dag phyag-rgya], 346; jeweled-casket [rin-chen sgrom-bu'i phyag-rgya], 348; Swirling Nectar [bdud-rtsi thabs-sbyor phyag-rgya], 348; vast-potency [rgya-chen shugs-ldan phyag-rgya], 349; comet-of-knowledge [ye-shes skar-mda'i phyag-rgya], 349; universal-sovereignty [dbang-sgyur 'khor-lo'i phyag-rgya], 350

Ghosts ['byung-po], 226, 296, 301, 344

Ghouls [grul-bum], 342

Gingkara [ging-ka-ra], 50

Giwam [gi-wam], 284, 291, 308, 309

Glances, four [lta-stangs bzhi], 304-305

Glorious Goddess [dpal-ldan lha-mo], 52, 54; Smoke-eater [dud-gsol-ma], 52, 54; Self-born Lady [rang-'byung-ma], 52, 54; Magic Weapon Army [dmag-zor-ma], 52, 54; Ekajaṭā [e-ka-dza-ti], 49, 52, 54; Firm Vajra [rdo-rje rab-brtan-ma], 52, 54

God of the Great Northern Plain [thang-lha]. *See* Protectors of the Law

Gods and ogres, eight classes of [lha-srin sde-brgyad], 294, 300, 353

Golden libation [gser-skyems], 325, 345, 355

Gonda, Jan, 144

Gongpo ['gong-po], 293, 294, 315, 316, 342, 356

Gönpawa [dgon-pa-ba], 172

Great Bliss [bde-ba chen-po], 127, 422; of the retinue, 113; and Emptiness [bde-stong], 132, 133, 134, 135, 136; in the Process of Perfection, 132-135. *See also* Innate Union

Great Kings, four [rgyal-chen bzhi]; replace owners of the earth, 295; guard solitary contemplation, 461

Great Liberation, ritual of [thar-pa chen-po'i cho-ga], 68

Great Manifestation [phyag-rgya chen-po], 107-108. *See also* Ritual Manifestation

Great Terrors ['jigs-pa chen-po]: eight, 198, 207, 229-230; sixteen, 231
Gross transgressions [sbom-po], 405
Ground, establishing for the initiation [gzhi-bsgrub-pa], 288, 289, 421-422
Grünwedel, Albert, 8
Guardians [srung-ma]: of the teachings [bstan-srung], 298, 314; of hidden texts [gter-srung], 314; of mantras [sngags-srung], 49; oath-bound [dam-can], 47, 298. *See also* Protectors of the Law
Guests [mgron]: four classes of, 165, 174, 217-222; inviting, 184; for the torma offerings, 217; evil spirits: creditors and hindering demons [gdon bgegs lan-chags mgron], 299, 300; tormas for, 324; for the multitudes [tshogs-mgron], 313
Gugü [gu-gul] incense, 263, 283, 416, 461
Guhyasamāja [gsang-'dus], 41, 44, 53, 54, 72, 82; Process of Generation, 111; great initiation, 401; three meditations of, 117-118; four limbs of, 106-108. *See also* High patron deities
Guhyasamāja Tantra, 53, 106-108, 119, 136, 157
Guru [bla-ma]: lineage of, 38-40, 399; offering to, 68; maṇḍala offering to, 167-170; evoking the heart of, 401; yoga with, 27, 441; service for, 232, 441, 464; eight manifestations of [gu-ru mtshan-brgyad], 38

Handbook [lag-len bshad-pa], 245, 433, 458
Hayagrīva [rta-mgrin], 42, 43, 351; generation in the flask, 413-415
Hearth [thab]: shape and color, 250, 265; drawing of, 265-266; corner lines [zur-thig], 266; Brahma lines [tshangs-thig], 265; round line [zlum-thig], 266; *muren* [mu-ran], 265, 268; *k'ach'er* [kha-khyer], 265, 268; marking thread [thig-skud], 265; combustibles [me-tshang] in, 265
Hermes, 93
Heruka [he-ru-ka], 42, 74, 263; of the ritual, 113; causal, 113; resultant, 113
Hevajra [kyai-rdor, dgyes-pa rdo-rje], 41, 53, 54, 83, 124; great initiation, 401; six limbs of, 115. *See also* High patron deities
Hevajra Tantra, 14, 27, 86, 94, 109, 112, 123, 304, 310; mantra of Kurukullā in, 14, 302
Hidden prophecy [gter-lung], 420
Hidden text [gter-ma], 292, 399; revealer of [gter-ston], 171, 399; guardian of [gter-srung], 314; of Tārā, 55
High patron deities [yi-dam], 40-45; general [spyi'i yi-dam], 40-42; particular [bye-brag yi-dam], 40, 42-45; of the Tantras [rgyud-sde yi-dam], 40-42; peaceful [yi-dam zhi-ba], 42; fierce [yi-dam khro-bo], 42-45; initiations of, 401
— Cakrasamvara [bde-mchog, 'khor-lo sdom-pa], 41, 42, 47, 53, 54, 68, 82, 112-114, 122, 130, 401; Guhyasamāja [gsang-'dus], 41, 44, 53, 54, 72, 82, 106-108, 111, 117-118, 401; Hevajra [kyai-rdor, dgyes-pa rdo-rje], 41, 53, 54, 83, 115, 124, 401; Kālacakra [dus-kyi 'khor-lo], 41; Buddhakapāla [sangs-rgyas thod-pa], 41; Caturpīṭha [gdan-bzhi], 41; Mahāmāyā [sgyu-'phrul chen-po], 41
— Hayagrīva [rta-mgrin], 42, 43, 351, 413-415; Yamāntaka [gshin-rje-gshed], 42, 44, 49, 53, 114-115, 124, 314-316; Ch'emch'og [che-mchog], 42, 44; Yangdag [yang-dag], 42, 44; Doje p'urpa, the Diamond Magic Dagger [rdo-rje phur-pa], 42, 44-45, 316; Diamond Prince [rdo-rje gzhon-nu], 44
Hindering demons [bgegs], 184, 199, 207, 217, 258, 263, 265, 269, 300, 344, 352, 356, 424, 426, 427, 428, 430, 437. *See also* Torma, for the

hindering demons; Torma, preliminary
Holmyard, E. J., 93
Holy Beauty [gzugs-mdzes dam-pa], 221, 351
Holy things, three [dam-pa rnam-pa gsum]: thought of enlightenment [sbyor-ba sems-bskyed dam-pa], 29; nonobjectifiable [dngos-gzhi dmigs-med dam-pa], 29; dedication of merit [rjes-su bsngo-ba dam-pa], 29
Hsüan Tsang, 8
Hungry ghosts [yi-dvags], 220, 342. *See also* Mantra, burning-mouth

Immeasurables, four [tshad-med bzhi], 30, 32-33, 125, 179, 276, 331, 379, 443
Increase [mched-pa]: at death, 140; as a real thing [dngos-por mched-pa], 138, 140; as the Clear Light ['od-gsal-du mched-pa], 142
Indrabodhi, 115, 117
Infusion of various grains ['bru-sna blugs-pa], 325. *See also* Golden libation
Initiation [dbang]: types of, 399-403; great [dbang-chen], 401; golden [gser-dbang], 401; as authorization for ritual service, 36-38, 398; as basis of the magical attainments, 363; as guarantor of lineage, 399; as magical function, 257; as empowerment from the deity, 402, 442
— torma [gtor-dbang], 394, 403, 430; evocation [sgrub-dbang], 402; self-entering [bdag-'jug], 402; into life [tshe-dbang], 15, 55, 375-398; explanation of [dbang-bshad], 386-388, 416-420; four [dbang-bzhi], 401, 424. *See also* Permission
Innate Union [zung-du 'jug-pa], 135, 136; body of [zung-'jug-gi sku], 130-131, 133, 141, 380, 454-457; of appearance and Emptiness [snang-stong zung-'jug], 80, 92, 101, 129, 135, 380; of Bliss and Emptiness [bde-stong zung-'jug], 133, 134, 135, 136; of Light and Emptiness [gsal-stong zung-'jug], 130, 131, 133, 134, 135, 137, 454; of understanding and Emptiness [rig-stong zung-'jug], 135
Insight [lhag-mthong], 454
Instructions [man-ngag, gdams-ngag], 400; on the ritual service, 245, 458-467
Intermediate state [bar-do]: between the birth and death of an event [skye-shi bar-do], 138-143; of dream [rmi-lam bar-do], 138; of waking [srid-pa bar-do], 138; of dissolution into Emptiness [stong-par nam thim-pa'i bar-do], 138; of dying ['chi-ka'i bar-do], 138, 139-141; illusory [sgyu-ma'i bar-do], 138. See also *Bardo*; *Gandharva*

Ja, Anecdotes of [bya-sgrung], 56
Ja, Teacher of [rgya-ston], 322
Jaling [rgya-gling], 40
Jampa tendzin tr'inle jats'o pezangpo [byams-pa bstan-'dzin 'phrin-las dpal-bzang-po], 395
Jamyang ch'entse wangpo ['jam-dbyangs mkhyen-brtse'i dbang-po], 6, 427
Jangbu [rgyang-bu]. *See* Tablets
Jangp'ek'ur [ljang-'phad-'khur] household, 57
Jāṅgulī, xiii
Jaspers, Karl, 45
Jepo [rgyal-po]. *See* King demons
Jewe jungne [rgyal-ba'i 'byung-gnas], 11, 12, 322, 387, 418
Jigme ch'öchi wangpo ['jigs-med chos-kyi dbang-po], 109, 110, 171
Jijang [gyi-ljang] district, 320, 321
Jonangpa [jo-nang-pa]. *See* Tāranātha
Jowo rinpoch'e [jo-bo rin-po-che], 6
Juk'ön [rgyu-'khon]. *See* Creditors
Jung, C. G., 89
Jungpo ['byung-po]. *See* Ghosts
Jütö [rgyud-stod] monastery, xiii
Juwa ch'ödar ['ju-ba chos-dar], 233

K'ach'er [kha-khyer]. *See* Hearth
K'achöpa [mkha'-spyod-pa, zhva-dmar karma-pa II], 172
Kadam [bka'-gdams], 14, 387
Kajegön [bka'-brgyad-dgon] monastery, 238, 239, 240
Kajü [bka'-brgyud], 12, 15, 41, 47, 55, 386; rituals of, 38-54; teachings on Clear Light, 137-143; lineage of White Tārā, 419, 430; initiations of, 402; style of altar, 377; prayer service of, 441
— Dragon [ʽbrug], 15, 27, 38, 40, 46, 47, 48, 49, 50, 51, 52, 53, 54, 238; great initiations, 401
— Karma [karma], 44, 49, 52, 54; lineage of Four Maṇḍala Offering, 172; lineage of White Tārā, 418; torma initiation, 430; great initiations, 401
Kajü drugje [bka-brgyud 'brug-rgyal], xv
Kajur [bka'-'gyur], xiv, 13, 44
Kālacakra [dus-kyi 'khor-lo], 41. *See also* High patron deities
K'am [khams], 16, 51, 63, 232, 238, 239
K'amgargön [khams-sgar-dgon] monastery, 16-21, 38, 44, 55
Kampa [kam-pa], 172
K'amtrü rinpoch'e [khams-sprul rin-po-che]: Ch'öchi nyima [chos-kyi nyi-ma, khams-sprul rin-po-che IV], 16, 19; Dönjü nyi-ma [don-brgyud nyi-ma, khams-sprul rin-po-che VIII], xv, 18, 19, 22, 40, 199, 232, 241, 323
Kamts'ang [kaṃ-tshang]. *See* Kajü, Karma
Karma Bakṣi [karma bakṣi, zhva-nag karma-pa II], 418, 419
Karmapa [karma-pa], 15, 425
Kat'og [kaḥ-thog]. *See* Nyingma
K'edrubje Geleg pezangpo [mkhas-grub-rje dge-legs dpal-bzang-po], 410
K'enpo [mkhan-po], 20
Kierkegaard, Soren, 92
Legpe sherab [legs-pa'i shes-rab], 322
Killing [bsad-pa], 304-305
King demons [rgyal-po], 294, 296-297, 373
Knowledge being [ye-shes sems-dpa'], 101, 103, 108, 115, 269, 273, 310, 332, 338, 379, 422; seated in sky, 336; asked to depart, 130, 333, 358; gathered in and absorbed, 129, 183, 223; sealed with a vajra cross, 396, 422, 423; installed in an image, 223-224, 359; conveyed to the hearth, 270-271; mantras and gestures of, 101-102. *See also* Symbolic being
Knowledge body [ye-shes sku], 129, 130. *See also* Mantra body
Kokila, 261
Kongtrü rinpoch'e [kong-sprul rin-po-che], 104, 243, 258, 261, 264, 278, 281, 284, 287, 290, 292, 308, 320, 321, 322, 407
K'ön konch'og jepo ['khon dkon-mchog rgyal-po], 13
Kulo [ku-lo], 320
Kunga doje [kun-dga' rdo-rje], 9, 293
Künzang dech'en [kun-bzang bde-chen], 57-58
Kurukullā [ku-ru-ku-lle], 14, 250, 264, 279, 301-310, 314; described, 302; mantra, 14, 302; functions, 302; magical devices, 309

Ladle: for liquids [dgang-gzar] and solids [blug-gzar], 266, 267, 269
Lady of the Goring Yak [g.yag-brdung-ma], 238-240
Lady of the Turquoise Lamp [g.yu-sgron-ma]. *See* Protectors of the Law
Lady who Accepts the Ceremonial Scarf [dar-len-ma], 6
Lagang [gla-sgang], 283
Laing, R. D., 83, 85
Lakṣmī, nun, 204
Lalou, M., 10
Lama [bla-ma]. *See* Guru
Langdarma [glang-dar-ma], 11, 304
Lechi doje [las-kyi rdo-rje], 395

Lenagpa [sle-nag-pa], 387, 418, 419
Lench'ag [lan-chags]. *See* Creditors
Lessing, Ferdinand, xi, 319, 327
Lévi, Eliphas, 88
Lha [lha], 293, 294, 295, 301, 342, 416
Lhagsam rabkar [lhag-bsam rab-dkar], 70
Lhak'ab Jigten lötang [lha-khab 'jig-rten blos-btang], 39
Lhat'og [lha-thog] district, 16, 18, 22, 241
Liberating [bsgral-ba]: as killing, 304, 305; proper objects of, 305; and offering as food, 316, 317. *See also* Lingam; Multitudes
Life: value of, 363-366; as magical attainment, 363, 432; magically transmitted, 375, 377-378, 398; absorbed from the life torma, 394; healing the degeneration of, 391-392; increasing with verses of good fortune, 397
— decay of [tshe-nyams], 367; power [klung-rta], 355; object [bla-gnas], 355; flask of [tshe-bum], 377; three deities of [tshe-lha rnam-gsum], 55; initiation into [tshe-dbang], 15, 55, 375-398; teaching [tshe-khrid], 378, 433, 441, 461, 463
— substances [tshe-rdzas], 375, 377, 383, 385, 310; pills of life [tshe-ril], 377, 385, 396; nectar of life [tshe'i bdud-rtsi], 377, 385, 396; life torma [tshe-gtor], 390-396; beer of life [tshe-chang], 377; silken arrow [mda'-dar], 377
Ligadur [li-ga-dur], 283
Limbs, six [yan-lag drug], 115-117, 118. *See also* Hevajra; Process of Generation
Limbs of approach and evocation, four [bsnyen-sgrub yan-lag bzhi], 106-108, 118, 445-446; approach [bsnyen-pa], 107, 445; near evocation [nye-bar sgrub-pa], 107, 446; evocation [sgrub-pa], 108, 446; great evocation [sgrub-pa chen-po], 109, 446. *See also* Guhyasamāja; Process of Generation
Limits [mtshams], 26; marked by stones, 461; guardians of, 461. *See also* Contemplation, solitary
Lineage [brgyud]: five types of [brgyud-tshul lnga], 399; thought [rgyal-ba dgongs-brgyud], 399; sign [rig-'dzin brda-brgyud], 399; ear-whispered [gang-zag snyan-brgyud], 399; entrusted [mkha'-'gro gtad-rgya'i brgyud], 399; initiation [dbang-lung man-ngag brgyud], 399
Lingam [ling-gam], 310-312, 314; in the iron house [lcags-khang], 315; demons cast down into form [gzugs-la bab] in, 315; demons summoned and made to enter [dgug-gzhug], 314; liberated and offered as food [bsgral-bstabs], 316, 317; corpse [ling-ro] offered up, 316, 317. *See also* Multitudes
Lion-faced [seng-ge gdong-ma]. *See* Ḍākiṇī
Loden sherab [blo-ldan shes-rab]. *See* Ngog, Translator of
Lodrö rabje [blo-gros rab-rgyal], 241
Lodrö t'aye [blo-gros mtha'-yas]. *See* Kongtrü rinpoch'e
Longdö lama [klong-rdol bla-ma], 38, 70, 244, 245, 246, 283, 290, 294, 305, 405, 406
Long-life Sisters, Five [tshe-ring mched-lnga]. *See* Protectors of the Law
Lord [mgon-po], 47-50, 52; room of [mgon-khang], 47; lama of [mgon-po bla-ma], 47; four-handed [mgon-po phyag-bzhi-pa], 48-49, 401; black-cloaked [mgon-po ber-nag-can], 49; of he tent [gur-gyi mgon-po], 49; hastening six-handed [myur-mdzad ye-shes mgon-po phyag-drug-pa], 49; four-headed [mgon-po zhal-bzhi-pa], 49. *See also* Protectors of the Law
— of Knowledge [ye-shes mgon-po]: Process of Generation, 111; great initiation, 401; golden initiation, 401

Lord of the Cemetery [dur-khrod bdag-po]. *See* Protectors of the Law
Lord of Death [gshin-rje], 369, 370, 390
Lord Ninth [rje dgu-pa]. *See* Wang-ch'ug doje
Lords of the soil [gzhi-bdag], 217, 220, 221, 294, 301, 324, 355; clear the road for the thread-cross, 345. *See also* Torma, white; Torma, *chog-dog*; Torma, for the lords of the soil
Lozang ch'öchi jets'en [blo-bzang chos-kyi rgyal-mtshan], 319
Lozang ch'öchi nyima [blo-bzang chos-kyi nyi-ma], 137
Lozang dragpa [blo-bzang grags-pa]. *See* Tsongk'apa
Lozang tenpe jets'en [blo-bzang bstan-pa'i rgyal-mtshan], 60
Lu [klu], 293, 294, 295-296, 301, 329, 335, 342, 373, 416
Lulle, Raymond, 88
Lunglag [lung-lag] fort, 387
Lungten togpa [lung-bstan rtogs-pa], 241
Lünpawa [lun-pa-ba], 172
Lutsen [klu-btsan], 329

Mach'en pomra [rma-chen spom-ra], 297, 298
Machig labdrön [ma-gcig slab-sgron]. *See* Ḍākiṇī
MacLeish, Archibald, 366
Magic: defined, 92-94; and reality, 85-86; in society, 23; Renaissance, 88-91; correspondences, 108-127
Magical attainments [dngos-grub], 245-255; eight great, 246, 252; general [spyi] and particular [bye-brag], 251; ordinary [thun-mong], 249-255; extraordinary [thun-mong ma-yin], 247-249; and functions, 245-255; long life as, 363, 432
Magic Weapon Army [dmag-zor-ma]. *See* Glorious Goddess
Mahākāla [nag-po chen-po]. *See* Lord
Mahāmāya [sgyu-'phrul chen-po], 41. *See also* High patron deities
Maitreya, 29, 73, 94, 98, 197
Male face [pho-tong], 327, 328, 352
Malinowsky, Branislaw, 144
Mamo [ma-mo], 44, 294, 342, 373, 390
Maṇḍala [dkyil-'khor]; Garbhakośa, 10; of residence and residents [rten-dang rten-pa'i dkyil-'khor], 72-75, 77, 168; radiation from the womb of the Mother, 114; in the body, 72-74, 101, 108; chief of [gtso-bo], 113; highest king of [dkyil-'khor rgyal-mchog], 117-118, 125, 127
— [maṇḍal] offering: to the guru, 167-170; to Tārā, 205, 215, 216; as thanksgiving [gtang-rag], 222-223, 398, 431; as fee [yon], 386, 410, 420; as a preliminary practice, 27, 437-441; at the end of the contemplative period, 463; visualization of, 169, 192-193, 437-441; piles of grain [tshom-bu] poured out, 168-169, 174, 206, 440; four-tiered tray for, 168; metal base used on altar, 168, 324, 408
— Four, Offering of [maṇḍal bzhi-chog], 55, 63, 170-226; outline of, 175-177; lineage of, 171-173; time of performance, 173; as a ritual of offering, 171, 259-260; as a ritual function, 257, 264; requires prior ritual service, 173
Mañjughoṣa ['jam-dbyangs], 29
Mañjuśrī ['jam-dpal], 44, 53, 73; as Slayer of Death, 315, 316
Mañjuvajra ['jam-pa'i rdo-rje], 53
Mantra [gzungs, sngags]: protective, 231; in folklore, 233, 236; praise used as, 145; as simulacrum of divine power, 94, 243; as instrument, 243; tasting the nectar of, 115; particles, 145; seeds [sa-bon], 145; as injunctions, 144-145, 186, 193; as formulas, 145; authorization to recite, 424; changing according to function, 231, 278
— thread [gzungs-thag], 411, 412, 413; vajra [gzungs rdo-rje], 409, 411, 413; guardian of [sngags-srung], 49

— visualization of, 208, 450, 462; recitation of, 36-37, 208-211, 280, 381, 450-452, 464; faults of recitation, 245, 451; requisite number of recitations, 210-211, 244, 467; verbal recitation [ngag-bzlas], 451, 462; settling recitation ['gog-bzlas], 450-451, 462; diamond recitation [rdo-rje bzlas-pa], 451, 462, 464; recitation with radiation and absorption of light [spro-bsdu-dang bcas-pa'i ngag-bzlas], 208, 381-383, 451, 462, 463-464; tasting the nectar of [bdud-rtsi myong-ba], 115

— contemplation of [gsang-sngags sgom-pa], 37, 38, 67, 208, 242-245, 255-261, 267, 277, 381, 433; effectuation of [gsang-sngags sgrub-pa], 37, 67, 207-211, 242, 245, 251, 255-261, 338, 384, 410; application of [gsang-sngags las-sbyor], 251, 242-245, 251, 255-261, 256, 275, 277, 280-283, 410-411

— 10-syllable, of Tārā, 211, 216, 217, 231, 243, 273, 289, 291, 308, 338, 391, 392, 393, 395, 396, 397, 412, 435, 440, 452, 456, 457, 460, 462, 463, 464; 100-syllable, of Vajrasattva, 144, 194, 223, 358, 385, 413, 435, 452, 464; heart of conditioned coproduction [rten-'brel snying-po], 146, 194, 223, 270, 286, 310, 381, 452, 460, 462, 464; burning-mouth [kha-'bar-ma'i sngags], 220, 221, 351; A-KĀRO, 146, 220, 221, 341, 343, 344, 345; ŚŪNYATĀ, 33-36, 104, 111, 112, 181, 276, 333, 443-44; AMṚTA, 143, 180, 218-221, 267, 313, 350, 380, 384, 385, 389, 411, 415, 421, 437; SVABHĀVA, 143, 180, 218-221, 267, 313, 350, 380, 384, 385, 389, 411, 415, 421, 437; OṂ ĀḤ HŪṂ, 218, 220, 221, 263, 313, 431, 385, 411, 415; JAḤ HŪṂ BAṂ HOḤ, 101-102, 105, 111, 112, 181, 276, 333, 444; of Hayagrīva, 414; of Kurukullā, 14, 302, 307, 310; fierce [drag-sngags], 185, 258, 263, 355, 356; for the offerings, 143, 144-146, 148; for the substitutes, 346-350. *See also* Appendix; Offering; Gesture

Mantra body [sngags-kyi sku], 129. *See also* Knowledge body

Manu [ma-nu], 289

Many Jewels [rin-chen-mang], 221, 351

Māra [bdud], 184, 196, 212, 303, 304, 336, 384, 414, 415, 420, 429, 431.

Maraini, Fosco, 48

Mark'am [dmar-khams] district, 8

Marpa of Lhodrag [lho-brag mar-pa], 12, 27, 81-82, 399

Masang [ma-sangs] Brothers, 293, 294

Meditations, three [ting-nge-'dzin gsum], 117-118; first preparations [dang-po'i sbyor-ba] 117, 118; highest king of the maṇḍala (dkyil-'khor rgyal-mchog], 117, 118, 125, 127; highest king of the ritual [las-kyi rgyal-mchog], 117, 118. *See also* Guhyasamāja; Process of Generation

Men [sman], 294, 301

Meyö [me-yol] stone, 266

Mila repa [mi-la ras-pa], 13, 27, 81-82, 399

Minyag [mi-nyag] language, 8

Miraculous image, 236-240, 242, 288. *See also* Thunderstone

Miraculous Manifestation ['phrul-snang] temple, 5

Misleading demons [log-'dren], 342

Monastery [dgon-pa]: described, 15-21; as service group, 23, 68; rituals of, 21-23, 38-54; roles available to residents, 23-25

— temple [lha-khang], 17; assembly hall [tshogs-khang], 17; room of the Lord [mgon-khang], 47; college [bshad-grva], 20; hermitage [sgrub-grva], 26; nunnery [a-ni dgon-pa], 375

— offices: altar server [mchod-bshams], 19; disciplinarian [chos-khrims], 19, 25; cook [ma-chen], 19; head monk [dbu-mdzad], 19, 25;

lama of the Lord [mgon-po bla-ma], 47; professor [mkhan-po], 20; teaching assistant [skyor-dpon], 20; storekeeper [gnyer-pa], 18-19; treasurer [phyag-mdzod], 240; Diamond Master [rdo-rje slob-dpon], 180
Monastic college [bshad-grva], curriculum of: ecclesiastical law ['dul-ba], 20; natural philosophy [mdzod], 20; logic and psychology [tshad-ma, sems-tsam], 20; metaphysics [dbu-ma], 20; wisdom literature [sher-phyin], 20
Monkey Alö, Anecdotes of [spre'u 'a-lod sgrung], 56
Mönpa [mon-pa], 320
Motong [mo-tong]. *See* Female face
Mu [dmu], 293, 294
Multitudes [tshogs], 312-318; circle of [tshogs-'khor], 312; upper [tshogs dang-po], 313; middle [tshogs bar-pa], 313; lower [tshogs tha-ma], 314; guests for [tshogs-mgron], 313; remainder [lhag-ma] of, 317; contract [chad-mdo bsgrags-pa] of, 317. *See also* Effigy; Lingam
Muren [mu-ran]. *See* Hearth
Music [rol-mo]: peaceful [zhi-rol], 181, 183, 191, 202, 203, 333, 336, 337; fierce [drag-rol], 343, 356, 416; gentle ['jam-rol], 422; inviting [spyan-'dren rol-mo], 351; three beats [gsum-brdungs], 341, 353, 355; training in, 24

Nachi rinch'en [nags-kyi rin-chen], 417
Nāgārjuna, xiii, 29, 35, 44, 80, 91, 93, 117, 136, 246, 254, 255, 287, 319, 320, 322, 333, 444
Nāgas, identified with *lu*, 295, 296
Nālandā, 8
Nangch'en [nang-chen] district, 22
Nangsa öbum [snang-sa 'od-'bum], 56-59
Nāro k'achöma [nā-ro mkha'-spyod-ma]. *See* Ḍakīṇī
Nāropa, 12, 170; six yogas of [nā-ro chos-drug], 136, 256, 257, 262, 452
Nart'ang [snar-thang] monastery, 203; hundred rites of, 172; Four Maṇḍala ritual of, 172
Natural flow [rang-bab], 131, 454. *See also* Process of Perfection
Natural state [rang-lugs], 454. *See also* Process of Perfection
Nebesky-Wojkowitz, René de, xi, 54, 165, 294, 297, 299, 303, 319, 327, 328
Nectar [bdud-rtsi], 283, 284, 288; as magical recipe, 283-284; of life [tshe'i bdud-rtsi], 377, 385, 396; taking vows with, 404; tasting with the mantra, 115; offering of the five, 158-159, 165
Nejorpa [rnal-'byor-pa], 419
Neuzurpa [sne'u-zur-pa], 322
Ngari [mnga'-ris] district, 11, 57
Ngarmi [ngar-mi]. *See* Portrait
Ngawang lozang [ngag-dbang blo-bzang]. *See* Longdö lama
Ngawang zangpo [ngag-dbang bzang-po], 137, 138, 141
Ngayam [nga-yam], 294
Ngog, Translator of [rngog lo-tsā-ba], 27, 417, 418
Nöjin [gnod-sbyin], 252, 253, 293, 294, 342, 416
No-na Hutukhtu, 232, 233
Nonobjectifiable [dmigs-med], 131, 357, 453. *See also* Emptiness; Holy things
Norma rowa [nor-ma ro-ba] village, 241
Norzang jats'o [nor-bzang rgya-mtsho], 395
Notes [mchan-bu] to ritual text, 177
Nyangtö jetse [myang-stod rgyal-rtse] district, 57
Nyangts'a sedrön [myang-tsha gsal-sgron], 57-58
Nyemozhu [snye-mo-gzhu] fort, 387
Nyen [gnyan], 294, 295, 329, 342
Nyen, Translator of [gnyan lo-tsā-ba], 13, 417
Nyeshing [nye-shing], 261

Nyet'ang [snye-thang] monastery, 11
Nyima dzepa [ṇyi-ma mdzad-pa], 318
Nyingma [rnying-ma], xiii, 14, 42, 44, 49, 51, 53, 54, 238, 239, 386; rituals of, 38-54; initiations of, 401; lineage of Four Maṇḍalas in, 171; Kat'og [kaḥ-thog] branch of, 171
Nyugrumpa [snyug-rum-pa], 419

Offering [mchod-pa]: ritual of, 66-68, 171, 175-177, 189-194, 202-203, 250, 257, 266, 267; as a ritual function, 250; to the gurus [bla-ma mchod-pa], 68; to the protectors, 22, 47, 68, 165
— standard pattern of, 149; as goddesses, 143, 148; mantras for, 143, 144-146, 148; gestures for, 146-164; filling in [mchod-bskang] of, 217-223; at end of the contemplative period, 464. *See also* Cleansing; Purifying; Empowering
— two waters [chu-gnyis], 148, 149, 174, 377, 409; five gifts [nyer-spyod lnga], 148, 149, 174, 269, 271, 274, 309, 333, 377, 409; outer [phyi-mchod], 148-157, 324; inner [nang-mchod], 157-159; secret [gsang-mchod], 159-164; specific [bye-brag], 165; general [spyi], 165; supreme [bla-na-med], 165; five fleshes [sha-lnga], 158-159; five nectars [bdud-rtsi lnga], 158-159, 165; five sense gratifications ['dod-pa'i yon-tan lnga], 157-158; seven precious gems of sovereignty [rgyal-srid-bdun], 151-154; eight signs of good fortune [bkra-shis brtags-brgyad], 154-157; space-vast treasury [nam-mkha'i mdzod], 154; medicine and blood [sman-rak], 165-167; Great Bliss [bde-chen], 165; Truth [de-kho-na-nyid], 164-165; flowers [me-tog], 193-194, 206-207; luminosity [rang-snang], 440; lotus seat, 149-150; clothing, 324, 337. *See also* Torma; Maṇḍala offering
Office, sevenfold [yan-lag bdun-pa], 30-32, 188, 203-204, 276, 341, 342, 358, 420, 439, 441, 460
Ogres [srin-po], 249, 293, 294, 300, 353, 416
Ojenpa [o-rgyan-pa], 419
Owners of the earth [sa-bdag], 294, 295, 301, 342

P'acho [pha-co], 320-321
Padmasambhava, 38, 47, 165, 171, 296, 298, 319, 399
P'amo drupa Doje jepo [phag-mo gru-pa rdo-rje rgyal-po], 395
Paolini, Fabio, 90
Parṇaśabarī, xiii
Parvatī, 229
Path [lam]: of the bodhisattva, 119-120; enacted in ritual, 30; of preparation [sbyor-lam], 122; of accumulation [tshogs-lam], 121, 122; of vision [mthong-lam], 122, 126; of development [bsgom-lam], 122, 126; beyond learning [mi-slob-pa'i lam], 126
P'awang k'awa [pha-wang kha-ba], 239
Pedendrö [dpal-ldan-gros], 172
Pehar [pe-har]. *See* Protectors of the Law
Peji doje [dpal-gyi rdo-rje], 304
Pema karpo [pad-ma dkar-po], 8, 73, 154, 159, 304
Pench'en lama [paṇ-chen bla-ma], 395
P'enyü ['phan-yul] district, 321
Pepung [dpal-spungs] monastery, 322
Pe p'ünts'og ch'ök'or ling [dpal phun-tshogs chos-'khor gling] monastery, 16
Permission [rjes-gnang], 375, 402, 407-431; as preparation for ritual service, 432; of body, 423; of speech, 424; of mind, 426; of qualities, 427; of function, 428-430; of emblem, 409, 429; of ornaments, 409, 427. *See also* Initiation
Personal gods ['go-lha], 373
Pico della Mirandola, 89, 90
Piling [pi-ling], 261

Pills, magic [ril-bu], 283, 284; around torma, 324; taking vows with, 404; of life [tshe'i ril-bu], 377, 385, 396; magical attainment of, 252-253

Pledges [dam-tshig], 403-407; individual to the five families [rigs-lnga so-so'i dam-tshig], 406; of Tārā, 407. *See also* Vows

Polluters [srul-po], 342

Portrait [ngar-mi], 325, 327, 330

P'otong [pho-tong]. *See* Male face

Pott, P. H., 288

Pound, Ezra, 69

Praises [bstod-pa]: as protection, 231-233; in folklore, 240-242; used as mantra, 145; arousing the heart with, 211-214

Prayers [gsol-'debs, gsol-kha]: to the protectors, 22; to the Buddhas, 194; to Tārā, 214-217, 242, 358; arousing the heart with, 214-217

Precious guru [gu-ru rin-po-che]. *See* Padmasambhava

Preliminary practices [sngon-'gro], 26-27, 258, 433, 434-442, 461

— ordinary [thun-mong-gi sngon-'gro]: the difficulty of attaining human birth [dal-'byor rnyed-dka'], 26; death and impermanence ['chi-ba mi-rtag], 26; the cause-effect pattern of karma [las rgyu-'bras], 26; the horrors of this world ['khor-ba'i nyes-dmigs], 26

— extraordinary [thun-mong ma-yin-gyi sngon-'gro]: visualization and recitation of Vajrasattva [rdor-sems bsgom-bzlas], 27, 434-436; going for refuge and awakening the thought of enlightenment [skyabs-sems], 26-27, 436-437; offering the maṇḍala [maṇḍal-'bul], 27, 437-441; yoga with the gurus [bla-ma'i rnal-'byor], 27, 441-442

Process of Generation [bskyed-rim], 66-67, 77, 100, 127, 132, 181-184, 271, 277, 389, 400, 410, 421, 445; as magical process, 110, 331; as simulacrum for Process of Perfection, 127-129, 131-132; defined, 103-104; four steps of, 104-106; four special properties of, 104; cleansing, perfecting and ripening [sbyang-rdzogs-smin] by, 109-110; as purifier [sbyang-byed], 126, 128; birth death and *bardo* as things to be purified [sbyang-gzhi] by, 104, 109-110, 119, 125, 126, 128; of Tārā, 104-105; of Cakrasamvara, 112-114; of Guhyasamāja, 106-108, 111, 117-118; of Hevajra, 115; of Yamāntaka, 114-115

— three rites of diamond [rdo-rje chog-gsum], 106; four limbs [yan-lag bzhi], 106-108; six limbs [yan-lag drug], 115; four realizations [mngon-byang bzhi], 109-110; five realizations [mngon-byang lnga], 111-112, 113, 119, 124, 125, 127, 128; four yogas [rnal-'byor bzhi], 114-115; three meditatoins [ting-nge-'dzin gsum], 117-118

Process of Perfection [rdzogs-rim], 127-143, 223, 443, 452-454; contemplative experiences in, 135; as soteriological function, 256, 262; as magical process, 133; in the ritual service, 259; in the six yogas of Nāropa, 136; and death, 139-143; and the Clear Light, 132-135, 137-143; and Great Bliss, 132; illusory body, 135; mantra body, 129; knowledge body, 129; authorization to perform, 427; of Tārā, 452-454; of Cakrasamvara, 130; with signs [mtshan-bcas], 132-133, 452-453, 462; signless [mtshan-med], 132, 453-454

— piercing the vital centers [gnad-du bsnun-pa], 132, 135; channels, winds and drop [rtsa rlung thig-le], 132, 141, 428; gathering in and arising [bsdu-ldang], 130, 132, 267, 453, 463; arising in the body of Innate Union [zung-'jug-gi skur ldang-ba], 130-131, 132, 141, 380, 454-457; transference of awareness ['pho-ba],

135; mystic heat [gtum-mo], 135; planting the magic dagger of life in the heart [snying-gar tshe-phur gdab-pa], 135, 452-453, 463, 464; four joys [dga'-bzhi], 132, 135, 136
Protections [srung-ba]: knotted [srung-mdud], 288; thread [srung-skud], 284; circle [srung-'khor], 284; carried on the person [gdags-'khor], 284; printed, 287, 288; against weapons, 288; against slander, 284, 285; at pregnancy and birth, 289; of averting, 280, 332; of pacifying, 280; dangers of, 290-291. *See also* Device, magical
Protectors of the Law [chos-skyong], 47-52; Ekajaṭā [e-ka-dza-ti], 49; Za [gza'], 49; Damchen Doje legpa [dam-can rdo-rje legs-pa], 49-50; Five Bodies [sku-lnga], 50; Pehar [pe-har], 50; Long-life Sisters, five [tshe-ring mched-lnga], 50; Lady of the Turquoise Lamp [g.yu-sgron-ma], 50; God of the Great Northern Plain [thang-lha], 50; Father-Mother Lords of the Cemêtery [dur-bdag yab-yum], 50. *See also* Glorious Goddess; Lord
Pure Sound [nā-da], 126, 130, 453
Purifying [sbyangs] with the SVABHĀVA mantra, 143, 380; the gift torma, 218, 219, 220, 221; the dwelling, 180; the excellent house, 350; the maṇḍala, 437; the multitude tormas, 313; the preliminary torma, 267, 415; the chief flask, 411; the disciples, 389, 421; the nectar and pills of life, 385; the offering torma, 385; the life torma, 384. *See also* Cleansing; Empowering; Offering; Mantra

Quicksilver [khro-chu]. *See* Yamāntaka
Quietude and benefit [dal-'byor], 365-366

Radiant arrow [mda'-bkra], 327
Radiant spindle ['phang-bkra], 327
Radreng [ra-sgreng] monastery, 387
Rāma, Legend of [rgyal-po ra-maṇa'i gtam-rgyud], 56
Rangjung doje [rang-byung rdo-rje, zhva-nag karma-pa III], 419
Ransom fee [blu-yon], 22
Ratnākaraśānti, 13
Ratnarakṣita, 123, 281
Ratnasambhava [rin-chen 'byung-gnas], 42, 73, 74, 115, 118, 348; pledge of, 406
Ravishing Goddess, Legend of [lha-mo yid-'phrog-ma'i gtam-rgyud], 56
Rawa [ra-ba] months, 458, 460
Re, Anecdotes of [re-sgrung], 56
Realizations [mngon-par byang-chub-pa], 109-112
— four [mngon-byang bzhi], 109-110; Emptiness [stong-pa-nyid], 109, 110; seed [sa-bon], 109, 100; perfected body [sku-rdzogs], 109, 110; syllables arrayed [yi-ge bkod-pa], 109, 110
— five [mngon-byang lnga], 111-112, 113, 119, 124, 125, 127; Suchness [de-bzhin-nyid], 111; kissing sun and moon [nyi-zla kha-sbyor], 112; seed [sa-bon], 111, 124; emblem [phyag-mtshan], 111, 124; perfected body [sku-rdzogs], 111, 124
Rech'enpa [ras-chen-pa], 419
Recipe [rdzas-sbyor], 250, 280, 283-284; against poison, 283; against leprosy, 283; as magical function, 250
Recollection of Purity [dag-dran], 80-81, 449, 461. *See also* Ego; Vivid appearance
Refuge, going for [skyabs-'gro], 26, 30, 178, 276, 378, 388, 436-437, 461
Remainder [lhag-ma]. *See* Multitudes
Repachen [ral-pa-can], 11
Resultant deity ['bras-bu'i lha], 113, 114, 126. *See also* Causal deity; Heruka
Rich, Adrienne, 84, 85
Richardson, Hugh, 237

Rigdzin zhigpo lingpa [rig-'dzin zhig-po gling-pa], 420
Rigpe wangch'ug [rigs-pa'i dbang-phyug], 76
Rinchendra [rin-chen-grags]. *See* Bari, Translator of
Rites of diamond, three [rdo-rje chog-gsum], 109; emblem [phyag-msthan], 106, 109; seed [sa-bon], 106, 109; perfected body [sku-rdzogs], 106, 109
Ritual: daily, 21-23; training in, 24-25; types of, 256-257
— general type, 256, 261-262; ritual type, 256, 262-275; magical type, 128, 256, 275-291; soteriological type, 128, 256. *See also* Function
Ritual Manifestation [las-kyi phyag-rgya], 107. *See also* Great Manifestation
Ritual service [bsnyen-pa], 26, 36-38, 67, 255-261, 277, 432-458; in solitary contemplation, 245; preceded by permission, 461: preceded by preliminary practices, 461; prerequisite to Four Maṇḍala Offering, 173; prerequisite to effectuation of the mantra, 208; prerequisite to magical attainments, 246; contemplation of the mantra in, 243, 433; Process of Perfection in, 259; as soteriological function, 257, 262; as life teaching, 433; equipment for, 460; bodily purity in, 460-461; requisite number of recitations in, 244, 467; requisite length of time in, 244, 465; signs of success in, 244, 466
Ritualization, 23-25; of moral attitudes, 29-33; of metaphysics, 33-36
Röpe doje [rol-pa'i rdo-rje, zhva-nag karma-pa IV], 418, 419
Rosary [phreng-ba], materials of, 451, 464
Rosen, George, 144
Ruegg, D. S., 136
Ruland, Martin, 89
Ruta [ru-rta], 283

Sacha [sa-skya], 13, 14, 41, 47, 49, 52, 53, 54, 249, 386; rituals of, 38-54; lineage of Four Maṇḍala Offering; 172; initiations of, 402
Sadag [sa-bdag]. *See* Owners of the earth
Sahajalalita, 466
Śākyaśrī, 171
Samantabhadra [kun-tu bzang-po], 73
Sangp'u [gsang-phu] district, 322
Śāntideva, 29, 189
Sato, Hisashi, 9
Schizophrenia, 82-86
Sealing [rgyas-'debs]: with the initiation, 106, 108, 115, 183-184, 379; the ritual with an earnest wish, 224, 358; with a vajra cross, 396, 422, 423
Self-born Lady [rang-'byung-ma]. *See* Glorious Goddess
Self-generation [bdag-bskyed], 67, 129-130, 208, 255-261, 257, 267, 330, 331, 378, 379, 410, 421, 442, 460, 461; and Process of Perfection, 129-130; in magical functions, 330-331; authorization to perform, 423. *See also* Generation, in front
Sendivogius, 89
Serag [bse-rag], 315, 316, 356
Sera [se-ra] monastery, xiii
Service [rim-gro, sku-rim], 232, 441, 464
Shak'ön [sha-'khon]. *See* Creditors
Shapiro, Karl, 367
Shastri, Hirananda, xii
Sheja [shes-bya] magazine, 240
Shinje [gshin-rje], 294, 320
Shinjeshe [gshin-rje-gshed]. *See* Yamāntaka
Shudag [shu-dag], 283
Si [sri], 299, 315, 316, 343, 356
Silts'il [bsil-tshil] cemetery, 318
Sinpo [srin-po], 293, 294, 416
Skull bowls [ban-dha, thod-pa], 159
Slayer of Death [gshin-rje-gshed] *See* Yamāntaka

Smoke-eater [dud-gsol-ma]. *See* Glorious Goddess

Snellgrove, David, xi, 21, 45

Söderk'a [gsol-sder-kha] monastery, 239

Sogdag [srog-bdag], 294

Songtsen gampo [srong-btssan sgampo], 5, 8

Śrīphalavajra, 35, 127

Stages [sa]: of the bodhisattva, 119-120; magically controlled, 104

Sthiramati, 97, 98

Stock [tshogs]: of knowledge [ye-shes tshogs], 33, 181, 276, 379, 443, 461; of merit [bsod-nams tshogs], 33, 177, 181, 276, 379, 443, 461

Subandhu, 7-8

Substitutes [glud], 324-326, 328-330, 346-350, 352, 353, 368; *ch'angbu* as, 324; around the thread-cross, 325-326; clothing and hair as, 326; cast into a river, 329; empowering with the six mantras and six gestures, 346-350; dispatching, 346-355

Subtle deities, deep contemplation of [phra-mo'i ting-'dzin], 72-74, 101. *See also* Empowering, the senses; Maṇḍala, in the body

Sumpa k'enpo [sum-pa mkhan-po], 4, 11, 293

Sun Ching-feng, 232

Surrealism, 86-88

Sūryagupta, xiii

Swirling Nectar [bdud-rtsi 'khyil-ba], 179, 180, 286, 348; mantra of, 143, 180, 218-221, 267, 313, 350, 380, 384, 385, 389, 411, 415, 421, 437; generated in the flask, 413; guards solitary contemplation, 461

Symbolic being [dam-tshig sems-dpa'], 101, 103, 107, 269, 271, 273, 333, 338, 379; generation of, 181-182; magical correspondences of, 108-127; generation in the hearth, 271; dwelling with the ego of, 130. *See also* Knowledge being

Tablets [rgyang-bu], 322, 327

Tagts'er [stag-tsher], 290

Tamdrin [rta-mgrin]. *See* Hayagrīva

T'angtön jepo [thang-ston rgyal-po], 342

Tantras [rgyud]: Practical [bya-ba'i rgyud], 417, 419; of the Highest Yoga [rnal-'byor bla-na-med-pa'i rgyud], 419; Father [pha-rgyud], 106, 109, 113; Mother [ma-rgyud], 109, 115; Nyingma, 44; of Tārā, 12-13, 417; proscribed in Tibet, 12

Tārā [sgrol-ma]: in folklore, 233-242; in drama, 55-59; in poetry, 59-63; in popular cult, 63; history of, in Tibet, 5-13; rituals for, 55; myth of origin, 64-66; Process of Generation, 104-105; maṇḍala offering to, 205, 215, 216; color of, 279; temple [sgrol-ma lha-khang], 11, 55

— forms of, 279; eight, 230; twenty-one, xiii, 320, 333-335; Khadiravaṇī, 320; Bhīmadevī, 292; Cintācakra, 378 and *passim*; Kurukullā, 301-310; Blue She-Wolf, 292; White, xiii, 231, 363, 418, 430; minor, xiii, 279. *See also* Vāgīśvarakīrti

Tāranātha, 4, 13, 417

Tara rinpoch'e [tā-ra rin-po-che], 375-398

Teaching [khrid], 400; deep [zab-khrid], 401; life [tshe-khrid], 378, 433, 441, 461, 463; textual transmission of [khrid-lung], 400

T'ebchu [theb-kyu]. *See* Buttons

Tendzin yongdü [bstan-'dzin yongs-'dul], xv

Tenjur [bstan-'gyur], xiv, 10, 204

Tenma [bstan-ma] goddesses, twelve, 318

Tenpe nyima [bstan-pa'i nyi-ma], 103, 109, 132

Tenpe nyinje [bstan-pa'i nyin-byed, situ VIII], 417, 418

T'eurang [the'u-brang], 294, 329

Textual transmission [lung], 399; of a teaching [khrid-lung], 400

Thought of enlightenment [byang-chub-kyi sems]: awakening [sems-bskyed], 177, 178, 189, 276, 331, 378, 388, 420, 442, 461, 436-437; actual [don-dam-pa'i sems], 29, 30-31, 34, 181, 436, 432; intentional [smon-pa'i sems], 26, 29, 30, 181, 436, 442

Thread-cross [mdos]: as demon trap, 327; as cosmogram, 329: as magical function, 257, 346; as magical device, 318; lineage of, 322; benefits of, 322-323; construction of, 326-327; ritual of, 318-359; dispatching [lam-du bskyal], 351, 335; space [nam-mkha'] of, 326, 329, 352

Thunderstone [gnam-lcags, thog-sku] image, 238-240. *See also* Miraculous image

Tilopa, 170

Tinglo [ting-lo], 266, 324

Toden rinpoch'e [rtogs-ldan rin-po-che], 75, 323

Torma [gtor-ma], 24, 82, 143, 165, 167, 217-222, 324-325, 340-346; decoration [rgyan-spros], 217, 324; materials, 175; initiation with, 403, 430; evocation, 383; offering, as a ritual function, 264, 340; magical employment of, 383; offered at end of contemplative period, 463. *See also* Buttons; *Ch'angbu*; *Tinglo*; Pills, magic

— three aspects of, 377, 430; as an offering [mchod-dus gtor-ma], 377; as an evocation [sgrub-dus lha], 377, 410; as a substance of magical attainment [dngos-grub zhu-ba'i rdzas], 226, 377, 431

— preliminary [sngon-gtor], 258, 262, 263, 265, 300, 410, 415-416, 461; round [gtor-zlum], 324; white [dkar-gtor], 324, 345, 355; round white [zlum-gtor dkar-po], 174, 266, 272, 377, 408; food [zhal-zas], 174, 217, 409; offering [mchod-gtor], 165, 174, 217, 291, 340-343, 376, 377, 385, 408; prayer [gsol-kha gtor-ma], 217; wordling ['jig-rten gtor-ma], 217, 274; fire-god [me-lha gtor-ma], 273; multitude [tshogs], 312; gift ['bul-gtor], 174, 217-222; for the hindering demons [bgegs-gtor], 217, 258, 263, 265, 300, 324, 343-344, 386, 461; for the creditors [lan-chags gtor-ma], 324, 344-345; *chogdog* [cog-rdog gtor-ma], 324; for the lords of the soil [gzhi-bdag gtor-ma], 324, 345; initiation [dbang-gtor], 376; life [tshe-gtor], 376, 384, 390-396, 410

Töt'ang [stod-thang] palace, 10

Tr'adrug [khra-'brug] monastery, 237

Trashilhunpo [bkra-shis lhun-po] monastery, 72

Tr'isong detsen [khri-srong lde-btsan], 10

Tr'itsün [khri-btsun], 5, 6, 8-10

True nature [gshis-lugs], 444. *See also* Process of Perfection

Truth: act of, 343-355; empowering by the strength of, 350; averting with, 355

Tsakali [tsa-ka-li], 377, 409

Tsang [gtsang] district, 57

Tsangpa jare [gtsang-pa rgya-ras], 15

Ts'ats'a [tsha-tsha], 288, 466

Tsebola [rtse-bo-la] district, 15

Tsen [btsan], 293, 294, 296, 297, 298, 300, 301, 329, 342, 373, 390

Ts'ewang norbu [tshe-dbang nor-bu], 171, 173, 174

Ts'ewang tobje [tshe-dbang stobs-rgyal], xv

Tsöndrü jats'o [brtson-'grus rgya-mtsho], 282

Tsongk'apa [tsong-kha-pa], 14, 27, 30, 33, 34, 35, 37, 69, 70, 75, 76, 77, 78, 79, 84, 101, 107, 108, 111, 112, 114, 116, 117, 118, 119, 120, 122, 126, 128, 129, 132, 136, 141, 177, 363, 402, 404, 452

Ts'ütr'im jewa [tshul-khrims rgyal-ba], 302

Tucci, Giuseppe, xii, 230, 294, 297

Ü [dbus] district, 57, 59, 321, 387

Ukar [dbu-dkar], 320-321
Urban VIII, Pope, 93

Vāgbhāṭa, 367
Vāgīśvarakīrti, xiii, 11, 12, 229, 363, 367, 387, 412, 417, 419, 430, 465, 467
Vairocana [rnam-snang], 42, 72, 74, 77, 115, 118, 142, 268, 348; seed of, 116; gate of, 125; pledge of, 406
Vajrabhairava [rdo-rje 'jigs-byed]. *See* Yamāntaka
Vajrakīla [rdo-rje phur-pa]. *See* Doje p'urpa
Vajrapāṇi [phyag-na rdo-rje], 43
Vajrâsana, 237
Vajrasattva [rdo-rje sems-dpa'], 27, 29, 74, 127, 144, 194; 100-syllable mantra of, 144, 194, 223, 358, 385, 413, 435, 452, 464; visualization and recitation [bsgom-bzlas] of, 27, 434-436; of the ritual, 113, 114; as diamond lust, 115, 116, 118
Vajravārāhī [rdo-rje phag-mo]. *See* Ḍākiṇī
Vajrayoginī [rdo-rje rnal-'byor-ma]. *See* Ḍākiṇī
Vasubandhu, 91, 95, 96, 97, 98
Vasudhara, 318
Vasundharā [nor-rgyun-ma], 279
Verses of good fortune [shis-brjod], 225, 397. *See also* Benediction
Vidyā [rig-sngags], 207
Virūpa, 135
Visualization [mos-pa, dmigs-pa], 36, 37, 68-76; ability in, 71-75; technique of, 75-79; as simulacrum of divine power, 242; application of, 250, 279, 280-283; distraction and drowsiness in, 70-71. *See also* Contemplation, states of; Mantra, recitation of
Vivid appearance [gsal-snang], 69-76, 103, 447-448, 461, 462. *See also* Ego; Recollection of purity
Vows [sdom-pa], 403-407; and pledges [dam-tshig], 37, 38; taking with nectar and beer, 404; of a holder of the mantra [rig-'dzin], 404; healing the degeneration of, 393-394. *See also* Pledges

Waddell, L. Austine, 8
Walker, Daniel, 92
Wangch'ug doje [dbang-phyug rdo-rje, zhva-nag karma-pa IX], 420, 430, 440, 441, 465
Wanglag [dbang-lag], 290
Wayman, Alex, 136
Wen-ch'eng kung-chu, 5, 6, 8-10
Wind running [rlung-sgom-pa], 256
Winternitz, M., 188

Yaje [ya-rgyal] district, 57
Yak [g.yag]: eagle [khyung-g.yag], 238; divine [lha-g.yag], 240; *dzomo* [mdzo-mo], 17
Yamāntaka [gshin-rje-gshed], 42, 44, 49, 124; four yogas [rnal-'byor bzhi] of, 114-115; Quicksilver [khro-chu], 44; Black Poison-faced [dug-gdong nag-po], 44; Black Master of Life [tshe-bdag nag-po], 44; Vajrabhairava, the Diamond Terrifier [rdo-rje 'jigs-byed], 44; Mañjuśrī, as Slayer of Death, 314-316. *See also* High patron deities
Yamshing [yams-shing] firewood, 266, 267, 270, 272
Yangdag [yang-dag], 42, 44. *See also* High patron deities
Yates, Francis, 88, 93
Year: ending in the number nine [dgu-mig], 299; when a death has occured [dur-mig], 299
Yeats, William Butler, 88
Yeshe jets'en [ye-shes rgyal-mtshan], 14, 67, 172, 173
Yeshe ts'oje [ye-shes mtsho-rgyal]. *See* Ḍākiṇī
Yoga [rnal-'byor]: with the gurus [bla-ma'i rnal-'byor], 27, 441-442; with the deity [lha'i rnal-'byor], 445; with the recitation [bzlas-pa'i rnal-'byor], 450

— four [rnal-'byor bzhi], 114-115; yoga [rnal-'byor], 114; further yoga [rjes-kyi rnal-'byor], 114; higher yoga [shin-tu rnal-'byor], 114; great yoga [rnal-'byor chen-po], 114. *See also* Yamāntaka; Process of Generation
Yogin [rtogs-ldan], 26
Yoginī [rnal-'byor-ma]. *See* Ḍākiṇī
Yülha [yul-lha], 294
Yungtönpa [g.yung-ston-pa], 419

Za [gza']. *See* Protectors of the Law
Za [gza'], 294
Zahor beṇḍa [za-hor beṇḍa], 320
Zangmar toden [zangs-dmar rtogs-ldan], 239
Zen [zan], 175, 325
Zen par [zan par], 326
Zhangtönpa [zhang-ston-pa], 172
Zhenji mit'ubpa [gzhan-gyis mi-thub-pa], 290
Zhidag [gzhi-bdag]. *See* Lords of the soil
Zhönnupe [gzhon-nu-dpal], 12
Zhuch'en [zhu-chen], 322